Lɪɴᴜx Companion for System Administrators

LINUX Companion for System Administrators

Jochen Hein

 Addison-Wesley

Harlow, England • Reading, Massachusetts • Menlo Park, California • New York
Don Mills, Ontario • Amsterdam • Bonn • Sydney • Singapore • Tokyo • Madrid
San Juan • Milan • Mexico City • Seoul • Taipei

© Addison Wesley Longman Limited 1999

Pearson Education Limited
Edinburgh Gate
Harlow
Essex CM20 2JE
England

and Associated Companies throughout the World.

The right of Jochen Hein to be identified as author of this Work have been asserted
by him in accordance with the Copyright, Designs and Patents Act 1988.

The programs in this book have been included for their instructional value. They have
been tested with care but are not guaranteed for any particular purpose. The publisher
does not offer any warranties or representations nor does it accept any
liabilities with respect to the programs.

Many of the designations used by manufacturers and sellers to distinguish their
products are claimed as trademarks. Addison Wesley Longman Limited has made
every attempt to supply trademark information about manufacturers and their
products mentioned in this book. A list of the trademark designations and their
owners appears on page xvi.

Translated and typeset by 46.
Cover designed by odB Design and Communication, Reading.
Printed and bound in the United States of America.

First published 1999. Reprinted 1999

ISBN 0–201–36044–6

British Library Cataloguing-in-Publication Data
A catalogue record for this book is available from the British Library

Library of Congress Cataloging-in-Publication Data
Hein, Jochen.
    Linux Companion for System A / Jochen Hein.
        p.   cm.
    Includes bibliographical references (p.   ) and index.
    ISBN 0-201-36044-6
    1. Linux. 2. Operating systems (Computers)   I. Title.
    QA76.76.063H4523   1998
    005.4'469--dc21   98-35977
                                                                    CIP

Preface

He who gives up functionality for ease of use
loses both and deserves neither.

Anonymous

LINUX is a UNIX-like operating system. Thus, a LINUX system has all the flexibility, but also all the complexity, of UNIX. This book is meant as a contribution to help users get to grips with this complexity and make efficient use of the flexibility.

LINUX is a free operating system. This applies not only to the kernel, but also to almost all the other programs. Free, as for the GNU General Public License (GPL), means that the source code is freely available. It does not refer to the sometimes free-of-charge distribution of LINUX via mailboxes or `ftp` servers.

In the freeware scene, there are basically four different kinds of license, all of which have their legitimation for specific purposes:

- the BSD or X copyright, which allows the code to be used also in commercial and proprietary systems;
- the GPL, which requires that the programs or improved versions derived from them continue to be free;
- programs whose commercial use or distribution is prohibited;
- programs that are not subject to any copyright, the so-called public domain programs.

These liberal licensing conditions made LINUX what it is today. A decisive role was played by the availability of GNU programs, which had already made the utilities of a UNIX system freely available. Another important issue was the X Window system port, which is today available as XFree86 for LINUX (and a series of other UNIX systems).

Free software is better software, because it gives the user the possibility of adapting, improving, and understanding the programs, or simply correcting errors. This opportunity is denied to users of proprietary software, who are at the mercy of software distributors, for better or for worse. Apart from the possibility of gaining complete insight into the system, this is the most striking argument in favor of LINUX or any other freeware system, such as NetBSD or FreeBSD. A further advantage for the user is that various suppliers can provide support for the system.

Besides the programs themselves, the corresponding documentation is also freely available. The LINUX Documentation Project has made it its business to write both HowTo documents and complete manuals. Some of these books are also available in bookshops. There are also projects to translate the HowTos into several foreign languages.

However, you do not have to be a programmer to employ LINUX efficiently. If errors occur, they are often found and corrected by programmers within a few hours or days. Especially if you have installed a 'stable' distribution of LINUX, the system will run steadily and reliably from the very first moment. Installation of new programs or an update to a new version is usually limited to the execution of a few commands.

This book has been written almost entirely with freely available software under LINUX. GNU Emacs and/or XEmacs were used as editors, together with the `auctex` package, which provides a powerful environment for the typesetting of texts with TeX or LaTeX. Typesetting was done in LaTeX 2_ε, making use of a series of additional styles. The stability and speed of LINUX together with the powerful UNIX environment have played a major role in the success of this project. This book is dedicated to all programmers (and users) of free software, without whom today's multitude of free software would not exist.

The English translation used AlphaLite (an Emacs equivalent under MacOS) as editing software and LaTeX 2_ε in the OzTeX implementation for MacOS for typesetting. Additional styles include proprietary display fonts for computer input/output and program listings.

Typographical conventions

Following the tradition of practically all computer books, I would like to dedicate a section to the presentation of typographical conventions. These are intended to improve readability and to avoid repeated explanations of basic features that are now presented once and for all.

- Computer output is set in a special display font (`Computer Display`).
- User input is set in the same font, but additionally highlighted by using **bold characters**.
- Variable input that has to be appropriately replaced by the user is shown in *italics*.
- To differentiate between various shells and privileged and non-privileged users, we use different shell prompts:
  - \# stands for the system administrator, who uses the `bash`.
  - > stands for a user with the `tcsh`.
  - $ stands for a user with the `bash`.

Let us look at an example produced by a `tcsh` user. The user `root` is used in this book only in places where it is definitely mandatory. The separation between user and system administrator is one of the fundamental concepts of UNIX and serves the security of user and system data and the stability of the system.

```
(Linux):~> echo 'This is an input' | sed s/in/out/
This is an output
```

Additional special formatting is used for shell or environment variables (`VARIABLE`). Names of programs and commands are set in display font (`program`), files are specified including the path (`/path/file`). Listings or excerpts from configuration files are set in display font (`Computer Display`), and so are names of computers. The use of key combinations is represented in the following form:

- ⒶＡ for the 'A' key, ⒹＤ∈Ｌ for the 'Del' key
- ⒸＴＲＬ-ⒸＣ for simultaneous pressing of 'Ctrl' and 'C'
- ⒺＳＣ,ⓍＸ for the key sequence 'Esc' followed by 'X'

Access paths for files

For every program package discussed, you will find an indication of where to find the programs or additional information. Possibly you may want to install an updated version of some software at a later stage; for this reason, a source where the software can be obtained is indicated with every program described.

Mailing lists

The LINUX operating system and the associated programs have been and are being developed by different programmers on the Internet. Communication takes place via different channels:

- The developers cooperate via private email. This is sensible as long as only a very limited number of programmers are working on a project.
- Use is made of (public or private) mailing lists. A special computer distributes all messages to the members of the mailing list.
- Part of the discussions takes place in newsgroups.

A series of mailing lists that are principally open to all interested parties is currently established on the computer `vger.rutgers.edu`. These lists are managed by means of the `majordomo` program package. For a first contact, you need to send a mail message containing the text `help` in the message body to the user `majordomo@vger.rutgers.edu`. You will then be sent instructions on how to use the management program.

Acknowledgments

First, I would like to thank all LINUX hackers and users and all programmers, without whom this book would not have been possible. I would also like to thank our proofreaders, who have detected many errors and inconsistencies and who have turned the book into what it is today.

Eberhard Mönkeberg, who developed the idea to write this book, and Harald Böhme deserve the same recognition as Carsten Schabacker, who laid the foundations for the chapter on UNIX *Tools*. Jörg Rade wrote the first draft of the chapters on *System start-up*, *X*, and the *World Wide Web*. Special thanks go to Sven Probst, who helped me by answering a great many questions on TCP/IP and networks. All remaining errors are my own responsibility.

If you have any questions or suggestions, you can reach me via email at the address `jochen.hein@li.org`. This address has been kindly provided by *Linux International*.

Clausthal-Zellerfeld, March 1996   *Jochen Hein*

Preface to the second edition

In the last few years and months LINUX has continued its almost unstoppable development. The kernel has been extended with new drivers, and its performance and suitability for SMP (Symmetric Multi-Processing) computers have been substantially enhanced. This meets the requirements of employing LINUX as a server system, though the average workstation user has not been forgotten either.

A special mention should be given to the effort that has gone into providing a powerful and flexible desktop. Three such projects are GnuStep, GNOME, and KDE. Futhermore, a series of applications have become available, such as StarOffice, ApplixWare, and Adabas. All in all, LINUX is beginning to leave behind its secretive status as an insiders' tool for hackers and programmers and is increasingly becoming a general use system.

The second edition contains many small improvements to practically all subjects, but also major changes to today's current areas, in particular the desktops and new network functions.

If you have any questions or suggestions, you can reach me via email at the address `jochen.hein@li.org`. This address has been kindly provided by *Linux International*. At this point, I would like to thank all readers of the first edition who have contributed with their questions and suggestions to further improving this book. I hope you will enjoy reading this book as much as I enjoyed writing it, and that you will learn as much as I did.

Kassel, December 1997   *Jochen Hein*

Preface to the English translation

LINUX is still an evolving system and a hot topic. I am glad to be part of that movement, and see LINUX being used widely. Once again I dedicate the book to all LINUX and GNU hackers around the world who made it possible.

I thank my editor Susanne Spitzer from Addison-Wesley Longman, Germany, for her on-going support and her efforts to get the English version started. Another big thankyou goes to Fiona Kinnear, Elaine Richardson, Lisa Talbot, and the staff from Addison-Wesley Longman, UK, who worked on the book. I also thank the translators from Goldshield Communications, who did a great job, especially Hans-Dieter Rauschner for his help with the English presentation. I hope you like the translation as much as I do.

If you have any questions or suggestions, you may reach me at `jochen.hein@li.org`.

Kassel, August 1998   *Jochen Hein*

Online resources

LINUX has been developed mostly on the Internet, so there are many servers dedicated to LINUX. The following list contains some useful starting points that you may or may not be aware of:

- `http://www.linux.org` is a central resource about LINUX, user groups, ongoing projects, and much more.
- `http://www.linuxhq.com` contains the latest and greatest kernels and a lot of useful patches and information.
- `http://freshmeat.org` announces information on many software projects.
- `http://slashdot.org` is a news and discussion server with lots of interesting things.
- `http://lwn.net` is a weekly newsletter completely dedicated to LINUX and Free Software.
- `http://www.debian.org` one of the best LINUX distributions, it is entirely built upon Free Software.

Contents

Preface   **v**

1 Linux – operating system of the future?   **1**

    1.1   Overview of LINUX features   2
    1.2   LINUX distributions compared   3
    1.3   The future of LINUX   9

2 The File System Hierarchy Standard   **11**

    2.1   Origins of the File System Hierarchy Standard   11
    2.2   Problem areas   12
    2.3   The root or / file system   13
    2.4   The /usr hierarchy   22
    2.5   /var – variable data   28
    2.6   The further development of the FHS   34

3 System start-up   **35**

    3.1   The Basic Input/Output System (BIOS)   35
    3.2   The LINUX boot loader   38
    3.3   Starting the kernel   46
    3.4   The init process   49
    3.5   Stopping the system   55

4 Configuration and administration   **57**

    4.1   Kernel and hardware configuration   57
    4.2   Configuring the hardware   67

4.3	Kernel modules	68
4.4	System configuration	71
4.5	User-definable system configuration	109
4.6	User-related configuration	113
4.7	Configuration of editors	116
4.8	Keyboard mapping	117

5 The Emacs editor — 119

5.1	Which Emacs should I choose?	120
5.2	Compiling the GNU Emacs	121
5.3	General aspects of working with Emacs	122
5.4	Configuration	128
5.5	Keyboard mapping	136
5.6	Emacs modes	137
5.7	Useful minor modes	142
5.8	Other extensions	144
5.9	Information sources	144

6 The X Window system — 145

6.1	Look and feel under X	145
6.2	History and concept	147
6.3	XFree86 server configuration	148
6.4	Window managers	153
6.5	General X11 command line options	156
6.6	Access control	157
6.7	Tools and other useful programs for X	160
6.8	Information and sources	161

7 Backup — 163

7.1	Why everybody needs backups	163
7.2	Surviving disk errors with RAID	166
7.3	Backup media	167
7.4	Backup strategies	169
7.5	Backup programs	172
7.6	Conclusion and additional information	183

8 National Language Support — 185

8.1	ASCII and ISO character sets	186
8.2	POSIX National Language Support	187
8.3	Names of locales	188
8.4	Categories used in NLS	189
8.5	Creating a locale definition	192

8.6   Creation of message catalogs with GNU `gettext`   193
8.7   Programming with NLS   194
8.8   Character set conversion   195

9   Localization   197

9.1   Console keyboard mapping   197
9.2   Using the ISO-Latin-1 character set   198
9.3   Keyboard assignment under X11   198
9.4   Use of foreign language characters at the shell level   200
9.5   Foreign language characters in editors   204
9.6   Special characters in mail and news   206
9.7   Adaptation of individual programs   209

10   UNIX tools   215

10.1   File management   216
10.2   Processing of text files   225
10.3   Search patterns (regular expressions)   231
10.4   Starting commands automatically   234
10.5   The AWK programming language   238
10.6   Processing text files with `sed`   244
10.7   Further useful utilities   247
10.8   The shell as a connecting link between programs   250
10.9   Processes and jobs   263

11   Tools (not only) for programmers   267

11.1   The `make` PROGRAM   267
11.2   The `imake` PROGRAM   270
11.3   Installation of programs   271
11.4   Editors   274
11.5   The Revision Control System (`rcs`)   276
11.6   Other version management systems   288

12   TEX and LATEX under LINUX   291

12.1   The `teTeX` package   291
12.2   Local extensions of the TEX system   294
12.3   Efficient use of TEX and LATEX   295

13   Emulators under LINUX   299

13.1   The BIOS emulator `DOSemu`   299
13.2   The Windows emulator `Wine`   312
13.3   The `iBCS` emulator   316

14 LINUX in a networked environment 321

14.1	Network software layers	322
14.2	Network hardware	323
14.3	Network-related kernel configuration	326
14.4	Activating the network devices	329
14.5	Assignment of IP addresses	331
14.6	All about `ifconfig`	334
14.7	All about `route`	336
14.8	The `netstat` program	337
14.9	The Address Resolution Protocol (ARP)	339

15 TCP/IP basics 341

15.1	Protocols	341
15.2	The `inetd` server	344
15.3	The TCP wrapper (`tcpd`)	345
15.4	The `ident` daemon	347
15.5	Adding new services	348
15.6	Remote procedure call	349
15.7	Architecture-independent data format	351

16 IP addresses and computer names 353

16.1	Correspondence between names and IP addresses in `/etc/hosts`	355
16.2	Domain Name Service	356
16.3	Using a name server with LINUX	356
16.4	Testing a name server	359
16.5	Reliability of name servers	362

17 Network applications 363

17.1	The `telnet` PROGRAM	363
17.2	The File Transfer Protocol (`ftp`)	364
17.3	Searching for files with `archie`	367
17.4	The r tools	369
17.5	The secure shell `ssh`	374
17.6	Sending warnings to remote computers with `rwall`	377
17.7	File transfer with `rdist`	377
17.8	Conversation between users with `talk`	379
17.9	Internet Relay Chat (`irc`)	380
17.10	File transfer with `sendfile`	380

18 Network File System (NFS) 383

18.1	LINUX as NFS client	383

18.2   LINUX as NFS server   385
18.3   The automounter   387

19   Anonymous FTP servers   **391**

19.1   Installing the `wu-ftpd`   392
19.2   Administration of an `ftp` server   394

20   Linux in a heterogeneous network   **397**

20.1   LINUX as a NetWare client and server   398
20.2   LINUX as an SMB client and server   405

21   Configuration and operation of a name server   **411**

21.1   The concept of Domain Name Service   411
21.2   General remarks on configuration of a name server   413
21.3   Primary name servers   413
21.4   The file `named.hosts`   415
21.5   The Masterfile format   415
21.6   The file `named.local`   421
21.7   The file `named.rev`   421
21.8   Secondary name servers   422
21.9   Slave name servers   422
21.10   Further information on the DNS   423

22   Network Information Service   **425**

22.1   Using NIS services as a client   426
22.2   NIS servers   428
22.3   Toward the future with NIS+   429

23   The `bootp` protocol   **431**

24   Connection via SLIP and PPP   **437**

24.1   Serial Line Internet Protocol (SLIP)   438
24.2   Point-to-Point Protocol (PPP)   441
24.3   Automatic connection with `diald`   446
24.4   ISDN instead of a modem   447

25   Linux and the World Wide Web   **451**

25.1   History and concept   451
25.2   The WWW and the Internet   452
25.3   Web browsers   454

25.4	Providing information	457
25.5	The use of LINUX in the Internet	459
25.6	Sources of information	460

26 Network administration 461

26.1	Troubleshooting in the network	461
26.2	Programs for network management	465
26.3	IP network management	471

Appendices 473

A The standard editor vi 473

B Generating passwords 477

C References 479

The LINUX Documentation Project	479
LINUX literature	480
GNU project documentation	480
General UNIX literature	481
General TEX/LATEX literature	483
Literature on UNIX networks	483
The World Wide Web	484
Miscellaneous references	485

D List of important RFCs 487

Index 493

Trademark Notices

Accelerated-X, Xi Graphics, Inc. ● AIX, International Business Machines Corporation (IBM) ● Alpha, Digital Equipment Corporation ● Amiga,Commodore Business Machines ● Apple, Apple Computer, Inc. ● Appletalk, Apple Computer, Inc. ● Dec, Digital Equipment Corporation ● Ethernet, Dec, Intel and Xerox ● IBM, International Business Machines Corporation (IBM) ● Intel, Intel Corporation ● IPX, Sun Microsystems, Inc. ● LAN Manager, Microsoft Corporation ● Linux, Linus Torvalds ● Macintosh, Apple Computer, Inc. ● Metro-X, Metro Link

Incorporated • Microsoft, Microsoft Corporation • Motif, Open Software
Foundation, Inc. • MS-DOS, Microsoft Corporation • NCP Novell Incorporated •
Netscape, Netscape Communications Corporation • NetWare, Novell Incorporated •
NFS, Sun Microsystems, Inc. • Novell, Novell Incorporated • OS/2, International
Business Machines Corporation (IBM) • OSF/1, Open Software Foundation • PC-
DOS, Microsoft Corporation • Pentium, Intel Corporation • POSIX, Institute of
Electrical and Electronics Engineers Inc. • PostScript, Adobe Systems Incorporated
• Red Hat, Red Hat Software, Inc • RPM, Red Hat Software, Inc. • SCO, The Santa
Cruz Operation Ltd (SCO) • Slackware, Walnut Creek CDROM and Patrik
Volkerding • Solaris, Sun Microsystems, Inc. • SPARC, Sparc International Inc. •
Sun, Sun Microsystems, Inc. • Token Ring, International Business Machines
Corporation (IBM) • ULTRIX, Digital Equipment Corporation • Unix, Licensed
through X/Open Company Ltd • Wabi, Sun Microsystems Inc. • Windows 95,
Microsoft Corporation • Windows NT, Microsoft Corporation • Windows,
Microsoft Corporation • Xenix ®, Microsoft Corporation • Xfree86, The Xfree86
Project, Inc.

LINUX – operating system of the future?

LINUX – in the narrow sense of the word – is 'merely' an operating system, meaning the part of a computer system's software that controls the hardware. In other (and simpler) words: the operating system is the system component that gives application software (such as word processing programs or news readers) access to the hardware facilities (such as printers, CD-ROM drives, and so on). Other operating systems which control widely-used PC hardware are, for example, OS/2, Novell NetWare, SCO, and Windows NT. DOS and DOS/Windows must also be considered as operating systems; however, since these systems allow application programs direct access to the hardware, there are reasonable doubts as to whether they should be put on the same level as the other systems mentioned above.

In a wider sense of the word, LINUX stands for something more. Usually, LINUX means a system which offers a comprehensive collection of UNIX tools and various application programs; one would typically think of such a collection when talking about a LINUX *distribution*. Differently emphasized distributions are put together by various parties, as they are tailored to the individual requirements of a user or user group: their bandwidth stretches from distributions that assemble only the most commonly needed tools on a few floppy disks (for example XLINUX) to distributions of several hundred megabytes in size, which provide a complete development environment and a large number of 'free' application programs (for example the Debian distribution).

These and other distributions are made available via `ftp` servers, but can often also be obtained on other media (floppy disks, CD-ROMs, tapes). Given the extent of the distributions, buying a CD is probably a better idea than spending a lot of time (even a day or more) downloading the software via `ftp` or modem. Together with the CD, many distributors also offer support and a manual describing the installation process and the first steps of using the system.

1.1 Overview of LINUX features

LINUX is a powerful operating system which during the past years has developed from a 'hacker system' to a general-use system, even for commercial applications. There are many reasons for this development. I would like to present some of these reasons, and give an overview of the possible applications of LINUX:

- LINUX is free; that is, practically the entire source code of the systems is accessible to everybody. This allows interested parties to implement improvements and eliminate errors, or simply to learn how the system works.
- LINUX is a UNIX-like system, with all the flexibility of UNIX. X11 is used as a graphical user interface, and both Motif and CDE are available for LINUX, as well as OpenLook (XView).
- LINUX complies with international standards such as POSIX and ANSI C. Furthermore, it supports many BSD or System V extensions. This greatly facilitates porting of many UNIX programs.
- LINUX is portable to other hardware architectures such as DEC Alpha, MIPS or Sun Sparc computers. This makes it one of the most portable systems currently available on the market.
- LINUX can be flexibly employed in TCP/IP networks. Besides this, several other protocols (IPX, AppleTalk, SMB) are supported.
- LINUX can still be run on 386 PCs with 4 Mbytes of RAM, whereas a system with 16 Mbytes can well be used as a workstation running X. Thus, in comparison with Windows NT, the hardware requirements are significantly lower.
- LINUX makes efficient use of memory (via shared libraries and demand loading) and modern processors (Pentium and Pentium Pro).
- LINUX can, without great expense, turn a PC into a workstation, an X terminal or a server.
- LINUX support is equally provided by distributors and developers, and even between users themselves. In fact, any interested party can offer commercial support, so the user has freedom of choice between many providers.
- LINUX is well adapted to common PC hardware, many drivers are available, and the system is comparatively fast.
- There are already many applications in the areas of program development, office packages, Internet servers and clients, as well as emulators of other systems such as Windows or IBCS2.
- The system is very well documented via electronic manuals (in /usr/doc), or man pages, and there are many books on the subject. If the documentation still leaves a question unanswered, you can always look for a solution in the source code itself, if the worst comes to the worst.

This list is certainly not complete and could be extended, with different users emphasizing different aspects. There is no system yet that would satisfy every possible user.

1.2 LINUX distributions compared

As already mentioned above, there is a large number of LINUX distributions. It is not easy to choose a 'good' distribution for individual use. In the following section, I will briefly present some distributions that I have tried out myself in the course of time and show their respective advantages and disadvantages. This list cannot be complete, because I did not have every distribution, and a reasonable test requires a lot of time. Furthermore, many test results have become useless with new versions of the corresponding distributions.

Each distribution should be supplied with corresponding installation instructions. These may come in the form of a README file, a booklet accompanying the CD, or a printed manual. Usually, such instructions describe the installation of the system in great detail, so in this presentation we will do without this kind of description. We will concentrate on highlighting the main differences between the distributions. It will be obvious that different distributions will match different requirements and that the suitability of a distribution will depend on the user's requirements.

Thanks to the GNU General Public License (GPL), to which many of the programs used under LINUX and the kernel are subject, every distributor is bound to supply the source code of the corresponding program together with the program or to provide it on demand. Therefore, many distributions also include the program sources on the CD. In case of problems, you can then recompile individual programs or find out with which options these programs were installed. This is an area where we can find significant differences between the distributions.

A further difference is to be found in the support given by the developers. Some CDs are offered without support, others entitle the user to support (via email, fax, or telephone) by the distributor. Often, vendors also maintain a mailing list in which special support is given for their distribution. More detailed information can be found in your distribution documentation.

To prevent excessive differences between the distributions, the *File System Hierarchy Standard* (see Chapter 2) was developed, which defines a LINUX directory structure. Most of the distributions presented here largely adhere to this standard, but some deviate from it in individual cases. These deviations are usually documented in the distribution manual.

Further information on the distributions presented here and on other distributions, such as, for example, the addresses of the distributors, can be found in the Distributions-HowTo. For practically every imaginable subject under LINUX, there is a HowTo file which introduces the subject and partly assumes the function of a FAQ (Frequently Asked Questions) list. Besides the HowTo documents, however, there is also a FAQ. In addition, a group of volunteers work on the LINUX Documentation Project (LDP), which produces man pages and manuals. These books are of good quality and some of them are also sold in bookshops. An overview of published titles can be found in Appendix C.

Before we come to the presentation of some distributions, I would like to explain in more detail the requirements that a distribution should fulfill. Important issues are the installation routines and the system itself, but we will also discuss the technical background.

None of the available distributions meets all of the requirements listed here. Nevertheless, all distributors learn something in the course of time and implement successful functions of other distributions. Here, the pressure exerted by the competition from many other (good) distributions has turned out to be an important impetus for developers.

- The installation routine should be able to do without a floppy disk, or use only one floppy, if the installation is carried out from CD, hard disk, or network. It is very helpful for newcomers or for PC users whose machine is not equipped with an operating system if any floppy disk that is required is readily supplied. This also presumes that only one floppy disk is required, without the need to select from a large number of preconfigured boot diskettes.

- The installation program should include an integrated help system. This makes it possible to display additional information during the installation and to provide the user with support.

- In case of input errors, it should be possible to carry out individual settings again without having to start over. This should apply to as many settings as possible.

- The selection of packages should take place before, not during, the installation. Available space should also have been checked at that point. This will make it possible to run the most time-consuming part of the installation without user interaction.

- The distribution should offer a choice between different 'standard installations' (for example with or without X, with or without TEX). These preselections can be very helpful for a beginner, since the number and variety of programs may be daunting.

- It should be possible to delete or add individual packages at a later time. Here, dependencies between the packages must be considered, because many packages build on others or mutually exclude each other.

- A powerful system administration tool can facilitate the installation. Not every user is interested in collecting the corresponding configuration files and adapting them with a text editor. Windows is a good example for showing how easy a system configuration can be with the aid of graphical tools.

- The distribution should include many application packages for mathematics, graphics, text processing, and so on. Here, a sensible subdivision into different application groups or series is useful.

- The distribution should include good documentation (description) of the packages at installation which should also be comprehensible to newcomers. After installation, complete documentation (README files, manuals and sample files) of the package should be available on the hard disk.

- The entire source code of the programs should be available and installable at the touch of a button.

- It should be possible to recompile the programs with one command in exactly the same way as they were compiled for the distribution.

- The original sources of the programs (for example, for use under other systems) and the adaptations for the distribution should be separated.

- The distribution should correspond to the file system hierarchy standard (FHS). If individual issues are not specified there, the principles to be followed should be clarity and the least amount of surprise for the user. Deviations from the FHS should be documented.

- The system should be based on a modularized kernel, so that initially the supplied kernel can be used.

- The distributor should get involved in the LINUX community, offering support and cooperation in projects, intensive cooperation with programmers to eliminate errors, and much more.

This list is not complete, but it does show the wide spectrum of requirements that distributions should meet. The effort of creating and maintaining a distribution is fairly high, so the market will hopefully stop growing in this respect.

1.2.1 The Slackware distribution

This distribution is available on the Internet via ftp. You can, however, also buy it on CD. Until recently, Slackware was something like the 'standard distribution' and has been installed in large numbers all over the world. This position is now jointly occupied by Red Hat and Debian.

The Slackware distribution is maintained by Patrick Volkerding and is usually very much up-to-date. Unfortunately, this is also the cause of (avoidable) errors for which bug fixes are not available or become available only slowly. This is a real problem in the detection of security loopholes. Other distributions, such as Debian, Red Hat, and Caldera, are much more user-friendly in this respect.

The installation program of the Slackware distribution is powerful and easy to handle. The program sources are partly only available in adapted form in the framework of the source tree, although this situation has improved significantly in the latest versions. Nevertheless, it is often unclear with which parameters and options the programs were compiled and installed.

1.2.2 The S.u.S.E. distribution

The S.u.S.E. GmbH has initially begun to adapt the international Slackware distribution to the German market. Recently, however, the developers have detached themselves from Slackware and have developed their own distribution. This was initially based on the Slackware package format, but has now shifted to using the format developed by Red Hat. This has significantly improved the technical side of this distribution.

This installation includes program descriptions (in German for the German language market) and a good installation program (`yast`) which can also be used for system administration. All settings are centrally stored in the file `/etc/rc.config` and from there are automatically converted into the appropriate configuration files. For many 'old hands,' this procedure is unusual, but it is very popular among new users.

Furthermore, many programs are preconfigured for German language users, so they too can immediately start working with the system. A special mention goes to the extensive installation manual and the rich choice of packages.

The installation is simple and easy to use and work with. If you buy the beginner's distribution, the distributor provides support. This distribution is probably the most widely used one in Germany; an American version is actively marketed as well.

Additional Information and Sources	
WWW server:	`http://www.suse.com/`
`ftp` server:	`ftp.cc.gatech.edu`
`ftp` path:	`/pub/linux/distributions/suse/`
Extent:	up to 500 Mbytes
Address:	`info@suse.com`

1.2.3 The Red Hat distribution

Another commercial distribution is the Red Hat distribution. It is available both via `ftp` and on CD. The installation program is also easy to handle. In contrast to Slackware, Red Hat uses another format (`.rpm`) for packages and has developed its own program (`rpm`) (Red Hat Package Management) for their management. This makes the use of the corresponding packages on other LINUX systems slightly more difficult; however, this format is quickly becoming established as the standard.

The `rpm` program implements some ideas that were realized for the first time in the BOGUS distribution. Thus, this distribution combines the technical advantages of the BOGUS distribution with great ease of use.

Under X, the Graphical LINUX Installation Tool (`glint`) is a user-friendly tool for installation and maintenance of packages. Besides package management, even part of the system maintenance can be carried out under X by means of an appropriate tool (`control-panel`). The aim of this distribution is to provide a stable platform for commercial developers and users.

This distribution can be installed via `ftp`. Furthermore, in the `contrib` directory it offers a large collection of useful programs that are not part of the standard system.

Additional Information and Sources	
WWW server:	`http://www.redhat.com/`
ftp server:	`ftp.redhat.com`

1.2.4 Caldera Open Linux

Based on the LST distribution, Caldera presents Caldera Open Linux (COL). Depending on the version, this includes a range of commercial packages in addition to the well-known free programs. The COL light version contains only the freely available packages and can be obtained via `ftp`. The COL base version includes the Looking Glass desktop (a graphical interface with file manager) and a font server that can handle TrueType fonts. The COL server version includes additional packages.

Furthermore, Caldera intends to provide a stable LINUX basis for other software enterprises. This basis is intended to induce other companies to port their programs to LINUX. Caldera distributes, for example, a port of WordPerfect and Corel-Draw. With this, Caldera wants to make LINUX usable in commercial environments; this is backed by an offer of support.

On the Caldera Solutions CD, several commercial programs (for example the Adabas database) are distributed. These can be unlocked by means of a license key.

The installation is simple and well-devised, many packages are included, and the system is immediately usable. If you are interested in commercial packages, Caldera is a good choice.

Additional Information and Sources	
WWW server:	`http://www.caldera.com/`
ftp server:	`ftp.caldera.com`
ftp path:	`/pub/OpenLinux/lite/1.2/`
Address:	Caldera Inc., 240 West Center Street
	Orem, Utah 84057 USA
	Tel.: 888 GO LINUX [465-4689]

1.2.5 Debian (GNU/Linux) distribution

The Debian distribution was initially developed by Ian Murdock. In the course of time, many other developers became involved with Debian. This made the Debian distribution a worldwide project that was also supported by the Free Software Foundation (FSF). The FSF considered this distribution a 'test case' for their own Hurd operating system.

The essential feature is that this distribution is free in the sense of the GPL. It can be copied and commercially employed within the framework of the GPL, even without buying a corresponding CD or other medium. Many developers have changed the copyright conditions of their programs to make them usable in this distribution without problems.

For installation and updates of program packages, a specific package format and a specific tool (`dpkg`) were developed. An important advantage is that the system or individual programs can be updated without problems, without having to format the hard disk and reinstall the software from scratch. The strategies developed for this purpose have recently also been adopted by other distributions (for example S.u.S.E. and Red Hat).

A further advantage is the consequent bug tracking, which is carried out by the developers via mailing lists. The list of open error messages is public and is regularly searched for errors that have remained untreated for too long. This makes the Debian distribution the most stable and error-free distribution. The developers also place great emphasis on the fact that the Debian distribution complies with the file system standard.

All sources, including the necessary patches, are part of the distribution. This also makes it possible for the user to recompile the system completely. In addition, the distribution is supplied with an extensive installation manual.

Development and support are essentially carried out via email, by establishing a series of mailing lists. You can subscribe to the lists `debian-user`, `debian-changes`, and `debian-announce` by sending an email to `debian-`*`list`*`-request@pixar.com` which contains `subscribe` in the message body.

Additional Information and Sources	
WWW server:	`http://www.debian.org/`
Mailing lists:	`debian-announce@pixar.com`
	`debian-user@pixar.com`
	`debian-changes@pixar.com`
	`debian-bugs@pixar.com` (bug reports only)
	`debian-changes@pixar.com`

1.2.6 Other distributions

Besides the distributions presented here, which I was able to test in more detail, several others exist. I have not been able to test every distribution, therefore the following brief overview contains only a little information on the individual distributions.

DLD The 'Deutsche Linux Distribution' is produced and maintained by the Delix company in Stuttgart. Delix is the distributor of the products Accelerated-X, Motif and CDE by X-Inside. Therefore they offer favorable bundle prices.

LST The distribution of the 'Linux Support Team' in Erlangen is also a German development. Caldera Open Linux is based on this distribution. LST now have the company name of Caldera Deutschland, therefore this distribution is expected to receive less publicity in the future, although it is included with several books.

Yggdrasil was one of the first CD distributions. It is quite widely used in the USA, but lately not much has been heard of it.

Unifix The Unifix company distributes the first POSIX-certified LINUX distribution. For many commercial developers, this is an important factor.

1.3 The future of LINUX

LINUX has, within a few years, changed from a hackers' system into a powerful UNIX system that is a worthy match even for commercial UNIX systems. But for how long is LINUX going to develop? There is really no answer to this question, because the answer depends on developers' available time and personal interests. We can, however, make some easy predictions:

- The ports to other architectures (68K, Sparc, MIPS, PowerPC, and DEC Alpha) are far advanced and are in part completed.
- For these architectures too there will be free and commercial distributions such as Debian and Red Hat. Some commercial products such as Motif have already been ported.
- The LINUX kernel contains support for symmetric multi-processing (SMP) for Intel processors. Support for other processor architectures is under development. A further project is the introduction of 'Fine Grained Locking,' so that as many processors as possible can be used to the best advantage.
- Support for threads and real-time processes is being implemented.
- The developers will continue their attempts to implement the current standards, such as POSIX and ANSI C.
- Installation will become even easier through the competition between the different distributions. Possibly, this trend will also continue with the applications.
- With the release of more commercial software, for example the StarOffice package, LINUX will open up still more areas for its application.
- For commercial application, good technical support is required. This is already offered by various companies.
- LINUX will gain more users, more programs will be available, and more hardware will be supported.
- LINUX will arrive on the desks even of inexperienced users because of its excellent desktop interfaces, but it will also gain more influence in the server environment because of projects like LINUX HA and many other improvements.
- With one of the next versions, IPv6 will be part of the standard distribution.

LINUX has already changed the world of 'personal computing'; it has become an accepted alternative to commercial operating systems. This is confirmed by a number of points:

- SCO give away their operating system to private users.
- Sun offers all research institutions very inexpensive access to the source code of Solaris – although not under the same conditions as is the case with LINUX.

- Even Microsoft produces LINUX software.
- Many hardware and software vendors already consider LINUX to be a mass market.
- More and more private users are showing an interest in the former 'hacker system.'

The file system hierarchy standard

2

The file system hierarchy standard (FHS) is a document that describes directory structure and file location under UNIX-like operating systems. The FHS was developed out of the LINUX file system standard, which was intended to standardize LINUX distributions. The new name is meant to emphasize the inclusion of the free BSD systems.

This chapter is intended to provide a guide through the jungle of the many files and subdirectories of a LINUX system. However, it goes further and attempts to clarify the background of this standard. This should enable a system administrator to decide how to install a package that does not (yet) correspond to the standard. Many reasons that have led to the establishment of the standard in its present form are discussed in some detail. The standard itself no longer contains these reasons because they are now viewed as generally recognized rules of system administration.

Additional Information and Sources	
Package:	`fhs-2.0.tar.gz`
`ftp` server:	`tsx-11.with.edu`
`ftp` path:	`/pub/linux/docs/linux standards/fsstnd`
Web server:	`http://www.pathname.com/fhs/`
Size:	about 150 Kbytes
Mailing list:	`fhs-discuss@ucsd.edu`
Subscribe:	`listserv@ucsd.edu`
	`ADD fhs-discuss` in the mail body

2.1 Origins of the file system hierarchy standard

As shown in the previous chapter, anybody interested in the subject can create a LINUX distribution. On the one hand, this has generated lively competition for topicality and completeness; on the other hand, it has created an inflation of new distributions.

The outcome of this is that almost no LINUX system resembles any other, so portability of applications becomes a problem between the different LINUX distributions. It also becomes practically impossible to answer questions about a particular distribution in a newsgroup if one cannot be sure that important configuration files are stored at the 'usual' location in the file system. Furthermore, the directory structure is often not comparable with the structures set forth in BSD, System V, or other UNIX systems.

When these problems became increasingly evident, a group of interested people, many of them experienced UNIX administrators, got together to set up a document that standardizes placement of files and programs within the file system. This brought to light a series of problems, and attempts were made to solve them. The file system hierarchy standard available today has been the most successful of these, and is currently supported by all major LINUX distributions.

The standard is not a binding rule for system administrators or distributors. It can only make suggestions which, if they are well-founded and as compatible as possible with the existing system, will be generally recognized and adopted. This objective has been achieved without problems.

At first sight, the directory tree of a LINUX system looks complex and unclear; in reality, however, it is well structured. The standard is intended to consolidate this structure and to explain it. Some understanding of this standard is quite helpful if you are looking for a specific configuration or data file.

Programs such as `find` or `locate` (Chapter 10) help find individual files. To obtain a quick overview, a file manager such as the Norton Commander clone `mc` (Midnight Commander) or the GNU Interactive Tool `git`, or the `dired` mode of the `emacs` editor (see also Section 5.6.3) can be useful.

2.2 Problem areas

The file system hierarchy standard not only tries to standardize the file system structure of the individual distributions, but also aims to solve a range of problems in the administration of LINUX systems – problems which became evident in the course of time.

No proper distinction was made between the directories `/bin` and `/usr/bin` in which most program files are stored, therefore, depending on the distribution, many programs could be found in either of the two directories. Furthermore, the `/bin` directory was often filled with many programs that should not necessarily have been stored in that location.

The directory `/etc` used to contain both configuration files and programs for system administration and network configuration. This caused the `/etc` directory to grow very large and difficult to handle, particularly on networked computers.

In the most common distributions, the `/usr` hierarchy could not be write-protected. This made it impossible to make a write-protected `/usr` file system available in a network via NFS. This would make a network more reliable, and the file server would not need to process the update operations of various computers. The use of a 'Life' file system on a CD was also only possible with great effort. Here, symbolic links were so often used to solve the problems that one quickly lost the overview.

No proper distinction was made between data that needed to be stored in a machine-specific way and data that could be shared by different computers. Especially with documentation, man pages, and voluminous packages such as X11 or TEX, much disk space can be saved in a network.

No proper distinction was made between machine-specific configuration and network-wide configuration, therefore maintenance of a large LINUX network was quite complicated. Thus, for example, the configuration of the kernel is typically machine-dependent, whereas the configuration of the `man` program can be the same for all machines.

Data can be static, remaining unchanged after the installation, or variable, changing all the time. Static data can be stored easily on a write-protected medium; variable data cannot. Table 2.1 shows a brief overview of some directories.

	Can be used in common	Cannot be used in common
Static data	`/usr`	`/etc`
	`/opt`	`/boot`
Variable data	`/var/mail`	`/var/run`
	`/var/spool/news`	`/var/lock`

Table 2.1   Directory cross-classification.

The file system hierarchy is in part quite different between LINUX and BSD systems. On the one hand, BSD can build on greater experience with several computer architectures; on the other, the two systems have simply been built by different developer groups. Occasionally, this makes it difficult to reach a consensus that is acknowledged by everyone involved.

2.3 The root or / file system

A UNIX file system is structured hierarchically. The starting point is the root directory, which is an anchor for a series of files and subdirectories, where the latter can in their turn contain files and further subdirectories. Unlike MS-DOS, however, UNIX does not use drive letters, but all partitions are 'mounted' into the directory tree. A user does not need to know which files are located on which partition; it is sufficient to know the path to the files.

The first file system that is mounted by the kernel at system start-up is the root or / file system. The kernel has no further information on the computer's other file systems, so all information and programs needed to proceed with system start-up must be present on this partition. The following functions are needed for system start-up or for repairs and must under all circumstances be able to be accessed from the root partition:

Mounting of file systems   At least the mount program is required, for example, to mount the /usr partition. With a /usr file system that is to be mounted by means of the NFS (Network File System), all necessary network programs, such as ifconfig, route, and ping, must be available too. On the one hand, because one wants to store as few programs in the root partition as possible, ping could also be stored under /usr/bin, but on the other hand, it is often very useful for error detection.

File system repair   In the case of a system crash, the file systems are automatically checked at the next system start-up. This is done by starting from a root file system which is only accessible for reading. All programs needed for the repair of file systems must therefore be stored in the root partition. More details on system start-up can be found in Chapter 3.

As an alternative, you can start the system from a second root partition, or use boot diskettes or an installation CD. Usually, however, you should be able to do without such aids.

Restoring a data backup   It is often sensible to store the programs and configuration files needed for data backups in the root partition, because this allows you to restore the lost data with a minimal system in case of an emergency. Chapter 7 on data backups deals with this subject in more detail.

Newcomers to LINUX might now be tempted to do without a /usr partition, or use only one partition for the entire LINUX system. In this case, all required programs would always be available, but there are a number of good reasons for keeping the root partition as small as possible and distributing the data across several partitions.

Susceptibility to errors   Errors in the root partition are a bigger problem than errors in other file systems, because they could damage the programs needed for file system checking, or other important programs, and make it necessary to use a boot or emergency floppy disk.

Since the / partition is constantly in write access, more inconsistencies than average occur during a system crash. This is specifically the case when the /tmp or /var directory is not stored on a separate partition and programs had only just created temporary files.

If mounting a partition results in a kernel error message, an Extended-2 file system can probably be mounted with the option check=none. In the event of such errors, however, only read accesses should be performed, for example for salvaging of data, and the file system should be checked as soon as possible or, if necessary, recreated.

For your peace of mind, it should be said that even after a system crash data are lost only very rarely. The programs for checking file systems, in particular the Extended-2 file system, are very powerful and reliable.

Separation of non-shareable data   The root partition cannot be shared by different computers, because too many system-specific items are to be considered, such as the drivers in the kernel, the host name, or the network address.

Several root **partitions** With small root partitions, only a little additional space is occupied on the hard disk if a second root partition is created for reasons of data security. This can then be used as an emergency or backup system.

Simple backup of user data Data can be separated for reasons of data security by distributing it across different file systems. Furthermore, the /home and /usr/local partitions can remain unmounted during a system update, so that these file systems survive a system update or reinstallation without damage. More information on the subject of data security can be found in Chapter 7.

Performance aspects A swap file is substantially slower than a swap partition, because the management functions of the file system must also be performed during swapping in and out of memory areas. A swap file in the root partition causes continuous activity of the disk and of the file system. This increases the probability of an error in the file system in the event of a system crash. Often, the /tmp directory is also stored in a separate partition or, on computers with a large amount of memory, in a RAM disk.

The access load can be distributed across different hard disks and partitions. Especially in systems equipped with several SCSI hard disks, this distribution can mean a significant gain in speed.

Current LINUX versions provide RAID levels 0, 1, and 5. This allows data to be distributed across several physical hard disks (RAID-0), to be mirrored (RAID-1), or to be secured by means of parity partition (RAID-5). RAID-0 can improve performance; RAID-1 and RAID-5 provide higher data security, since one hard disk can fail without any data being lost. More on this subject can be found in the file README.md in the kernel sources.

Using important partitions less frequently A /var partition, as well as a /tmp partition, can help reduce continuous changes to the root partition, thus minimizing the danger of loss of data.

However, distribution of the LINUX system across several partitions also has its disadvantages. On each partition there is usually some disk space that remains unused. This wastage can in the end add up to the space needed to install another program package. However, since the size of a partition can only be changed by deleting and recreating the partition, modification of partition sizes is quite laborious.

The following subsections present a detailed description of the individual directories of Table 2.2 and an explanation of the background of why the directories are created and used in this form. This includes a presentation of the ideas of the file system hierarchy standard and the directory hierarchy as a whole.

2.3.1 /bin – programs needed for system start-up

The directory /bin stores all programs that are needed for system start-up and which are also needed by non-privileged users. All programs that are needed only by the system administrator should be stored in /sbin (programs needed to proceed with system start-up) and /usr/sbin (daemons and system administration programs).

/	The root directory
/bin	Programs needed for system start-up
/boot	Files for boot loaders (for example LILO)
/dev	Devices
/etc	Machine-dependent system configuration
/home	Home directories of the users
/lib	Shared libraries (libc.so.*, libm.so.* and ld.so)
/mnt	Temporary mounting opportunity
/opt	Additional applications
/proc	Pseudo file system containing process information
/root	Home directory for the system administrator root
/sbin	System programs needed for system start-up
/tmp	Temporary files
/usr	The /usr hierarchy (see Table 2.3)
/var	Variable data
vmlinuz	Linux kernel image

Table 2.2   Overview of the root or / directory.

Programs not necessarily needed for system start-up but installed by the distribution are stored in the /usr/bin directory. Programs installed locally for the computer or network in question can be found in /usr/local/bin.

The file system hierarchy standard contains a detailed list of the (absolutely) needed programs. This list is divided into programs that should be found in /bin on every LINUX system, programs that are needed on networked computers, and a list of optional programs for backing up and restoring data.

2.3.2 /boot – the boot loader

The /boot directory stores all the data needed for the boot loader (for example LILO). This consists of boot sectors which allow other programs to be started, and backup copies of the old boot sectors.

Here, you also find the map file which contains the numbers of the sectors in which the kernel is stored. This information is needed by the LILO boot loader in order to load the kernel directly. At that point, access by means of the functions of the file system is not possible. Therefore, lilo must be newly executed every time a new kernel is installed (and consequently, the sectors in which the kernel is stored have changed). For other boot loaders, such as grub, this is not always needed.

It is also possible to store the kernel in this location. Otherwise, the kernel is found in the / directory as vmlinuz. The data stored here is machine-specific and cannot be shared by different computers. Further information on the start of a LINUX system and the different boot loaders can be found in Chapter 3.

2.3.3 /dev – device files

The /dev directory contains special files needed to access the hardware of a UNIX system. This directory is mandatory for the operation of a UNIX system and must therefore not be deleted.

Device files (devices) are created by means of the mknod program. The script to generate all device files is MAKEDEV in the /dev directory, which also sets the correct access rights. Device files set up locally by the system administrator should be entered in the script MAKEDEV.local, so these files too can be automatically created with the correct access rights.

Device files are used for communication between application programs and the kernel. A device is uniquely identified by its type (block-oriented or character-oriented), and its major and minor numbers. Block-oriented devices include, for example, hard disks, diskettes, and CD-ROM drives. Character-oriented devices include, for example, serial and parallel interfaces, the keyboard, and tape drives. The major number selects the corresponding kernel driver; the minor number is used for different purposes, depending on the device. A list of all reserved device numbers can be found in the LINUX device list in the kernel sources (./Documentation/devices.txt).

If the root file system is full, it is often worth looking in the /dev directory. It is likely that someone has tried to redirect the output of a command to the printer[1] or specify a non-existing device during file backup with tar or similar programs, which may have generated a large file in this location. Such files can usually be deleted.

2.3.4 /etc – local system configuration

Today, only configuration files are stored in the /etc directory. All programs stored here in older UNIX or LINUX systems can now be found under /sbin or /usr/sbin. Thus, even the user root no longer has the /etc directory in the search path for programs, but the directories /sbin and /usr/sbin.

With the aim of further structuring, the following subdirectories are proposed by the standard for a range of programs:

- The /etc/rc.d directory contains the scripts executed during system start-up. This applies both to the System-V-like init which is installed, for example, by the Slackware distribution, and to the 'true' System V Init. The functioning of system start-up and the different configurations are discussed in more detail in Chapter 3.

- /etc/skel contains the files copied by the adduser program into the home directory of a new user. This allows a special environment to be set up for new

---

[1] A better alternative would be using the UNIX printing system; see also Section 4.4.4.

users before their first login. A sensible selection of files might be `.profile`, `.login`, `.fvwmrc`, `.emacs`, and `.inputrc`, so paths can be set and users can find an environment that they can start to use without modifications. This may be, for example, a system-wide or network-wide standard configuration which facilitates new users in their first contact with the system and simplifies user support.

- `/etc/X11` is reserved for the machine-specific X configuration, among others for the file `XF86Config`. XFree86, however, will not be able to find the file in this location, therefore a corresponding symbolic link must be established (for example from `/etc/XF86Config`). In addition, subdirectories for the individual window managers and the X display manager `xdm` can be created. The `/etc/X11/xdm` directory then stores the configuration files which could previously be found under `/usr/lib/X11/xdm`. More details on `xdm` configuration can be found in Chapter 6.

- `/etc/opt` contains the configuration of packages installed under `/opt`.

For the `/etc` directory, the file system hierarchy standard lists a series of files that should be stored here, depending on whether the computer is networked or not, or whether, for example, the system is equipped with shadow passwords. Here, the passwords are stored in the file `/etc/shadow`, which can only be read by the user `root`. The file `/etc/passwd`, which can be read by all users, no longer contains encrypted passwords, so password decryption by means of dictionaries is no longer possible.

2.3.5 /home – the users' home directories

Apart from his or her own home directory, a user possesses write access rights only at very few points in the file system. If at all possible, home directories should be stored on a separate partition, so that this data is not affected by a reinstallation of the system. This solution also provides good separation between system data and user data for backup purposes.

A further advantage is the 'hardware quota,' which ensures that users can only fill their own `/home` partition up to the brim with data. The overall performance of the system is maintained. With a full `root`, `/tmp` or `/var` partition, system performance can be hampered. Therefore, the Extended-2 file system creates a `root` reserve which can only be used by the system administrator. The `tune2fs` program can be used to specify the percentage of reserved blocks and the user who is allowed to use these blocks.

With kernel version 2.0, the long-desired quota support has been incorporated into the standard kernel. This makes it possible to assign individual users or user groups only a given part of the hard disk space. A distinction is made between a soft limit, which can temporarily be overdrawn, and the hard limit, which prevents further writing attempts. On many computers (with reasonable users) these functions are not needed, but with a large number of users and limited disk space, the use of quotas can be a sensible precaution.

The use of /home directories is a special feature of LINUX, but it is widely employed, and the meaning is obvious. Other UNIX systems often use /users, /usr/users or similar directories. These directories are often further subdivided, for example, into different user groups, such as students, staff, or system administrators. The final subdivision is, however, a decision that system administrators should make on the basis of local requirements.

Programs (and users) should not directly refer to the home directory by name, but should use the shell variable HOME or, depending on the shell, the short form with the tilde character (˜). In C programs, the function getpwent() should be used.

2.3.6 /lib – shared libraries

This is the storage for all shared libraries that are needed for system start-up. All other shared libraries (for example those of X11 or of the SVGA library) should remain in the /usr partition so long as they are not mandatory for system start-up. For reasons of compatibility with other systems, a link /lib/cpp to the C preprocessor is required because some programs start the C preprocessor with this name.

The /lib/modules subdirectory stores the kernel modules that can be loaded dynamically at runtime. The file system hierarchy standard does not contain a more precise specification; in the current kernel implementation, for each kernel version a corresponding directory is created, where the modules are stored ordered by subsystem.

2.3.7 /mnt – temporary mounting opportunity

Frequently, the system administrator must 'just quickly' mount an additional file system. This may be a further hard disk partition, a floppy disk, or a network directory mounted via NFS. For this purpose, the directory /mnt can be used. As a rule, no other file systems should be mounted here.

Installation programs should use another directory to prevent overlaps and other problems. Separate directories should be created for devices that are mounted continuously and even by normal (non-privileged) users. Then, the corresponding options for the mount command can be entered in the /etc/fstab file. Thus, these options need no longer be specified every time; it is sufficient, for example, to indicate the device or the mount point. More information on this subject can be found in Section 4.4.3.

On my own systems, I have either fixed mounts in various subdirectories under the /mount directory, or I use the automounter amd to carry out the corresponding mounts. The current kernel version additionally includes the autofs function, which implements an automounter in the kernel.

2.3.8 Additional software packages in /opt

The /opt directory is used for the storage of larger program packages which are installed in addition to the system itself. For each software package, a separate directory /opt/*package* should be created which contains the static data of the package. The executable programs are stored under /opt/*package*/bin, the man pages in the corresponding man directory.

Locally, the system administrator can create the directories /opt/bin, /opt/man, and so on (in analogy to /usr/local), for example, to install scripts for calling the installed packages or other front ends.

Variable data of packages should be stored under /var/opt, configurations under /etc/opt. Lock, PID, and device files are stored in the usual UNIX directories.

Usually, /opt is used to store programs not supplied with the distribution, but which originate from a source that system administrators do not necessarily have under their control. Thus, packages such as StarOffice, WABI, or KDE are installed under /opt. Programs compiled and installed by system administrators will still be stored in /usr/local.

2.3.9 /proc – process information

The /proc file system does not really exist and therefore does not take up any space on the hard disk. Here, the LINUX kernel makes internal information available to other processes. Thus, for example, the ps program reads the /proc file system to obtain the required information on currently running processes.

Programs that display network statistics often use the /proc file system. Therefore, this file system should be available on all LINUX computers, and should be mounted at this precise point. To achieve this, you must answer the question '/proc file system support' with 'y', and the file /etc/fstab should contain a corresponding entry. This is the case with all current distributions.

This file system makes kernel-related programs largely independent of the kernel version and of the internal data structures used. The ps program, which reads this information from the device /dev/kmem (kernel memory), always depends on the kernel version used and must readapt its data structures to the new kernel after each kernel update. After internal changes in kernel structures, this program is often no longer operational, so most users employ the /proc file system.

A further interesting application of the /proc file system is the possibility of watching a running LINUX kernel in the debugger. Although you cannot set breakpoints, you can still look into internal data structures:

```
(Linux):~# gdb /usr/src/linux/vmlinux /proc/kcore
```

For compatibility with other systems, you can establish a symbolic link named /dev/core to the (virtual) file /proc/kcore. This file contains a kernel memory image in the 'core' format used by the debugger.

2.3.10 /root – the system administrator's home directory

Traditionally, the user root had the home directory /. This led to the practically unavoidable consequence that several files were created in / which made the root directory too large to retain a clear overview. In order to keep this directory small with regard to the number of directory entries, today the /root directory is often used as the system administrator's home directory.

This directory should, however, be located in the root partition to allow the system administrator to log in even if no further partitions are mounted. There are login programs which use / automatically as the home directory when the directory specified in the file /etc/passwd is not available, but there are also programs that refuse a login. In this case, even the user root would be locked out from the system.

Electronic mail for the user root should be redirected to a normal user; this can be done by creating a file ~/.forward which contains the name of the user who is to receive the mail. Alternatively, a sendmail alias can be created. Similarly, the user root should not be used to read or write news, or to work on the system on a day-by-day basis.

2.3.11 /sbin – system programs needed for system start-up

The /sbin directory contains all the programs required for system start-up before the /usr file system is mounted, plus programs only needed by the system administrator. Programs that are also needed by non-privileged users should be stored in either /bin or /usr/bin, to prevent these users from having sbin directories in the search path. Important programs installed in the /sbin directory include, among others:

- The init program is responsible for system start-up. The system administrator can use it to change the runlevel – that is, the mode of operation of the LINUX system – for example, to switch the system into network server mode.
- Programs for file system maintenance and repair, such as, for example, mkfs*, fsck*, and fdisk. This group also includes the mkswap and swapon programs. Especially with computers with only a small amount of main RAM, it is often necessary to create additional virtual memory before creating or checking file systems.
- Essential network programs, such as ifconfig or route, are used to initialize the network at system start-up and ensure that the /usr partition can also be mounted via NFS.

Programs that can also be employed by normal users in everyday operation, such as ping, shells, or tar, should be installed in the /bin directory if they are required for system start-up or for restoring operations. The /bin and /sbin directories were not separated for reasons of system security. Therefore, these directories can (and should) be readable by all users, and the programs contained in them should be executable. Exceptions are obviously sensible for setuid or setgid programs (see Chapter 4).

2.3.12 /tmp – temporary files

Here is where programs can create temporary files. It is, however, not specified how long these files should be kept. On computers with a large amount of memory, the /tmp directory can be located on a RAM disk. The FHS recommends that the /tmp directory should be deleted at every reboot.

In other UNIX systems, it is standard practice for the /tmp directory to be deleted at every system start-up or at given intervals. For the latter, you may want to adapt the script shown in Listing 2.1 to your specific requirements. This shell script deletes files that have not been read during the past three days, and old, empty directories.

```
if [ -d /tmp ]; then
cd /tmp && {
find . -type f -atime +3 -exec rm -f -- {} \;
find . ! -name . -type d -mtime +1 \
    -exec rmdir -- {} \; >/dev/null 2>&1; }
fi
```

Listing 2.1   Deleting the /tmp directory.

Please note that this script was not designed with security in mind and that it can induce non-privileged users of the system to delete arbitrary files. The Red Hat distribution contains the tmpwatch program for this purpose, which was developed with regard to security. For your home computer, the simple script is certainly sufficient, but in more complex environments it is definitely not secure enough.

The /tmp directory must be writable for all users, because many programs use it to create their temporary files. Examples are crontab or mail readers when an external editor is called. If the /tmp directory is not writable, a great many programs will simply quit, often leaving it unclear that this was the reason. For security reasons, the t bit should be set for this directory, so that users can only delete their own files.

It is equally annoying, however, if the tmp directory is full. If your computer is behaving in a strange way, have a look at the contents and access rights of the /tmp directory and the available disk space.

2.4 The /usr hierarchy

On many LINUX systems, the /usr file system occupies the lion's share of disk space. This is where most programs that are supplied with a distribution are installed. The same structure as the one described here could (and should) be recreated under /usr/local. That is where the system administrator installs all programs needed locally for the computer or local network of computers in addition to what the distribution already supplies. Immediately after a first installation, /usr/local should not contain any files.

The /usr file system contains data that can be used by different computers but that do not need to be write-accessible. This allows the /usr file system to be mounted write-protected via NFS, or with a 'live' file system from a CD. This is an alternative to buying a new hard disk, especially for 'nosing around' in LINUX and when little hard disk space is available. The disadvantages are the slow access to data and programs, and a certain loss of functionality, because the CD must be permanently inserted.

For large program packages such as TEX or emacs, no directories should be created directly under /usr, but a new directory under /usr/lib should be used. This is intended to prevent the /usr directory from becoming too large and complex. Table 2.3 shows an overview of the directories usually found under /usr.

/usr	The /usr hierarchy
⊢ X11R6	The X Window system
⊢ bin	Practically all programs
⊢ games	Games
⊢ include	Header files for C programs
⊢ lib	Libraries and program packages
⊢ local	Local installations (initially empty)
⊢ sbin	Programs for the system administrator
⊢ share	Architecture-independent data
⊢ src	Source code of various programs

Table 2.3   Overview of the /usr hierarchy.

Until all programs have been adapted to the file system hierarchy standard, symbolic links such as those shown in Table 2.4 should be established. Once all programs that use a directory of the old, now obsolete, structure have been recompiled, these links can be removed. This is generally the case with today's distributions.

Old directory	New directory
/usr/adm	/var/adm
/usr/preserve	/var/preserve
/usr/spool	/var/spool
/usr/tmp	/var/tmp
/var/spool/locks	/var/lock

Table 2.4   Compatibility links for /usr and /var.

2.4.1 The /usr/X11R6 directory

In this directory, Release 6 of the X Window system is installed. This is both the path in which the binary distribution of the XFree86 team is installed and the default path if you want to compile X11R6 yourself. To facilitate system management and installation of additional X programs, and also compatibility with other systems, the symbolic links specified in Table 2.5 can be established.

Symbolic name	Real name
/usr/bin/X11	/usr/X11R6/bin
/usr/lib/X11	/usr/X11R6/lib/X11
/usr/include/X11	/usr/X11R6/include/X11

Table 2.5 Compatibility links for X.

2.4.2 /usr/bin – programs

The /usr/bin directory is the primary directory for programs in a LINUX or UNIX system. An exception is constituted by programs that are exclusively destined to be used by the system administrator (these programs are stored in the corresponding sbin directory), programs that have been locally installed by the administrator in /usr/local for the system in question, and the programs required for system start-up, which must be located in /bin.

When creating scripts that are started via the #! mechanism, you must specify the complete path to the corresponding interpreter. The character sequence #! tells the kernel that the program cannot be started directly, but has to be processed by an interpreter. Thus, the interpreter is loaded and passed the script.

The absolute path is no problem for sh or csh scripts since these programs can be found in the /bin directory in every UNIX system. More problems are caused by interpreters, such as perl, tcl, or python, which are often installed in different locations. Thus, scripts that use these interpreters can often not be ported unchanged from one system to the other, because the path in the first line of the script must be modified. Here, the file system hierarchy standard recommends that these interpreters should be installed in the /usr/bin directory, or that symbolic links to the programs should be established. Then scripts can reference the interpreter in /usr/bin, independently of the directory in which the programs are actually installed.

2.4.3 /usr/include – include files

This directory contains the header or include files for the C library libc. It contains a series of subdirectories in which the header files for different subsystems are stored. The header files belonging to libc are not complete; the kernel-specific header files are missing. Here, the symbolic links in the kernel sources (generated by means of `make symlinks` in the kernel directory) are of the utmost importance, otherwise many system-related programs cannot be compiled.

2.4.4 /usr/lib – libraries and program packages

This directory stores the libraries and object files required for programming, but also internal programs of the GNU C compiler `gcc`. In addition, there is a range of other static data. Each program package that needs static, processor-type-independent data should install this data in a subdirectory under `/usr/lib`.

Old `sendmail` versions used to be installed as `/usr/lib/sendmail`. Therefore, this path is hard-coded in many other programs. The `sendmail` program is now installed in the `/usr/sbin` directory. For reasons of compatibility, you should therefore create a corresponding symbolic link. The `/usr/sbin` directory should be readable for all users, and the `sendmail` program should be executable for all users. The `smail` program is also installed in `/usr/sbin`, but you must also create a symbolic link with the name `sendmail`.

2.4.5 /usr/local – locally installed software

Here, you can and should create essentially the same hierarchy as under `/usr`. The system administrator can install local programs which are not part of a distribution (see Table 2.6). After the installation of a distribution, this hierarchy should be empty except for the names of directories, so that programs belonging to the distribution and subsequently installed programs can be identified. This separation facilitates system maintenance both when installing or updating a distribution and when installing other programs.

/usr/local	The /usr/local hierarchy
├ bin	Locally installed programs
├ games	Games
├ include	Header files for C programs
├ lib	Libraries and program packages
├ local	Local installations (initially empty)
├ sbin	Programs for the system administrator
├ share	Architecture-independent data
└ src	Source code of various programs

Table 2.6   Overview of the /usr/local hierarchy.

When updating a distribution, you must be aware that program files in `/usr` or `/` may be overwritten. By definition, the `/usr/local` directory is the complete responsibility of the local system administrator and is therefore not modified. For safety, you can also simply unmount this directory (and remove it from the file `/etc/fstab`).

2.4.6 /usr/sbin – **further system programs**

Here, the system administrator will find a series of programs for system management. These programs, however, are not needed in emergencies, but only during normal operation. This is usually where you will find network daemons, programs for system administration, and servers started in the so-called multi-user mode. Locally installed programs for the system administrator should be stored in the /usr/local/sbin directory.

2.4.7 /usr/share – **architecture-independent data**

In the initial stage of LINUX, only Intel-based PCs were supported. Therefore, there was no distinction between processor-dependent data and processor-independent data. Today, ports for practically all hardware platforms are available or under development, so this situation has changed. In the /usr/share directory, you will find data that are static and can be shared by different computers with different processor architectures.

Many of the data stored here could previously be found under /usr/lib, /usr/man, or /usr/doc. For reasons of downward compatibility, individual directories may still be installed under /usr/lib; this depends on the distributor.

Table 2.7 shows an overview of the directories allowed here. Since this directory has only been incorporated into the FHS with version 2.0, this hierarchy is still seldom used. Once version 2.0 has been accepted by all developers and distributors, this will change very quickly.

/usr/share	The /usr/share hierarchy
├ dict	All kinds of dictionaries
├ doc	Documentation for packages and FAQs
├ games	Static data for games
├ info	Online documentation of the GNU programs
├ locale	Data for National Language Support
├ man	Online manual
├ nls	National Language Support
├ misc	Various data
├ terminfo	The terminal database
├ tmac	troff macros lacking with groff
└ zoneinfo	Time zone information

Table 2.7   Overview of the /usr/share hierarchy.

Many of the ideas incorporated into the design of the /usr/share directory originate from BSD projects. These equally freely available systems were ported quite early to different hardware platforms, therefore some experience was gained. Time will show how useful this directory will be under LINUX.

The /usr/share/dict directory

In this directory, dictionaries are stored, for example for ispell. These dictionaries should bear the English term for the language and preferably use a unique character set. It is not defined how a dictionary not stored in an ISO character set is to be marked.

/usr/share/man - online documentation

In this directory tree, the man pages are stored. The structure presented here can also be found under /usr/local/man for locally installed programs and under /usr/X11R6/man for man pages on the X Window system. The online documentation is subdivided into the following sections, where one subdirectory mansection exists for each section:

- 1 – **Commands**: documentation of the commands that a user can call at the shell prompt.
- 2 – **System calls**: operating system calls which are processed by the kernel.
- 3 – **Functions of the C library**: the documentation of many functions of the standard C library.
- 4 – **Device files**: description of many special files (devices) from the /dev directory.
- 5 – **File formats and conventions**: description of syntax and meaning of many configuration files, for example, /etc/passwd and /etc/syslog.conf.
- 6 – **Games**: description of the installed games.
- 7 – **Macro descriptions and standards**: hints on and documentation of macro packages (for example groff) or standards (for example character sets).
- 8 – **Commands for the system administrator**: description of the commands which are used only by the system administrator for system management.

The /usr/share/man directory is the primary manual directory. Here, you will find all man pages for the programs contained in / and /usr.

In directories other than /usr/share/man, individual sections can be omitted if no manual pages are needed for these sections. This applies, for example, to category 4, device files, which usually exists only under /usr/share/man, but not under /usr/local/man.

Man pages are currently distributed in English. It is, however, desirable that programs should in future also be supplied with translated man pages. A group of committed users working with Martin Schulze is doing just that for German translations.

For an ordered, language-dependent access, you need to create a subdirectory for each new language in which the above-mentioned structure is created again. For manual pages in English, you can still use the path `/usr/share/man/mansection`; German manual pages would be found under `/usr/share/man/de_DE.88591/mansection`. The names of the directories are derived from the POSIX.1 standard; a precise explanation can be found in Section 8.3.

If a distribution installs preformatted man pages, this can be done in the `catman` directory. Installing only preformatted man pages is generally considered poor style. Users can view this documentation only on screen, but cannot output it as a PostScript or DVI file. This makes a visually appealing printout impossible.

/usr/share/misc – miscellaneous

Many programs have only one or a few files that can be stored under `/usr/share`. Since it is not worth creating a separate subdirectory for each program, it has been decided to propose this directory. The FHS contains a list of files that are likely to be found here.

2.4.8 /usr/src – source texts of programs and the kernel

This is where all (non-local) source texts that are needed for the compilation of programs or of the kernel should be stored. The `include` files of the kernel are particularly important, because these are often also required for the compilation of applications. Each distribution that installs the C compiler should at least store the `include` files in this directory.

The kernel sources can usually be found in the `/usr/src/linux` directory. It is very important that the `include` files belonging to the kernel are not copied into the `/usr/include` directory, but that a symbolic link is established from `/usr/include/linux` to `/usr/src/linux/include/linux`. Similarly, a link for the `asm` directory must be created. If the `include` files are copied, the result is likely to be a mixture of old and new files, which can cause the most peculiar errors. For system-related programs such as `DOSemu`, it is definitely required that the kernel itself is recompiled. At the very least, in any case, a `make config` should be executed.

The `/usr/src/linux` directory (or even `/usr/src` itself) can be a symbolic link, for example to `/var/src`. This is sensible for a write-protected `/usr` file system, such as a 'Life' file system on a CD.

Subdirectories can be created in this directory. Thus, the BOGUS distribution structures the subdirectories, in accordance with the installation target directories, into directories such as `bin`, `usr.bin` or `sbin`. This certainly facilitates maintenance of the distribution.

2.5 /var – variable data

This directory hierarchy contains variable data. Since this hierarchy has only found a wider audience with FHS-compatible distributions, many older systems still do not have a clean separation between /usr and /var. This separation is sensible if we wish to avoid the LINUX partition that is often the largest (/usr) having to be mounted with write access. Modern distributions usually follow the rules of the FHS.

With version 2.0 of the FHS, a great many changes have taken place, but it will be some time before they become an accepted part of the distributions. Basically, these changes are a consequence of LINUX getting closer to other UNIX systems.

Many of the directories were introduced to avoid individual programs or program packages requiring a writable /usr partition. Therefore, some of the directories presented here are optional for many systems, while others must be created by the system administrator for new software. So long as not all programs have been completely adapted to this standard, the system administrator will always have to think about how individual programs can sensibly be configured and installed.

/var	Variable data
├ account	Accounting data (process accounting)
├ cache	Cache for application data
├ games	Variable data of games
├ lock	Lock files
├ log	Log files and directories
├ mail	Mail boxes of the users
├ opt	Variable data from /opt
├ run	PID files of processes
├ spool	Directories for waiting queues
├ state	Status information
├ tmp	Temporary files
└ yp	Network Information System

Table 2.8   Overview of the /var hierarchy.

In very old distributions, /var used to be a symbolic link to the /usr directory. This made a separation of the two directory hierarchies impossible, since some programs used /var and others /usr to access the same file. If it is necessary to represent /var by a symbolic link, for example because no separate /var partition was created or the space in the root partition is not sufficient, this link should, for example, point to the /usr/var directory.

2.5.1   Process accounting (/var/account)

This directory contains the variable data of the process accounting, provided the distribution supports it. Accounting can establish, for example, when a certain user executed a command and which resources were needed. For many private systems, this is not necessary, but many commercial computer centers invoice, for example, for CPU time used.

If your distribution does not supply the corresponding tools, then you can find them on every GNU mirror as `acct-6.3.tar.gz`. Please note that the raw data can grow to a great extent. Therefore, you should convert this data periodically into a sum.

2.5.2 /var/cache – cache for applications

This directory hierarchy was newly introduced with version 2.0 of the FHS. This is the storage for data created by time-intensive calculations or other complicated operations. If this data is available in later runs, calculations need not be performed again, because the existing data can be used.

One could think, for example, of WWW proxy caches, TEX fonts, or pre-formatted man pages. The applications can organize deletion of obsolete data, but the administrator too can delete this data (almost) without problems, for example, if disk space is running out.

This directory has been introduced to allow administrators to define, for example, their own backup rules specially for this kind of data. For many private systems, this is a secondary issue, but for publicly accessible computers on which many users work with TEX, it might be a good idea to store the generated fonts.

/var/cache/man – locally formatted man pages

This (optional) directory is designed to contain the locally formatted man pages where there is a write-protected `/usr` partition. Storing the formatted man pages is often worth while, because with large man pages, formatting can take a relatively long time. If the `/usr` partition is writable, the formatted man pages could also be stored directly in `/usr/man/cat[1-9]`; however, it is recommended that one of the following procedures be used:

- All man pages can be formatted by means of the `catman` program and then stored in `/usr/man/cat[1-9]`. Thus, the `nroff` formatting program for man pages is no longer called when a user wants to look at the documentation.

- No formatted man pages are stored. This causes reformatting of the corresponding man page at each call of the `man` program. On relatively slow computers, this can lead to annoying delays if a large man page is reformatted several times in a row.

- The formatted man pages can be stored under `/var/man/catman`. This directory then serves as a cache for formatted man pages.

The structure under `/var/catman` must now also reflect the availability of translated man pages and the different directories in which man pages are stored. If you ever get into the situation when you have to create these directories yourself, you will find a proposal for a possible structure in the FHS.

2.5.3 /var/games – variable data of games (high scores)

Here, only variable data of games are stored, such as results or high-score lists. Often it is sensible to create a special group (for example games) and make this directory writable for this group. Static data, such as levels or help texts, are stored in the /usr/lib/games directory.

2.5.4 /var/local – variable data from /usr/local

This directory is intended to store variable data for programs installed locally by the system administrator. Since the authors of the FHS do not know which programs will be installed locally, no further subdivision of this directory is proposed. The use of this directory is the system administrator's business.

If, however, the files fit into a category introduced here, they should be stored in that location. This applies, for example, to lock files, which should be stored in /var/lock.

2.5.5 /var/lock – lock files

All lock files used for locking devices against multiple use should be created in the /var/lock directory. No lock files should be created in the /usr partition to allow this partition to be mounted write-protected.

The name of a lock file begins with LCK.., followed by the name of the device to be locked. Thus, to lock the device /dev/ttyS0, the file /var/lock/LCK..ttyS0 is used.

All lock files should be readable for every user and contain the process number of the process to be locked in clear text. Thus, each program can check whether the process that created the lock still exists.

It is sensible to do without the symbolic link /dev/modem and to use the true device instead. Lock files can then be created exclusively for true devices. On the one hand, a device is not going to be addressed under two different names; on the other hand, for symbolic links, the semantics of the chown system call under LINUX does not correspond to that of other systems.

Standardization of this directory should sensibly increase the cross-functionality between different programs whose synchronization is carried out via lock files. This is, first, because *all* programs create their lock files here, and, second, because the FHS specifies a standard format for the contents of these files.

2.5.6 /var/log – all kinds of log files

Even without programs such as syslogd, a UNIX system always writes a series of log files. These are used for system monitoring and error detection. Examples of such files are lastlog for the date of the last user login and wtmp for the times of all login and logout processes.

Log files created by root processes can be directly stored in this directory. If log files are generated by systems such as news and UUCP which run under their own user IDs, a separate directory should be created for each ID, which is writable for exactly this ID.

2.5.7 /var/mail – mailboxes of the UNIX users

The /var/mail directory contains the mail of the users in UNIX format (mbox). This directory has been shifted from /var/spool/mail to improve cross-functionality with many other systems.

2.5.8 /var/opt – variable data for programs from /opt

This directory is used to store variable data of the packages installed under /opt. As under /opt, a separate subdirectory should be created for each package.

2.5.9 /var/run – PID files of processes

Here, the PID (process id) files for daemons are stored, so that the process number of a background process can be identified easily. These files should be called *program*.pid and should contain the process number in clear text. This facilitates sending a signal to a background process, for example the syslog daemon (see also Listing 2.2).

```
(Linux):~# kill -HUP `cat /var/run/syslog.pid`
```

Listing 2.2   Use of lock files at the shell prompt.

This directory should also be employed for UNIX domain sockets that are used for communication between programs. Since daemons are started under different user IDs (the news daemons, for example, run under the user name news) this directory must be writable for all users. For reasons of security, however, the t bit should be set as with the tmp directories. Thus, users can only delete a file that they themselves own. An alternative could be for appropriate subdirectories to be created, which would then be writable only for the corresponding user or for a special program.

2.5.10 /var/spool – directories for waiting queues

The /var/spool directory is used for temporary storage of uucp jobs, printer outputs, or other tasks that the system must carry out at a later time. Often, the data is automatically deleted after the task has been executed. The precise structure of this directory is determined by the system administrator, on the basis of the available hardware and software environment. Table 2.9 shows an overview of subdirectories which might exist in /var/spool.

/var/spool	Spool directories
├ cron	Tasks for cron and at
├ lpd	Waiting queues for the printing system
├ mqueue	Waiting queue for outgoing electronic mail
├ news	Directory for news storage and delivery
├ rwho	Working files of the rwho daemons
├ smail	Waiting queues for smail
└ uucp	Waiting queues for UUCP

Table 2.9 Overview of the /var/spool directory.

2.5.11 Variable status information – /var/state

This directory contains variable information about the status of individual applications. Users should never get into a situation where they have to modify one of these files.

In old versions of the FHS, there used to be the directory /var/lib, which was replaced with /var/state. Data stored here are persistent and are preserved even after a reboot of the system.

Examples are the database of the package management of a distribution or the locate database. No log files or spool data should be stored here.

For individual packages, separate directories can and should be created. The FHS provides several examples which are of particular interest for distributors and system integrators.

2.5.12 /var/tmp – temporary files

Like /tmp, the /var/tmp directory is a directory for temporary files. It is used to keep the root partition, which also contains the /tmp directory, as small as possible. Here too, it is up to the system administrator to decide how long the data is kept in /var/tmp. However, the data should be kept for at least as long as the data in the /tmp directory.

2.5.13 /var/yp – Network Information Service (NIS)

The Network Information Service (NIS) was formerly known under the name of Yellow Pages (YP). With this service, files such as passwd or group can be centrally maintained on a NIS server; all clients receive this data via the network. The /var/yp directory is used to store the corresponding data. More details on the configuration of the Network Information Service are given in Chapter 22.

NIS should not be confused with the extended version NIS+. NIS+ uses /var/nis as its directory.

2.6 The further development of the FHS

In today's form, the file system hierarchy standard is generally recognized among LINUX users as a sensible and reasonable agreement. Nevertheless, there still are (and will probably continue to be) significant differences between the individual distributions.

Whenever these differences (may) lead to problems, there will be a discussion in the corresponding mailing list. At present, there is a discussion about the integration of (commercial) packages into the standard, and the use of the file hierarchy standard for the *BSD systems as well.

Although different opinions are brought forward about many issues, which occasionally cause lively 'flare-ups,' the mailing list is a very productive institution. Because of the very extensive discussion going on, traffic is very high when compared to other mailing lists, with regard to both the number and the extent of the messages.

System start-up

3

When a computer starts up, it is as though something magic happens. The process is commonly known as 'bootstrapping.' The image this gives is of someone pulling himself up by his own bootstraps. But there are logical explanations which show that each step of the process assumes specific outcomes from the previous steps, so that there is always a solid base for the next step. The start-up of a LINUX PC has the following phases:

- Execution of the Power On Self Test (POST) of the Basic Input/Output System (BIOS); this is often stored in ROM or flash EPROM.
- Execution of a boot loader from a floppy disk, hard disk, or recently also from a CD-ROM drive.
- Start of the kernel by means of the boot loader.
- Processing of the individual configuration via `init`.

3.1 The Basic Input/Output System (BIOS)

The first part of the boot process is performed by the BIOS of the main board. This software, which is mainly stored in EPROMs (and recently also in flash EPROMs) contains a series of functions, the so-called BIOS interrupts, for example `0x10` for screen control or `0x13` for diskette and hard disk access. This means that minor deviations in hardware control can be adjusted by means of corresponding adaptations of the BIOS – this was one of the reasons for the success of IBM-compatible PCs.

Any expansion board or component designed to be IBM-compatible must react to appropriate calls, for example initialization by the BIOS, in a well-defined manner. This created a certain independence from specific peripheral devices, which substantially contributed to the development of the market for IBM-compatible components. Properly speaking, the compatibility is with Intel, more precisely with

35

the Intel 8088/86 processor, since the software burnt into the BIOS chips consists of instructions for this processor.

There is a multitude of BIOS versions, practically one for each type of motherboard. How individual functions are implemented and in which order they are processed is, to a certain extent, the business of the manufacturer. The following overview of a BIOS start-up should therefore be seen only as an example.

After switching the power on, the BIOS is, via hardware, loaded into the memory area from 0xF000:E000 to 0xF000:FFFF, and the program counter is set to the address 0xF000:FFF0, which starts the execution of the BIOS codes. The processor starts in the so-called real mode, thus only the memory below 1 Mbyte is available. Usually, the BIOS only contains code for this mode, so it cannot be used by protected-mode systems such as LINUX.

Before the BIOS begins to test itself and the computer's periphery, it checks the memory area between the graphics adapter on address 0xA000 and its own starting address for BIOS extensions of other plug-in boards, for example network cards. Cards with their own BIOS are recognized from the BIOS signature 0xAA55 or 0x55AA at the end of a 32K block.

The BIOS then executes the 'Power On Self Test' (POST): the functions of the processor itself, the registers, and several commands are checked; if the processor is defective, the PC is halted, logically without displaying a message. With some errors, some BIOS versions produce acoustic signals which, according to the number of beeps, provide information on the nature of the error. Then, checksums are made over the ROM itself and compared with the stored values to detect possible defects in the ROM BIOS or, if it was already copied into RAM, in the corresponding RAM component.

Subsequently, further components of the motherboard, such as interrupt and DMA controllers and main memory, are tested and initialized. The POST continues with checks of keyboard, diskette, and hard disk drives. The results of this test are stored in BIOS variables, and the interrupt vector table is initialized. By means of the BIOS interrupt 0x19, the boot process itself is initiated or the 'bootstrap loader' is called.

The early initialization of the extension cards makes it possible for a network card to take over the function of the boot loader during the further course of the boot process. This function is used if one wants to boot a computer via a network. This has several advantages:

- Even when the computer is switched off, you can carry out configuration adaptations on the boot server.
- The computer needs no hard disk or only a small one for swapping. This makes it very quiet.
- A computer can be reconfigured relatively easily, for example with a new IP address or a new kernel.

Obviously this function has some disadvantages: the network load increases and some accesses are slower via NFS than on a local hard disk. If you wish to use this function, you can find additional documentation in the file `Documentation/nfs-root.txt` in the kernel sources and in the Mini-HowTos `NFS-Root` and `NFS-Root-client`.

3.1.1 Loading from floppy disk or hard disk

In a sequence which is the same for all operating systems, attempts are made to read the first sector of `/dev/fd0` (drive `A:`) and then of `/dev/hda` (drive `C:`). More recent BIOS versions allow a different order to be specified via a setup; this changed order is then stored in the CMOS RAM. With floppy disks, this first sector is called the boot sector; with hard disks, it is called the Master Boot Record (MBR). The size is always 512 bytes. You can only boot from SCSI disks if no IDE disks are installed in the system, because the BIOS does not support this function.

Many UNIX workstations can also be booted from tape or from CD; these functions too are only implemented in more recent PC BIOS versions or in the BIOS of the SCSI controller. If your BIOS supports this function, you can boot directly from a LINUX CD and install the system – without diskettes.

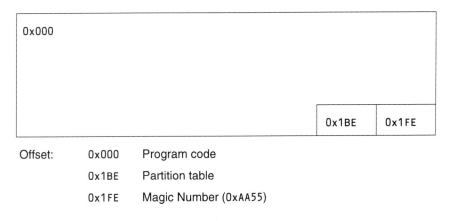

Offset: 0x000   Program code

                0x1BE   Partition table

                0x1FE   Magic Number (0xAA55)

Figure 3.1   Structure of a Master Boot Record.

The MBR (see Figure 3.1) of a hard disk contains four entries of 16 bytes each, that is one for each of the four possible (primary) partitions. If a primary partition is further subdivided, it is called an extended partition; up to four so-called logical drives can be created per (extended) partition; that is, you can have a maximum of 16 logical drives per hard disk. For reasons of simplicity, the structure of the first sector of an extended partition corresponds to the structure of the MBR.

Besides specifications regarding the type of partition (for example: Linux = 0x83, Linux Swap = 0x82) and start, end, and size of the partition, each of the four partition entries of the MBR also contains a boot flag which indicates whether the partition is 'active' and therefore used for booting. Only one partition at a time can be marked as active by the boot flag; this is then booted from the standard MBR.

The program code located before the partition table of the MBR loads the boot sector of the partition marked as active and is therefore called the boot loader. Independently of the operating system used, a boot loader when booting from a hard disk has the task of determining the active partition and loading the boot sector of this active partition by making use of the BIOS routines. This is also the function of the standard MS-DOS boot sector. Whenever possible, you should leave the MBR unchanged and install, for example, LILO into the boot sector of the root partition instead.

In the beginning, there were only primary partitions under MS-DOS – therefore, the MS-DOS `fdisk` can only activate primary partitions. Modern boot loaders under LINUX, in contrast, offer many more possibilities; among others you can also boot from logical drives in extended partitions. The MS-DOS boot sequence is as follows:

MBR	Boot sector	Operating system
DOS-MBR →	DOS boot sector →	MS-DOS (IO.SYS, MSDOS.SYS)

Recent LINUX versions are so large that they can no longer be loaded into the first megabyte of memory. Possible solutions are kernel modules or the generation of a `bzImage` which is already loaded in protected mode.

3.2 The LINUX boot loader

In contrast to the MS-DOS process, modern boot loaders such as LILO under LINUX offer many more possibilities; for example, booting of other operating systems, changing between different versions of an operating system, and passing of parameters at the start of the kernel.

The three most important boot loaders for LINUX are: LILO, `loadlin`, and `syslinux`. All three boot loaders share the capability for accepting parameters or arguments passed quasi 'by hand' at the call or at a certain point of time during loading. These parameters either affect the boot loader itself, the kernel or the `init` process, or they are stored as environment variables and can thus be used for the configuration of the process to be started. These specifications are often called kernel command line parameters – the name boot parameters would, however, be more appropriate since many system administrators encounter them primarily in special configuration files.

The parameters for the boot loader itself contain information such as the name and path of the kernel file to be loaded and an indication of the partition on which it can be found. All parameters which the boot loaders do not understand are simply passed to the kernel; what the kernel itself or a device driver evaluates mostly regards presence and, if needed, configuration of detected hardware. The kernel in turn passes the parameters it does not know, or those it recognizes but does not process, on to `init`. The values that even `init` does not recognize are stored as environment variables in the format `variable=value` and can thus be evaluated by a shell or any other program.

This flexibility of the various programs involved in handling the boot parameters, however, also has the consequence that options are not only passed but
sometimes overwritten. This is, for example, intentional when values hard-compiled
into the kernel, such as the interrupt and port of a network card, turn out to be incorrect at a later stage.

A current development is the boot loader grub (Grand Unified Bootloader).
This program is substantially more flexible than LILO and can boot many other systems besides LINUX. The use of grub still requires changes to the kernel, but once
these have been incorporated into the standard, this could become the boot loader of
choice. At boot time, grub can read and boot arbitrary files from an Extended-2 file
system, so it is much safer and more flexible than LILO.

3.2.1 The LINUX loader LILO

LILO by Werner Almesberger is the most widely used and flexible boot loader for
LINUX. The abbreviation LILO stands for LINUX loader; LILO can, however, load
other operating systems too. Many LINUX users notice LILO for the first time after
the installation of a LINUX distribution, when they see the text LILO appear on the
screen after a restart of the system. After pressing one of the keys Shift, Ctrl or Alt,
or if either ShiftLock or ScrollLock is activated, LILO shows the boot: prompt and
waits for an action by the user, that is, waits for the user to enter the name of a boot
configuration to be loaded. By pressing Tab, a list of the available configurations is
displayed on screen (via BIOS function 0x10).

The LILO package consists of two parts which are interdependent in some way.
These parts are:

- The program /sbin/lilo which must be called after each modification to the
  kernel files (usually /vmlinuz) if LILO is used as the boot loader. This program
  determines the sector numbers in which the kernel image is stored and keeps
  this list in the map file.

- Various boot sectors which can start other operating systems (even from the
  second disk) or load a kernel image. Since these boot sectors have no information on the internal structure, for example, of the Extended-2 file system, they
  need an up-to-date map file.

This is also the biggest disadvantage of LILO: after each modification to the
kernel, the lilo program must be called to update the map file. In addition, the system
administrator must ensure that a backup kernel is always available and linked into
the LILO configuration. The function known from *BSD systems, to boot an arbitrary
kernel from the file system, is unfortunately not available.

LILO can boot up to 16 different configurations and can be installed both in the
MBR and in the boot sector of primary partitions. LILO can

- serve as a boot sector on a LINUX floppy disk,

- function as the MBR on the first hard disk, and

- be installed as the boot sector in arbitrary primary partitions (except for swap) of the first hard disk.

In contrast, it can *not*

- be installed on an MS-DOS floppy disk (or any other non-LINUX floppy disk),[1]
- be installed in a logical partition, or
- be installed on another disk which is not the first hard disk.

This latter limitation is, however, not a real restriction for the design of a boot configuration, since LILO can load a kernel image from another disk which is not the first hard disk; it can also use arbitrary partitions, including logical drives, on additional hard disks as the root file system.

The installation of LILO into the MBR or the boot sector evidently requires root privileges. LILO is configured via the file /etc/lilo.conf. Before a final installation, you should first use /sbin/lilo -t to check whether the commands contained in the configuration file are known and syntactically correct, and whether the specified kernel files could be found and the specified partitions exist.

Configuring lilo

True, LILO also accepts parameters entered at the boot prompt, but in the normal case of a readily configured system, permanently required settings are passed via the configuration file /etc/lilo.conf. An example of this file is shown in Listing 3.1.

```
boot = /dev/hda2
compact
image = vmlinuz
image = vmlinuz.old
other = /dev/hda1
  table = /dev/hda
  label = msdos
```

Listing 3.1   A very simple LILO configuration.

The LILO options can be divided into global and image-specific options. Global options concern all kernel files and function independently of the selected configuration; the other options only concern one of several bootable configurations. In the example, the global options are ranged left, the image-specific options are indented by two characters. A block of image-specific options is initiated either with image= or with other=; up to 16 different blocks are allowed – including several other= blocks. LILO has the following global options:

---

[1] For this purpose, syslinux can be used.

backup=*backup_file*
> A backup copy named *backup_file* is made of the original boot sector. If the file
> /boot/boot.*device* does not exist, the old boot sector is saved there by default.

boot=*boot_device*
> Specifies the hard disk or the partition that contains the boot sector of LILO. If
> you use the NT loader, you can also create a 512-byte file and include this in the
> file boot.ini.

compact
> Tries to bundle read requests for neighboring sectors on the drive. This can sig-
> nificantly reduce the loading time, especially when loading from diskettes.

default=*name*
> The specified image file is entered as the default value. If no specification is made,
> the first image-specific entry is used as default.

delay=*tsecs*
> Waiting time in tenths of seconds before LILO loads the default image. If no delay
> is specified, booting is carried out immediately.

disk=*device_name*
> Specifies geometry values (heads, cylinders, and sectors) of the boot device. You
> should only use this function if you partitioned the disk with parameters other
> than those the disk itself communicates to the BIOS and thus to LILO.

fix-table
> Allows LILO to correct three-dimensional sector, head, and cylinder addresses
> in partition tables. Please note that this can possibly trigger most unwelcome
> interactions with other operating systems.

force-backup=*backup_file*
> Same as the backup option, but an already existing backup file is overwritten. If
> force-backup is specified together with backup=, only the force-backup option
> will be operational.

ignore-table
> Instructs LILO to ignore defective partition tables.

install=*boot_sector*
> Installs the specified file as the new boot sector. If no specification is made, the
> file /boot/boot.b is used as the LILO boot sector.

linear
> Linear sector addresses are to be used instead of sector/head/cylinder addresses.
> Linear addresses are converted at runtime and do not depend on the hard disk's
> geometry. Boot diskettes created using linear may not function correctly be-
> cause the BIOS functions for determining hard disk parameters do not work
> reliably for diskette drives.

map=*map_file*

Specifies the absolute path and name of the map file to be used; the default value is /boot/map.

message=*message_file*

Specifies a file containing the messages to be displayed on screen. These messages are displayed before the boot prompt. A 0x0C character (⎡Ctrl⎤-⎡l⎤) in this file clears the screen. The maximum size of the file is 64 Kbytes. If the message file is modified, the map file must be recreated by calling lilo.

nowarn

No error messages regarding possible problems are displayed.

optional

Makes all images optional, so no checks are carried out.

password=*password*

Sets a password for all images.

prompt

Displays the boot prompt without any key having to be pressed beforehand. If, in addition, timeout is not set, the computer halts at this point and waits for input.

restricted

Cancels some of the restrictions set by password. Any configuration can be booted, but no input of parameters is allowed. You can use this option, for example, to prevent activation of the single-user mode.

serial=*parameter_string*

Allows system control via a serial connection, that is, LILO accepts input both from the keyboard and from the connected terminal. Sending a ⎡Break⎤ via the connection corresponds to pressing the ⎡Shift⎤ key at the console and causes the boot: prompt to be displayed on the screen.

When access via a serial connection is activated, all configurations should be protected by means of password if access via the serial line is less secure than access to the console itself; for example, when a modem is connected to the serial interface. The format of the *parameter_string* has the following syntax: *port,bpsparitybits*. The last three specifications can be omitted; if one of these three specifications is not made, the subsequent ones must also be omitted. If only the *port* is specified, the comma must be omitted too. On my system, I use serial=1,9600n8 for a 9600-baud terminal on /dev/ttyS1.

When serial= is set, the value for delay is automatically set to 20 tenths of a second. With the setting serial=0,2400n8, the first serial interface is initialized with the default values. Together with some kernel modifications and adaptations of the init program, it is thus possible to use a simple terminal as the console.

timeout=*tsecs*

Determines the time LILO waits for keyboard input. If no key is pressed within the specified time, the default image is loaded; if no specification was made for `default=`, this is the first image listed. Correspondingly, the password check is also aborted if during this time no input was made. The default value for `timeout=` is infinite.

`verbose=`*level*
> This is used to activate error and diagnostic messages. The higher this value, the more messages are output.

Image-specific options

The globally effective options can also be used inside the image-specific configuration blocks. Besides the global options, `LILO` provides the following additional options, which can *only* be used inside image-specific blocks.

`append=`*string*
> Appends the string to the kernel command line.

`literal=`*string*
> Sets the kernel command line to string.

`ramdisk=`*size*
> Creates a RAM disk of corresponding size (in Kbytes).

`read-only`
> Causes the kernel to mount the `root` file system read-only. Thus, an `fsck` can be carried out on this file system too. This is standard with all distributions. After the file system has been checked, it is remounted with write access. The parameters for number and intervals of the checks can be configured by means of the `tune2fs` program.

`read-write`
> The `root` file system is mounted in read/write mode.

`root=`*root_device*
> The specified device is used as `root` file system.

`vga=`*mode*
> Allows the screen resolution of the console to be changed. At runtime, you can also use the `SVGAtextmode` program for this purpose.

`initrd=`*image*
> The file *image* is loaded as RAM disk. If this is not desired, you can specify `noinitrd` at the `LILO` prompt.

It is possible to have several configurations for the same image file, because `LILO` does not store the configurations in the image, but in so-called image descriptions. An additional name can be assigned to an entry by means of `alias=`*alias*.

The use of `LILO` together with a `UMSDOS` file system is possible, but problematic. If a defragmenter is called under DOS, a kernel image can be moved to a different location on the hard disk. Subsequently, LILO may no longer find the kernel image to be booted, and the start of the system fails. In this case (of emergency), you can start the system with loadlin and reinstall LILO.

Additional Information and Sources	
ftp server:	sunsite.unc.edu
ftp path:	/pub/Linux/network/boot/lilo
File name:	lilo.20.tar.gz
Size:	about 165 Kbytes

The GRUB boot loader

A recent development is GRUB (Grand Unified Bootloader). Like LILO, it essentially consists of a boot sector, and there is no easy-to-handle configuration program (yet). The substantial advantage of GRUB is that it is capable of booting many systems directly and that it has information on the corresponding file systems.

With LILO, it is only possible to start previously specified kernel images. GRUB can browse through the file system at the boot prompt and dynamically load different kernels. For daily use, you can set up a menu, but it is always possible to select other kernels or options dynamically.

Additional Information and Sources	
ftp server:	ftp.uruk.org
ftp path:	/public/grub
File name:	grub-0.4.tar.gz
Size:	about 210 Kbytes
WWW page:	http://www.uruk.org/~erich/grub/

3.2.2 The loadlin boot loader

loadlin and loadlinX by Hans Lermen are programs that run under MS-DOS and allow you to start LINUX from MS-DOS. loadlinX[2] is a preprocessor for loadlin which carries out a conversion of the command line parameters. Together with the UMSDOS file system, loadlin allows you to 'nose around' in LINUX without the need to repartition the hard disk. Particularly for LINUX newcomers, this possibility represents a simpler and safer alternative to LILO. loadlin is also useful when, for example, a sound card must first be initialized by means of a special program under DOS before it can be used under LINUX.

The combination of loadlin as boot loader and UMSDOS as file system is, for example, used in Mario Valente's MINILINUX distribution. Pat Volkerding's Slackware distribution also allows you to choose UMSDOS as file system and loadlin as boot loader.

---

[2] Even DOS 6.2 does not distinguish between upper and lower case in commands; the upper-case X in loadlinX is only meant to emphasize the different program names.

To be able to use `loadlin`, LINUX must be installed first, for example via a Slackware distribution. The step that follows in most distributions, namely installation of `LILO` into the boot sector, is skipped. Creation of a boot diskette, instead, must be carried out to allow LINUX to be initially booted from the floppy disk. The kernel (`/vmlinuz`) is then copied to the DOS partition. If the DOS partition has not yet been mounted by the installation routine, this can be done manually by means of, for example, `mountt -t msdos /dev/hda1 /mnt`.

The `loadlin` program is passed the DOS file name of the kernel image to be started as the parameter, for example `c:\linux\vmlinuz`. The second argument, for example `root=/dev/hda2`, contains the partition to be used as `root` file system. The only further specification needed is whether the root partition is to be mounted read-only (`ro`) or read/write (`rw`). A typical command line would be:

```
C:\> c:\linux\loadlin c:\linux\vmlinuz root=/dev/hdb2 rw
```

If UMSDOS is used as the file system, care should be taken to employ the `loadlinX` preprocessor instead of `loadlin`. When using `loadlinX`, only the drive to be used, for example the primary DOS partition `C:` or one of the disk drives `A:` or `B:`, is passed as an argument in the `root=` parameter. A command line making use of `loadlinX` could look like the following:

```
C:\> c:\linux\loadlinX c:\linux\vmlinuz root=c: rw
```

It should be noted that when using UMSDOS, write-protected mounting of the file system (`ro/read-only`) is not possible. There are no special boot parameters to be used exclusively with `loadlin`.

An essential advantage of `loadlin` is that neither the MBR nor the start sector of the LINUX partition needs to be modified. This allows you to switch between different systems without problems and also to update them. If you have `LILO` installed in the MBR, it will be overwritten, for example, by the NT or Windows 95 installation, although it remains as a disturbing presence even when you remove LINUX.

To automate loading with `loadlin`, you can use a boot selector under DOS, such as `BOOT.SYS`. Under LINUX, you should create a script `/sbin/installkernel` that copies the kernel to the DOS partition during `make install`.

Additional Information and Sources	
`ftp` server:	`sunsite.unc.edu`
`ftp` path:	`/pub/Linux/distributions/slackware/setup`
File name:	`loadlin.exe`
Size:	about 15 Kbytes
File name:	`loadlinx.exe`
Size:	about 15 Kbytes

3.2.3   The `syslinux` boot loader

`syslinux` by H. Peter Anvin is a boot loader which replaces the MS-DOS boot sector or IO.SYS and MSDOS.SYS on diskettes. `syslinux` itself is an MS-DOS program used to create LINUX boot diskettes from MS-DOS formatted diskettes. Under DOS (or via `mcopy`), one or more kernel files are copied to the MS-DOS floppy disk, then the DOS command:

```
c:\> syslinux a: vmlinuz root=/dev/hda1
```

is used to specify the image in the file `a:vmlinuz` as the kernel image to be loaded and the boot parameter `root=/dev/hda1` as the argument to be passed. `syslinux` modifies the boot sector of the floppy disk and transfers the file `LDLINUX.SYS` to this disk.

When starting from a boot diskette generated by means of `syslinux`, a boot prompt is displayed, similarly to `LILO`, after pressing one of the keys ⌨Shift⌨, ⌨Alt⌨, ⌨ShiftLock⌨ or ⌨ScrollLock⌨. At this point it is possible to specify parameters other than the default boot parameters and a kernel file name different from the hard-wired one, provided it is contained on the diskette.

If a file named `LINUXMSG.TXT` exists on the floppy disk, its contents are displayed during the start-up. In this case, the boot prompt is also displayed even if none of the above keys has been pressed.

Boot diskettes generated with `syslinux` can be easily copied with the DOS program `DISKCOPY`. Since, however, more and more distributions are equipped with bootable CDs, this process is now relatively seldom used.

Additional Information and Sources	
`ftp` server:	`sunsite.unc.edu`
`ftp` path:	`/pub/Linux/Linux-boot`
File name:	`syslx120.zip`
Size:	about 50 Kbytes

3.3 Starting the kernel

After one of the boot loaders has loaded the kernel image, for example `/vmlinuz`, from the active partition into RAM, the kernel must first be decompressed because, since version 0.99pl12, all kernels are created in a compressed form. The additional load of the CPU does not count because at that time it is mostly 'twiddling its thumbs,' waiting for data to arrive from the disk I/O 'bottleneck.' The net loading time of compressed data is even lower. If, in contrast, the CPU represented the bottleneck, using uncompressed data would be more advantageous; at the current state of the art of bus and hard disk technology, however, this is not to be expected in the near future. Another advantage of compression is the saving of disk space, but in this case this is not too important.

The use of compressed kernels has become necessary, because in an uncompressed form they became bigger than 704 Kbytes (640 Kbytes of 'conventional DOS memory' plus 64 Kbytes of unused data area of the graphic boards under DOS), and the processor is at that point still in real mode, in which only memory addresses below 1 Mbyte are available.

The introduction of compressed kernels has only obfuscated the real problem. Because of the large number of drivers that can now be linked into the kernel, one once again reaches the limits of the real mode, which requires the kernel to be loaded initially into the memory below 1 Mbyte. Sooner or later, the boot loader will run in protected mode, so the size of the kernel will only be limited by the real amount of RAM.

The last official act of the boot loader is to pass program control to the unpacking (and logically not compressed) 'prefix' which was attached during compilation of the system by means of the programs `xtract` and `piggyback` contained in the directory `/usr/src/linux/arch/i386/boot/compressed`. The processor is now switched into protected mode to allow the decompression routine to unpack the image to (virtual) addresses from three gigabytes (`0xC0000000`) onward. The program counter is set to this address, and once again program control is passed, this time to the kernel itself.

Viewed under the aspect of configuration possibilities, two stages can be identified during the system start, after having selected the operating system:

- determination and checking of the hardware configuration, and
- processing of the configuration files and automatic starting of programs.

During the first stage (see `arch/i386/boot/setup.S`) parts of the hardware configuration are detected even before unpacking the kernel. The corresponding BIOS variables (for diskette and hard disk parameters plus the connected graphics card) are read and stored in a safe place in main memory. Further hardware tests are carried out after switching into 32-bit mode; more about this later (for the exact sequence cf.: `./linux/init/main.c`). First, however, internal functions and tables of the system are initialized:

- the table for memory management,
- the assignment of error interrupts and IRQs,
- the process table.

Subsequently, the scheduler is started and the screen is initialized; from now on messages are not only displayed on screen, but are also managed by means of `syslogd` and are possibly stored in a file. More about the use of `syslogd` can be found in Section 4.4.5. These messages can later be redisplayed by means of the `dmesg` program.

At this point, together with the initialization of the corresponding device drivers, the previously mentioned second phase of the hardware tests begins. The hardware is checked by means of various tests (so-called auto-probing or autodetect). By looking at the screen messages, you can trace which devices were found. If in this phase no message is displayed or there is an erroneous message (for example, different I/O ports or interrupts) for a controller card, you will not be able to access this device later. One likely cause of such problems is that several cards are set to the same interrupt or I/O port (either via jumpers or via software configuration). The automatic hardware detection can be influenced by means of command line parameters for the kernel. Please also consult the up-to-date `README` files in the kernel sources.

Now, the processor is switched from privileged (or kernel) mode into non-privileged mode[3] (or user mode); from now on, the first LINUX process runs (with process number 0). This process is in principle not different from all other LINUX processes, but it runs only if no other process is active. Process 0 is the so-called idle process, which in the case of non-use of the processor occupies 100% of the system resources.

Process 1 is started from process 0 by means of the system call fork().[4] This process in turn initiates the further initialization of the system. Here, the hardware is basically initialized, the root partition is mounted, and the init program is executed. In UNIX systems, init is often called the parent of all processes, which for LINUX is not entirely correct; here, by right, it would be the idle process with the number 0. One further process is started which takes care of regular updates of the internal information about the file system on the hard disk. The behavior of this process can be influenced by means of the bdflush program.

According to the file system hierarchy standard (FHS version 2.0), the init program should be located in /sbin/init. The actual search order established in linux/init/main.c is, however, /etc/init, /bin/init, and /sbin/init. If init is not found there, an attempt is made to start /etc/rc or /bin/sh to allow the repair of such a 'disorderly' system. With current kernel versions it is possible to use the command line parameter INIT=/bin/sh to start a shell instead of init.

To conclude the initialization, the kernel reports its version number and creation date. First, however, one of the three init programs normally used under LINUX is started. This concludes the system start-up from the point of view of the kernel. However, the system can still not be used at this point because no login can take place and no background processes (daemons) have been started.

3.3.1 Kernel parameters

Many initializations (for example I/O addresses for expansion boards) of the kernel can be influenced by means of command line parameters. These parameters are passed to the kernel by the boot loader.

debug
> Sets console_loglevel to 10, thus activating 'verbose' console messages.

mem=*size*
> Sets the end of the physical memory. This may be necessary when the RAM size cannot be determined automatically, for example in computers with more than 64 Mbytes of RAM.

no387
> A possibly existing math coprocessor is not used.

---

[3] The privileged mode must not be confused with the protected mode.

[4] This fork() works in a different way as process 0 has a special role: it works with the same memory area as process 1, in particular with the same stack. Therefore, process 0 only carries out operations that do not use the stack. Quoted after Beck, M. *et al.* (1997).

no-hlt
> Prevents use or execution of the HLT instruction of more recent Intel (-compatible) processors when the system is idle. When this instruction is used, the CPU is less heated and laptops consume significantly less power, but some machines may hang.

reserve=*port1,num1[,portn,numn]*
> Excludes I/O ports and zones from auto-probing. This is needed, for example, when auto-probing leads to 'hanging' of the system. *port1* represents the first address, *num1* indicates the number of the addresses to be excluded from *port1* onward.

root=*device*
> Changes the device used as root file system. This overwrites the specifications stored in the kernel image. *device* is either a device name such as /dev/hda3 or a hexadecimal device number.

ro or rw
> The root partition is mounted into the directory tree read-only or read/write.

3.4 The init process

The started init program processes its configuration file /etc/inittab and starts the specified programs and processes. If no init program is found, the kernel tries to start a shell and execute /etc/rc in it. The format of /etc/inittab is different for simpleinit and the other two init strategies.

Mixing different inits and inittabs can make the system unusable. Before changing from one init method to another, it is highly recommended that backups of the affected files and programs be created and both a boot diskette and a root diskette including an editor be produced. Usually, the following parameters are passed to init.

3.4.1 Parameters for init

The following parameters are recognized by all init variations used under LINUX. These parameters can be passed to init by the kernel.

single
> Starts the system in single-user mode. All init programs available for LINUX recognize at least the parameter single.

auto
> Starts the system in the way specified in the /etc/inittab configuration file.

3.4.2 The `simpleinit` program

The `simpleinit` program is used in the `util-linux` package by Rik Faith and thus also in the BOGUS distribution. `simpleinit` was written by Peter Ørbæk. Parts of the single-user mode are due to Werner Almesberger. Although `simpleinit` must be called as `init` (it is recommended that a link is created or the program is saved as `init`), it is usually called `simpleinit` to differentiate it from other `init` programs.

`simpleinit` has basically only two different modes to which it can set the system. The normal multi-user mode is started by processing `/etc/rc` and starting the processes specified in file `/etc/inittab`. The other mode is the single-user mode for system administration. This mode is started if one of two conditions is satisfied: either `init` is passed the argument `single` when it is called, or it finds the file `/etc/singleboot` during the start. In both cases, input of the `root` password is required, if the file `/etc/securesingle` exists, or if the file `/etc/passwd` exists and contains a password for `root`.

```
# Comments begin with a hash character
# Empty lines are ignored

# The format scheme of simpleinit is as follows:
#tty line:termcap entry:terminal program
#    |                |                        +- program call
#    |                +--------------------- entry to be used
#    |                                          from /etc/termcap
#    +---------------------------------- device to be used

# Entry for the first virtual console
tty1:linux:/sbin/agetty 9600 tty1
#           |                |    +- 2nd parameter: device
#           |                +------ 1st parameter: baud rate
#           +-------------------- absolute path to the program

# Additional consoles
tty2:linux:/sbin/agetty 9600 tty2
tty3:linux:/sbin/agetty 9600 tty3
tty4:linux:/sbin/agetty 9600 tty4

# A serial terminal on the first serial interface
ttyS0:dumb:/sbin/agetty 9600 ttyS0
```

Listing 3.2   The `/etc/inittab` file for the `simpleinit` program.

The format of the `/etc/inittab` file for `simpleinit` is substantially different from the format used by the System V and the System V-like `init`s. The initialization table of `simpleinit` cannot be used for the System V `init` and vice versa. An `/etc/inittab` file for `simpleinit` may, for example, look as shown in Listing 3.2.

The configuration options of simpleinit are thus limited to virtual consoles and serial terminals. The two System V init variations, in contrast, also provide the possibility of starting further processes, depending on the situation and in different combinations.

3.4.3 The System V-like init

The System V-like init procedure used by the Slackware distributions is modeled on the procedure of HP-UX. It is somewhat easier, but also less flexible, than the true System V init. By means of the configuration entered in /etc/inittab, various other processes are started, for example one or more of the different getty programs waiting for user logins and input on the virtual consoles and the serial lines. With both the true System V init and the System V-like init, the scheme of an inittab entry looks as follows:

```
id:runlevel:action:process
```

id
    Stands for a unique code for identifying an entry.

runlevel
    Can assume values from 1 to 6, plus S and A to C (upper- and lower-case spelling is ignored). S, for example, stands for the single-user mode in which the system administrator usually carries out system maintenance chores. If init is called as telinit, the additional runlevels A, B, and C are available which can be used to call special settings via inittab. This can be used for starting or stopping different services.

action
    Specifies what happens to the process at a restart (of the system) or its termination (for example, restart of the process). Table 3.1 shows an overview of the possible actions.

process
    Contains the name of the program to be started, together with the parameters to be passed at the start.

Listing 3.3 shows an example for the /etc/inittab file. Extensive documentation of the format can also be found in the man page on inittab(5).

The telinit program is a link to init and provides an extended possibility to control the system via the additional arguments a, b, and c: only the entries with a runlevel of a, b, and/or c are accessed. Thus, for example, only the programs of the special runlevel a can be restarted. It is also possible to use the telinit program to switch between the numeric runlevels (1–6). The parameter q causes the init program to reread the file /etc/inittab.

Action	Description
respawn	The process is restarted after termination.
wait	init waits for the end of the process.
once	The process is started at a change into this runlevel.
boot	The process is generated at system start-up.
bootwait	As boot, but init waits for the end of the process.
off	Entry without function.
ondemand	Start at request for the runlevel, but no change of runlevel.
initdefault	Default runlevel.
sysinit	Start before boot or bootwait.
powerwait	Signal of the UPS about a failure in the power supply. The powerd daemon must be run.
powerfail	As powerwait, but init does not wait for process termination.
powerokwait	Power supply is OK again.
ctrlaltdel	[Ctrl]-[Alt]-[Del] was pressed at the console.
kbrequest	Processing of a special key combination.

Table 3.1   Actions in inittab.

3.4.4 System V init

The widespread Slackware distribution uses only a fraction of the possibilities of the System V init. Other distributions, such as, for example, Red Hat, the Caldera Network Desktop based on it, and Debian, use this init in the same way as other (System V) UNIX systems. Some runlevels are reserved, others have a historical meaning. Table 3.2 shows a brief overview.

The different use of the various runlevels allows a simpler and more flexible control over the initialization of the system. Furthermore, it is much clearer which daemons are to be started or stopped at which runlevel. Runlevels can be edited by means of the tksysv program, which is part of several distributions.

The sequence of a system start-up is at first similar to the one outlined in the previous sections. After loading the kernel and starting init, the file systems are checked and the necessary daemons are started. Subsequently, the /etc/rc script is started. This script contains the required runlevel as a parameter. The corresponding call in the inittab file can be found in Listing 3.4.

For each runlevel, there is a directory /etc/rc.d/rcRunlevel.d. Each of these directories contains links to so-called start and kill scripts. The names of the start or stop scripts begin with S or K, followed by a two-digit number. The scripts are started in ascending order of these numbers. This makes it possible to activate the network interface first and then start the client and server processes. The last part of the name usually describes the type of service controlled by this script. The scripts themselves are stored in the /etc/init.d directory.

```
# /etc/inittab: this file determines the sequence of the
#               system start-up and what must happen
#               at each runlevel.

# Runlevel 5 is started if nothing else is specified.
id:5:initdefault:

# System initialization, is executed at each system start-up.
si:S:sysinit:/etc/rc.d/rc.S

# Switch to single-user mode.
su:S:wait:/etc/rc.d/rc.K

# Switch to multi-user mode.
rc:123456:wait:/etc/rc.d/rc.M

# If <Ctrl><Alt><Del> is pressed on one of the virtual
# consoles, a shutdown is executed. Authorized
# users are registered in the file /etc/shutdown.allow
ca::ctrlaltdel:/sbin/shutdown -t3 -rf now

# Virtual consoles
c1:12345:respawn:/sbin/agetty 38400 tty1
c2:12345:respawn:/sbin/agetty 38400 tty2
c3:45:respawn:/sbin/agetty 38400 tty3
c4:45:respawn:/sbin/agetty 38400 tty4
c5:45:respawn:/sbin/agetty 38400 tty5
c6:456:respawn:/sbin/agetty 38400 tty6
```

Listing 3.3   An example for the System V-like init.

Runlevel	Meaning
0	Shutdown (reserved)
1	Single-user mode (reserved)
2	Multi-user mode
3	Multi-user mode as network server
5	X workstation (xdm)
6	Reboot

Table 3.2   The different runlevels and their meaning.

```
# Default runlevel.
id:5:initdefault:

# System initialization before anything else.
si::sysinit:/etc/bcheckrc

# /etc/rc takes care of runlevel handling.
l0:0:wait:/etc/rc 0
l1:1:wait:/etc/rc 1
l2:2:wait:/etc/rc 2
l3:3:wait:/etc/rc 3
l4:4:wait:/etc/rc 4
l5:5:wait:/etc/rc 5
l6:6:wait:/etc/rc 6
```

Listing 3.4   Changes to the /etc/inittab file.

The scripts are called with the parameter start or stop and start or stop the corresponding subsystems. Listing 3.5 shows an overview of the scripts used on my system. Special importance must be attributed to the kill scripts which stop specific services at a switch of runlevels. The names of the kill scripts begin with K. Within a runlevel, scripts are processed by ascending numbers.

```
(Linux):/etc> ls rc*
rc0.d:
S20halt@

rc1.d:
S20single@

rc2.d:
K51syslog@   K60lpd@       S51syslog@   S60lpd@
K55cron@     K95gpm@       S55cron@     S95gpm@

rc5.d:
K51syslog@   K60lpd@       S51syslog@   S60lpd@
K55cron@     K95gpm@       S55cron@     S95gpm@

rc6.d:
S20reboot@
```

Listing 3.5   Scripts for the System V init.

Usually, it is not worth changing to another `init` procedure. On the other hand, compatibility with other (commercial) systems is certainly sensible, in particular if one continuously changes between different systems. In this case it does make sense to assign the runlevels in the same way as one normally does for other systems.

On computers with only a small amount of RAM it may be better to start only a few and small daemons. In this case, the choice could be, for example, a combination of `simpleinit` and a slimmed-down `bdflush` (an extended `update` daemon), instead of a System V `init` with the normal `bdflush`. Both programs are included in the `util-linux` package.

If you want to change your system from one variation of the `init` program to another, do not forget to have a boot and a root diskette ready, just in case. But remember that you will not get very far with a boot diskette, because the `init` program on the hard disk may not work. In the worst case, you will not even be able to start the system in single-user mode, and you will have to boot from a diskette. Luckily enough, when changing from the System V-like `init` to the System V `init`, you need only modify the `/etc/inittab` file (and possibly undo these changes). All other affected files are replaced with completely different files with entirely different names.

The `init` used under LINUX deviates from those of other systems in one regard: it switches directly to the required runlevel without running through the minor runlevels one after the other.

Additional Information and Sources	
Man pages:	`init(8)`, `inittab(5)`
`ftp` server:	`ftp.cistron.nl`
`ftp` path:	`/pub/People/miquels/SysVinit`
File name:	`SysVinit-2.58.tar.gz`
Size:	about 50 Kbytes

3.5 Stopping the system

As in every other UNIX system, under LINUX, many processes run in the background. Before the system is switched off, these processes must be terminated, because otherwise data might be lost. A further reason for an ordered shutdown of the system is that LINUX also buffers write accesses in main memory. Thus, after the termination of a program, the data has not yet been permanently written to the hard disk. This is only carried out after a `sync`, which is, however, periodically executed by the `update` daemon.

The standard way to stop a UNIX system is to call the `shutdown` command. Depending on the command line parameters, the system can react in various ways. A mandatory parameter is the time after which the system is shut down. The specification `now` stands for immediate stopping of the system, otherwise the time is specified in minutes. Before the shutdown, all logged-in users are warned that system maintenance is imminent.

With the additional parameter -h (halt), the system is halted; the parameter -r (reboot) restarts the system. If the parameter -f is specified, a fast reboot without checking the file system is performed. This is often no longer implemented in the rc scripts, because the Extended-2 file system has its own flag for an orderly system shut down.

For reasons of simplicity, abbreviations exist for frequently occurring tasks. Thus, depending on the init, reboot or init 6, for example, stand for a restart; halt or init 0 stand for halt. These programs are part of the corresponding init systems. Additional information can be found in the appropriate man pages.

Many PC users have grown accustomed to the key combination ⌈Ctrl⌋-⌈Alt⌋-⌈Del⌋ to restart their systems. This key combination can also be used under LINUX. With the ctrlaltdel command, the behavior of the system can be specified. When pressing the three magic keys, the option hard triggers a sync and restarts the system (hard_reset_now() in the kernel). The option soft causes the signal SIGINT to be sent to init, which then controls the further shutdown.

To ensure that the system cannot be stopped by any user, you can make the functioning of the restart dependent on an authorized user being logged on. The names of the authorized users are simply registered in the file /etc/shutdown.allow. Such limitation to individual users only makes sense if the system cannot simply be switched off, that is if the reset and power supply switches are out of reach.

Configuration and administration

4

Adapting a LINUX system to user-specific hardware and requirements, also known as configuration, involves a series of completely different aspects. In this chapter, we present the most important configuration alternatives for each major area not addressed in a separate section of this book.

Many things can be configured by the system administrator for all users of the system as well as by each user individually. This possibility is a great advantage over single-user systems such as DOS or OS/2 where a configuration generally applies to the entire system, independently of whether other users of the computer will be affected or not. Who has not been annoyed more than once by misadjusted colors under Windows or absurdly disarranged icons under OS/2?

However, before you begin with the configuration of your system, please read Section 11.5 on the *Revision Control System* and Chapter 5 on *Emacs* first, so that you will not only be able to implement the modifications but also have the opportunity to document changes made in a way which can be traced back. The possibility of easy tracing of changes is an advantage over DOS and Windows systems, where practically every program changes system-wide settings in the files `CONFIG.SYS` and `AUTOEXEC.BAT`, and in Windows' `*.INI` files. Do not throw away this possibility by making hasty changes before you have learnt more about the Revision Control System.

4.1 Kernel and hardware configuration

During system start-up (see also Chapter 3), the kernel checks the hardware and, if necessary, initializes it. Usually, this does not cause problems as many drivers carry out so-called auto-probing. This is a check as to whether an appropriate interface or board is present at a determined I/O address or interrupt.

Devices for which no drivers are present in the kernel are not initialized and cannot be addressed. Drivers whose corresponding device is not installed take up unnecessary RAM space. Since, in the case of low memory, the kernel cannot be swapped out from real memory to hard disk as with normal application programs, this memory space is not available for applications or buffers.

The large number of drivers previously linked into the distribution kernels often occupied a substantial amount of memory and, in addition, significantly increased the time the operating system needed for booting. With the use of dynamically loadable modules, which can also be removed from memory again, this aspect is losing importance. Thus, in many cases, the distribution kernel can be permanently employed without problems.

Some NE2000-compatible network cards are known for the effect they have of halting the computer (more precisely, the bus) when other drivers search for devices on their addresses. Therefore, only the necessary drivers should be linked into the kernel. This also prevents or at least reduces conflicts during initialization of the cards. For this reason, it is always sensible to generate a new kernel specially adapted to one's own hardware.

For many functions, options, or drivers, you will find additional information in the kernel sources. Generally, it is stored in the `./Documentation` directory, where you may also find information on additionally required programs and where to obtain them, together with references to more in-depth documentation.

4.1.1 Configuring the kernel

The kernel's source code is located in the `/usr/src/linux` directory. There, the kernel is first configured and then compiled. Kernel configuration is carried out interactively and consists of a series of questions about the hardware and software used. You start the configuration process with the `make config` (in text mode), `make menuconfig` (menus in text mode) or `make xconfig` (under X, you need Tcl/Tk) command. You are asked a series of questions; each question is associated with an online help text which you can access by typing ? or by selecting the help button.

The following section is limited to a discussion of general kernel configuration; information on special settings can be found in the corresponding chapters (*Networks*: Chapter 14, *File systems*: 4.1). Further information on the kernel and installation can be found in the `README` file in the `/usr/src/linux` directory and in additional `README` files in the kernel sources. In addition, there is a kernel configuration HowTo which can also be consulted.

Several development tools are needed to compile the kernel. First, you need the GNU C compiler GCC together with its `binutils` (among others, the assembler `gas` and the linker `gld`). Generating the kernel's boot sector requires the 16-bit assembler `as86`. The compilation process is controlled by means of the `make` program, which is discussed more in detail in Chapter 11. Dependencies are generated by means of a simple C program which fulfills this task faster than the corresponding function of the C compiler. Compilation of the NCR SCSI driver also requires `perl`.

Loadable module support

Provided they are not needed for start-up, many parts of the kernel can be compiled as modules. For these parts, no RAM memory is required so long as they are not loaded into memory by means of `insmod`. More information on handling modules can be found in Section 4.3.

The following list corresponds to the questions asked during configuration of a LINUX kernel version 2.0. In the current developers version 2.1, some of these questions are substantially different, whereas others have remained unchanged.

Prompt for development and/or incomplete code/drivers   The standard kernel, even though it has been declared as stable, often contains new or modified functions which still have to be extensively tested. These special functions are only made available when this question has been answered with 'Y'.

Enable loadable module support   Should loading of modules be at all possible? As a rule, this option should be activated.

Set version information on all symbols for modules   Modules can only be loaded into a kernel into which they fit. The only way to be absolutely sure about this is that the kernel version used is exactly the same. If the internal structures of the kernel have not changed, different version modules may still function. Version information on modules can be used to check compatibility with other kernel versions.

Kernel daemon support   With the kernel daemon contained in the `modules` package, the kernel can trigger a user process (for example, `kerneld`), which then carries out specific functions. Thus, for example, when accessing the CD drive, it may load first the corresponding CD-ROM drivers and then the ISO-9660 file system. More about this subject can be found in Section 4.3.

General setup

The next section of the kernel configuration asks for general settings. For each question, an explanatory text is displayed, followed by the corresponding configuration variable (in parentheses) and its default value (in square brackets). All inputs are stored at the end of the configuration and are proposed as default settings in the next configuration. The default value is accepted by pressing the ⌐Enter⌐ key.

Kernel math emulation   Emulation should only be activated if the computer contains an i386 or i486SX processor without a math coprocessor, which will then be emulated by calling the corresponding kernel routines (penalizing speed). This can be useful for installation or emergency floppies and for testing purposes. Use of an existing coprocessor can be prevented by means of the `LILO` option `no387`. More about `LILO` and available options can be found in Chapter 3.

Networking support   If your computer is integrated into a network or you want to use SLIP or PPP, you select this option. This also applies if you only want to use the loopback device. Many programs, for example `lpd` or `syslogd`, internally use network functions, thus you should activate this function in any case. More about network configuration can be found in Chapter 14.

Limit memory to low 16 MBytes   Because of its design limits, PC architecture often has the problem that memory above the 16-Mbyte limit cannot be used at all or only incompletely. This is the case when so-called BIOS extensions map memory into RAM shortly below the 16-Mbyte limit. This option allows us to ignore memory above the 16-Mbyte limit, since only contiguous memory can be used. However, it is more reasonable to configure your hardware to use as much memory as possible. All additional available memory can be used by LINUX in some way or other, be it as cache or for programs or data. Because of BIOS limitations, you must pass the kernel the size of your memory in a kernel command line (for example `mem=128M`) if you have more than 64 Mbytes of memory.

PCI BIOS support   Modern PCI bus computers have a BIOS which can be used to control the hardware under LINUX as well. If this option is activated, you will also be asked for experimental support of PCI bridges. This question can without hesitation be answered with 'n'. More about this subject can be found in the PCI HowTo.

System V IPC   This option allows application programs to exchange data by means of IPC (Inter Process Communication). Since this option only requires a little additional memory and is used by several programs (for example databases and the DOS emulator), this option should be selected.

Kernel support for ELF binaries   Traditionally, LINUX used the `a.out` format. Creating shared libraries, however, was fairly expensive. This and the limitations of the `a.out` format led to the implementation of ELF (Executable and Linkage Format) under LINUX. This option should definitely be answered with 'y'.

Kernel support for JAVA binaries   This is a 'marketing stunt' which made LINUX the first system capable of executing Java programs directly. In version 2.1, this option is replaced by a more flexible function for loading arbitrary programs. This allows direct execution of Windows, DOS, or (on the Alpha platform) Intel programs.

Compile kernel as ELF   It makes no difference at all for the usage of ELF if the kernel itself is present in ELF format or not. If you use an ELF compiler (GCC version 2.7.x or higher) you should answer with 'y'.

Processor type   Depending on the processor, different optimizations can be carried out on the basis of further developments or bug fixes. Kernels optimized for 386 processors run on all processors, whereas kernels optimized for 486 and Pentium cannot be used on 386 processors. Select the CPU you are actually using.

Floppy, IDE, and block devices

Normal floppy disk support   Support for floppy disk drives is needed if, for example, the `root` file system is stored on a floppy disk or loaded from a floppy disk into the RAM disk. Otherwise, the drivers can be loaded as modules at a later stage. More about modules can be found in Section 4.3.

Enhanced IDE/MFM/RLL disk/cdrom/tape/floppy support   This is the driver for IDE hard disks, new IDE CD-ROM drives (ATAPI), and corresponding tape or floppy disk drives. If you select this driver, you have the choice between an old, well-proven driver or a new development. If you use the new development you are also asked for the driver for IDE/ATAPI CD-ROM drives. This driver is not designed for SCSI CD-ROM drives or older drives which use a separate controller board or are connected to a sound card (not to the IDE port).

Additional block devices

Loopback device support   The loopback device can be used to mount an arbitrary file as a block device and to access its file system. This is frequently used to create boot and root disks, write CDs and access disk images for the DOS emulator.

Multiple devices driver support   Since version 2.0, LINUX supports the options RAID-0 (Striping) and RAID-1 (Mirroring); in version 2.1 this has been extended to include RAID-5. This driver is responsible for their implementation.

RAM disk support   The kernel can reserve part of the main memory for a RAM disk. This is sensible for boot or emergency floppies. Further information is contained in the documentation, in the file `ramdisk.txt`.

XT hard disk support   Used for the support of (old) 8-bit hard disk controllers with their own BIOS, as they were used in PC/XTs. If you have such a hard disk in your computer, you know what this means.

Networking options

If you selected network support, you must now answer some questions regarding the network. A detailed explanation of these values can be found in Chapter 14.

SCSI support

This section of the configuration is exclusively concerned with the configuration of SCSI host adapters and devices. If your computer is not equipped with SCSI, you can skip this section by answering this question with 'n'. Otherwise, further questions are asked. Since one SCSI controller can usually control up to seven devices without problems and these controllers are generally faster and more powerful than traditional AT bus disks or streamers, you should take SCSI into serious consideration when buying a new UNIX system. Further information on operation of SCSI devices under LINUX can be found in the SCSI HowTo.

SCSI disk support   When you are using SCSI hard disks you must set this option. Otherwise you will not be able to access these hard disks under LINUX.

SCSI tape support   Must be selected when you want to use a SCSI streamer under LINUX. Because of the lack of data security, the use of so-called floppy streamers (see also Chapter 7) under LINUX must only be regarded as an emergency makeshift solution.

SCSI CDROM support   Used to support CD-ROM drives connected to the SCSI controller. Without this option, you cannot use these drives.

SCSI generic support   Allows operation of SCSI devices which are not specially supported, using low-level SCSI commands. This driver is used for accessing scanners or functions that are not implemented in the standard drivers.

Hardware drivers   Subsequently, you must link the drivers that match your SCSI controller into the kernel. Otherwise, all devices connected to this controller and the controller itself will not be recognized and cannot be used.

SCSI error messages   At the very end of the kernel configuration you can specify that SCSI error messages will be displayed with explanatory text. This option takes up some memory, but should usually be selected.

Drivers for network cards

The choice of drivers depends on your hardware and the connection used. More detailed information can be found in Chapter 14.

The ISDN subsystem

Under LINUX, a series of widely used ISDN cards can be employed. Here you can select the corresponding drivers and the protocol of the connection (Euro ISDN or national ISDN). Furthermore, you can determine which application protocols should be supported by the ISDN subsystem.

Drivers for CD-ROM drives

These drivers are only suitable for CD-ROM drives that are not connected to a SCSI or IDE controller (ATAPI). A range of drives are supported (for example Sony, Mitsumi, Panasonic, and Aztech). Depending on the drive, you may be required to notify the kernel of the controller's address either in the kernel sources or via a `LILO` command line.

File systems

LINUX supports a series of file systems, each of which can either be directly compiled into the kernel or loaded as a module at runtime. Frequently used file systems should be directly incorporated into the kernel; rarely used ones can be loaded later as modules (see also Section 4.3). The file system used to format the `root` partition must in any case be incorporated into the kernel, because otherwise this partition cannot be accessed.

Quota support   On a computer with many registered users, often a few individual users may occupy most of the available space. Even the `root` reserves do not prevent all other users being hampered in their work. With the `quota` system you can restrict the amount of memory a user can occupy. For this purpose, you need the `quota` programs.

Standard (minix) fs support   LINUX was originally developed under Minix, so for the purpose of a simple data exchange it was reasonable to be able to read and write this file system as well. This file system is extremely stable since it was supported by LINUX from the very beginning. An essential limitation is that only partitions of less than 64 Mbytes are allowed. Furthermore, file names were originally limited to a length of 14 characters[1]; now up to 30 characters are allowed. This file system is still used for data exchange on floppy disks, and so is `xiafs`.

Extended fs support   Because of the limitations of the Minix file system, a new file system was developed quite quickly, the so-called extended file system. This file system became the standard file system for many LINUX distributions, since the limitations in both partition size and name length were substantially less restrictive. This file system was replaced by the extended-2 file system and exists only for reasons of compatibility. In version 2.1, the source code for this file system was removed from the kernel.

Second extended fs support   This file system is today's standard for LINUX. It supports large partitions (more than 2 Gbytes) and big files; file names can be up to 255 characters in length. This file system has been newly developed on the basis of the experience with the extended file system. It offers space for extensions and has been implemented with specific consideration to data security. This file system is well maintained and has a very powerful `fsck` program for consistency checking. Some of its features (for example, the `root` reserve) make it poorly suited to floppy disks.

xiafs file system support   When the limitations of the Minix file system became apparent, but before development of the extended file system was complete, this file system was developed on the basis of the Minix file system. Therefore it is also very stable, but it does not possess the features of the extended-2 file system.

DOS FAT fs support   In the LINUX kernel, the DOS-based file systems form a whole family of file systems, which are partly based on the same code. Here, general support is requested.

msdos fs support   This file system is particularly well suited for the exchange of data with other computers or operating systems. Furthermore, it allows you to mount DOS partitions nearly transparently (DOS does not recognize users and permissions) into the LINUX file system.

umsdos: Unix like fs on top of std MSDOS FAT fs   This file system originated from the desire to install LINUX on an existing DOS partition without repartitioning the disk. Speed and data security are not as high as with the extended-2 file system, but it offers the chance to try out LINUX without having to repartition.

---

[1] 14 characters is the maximum file name length under System V.

VFAT (Windows 95) fs support   With this file system you can also access partitions with file names conforming to Windows 95. However, under version 2.0, the 32-bit extension of Windows 95b is not supported.

/proc file system support   Many programs (such as, for example, ps) must access internal data of the kernel. Prior to the development of the /proc file system, these programs had to access the corresponding kernel addresses. For this purpose, they had to be given access to the /dev/kmem device and understand the internal data structures of the kernel. With the /proc file system, these programs receive the necessary data provided by the kernel in a digestible format and are thus no longer directly dependent on kernel versions.

NFS file system support   When your LINUX computer is linked into a network, the *Network File System* allows you to use data from other computers in the same way as if they were stored on your own computer. More detailed information on NFS configuration can be found in Chapter 18.

SMB file system support   With this file system, you can mount shares of Windows for Workgroups or Windows NT under LINUX. With the samba package, LINUX can also be employed as an SMB server.

NCP file system support   If you have activated IPX as the network protocol, you can use this file system to access Novell NetWare servers. NCP stands for NetWare Core Protocol. With the lwared or mars_new packages, LINUX can also be used as a NetWare server.

ISO9660 cdrom file system support   If you have selected support for a CD-ROM drive, you can use the ISO9660 file system to mount CDs into the LINUX file system. This standard defines the storage of data on CDs. LINUX supports the Rockridge extensions, which allow you to store UNIX file names and permissions on CDs.

OS/2 HPFS file system support (read only)   With this file system, you gain read access to OS/2 partitions formatted with HPFS (High Performance File System).

System V and Coherent file system support   If you have installed another UNIX system on your computer, you might be able to access its data by means of this file system.

Further file systems in the standard kernel are the Amiga file system and the Unix File System (UFS). New additions to the developers kernel are the driver for the NT file system (NTFS) and the Jolliet extensions, which allow long file names on Windows CDs.

Character devices

The following section deals with configuration of individual character oriented devices. Partly, these are special serial cards (so-called multiport cards), but also printers and mice not connected to a serial interface.

Standard/generic serial support   The normal serial driver can be compiled as a module if you do not have a serial mouse or if you use the interfaces only rarely.

Digiboard PC/Xx support   Compiles the driver for a special interface card.

Cyclades async mux support   Activates the driver for the corresponding Cyclades multiport card.

Stallion multiport serial support   Activates the driver for the corresponding Stallion products.

SDL RISCom/8 card support   Is the driver for an additional interface card.

Parallel printer support   If you have connected a printer to your computer's printer port (parallel interface), you can compile the corresponding driver into the kernel by activating this option. Otherwise, this driver is compiled as a module and can be loaded into memory at runtime.

Bus mouse support   There are LINUX drivers for several widely used bus mice. Their exact installation is extensively described in the bus mouse HowTo.

Support for user misc device modules   To avoid having to reserve a separate major number for each driver, programmers can use this point to link simple drivers which, for example, need only one or two minor numbers.

Advanced Power Management BIOS support   Many laptops are equipped with energy saving functions. These can be used under LINUX when you activate this function.

Watchdog Timer support   This option is used to activate a software watchdog. This may be used to reboot an unusable computer quickly and without supervision. Please refer to the file `watchdog.txt`. If you want to supervise a server, you should install a corresponding interface card, which is a much better approach than using a software solution.

Sound

The configuration of a sound card under LINUX is quite an enterprise. Therefore, I can only refer you to the Sound HowTo, because I do not have a sound card myself.

4.1.2 Compiling the kernel

After the above configuration, the source text of the kernel must be compiled. For safety, you should not install the new kernel with `LILO` (the boot loader) straight away, but you should generate a boot floppy. If the system works correctly with the new kernel, it can be installed by means of `make install`. Further information on the use of `make` can be found in Chapter 11. The commands needed for compiling the kernel are listed in Listing 4.1. Additional information can also be found in the file `/usr/src/linux/README`. Depending on the processor and available memory, compiling the kernels takes between a few minutes (on a fast Pentium) and several hours (on a 386SX with 4 Mbytes of memory).

You should reboot with the newly created floppy disk and, after a successful trial, execute the `make install` command to install the new kernel. If the `LILO` boot

```
(Linux):/usr/src/linux# make dep
(Linux):/usr/src/linux# make clean
(Linux):/usr/src/linux# make
(Linux):/usr/src/linux# make zdisk
(Linux):/usr/src/linux# make modules
(Linux):/usr/src/linux# make modules_install
```

Listing 4.1   Compiling the kernel.

loader is installed on your system, this command is equivalent to the command make zlilo. If, however, you use a different boot loader, such as loadlin, for example, you can create a script /sbin/installkernel which will automatically execute all operations needed for the installation of the new kernel.

4.1.3 Updating the kernel

A kernel update can be carried out in two ways. You can either install a completely new kernel, or the changes in the source code can be transferred to the kernel sources by means of the patch program (see also Chapter 10).

Complete installation of the kernel

Installing a complete new kernel is quite easy. First, the old kernel sources should be saved, so that the old kernel can be used again in case an error occurs. If you have enough hard disk space, it is sufficient to rename the complete path. Otherwise, it would be sensible to execute make clean and then store the kernel in a (compressed) archive (for example, by using tar). Subsequently, the new kernel sources can be unpacked and the already known process of kernel configuration and compilation can be run. Many system-related programs depend on the fact that at least the make config step is performed. The necessary commands are listed in Listing 4.2.

```
(Linux):/usr/src/linux# make clean
(Linux):/usr/src/linux# cd ..
(Linux):/usr/src# mv linux linux.old
(Linux):/usr/src# tar zxvf /tmp/linux-1.2.2.tar.gz
(Linux):/usr/src# cd linux
(Linux):/usr/src/linux# make config
...
```

Listing 4.2   Complete kernel update.

Patching the kernel

The second method of updating the kernel is the so-called patching of the kernel. Since the source code of two kernel versions is often nearly the same, much less data need to be transferred for an update. A patch only contains the changes from one version to the next. Thus, if you want to use a kernel that is several versions more recent, it is often easier to obtain the new sources than to execute all patches in the correct order.

If these aspects are taken into consideration, updating the kernel is quite simple. As an example, we show the update from kernel version 1.2.1 to version 1.2.2. The essential advantage of patching is that you find all changes to the source text in a relatively well-structured way. If you have some programming experience, you should definitely have a good look at the patches before you install them. The zmore program used in the present example is not contained in the widely used Slackware distribution; you will have to use zless instead. The necessary commands are listed in Listing 4.3. Besides all working files, the command make mrproper also deletes the old kernel configuration.

```
(Linux):/usr/src/linux# zmore /tmp/patch-1.2.2.gz
(Linux):/usr/src/linux# zcat /tmp/patch-1.2.2.gz|patch -p1
(Linux):/usr/src/linux# make mrproper
(Linux):/usr/src/linux# make config
...
```

Listing 4.3   Kernel update with patch.

After a patch, you should look for failed modifications. This can be done by using the find program (see also Chapter 10) to search for the corresponding backup files. Depending on the patch version, these files are named *.rej or *#. Failed modifications are a bad sign; depending on your experience, you should either install a completely new kernel or perform the modifications manually using an editor. This kind of problem tends to occur if you have modified the kernel yourself or installed additional patches.

Backup copies are also created for files that have been successfully modified. Depending on the patch version, these files are named *.orig or *~ and can be deleted later. Further information on the patch program can be found in Chapter 10.

4.2 Configuring the hardware

Many drivers use auto-probing to find and initialize the corresponding hardware by searching various I/O addresses (ports), interrupts or DMA channels for typical signatures. This can crash your computer, but it may also happen that installed devices are not found. In such cases you can either change the list of the addresses or interrupts to be checked in the kernel, or you can set the corresponding parameters by means of kernel command lines. This presumes, however, that you use an appropriate boot loader (see also Chapter 3). The syntax of the kernel command line option depends on the individual driver, therefore you will find its documentation in the corresponding HowTo or README files.

Often, multi-serial cards are not correctly recognized. The corresponding parameters (I/O address and IRQ) can be set with setserial. In the widely used Slackware distribution, examples can be found in the file /etc/rc.d/rc.serial.

Some drivers, for example CD-ROM drivers, support the configuration of the behavior of the devices via the ioctl() function. Here, for example, automatic ejection of the media when unmounting a CD-ROM file system can be switched on or off. An example that can be employed directly is the cdeject package. Parameters for a QIC-02 compatible tape drive can be set by means of the setqic2 program if you have not programmed them directly into the kernel.

4.3 Kernel modules

One of the criticisms of LINUX is the use of a monolithic kernel instead of today's 'modern' micro kernel. This criticism is, however, only partly justified. Interested readers should refer to a discussion between Linus Torvalds and Andrew S. Tannenbaum, author of Minix and operating system specialist, on the advantages and disadvantages of the new development of LINUX. You will find the discussion that took place in the comp.os.minix newsgroup in the file linux_is_obsolete in the doc directory of the LINUX ftp server.

A micro kernel (such as, for example, Mach) is a minimal kernel which contains only the most important functions (such as memory and process management or hardware drivers). File systems, personalities (such as a BSD or UNIX interface), or other functions are loaded later and can be implemented in the user space, that is, by means of normal programs. This allows greater flexibility, but at the expense of a higher management cost. Since LINUX was originally developed on relatively slow (by today's standards) 386 PCs, Linus Torvalds had to make do without 'modern' concepts such as a micro kernel.

During the course of time, however, several disadvantages of the original concept came to light. The kernel must be almost completely recompiled in order to accommodate a new driver. During the development of a driver, the kernel must be rebooted after each change, which entails a restart of the whole computer. Thus, the development of drivers takes more time, and the user misses the flexibility of other systems.

These problems led to the development of the concept of kernel modules. Here, drivers or other functions are added to or removed from the kernel (by means of the programs insmod and rmmod, respectively) at kernel runtime (without restarting the computer). A list of loaded modules can be displayed by means of the lsmod command.

A module is a (nearly) normal object file generated by a C compiler. Since a module cannot function on its own, but must have access to some internal kernel structures, these symbols must be exported within the kernel. All of these symbols must be defined in the file linux/kernel/ksyms.c. If a symbol is missing, the module cannot be loaded. In the same way, the kernel version must either match exactly (if the kernel was compiled without CONFIG_MODVERSIONS) or the module version must be compatible with the one in the kernel. These checks are carried out by means of checksums by the insmod command when loading the module.

In the second step the module is initialized; that is, a driver can search, for example, for the corresponding hardware. If initialization fails, the module is removed from memory. Otherwise, the module runs in the kernel space as if it had been compiled into the kernel in the first place. This allows full access to the entire hardware, so the same caution (data backups, defensive programming) applied to kernel programming itself should also be applied to the programming of a new module.

After having been used, and provided they are no longer needed, modules can be removed from kernel memory by means of the rmmod command. This also calls a clean-up function which frees occupied resources, such as memory, I/O ports, or interrupts. Modules that are still active cannot be removed.

While loading modules, variables such as, for example, I/O ports or interrupts to be used, can be specified as parameters. These variables are modified by insmod prior to the module's initialization. This prevents longwinded and sometimes dangerous auto-probes. An example for loading and removing a module is shown in Listing 4.4.

```
(Linux):~# insmod sbpcd.o sbpcd=0x300,1
sbpcd.c v3.6-1 Eberhard Moenkeberg <emoenke@gwdg.de>
Scanning 0x300 (LaserMate)...
Drive 0 (ID=0): CR-562 (0.80) at 0x300 (type 0)
data buffer size: 8 frames.
(Linux):~# lsmod
modules:        #pages:  Used by:
minix               5
sbpcd              10
...Usage of the module...
(Linux):~# rmmod sbpcd
sbpcd module released.
```

Listing 4.4   Use of a kernel module.

Modules selected during kernel configuration are compiled with the command make modules and installed with make modules_install into the directory /lib/modules/kernelversion. These modules can be loaded in different ways:

- The system administrator can load modules with the insmod command.
- The depmod command can be used to generate a kind of Makefile which contains dependencies of modules. Subsequently, the modprobe program can be used to load a single module or a whole batch of modules.

- By means of the `kerneld` daemon, the kernel can automatically load a module when it is needed.

The programs `depmod`, `modprobe`, and `kerneld` read the configuration file `/etc/conf.modules`. In this file, aliases for modules and parameters for loading modules can be specified. This allows us to compile only the most important drivers and functions into the kernel and leave the remainder to the `kerneld` daemon. An example for the `conf.modules` file is shown in Listing 4.5.

```
# The dummy device for the network
alias dummy0 dummy
#options dummy -o dummy0

# Alias names for the ISO file system (CD)
alias iso9660fs isofs
alias cdfs isofs

# Alias names for the Soundblaster CD-ROM driver
alias block-major-25 sbpcd
options sbpcd sbpcd=0x300,1

# Alias names for a.out
alias binfmt-204 binfmt_aout
alias binfmt-267 binfmt_aout

# ftape driver
alias char-major-27 ftape
```

Listing 4.5 The `conf.modules` file.

Comments begin with a hash character (#) and end with the line end. The keyword `alias` is used to define an alias name for a module. Thus, for example, when accessing a character-oriented device with the major number 27 (alias), the `ftape` module (real name) will be loaded. If `off` is specified as the real name, the module will not be loaded by `modprobe` or `kerneld`.

`options` allows us to specify options that will be used when loading the module. Thus, the internal name of a module can be changed (option -o) or a variable can be set. The keywords `path` and `depfile` specify the path in which the modules or the file containing the dependencies is stored. In general, you are not required to change these settings.

During system start-up, `depmod -a` is used to create the file `modules.dep` which contains the dependency structure of the modules. Subsequently, a module can be loaded with `modprobe` *module*; any additionally required modules are automatically loaded beforehand.

The use of `kerneld`, which performs this function automatically and in a way that is completely transparent to the user, is much easier. A further advantage of `kerneld` is that unused modules are automatically removed from memory. `kerneld` needs the file `modules.dep` and the configuration file `/etc/conf.modules`. Today, most distributions contain the `kerneld` daemon, which takes over management of the modularized kernel.

Thanks to the implementation of the module interface, it has become possible for hardware providers to release drivers for their hardware only as binary code. The hope of all LINUX developers is, however, that because of incompatibilities with future kernel versions and for easier maintenance of drivers in the standard kernel, manufacturers will nevertheless release the source code.

Many distributions contain only one boot diskette for all systems. Thus, it is no longer necessary to choose a (hopefully) matching boot diskette. This single floppy now includes *all* hardware drivers as modules. After installation, a modular kernel is copied to the hard disk together with the corresponding modules.

But what happens if the root file system is located on a medium that can only be addressed by means of a kernel module? Here, `initrd` is employed. This creates an initial RAM disk which contains all drivers. When mounting the root file system, all required modules are loaded and, subsequently, the RAM disk is released.

Additional Information and Sources	
Man pages:	`insmod(1)`, `rmmod(1)`, `lsmod(1)`, `ksyms(1)`
	`depmod(1)`, `modprobe(1)`, `modules(2)`
`ftp` server:	`sunsite.unc.edu`
`ftp` path:	`/pub/Linux/kernel`
Package:	`modutils-2.0.0.tar.gz`
Size:	about 115 Kbytes

4.4 System configuration

Some settings can only be carried out by the system administrator, for example the administration of user IDs, file systems, network connections, and other settings. Here, we present the areas that are not discussed in separate chapters (such as, for example, the network configuration, see Chapter 14).

4.4.1 User IDs and permissions

As opposed to single-user systems, such as MS-DOS or MS Windows, UNIX utilizes a series of security mechanisms which on the one hand prevent modification of system files, and on the other allow storage of private data. It is also possible to create user groups for special tasks or projects. The access right check is carried out on the basis of the assigned group and user ID for files, directories, and processes inside the kernel.

After its installation, a LINUX or UNIX system has no user IDs that could be directly used by new users. Furthermore, all existing IDs, such as for example `daemon`, `uucp`, or `news`, should either be given a password, or a login should be forbidden. The next step after installation should be the creation of a non-privileged user ID. The new ID must be registered in the file `/etc/passwd`. Depending on the system, this can be done in various ways.

- A new ID can simply be inserted with an arbitrary editor. However, this does not lock the file against modification by another user, and therefore access conflicts can arise when several system administrators work on the password file at the same time. For a single-user system, however, this plays no role.

- A special version of an editor can be used which creates a lock file so that during this time no other users have write access to the `/etc/passwd` file. The `util-linux-2.5` package contains the program `vipw` which can be used to edit the password file.

- The new ID can be created by means of the `useradd` program. This automatically creates the home directory for this user and, if they exist, copies standard configurations from `/etc/skel` into this directory. Especially when creating a large number of IDs, this feature offers the advantage that all users start with a uniform environment.

- In many distributions, this function is integrated into the included administration tool. You will find more information on these tools in the documentation accompanying your distribution.

Each ID consists of exactly one line in the file `/etc/passwd`. Each line is subdivided into a series of colon-separated fields, each with its own special meaning. The corresponding documentation can be found in the man page `passwd(5)`.

`ID:password:uid:gid:name:directory:shell`

- The name of the user ID must consist of one word and must not contain special characters; that is, it must be composed exclusively of letters and digits. The use of foreign language characters, such as umlauts or accented letters, may cause a variety of effects. One essential aspect is that many mail systems will garble an address which, for example, contains umlauts. The user ID name must be unique within the system. Common IDs are first or second names in lower case letters, or nicknames. Some organizations employ numerical or otherwise structured IDs.

- During creation of a new user ID, this field, which contains the encrypted password, should initially remain empty. Using the `root` login, the password can be initially set with the `passwd ID` command. If a user ID is to be created under which no login will be allowed, an asterisk (*) can be entered instead of the encrypted password.
  When shadow passwords are used, the password is not stored here, but in the file `/etc/shadow`. In order to prevent security problems, an asterisk (*)

should be entered in any case. The password is encrypted with the libc function crypt() whose source code is freely available too. Passwords should not contain any foreign language special characters.

- The uid number (user identification) is the unique ID of a user which is also used internally by the kernel to check the access rights. The entries in the /etc/passwd file should be sorted in ascending order by this number, so that the useradd program can automatically find the next available number.

- The gid number (group identification) specifies the membership of a user in a user group. This makes it possible for a group of users to work on files together or allows individual users to use specific programs.

- The name should be the full (real) name of the user. This is sensible for programs such as finger, but also for the use of mail and news. The name entered here can be changed by means of the chfn program. This field, which is also known as the gecos field, can also accommodate the office number and the office and private phone numbers.

- Each user is associated with a home directory which becomes the current directory when the user logs in to the system. This directory should be executable for all other users so that, for example, the finger daemon can change into this directory. Only the owner, however, should have write access. If the user wishes to protect data against access by others, then those files should be stored in subdirectories of the home directory for which the corresponding access rights are set. If this directory does not exist, the user is assigned the / directory as the home directory or the login is not executed, depending on the login used.

- After successful login to the system, the shell specified in the last field is started. The shell can be changed by every user by means of the chsh program. However, only those shells are allowed that are listed in the file /etc/shells. The shell should exist, because otherwise no further login is possible. This is particularly awkward if the system administrator root has no valid shell. A valid shell is also required for access via ftp (see also Section 17.2).

```
root:4IIeEz9nkoE:0:0:system administrator:/root:/bin/bash
uucp:*:5:5::/usr/uucp:
jochen:EgIrRB.hrBU:40:6:Jochen Hein:/home/jochen:/bin/tcsh
guest::41:14:guest account:/home/guest:/bin/tcsh
nobody:*:65534:65534:Nobody:/:/bin/false
```

Listing 4.6   Example of a password file.

Listing 4.6 shows an excerpt of a password file. The system administrator root has a password and is always assigned user and group number 0. This number is used by the kernel for checking of access rights, and the value 0 as the user identification means superuser privileges. Thus, under UNIX no further subdivision of administrator rights is possible. POSIX.1e is, among others, supposed to define a standard for the above; more about this subject can be found in Section 4.4.2.

/root is used as the home directory, and the bash is used as the shell. The home directory should in any case lie on the root partition so as to allow the user root to log in and work in single-user mode. When you change the shell of the user root, please make sure that you can log back in with the new shell, before you completely log out.

The second line contains a user ID for uucp. For this user, an asterisk (*) was registered as the password, thus logging in to the system with this ID is not possible. Such an ID is used for administration of a UUCP installation. The system administrator uses the su – uucp command to change to this user ID before starting to carry out modifications to the configuration files of the UUCP system.

The user jochen has a unique, non-zero user number and is a member of group 6. In the file /etc/group shown in Listing 4.13, this group number is associated to the denomination users. This association is not standardized; in a network in which you use NFS, the files /etc/passwd and /etc/group should as far as possible match between the different computers. The easiest way to achieve this is by means of NIS, the Network Information System. More about this subject can be found in Chapter 22.

In the last line, you will find a guest access which is not protected by a password. This kind of access is sensible only in special cases, since it allows at least read access to a large number of system files. Many (known) security gaps presume that there is at least one local access to the system, which is obviously the case with a user ID without a password.

Now is the time to create the home directory of the user, if this has not already been done by scripts or programs such as adduser. This directory must be owned and writable by this user. For other users and daemons this directory should be executable, since, for example, the finger daemon changes into this directory and reads the files .plan and .project from the user's home directory. A further advantage is that users can read each other's configuration files and thus adapt their own environment to their requirements more easily.

Configuration files can be copied into the home directory, so that new users will find a preconfigured environment. The home directory of a user must only be writable for this user. Otherwise, another user could create files there and thus obtain the privileges of this user. This applies also (and in particular) to pseudo users such as uucp, mail, and news.

Shadow passwords

In the standard UNIX variant, the encrypted passwords are stored in the file /etc/passwd. Since the algorithm used for the encryption is known (interested readers will find the sources of the crypt() function in libc) and regarded as secure, it is only possible to 'guess' a password. To do this, select words from a dictionary, encrypt them, and compare the result with the password stored in the file /etc/passwd. If both character strings are the same, you have guessed the password.

There are programs (for example `crack`) which perform this function. A number of easily configurable rules can be applied, which generate possible passwords from dictionary words via different distributions of upper- and lower-case letters and/or appending of digits. Thus, all passwords that could be found in a dictionary (even a foreign language one) are on the whole insecure. The `npasswd` program tries to apply the tests that `crack` performs at high cost by using the `crypt()` function during input of the password. This procedure requires much fewer system resources.

Secure passwords can be generated in different ways. For most users, it is sensible to select a quotation or a sentence from a book and then use the initial or final letters of the words of this sentence. Furthermore, it is possible to change between upper and lower case and to insert digits or special characters (such as, for example, `,` or `;`). Differently ordered or swapped letters offer additional protection against easy decoding of the password.

It should be noted that often the national keyboard mapping is not yet activated at this point, and that several special characters cannot be entered by pressing the keys bearing their symbols. For this reason it is recommended not to use umlauts or accented letters in passwords. Furthermore, some systems restrict the password length to eight characters. Security-relevant passwords are best generated in a haphazard way by throwing dice or by using a random number generator. A table set up for this purpose can be found in Appendix B.

Make sure that you do not write down your password or make it accessible to other persons in some other way. A different rule applies to the system administrator's password which should also be available in his/her absence, for example deposited in the company's safe. Often just standing behind a person while he/she is logging in is enough to see and therefore compromise a password. In such a situation, it is polite to look away discreetly.

The `/etc/passwd` file must be readable for all users so that, for example, the `ls -l` command can display the names of the users instead of their numeric user identification. When the passwords are stored in another file which is readable only by the system administrator, all programs can still use the data stored in `/etc/passwd`, but they have no access to the encrypted passwords. All programs that carry out logins run under the `root` ID, so that they can also read the encrypted password.

This function is implemented in the shadow password suite; the passwords are stored in the file `/etc/shadow`. Further functions of the shadow system are passwords which expire after a certain time, so that a new password must be selected. The validity period of passwords should not be set too short. If the validity period is one month, users tend to choose one password and only append the number of the current month. This certainly does not improve system security; in such cases it seems more reasonable to set the validity of passwords to about six months.

Shadow passwords make a UNIX system more secure, but may inadvertently cause new security problems. Each program concerned with users logging in and out of the system must use the shadow routines. Therefore, although this is not required for shadow programs, an asterisk (`*`) should be entered in the password field of the `/etc/passwd` file. If there is no password, and a program does not use the shadow routines but the regular password file, login can be carried out without a password.

Network Information Service – NIS

A further possibility for administration of user IDs is the Network Information System NIS or NIS+, formerly known as YP (Yellow Pages). Here, the IDs are created on a NIS server and then called upon by the NIS clients via the network. This allows us to create and maintain user IDs only once for the entire network. More detailed information on the setup and use of NIS or NIS+ can be found in Chapter 22.

Pluggable Authentication Modules

On a UNIX system, many different programs must carry out a user check. This begins with login, followed by xdm and various other programs for logging in under X, and does not end at all with, for example, the ftpd daemon. If you want to adjust your system for the use of shadow passwords, you must check all these programs and newly compile and/or link them.

Modification or extension of the user check is very expensive, but it is often necessary. As a solution to this problem, the method of Pluggable Authentication Modules (PAM) was developed. Here the consumers, that is, the programs that want to carry out user checks, are taken out of the checking process as such. This allows us to add or remove dynamically an additional check without the individual programs being directly affected. Figure 4.1 shows the structure from the programmer's point of view.

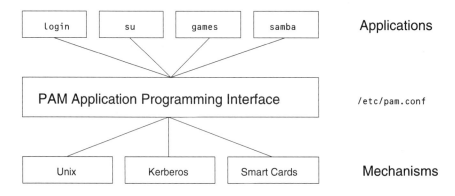

Figure 4.1   Structure of the user check with Pluggable Authentication Modules.

All programs concerned with authentication use the unique PAM-API (Pluggable Authentication Modules Application Programming Interface) which is completely independent from the authentication method used. By means of the file /etc/pam.conf or the files contained in the directory /etc/pam.d, the system administrator can determine methods to be used. This allows great flexibility in choice and configuration.

Before we address the configuration, some words about the possibilities of PAM. As well as authentication, PAM deals with password and user or session management. The individual modules are exchangeable, can be 'stacked,' create log

```
# ftp authorization
# Service Type   Control   Module
ftp    auth      required   /lib/security/pam_listfile.so \
       item=user sense=deny file=/etc/ftpusers onerr=succeed
ftp    auth      required   /lib/security/pam_unix_auth.so
ftp    auth      required   /lib/security/pam_shells.so
ftp    account   required   /lib/security/pam_unix_acct.so
ftp    session   required   /lib/security/pam_unix_session.so
```

Listing 4.7   Excerpt from the file /etc/pam.conf.

entries, and allow us to operate a 'single logon.' The ideas that stand behind PAM and the definition of the interfaces are discussed in rfc86.0.txt of the Open Software Foundation.

The free-standing implementation of PAM under LINUX is documented in the files pam.txt, pam_modules.txt, and pam_appl.txt. The project is still under development, so some changes might be expected. However, because of its flexibility, this approach could advance quickly under LINUX.

The configuration of PAM can be individually adapted to each application. You can either maintain the central file /etc/pam.conf or, for each application, create a file with the corresponding name in the directory /etc/pam.d. Both solutions have their advantages and disadvantages; I myself tend to store individual files in the /etc/pam.d directory. If you make a mistake here, at most one service is affected, and the files are smaller and more clearly structured. Listing 4.7 shows the entry for the ftp service in the file /etc/pam.conf.

The first column contains the name of the service. If you use the /etc/pam.d directory, the file /etc/pam.conf is ignored and the file ftp is read instead. Besides the missing first column, the format of this file is identical to that of the file /etc/pam.conf. If no entry exists for the required service, the entry OTHER or the file /etc/pam.d/other is sought and the settings defined there are used.

The second column of Listing 4.7 determines to which part of PAM the entries should apply. Possible alternatives are auth, account, session, and password.

auth
: The application reads user name and password; the corresponding modules of PAM check the 'authenticity' of the user. In the simplest case it is possible to carry out no check at all, which is obviously not particularly recommended. There are modules that can emulate the behavior of UNIX or go even further.

  Another function of these modules is the so-called 'Credential Granting.' This means that the user is granted the right to use specific services.

account
: The account management can, for example, be used to specify login restrictions. These can be limitations to the time when the service can be used or restriction

to specific terminals. It is also possible to monitor system resources, for example, to prevent a user logging in with multiple sessions.

For many private systems, these functions are not necessary, but for intensively used, publicly accessible systems, use of such procedures makes a lot of sense.

`session`

The modules listed under this heading are responsible for opening and closing of the session. Here, environment variables can be set or other settings, such as the maximum number of processes, can be defined. Furthermore, it is a good idea to protocol the beginning and end of each session.

`password`

Used for changing and managing passwords. This module can, for example, be used to simulate a single login where all passwords are managed centrally.

The third column in the file `/etc/pam.conf` describes when and how a module is used. Here 'stacking' modules can be set by assigning more than one entry to one application. Some examples will be shown in the following paragraphs.

`required`

This entry means that a successful pass through this module is required for a successful check of this type. The user cannot identify in which module his/her login failed because all other modules are passed as well.

`requisite`

A successful pass through this module is required as with `required`. A failure in this module, however, causes further processing to be aborted. Such a procedure can be sensible if one does not want a complete user check to be carried out any more. It is, however, possible that because of the different behavior, an aggressor can gather information about the system and already registered user IDs.

`sufficient`

Success of this module successfully terminates the whole procedure. Failure is not definitive, so that in this case further modules can be called.

`optional`

This module is not essential for success of failure of the login. It can, however, influence the application's response to the login attempt.

The file name in the fourth column of the file `/etc/pam.conf` determines which module carries out the required function. LINUX PAM contains a series of modules which allow you to specify a behavior of PAM similar to the known UNIX procedures. In addition, many other things are possible, including time restrictions. More detailed and up-to-date documentation can be found in the file `pam.txt`.

The line can be continued with a backslash \ ; this increases readability if additional parameters are to be specified, as can be seen in the first lines of Listing 4.7. Listing 4.8 shows the file `/etc/pam.d/ftp` for comparison.

```
#%PAM-1.0
auth       required    /lib/security/pam_listfile.so \
     item=user sense=deny file=/etc/ftpusers onerr=succeed
auth       required    /lib/security/pam_pwdb.so shadow nullok
auth       required    /lib/security/pam_shells.so
account    required    /lib/security/pam_pwdb.so
session    required    /lib/security/pam_pwdb.so
```

Listing 4.8   The file /etc/pam.d/ftp.

The example in Listing 4.8 shows how several modules can be used. Documentation on all available modules can be found in the file pam.txt, once you have installed the PAM system.

In the first line, all user IDs whose names are listed in the file /etc/ftpusers are sorted out. Usually, this file includes IDs such as root and various other system IDs. The module pam_listfile is used which is passed the name of the file and several other parameters. The crucial point is that by means of the parameter onerr=succeed the condition is changed in such a way that all users not included in this file can log in.

The second line uses the password file (or the shadow file) to check the validity of the user ID. The third check to be passed during login via ftp is the validity of the shell. Thus, three relatively simple modules are sufficient to implement the behavior of a normal ftp login.

The next example in Listing 4.9 shows the configuration for the rlogin program (see also Section 17.4.2). A check is made as to whether the login comes from a permitted terminal. In the second line the module pam_rhosts_auth checks on the basis of the /etc/hosts.equiv or ~/.rhosts files whether a login without a password is allowed. If this is the case, the user check terminates at this point.

```
auth        required     /lib/security/pam_securetty.so
auth        sufficient   /lib/security/pam_rhosts_auth.so
auth        required     /lib/security/pam_pwdb.so \
            shadow nullok
auth        required     /lib/security/pam_nologin.so
account     required     /lib/security/pam_pwdb.so
password    required     /lib/security/pam_cracklib.so
password    required     /lib/security/pam_pwdb.so \
            shadow nullok use_authtok
session     required     /lib/security/pam_pwdb.so
```

Listing 4.9   The file /etc/pam.d/rlogin as a second example.

If a login without a password is not possible, the normal password routine of the UNIX system is used. Again, a few and relatively simple modules are sufficient to emulate the behavior of traditional UNIX systems. It is expected that more and more LINUX distributions and other UNIX systems will include this library. However, I would not recommend a manual change without the aid of a distribution.

Additional Information and Sources	
ftp host:	tsx-11.with.edu
ftp path:	/pub/linux/ALPHA/PAM/
PAM RFC:	http://www.pilgrim.umass.edu/\
	pub/osf_dce/RFC/rfc86.0.txt
LINUX PAM:	http://parc.power.net/morgan/Linux-PAM/

User groups

In the /etc/passwd file, a user ID is assigned to a group. Which group this is can be discovered by means of the id command or can be read from the password file. This group is the standard group of the user and is used, for example, when a new file is created. The group membership of a file can be changed with the chgrp *group file name* command.

The owner of a file can be changed (*only* by the user root) by means of the chown command. This makes it impossible to 'donate' files, which may create security gaps or circumvent quotas.

A user can be assigned to several groups. The corresponding user name is entered in the file /etc/group after the group it is joining in addition to the group specified in the /etc/passwd file. The format of the group file is similar to that of the password file; the meaning of the individual fields is explained in more detail in the following paragraphs. By means of the newgrp command, a user can make another group his/her default group for the current session.

group name:password:gid:user IDs

- As for the user ID, the group name is a word that does not contain special characters and uniquely identifies the group.
- If no password is specified, it is possible to switch to this group without a password, provided the user is already a member of this group. If a password exists, it is checked by the newgrp program in case a user who is not a member attempts to switch to this group. This password is encrypted with the same algorithm as the password file.
- The group number is the unique identification of a group. This number is used by the kernel for checking access rights.
- In the last field, a list of user IDs can be specified that are associated to this group at login time.

All groups associated to the logged-on users can be displayed by means of the id or groups commands; an example is shown in Listing 4.10.

```
(Linux):~> id
uid=40(jochen) gid=6(users) groups=6(users),7(project)
(Linux):~> groups
users floppy
```

Listing 4.10   The id and groups commands.

In Listing 4.10 first the user ID and then the primary group are displayed. This group usually determines the group to which a newly created file belongs. You can change this group by means of the newgrp command. Listing 4.11 shows an example.

```
(Linux):~> id
uid=40(jochen) gid=6(users) groups=6(users),7(project)
(Linux):~> newgrp project
(Linux):~> id
uid=40(jochen) gid=6(project) groups=6(users),7(project)
```

Listing 4.11   Changing the primary group with newgrp.

Manual switching between different groups is, however, awkward, and the procedure is relatively error-prone when several users are working together in different groups or projects. Later in this chapter, we will introduce a much easier solution for this task.

Permissions for files

The breakdown of users into different groups can be used for various purposes. As an example, let us look at the following password and group files (Listings 4.12 and 4.13).

```
root:4IIeEz9nkoE:0:0:system administrator:/root:/bin/bash
jochen:EgIrRB.hrBU:40:6:Jochen Hein:/home/jochen:/bin/tcsh
karl::41:6:Karl Eichwalder:/home/karl:/bin/tcsh
michael::42:6:Michael Kohl:/home/michael:/bin/tcsh
```

Listing 4.12   Excerpt from a password file (/etc/passwd).

Users karl and jochen work on a common project and are therefore associated to the project group. The group membership is displayed by means of the id command. The value gid is the primary group of the user; after groups you will find the additional groups to which the user is associated in the file /etc/groups.

Files to be worked on in common are stored in the directory /home/project. The access rights are set in such a way that other users (for example michael) cannot

```
root::0:root
admin::3:root,bin,sys,adm,jochen
users::6:
project::7:jochen,karl
```

Listing 4.13 Excerpt from a group file (/etc/group).

delete or modify these files. The access rights can be set by means of the chmod program. Listing 4.14 shows an example of the id command and the assignment of permissions to directories.

```
(Linux):/home> id
uid=41(karl) gid=6(users) groups=6(users),7(project)
(Linux):/home> ls -ldF jochen project
drwxr-x--x  16 jochen  users    2048 Apr 04 21:44 jochen/
drwxrws--t   2 jochen  project  1024 Mar 23 08:22 project/
```

Listing 4.14 Example for assignment of permissions.

The first field (for example drwxrws--t) shows the type of the file in the first column; a list of all types can be found in Table 4.1. In Listing 4.14, both directory entries are subdirectories in their turn.

File type	Meaning
–	Normal file
d	Subdirectory (directory)
p	Named pipe
s	Socket
l	Symbolic link
c	Character device
b	Block device

Table 4.1 Types of files in the file system.

The other nine characters, subdivided into groups of three, specify the access rights of the owner, the group, and all other users. Permissions for access to directories and access to files must be differentiated. Table 4.2 lists the possible permissions for files together with brief explanations.

The s bits can be set with the owner or with the group. Then, the program is not started under the ID of the logged-in user, but under that of the owner or the group of the file (setuid). This can be a security problem, particularly if the user root is owner of the file. Therefore, at least the execution of scripts under different IDs is not

Access mode	Numeric	Meaning
r	4	Read access
w	2	Write access
x	1	Program execution allowed
s	4	Start under different user ID (s bit)
s	2	Start under different group ID (s bit)
t	1	Swap instead of demand loading

Table 4.2 Permissions for files

implemented, since this *always* constitutes a security risk (additional information on this question can be found in the UNIX FAQ and in the Security FAQ).

Often it is possible to obtain missing permissions via an additional group. Thus, for example, the devices for floppy disks (/dev/fd*) can be associated to a group, floppy, which is also given write permission for these devices. Subsequently, one can make the required users additional members of this group.

In some UNIX systems, the t bit for programs causes the program not to be reloaded from the file system when real memory runs short, but from the swap space. Under LINUX this function is not implemented, because with today's fast hard disks, this will not give a noticeable increase in speed. It might make a difference in speed when running large programs from slow CD-ROM drives.

As opposed to binary programs, shell scripts must be both executable and readable, since for their execution they must be read and interpreted by the shell. For shell scripts, the setuid or setgid bits are ignored by the kernel for security reasons. Thus, you may either write a small C wrapper or implement the script by means of Perl which internally provides the setuid mechanism and performs many security checks.

Programs started with setuid or setgid should, if possible, not be readable for users, in order to make life for intruders less easy. Otherwise, for example, strings could be used to find out which files are read and written, or the program could be disassembled.[2]

Table 4.3 lists the possible permissions for directories with corresponding explanations. The s bit for the group ensures that all newly created files in this directory automatically get the same group as the directory. Therefore this bit is set in the example in Listing 4.14.

A file can be deleted if the user has write access to the corresponding directory. This means that he/she must *not* necessarily be allowed to read or change the file. Therefore, in globally writable directories such as /tmp the t bit is set. Thus, only the owner of the file or the owner of the directory can delete a file.

In Listing 4.14, the access rights can be set with the program chmod; the exact parameters for these permissions are listed in Table 4.4 in both numeric and textual form. Which of these forms you use is a matter of personal taste and experience.

---

[2] Since the source code of most LINUX programs is freely available, one doesn't need to do it anyway.

Mode	Numeric	Meaning
r	4	Read access
w	2	Write access
x	1	Changing into the directory allowed
s	2	Files automatically belong to the same group
t	1	Only owner may delete (t bit)

Table 4.3 Permissions for directories.

Directory	Numeric mode	Textual mode
jochen	751	u=rwx,g=rx,o=x
project	3771	+t,u=rwx,g=wrxs,o+x

Table 4.4 Setting of permissions.

More information on assignment of permissions can be found in the man page on chmod(1).

After this excursion into the UNIX access right concept, let us get back to Listing 4.14. The second column specifies the link count of the file or of the directory. Most files have a link count of 1; this value is increased by 1 for each hard link pointing to this file. Directories always contain the entry ., which is a hard link to the directory itself. Therefore, each directory has at least a link count of 2. If a directory contains a further subdirectory, the link count is increased by 1, because each subdirectory contains an entry .. which points to the higher directory.

The third field indicates the owner of the file. The group membership can be found in the fourth field. The fifth field specifies the size of the file or of the directory. Next, the date of the file's last modification is displayed. If the modification date is relatively recent (less than six months), the time of day is indicated, otherwise the year. The last field contains the file or directory name.

Default values for access rights

New files always belong to the creating user. Their group is the default group assigned to the user in the /etc/passwd file. The group used for creation of files can be changed with the newgrp command. In the main, text files are assigned rw permission (666 or a=rw), whereas programs generated by the compiler or linker are assigned rwx permission (777 or a=rwx). Bits set in umask are removed from these values. With a umask of 027, the final permissions would be 640 or u=rw,g=r,o= for text files and 750 or u=rwx,g=rx,o= for programs.

The current setting of umask can be displayed and modified by means of the umask command. If the bash is used as the shell, it is also possible to use the symbolic notation instead of the inverted bit notation. For a symbolic output, the -s option must be specified, whereas in the input the symbolic notation is recognized automatically.

Thus, calculation of the bit mask used for masking the unwanted permissions is no longer necessary. The notations used in Listing 4.15 are equivalent.

```
(Linux):~$ umask 027
(Linux):~$ umask u=rwx,g=rx,o=
(Linux):~> umask 027
```

Listing 4.15   Examples for setting the umask.

Permissions and groups in operation

You can view a group also as a role in which a user appears. Each time he/she changes role, for example, working on another project, he/she also changes (the primary) group. This can be achieved, for example, with the newgrp command, but one must not forget to set a corresponding umask as well.

The Red Hat distribution uses the concept of 'User Private Groups.' As his/her primary group, each user is assigned a separate group, preferably with the same name as his/her user ID. This symbolizes that the user initially appears in the role of a private user.

The default umask is 002. Thus, all files are readable and writable by the user and his/her own group. Since each user initially has a private group, the permissions are not set wider than with other schemes without a private group and umask 022. But this trick can be used to set the umask always to a value with which all files and directories are group readable and writable.

Usually, files worked upon in common by a group of persons in their individual roles will be stored in special directories. If it is now ensured that this directory belongs to the group and is writable for the group, all members of the group can use it to store files. The second trick is to give this directory the s bit for the group, so that all newly created files automatically belong to the same group as the directory.

Thus, this method can be used to ensure that each user can continue to store private files, but that as soon as he/she appears in a new role, all data is stored with the corresponding permissions. For normal work at the shell prompt, these settings are sufficient, but you should probably adjust the umask of the ftpd programs in /etc/inetd.conf. If you export group directories by means of Samba, you should enter the corresponding umask in /etc/smb.conf as well.

Additional file permissions

Permissions for files introduced up to this point do not satisfy all requirements for being put on a system. Therefore, in the extended-2 file system, further access rights were implemented in Access Control Lists (ACL). In this list, additional file access options can be set for each individual file. Table 4.5 shows the complete list of possible attributes in an ACL. These attributes can be displayed with lsattr and modified by means of chattr.

Attribute	Effect
a	Only append allowed (APPEND)
c	Compress file (not implemented)
d	File is not saved by dump
i	File is immutable:
	no deletion, renaming, writing, and linking
s	Secure deletion of file
S	Synchronous writing of modifications
u	Allow undelete (not implemented)

Table 4.5 Attributes for Access Control Lists.

These features allow better and more flexible protection and more meaningful treatment of individual files. Thus, log files generated by the syslogd daemon can be given the attribute a to protect them against changes with an editor. However, this attribute prevents processing of log files with prune or similar programs. Another important attribute is S for synchronous writing which ensures that possibly all messages are immediately stored on the hard disk. Thus, after a system crash, one may hope to find the very last message, which could give some idea as to the cause of the breakdown.

4.4.2 Finer subdivisions of rights, or the almighty user root

Under UNIX, there is generally only one user with special privileges: the system administrator, known as the user root, identified by user number 0. In practice, this has proved to be far too inflexible, since quite often other users should be able to (orderly) terminate processes, control printers, or start the system.

If you cannot (or do not want to) shake up the fundamental division into system administrator and 'normal' users under UNIX, you can use the program sudo. This program is configured by means of the configuration file sudoers, which specifies which users can execute which programs under which conditions.

With all its advantages, this system has some serious disadvantages as well. First, the main advantages:

- Purposeful assignment of permissions to users, controlled via the program names.
- Protocoling of all activated commands by means of syslogd.
- No password check for specified users or user groups.
- Additional authentication via renewed input of the password of the calling user.
- Significant facilitation of 'quickly logging in as root.'

However, one must still keep the disadvantages in mind. UNIX and its programs are not designed with the aim of distribution of permissions. This is the source of the most important inconveniences:

- The access rights check is carried out in an application program and not in the kernel where it should belong.
- One trusts the security of the permitted program. Since this has never been the aim of the design, one must expect extreme security problems.
- The last point suggests that sudo can only be employed in a relatively controllable environment without leading to massive security gaps.
- It is not guaranteed that the permissions remain limited to the assigned programs. It is conceivable for a user to gain access rights to further programs by using those of the permitted program.

In the information box at the end of this section, you will find the URL of this program. I myself employ it in a controllable environment, but I think that the security problems caused by its use should not be neglected. What is still needed is a rethink and an improved access rights concept attuned to the requirements of everyday practice.

Other systems, such as Windows NT or VMS have a whole series of individual permissions that can be individually assigned and revoked. Under VMS, a user can even have the right to procure specific permissions, but these are not active at a normal login. This provides far better control over the system.

In the framework of POSIX standardization, a special standard for UNIX security is under development. This standard is known as POSIX.1e (formerly POSIX.6) and, after many years, has not yet been passed.

The standard defines a series of security interfaces, such as for example auditing, access control lists and subdivision of the root privileges. Under LINUX, a project (LINUX Privs) exists which implements these features in the kernel and the corresponding user programs. These functions are still under development, but I hope that they will find their way into the distributions as quickly as possible.

Additional Information and Sources	
ftp server:	ftp.courtesan.com
ftp path:	/pub/sudo/
File name:	cu-sudo.v1.5.3.tar.Z
Size:	about 300 Kbytes
Home page:	http://www.courtesan.com/courtesan/- products/sudo/
LINUX Privs:	POSIX.1e for LINUX
Home page:	http://parc.power.net/morgan/- Orange-Linux/linux-privs/index.html

4.4.3 File systems and data media

UNIX does not utilize drive letters. All data is integrated into one directory tree, and can be accessed in this tree. For the user, it makes no difference at all on which physical hard disk or on which file server the data is stored. When the access paths to the files are the same on all computers in the network, the user will notice no difference between being logged on to the file server or an arbitrary client.

Mounting the file systems and building up the directory hierarchy is normally a task for the system administrator. Nevertheless, it is quite common for even non-privileged users to access their own data media, such as floppy disks, magnetic tapes, or CD-ROMs. Depending on data media and file system, various options are possible.

The mtools package for DOS file systems

DOS diskettes or hard disk partitions can be accessed by means of the mtools package. For this purpose, the existing drives or partitions that are to be made available are entered in the file /etc/mtools.conf. Alternatively, it is possible to use the file ~/.mtoolsrc or the file whose name is stored in the environment variable MTOOLSRC.

To use the mtools, the user must have access rights to the corresponding devices. These can be obtained, for example, by assignment to a special group in the file /etc/group, which then also has read and write permissions on the corresponding device files. All users who are using floppy disk drives are additionally registered in the floppy group.

```
(Linux):~# chgrp floppy /dev/fd[01]*
(Linux):~# chmod 660 /dev/fd[01]*
```

The commands for accessing DOS data media are the ones known from DOS, with an 'm' put in front of the command name to differentiate it from other commands (mcopy, mformat, mtype, mcd, and so on). In all programs of the mtools, except for mformat, the corresponding device can be used with automatic recognition of the data media size. Since the formatting program cannot determine the size by itself, the matching device must be used. An example for the file /etc/mtools.conf is shown in Listing 4.16. The corresponding file systems must not be mounted at the same time; otherwise the file systems might be damaged.

On most of the supported platforms, the mtools can be used without further configuration. In the example in Listing 4.16, the DOS partition and the virtual floppy disk and hard disk for the DOSemu are made available as well. Further information on configuration of the mtools can be found in the extensive info documentation.

The current version of the mtools supports the VFAT file system. This allows storage of long file names on diskettes as well, making it finally possible to transport such files too without any problems. As opposed to diskettes created with tar or cpio, these diskettes are also readable on a DOS or Windows PC.

```
drive a: file="/dev/fd0" exclusive
drive b: file="/dev/fd1" exclusive

# First SCSI hard disk partition
drive c: file="/dev/sda1"

#dosemu floppy image
drive m: file="/var/lib/dosemu/diskimage"

#dosemu hdimage
drive n: file="/var/lib/dosemu/diskimage" offset=3840
```

Listing 4.16   Excerpt from the file /etc/mtools.conf.

	Additional Information and Sources
ftp server:	ftp.gnu.org
ftp path:	/pub/gnu
File name:	mtools-2.0.7.tar.gz
Size:	about 60 Kbytes

The mount program

Another possibility for accessing a data medium is to mount it into the LINUX directory tree. Most partitions are automatically mounted at system start-up and can be used by all users. For this purpose, the start scripts call the mount program, which evaluates the file /etc/fstab.

However, the mount command is a privileged command which can only be executed by the system administrator. Thus, a non-privileged user cannot use it to mount additional file systems. The program usermount or mount from the util-linux package is setuid-root installed and carries out a series of additional checks. However, users can only mount those file systems that are registered in the file /etc/fstab with the user option, and it is not possible to specify any further options.

It must be ensured that these file systems are provided with a series of additional options to prevent security problems. The options nosuid and nodev are particularly important. If the corresponding file systems are not to be mounted at system start-up, the option noauto must be specified.

If a file system is registered in the file /etc/fstab, most options are superfluous when mounting it into the LINUX directory hierarchy. The commands shown in Listing 4.18 are equivalent to the /etc/fstab file specified in Listing 4.17.

In /etc/fstab, a series of additional options can be specified; for example, the uid and gid under which DOS file systems are mounted (DOS does not have user IDs). The fifth field specifies the frequency with which the file system is saved by

```
# Device     Directory     Type      Options            Freq Pass
/dev/hda3    /             ext2      defaults           1    1
/dev/hda5    /usr          ext2      defaults           1    2
/dev/sbpcd   /mount/cdrom  iso9660   user,nodev,ro,noauto
/dev/fd0     /mount/fd0    msdos     user,noauto
/proc        /proc         proc      defaults
/dev/hda2    none          swap      sw
```

Listing 4.17   Excerpt from the file /etc/fstab.

```
(Linux):~# mount -t msdos /dev/fd0 /mount/fd0
(Linux):~# mount /dev/fd0
(Linux):~# mount /mount/fd0
```

Listing 4.18   mount commands using the file /etc/fstab.

means of dump. The sixth field indicates the order in which the file systems are to be saved. Often the root file system is marked with a 1 and all other file systems with a 2.

The mount program understands a series of options that are indispensable for system security. Other options are important for the convenience and security of non-privileged users. Some of the more important options are discussed below. They can either be entered in the file /etc/fstab or can be specified after the option -o in a call of the mount program.

- nodev prevents a device file from being used on a data medium that has enough access permissions to endanger system security. All hard disk devices (/dev/hd* and /dev/sd*) should only be readable (and writable) for the system administrator (and, if needed, a corresponding group). Otherwise, a user could read (or even manipulate) all data on this hard disk. Therefore, this option should be set for all removable media (including CD-ROMs). The opposite of this option is dev.

- Execution of programs from this device can be forbidden by means of the noexec option. The exec option, on the other hand, allows execution of programs.

- Generally, execution of programs can be allowed, but the particular use of suid programs can be forbidden by means of the nosuid option. The suid option, instead, allows execution of suid programs.

- Some partitions are automatically mounted at system start-up, others are not. This is achieved by means of the keywords auto and noauto, which only make sense in the /etc/fstab file.

- File systems can be mounted either with read/write access (rw) or with read-only access (ro). For CD drives, it is mandatory to specify the ro option.

- The `root` partition cannot be unmounted; thus at system start-up, it is initially mounted `readonly`, and only after the file system check is carried out is the access mode changed to write access by means of the `remount` option. At system shutdown, the `remount` option is used again to change the mode back to `readonly` operation.

- Partitions can be mounted with the `sync` option, which prevents modifications from being temporarily stored in the buffer cache. The default is `async`, which allows buffering. For diskettes, it may be sensible to write all data unbuffered before the user removes the floppy disk from the drive.

- Non-privileged users too should be allowed to mount diskettes or CD-ROMs. This is achieved by entering the `user` option in the `/etc/fstab` file. Then the system uses the options `noexec`, `nosuid`, and `nodev` as the default. The system administrator can overwrite these options in the `/etc/fstab` file.

- The `defaults` option implies the options `rw`, `suid`, `dev`, `exec`, `auto`, `nouser`, and `async`, as discussed above.

Individual file systems may have additional options. Thus, neither the DOS FAT file system nor HPFS has user IDs. Therefore, a user and group ID can be globally assigned to the whole file system when it is being mounted. This is done by means of the `uid=` and `gid=` options, each followed by the numeric identification. Assignment of permissions too can only be carried out for the entire file system, by specifying the corresponding `umask=` during mounting. Further options are extensively described in the man page for `mount(8)`.

The automounter amd

The easiest solution for the user is the automounter (`amd`) which, every time a user changes directory, temporarily mounts the corresponding file system. If the file system is not used for a certain time, it is automatically unmounted. It is, however, also possible to trigger the unmounting in such a way that a user can remove a data medium from the drive immediately after usage, without having to wait for the time-out. The full power of the automounter, however, is only unleashed in network operation; more detailed information on this subject is given in Section 18.3. The latest kernel version integrates `autofs` which is supposed to replace the automounter in the near future.

4.4.4 Printing under LINUX

Before we can start printing under LINUX, the kernel must first recognize and initialize the corresponding printer port, for which either a parallel or a serial connection can be used. Here and in the following chapters, we assume that the printer is connected to the parallel port. The driver for this port can either be compiled into the kernel during kernel configuration or can be loaded later as a module (see also Section 4.1.1). If the driver was compiled into the kernel, a message similar to the one shown in Listing 4.19 should be displayed after a restart of the computer.

```
lp1 at 0x0378, using polling driver
```

Listing 4.19   Initialization of the parallel port by the kernel.

With this, the kernel has recognized and initialized the interface. Some interface parameters can be modified by means of the `tunelp` program. Initially, the driver is operated in the so-called 'polling mode,' which does not use interrupts to control the parallel interface. However, the system as a whole is less strained if the printer port is used in interrupt mode. This, however, requires a free interrupt, and the corresponding interface card must support this function.

Another useful option of `tunelp` is `-C`, which requires particularly careful checks before printing. This means that the printer may initially be switched off, the data to be printed is buffered and is printed only when the printer is switched on. More detailed information on `tunelp` can be found in the corresponding man page. Additional information on printing under LINUX can also be found in the Printing HowTo.

First, a test should be carried out as to whether the printer can actually be accessed from LINUX. As `root`, you can simply perform this check by means of the command `cat /etc/passwd > /dev/lp1`. Immediately after this command, the printer should begin to print. Depending on the printer type, different problems may occur.

One phenomenon occurring with many printers is the so-called staircase effect. This means that a new line is not started in the first column of the next line, but after the last character of the previous line. This is because under LINUX (and UNIX) the individual lines of a text are separated by means of the character LF (line feed). In texts under DOS, this separation is instead carried out by means of the character combination CR and LF (carriage return and line feed). Many printers are configured in such a way that the CR and LF characters are mandatory to begin a new line. This problem can be solved in two ways:

- Before printing, the text can be converted, for example by means of the `recode` program (see also Section 8.8) or a short `sed` script (see Section 10.6).

- The printer can be configured in such a way that the LF character is interpreted as CR+LF, either by means of a control sequence or with a changed setting of the printer's DIP switches. Even when used under DOS, this setting has no negative consequences since the second CR is ignored. Please consult your printer manual.

A further problem is that LINUX uses the ISO-Latin-1 character set, whereas DOS generally uses code pages 437 or 850. Thus, umlauts and other special characters are coded differently, so that printouts containing these characters are incorrect. Here, you can either reconfigure the printer by means of an appropriate control sequence or the DIP switches, or you can convert the text accordingly, once again using the `recode` program.

Directly accessing the printer interface, as we did for testing, has several disadvantages:

- The interface must be writable for all users.
- Simultaneous access of several users is not coordinated.
- The output must always be readily prepared for the printer.
- The printer must be switched on for printing actually to occur.

All of these problems can be solved by means of the lpr system. LINUX uses this system, which is also known from BSD systems, instead of the lp system of System V. The following section discusses how the printer is linked into the system and how the output is prepared.

The lpr/lpd system

The BSD printing system consists of a series of programs and files used for the management of print jobs in waiting queues. Print jobs are created by means of the lpr program; they can later be deleted by means of lprm. Queued print jobs are displayed by means of lpq; the system administrator can use the lpc program to control the whole printing system. The central configuration is stored in the file /etc/printcap. To allow the use of lpd, you may need to carry out a minimum configuration of the network system (for loopback). Suggestions on how to do this can be found in Section 14.4.

The file /etc/printcap   This is the central configuration file of the BSD printing system. It has a similar format to the file /etc/termcap; the individual fields are separated by colons, and long lines are continued by means of a backslash (\) at the end of the line. This file specifies which waiting queues are responsible for which printer and how printing data is to be processed. Such an entry is also called a stanza.

Listing 4.20 shows an excerpt of the /etc/printcap file. This excerpt contains only the most important entries, which will be discussed first, before more complex entries are created.

```
lp|standard printer:\
        :lp=/dev/lp1:\
        :sd=/var/spool/lpd/lp1:\
        :sh:\
        :mx#0:\
        :lf=/var/log/lpd:\
        :lo=/var/spool/lpd/lp1/lock/lpd.lock
```

Listing 4.20   Excerpt from the file /etc/printcap.

A single entry (capability) consists of a two-character code. These codes are described in the man page printcap(5). Codes that need a string as a parameter are followed by an equals sign (=), whereas numeric parameters are separated by a hash (sharp) character (#).

- The first field specifies the name of the printer. Several alternative names for the same printer are separated by vertical bars (|). The last name is usually the longest.

- The value lp (line printer) specifies the interface to be used for printing. Here, a local interface is used.

- The value sd (spool directory) defines the directory in which print jobs are buffered. A separate directory should be used for each queue.

- The value sh (suppress header) suppresses printing of the header page. This is sensible for single-user systems, whereas printers used by several users should at least print a brief header line (sb = short banner). If a printer is used by a large number of users, printing a separation page between the listings is definitely a good idea.

- By default, the printing system accepts only jobs that are smaller than 1 Mbyte. This size limit can be changed by setting mx to a different value, where 0 stands for unlimited size. Another possibility for printing large files is to use the -s option when printing with lpr. You must neither modify nor delete such a file until it has completely finished printing.

- The value lo specifies the name to be used for the lock file.

- The file /var/log/lpd is used as a log file. The name is determined by means of the capability lf.

Many (different) printers can be included in the /etc/printcap file. A system default printer is usually called lp. By means of the environment variable PRINTER, each user can set another printer as the default. Furthermore, another printer can be selected when calling lpr with the -P option. More detailed information on the printing system and its configuration can be found in the manual pages of lpr(1), lpq(1), lprm(1), lpd(8), lpc(8), and printcap(5), and in the Printing HowTo.

Printing on remote computers   The lpr system also provides the ability to print on remote computers. Obviously, a network connection must exist between these computers. More on the subject of networks can be found in Chapter 14.

The print server (the computer to which the printer is physically connected) must allow other computers to access the printer. Names of authorized computers are registered in the file /etc/hosts.lpd. Further access rights can be entered in the file /etc/hosts.equiv, but this is only sensible in very rare cases.

Now, the remote printer must be set up in the /etc/printcap file of the client computer (see Listing 4.21). This is done by means of the entries rm (remote machine) and rp (remote printer).

There are lpr programs that ignore printer filters (as described below). If you need that feature you may be forced to change to another lpr system, such as plp or lprng.

```
server|Printer connected to the server:\
      :lp=:\
      :rp=printer:\
      :rm=server:\
      :sd=/usr/spool/server:
```

Listing 4.21 printcap for a printing client.

Additional Information and Sources	
ftp server:	linux.org.uk
ftp path:	/pub/linux/Networking/NetKit/base
File name:	NetKit-B-0.06.tar.gz
Size:	about 1.2 Mbytes

Printer filters

Under UNIX, the use of PostScript as default format for print jobs has become a standard. The advantage of this format is that printouts look almost identical on all printers and that PostScript files can be viewed on screen.

Many PC systems, however, are only connected to a normal dot matrix or inkjet printer which is not PostScript capable. The GNU program GhostScript contains drivers for many widely used printers which allow PostScript files to be output on these printers as well. For this purpose, the output of the gs can be output on the printer with lpr. In the long run, this solution is not satisfactory since it always requires intervention by the user.

To solve this problem, a so-called printer filter can be used to convert the printing data. An input filter tries to determine the file type by means of the file command and to convert the output accordingly. An input filter is started afresh for each printing job, whereas an output filter, which at first sight appears to be just as suitable, is started only once and further printing jobs are handled by the same process.

When creating printer filters, great care must be taken not to compromise system security, since all these programs run under the ID of root. The use of GhostScript (gs) in particular can lead to security problems, as PostScript is a complete programming language and thus allows access to arbitrary files. Therefore, to prevent at least these security problems, you should definitely set the –dSAFER option.

One printer filter which can be easily installed is the magicfilter package by H. Peter Anvin. Compilation and installation follow the GNU standard. The ./configure program checks the system for available programs and adapts the filter correspondingly. The programs are compiled with make and installed with make install. The command make install_filters installs all filters in the /usr/local/bin directory, but often one or two filters are sufficient for the connected printers, so it is sensible to copy just these filters manually. These filters are configuration files for the `magicfilter` program, which decides on the basis of the first few bytes of the printing data how to convert the data for printing.

Another printer filter is `apsfilter` by Andreas Klemm. The basic principle of this filter is similar to that of `magicfilter`, but the implementation looks slightly different. Essentially, the differentiation between the various file formats is based on the `file` program, which reads its data from the file `/etc/magic`. Thus, `apsfilter` depends on the completeness of the file `/etc/magic`.

For each printer, `apsfilter` creates a series of entries in the file `/etc/printcap`. With these entries, you can either print with the automatic filter or request special treatment by specifying the corresponding printer entry from `/etc/printcap`. This is, for example, required for the printing of texts containing umlauts or accented letters, since `file` erroneously identifies these files as `data`.

Additional Information and Sources	
`ftp` server:	`sunsite.unc.edu`
`ftp` path:	`/pub/Linux/system/printing`
File name:	`magicfilter-1.2.tar.gz`
Size:	about 53 Kbytes
`ftp` server:	`ftp.informatik.rwth-aachen.de`
`ftp` path:	`pub/Linux/local/packs/APSfilter`
File name:	`aps-48.tgz`
Size:	about 130 Kbytes

Printing on other network printers

In many networks, not all printers can be accessed via TCP/IP; often they can only be accessed via the NetWare protocol or the protocol of the Windows network. Since LINUX can be integrated into both networks, it is possible to use these printers as well.

If the IPX system is installed and configured (see Section 20.1), it is possible to print to NetWare printers by means of the command `nprint`. If you include the `nprint` call in an input filter of the `lpr` system, you can use a LINUX computer as a gateway between the different systems.

Printers on a Windows network can be accessed by means of `smbclient`. This program is part of the `samba` package; more information on this package can be found in Section 20.2.

4.4.5 System logs

Every UNIX system keeps a series of log files for the purpose of system behavior monitoring and error detection. A generally accessible interface by means of which programs can write log files is the `syslogd` daemon. This daemon is configured by entries in the file `/etc/syslog.conf`. Depending on their origin or importance, it allows messages to be displayed or redirected into different files. In networked environments it is possible to have the log files kept by a special computer, the so-called log host.

Depending on their importance and origin, the log entries can be treated in different ways. Table 4.6 describes the different origins (or facilities).

Origin	Description
auth	Security/authorization messages
authpriv	Private security/authorization messages
cron	Messages from cron and at
daemon	Other system daemons
kern	Output of the kernel
lpr	Logs of the lpr system
mail	Messages of the mail system (sendmail etc.)
mark	Inclusion of marks in the log files
news	Output of the news system
syslog	Messages of the syslogd daemons
user	General messages (default)
uucp	Logs of the UUCP system
local0-7	Origins for local use

Table 4.6   Origins of syslogd messages.

For each of these origins, the message can have a different importance. Table 4.7 contains various settings ordered by decreasing importance.

Importance	Description
emerg	An emergency is signaled
alert	'Yellow alert, activate shields!'
crit	A critical situation has occurred
err	An error situation has been recognized
warning	A warning
notice	A notice
info	Informative messages
debug	Output for error detection

Table 4.7   Importance of syslogd messages.

Listing 4.22 shows an explanatory example of a syslogd daemon configuration. It should be noted that message origin and destination must be separated by tabs. Also, many syslogd implementations do not allow spaces before or after the destination.

All messages generated by the UNIX kernel (kern.*) are written into the file /var/log/kernel. The slash (/) as first character tells the syslogd daemon that this destination is a file or a device. Kernel messages that signal an emergency are sent to

```
# Facility.Level              Destination
kern.*                        /var/log/kernel
kern.emerg                    *
*.err                         /var/log/errorlog
*.emerg                       /dev/console
*.=debug                      /var/log/debug
*.=crit                       root,jochen
*.crit                        @loghost
```

Listing 4.22   Excerpt from the file `/etc/syslog.conf`.

all users (`*`) currently logged in. All messages of all systems that are of importance `err` or higher are protocoled in the file `/var/log/errorlog`. Messages that signal an emergency are in addition protocoled on the console.

If you want to prevent more important messages from being included in a protocol, you can specify the importance with an equals sign (`=`). Thus, all messages concerning error detection (and no others) are protocoled in the file `/var/log/debug`. The last two lines demonstrate the notification of users `root` and `jochen` in the case of critical messages, together with the transmission of these messages to another computer (`loghost`) for protocoling.

If you want to store messages on a log host, you start the host's `syslogd` process with the command line option `-r`. Otherwise, no messages are accepted from remote computers to prevent users filling the hard disk by means of the `logger` program. Other useful options are `-l` followed by a list of computers whose domain names should not be stored and `-s` followed by a list of domain names which should also not appear in the log.

On a private system it can be sensible to display all messages on an unused virtual console, for example `/dev/tty12`. Then, at the touch of a key, the last log entries can be viewed and the necessary measures can be taken. The appropriate entry in the file `/etc/syslog.conf` is shown in Listing 4.23. Please note that not all UNIX systems support this kind of entry.

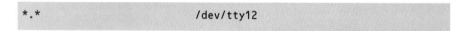

```
*.*                           /dev/tty12
```

Listing 4.23   All messages are directed to the virtual console `/dev/tty12`.

The output files must exist at the start of the `syslogd` daemon. If a file has not yet been created, the daemon displays an error message. The corresponding file can then be created by means of the command `touch file_name`.

After a modification of the configuration file `/etc/syslog.conf`, the daemon must be reinitialized. This can be done by sending the `HUP` signal to the running `syslogd`, for example by means of the command

```
kill -HUP `cat /var/run/syslog.pid`
```

If you want to know whether the required message is correctly protocoled, you can verify this by means of the command

```
logger -porigin.importance "text"
```

However, this also allows confusing messages to be generated and the size of the log files to be significantly increased.

Protocol files have the annoying property that they continue to grow and need ever increasing disk space. Therefore, log files should be emptied at regular intervals. To prevent older messages from being deleted immediately, it is a good idea to send the logs to the system administrator via mail or to create a backup copy. In part (for example in the news system or in UUCP), this is already done by scripts which belong to the system. For the other log files, you can either use your own script or resort to the `prune` package.

In a multi-user system it is necessary and sensible that not all users can read all log files. Thus, for example, login error messages in which user names or passwords might appear should be readable only for the system administrator. During creation of a protocol file with `touch`, the permissions are set according to the specified `umask`. These might be incorrect permissions; therefore log files should not simply be deleted and newly created with `touch`. It is much better to reset the files by means of output redirection, for example with the command `echo -n > Logfile`.

The Red Hat distribution contains the `logrotate` program, which can be used to shorten log files on a regular basis. Before and after shortening, commands can be executed, for example a restart of the `syslogd` daemon. In addition, the file permissions can be specified and version management can be set up. In this way, you always have an up-to-date log file plus one or more older versions of which the oldest will be deleted.

4.4.6 Shared libraries

The shared libraries used under LINUX are loaded into memory only once, even if several programs use them. Thus, the available memory can be used for other things, such as additional processes or disk cache. This is why it is still possible to work reasonably even with a LINUX system with as little as 8 Mbytes of RAM. Shared libraries are upwardly compatible as long as the first digit of the version number (the main or major version) does not change. This makes using a new, improved library, relatively easy.

However, the use of shared libraries also has its disadvantages. For example, the required libraries must always be available on the system. If a system administrator has deleted these libraries or if they have been damaged during a system crash, it may become necessary to boot the system with an emergency floppy and carry out the appropriate repairs. To avoid such problems, a series of programs can be linked statically, that is, without needing to access shared libraries. Since these programs occupy substantially more disk space, they are usually restricted to a limited series of important programs, for example, to a small, but powerful shell such as `sash` and utilities such as `ln`. A statically linked `ln` can often be found under the name of `sln`.

Linking shared libraries at program runtime is carried out by the dynamic linker ld.so, which is itself a shared library. The libraries needed by the program are sought at runtime and loaded into the address space of the process. Libraries required by a program can be displayed by means of the ldd *program* command. An example of this command is shown in Listing 4.24.

```
(Linux):~> ldd /usr/X11R6/bin/xterm
libXaw.so.6 (DLL Jump 6.0) => /usr/X11R6/lib/libXaw.so.6.0
libXt.so.6 (DLL Jump 6.0) => /usr/X11R6/lib/libXt.so.6.0
libX11.so.6 (DLL Jump 6.0) => /usr/X11R6/lib/libX11.so.6.0
libc.so.4 (DLL Jump 4.5pl26) => /lib/libc.so.4.6.20
```

Listing 4.24   Output of the ldd command.

The first column displays the library version linked with the program. The precise version number is shown in parentheses. On the right-hand side we see the libraries found at runtime. In Listing 4.24 the program xterm was linked with the library libc-4.5.26; at runtime the (more recent) version libc-4.6.20 is available.

The dynamic linker searches a series of directories to find all required libraries. In particular, the following directories are searched:

- First, the directories listed in the environment variable LD_LIBRARY_PATH are searched. This variable is ignored for programs that are setuid or setgid. Otherwise, any user could execute arbitrary functions under the ID of the file owner.

- A list of libraries and directories is stored in the file /etc/ld.so.cache. This is done by means of the ldconfig program.

- The file /etc/ld.so.conf contains a list of directories which are searched for the matching libraries by ld.so and ldconfig.

- Finally, libraries are searched for in the system directories /usr/lib and /lib.

Updating of shared libraries

A further advantage of shared libraries is that a new, improved version of a library can be installed without major problems and that programs can use the new, usually more powerful and stable, version. However, since the shared libraries are indispensable for the operation of the system, the system administrator must take adequate care during installation of new libraries.

The libc library is accessed with the name libc.so.4 (see also Listing 4.24). However, this is not the library itself, but a symbolic link pointing to the current library. A new library is activated by setting the symbolic link to the new version. The link must not be deleted and then recreated, because the ln program is not linked statically and the shared library cannot be loaded without this link. Also, the use of ln is not really required; a library update is more sensibly carried out by means of the (statically linked) program ldconfig.

When updating the libc library, further points must be considered. You should read the corresponding release notes, and understand and follow the instructions. At that point, the corresponding header files of the C compiler and additionally required libraries are installed, such as, for example, new versions of the dynamic linker ld.so.

4.4.7   User login

A user logs in to a LINUX system with his/her name and password. This can be done, for example, at the console, at a serial terminal (or a serially connected PC with a terminal emulator such as Telix), via the network with telnet or rlogin or under X with xdm. At the console, several virtual screens are available between which the user can toggle with ⌐Alt⌐-⌐Fn⌐. On a terminal, a similar functionality can be achieved with the screen program. This program can be found on all GNU mirrors.

In the simplest case, the init program, controlled by the /etc/inittab file, starts the getty program on several virtual consoles. This program initializes the corresponding device (tty) and outputs either the file /etc/issue or another message. Subsequently, the login: prompt is displayed and the user name is read. Only then is control passed to the login program, which checks the identity of the user by comparing the entered password with the one registered in the /etc/passwd file.

In practice, things are not always as simple as described above, because there are different getty programs under LINUX which are suited to different situations. In the following paragraphs, the most widely used getty versions will be introduced and their advantages and disadvantages in various application areas compared.

When modifying getty settings it may easily happen that logging in becomes impossible; therefore you should always have an emergency boot floppy available. Another solution is to run at least one virtual console with an older version or a completely different getty. As a simple alternative, you could use the program agetty or the internal getty of the System V init.

The use of a larger number of getty programs is not recommended since on the one hand, many processes need RAM memory and on the other hand, the password must be entered again at each login. With the program open, any program can be started on an additional virtual console without having to log in or starting a new getty.

The agetty program

The agetty program has been developed by W. Z. Venema and ported to LINUX by Peter Ørbæk. It is distributed with the util-linux collection by Rik Faith and is a relatively simple getty. This reduces the possible errors during installation, but makes the application relatively inflexible. The use of agetty on virtual consoles in combination with simpleinit is without problems. However, when connecting serial terminals or dialing in via modem, other gettys are often more suitable.

The `agetty` program should only be used in combination with `simpleinit`, since the correct setting of the environment variable `TERM` is carried out by `init`. Expected parameters are the baud rate of the connected device and the `tty` to be used. The order of parameters should play no role in this `getty`. The following example shows the use of `agetty` in combination with `simpleinit` for a virtual console and a directly connected `vt100` terminal.

```
tty1:linux:/sbin/getty 9600 tty1
ttyS1:vt100:/sbin/getty -L 19200 ttyS1
```

In front of the `login:` prompt, the file `/etc/issue` is displayed unless the `-i` option was specified. In the display, some special character sequences are substituted with the corresponding values so that, for example, the current kernel version could be shown. The complete list of possible variables is shown in Table 4.8.

Character sequence	Substitution with
\s	name of the operating system (Linux)
\n	name of the computer (host name)
\r	release of the operating systems (for example 1.2.3)
\v	additional version information
\m	computer architecture (i386)
\o	domain name
\d	current date
\t	current time
\b	baud rate

Table 4.8 Substitutions in the `/etc/issue` file.

Some distributions newly generate the `/etc/issue` file at each system start-up in the script `/etc/rc.local`, entering the current kernel version. In the system-specific adaptation of the `/etc/issue` file, this 'feature' should be disabled.

When connecting a serial terminal, the `-L` option must be specified to make the `agetty` program recognize the terminal as being locally connected. In addition, different baud rates can be specified, separated by commas, between which the user can toggle by means of (Break).

The internal `getty` of the System V Init

There is a patch for the System V Init which integrates a simple `getty`, derived from `agetty`, into the `init` program. A simple `login` is integrated as well, so that a series of error sources can be excluded. On the one hand, this makes the configuration easier; on the other hand, a good portion of RAM can be used for other purposes, particularly if many `getty` programs must be started and the computer has only a small amount of RAM.

To use the internal `getty`, the new keyword `igetty` was introduced into the `inittab` configuration. The following example shows its use in the `inittab` file.

```
i1:123456:igetty:tty1
```

This internal `getty` is not suited for terminals or modems because it does not include configuration options for baud rates and similar things. It is, however, a reasonable alternative for virtual consoles, if many `getty` programs will be started.

The program getty_ps

The `getty_ps` program was originally developed by Paul Sutcliffe and is maintained by Kris Gleason. This program is suited for operation both on virtual consoles and on incoming and outgoing connections via modem. Because of its greater flexibility, configuration is slightly more complicated than with the simple `agetty`. Nearly all the configuration takes place at runtime. The only decision to be made for the compilation of `getty_ps` is whether the program is to be configured and installed according to the file system hierarchy standard. Table 4.9 shows an overview of the paths and files used.

Function	Default path	FHS path
gettydefs	/etc/gettydefs	/etc/gettydefs
Configuration	/etc/defaults/getty	/etc/conf.getty
Local configuration	/etc/defaults/getty.*Line*	/etc/conf.getty.*Line*
Lock files	/usr/spool/uucp	/var/lock

Table 4.9 Paths and files for `getty_ps`.

First, the `getty` must be included in the `/etc/inittab` file. It is important that at least the order of parameters is correct. Instructions can be found in the man page; furthermore, it is possible to try out the program on a free console without entering it in the `inittab` file by directly inputting the part after the third colon as a command. As parameters, the `getty` program expects at least the `tty` on which the login is to take place. Optional parameters are the specification of the speed and of the terminal type which has an entry in the `/etc/termcap` file. The following example shows two entries in the `/etc/inittab` file for the System V `init`, one for a virtual console and one for a serial terminal.

```
1:12345:respawn:/sbin/getty tty1 VC linux-28
S1:2345:respawn:/sbin/getty ttyS1 DT9600 vt220
```

As a second step, the file `/etc/gettydefs` must be adjusted. The format is documented in the man page `gettydefs(5)`. The `getty_ps` program sources include an example which can initially be employed without modification. It contains the default configuration for the initialization of the connections and the selected speeds. The individual lines have the following format:

```
speed# init-flags # final-flags #login-string#next-speed
```

After each entry, an empty line must be inserted; the first line is the default setting if no speed is specified at the call of getty. Comments are marked by a # at the beginning of a line. When changes have been made to this file, the command getty -c should be used to check the syntax of this file because in the event of syntax errors in this file, no login to the system will be possible.

speed is the symbolic specification of the speed specified as a parameter at the call of getty. If the same value is entered for next-speed, the speed cannot be changed. Otherwise, the (Break) key can be used to toggle between the different speeds.

The init-flags and final-flags values determine the initial and final TERMIO settings. Usually, no modification is needed. However, for my own terminal, the XON/XOFF protocol had to be switched off; thus I included the additional settings -IXON -IXOFF in the final-flags. The flags to be specified here are exactly the same parameters as the ones known to the stty program. Interested users should refer to the man page for stty(1).

login-string contains the text displayed as the login prompt. As with the output of the /etc/issue file, a series of special character sequences are substituted. Table 4.10 shows a list of these character sequences and their substitutions.

Character sequence	Substitution with
@B	Baud rate
@D	Current date (MM/DD/YY)
@L	Current tty
@S	Name of the computer (host name)
@T	Current time (HH:MM:SS)
@V	Version of the operating system
@@	One single @ character
\\	One backslash (\)
\b	One backspace (Ctrl-H)
\c	Prevents line feed
\f	One form feed (Ctrl-L)
\n	One new line (Ctrl-J)
\r	One carriage return (Ctrl-M)
\s	One single space
\t	One tab (Ctrl-I)
\nnn	ASCII character with octal value nnn
\@	One @ character

Table 4.10 Substitutions in getty_ps.

In the last step, the program can be specially configured for each connection. This concerns not only the file issue, but also speeds and extended functions. Configurations that apply for all connections are set in the file /etc/conf.getty (or /etc/defaults/getty); for a special connection, the file is called /etc/conf.getty.Line (or /etc/defaults/getty.Line). With the option -d, another file can be specified. This is often done when testing modifications; thus, the remaining `getty` programs will in any case be able to run.

The configuration files contain lines of the form `NAME=value`; there is a whole series of values that can be changed at runtime in this way. The most important values are presented in the following paragraphs; a more detailed discussion of all possible settings can be found in the man page for `getty(1)`.

`SYSTEM=name`

> The character sequence `@S` is usually substituted with the host name. With this setting, a different name for the `getty` can be set.

`VERSION=string`

> The character sequence `@V` is usually substituted with the version of the operating system. Here, the specified text can be used instead. If the text begins with a slash (`/`), the contents of the specified file are displayed.

`ISSUE=string`

> At start-up, `getty` displays the contents of the file `/etc/issue`. Here, you can either specify another text or, if the string begins with a slash (`/`), another file.

`LOGIN=name`

> `name` is the complete path to a program, which is to be used instead of the normal `/bin/login`. As a parameter, the entered user name is passed.

`CLEAR=value`

> `getty` deletes the screen before the file `/etc/issue` is displayed. If the value `NO` is entered here, the screen is not deleted.

After the general settings, there is a series of configuration options for the use of modems or serial terminals in connection with `getty_ps`.

`INIT=string`

> At the start of `getty`, the modem can be initialized with this value, for example, with the entry `INIT="" ATZ\r`. The characters are interpreted as 'Chat-script', beginning with a text which is expected by the modem.

`HANGUP=value`

> Usually, `getty` hangs up when it starts, so that after three unsuccessful attempts or after logging out, the line is interrupted. If the value `NO` is entered here, the phone is not hung up, but a new login prompt is displayed. The same function is carried out by the command line option `-h`.

`WAITCHAR=value`

> `getty` waits with the display of the login prompt until a character has been entered. This is sensible for directly connected terminals or modems which always display `Carrier Detect`.

DELAY=*seconds*
> Normally, there is no delay between the first character entered and the display of the login prompt. With this option (or the command line option -r), a delay can be set.

TIMEOUT=*number*
> getty waits indefinitely for a user name. For dial-in connections, it may be sensible to set a timeout. In this case, however, the line should be interrupted at the end or a restart of getty.

CONNECT=*string*
> Here again, a sequence of strings and modem commands can be specified by means of which the connection between modem and getty is established. Automatic setting of the transmission speed has not proven reliable in this case.

WAITFOR=*string*
> Similar to WAITCHAR, this parameter is used to wait for a character sequence. The getty program continues only after this character sequence has been recognized. In the following example, getty waits for a call which is signaled by the modem by means of the string RING. Subsequently, it opens the line (ATA) and waits for the character sequence CONNECT issued by the modem. The character sequence "" stands for 'do not wait.'

```
WAITFOR=RING
CONNECT="" ATA\r CONNECT
```

For modem operation it is possible to allow a login only at specific times or a predefined sequence of ringing and recalling. These settings can be controlled by means of the following keywords:

RINGBACK=*value*
> If this value is set to YES, a login is only allowed if the phone rings one to three times, then it hangs up, and a new call is made within 60 seconds. This value can be modified by a series of additional parameters. MINRINGS and MAXRINGS determine the minimum and maximum number of rings for the first call. The values MINRBTIME and MAXRBTIME indicate the minimum and maximum time between the first and the second call.

SCHED=*range1 range2 range3* ...
> getty allows logins only in the time intervals specified by *range*. Outside these times, getty sends the OFF string and waits for the next on-time. An allowed time span is specified in the form d:hh:mm-d:hh:mm. Here, d is the day of the week (0 = Sunday, 1 = Monday, and so on), hh is the hour, and mm is the minute where a time span begins or ends.

OFF=*string*
> The format of this setting is the same as for the INIT string. This string is sent to the modem when the connection no longer allows logins. It can be used, for

example, to switch off the modem auto answer function or to unhook, so that callers receive a busy signal.

The `getty_ps` program is also capable of cooperating with a Fido mailer. Interested users will find more information in the man page for `getty(1)`.

The `getty_ps` program is a flexible and powerful `getty` which, however, conceals a series of pitfalls during configuration. Nevertheless, the higher expense is definitely worth it for the use of modems or serial terminals, because practically any configuration requirement can be satisfied. A particularly useful feature is the capability to configure individual connections differently and thus operate them in different ways.

Additional Information and Sources	
ftp server:	`sunsite.unc.edu`
ftp path:	`/pub/Linux/system/serial/getty`
File name:	`getty_ps-2.0.7f.tar.gz`
Size:	about 85 Kbytes

The `uugetty` program

The `uugetty` program is part of the `getty_ps` package and is essentially configured in the same way. However, since lock files are created that prevent multiple simultaneous use, it allows cooperation with programs such as `uucp` via a serial line.

LINUX provides two devices to communicate with a serial interface. These are the `/dev/ttyS*` devices, which are designed for incoming connections, and the `/dev/cua*` devices, designed for outgoing calls. With this, the kernel itself can carry out the lock management. However, this system functions only if the modem is in auto answer mode. This means that after a specified number of rings, the modem answers the call even if the computer is not ready or no login is allowed. If the `getty` itself answers the call, the `/dev/ttyS*` device must be used for both kinds of connection, and the applications must take care of the lock management themselves.

The file system hierarchy standard (see also Section 2.5.5) specifies that lock files are stored in the `/var/lock` directory. Not all programs use this directory, thus care must be taken. Only if all programs create and/or search for the lock files in the correct directory, and the files have the correct format, does the lock management function reliably. Some distributions, for example, use the `/dev/modem` device to access the serial interface to which the modem is connected. Then all programs too must use (and lock) this device. In the long run, it is more sensible to specify the real device (`/dev/ttyS*`) in order to avoid these problems.

After these general remarks, back to `uugetty`. If a valid lock file is found during the start, `uugetty` waits until the process releases this lock and terminates. Subsequently, `init` starts a new `uugetty` which can reinitialize the line. If an invalid lock is found (that is, the process which generated the file no longer exists), this file is deleted and `uugetty` continues to work as usual.

At runtime, when a call is expected, a search for lock files is carried out at regular intervals, for example by means of uucp. Then uugetty terminates, and the program newly started by init can reinitialize the modem.

If no lock file is found, uugetty waits for incoming calls without creating a lock file. This makes it possible to use the modem for outgoing calls. If a call comes in, the corresponding lock file is generated. When the RINGBACK function is used, lock files are already created at the first call, so that the expected second call cannot be disturbed by outgoing calls.

The mgetty program

The mgetty program was developed by Gert Döring and is distributed in one package together with sendfax. This allows both incoming and outgoing calls and can differentiate between data and fax connections. An additional program (vgetty) turns your modem into an answering machine, provided it supports this function.

To install mgetty, you must copy the file policy.h-dist as policy.h and adapt it to your system, paying special attention to the correct lock files. The file is extensively commented and contains lots of useful information for the operation of fax modems. The detailed Texinfo manual of mgetty contains additional hints for special modem types.

Since many configurations must be carried out at compile time, you should compile mgetty and keep the sources available for some time, so that you can carry out further adaptations. Once you are happy with your configuration, you save your changes by permanently storing a context or unified diff between the files policy.h-dist and policy.h. When a new version is installed or adjustments are required, you can directly recall your changes (either manually, using the emacs mode ediff, or by means of the patch program).

Additional Information and Sources	
ftp server:	sunsite.unc.edu
ftp path:	/pub/Linux/system/serial/getty
File name:	mgetty+sendfax-1.0.0.tar.gz
Size:	about 590 Kbytes

Working at a terminal or via a modem connection

If you have a serial terminal connected to your computer, or use a PC as a terminal, or log in to another system via a modem, you no longer have the convenience of the virtual consoles under LINUX or the possibility of using gpm to transfer data between the consoles by means of your mouse. In some cases, Emacs can be of some help, but more often than not this is not a good idea.

In this case you should definitely have a look at the GNU program screen. On practically any terminal type, this program emulates a VT100 and manages several sessions in parallel. You can switch between the different sessions with a few keystrokes and transfer textual data between the simulated terminals. Table 4.11 shows an overview of the most important key combinations.

Key	Meaning
`Ctrl`-`A`	Escape
`Ctrl`-`A`, `?`	Display help
`Ctrl`-`A`, `a`	Send a Ctrl-A to the application
`Ctrl`-`A`, `[`	Copy
`Ctrl`-`A`, `]`	Paste
`Ctrl`-`A`, `d`	Detach
`Ctrl`-`A`, `0-9`	Select terminal 0-9

Table 4.11   Key combinations for `screen`.

In addition, you can log in once, use `screen` and, when you log out, send it into the background without terminating it. Then you can resume your session at another terminal by means of `screen -r`.

4.4.8 User information

After logging in, the `login` program displays the file `/etc/motd` (message of the day) before the user's shell is started. This file is often used for information messages about system availability or new software.

If you use `xdm` on your system, you can use the `xmessage` program to display a message. Other programs for this purpose are `xbanner` and `xmotd`.

4.5 User-definable system configuration

The following section discusses how a user can modify system-specific settings for his/her login, although this would normally be a task for the system administrator. This possibility is an essential advantage of a UNIX system, since many problems can well be solved without the system administrator having to intervene.

With many features, in particular with regard to implementation, a range of security considerations need to be observed. However, as the source code of the entire system is available, it is possible for experienced UNIX specialists to detect security gaps by studying the program sources and then to eliminate them. In general, systems whose source code is available and thus verifiable are considered more secure than systems that are not verifiable from outside (security by obscurity).

4.5.1 Terminal configuration

Under UNIX, screen devices (terminals and the console) are controlled by means of libraries which keep the programs independent from the hardware used. These libraries read the descriptions of the terminals with their capabilities and command sequences from so-called terminal databases.

In the old days, UNIX systems were controlled via teletype terminals (typewriter, TTY). When the first screens came about, it became necessary to support these devices too. Since there was a large number of different and obviously incompatible terminals, a method was sought that allowed programs to remain independent from the terminal used. In the framework of the BSD system, the termcap library was developed, whereas on System V systems, the curses library was written. Today's UNIX systems usually support both libraries.

The termcap database

A widely-used database is /etc/termcap (terminal capabilities). This is a text file where the system administrator can add new entries or modify existing entries by means of an editor. However, since there is such a large number of terminals around, on many systems this database is not particularly up to date or well maintained. In case of problems with this database, one can try to use a widespread standard (for example, by setting the environment variable TERM to the value vt100), provided this terminal is emulated. In this way, however, one loses access to possible extensions or improvements of the device with respect to the standard.

Because of these problems, it is often sensible for individual users, either as a trial or permanently, to use a different terminal database. A user has various possibilities for influencing the choice of the database:

- The user can use the system database /etc/termcap by just setting the environment variable TERM to the correct terminal type.
- If the system database is not suited, a user can create and activate his/her own database in the home directory:

```
(Linux):~> cp /etc/termcap .termcap
(Linux):~> setenv TERMCAP $HOME/.termcap
```

- The termcap database entry can be copied into the environment variable TERMCAP and then modified.

Listing 4.25 shows an example of a termcap entry. The format is the same as in the file /etc/printcap. The meaning of the individual entries can be found in the man page of termcap(5) or in the corresponding info documentation. If you do not want to spend entire evenings engulfed in terminal configuration, you had better keep your hands off this.

```
d0|vt100|vt100-am|vt100am|dec vt100:\
        :do=^J:co#80:li#24:cl=\E[;H\E[2J:sf=\ED:\
        :le=^H:bs:am:cm=\E[%i%d;%dH:nd=\E[C:up=\E[A:\
        :ce=\E[K:cd=\E[J:so=\E[7m:se=\E[m:us=\E[4m:\
        :ue=\E[m:md=\E[1m:mr=\E[7m:mb=\E[5m:\
        :rs=\E>\E[?3l\E[?4l\E[?5l\E[?7h\E[?8h:\
        :ks=\E[?1h\E=:\
        :ku=\E0A:kd=\E0B:kr=\E0C:kl=\E0D:kb=^H:\
        :ho=\E[H:k1=\E0P:k2=\E0Q:k3=\E0R:k4=\E0S:sr=\EM:\
        :ke=\E[?1l\E>:vt#3:xn:me=\E[m:is=\E[1;24r\E[24;1H:\
        :sc=\E7:rc=\E8:cs=\E[%i%d;%dr:pt:
```

Listing 4.25   An example of a `termcap` entry.

Additional Information and Sources	
ftp server:	ftp.gnu.org
ftp path:	/pub/gnu
File name:	termcap-1.3.tar.gz
Size:	about 300 Kbytes

The `terminfo` database

Another database for controlling terminals which is present on practically every UNIX system is the `terminfo` database. This database is used by the `ncurses` library. The system-wide `terminfo` database is located in the directory `/usr/lib/terminfo`.

For faster access to the individual entries of the database, there is one subdirectory for each letter, in which the terminal descriptions beginning with this letter are created. These files are created out of the corresponding source text of the terminal descriptions by means of the `tic` (TermInfo Compiler) program. If this database is incomplete or incorrect, each user can create his/her own database in the home area:

```
(Linux):~> cp -dR /usr/lib/terminfo terminfo
(Linux):~> setenv TERMINFO $HOME/terminfo
```

The default path for a user-defined `terminfo` database is the `~/.terminfo` directory. This path is used, for example, by `tic` if you want to compile a `terminfo` entry as a non-privileged user. Compiled entries can be reconverted into a readable format by means of the `infocmp` command.

Additional Information and Sources	
ftp server:	ftp.gnu.org
ftp path:	/pub/gnu
File name:	ncurses-1.9.8a.tar.gz
Size:	about 550 Kbytes

4.5.2 **Documentation**

Under UNIX, the man program is an important source for documentation. This program reads existing documentation, formats it, and displays it on screen. The system administrator can set the search path for man pages in the file man.config or man-path.config in the /etc directory. However, each user can define his/her own path by setting the environment variable MANPATH.

```
(Linux):~> setenv MANPATH $HOME/man:$MANPATH
```

The man pages can usually be found in the directories /usr/man, /usr/local/man, and /usr/X11R6/man. Since formatting larger man pages takes a relatively long time, the most widely-used man programs are able to store the formatted pages as cat pages and then read these directly.

man pages can also be converted into PostScript or DVI files by means of groff. This allows a visually more acceptable output. The precondition is, however, that the nroff sources of the man pages are installed. The following command formats a man page and stores it in a PostScript file.

```
(Linux):~> groff -Tps -mandoc /usr/man/man1/ls.1 > ls.ps
```

man pages are used for quick information about options and usage of the programs. They often contain a section with examples, but rarely a tutorial.

If you do not know what a command does, you should read the man page before trying it out. If you are looking for a command for a specific function, try apropos *keyword*. A telegram style description of a command can be displayed by using whatis *command*. There is a man page for practically every command under LINUX, which usually answers most questions.

Another documentation system is used by the GNU project. This system (texinfo) allows you to use the same source text to generate a document (a so-called Info file) by means of the makeinfo program, that can be read online with the info program, and to print the documentation using TeX. This is the standard format for the documentation of GNU programs. This documentation is designed as extensive user documentation with examples. In its printed form, the documentation can be read as a book, the layout, too, being visually quite appealing.

The online Info files can be found in the /usr/info or /usr/share/info directory; however, the search path for these files can be changed by means of the environment variable INFOPATH. Info files can be read using either Emacs Info mode or the info or xinfo program.

```
(Linux):~> setenv INFOPATH $HOME/info:$INFOPATH
```

Further information on individual programs can also be found in the /usr/doc directory. There, you will often find README files or extensive instructions. Many programs display a brief list of instructions when called with incorrect parameters or with the -?, -h, or --help option.

4.5.3 Libraries

As already discussed above, LINUX makes use of shared libraries. These libraries are mapped into the address space of a process and are loaded only once for all processes. It is, however, possible for a library to contain errors that cause a user's programs to crash. In such cases it is sensible temporarily to use one's own shared library, for example to test a bug fix. The search path for such libraries can be set by means of the environment variable LD_LIBRARY_PATH.

```
(Linux):~> setenv LD_LIBRARY_PATH $HOME/lib:$LD_LIBRARY_PATH
```

When starting programs that do not run under the normal ID of a user, but under an ID set with `setuid` or `setgid`, the path set in the variable is ignored, otherwise one could activate arbitrary functions under a `setuid` ID.

Furthermore, the user can use the environment variable LD_PRELOAD to define an additional library which will be loaded after all other libraries. This library can, for example, be used to overwrite existing functions from other libraries, which is an easy way to modify and test individual functions.

4.6 User-related configuration

UNIX systems provide many features by means of which each user can individually configure his/her working environment. The system administrator's task is to allow users reasonable working conditions from the very start. Therefore, when a new user ID is created, a standard environment should be installed. The required files should be stored in the directory /etc/skel and can be copied either manually or by means of a script (see also the `useradd` program) into the home directory of the new user. Obviously, the new user should also become the owner of these files so that he/she can later adapt them to his/her personal requirements.

Modern shells use the tilde character (~) to refer to the home directory of a user. However, only access via the environment variable HOME is portable (and thus, for example, usable in sh scripts). The cd (or chdir, change directory) command without parameters always changes back into the home directory, so the pwd command (print working directory) must be used to display the current directory. This command is often an internal command of the shell, but for reasons of compatibility with the POSIX.2 standard, there is also a program /bin/pwd.

The names of most configurations files begin with a dot (.), so that these files are not shown by ls. To display all files, the –a option (or --all with GNU ls) must be specified.

4.6.1 Selection of an interactive shell

When logging in at a text terminal or console, the shell specified in the file /etc/passwd is started. This will usually be a program, such as the bash or the tcsh. This shell is also started by the xterm program if no program name is specified as a parameter. The shell is the first user interface a user encounters on a UNIX system. Therefore, the use of an appropriate shell is very important for efficient work.

For interactive work, generally a shell is used which allows editing of the command line and which has a history function. Command and file name completion are additional useful functions. Frequently, alias names are used to abbreviate long commands or automatically specify special options.

The csh or tcsh

The csh (or tcsh) is often used as a login shell. It is well suited for interactive work and has practically all functions one would expect from a shell. However, it is not the 'optimum' shell, since there are tasks which this shell cannot perform. An extensive description of the disadvantages of the csh can be found in the text 'Why csh is considered harmful' by Tom Christiansen (tchrist@mox.perl.com). This text is posted regularly, for example, in the newsgroup comp.unix.shell and can be found in the FAQ archive of rtfm.with.edu.

It is especially worth mentioning that the tcsh has a programmable completion function. This can be used, for example, to program compiler flags or other parameters which are only available for these commands. An extensive example is included in the sources of the tcsh.

The bash

The bash is the shell of the GNU project and on many LINUX systems, it is the standard shell. This shell too has history functions and completion of program and file names.

There are several other (also freely available) shells such as, for example, the pdksh or zsh. The choice of a special shell will always depend on the users' experiences and expectations.

Some systems offer no possibility of changing the shell, because either the command chsh does not exist or not all shells are registered in the file /etc/shells. A makeshift solution is to start the new shell in an initialization script of the login shell. This should be carried out by means of the command exec *new_shell*, so that at the end of the shell, the session is terminated as well and no unnecessary memory is wasted for a second shell. The exec command replaces the currently running shell with the program specified as a parameter. Provided you have at least started another interactive shell, you can still use this command to start a program, even though the message no more processes is displayed.

The most powerful shell – zsh

Another widely used shell is the zsh. It is relatively compatible with the Bourne shell, but has many extensions of the csh and tcsh built in. If you are looking for a sh compatible shell with programmable completion, the zsh is precisely what you want.

4.6.2 Non-interactive shells

Usually, the Bourne shell sh is used for programming shell scripts. This shell can be found on practically all UNIX systems. Under LINUX, the shell /bin/sh is often a symbolic link to the /bin/bash. This is fairly inconvenient if one wants to develop shell scripts that also run on other UNIX systems, because the bash, even if called under the name of sh, provides a series of useful extensions. In such cases, use of the ash shell is recommended, which is, however, seldom used in interactive operation. Here, the bash is easier to handle, since it has history and extension functions. On average LINUX systems, however, a certain number of scripts (even some needed for system start-up) are written making use of special features of the bash, but they generally call the /bin/sh.

It is better not to use the csh for programming scripts, because here too one reaches the limits of the shell. More information on this subject can again be found in the text 'Why csh is considered harmful.'

4.6.3 Shell initialization

Depending on the shell, different files are read during initialization. Here, we introduce the configuration files for the widely used shells bash and tcsh.

If at all possible, the system administrator should not define any alias names for programs in the system profiles. This is a highly user-specific configuration which, accordingly, users should carry out by themselves. Nevertheless, it is occasionally sensible for the system administrator to create alias names (such as dir), for example, to prevent common errors or to make the system as a whole more user friendly.

Initialization of the tcsh

First of all, the tcsh reads the file /etc/csh.cshrc. When a login shell is started, the file /etc/csh.login is read too. This concludes the initialization because of the system-wide predefined settings. Users can create a series of files in their home directory that can be used to carry out additional personal settings. First, the file ~/.tcshrc is read. If this file does not exist, the shell reads the file ~/.cshrc. If this shell is a login shell, the file ~/.login is processed as well.

When leaving a login shell, the files /etc/csh.logout and ~/.logout are read and the commands specified in these files are executed.

Initialization of the bash

The bash too has a series of initialization files. Depending on the kind of shell and the specified command line parameters, different files are executed.

When the bash is started as a login shell, the file /etc/profile is processed first. If the file ~/.bash_profile exists, this file is read. Otherwise, the file ~/.bash_login is processed, provided it exists. If none of these files exists in the home directory, the file ~/.profile is read, if it exists.

When logging out of the system, the file ˜/.bash_logout is processed. Here, for example, work files may be deleted or the processed data may be backed up onto floppy disks.

The sh only reads the files /etc/profile and ˜/.profile; therefore, functions which are to be used only by the bash or which need the bash for execution, should only be called in the other above-mentioned files. Otherwise, the corresponding scripts will no longer be usable in a heterogeneous environment.

If the bash is started as an interactive shell, the file ˜/.bashrc is read. If aliases are also to be used in shells that are to be started under X, an appropriate call should be included here.

Finally, the bash can also be started as a non-interactive shell by means of the option −posix. Then, those initializations are carried out that are contained in the files specified in the environment variable ENV.

Initialization of the zsh

Initialization of the zsh is similar, with one or two differences. First, the file /etc/zshenv is read. In this file, the option RCS can be set, which prevents reading further configuration files.

After the file /etc/zshenv, the file .zshenv is read which is searched for either in the ZDOTDIR or in the HOME directory. If the zsh is started with the option −l or the first character of the program name ($0) is a minus sign, the files /etc/zprofile and .zprofile are read.

If the zsh is interactive, the files /etc/zshrc and .zshrc are processed. If the zsh is started as a login shell, the files /etc/zlogin and .zlogin are read.

When logging out, the files /etc/zlogout and .zlogout are processed, provided they exist. As you can see, the user of the zsh can choose between many different configurations .

4.7 Configuration of editors

Since the use of editors depends strongly on personal taste, users should determine their default editor which will then be used by (nearly) all programs (such as, for example, tin or crontab). If neither of the environment variables EDITOR or VISUAL is set, the default editor vi is used. Many users, however, prefer other editors, such as joe or Emacs (Listing 4.26).

```
(Linux):˜> setenv EDITOR emacs
(Linux):˜> setenv VISUAL emacs
```

Listing 4.26   Setting of the default editor.

Finally, practically any editor can be adapted to the special preferences and requirements of the user. The following paragraphs simply introduce the configuration files, without discussing the configuration itself in more detail.

In the same way, the program more is used for the display of man pages. Each user can choose another program for the display by setting the environment variable PAGER to an appropriate value (Listing 4.27). Frequently, the less program, which is much more powerful than more, is entered here; other systems have a program pg.

```
(Linux):~> setenv PAGER less
```

Listing 4.27   Selecting the default pagers.

4.7.1 The editor emacs

More detailed information on configuration and application of this powerful editor is given in Chapter 5. The user-specific configuration can be found in the file ~/.emacs.

4.7.2 The editor joe

The joe editor is an easy-to-handle WordStar clone programmed by Joseph H. Allen (jhallen@world.std.com). For many people used to DOS, this editor will initially be the easiest one to handle. The editor is configured by the system administrator by means of the file /usr/lib/joerc. Users can copy this file as ~/.joerc and modify it to their personal liking.

The author has created additional configurations for a better emulation of the WordStar or Turbo C editor (jstar) and a still fairly primitive emulation of Emacs (jmacs). All sample configurations are well-documented text files which can be processed with any editor.

4.8 Keyboard mapping

Under LINUX, keyboard mapping can be adapted to personal requirements in a very flexible way. This applies both for working at the console and working under X. This section only deals with console keyboard mapping; information on remapping keys under X can be found in Section 6.3.3.

Keyboard mapping for the LINUX console is carried out by means of the load-keys program. If a file name is specified as a parameter (for example, loadkeys de-latin1.map), the file is read and the keyboard mapping is modified accordingly. However, the loadkeys program can also read its input from the standard input. This is useful if the keyboard mapping is stored in compressed form (for example, on a boot or emergency floppy disk). Then, the call could look like, for example:

```
zcat /etc/keytables/de-latin1.map.gz | loadkeys
```

The `kbd-0.95.tar.gz` package which can be obtained anywhere where an up-to-date LINUX kernel is available, includes a series of keyboard tables, three of which describe German keyboards. These keyboard tables are installed in the directory `/usr/lib/kbd/keytables`.

- `de.map`: Here, the umlaut keys are mapped to the following special characters:

Key	Character	Shift-Character
ö	[	{
ä	]	}
ü	@	\
ß	\	?

- `de-latin1.map`: With this keyboard mapping, the umlaut keys produce the expected umlauts. It should, however, be noted that the program used to test the keyboard mapping must be 8-bit clean (see also Chapter 9). This does not, for example, apply directly to the `bash`. The `vi` clone `elvis` is quite suitable for a quick check of a new keyboard mapping, since the program is 8-bit clean.

- `de-latin1-nodeadkeys.map`: In contrast to the keyboard mapping `de-latin1.map`, here the accent keys are not defined as `dead-keys`. Thus, these keys do not act as modifiers, as under `de-latin1.map`, but output the corresponding character directly.

The keyboard mapping is initially loaded at system start-up by means of the `loadkeys` program. Users can, however, use the `loadkeys` programs to remap the keyboard according to their own requirements. This can also have the effect of putting the keyboard into an unusable state. The file `de-latin1.map` can serve as an example of how to modify the keyboard mapping.

Additional Information and Sources	
Man pages:	`loadkeys(1)`, `dumpkeys(1)`, `keytables(5)`, `showkey(1)`, and several others
ftp server:	`ftp.funet.fi`
ftp path:	`/pub/Linux/PEOPLE/Linus/`
Package:	`kbd-0.95.tar.gz`
Size:	about 398 Kbytes

The Emacs editor

5

Emacs Makes All Computing Simple
One solution of the acronym Emacs

In its documentation, Emacs is called an extensible, customizable, user-friendly, self-documenting editor. These are big words which, however, are not exaggerated when comparing Emacs with other editors. This chapter presents some of the functions of Emacs that make it so special.

The Emacs editor was originally written by Richard M. Stallman, founder of the Free Software Foundation (FSF) and initiator of the GNU project. The origin of this editor goes back as far as pre-UNIX times: the first Emacs (Editor MACroS) was a macro package for TECO (Text Editor and COrrector) and ran on DEC's legendary PDP-11.

This editor has given rise to a whole family of Emacs-like editors which are distributed both commercially and for free. The central focus in this family is the GNU Emacs which is still maintained by its author, Richard M. Stallman. Other family members are, for example, XEmacs, developed on the basis of a prerelease of the GNU Emacs 19, `jed`, MicroEmacs, and `jove`.

Emacs is fairly large and on several computers (in particular those with little memory and CPU power) it is relatively slow. On such computers, running an Emacs clone does make a certain sense. However, the way clones operate differs in many details from the original, and therefore a continuous switch between two Emacs-like editors is quite tiresome. Furthermore, many Lisp packages simply cannot be employed unless (X)Emacs is used.

Many operating system and computer vendors supply Emacs as an additional software package with their products. Otherwise, Emacs can be compiled on practically every UNIX system around because, as with all GNU programs, it is automatically configured by means of `./configure`. Emacs demands a lot from the operating system, both during compilation and execution – but it is quite portable.

The Emacs editor is very powerful; it is, indeed, a Lisp interpreter which knows how to handle texts. The Lisp dialect of Emacs is a (fully-fledged) Lisp: the Emacs Lisp (in short, elisp). Thus, during execution of macros, the novice user will be surprised by strange messages such as: `Garbage collecting....`

This message tells the user that an internal function of the Lisp interpreter is running which releases memory that is no longer used. Since Lisp does not have explicit allocation and release of memory, this function is called periodically (or when more memory is needed).

There is a large number of adaptations, extensions, and macros for Emacs written in elisp; these macros are stored in files with the extension `*.el`. `*.elc` files are the corresponding (byte-)compiled versions which the Lisp interpreter can execute much faster. These Lisp programs, together with the really extensive and well-written documentation, are the reason for the huge space requirements of Emacs.

5.1 Which Emacs version should I choose?

The Emacs editor family consists of a huge number of variations and more or less compatible clones. This multitude makes the choice of a version relatively difficult, but there are always good reasons for choosing one or the other variation.

The probably most widespread version is the GNU Emacs which is directly developed by the FSF under the direction of Richard Stallman. This version includes a fairly good selection of additional Lisp packages and runs both under X and on a terminal. Under X, different fonts and colors can be used. If required, texts can be stored in RTF (Rich Text Format) including the attributes.

The biggest competitor is the XEmacs. This version was originally developed to improve the X interface, but it can now also be used on a terminal. Here, special functions are the use of colors on color terminals and under X, together with the possibility of addressing one XEmacs process both from a terminal and under X. A further advantage is that more Lisp packages are supplied than with Emacs. These packages are also stored in a better structured way.

One disadvantage of the XEmacs is that the Lisp interpreter and some functions are not compatible with the GNU Emacs – XEmacs is just not the 'standard Emacs.' Therefore, many Lisp extensions run only with the GNU Emacs or an older version of the XEmacs. XEmacs needs significantly more memory and CPU power than the GNU Emacs. The increase in power comes at a price.

When we talk about Emacs in the following sections, we mean both GNU Emacs and XEmacs. In most cases, these two have very similar or even identical behavior, so that differentiating between them makes little or no sense. However, where there are differences between the two versions for the user or the configuration, these differences will be explained.

In addition, there is a whole series of (simple) Emacs clones. These programs generally have the advantage that they take up substantially less space on the hard disk or in memory. However, they lack several features of the 'true' Emacs:

- Some clones do not have an integrated programming language, others use their own language and others again use a reduced and incompatible Lisp version.
- Configuration is carried out by means of different files and a different syntax.

- There are far fewer extensions than for the GNU Emacs.

Wherever disk space or available CPU power is limited on a computer, it may be sensible to employ at least an Emacs clone. For the inexperienced user, these programs are substantially easier to handle than, for example, vi. Because of the rather high memory consumption of Emacs, computers shared by several users tend to end up swapping and thus become unbearably slow.

5.2 Compiling the GNU Emacs

Although the GNU Emacs is available in source code (it is distributed under the GPL), there are very few people who would compile it under LINUX themselves. This is due on the one hand to the extent of the source code (about 10 Mbytes compressed), and on the other hand to the fact that readily compiled binary versions exist for many systems. Compilation of the GNU Emacs takes about 60 Mbytes of disk space (about 30 Mbytes for the source code and about 20 Mbytes for the installation).

Space requirements for the XEmacs are slightly higher, since many additional elisp packages are included in the distribution. Personally, I prefer XEmacs because of the wider choice of elisp packages and the capability of representing different fonts (under X) and different colors on the console. However, this is a personal preference, and one must weigh the additional functions against the higher hardware requirements.

Only a relatively small part of Emacs is written in C, namely the Lisp interpreter and the most important operations on text, the so-called primitives. Thus, the central functions are relatively fast.

All further functions are implemented in Emacs Lisp. This high-level language allows you to adapt Emacs relatively easily to your own requirements or to develop your own Lisp extensions. Direct execution of the Lisp programs by the interpreter is relatively slow; therefore, nearly all Lisp files are processed with the 'byte compiler.' The byte code generated in this way can be interpreted more easily (and thus more quickly).

As with the other GNU programs, Emacs is adapted to the system by means of the `configure` command and can be compiled with `make` and installed with `make install`. Many of the options can be set with `configure`. Some of the more important ones will be presented here; the complete list can be found in the file INSTALL:

- `--prefix` specifies the installation prefix. The binary versions included in the distributions have mostly been compiled with `--prefix=/usr`; the default value is `/usr/local`.

- `--with-x-toolkit` includes the X interface, provided it exists on the computer, so that under X it is possible to work more comfortably (for example with mouse-selectable menus, additional mouse functions and syntax highlighting). One option that should be used is `--with-x-toolkit=lucid`, which includes highly operational and good-looking menus. Without the addition `=lucid`, the X toolkit would be used and its menus do not look very convincing.

If you encounter problems with the compilation of (X)Emacs, you should look into the files `./PROBLEMS` and `./etc/MACHINES`. They document many problems and offer solutions for different types of computers and operating systems. Some older C compilers had real difficulties in compiling Emacs. Partly, these could be solved by compiling individual modules with or without optimization, while others needed changes in the source code. In general, however, the editors of the Emacs family can be installed quite easily.

First, the C kernel is compiled. Subsequently, a minimal Emacs (`temacs`) is started which loads the most important Lisp extensions. This program is then dumped from memory to disk. This makes loading Emacs faster than loading first the interpreter and then the Lisp packages at each start of Emacs. Additional Lisp packages can be loaded if they are specified in the file `./lisp/site-init.el`.

After installation into the appropriate directory, Emacs is ready to be used. If you are unable or unwilling to install Emacs in a system directory, you can specify the option `--run-in-place` in `configure` and run Emacs directly from the compilation directory. This can be sensible if you want to test a new version and do not want to install it system-wide.

All configuration options for the compilation of Emacs are documented in the INSTALL file. In addition, you will find further information on many computer and operating system variations, together with hints and tips and bug fixes in the file `./etc/MACHINES`. Furthermore, this directory includes a series of interesting files, such as the Emacs FAQ, additional documentation on Emacs and the GNU project, and some man pages which you do not need to take too seriously.

5.3 General aspects of working with Emacs

Emacs is a 'self-explanatory' editor. Even without a printed manual and a computer wizard sitting next to you, you can work with Emacs. At start-up (Figure 5.1), Emacs tells you how you can obtain further help. You can read the documentation directly in Emacs, and use many Emacs commands (for example, for searching) in the buffers. The documentation is well-written and very exhaustive.

In addition, you can print the documentation written in Texinfo format yourself, or you can order it from the FSF. Texts written in this format can be displayed on screen (for example using the `info-mode`), can be printed as a book, or converted into HTML. Thus, the authors have to maintain only one document, the contents of the different media are consistent, and the printed version is properly set and easy to read.

Pressing ⎡Ctrl⎤+⎡h⎤, ⎡t⎤ starts the tutorial which introduces you to the most important Emacs terms and functions. Working through the tutorial should not take you longer than half an hour; then you should be able to use Emacs without problems for simple editing tasks. Foreign language versions of the tutorial are currently under development.

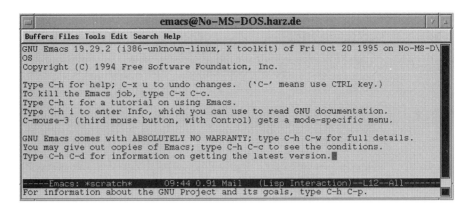

Figure 5.1   The Emacs welcoming screen.

The info documentation on Emacs and practically all GNU programs can be viewed by pressing Ctrl+h, i. This representation was generated from the same files as the printed manual. In the display, the cross-references are used to navigate through the documentation. If you use Emacs under X, you can follow individual links in the hypertext by pressing the middle mouse button.

5.3.1 Concepts and terms

Emacs manages a loaded file in a buffer. Buffers are also used internally, for example, to display a selection list. A buffer is displayed in a window. A window is a section of an Emacs window (under X) or a part of the screen, which represents a buffer. Under X, Emacs can open several windows (called frames). In Figure 5.2 you will find two Emacs frames, with the frame in front containing two windows.

Inside a buffer there are two important positions: the position of the (insertion) point (between the character on which the cursor is placed and the following character) and the position of the mark. The area between point and mark is called the region. Many commands are designed to be executed on regions.

By default, GNU Emacs does not show the set region. If you want to have the region represented visually, you can activate the transient mark mode (M-x transient-mark-mode). XEmacs, on the contrary, shows the region, as opposed to GNU Emacs, even on the text console. You can also adapt the representation of the active region as you like by means of the variables shown in Listing 5.1.

```
(set-face-background 'zmacs-region "red")
(set-face-foreground 'zmacs-region "yellow")
```

Listing 5.1   Changing the representation of an Emacs region.

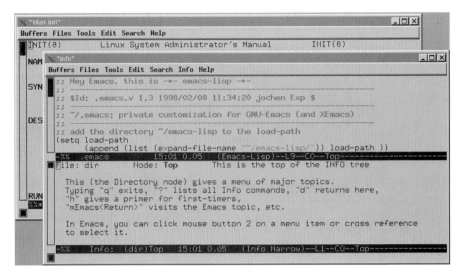

Figure 5.2 Emacs frames and windows.

Under each window you will find the mode line, which displays information on the current file and the set modes. There you can find the name of the loaded file or the name of the buffer, the modes used and some additional information. Thus, for example, the characters ** at the left-hand border stand for a modified buffer, the characters %% for a write-protected one. The contents of the mode line can (obviously) be adapted to the requirements of the user by modifying the variable modeline-format. You can obtain a description of this variable by means of C-h v modeline-format.

The last line of the frame is used to communicate with the user via the minibuffer. Here, messages are displayed (as shown in Figure 5.1) or the user is prompted for input. If a function is called from a menu by means of the mouse, a dialog box is opened under X. This makes Emacs relatively easy to handle with the mouse, but experienced users can write with the sole use of the keyboard.

In addition to the key combinations, under X Emacs can also be operated by means of the menus shown in Figure 5.1. More recent versions of GNU Emacs have a menu even on text terminals, which can be activated by pressing the F10 key (tmm-menubar or M-`). Unfortunately, this menu is completely different to use compared to other commonly used systems (for example SAA). If you want to switch the menu on or off, you need to call the function menu-bar-mode. XEmacs does not provide menus on text terminals and can be used only with the keyboard.

Emacs provides special support for many file formats (modes) by means of additional key combinations and functions. Modes exist for practically all programming languages, but also for execution of the most disparate tasks. Each buffer is always in exactly one major mode, such as, for example, text or emacs-lisp.

In addition, there are minor modes which can further influence the behavior of the buffer. Frequently used minor modes are auto-fill (for automatic line breaking) or `font-lock` (for colored highlighting of comments, strings, or key words). Several minor modes can be active in one buffer. For me personally, the large number of usually very useful modes is *the* argument in favor of Emacs.

5.3.2 Call and command line options

As with any other editor, Emacs can be passed the name of one or more files to be edited as an argument of the call. These files are loaded and displayed in different windows. When Emacs is called without arguments and options, it starts by default with the message shown in Figure 5.1, which informs the user about the tutorial, the help function and the license conditions.

(X)Emacs can be used both on a text terminal and under X. If Emacs is started under X, the X interface is used by default. If, under X, the text interface is to be used instead, Emacs must be started with the option `-nw`. If a different X display than the one specified by `DISPLAY` is to be used, this can be indicated after the option `-display` (or `-d`).

If Emacs is started with a directory as an argument, it switches automatically into the `dired` mode (the buffer contains something like the output of `ls -la`). This mode can also be used to load, delete or move files. More about the `dired` mode can be found in Section 5.6.3.

It is also possible to specify functions to be executed during the start, for example, `-f ispell-change-dictionary`. With appropriate parameters, Emacs can also be run in batch mode, without user interaction, for example, to generate a new file on the basis of a text file and a file with registered user actions (individual key strokes). This is sensible to do when an editing session has crashed. There are even those who maintain that following this on screen is more entertaining than many TV programs.

Emacs can also be passed a line number as an argument (for example, `+10`), causing it to jump to the specified line of the corresponding file. This is used, for example, by programs such as `elm` or `tin`. The option `-q` is used to prevent loading of the user's configuration file (`~/.emacs`), if this contains an error which must first be corrected. Also, no user-specific configuration should be used for a bug report, if one wants to be able to reproduce the error with the original settings.

5.3.3 Operation: Escape, Meta, Alt, Control, and Shift

Another solution of the Emacs acronym is *Escape, Meta, Alt, Control, and Shift*. This refers to the operation of the editor via key combinations. Apart from many key combinations, practically all functions can also be called by means of their full names. If you use Emacs under X or GNU Emacs, you can select several functions from menus as well. Beginners will often select functions from the menu. Experienced users learn many commands and key combinations in the course of time, thus increasing their working speed. The reference card supplied with Emacs contains the most important commands – it is also available in several foreign language versions.

In the remainder of this chapter, key combinations, that is, pressing two keys simultaneously or in rapid sequence, are represented in the form C-x or M-<. C-x means: press the Ctrl key and the x key together, that is, press the control key and keep it depressed while you briefly press the x key. The meta key can also be labeled Alt or ◇.

If such a key does not exist (or does not function, because it is not appropriately configured), the Esc key can be used. It must be noted, however, that the Esc key must only be pressed briefly (as when typing a single letter), followed by the second key of the key combination. This notation is only used for the Emacs chapter to remain consistent with the Emacs documentation.

Table 5.1 shows a brief overview of the most important key combinations. Furthermore, there is an (English language) reference card which you can find in the file /usr/lib/emacs/19.34/etc/refcard.tex. At the end of this chapter, you will also find the source for a German reference card.

As well as these keyboard combinations, you can also use the key combination M-x (execute-extended-command) to call many commands directly. Subsequently, you can enter the appropriate command in the minibuffer. As with loading of files, both a completion and a history function (Tab/Space and M-p/M-n or the cursor keys) are available.

In the minibuffer, Space (written as SPC in the Emacs documentation) completes names up to the next hyphen. The Tab key completes names up to the next ambiguity; the Enter key (RET) completes names in the same way as Space, but executes a complete command immediately.

The function and variable names used inside Emacs are extensive and clear, which, however, does not impair the use of Emacs. On the contrary, the documentation is very good, so you can easily find any required function by means of apropos, while the typing effort is greatly reduced by the completion functions. In the following sections, the key combinations are always integrated with the corresponding commands in parentheses. For each key combination, you can view the command to be executed and brief documentation by pressing C-h k (describe-key).

If, against all expectations, the system or the Emacs editor crashes, the currently processed data is not lost. Emacs periodically saves its data in an auto-save file (#file name#) which can be used to restore the data after a breakdown. When loading a file for which an auto-save file exists, users are advised that they can restore modifications by means of the M-x recover-file command. If you have edited many files, you can restore the whole session with M-x recover-session. Emacs presents a list of the previous sessions from which you can choose by moving the cursor to the corresponding line and pressing C-c C-c.

Creation of backup copies can be configured by means of a series of variables. If the variable auto-save-default is not nil, the auto-save function is activated for every new buffer. The value of the variable auto-save-interval specifies after how many typed characters a backup copy is created. The variable auto-save-timeout is used to determine after how many seconds without user input an auto-save file is written.

Action	Keys	Description
Exit	C-x C-c	Quit Emacs
Save	C-x C-s	Store contents of buffer
Execute	M-x	Execute Lisp functions
Cursor movement	C-n, C-p	Next/previous line
	C-f, C-b	Next/previous column
	C-a, C-e	Beginning/end of line
	M-a, M-e	Advance/go back one sentence
Abort	C-g	Abort last/current command
Undo	C-x u	Undo last command
Help	C-h	
Quoted-Insert	C-q	Insert special characters
Prefix	C-u	Start next command without parameters
Window commands	C-x 2	Split current window horizontally
	C-x 1	Delete other window
	C-x 0	Delete current window
	C-x o	Change to next window
Search	C-s	Incremental search forward
	C-r	Incremental search backward
	M-%	Search and replace
Macros	C-x (	Begin recording
	C-x)	End recording
	C-x e	Execute last macro
Kill and yank	C-k	Delete up to line end
	C-w	Delete region
	C-y	Insert last deleted element

Table 5.1   Important Emacs keyboard shortcuts.

Normally, the auto-save function is active when Emacs is started, and the variable `auto-save-interval` has a value of 300. If many characters were deleted in a buffer, Emacs deactivates the auto-save function, because it would be wasteful. You can, however, delete the buffer and reload the file, so that Emacs can again create auto-save copies.

5.3.4 Tutorial, help, and info mode

Before you make a decision about using Emacs as your editor, you should definitely work your way through the tutorial (C-h t; M-x help-with-tutorial). You will also learn about other Emacs features, such as the use of macros. After the tutorial, you should be familiar with the most important functions, such as navigating in the buffers, switching windows, and searching and replacing.

Emacs is very well documented. First, the whole manual is available in info format, so that you can read it with Emacs' built-in info browser (C-h i; M-x info). You can also print the documentation with TEX or buy an appropriately relevant book.

This documentation, however, is only one part of the entire documentation. Additional information on most of the variables can be obtained by means of the describe-variable command. To execute this function, you can use either of the key combinations C-h v or M-x describe-variable. You need not type the full name of the function or the variable. The TAB or SPC keys will automatically complete the name as far as possible.

Documentation on Lisp functions is obtained via the key combination C-h f (describe-function). If you do not know the name of the variable or function, you can use C-h a (apropos) to search for functions or variables whose names contain a specified character sequence. The search results are displayed in a buffer you can search with the normal Emacs functions. If your cursor is placed on a function or variable name, you can view the corresponding documentation by pressing RET.

The key assignments of a given mode can be viewed by means of the key combination C-h m (describe-mode). The function called by a specific key is shown by C-h k (describe-key). With these aids and the sources of the Emacs Lisp packages which frequently contain information on configuration, you should be able to adapt Emacs completely to your requirements. Some sample adaptations will be shown later in this chapter.

The assignment of clear names for variables and functions makes searching with the apropos command quite easy. The names of variables and functions usually follow specific conventions, so that a search is very often crowned by success. This is one of the reasons for calling Emacs a 'self-documenting' editor.

5.4 Configuration

Since Emacs is largely programmed in Emacs Lisp, it is extremely flexible and can practically be adapted to any requirement. Ready-made packages, which are collected in the Emacs Lisp archive, are already available for many tasks. The address of the archive can be found in the info box at the end of the chapter. Nearly all packages have their own configuration variables which users can set to their liking.

5.4.1 Configuration files

When Emacs is loaded, the file ~/.emacs is read first. This file contains Emacs Lisp commands that can be used to modify the behavior or the appearance of Emacs. In this file, users can configure the editor to suit their preferences. Subsequently, if the variable `inhibit-default-init` is not `nil`, the file `default.el` is loaded.

In addition, there may be a system-wide configuration file (`site-init.el`) which is loaded before `~/.emacs`. Loading this file can be prevented with the command line option `-no-site-file`. However, this should only be necessary in rare cases, for example, for error detection purposes.

Each of these files contains Lisp code. As a rule, you need not be a Lisp expert, because for many applications, appropriate suggestions for configuration can be found in the (X)Emacs FAQ, in the info system or in the Lisp files of the corresponding modes. Whatever else you need to know about Lisp will be shown in the following sections.

The name Lisp is an abbreviation of 'List programming.' Lists (please note: programs or Lisp functions are nothing but lists, too) are enclosed in parentheses. Therefore it quite often happens that several closing parentheses appear at the end of a line or function. When inserting a new closing parenthesis, the corresponding opening parenthesis is highlighted in `lisp-mode`. This is of great help for the programmer or user. The Emacs FAQ contains more hints and tips on this subject.

Comments in Lisp begin with a semicolon (`;`) and end with the line end. The Lisp mode of Emacs (not the Lisp interpreter) differentiates between comments that begin with one, two, or three semicolons. These mark comments which are to be indented at different levels. One semicolon means indent to column 40, two stand for the same indent as the current code and comments, and comments starting with three semicolons stay exactly where they are. By using the `Tab` key (`lisp-indent-line`), a line can be formatted accordingly.

Emacs provides some functions which make Lisp programming almost a pleasure. Highlighting corresponding pairs of parentheses is only one example. You can process a configuration file without leaving Emacs by using the `eval-buffer` command. You can pass a region to the Lisp interpreter with `eval-region`. These functions are available in `elisp-mode` and in the `*scratch*` buffer. The `*scratch*` buffer is found in the `Lisp Interaction` mode, in which commands can be entered and executed.

Further useful functions are `eval-defun` (`M-C-x`, evaluation of the function definition in which the cursor is located) and `eval-last-sexp` (`C-x C-e`, execute the last Lisp expression). In many cases, this allows interactive programming and/or testing of new configuration settings.

Listing 5.2 contains some commands that you may want to include in your `~/.emacs` file. Before we carry on with more complicated configurations, we will first explain the individual commands in Listing 5.2. Lisp consists of expressions which are enclosed in parentheses. These expressions can also be interpreted as lists. Directly after the opening parenthesis, we will find the function to be executed, followed by the function's parameters. Some functions return a value, which in turn can be the parameter for another function call.

Variables are modified by means of the function `set` or `setq`. The function calls shown in Listing 5.3 are equivalent (the 'q' in `setq` stands for 'quote,' that is, the single quotation mark '). A quote is used to prevent the evaluation of the following

```
;; do not extend buffer after last line
(setq next-line-add-newlines nil)
;; include line number in the mode line
(setq line-number-mode 't)
;; highlight search results
(setq search-highlight 't)
;; standard mode is "text-mode"
(setq default-major-mode 'text-mode)
;; automatic line breaking
(add-hook 'text-mode-hook 'turn-on-auto-fill)
```

Listing 5.2   Simple commands for the file `~/.emacs`.

```
(setq next-line-add-newlines nil)
(set 'next-line-add-newlines nil)
```

Listing 5.3   Comparison of `set` and `setq`.

expression. In Listing 5.2, the values `t` and `nil` occur several times. These values have a special meaning in Lisp and stand for TRUE and FALSE (or for the empty list, *not in l*ist).

Back to the examples in Listing 5.2. Emacs automatically appends lines to the buffer when the cursor is placed past the end of the file. This can be somewhat disturbing (the buffer is modified although no 'real' changes have been made) and is often not desired. The first Lisp expression switches this behavior off.

You should document your adaptations extensively, so that others can profit from your experience and you yourself keep things under control. My own Emacs configuration files change relatively often; therefore they are managed with the Revision Control System (see also Section 11.5). This requires some discipline, but keeps track of modifications.

The last two expressions control the behavior of Emacs if no special mode exists for a buffer. Usually, such a buffer will be in the `fundamental-mode`. Often it only contains natural language text, so that the `text-mode` would be more appropriate. With the last but one expression, this mode is used as default if no special adaptations are available.

In many applications it is sensible to break a text automatically at word boundaries. This behavior is implemented by means of a minor mode (`auto-fill-mode`). The last Lisp expression of Listing 5.2 switches into this minor mode every time a buffer is put in `text-mode`.

It is not always sufficient to adjust the values of individual variables. In many places, Emacs provides so-called hooks which users can employ to carry out special functions. Thus, whenever a file is read, the hook `find-file-hook` is called, and the commands contained in it are executed. Many other Lisp packages allow flexible extensions of their functionality by means of a series of hooks. The names of the hooks and their meaning can be found in the documentation of the corresponding mode.

```
;; direct inclusion in the hook
(add-hook 'text-mode-hook 'turn-on-auto-fill)

;; include unnamed function in the hook
(add-hook 'text-mode-hook
    (lambda ()
        (turn-on-auto-fill)))

;; include named function in the hook
(defun my-text-mode-hook ()
    (turn-on-auto-fill))
(add-hook 'text-mode-hook 'my-text-mode-hook)

;; delete hook; remove-hook deletes single calls
(setq text-mode-hook nil)

;; set hook to a defined value
(setq text-mode-hook 'turn-on-auto-fill)
```

Listing 5.4   Extending and setting of hooks.

In general, users will add additional functions to the hook. This can be done by means of the add-hook function. If not only one function is to be executed, a (named or unnamed) function must be created which is added to the hook. Examples for the use of hooks are shown in Listing 5.4. Direct setting of a hook, which is indeed nothing but a variable, by means of setq should only be carried out in truly exceptional cases, because it might lead to unintentional changes in other settings.

Some other things can be configured by making use of X resources (~/.Xresources). A complete list of modifiable resources can be found in the man page. With GNU Emacs, these are essentially the size of the window, the font to be used, and the colors. XEmacs uses many more features of the X Window system; thus, significantly more adaptations can be made. For XEmacs, these are all colors, the fonts to be used, and various settings for the mouse.

Together with XEmacs, the sample files sample.emacs and sample.Xdefaults are installed which contain many tips and hints for the configuration of XEmacs. Many simple configuration tips can also be found in the Emacs (or XEmacs) FAQ.

5.4.2 Large configuration files

If you employ Emacs for many tasks, you will probably create separate configurations for many modes. Most modes can be used without previous configuration, but sometimes another add-on package needs to be integrated or special functions are to be used. In all of these cases, you will need to add some entries in your ˜/.emacs file.

Simple editors do not offer this flexibility. However, at least at the beginning, you should only change very few settings and gradually discover the functions of Emacs. Above all, it does not make sense simply to use the configuration of another Emacs user, because then you have no guarantee that all Emacs functions work as described in the manual.

If many different adaptations are included, the ˜/.emacs file becomes too large and complex, and loading and executing the file takes relatively long. One solution to this problem is to incorporate the configurations into another file than .emacs and then to compile this file (with byte-compile-file).

In practice it becomes useful to create a separate, relatively small, configuration file for each major Lisp package and to have this file automatically compiled at every start of Emacs. This makes the configuration clearer and much easier to maintain. Related settings are stored together in a relatively small file. If you keep all of these files under a version management, you will always be able to trace your modifications. This can be very useful if you change frequently between GNU Emacs and XEmacs and different computers. Listing 5.5 shows an example of a .emacs file.

```
;; include the directory ~/emacs-lisp in the load path
(setq load-path
      (append (list (expand-file-name "~/emacs-lisp/"))
              load-path))

;; trick to recompile the .el file
;; if it is newer than the .elc file
(defun byte-compile-if-newer-and-load (file)
   "Byte compile file.el if newer than file.elc"
   (if (file-newer-than-file-p (concat file ".el")
                               (concat file ".elc"))
       (byte-compile-file (concat file ".el")))
   (load file))

;; compile and load init file if needed
(byte-compile-if-newer-and-load "~/emacs.init/emacs.init")
```

Listing 5.5 A minimal .emacs file.

Thus, the file ˜/.emacs contains a series of simple global settings, such as those shown in Listing 5.2, and a call of the function byte-compile-if-newer-and-load for each major package, which is configured via a series of variables and hooks. Even byte compiling of the modified configuration files is fairly quick, because the individual files are very small. Furthermore, this way of proceeding has the advantage that the configuration instructions belonging to one package are not spread across the whole `.emacs`.

Bundling all adaptations into one mode or package allows you to survey them at a glance. This is quite useful for error detection and allows you to distribute your settings to other users without much effort. Do not simply copy the files, because they frequently contain idiosyncratic settings.

5.4.3 File-specific configuration

Besides the configuration specified in the initialization files, Emacs permits buffer- or file-specific configurations. Often these are variables that can assume a different value for each buffer, for example, keyboard mappings, settings of the auto-save function and many others. With many file types, you can store these (and other) variables permanently in the file as local variables.

Local variables are stored at the end of the file, usually in a comment of the programming language used. The block of local variables initiates with text `Local variables:`, the end of the block is marked with `End:`. Between these keywords, you will find the name of a (buffer-specific) variable, followed by a colon and the new value of this variable. This can be used to define a special indentation style for given files, for example.

```
% Local variables:
% mode: latex
% TeX-master: "master"
% End:
```

Listing 5.6   An example of local variables in a LaTeX source text.

Listing 5.6 shows an example of local variables in a LaTeX source text. These variables are evaluated by the `auctex` mode, which unfortunately is not part of the standard delivery of GNU Emacs; XEmacs includes this package. This mode can be used for TeX and LaTeX files, the `mode` variable always selects LaTeX mode for this file. The above file is one of several files that constitute a document; the main file to be processed by LaTeX is called `master.tex`.

If the variable `enable-local-variables` is `t`, local variables are always taken into account; if the value is `nil`, the variables are ignored. Any other value leads to the corresponding block being displayed, while the user is asked whether the variables are to be set or not.

This mechanism also allows macro viruses to be implemented in Emacs, because many Emacs functions are influenced by variables and, in the end, hooks are simply variables with special contents. Therefore, one should not blindly take over local variables from foreign documents, but check them and, if necessary, deny the request.

The variable `ignored-local-variables` can also be used to exclude specific variables from being modified. As an example, Listing 5.7 contains the default setting of XEmacs. This setting can prevent an initial prompt to be issued for one file and then to be deactivated for all subsequent files. Additional variables may be included in the list.

```
;;; The following variables cannot be buffer-specific.
(setq ignored-local-variables '(enable-local-eval))
```

Listing 5.7   The variable `ignored-local-variables`.

5.4.4 Emacs as server – one for all

Various programs, for example `elm`, `tin`, and `crontab`, can call an arbitrary editor for editing mail or texts. Usually, these programs use the environment variables `EDITOR` or `VISUAL` which contain the name of the editor. If these variables simply contain `emacs`, a new Emacs process is started at each call. This is not very practical because it costs time and memory; furthermore, the Emacs processes cannot access each other's buffers. Therefore, true Emacs users do nearly everything inside Emacs, which they start once when logging in and do not terminate until logging out.

It is possible to use a running Emacs as an editor for a new buffer, for example from within `elm`, by configuring Emacs as a server. For this purpose, the function `server-start` must be called from within Emacs. This can be automated by means of an appropriate entry in the file `~/.emacs`. The environment variable `EDITOR` must then be set to `emacsclient`.

This has the consequence that, whenever an application calls `emacsclient`, a message is sent to the Emacs server in which this is asked to load a specific file into a new buffer. The client issues the message `Waiting for Emacs` and waits for the end of the corresponding server session. If you work with virtual consoles, you must switch to the console running Emacs; under X, you activate the corresponding window.

When you have finished editing the text in the server, you leave the buffer with `C-x #` and, if present, the previously edited buffer is again displayed in the window. Then, a message is sent to the `emacsclient` program, asking it to terminate itself. The programs that use `EDITOR` or `VISUAL` wait for the underlying `emacsclient` to be terminated. Thus, these programs see no difference from a direct call to an editor.

The whole process also works on text consoles. Here, however, it is more practical to start Emacs on one virtual console and the mail program on another, because it is faster to change console than to load Emacs completely. XEmacs in particular takes a long time to load the configuration, so this procedure is worth while.

5.4.5 XEmacs as server – even more features

The functions provided by GNU Emacs as a server are not always sufficient. Thus it is not possible to have the running process evaluate individual Lisp expressions. Furthermore, it is not possible to access the Emacs process 'en passant' on another screen, for example at the workstation of a colleague, or via a modem connection. All this is, however, implemented in the current version of XEmacs.

To avoid clashes between GNU Emacs and XEmacs, XEmacs uses different Lisp functions and programs. You should, however, write your Emacs Lisp files in such a way that you can use them with both editors. This is useful if on a new computer XEmacs is not (yet) installed or if you frequently have to switch between the two environments.

In XEmacs, the server is started by means of the function gnuserv-start. Listing 5.8 shows an example of how to differentiate between GNU Emacs and XEmacs inside Lisp functions.

```
;; Which one is running, XEmacs or GNU Emacs?
(defvar running-xemacs
        (string-match "XEmacs\\|Lucid" emacs-version))

(cond
  ((not running-xemacs)
  ;; GNU Emacs-specific code
  (server-start))
 (t
  ;; XEmacs-specific code
  (gnuserv-start)))
```

Listing 5.8   Automatic start of the Emacs servers for GNU Emacs and XEmacs.

Subsequently, you can work with the gnuclient program in exactly the same way as with emacsclient. The only difference is that processing the buffer can also be carried out from a different computer. For this purpose, either a host-based authentication or, better, a password check must be carried out. If Emacs was installed correctly, the xauth program can be used; the display number is 999.

Particularly interesting extensions of the GNU Emacs are the programs gnuattach and gnudoit. With gnuattach, an already running XEmacs process can be persuaded to accept additional input on the current terminal. This is useful if one is logged in via a modem or sitting at a colleague's workstation, and one cannot or does not want to start a new XEmacs. It may, however, happen that the keyboard mappings and the colors do not match the current terminal, since these settings are often carried out only once at the start of XEmacs.

The program gnudoit is used to have Lisp expressions evaluated by XEmacs. Examples for the call can be found, for example, in the man page for gnudoit. With this method you can control a running XEmacs from outside – the security implications are the same as with gnuattach.

5.5 Keyboard mapping

Besides the call of functions via menus (under X), keyboard shortcuts, and the call by means of M-x *command*, practically all keys can be associated to functions. Emacs differentiates between a global mapping that applies to all modes and a local mapping, possibly adapted to individual modes.

Please note that many modes redefine individual keys in a local table, so that the mapping can change between buffers and a global adaptation will possibly not be working in one particular mode. Listing 5.9 shows examples for the adaptation of the global and one local keyboard table. Please note that the representation of many keys differs between GNU Emacs and XEmacs; this will probably not change in the near future.

```
;; global adaptations
(global-set-key [home]          'beginning-of-line)
(global-set-key [end]           'end-of-line)
(global-set-key "\C-cg"         'goto-line)

;; adaptation of the LaTeX keyboard map
(defun my-latex mode-hook ()
    (define-key LaTeX-mode-map '[delete] 'delete-character))
(add-hook 'latex-mode-hook 'my-latex-mode-hook)
```

Listing 5.9   Adaptation of the keyboard map.

First, the keys ⌷Home⌷ and ⌷End⌷ are mapped in such a way that the cursor is moved to the beginning of the line or the end of the line. The Emacs default setting is that the cursor jumps to the beginning or the end of the buffer. Here, symbolic names are used for the keys ([home] and [end]) which Emacs maps internally to the corresponding keys of the terminal. This allows you, by relatively simple means, to specify a uniform keyboard mapping for different terminals and keyboards.

Please note that some key combinations, such as ⌷Shift⌷-⌷F1⌷, are only uniquely defined under X. Furthermore, a number of keys are not available on various terminals or terminal emulations. However, Emacs includes configurations for the most widely used terminals; in addition, the terminfo or termcap database is read.

In the third line of Listing 5.9, the command goto-line is mapped to the key combination c-c g. All mappings discussed until now refer to the global keyboard table. To set these mappings, the elisp function global-set-key is used, which you can also call interactively.

In addition to the default keys, many modes use additionally mapped keys. These modifications are stored in a mode-specific keyboard table. All keys not changed in that table keep their global mapping. Some special modes, such as the dired mode, modify the functioning of a large number of keys.

In the second part of Listing 5.9, the (Del) key in LaTeX mode is mapped to what one is used to from other editors. In the current version of AUCTeX, this setting is no longer required. The mapping of the (←) (backspace) and (Del) (delete) keys under UNIX is unfortunately not consistent and is in fact highly controversial.

Particularly in the use of special keys (such as function keys and the Shift and Control keys) the keyboard mapping syntax is different in XEmacs and GNU Emacs. These differences originate in the different implementations of the two versions and will probably not disappear in the near future. An example for this is shown in Section 5.6.2.

If you want to know the mapping of a key, you can obtain it by means of C-h k (describe-key). Documentation on a function is called up with the key combination C-h f (describe-function). If you are looking for the key that calls a specific function, you may use C-h w (where-is). You are asked for a function name and get a list that shows all keys associated to this function.

5.6 **Emacs modes**

Emacs gets its particular processing power from the large number of available modes. With these modes, Emacs is specially adapted to different file types or tasks, which gives Emacs users many advantages through additional functions or key combinations. Often, Emacs can help with the syntax of files, so that common errors such as a missing closing parenthesis can be avoided.

Based on the syntax, Emacs can also create colored highlighting of keywords, comments, and literals. This often makes it much easier to find one's way around foreign programs or texts.

To describe all available modes would exceed the scope of this book and upset the balance within topics; therefore only a small selection will be presented in the following section. Many modes already belong to the standard configuration of Emacs, and from version to version they are becoming more numerous. Furthermore, you can obtain additional modes from the Emacs Lisp archive (the source can be found at the end of this chapter). Experienced Emacs users can also develop modes themselves; more information on this subject can be found in the Emacs Lisp manual.

Emacs often recognizes which mode should be used, for example, on the basis of the file name or the extension. However, you can give Emacs some support by including the text -*- mode -*- in the first line of the file. In the source texts for this book, I use the following text:

```
% Hey Emacs, this is -*- LaTeX -*-
```

The character string -*- tells Emacs that the name of the mode to be used will follow. The name is again terminated with the character string -*-, the initial text is only a comment. In the above example, the auctex mode is instructed to consider this file as LaTeX source text. Often enough, Emacs recognizes this by itself on the basis of the beginning of the file; this, however, does not always work.

5.6.1 The `fundamental-mode`

If Emacs is started with a file for which no special mode is available, it changes into `fundamental-mode`. This mode provides practically no special functions. Thus, one can regard all other modes as extensions and adaptations of the `fundamental-mode`.

Many users use the `text-mode` as default mode. An example for this setting is shown in Listing 5.2 on page 130.

5.6.2 The `text-mode`

Emacs understands certain characteristics of a text. First of all, it knows words and can perform various commands on words: delete words (`kill-word`), skip words (`forward-word`), or check their spelling (`ispell-word`). This does not differentiate Emacs from other editors.

Furthermore, Emacs also recognizes higher-level constructions of a (natural language) text, that is, sentences and paragraphs. A sentence is terminated by a punctuation mark followed by two spaces; this is an American typesetting convention. This makes it possible to apply commands (such as, for example, `kill-sentence`) to sentences or to move through the text by sentences (`backward-sentence`) and `forward-sentence`). These functions can obviously be mapped to appropriate key combinations (for example meta cursor keys).

Listing 5.10 shows an example of the corresponding keyboard assignments in GNU Emacs. It should be noted that these keyboard combinations are supplied only under X in a format that can be evaluated by Emacs. Therefore, this mapping will not work on the console.

```
(global-set-key [C-up]   'backward-sentence)  ; M-a
(global-set-key [C-down] 'forward-sentence)   ; M-e
(global-set-key [M-up]   'backward-paragraph) ; M-{
(global-set-key [M-down] 'forward-paragraph)  ; M-}
```

Listing 5.10   Keyboard assignments of GNU Emacs.

Listing 5.11 shows the adaptations for XEmacs. This syntax is clearer than that of GNU Emacs, however, the two lines of development cannot be expected ever to meet again.

```
(global-set-key [(meta up)]      'backward-paragraph)
(global-set-key [(meta down)]    'forward-paragraph)
(global-set-key [(control prior)] 'beginning-of-buffer)
(global-set-key [(control next)]  'end-of-buffer)
```

Listing 5.11   Keyboard assignments of XEmacs.

One extension with respect to the `fundamental-mode` is the Lisp function `ispell-complete-word` (`M-TAB`) which automatically completes a word if it is contained in the `ispell` dictionary. The `text-mode` already provides some simple text formatting functions:

- `TAB` to jump to the next tab stop,
- `M-s` to center a line, and
- `M-S` to center the whole paragraph.

On my system, the `auto-fill-mode` is activated. This is sensible for processing normal texts, but for processing configuration files or other specially formatted texts, such as mail headers, this function is not really helpful.

5.6.3 The `dired` mode

The `dired` (directory editor) mode represents a directory in an Emacs buffer, in which this directory can be 'edited.' Files can be displayed, renamed, edited, or copied. In addition, many other functions are available, such as `chmod`. The `dired` mode can be accessed in different ways:

- by calling Emacs with a directory as an argument, for example, by means of `emacs .` in the simplest case,
- by calling the `dired` function (by means of `M-x dired`),
- by means of `C-x d` (not to be confused with `C-x C-d`, which results in a short directory listing), or
- by selecting the appropriate menu entry.

In `dired` mode, the buffer shows more or less the same information that would be output on a text console by the command `ls -la`. The output format can be changed by means of the variable `dired-listing-switches`. Changing the text in this buffer is not sensible, since many keys are assigned to special commands. An overview of the most important commands is shown in Table 5.2. Like any normal text buffer, this buffer also allows searching for strings (for example, file names).

The `dired` mode works with file marks. If no file is marked, the current file is used. The current file is determined by the cursor position. Marks are set by means of the key `m`. An (incomplete) overview of possible key combinations is shown in Table 5.2; the complete documentation can be found in the info system.

In addition, `dired` understands further commands for processing directories (creation, insertion into the listing). Thus, full file management can be carried out by means of the `dired` mode, without having to use any other tools. Thus, one can remain in the usual environment and, compared to many other X file managers, the `dired` file management is very fast. Additional information on the use of `dired` and its configuration options can be found in the info system.

Key	Function
g	Rebuild directory
k	Delete file from listing
M-k	Delete all marked files from listing
m	Mark file or directory
u	Delete mark
M-DEL	Delete all marks
c	Copy file
r	Rename file
d	Mark file for deletion
x	Execute deletion
X	Delete files marked with *
#	Mark auto-save files for deletion
~	Mark backup files for deletion
!	Execute shell command
C/U	Compress/uncompress file
M	Change access rights of file
O	Change owner of file
G	Change file group
f	Edit file (or e)
v	Display file

Table 5.2   The most important dired commands.

5.6.4 Processing files on a remote computer with ange-ftp

The Emacs editor is not only capable of processing locally stored files, but provides both an interface for the ftp program and the possibility of processing files on remote computers. For this purpose, an ftp connection to the corresponding computer is established, and the remote directory is displayed in a dired buffer. This allows easy working with files on remote computers too.

In the simplest case, no further configuration is required. The name of the file to be processed is specified in the form /user@computer:file. ange-ftp asks for the user's password and transfers the file to the local computer. Subsequently, the file can be processed as usual and, when being saved, is transferred back to the remote computer via ftp.

This mode also cooperates with the dired mode, so that it is also possible to perform file management on remote computers – transferring a file with ftp functions in exactly the same way as local copying. If you specify ftp or anonymous as your user name, you can also look at public ftp servers.

If the connection is interrupted because of a timeout, ange-ftp reestablishes it automatically. For the user, the remote file looks like a completely normal buffer.

Thus, all commands that work on Emacs buffers can be used. The only difference is slower transmission of files via the network.

Even if you can reach remote computers only via a gateway, you can still use `ange-ftp`. You simply enter the name of the gateway in the variable `ange-ftp-gateway-host`. More about gateway configuration can be found in the info documentation.

Even if you do not have an Internet connection, using `ange-ftp` will make sense. Many users usually work only under X and use `xauth` (this is the LINUX default) for authorization of the client. This means that after having issued the `su` command to obtain superuser privileges, no X client can be started from an `xterm`. You can either use `xauth` to transmit the magic cookie (see also Section 6.6) or allow access to all local clients with `xhost`.

In a larger network, the use of `xhost` is not recommended, and the transmission of the X authority is not particularly easy. In this case, you can allow a login of the user `root` via `ftp` and use `ange-ftp`. For security reasons, however, most computers exclude `ftp` access as `root`. My tip in such cases is to use the `ssh`; more about this can be found in Section 17.5.

5.6.5 The `outline-mode`

When processing larger files, it is easy to lose the overall perspective and go on browsing through the text. Another problem is that the contents structure is barely reflected in the file. Here, help is provided by the `outline-mode`. This mode can be used both as major and as minor mode, so that even inside Lisp, LaTeX, or C files, the functions of the `outline-mode` can be used.

5.6.6 Miscellaneous Emacs modes

Many other modes exist besides the ones presented above, some of which are now included in the standard set of Emacs. These include, among others, a mode for the display of man pages (`M-x man`), the `shell-mode`, and a calendar (`M-x calendar`). Each of these modes is available as Lisp source code and can be configured to the users' requirements. Examples of modes I employ on my own computer are:

- `Gnus` as mail and news reader; special features are splitting mail into various groups (for example, mailing lists), reading from remote news servers and sophisticated scoring.

- `psgml` for editing of SGML documents, for example, HTML pages (included in the standard set of XEmacs), however, arbitrary DTDs can be processed.

- `bbdb` (Big Brother's Database) as small address management which is integrated in `Gnus` for handling mail addresses and signatures.

- `calendar/diary` as an agenda with alarm function,

- `zenirc` as an IRC client, and

- modes for various programming languages, such as C, Lisp, Java, Perl, AWK, and COBOL.

Extensive documentation of these modes can be found in the info system and in the Lisp sources of the modes. Even if you do not know Lisp, you will find many hints and new ideas for possible configurations in the comments.

5.7 Useful minor modes

In addition to the major mode, each buffer can be put into a series of minor modes which are able to provide special functions that may be useful in more than one mode. In the following section, I would like to introduce some of these minor modes which can make the life of a UNIX user significantly easier.

5.7.1 The auto-fill-mode

Many users require typed-in text to be automatically word wrapped at the end of the line. In `auto-fill-mode`, lines are broken when the `Space` or `Return` key is pressed and the cursor is located behind the `fill-column` position. If no automatic line breaking is desired in spite of an activated `auto-fill-mode`, `C-q` (`quoted-insert`) must be pressed prior to the Space or Enter key. Thus, the special meaning of the keys is annulled.

The right-hand margin can be set by positioning the cursor in the appropriate column and pressing `C-x  f` (`set-fill-column`). If you require a left-hand margin, you can define a fill prefix. Write the prefix at the beginning of a line, position the cursor to the end of the prefix, and press `C-x  .` (`set-fill-prefix`). This prefix is automatically taken into consideration in all newly inserted lines. Also the `M-q` (`fill-paragraph`) command respects this setting.

Another useful function is `M-s` (`center-line`) for centering a line. Additional functions are `center-paragraph` and `center-region` which center a paragraph or a region.

Sometimes it can be useful to store a text in an aligned format. Usually, text processors are used for such a purpose, but Emacs also possesses the relevant functions. With `set-justification-`*option*, the paragraphs in a region can be formatted. Legal values for *option* are `left`, `right`, `center`, `full`, or `none`.

5.7.2 The abbrev-mode

Another useful mode is the `abbrev-mode`, a minor mode which expands user-defined abbreviations and can thus significantly reduce typing effort. Thus, for example, the input `br M-Space` could be expanded to 'Best regards.' Both global (that is, valid in all modes) and mode-specific abbreviations can be defined.

A global abbreviation can be defined by means of `C-x  a  g` (`add-global-abbrev`). This function reads the word ending with the point and searches the minibuffer for a possible expansion. If you want to abbreviate several words (for example, three), you must specify the number by means of a prefix: `C-u  3  C-x  a  g`. Mode-specific abbreviations can be defined by means of the key combination `C-x  a  l` (`add-mode-abbrev`).

Abbreviations are stored in the file ˜/.abbrev_defs. You can change the name of the file by storing the required file name in the variable abbrev-file-name. With the Emacs command write-abbrev-file, you store your abbreviations for the next session.

If the buffer is not in abbrev-mode, abbreviations are only expanded by means of the key combination M-Space. If the buffer is in abbrev-mode, the abbreviation is expanded if it is immediately followed by a space, a full stop (.), or another punctuation mark. This is not always a desired outcome, so expansion can be prevented with the key combination C-q (quoted-insert). If an abbreviation was inadvertently expanded, you can undo the expansion by means of the key combination C-x u (advertised-undo) or the M-x unexpand-abbrev command.

To obtain an overview of the defined abbreviations, you can use the functions list-abbrevs and edit-abbrevs. Further information on the use of abbreviations can be found in the info system.

Although the abbreviations introduced above are created by the user, they are still relatively static. Emacs, however, also supports so-called 'dynamic abbreviations.' In this case the buffer is searched for a word that starts with the same character sequence as the string to be expanded. Expansion does not happen automatically, but must be triggered manually with M-/ (dabbrev-expand).

5.7.3 Colored highlighting

Under X, Emacs can highlight (and XEmacs can do so even on the console) for example keywords, comments, or strings in different colors, according to the syntax of the file. This is particularly useful with files that must obey a certain syntax, such as program sources, LATEX files, or nroff files. With GNU Emacs, the simplest way is to use the hilit19 package; a sample entry for the .emacs file can be found in Listing 5.12. Unfortunately, this package is rather slow.

```
(cond (window-system
       (setq hilit-mode-enable-list  '(not text-mode)
             hilit-background-mode    'light
             hilit-inhibit-hooks      nil
             hilit-inhibit-rebinding nil)
       (require 'hilit19)))
```

Listing 5.12   Activation of hilit19.

A faster and more convenient solution is to use the font-lock-mode. This mode is used by XEmacs as a default and can be configured with the 'options' menu. Under GNU Emacs, you must carry out a separate manual configuration for every single required mode. Since font-lock too takes a while to run on slow computers, you should immediately install the lazy-lock mode. An example is shown in Listing 5.13.

```
; activate font-lock for the required modes
(add-hook 'emacs-lisp-mode-hook 'font-lock-mode)

; activate lazy-lock
(autoload 'turn-on-lazy-lock "lazy-lock"
    "Unconditionally turn on Lazy Lock mode.")
(add-hook 'font-lock-mode-hook 'turn-on-lazy-lock)
)
```

Listing 5.13   Activation of font-lock-mode.

5.8 Other extensions

The presentation of some modes supplied together with Emacs was supposed to give you a taste of what can be done with Emacs. In the following chapters, it will be mentioned when an Emacs mode is available for a determined purpose.

Since there are many Emacs users in the world, many Emacs Lisp extensions have been written. To make locally created functions and modes accessible to others, they can be stored in the Emacs Lisp archive. There you should be able to find almost anything you might want when talking about Emacs extensions. Obviously, there is also a special Emacs mode for searching through this archive.

5.9 Information sources

This is a synopsis of possible sources of information on Emacs and Emacs modes.

Additional Information and Sources	
Man page:	emacs(1)
Info system:	Emacs
FAQs:	Emacs or XEmacs
Newsgroups:	comp.emacs, gnu.emacs.help
ftp server:	ftp.gnu.org
Path:	/pub/gnu
File:	emacs-19.34.tar.gz
Size:	about 10 Mbytes
ftp server:	ftp.xemacs.org
Path:	/pub/xemacs
File:	xemacs-20.4.tar.gz
Size:	about 15 Mbytes
Elisp archive:	cis.ohio-state.edu
German Refcard:	http://www.inf.tu-dresden.de/~sr1/-projects/emacs-refcard/index.html

The X Window system

6

The X Window system, often incorrectly referred to as X-Windows, is *the* platform-independent and network transparent graphics system. This may sound rather boastful, but the boasting is totally justified.

X is platform-independent, because there are ports for all commonly used platforms. Originally designed to work under UNIX and VMS, there are now versions for all kinds of Windows and OS/2.

X programs can even run on a computer other than the one where the user interaction takes place. It does not matter at all if the two computers have different processors and operating systems. A remote X program can be completely integrated into the local desktop, so that even the user does not (have to) know about this.

X is based on a client/server concept, that is, a separation between the part of the software that carries out the 'calculation' of the screen contents (*X client*) and the part that carries out the display of the screens (*X server*). Communication between X server and X clients takes place by means of the X protocol. This can be used locally on one computer or transmitted across the network by means of TCP/IP.

As a service, the X server provides abstract access to the hardware (graphics card, mouse, and keyboard). An X server runs, for example, on a personal workstation or an X terminal; the client, that is, the application program that uses the services, runs, for example, on a powerful computer.

6.1 Look and feel under X

X does not enforce any special look and feel of the interface. Windows are areas on the screen whose look and handling is determined by the X client itself. The frames around these windows are managed neither by the client nor by the X server; this task is the responsibility of a special client, the *window manager*. X provides the technology and does not prescribe a policy. This makes X very flexible, but it also has its disadvantages.

As a consequence, the clients (application programs) under X do not look as uniform as, for example, on the Macintosh or under MS Windows. Standard X has no style guide, although such guides are often part of user interfaces based on X technology. Usually, such interfaces also carry their own programming interface.

The 'Athena widgets' used to be supplied as a sample interface. With respect to their look, they can today only be described as obsolete. The feel needs getting used to. Although some ideas, such as the handling of scroll bars, differ quite substantially from current common schemes, fast and precise use is possible. This example has not succeeded in becoming a standard for the most varied reasons, but many free X programs actually do employ this user interface.

One (still) widely used interface is OpenLook, originally developed by Sun and today freely available (also for LINUX). Sun has discontinued further development of this interface, so practically no new applications are developed for OpenLook.

Most commercial systems today use OSF/Motif as their user interface. Motif is not freely available; however, lesstif provides a free implementation of the Motif standards which can run on practically all platforms. Furthermore, you can get a Motif license from almost all distributors, either for the developer version which allows development (and compilation) of Motif programs, or for the runtime version which only contains the Motif window manager (mwm) and the shared libraries.

Recently, the Common Desktop Environment (CDE) has developed with a view to becoming a standard for commercial systems. This user interface is based on Motif, but it contains several additional features. This product is commercial, but it is possible to acquire a LINUX port.

The lesstif project has begun with the implementation of this interface; however, it is not known when it will reach the operational stage.

Much is happening in the world of free software, particularly in this area. The KDE (K Desktop Environment) project has started to implement a complete desktop. KDE is based on the qt tool kit by Troll Tech, which can be used free of charge only in free software. Here, the emphasis is on the requirement that programs have a unique control interface, that they can be easily configured with the aid of menus, and that they offer the user the total comfort of a modern GUI.

It should, however, neither be forgotten nor should it be hidden that underneath KDE, the work is done by some kind of UNIX, and that the user will still be able to benefit from its advantages. KDE is not restricted to running under LINUX, although it is mainly implemented in LINUX systems. Thus, for the first time today, the world can enjoy a free, stable, and modern user interface as free software.

Because of the licensing conditions, which prohibit distribution of a modified qt version, some users are not happy with this situation. This has led to the development of yet another desktop project, GNOME (GNU Network Object Model Environment). This project is based on the gtk tool kit which has been developed in the framework of the GIMP. Unlike KDE, only free software is used.

Both desktop projects include a style guide which prescribes how applications should look and how they are to be controlled. This is one of the first steps towards a consistent desktop which is easy to use even for beginners. In spite of the relatively short time that has elapsed since the start of these projects, there are already quite a lot of things to be seen and tried out.

Additional Information and Sources	
Lesstif:	`http://www.hungry.com/products/lesstif`
The K Desktop Environment:	`http://www.kde.org`
The GNOME desktop project:	`http://www.gnome.org`

6.2 History and concept

The X Window system has been developed since 1984 at the Massachusetts Institute of Technology (MIT) within the framework of the 'Athena' project in cooperation with Digital Equipment Corporation. Early in 1986 the X10 system, the predecessor of X11, was released; the first version of the X11 system, X11R1, was published in September 1987. The current version is X11R6.4. The X Consortium, which had taken on the development of X, has now discontinued this and has started to work on new projects on the basis of X.

The aim of the X11 development is the creation of standard interfaces on all levels of the X Window system in the framework of cross-company cooperation. In the X Consortium, which controls the development of X, practically all companies are represented that are active in the UNIX area, so a unique development is guaranteed. Thus, clients and servers of different manufacturers cooperate well enough, even between different versions of X.

Primarily, X is only the specification of a protocol for network-transparent representation and transmission of graphics and events. This protocol is implemented in the Xlib and is documented in a freely accessible way for all interested parties. The release distributed by the X Consortium is a sample implementation of the protocol and several X servers. At first, the participating companies developed only sample servers for their own hardware, but the number of servers grew with every new release.

In 1988, with the R2 release, the X Consortium took over the leadership of the X11 development from the MIT. Many well-known companies participate in the X Consortium: as well as DEC, there are also IBM, Sun, Hewlett Packard; the list of members reads like the hall of fame of the computer world. Most of the activities of the X11 Consortiums are carried out via email; proposed specifications undergo a public 'review' which recalls the RFC procedure on the Internet. Interested parties can find more detailed information under `http://www.x.org/ftp/pub/DOCS/XConsortium`.

At that time, X was practically exclusively available for (larger) UNIX workstations. X made (for those days) high demands on the hardware and the operating system. In May 1990, Thomas Röll published a freely available X11R4 server for PC UNIX systems as part of the X386 project. Based on this server, SGCS (Snitily Graphics Consulting Services), for whom Thomas Röll subsequently worked, produced a follow-up version which, however, turned out to be unstable.

This led to the development of 'The XFree86 Project' which aimed to improve version 1.2 of the X386 server. Today, XFree86 is freely available for many different operating systems. Several commercial UNIX vendors supply the XFree86 system instead of their own version of X. To be able to participate in the further development of X, the non-profit organization 'The Xfree86 Project, Inc.' was founded, which then became a member of the X Consortium. The Xfree86 project is exclusively financed by donations. Further information on XFree86 can be found on the WWW under `http://www.xfree86.org`.

X servers do not only exist for UNIX. Even for OS/2 and Windows, there are ports that can be used. However, if you generally work with UNIX systems and use your PC only as an X terminal, then XFree86 is certainly a better choice than any Windows version with a corresponding add-on.

The X software is neither subject to the GPL, nor is it public domain – the copyright is owned by the different organizations participating in the development. Nevertheless, the X distribution is freely available and can be redistributed without licensing fees. This shows clear parallels to the GPL conditions. In contrast to the GPL, however, these programs can also be used in proprietary systems without the source code having to be available. Individual applications and add-on programs, in particular from the `/Contrib` area, however, may well be public domain, and/or subject to the GPL or other licensing conditions.

Because of the licensing conditions and the power of this concept, X11 became the standard graphics system for UNIX workstations. Practically all manufacturers supply a (possibly adapted) X11 together with their systems. The sources are, however, freely available (for example via `ftp.x.org`), so individual system administrators can also compile and install the Window system themselves. This is not too difficult, because the procedure is well documented; however, you will need a relatively high amount of free disk space.

Besides the X system itself, the X Consortium also distributes some programs as 'contributed' software. These programs are not maintained by the X Consortium, but are only distributed through this channel. Before each new release, a collection of programs and tools is put together which are already adapted to the new version. These are then distributed together with the X sources on tape or CD-ROM. Users with a good Internet connection can also obtain the programs via `ftp` from `ftp.x.org`.

6.3 XFree86 server configuration

In previous versions, configuration of an XFree86 server used to be a laborious exercise. If you adapt the configuration file `/etc/XF86Config` manually, the X server can exploit the hardware (graphics card and monitor) up to the limits (and further). However, this presumes an in-depth knowledge of the hardware and the procedures used, and is, in short, not to be recommended for the average user.

With release 3.2 of Xfree86, a graphical tool for the configuration of the server is now supplied in the form of `XF86Setup`. This tool guides you through the configuration by means of menus. The only important issue is that you know the hardware you are using (mouse, graphics card, and monitor), and that you have the technical data ready, which you will find in the corresponding manuals.

If during this procedure you enter values that exceed the specifications of your graphics card or your monitor, you may damage these devices. However, if you are more deeply interested in the configuration, you can edit the XF86Config file with any editor. Format and possible settings are documented in the man page XF86Config(5).

Some important key combinations may help you with the configuration (and also later on). Thus, for example, Ctrl-Alt-Backspace can be used to abort the X server process. If your monitor cannot synchronize the image, you should immediately terminate the X server to prevent your monitor from being damaged.

During configuration you can set different resolutions (for one color depth). You can toggle between these resolutions with Ctrl-Alt-keypad + and Ctrl-Alt-keypad -. To change between the different color depths, you must unfortunately terminate the server and then restart it (for example, with startx -- -bpp 16 for a color depth of 16 bits.

You can also start several X servers on one computer by specifying the screen to be used as a parameter. The first X server (automatically) becomes screen :0, the second server can be started with startx -- :1. Obviously, you may use different color depths for each screen.

6.3.1 Configuration of commercial X servers

Besides XFree86, there are also commercial X servers (Metro-X and Accelerated-X) for LINUX. These are sometimes faster than comparable XFree86 servers. Use of such programs can be sensible if the chip set on the graphics card is not (yet) supported by XFree86. However, these servers use all the other X programs of the normal XFree86 distribution.

Also the commercial X servers available for LINUX have appropriate, easy-to-handle configuration programs. Here too you need the relevant information about your hardware; using these is as simple as with XF86Config. You will find more about this subject in the manual of your X server.

6.3.2 Software configuration

The X Window system defines only the interface between the X clients and the X server. Practically no assumptions are made about the 'look and feel' of the applications or of the system. This makes it very flexible on the one hand, but not easy to configure on the other. Furthermore, the X interface may look totally different for two users on the same system, and also show significant differences in handling.

Basically, there are two ways to start the X Window system. Both ways have their legitimation and are configured differently. Nevertheless, both variations may be used in parallel on the same system.

Starting the X Window system with `startx`

Every user who is logged on to the system can start the X Window system by means of the `startx` command. The file `~/.xinitrc` which is read by the `xinit` program determines which clients (applications) are to be started. These could be, for example, an XTerm and the window manager.

If the user has not got this file in his/her home directory, the system file `/usr/X11R6/lib/X11/xinit/xinitrc` is used. This procedure is sensible if no X server should be continuously running, for example because the computer has relatively little RAM. Unfortunately, the standard programs of XFree86 do not check whether the user is actually logged in at the console, so even users logged in via the network can start an X server on the console. This can be rather confusing for a user logged in on the console, and it is a security problem.

During the start via `startx`, the server can be passed additional options. Thus, for example, with `startx -- -bpp 16 :1` a second server with a higher number of colors can be started. All options available for calling an X server are documented in the `Xserver(1)` man page. Another good introduction is the general introduction in the man page `X(1)`.

Starting the X Window system with `xinit`

Which server is started by `xinit` can be determined by a series of possibilities:

- By default, the `X` program is started. This can be a link to the correct server.
- If the file `/usr/X11R6/lib/X11/xinit/xserverrc` exists, it is executed. The file name used can be overwritten by means of the environment variable `XSERVERRC`.
- Each user can create the file `~/.xserverrc` in his/her home directory, which is used to start the X server.

Logging in under X with the X Display Manager

As an alternative to a login at the console, it is possible to use the `xdm` program (X Display Manager) to carry out the login directly under X. The configuration file used to start the client is `~/.xsession`. If this file does not exist, the default settings in the file `Xsession`[1] are used.

If a login is not possible, for example because of errors in the file `~/.xsession`, an emergency session can be started if the password is not confirmed with (Enter), but with (Alt)-(F1). With this kind of login, possible error messages can be found in the file `~/.xsession-errors`. Even if you normally do not notice any peculiarities, you should still have a look at this file from time to time.

A login under X only makes sense for computers with sufficient RAM and a good monitor. In such cases, one achieves great similarity to commercial operating systems on workstations, or rather, the systems are practically indistinguishable.

---

[1] Depending on the distribution, this file can be found in the directory `/etc/X11/xdm` or `/var/X11/xdm`.

Apart from starting a session on the local computer, LINUX can also be used as an X terminal. On an X terminal, you only run an X server which manages the hardware. The login is carried out on a (remote) UNIX computer somewhere in the network.

The selection of the computer on which the login takes place is carried out by means of the `chooser`. On the remote computer the X Display Manager `xdm` must be started and logins must be allowed. This is the case by default and is configured in the file `/etc/X11/xdm/Xaccess`.

Depending on the requirements, there are different possibilities for starting the X server on the X terminal. In particular, these are:

- `X -broadcast`, to search the local subnetwork for computers with a running `xdm`. If an `xdm` is running on the local computer as well, local logins are possible too.

- `X -query` *host*, to obtain the login screen of a specific computer, and

- `X -indirect` *host*, to fetch the list of possible systems from computer *host*.

There are commercial X terminals based on LINUX. Furthermore, it is possible to boot a LINUX kernel via the network, and to mount the root file system by means of NFS. This allows diskless systems to be implemented, which can also serve as X terminals.

With the availability of the Java Development Kit and the direct support of Java in the kernel, LINUX systems are suited to be used as network computers. The advantages over other solutions are the use of standard PC hardware and the possibility of growing into a 'true' LINUX workstation.

Logging in to special desktops

If you have acquired CDE or know it from other systems, you will have noticed that the login is also carried out under X, but that a separate interface is used for this purpose. This is done by not starting the `xdm`, but rather the `dtlogin` program. This reads its configuration files from `/usr/dt/config`, and for the rest it behaves like `xdm`.

The KDE project follows a similar approach with the `klogin` program. The use of a separate login form has the advantage that the correct look and feel is used already at that stage, and that, furthermore, additional settings can be made.

6.3.3 Keyboard mapping under X

The keyboard mapping too can be extensively modified under X. This is done by means of the `xmodmap` program. Usually, you will not have to make many changes to the keyboard map, because XFree86 takes over the keyboard assignments of the console. If in spite of this you plan substantial changes, we recommend the use of `xkeycaps`, which you can find in the `Contrib` directory on `ftp.x.org`. Another useful tool is the `xev` program which displays the full text for all events it receives (events, key strokes, mouse movements).

Especially in X applications that employ the Motif libraries, frequent use is made of special keyboard assignments which are not present in statically linked applications. These applications should then contain a file XKeysymDB in which the missing link between keys and functions is established. This file is stored either as /usr/lib/X11/XKeysymDB or as /usr/openwin/lib/XKeysymDB. By assigning an appropriate path to the environment variable $XKEYSYMDB, another file can be used. Without this file, or in case of missing entries, you may be faced with error messages such as 'unknown keysyms'.

With the xmodmap program, you can also reconfigure your mouse as left-handed. Since all standard scripts evaluate the file ~/.xmodmap at the start of an X session, you enter the line from Listing 6.1 into this file.

```
pointer = 3 2 1
```

Listing 6.1   Swapping mouse buttons for left-handed users.

6.3.4 X resources

Not only can X itself be widely adapted to the requirements of the users in its look and feel, but also the individual X clients can usually be configured in a very flexible way. This is done by means of so-called resources. Resources store values which are either set system-wide or which can be overwritten by the user. System-wide valid resources are stored in the directory /usr/X11R6/lib/X11/app-defaults. There you can find a resource file for practically every X client.

The resources which are read by an application program and can be used for its configuration are documented in the corresponding man page in the RESOURCES section. Some of these settings can also be passed to the client as command line options at the start. Each user can, however, specify his/her own settings by creating the file ~/.Xresources. This file is loaded at the start of X (or after the login).

Modifications to this file do not become automatically active in an ongoing session, but must first be read into the X11 system by means of a command, for example xrdb -merge .Xresources. Technically, this data is stored in the X server which supplies the applications with the appropriate values.

Resources can be specified in a series of different formats, where more specialized ones are preferred to less specialized ones. The specification of:

```
rxvt.background:        lightblue
```

causes the program rxvt to use the color lightblue as background color. With the entry:

```
*background:    white
```

the background color is set to the color white for all clients. If both entries are present in the resources, rxvt uses the color specified for it, whereas all other clients use white as background color.

If you cannot install programs in the system directories, you can specify the directories to be searched in the environment variable XAPPLRESDIR. All in all, this configuration method has a do-it-yourself aspect, and does not compare favourably with the easy-to-use modern systems. On the other hand, the system is very flexible and is available on every X server.

6.3.5 Other configuration possibilities

Another program to adapt X to users' requirements is xset. You can switch the keyboard click on and off and change its volume. If you want to change the tracking speed of the mouse, you also need to use xset. In addition, you can use this program to modify search paths for fonts dynamically.

6.4 Window managers

The appearance (the 'furniture') and the behavior of the windows distinctly characterize the look and feel of a Window system. Under X, this part is implemented by means of the so-called window manager. The window manager under X is not a part of the X Window system itself, but a client (application program), like any other.

This has the advantage that X itself does not (and cannot) make any prescriptions about look and handling, and that even with a 'busy' X client the system still reacts correctly. In Windows NT too an application can move or resize its own window to prevent the user feeling that the system is 'standing still.'

Window managers determine the layout of the window's title bar, window frame, type of icons and, if needed, number and position of several virtual desktops. In addition, the window manager is responsible for the keyboard focus, that is, which application receives keyboard input. Depending on personal preferences, one can require a click in the window or on the title bar to transfer the keyboard focus. Personally, I prefer the option in which the focus always belongs to the window where the mouse pointer is located.

There is a whole series of window managers with rather different properties; with the more recent ones mostly following the 'Inter-client Communication Conventions Manual' (ICCCM). The ICCCM is one of the official documents of the X Consortium which define the X Window system or the X environment. In its current version 2.0, this document is part of X11R6. This documentation can be found on the Internet under ftp://ftp.x.org/xc/doc/specs/ICCCM. The ICCCM specifies the conventions which applications have to follow in order to cooperate with other clients (on the same server); the specifications laid down in the ICCCM can also be seen as a protocol. Particularly critical points in this context are the interaction between window manager and applications, plus the selection mechanism (cut and paste).

Each of the available window managers has special functions and thus advantages and disadvantages. One useful feature is the representation of virtual screens or desktops which allows many windows to be neatly arranged even on small monitors. Table 6.1 shows an overview of a series of widely used window managers. LINUX

Program	Description
twm	'Tab Window Manager': standard window manager in X11
awm	'Ardent Window Manager': preferred by hackers, has features (dynamic menus) that others do not offer
olwm	'Open Look Window Manager': Sun's window manager
mwm	'Motif Window Manager'
fvwm	'? Virtual Window Manager': slim, configurable window manager (mwm emulation)

Table 6.1 Overview of different window managers.

systems frequently use a program of the fvwm family, which will be described in more detail in the next section.

Which window manager you use depends entirely on your personal preferences. The only window manager which is present in all (including commercial) UNIX systems, is twm. This is initially the only option for a unique system environment although its look and handling are no longer state of the art.

For commercial systems, the Motif window manager is currently the standard. Under LINUX you can either use fvwm in Motif compatibility mode, or the Motif clone lesstif, or you can employ a commercial mwm. On the other hand, it might also be sensible to install fvwm on the other systems; often, however, this is not possible.

6.4.1 The window manager fvwm

LINUX systems very often use fvwm, the new version fvwm2, or the special variation fvwm95. This window manager is derived from the standard twm, but needs significantly less memory. Nevertheless, this window manager is very powerful; it is able, for example, to represent a virtual desktop, and is flexible in its configuration, which implements nearly any option you can think of. The system-wide configuration can be found in the file /usr/X11R6/lib/X11/fvwm/system.fvwmrc, whereas each user can specify his/her own setting in the file ~/.fvwmrc.

In this section, we introduce the configuration of fvwm version 2. Since the order of the entries is significant, the various options will be presented in the order specified in the default system.fvwmrc. We will discuss this later, but it should be briefly mentioned that besides fvwm itself there is a series of add-on programs, the so-called modules, whose configuration is equally carried out in .fvwmrc. The default file is extensively commented, therefore, together with the man page for fvwm, the configuration is relatively easy to master.

- Under X, there are two alternatives for how windows get the focus, that is, become the current window. fvwm normally uses 'focus follows mouse'; alternatively, the keyword ClickToFocus can transfer the focus via clicking in the window. Active windows are automatically brought to the foreground after the number of milliseconds specified after AutoRaise has expired.

- fvwm can manage several desktops. The size is specified by means of the entry DeskTopSize. You can toggle between the various desktops by means of the keyboard ([Ctrl]-arrow key) or the mouse. The mouse pointer must be moved to the screen border. After the lapse of time specified after EdgeResistance, the screen is scrolled by EdgeScroll percent. The second parameter after Edge-Resistance specifies how long one has to wait when a window is moved as well.

- Some settings can be made for reasons of compatibility with mwm (Motif Window Manager).

- Positioning of the windows can be influenced via different settings.

    – Interactive positioning of the windows is the default.

    – RandomPlacement stands for arbitrary positions.

    – SmartPlacement tries to find a free area on the screen. If this fails, interactive or random placement is used.

    – StubbornPlacement prevents covering up of iconized programs.

- The menus which appear on the background (the root window) can also be arbitrarily modified.

- Together with fvwm a series of modules is installed which are also configured in the .fvwmrc. A more detailed presentation of some of the modules follows in the next section.

- Many functions of fvwm can also be triggered by function keys. This can be useful for transferring the focus, for example by means of [Alt]-[Tab].

After changing the configuration, fvwm must be restarted. For many other window managers this would require termination of the session, but fvwm can simply be restarted by means of a menu option.

6.4.2 The fvwm modules

Many functions required by some users need large amounts of memory which can be saved without problems for all other users. fvwm supports this via the use of modules that carry out special functions.

- GoodStuff
  This module generates an icon bar which allows frequently needed programs to be started with a click of the mouse. This bar can be easily configured by each user and can be positioned anywhere on the screen. To make the bar appear, fvwm must be started together with this module.

- FvwmAudio
  This module allows you to associate sounds to specific window actions, for example, every time the close button is selected, you hear the sound of a breaking glass pane (provided a sound driver plus hardware exists and is activated).

- FvwmBacker

  Allows you to associate each desktop to a separate screen background and to display it when desktops are changed. Any available program may be used for this purpose, for example xv, xsetroot, xpmroot, xearth, and so on.

- FvwmBanner

  Shows the fvwm logo in the middle of the screen for five seconds. Can also be called from the command line.

- FvwmIconBox

  Manages a box containing the icons of the started programs.

- FvwmPager

  Allows you to switch between the virtual desktops by means of a simple click in an overview window. This window can also be integrated into the icon bar of GoodStuff.

- FvwmSave

  Allows the layouts (sizes and positions) of the active applications to be stored in the file ~/new.xinitrc. Obviously, this file must then be used by ~/.xsession or ~/.xinitrc.

- FvwmWinList

  Displays a list of open windows. A window can be activated by clicking on the corresponding entry in this list.

6.4.3 Other window managers

If you use Motif, you will find that it includes mwm. This is a window manager which harmonizes with other Motif applications and is described by the style guide. This window manager is currently not very often employed, since commercial systems are usually equipped with CDE.

The lesstif project contains a free implementation of mwm which is based on fvwm. This has kept its capability of handling virtual desktops, but the syntax of the configuration file was made compatible with the original. Both programs read the file ~/.mwmrc.

CDE and KDE also include their own window managers. CDE uses dtwm, which is based on mwm, whereas the KDE project uses kwm.

Further window managers worth looking at are AfterStep, which emulates the look and feel of the OpenStep system, and Enlightenment, which is particularly eccentric in its graphics. Whichever window manager you choose, you will certainly be able to find one under LINUX that meets your requirements.

6.5 General X11 command line options

Many X11 application programs, including all programs developed by means of the X tool kit (libXt), 'inherit' some command line options. Even if, according to its man page, an application program is unable to specify size and position of a window at the call, for example, this is nevertheless possible because the passed options are first evaluated and also understood by the X tool kit. The following points briefly present some of these generally applicable command line options. All options are described in the man page for X(1).

- Screen
  With –display, host name and screen number of the server are specified; thus, for example, 'display' corresponds to dorin:0.0. More details on the use of X in the network can be found in Section 6.6.

- Size and position of windows
  The option –geometry is used to specify the initial size and position of a window. A valid 'Geometry' could be, for example, –geometry 81x24+0+0, which would open a window of 81 chars by 24 lines in the upper left corner of the screen. The xwininfo program displays this (and further) information.

- Colors
  Both the foreground and the background color of an X client can be modified with the option –fg or –foreground, or –bg or –background.

- Fonts
  The font to be used can be specified with the option –fn or –font.

- Window title
  For a better distinction between windows of the same program, these can be assigned different titles by means of the option –title.

- X resources
  At the start of the program, individual resources can be overwritten by means of the option –xrm, for example, to test different settings. For permanent use, these settings should be entered in the file ~/.Xresources.

6.6 Access control

X is a network-transparent window system. Programs can run on one computer (for example, a powerful workstation) and display their windows on a simple X terminal, a LINUX computer, or an X server under Windows. The server that displays the windows can be determined by means of two procedures:

- Setting of the environment variable DISPLAY. Here, the host name of the server is specified, followed by the number of the display. After the command export DISPLAY=dorin:0, the newly started clients will display the windows on the computer dorin, using the first X server started there.

- The standard command line option –display for the specification of the X server. The command xterm –display dorin:0 opens a shell window on the computer dorin. The shell itself (and the xterm program) run on the local computer.

It is, however, not sensible that any user can access any server – unfortunately, this is still the standard with many commercial X servers or X terminals. On the one hand, screen output and keyboard input can be monitored; on the other hand, keyboard input can even be foisted on clients. This can become a real security problem, because as a user, one is not always aware of such proceedings.

Especially if you need to enter a password under X (for example, if you execute su), you should select the option 'secure keyboard' ([Ctrl]-left mouse button) in xterm. This is the only way to ensure that only a program can receive your input.

6.6.1 Allowing computerwise access with xhost

To maintain flexibility despite the security concerns, sophisticated security mechanisms are needed. Up to release 4 (X11R4) access control was only possible via the computer name. Because, even today, many computers with X11R4 are still around, we briefly explain this procedure. With more recent X releases, you should use the xauth procedure presented in the next section.

By default, access from other machines is not allowed; entering the command xhost + allows access from arbitrary computers. Some commercial X terminals use this setting, which leaves the doors open for manipulation. If you come across this setting, you should immediately remove it. It may be easier to forget about these things, but it ruins the security of the whole system.

The command xhost – prevents general access. Usually, you will authorize access only for a specific computer with the command xhost *hostname*. Immediately after the client has opened its window, you can prevent the opening of further windows from this computer by means of xhost *-hostname*. With this method, you can reduce the lapse of time during which you are vulnerable, but the procedure is still far from being secure.

6.6.2 Allowing user-specific access with xauth

As already mentioned above, this procedure is not particularly secure. Every user with an account on the corresponding computer can gain access to this X server. Therefore, another authorization procedure was implemented with X11R5. Here, the access right is not determined by the computer name, but by a type of password (a 'magic cookie'). Management of access rights is carried out by means of the xauth program. During the start of the X server (or the login with xdm), a random key is generated and stored in the file ~/.Xauthority.

Each client knowing this cookie is authorized to access the server. Thus, if you transfer the magic cookie to another computer, it can be monitored with a packet sniffer and used for breaking in. The magic cookie is newly generated by xdm with each login, so an old access authorization cannot be used a second time.

If you have the same home directory on the corresponding computers (for example via NFS), client and server have direct access to the key. If the client runs on a computer which has no access to the key, then the key must previously be transferred. Listing 6.2 shows an example for the application of xauth. If you often work

```
(Linux):~> xauth list
No-MS-DOS/unix:0  WITH-MAGIC-COOKIE-1 66e15be3b61c812e0df5
(Linux):~> xauth extract - | rsh dorin xauth merge -
(Linux):~> rsh dorin xterm -display 'hostname -f':0
```

Listing 6.2   Usage of xauth.

with different computers, you can define appropriate aliases. Please note that magic cookies should not appear in the command line for xauth. Otherwise, the key can be read, for example, from the process list.

6.6.3 Secure shell under X

As we have seen, the secure use of X requires some effort. Many users write scripts which first transfer the magic cookies to a remote computer and then start the corresponding program via remote shell, taking care that the DISPLAY variable must be adapted correspondingly.

In principle, this script for special applications is relatively simple. However, if it is supposed to work under several systems and across domain boundaries (which can again lead to security problems), the script soon becomes fairly complicated.

If you are frequently using display redirection, you should in any case use the ssh. Unfortunately, this is not a part of standard UNIX systems, but the installation effort is always worth while.

First of all, authentication is improved, because it no longer uses the IP address, but a public key method. The second important aspect is that the whole session is encrypted, so even with a packet sniffer, no data can be detected. The encryption also applies to the X redirection which is automatically used by the ssh. And, last but not least, ssh is call-compatible with the rsh, so your users do not have to change their habits.

Additional Information and Sources	
Home page:	http://www.ssh.fi
ftp server:	ftp.cert.dfn.de
ftp path:	/pub/tools/net/ssh
File name:	ssh-1.2.21.tar.gz
Size:	about 1 Mbyte

6.7 Tools and other useful programs for X

Not only are there many applications, such as text processing, editors or spreadsheets, available for X, but there is also a series of important tools which are continuously needed in day-to-day operation. Many of these tools belong to the standard distribution of X11, others to the so-called Contrib software; others again are distributed through other channels.

6.7.1 Standard tools

The standard tools are part of the X distribution. Some vendors partly replace these programs with their own programs or do not supply a corresponding tool. Thus, the standard XTerm, that is, the shell window under X, is often substituted (aixterm under AIX, dxterm under Digital UNIX or ULTRIX). Unfortunately, these terminals are often not correctly entered in the Termcap or Terminfo files of other systems. Therefore, only the existence of the standard tools allows a unique working environment in a heterogeneous network.

- xterm is used as shell window.
- The xprop program displays information (properties) about clients.
- The properties of a window are shown by xwininfo. For the root window (the background), this information also includes the currently used color depth.
- The xwd program can be used to store the current screen contents in a file.
- Various settings such as keyboard click, sound, or the screen saver, can be set by means of the xset program.
- Information about the X server is displayed by xdpyinfo.
- The editres program can be used for displaying and editing of X resources.
- xev displays the X events which are, for example, generated by key strokes.
- xmodmap can be used to change the keyboard mapping. A graphical front end is xkeycaps which, however, does not belong to the X core, but is distributed as Contrib software.
- xman is a simple program for the display of man pages. Many users employ tk-man which, however, presumes Tcl/Tk, a script language with an X connection.
- With xmag, you can magnify parts of the screen.
- If you wish to obtain information on your server, you should run the xdpyinfo program. Information on a client can be obtained by means of the xwininfo program.

6.7.2 Contributed tools

As well as the tools from the X distribution, there is a series of additional useful programs. Many of these programs were 'contributed' and are distributed by the X Consortium. Only a minimum part of these programs is usually supplied by the vendor, but you are free to install them yourself. Please also refer to Section 11.2.

- XTrap is implemented as a server/library extension and can be used to record and replay an X session. It is available from `ftp.x.org:` under `/contrib/XTrapV33_X11R5.tar.Z`.

- `xcb` is a multiple cut and paste buffer.

- `xse` (version 2.1) is an interface to the Xlib routine Xsendevent and allows an X window or the application running in it to be sent specific keyboard or mouse events, thus emulating the input of a user.

- `xgrab` allows easy generation of screen shots. The screen shots of this book were stored as PostScript files by means of this tool and then integrated into the LaTeX document.

6.8 Information and sources

Additional Information and Sources	
Man pages:	`X(1)`, `XF86config(5)`
Newsgroups:	`comp.windows.x`
Mailing list:	`xpert[-request]@x.org`
	gatewayed with `comp.windows.x`
Name:	`comp.windows.x FAQ`
Size:	about 240 Kbytes
Name:	`comp.windows.x x-faq/speedups`
Size:	about 670 lines

Backup

7

Only wimps use tape backup:
real *men just upload their important stuff on ftp,*
and let the rest of the world mirror it.

Linus B. Torvalds

7.1 Why everybody needs backups

For many users, making backups falls under the category of annoying, because unproductive, chores. Nevertheless, a system administrator – and whoever runs a one-user system is a system administrator too – should dedicate some serious thought to the security of their data. A series of user errors and problems can be responsible for data being lost or corrupted.

A good backup must satisfy a set of criteria: the backup should as far as possible run without supervision; the backup media should be managed by the programs themselves; and restoring data should be easy and reliable. In any serious computer use, backup is indispensable if one does not want to run the risk of painful data loss.

Substantial amounts of data can be lost through negligence in the use of 'dangerous' commands. Under UNIX, a complete directory tree can simply be deleted without confirmation by means of the command `rm -rf *`.

To avoid such problems, aliases with more prudent settings can be used instead of the dangerous commands. Examples for the programs `rm`, `cp`, and `mv` can be found in Listing 7.1.

The option `-i` (`--interactive`) forces a prompt for confirmation when attempting to delete or overwrite files. The option `-v` (`--verbose`) causes the file name

```
(Linux):~> alias rm 'rm -i -v'
(Linux):~> alias cp 'cp -i -v -b'
(Linux):~> alias mv 'mv -i -v -b'
```

Listing 7.1   Examples for aliases.

to be displayed. In the commands cp and mv, additional creation of backup copies can be triggered with the option −b (or −−backup). You can also keep several versions of a file as backup copies. The exact management of backup copies can be specified by means of the environment variable VERSION_CONTROL or the option −V (or −−version−control). More detailed information can be found by calling man cp.

The rm program deletes files irrevocably. There is no undelete program under LINUX. This functionality can be achieved either by means of some shell scripts or aliases, or via a special delete/undelete system (for example the MIT one). Unfortunately, practically all solutions to this problem, unless they have been implemented in the kernel, have their disadvantages, so many users just learn to live with permanently deleted files.

An additional problem is that a simple shell function, namely the output redirection, overwrites a file without prompting for confirmation. In the bash, this can be prevented by means of the setting set −o noclobber. An existing file can only be overwritten with the specification of >| instead of >. Users of the tcsh can use the command set noclobber to prevent files from being overwritten through output redirection. The file is overwritten if the character sequence >! is used instead of >. The combination >| causes the tcsh to redirect both the standard output and the standard error output together.

Under UNIX, the system administrator can delete or modify all files. Therefore, the user ID root should only be used for system administration, but not for daily work. A non-privileged user can only delete or modify a limited number of files, so the danger of complete loss of all data is simply not there.

Many UNIX neophytes employ the user ID root also for their daily work. When using a non-privileged user ID, one sometimes receives the message 'Permission denied.' If this message appears at the start of programs that should be executable for every user, the system is incorrectly configured. The work invested in correct configuration pays off in the long run through the increased security achieved by the access right checks of the kernel.

A system administrator should always check the command line several times, particularly prior to 'hazardous' actions, before actually executing the command. Thus, when creating loops or other instructions that are to process many files, you should definitely use the possibility to run them 'out of the wood' by inserting an echo in front of the command proper (Listing 7.2).

The first command displays the list of all files to be processed; in the second command, these files are actually deleted. Another possibility for using the output of the first command is to redirect the output into a shell. The third command

```
(Linux):~# find . −name \*~ −exec echo rm {} \;
(Linux):~# find . −name \*~ −exec rm {} \;
(Linux):~# find . −name \*~ −ok rm {} \;
```

Listing 7.2   Dry execution of dangerous commands.

```
(Linux):~# find . -name \*~
(Linux):~# rm $(find . -name \*~)
```

Listing 7.3   Dry execution of dangerous commands, another way of doing it.

in Listing 7.2 ensures that for each file found the user is prompted to confirm that the command should actually be executed. A further alternative for the deletion of backup copies is shown in Listing 7.3.

In case of a power failure or a system crash, sometimes not all data is written to the hard disk. LINUX, like other UNIX systems and modern versions of the MS-DOS cache `smartdrv`, implements a write cache, in which write accesses are buffered before the data is actually written to the hard disk. This makes writing to the hard disk substantially faster for the application, which therefore has more time to carry out other functions.

After a system crash, the file system may be in a non-recoverable state, so that some data is lost. In the worst case, even a total loss of data is imaginable, if the internal structure of the file system is no longer consistent. The Extended-2 file system, widely used under LINUX, has been implemented with a view to far-reaching reparability, so these problems occur relatively seldom. Most of the errors of this kind have up to now been caused by defective hardware.

The first superblock of the file system, which contains the most important information on this file system, could be damaged. The program for checking Extended-2 file systems, `e2fsck` or `fsck.ext2`, can be instructed to use a backup copy of the superblock via the command line option –b. Listing 7.4 shows a possible way of proceeding. The first superblock is located in the first block, further superblocks can be found every 8192 blocks of the partition.

With the structure of the LINUX directory tree and the powerful utilities, it is relatively easy to save the user and configuration files. Even in the standard

```
(Linux):~# fsck.ext2 -f -v /dev/hdb1
e2fsck 0.5b, 14-Feb-95 for EXT2 FS 0.5a, 94/10/23
e2fsck: Bad magic number in super-block while trying to
open /dev/hdb1

The file system superblock is corrupt. Try running e2fsck
with an alternate superblock using the -b option. (8193
is commonly an alternate superblock; Hence,
'e2fsck -b 8193 <device>' may recover the file system.)
(Linux):~# fsck.ext2 -f -v -b 8193 /dev/hdb1
```

Listing 7.4   Example of a corrupted superblock.

installation, the necessary tools are available, for example, if you store /home in a separate partition.

It is, however, important that not only the backup is executed on an error-free medium. The system administrator should also check the restoring of individual files and, if at all possible, also of the entire system. Only after such a check can you be sure that the data was effectively backed up and can also be restored. This test should obviously be rerun if changes are made to the system software used (kernel, hardware drivers, libraries, backup system) or to the hardware.

In particular, it is sensible to create an emergency diskette which contains all drivers and programs needed to restore the system. Then, a minimal system can initially be booted from the floppy disk, so that no data from the hard disk is needed. This makes it practically always possible to restore a backup, even if the system on the hard disk is in no condition to run.

There are several freely available packages for the creation of emergency diskettes, which must be adapted to local requirements by the system administrator. If in doubt, the boot and root diskettes of the corresponding distribution are a good starting point; modern systems and distributions can also boot from CD, which makes things particularly easy. Some packages for creation of emergency and boot diskettes can be found on the ftp server sunsite.unc.edu in the directory /pub/Linux/system/Recovery.

7.2 Surviving disk errors with RAID

From the point of view of the operating system, modern hard disks are error-free for a relatively long time. If, however, the first error is signaled, it is time to replace this disk. Usually, you will carry out a last backup and then restore this onto the new hard disk.

During the time in which the data is backed up and restored and the hard disk replaced, no system operation is possible. Thus, it is the aim, even in the case of disk damage, to run the system until the next period of reduced activity, to replace the disk in peace and quiet. Some modern SCSI adapters and disks are 'hot-plug' capable, that is, they can be replaced during normal operation, but this is not always possible.

With the RAID technology (Redundant Array of Inexpensive Disks), a procedure has been developed which is capable of surviving the failure of one or more disks without loss of data. Unfortunately, this technology does not help against accidental erasure or inconsistencies after a system crash.

The RAID technology has a series of levels which describe the kind of data storage in more detail. Currently, the following are the most widely used levels:

- RAID-0 is used to combine several disks or partitions into one larger (virtual) partition. There are two variations, the simple concatenation of the parts (concat) and the so-called striping. In striping, consecutive blocks are not put on one disk one after the other, but are distributed in stripes across all disks involved. This achieves a higher performance, in particular if the hard disks are connected to different SCSI adapters. Data security, however, decreases, so loss of data must be expected if one of the disks is defective.

- Data security is improved with RAID-1, the so-called mirroring. Here, each block is written in parallel to two or more disks, so that in case of failure of one hard disk, the data can still be accessed. When reading, the load can be distributed across several disks, and thus a higher data throughput can be achieved. The cost of this solution is relatively high because all hard disks must be doubled.

- In RAID-4, in addition to the data, a so-called parity is stored. If one disk of the array fails, the data can still be reconstructed from the other disks. The disadvantage of this solution is that each write process must also take place on the parity disk. The advantage is that comparatively few additional hard disks are needed.

- Most frequently, RAID-5 is used which combines the advantage of RAID-4 with a parity distributed across all disks. Thus, data throughput does not decrease to the same extent as with RAID-4.

All of these solutions can be realized by means of special hardware (a SCSI adapter with a corresponding disk array) or software. The current developers' versions of the LINUX kernel implement these functions.

Before you rejoice – RAID is not the solution to all problems. With RAID, you can protect yourself against the failure of one hard disk. If, however, the corresponding hard disk controller gives in, the most reliable mirror is good for nothing. In the same way, RAID does not protect you against system crashes or accidental erasure of data. Therefore, you should carry out periodical backups even with RAID.

Additional Information and Sources	
ftp server:	`ftp.kernel.org`
ftp path:	`/pub/linux/daemons/raid`
File:	`raidtools-0.41.tar.gz`
Size:	about 40 Kbytes
Home page:	`http://linas.org/linux/raid.html`

7.3 Backup media

With today's hard disk sizes, a complete backup on diskettes has become practically impossible. The expense in time and backup media is out of all proportion to the security to be expected. Nevertheless, backups on diskettes of small amounts of data which need frequent backing up are possible and make sense. The text of this book was backed up on diskette after each change.

For a convenient and automatic backup it is necessary for the data of a backup to fit on a medium, so that the presence of the system administrator (for example, for changing tapes) is not required. This allows backups to be carried out overnight without human intervention.

Frequently, magnetic tapes are used as backup media. Tapes are inexpensive and, despite the sequential access, sufficiently fast. There are several different standards for magnetic tapes and the corresponding drives or interfaces to which the drive can be connected. The most well-known standards are the QIC (Quarter Inch Cartridge) standards.

7.3.1 Floppy streamers

On PC systems, floppy streamers that can be connected to the floppy disk controller are very popular. These devices can read and write magnetic tapes in QIC-40 or QIC-80 format. Recently, systems with higher capacity have appeared.

This kind of streamer must be synchronized very precisely, which is not always feasible under a multitasking operating system. Therefore, data security often leaves much to be desired. For a new acquisition, you should seriously think about a SCSI or DAT streamer (DAT = Digital Audio Tape). Even the capacity of QIC-80 tapes of 120 Mbytes without compression is much too small for today's hard disk and partition sizes. The capacity value of 250 Mbytes with compression which is quoted by manufacturers and dealers is unattainable, in particular for already packed data.

To operate such a streamer you need the `ftape` driver. This driver is contained in the standard kernel and can either be permanently compiled or loaded into the kernel at runtime as a module. Since tapes are not usually needed constantly, you can automatically load the driver by means of `kerneld`.

QIC-40/80 magnetic tapes must be formatted. Under LINUX, this is not possible as yet, so you must either buy preformatted tapes or format them under DOS.

Under LINUX, the device files for the floppy streamer are called `/dev/rft0` to `/dev/rft3` or `/dev/nrft0` to `/dev/nrft3` for no-rewind devices. For reasons of compatibility with older systems, you can also often access the floppy streamer under `/dev/ftape` or `/dev/nftape`.

7.3.2 QIC-02 streamers

Another interface standard is QIC-02. Here, the tape drives are connected to an additional controller card. Thus, the timing problems of the floppy tape driver no longer apply, but in return you need a free interrupt, a DMA channel, and a free I/O address. The capacity of the tapes is higher than the above-mentioned 120 Mbytes.

7.3.3 SCSI streamers

For SCSI streamers too there is a range of standards (QIC-150/520/625). They differ in capacity, recording method, and sizes of cassettes. For LINUX, it makes practically no difference which drive type is used; only the SCSI controller must be supported.

Today's most fashionable devices are (SCSI-) DAT drives, which have a very high capacity (up to 4 Gbytes). Thus, even larger partitions can be backed up without changing tapes. Unfortunately, after using the cassettes several times, data security suffers through the very high abrasion during operation. You should therefore regularly clean the drive and replace a tape after a certain number of write operations. DLT drives do not have this problem, but are significantly more expensive.

In order to be able to use SCSI tape drives, the support for the corresponding SCSI controller and the support for SCSI tape drives (`SCSI tape support`) must be selected during the kernel configuration. The tape drive can be accessed under `/dev/st0` or `/dev/nst0`. On other UNIX systems, tape drives are frequently accessed as `/dev/rmt0`.

7.3.4 Backup via network

Under LINUX, as under any other UNIX, the backup can be carried out on a tape drive that is connected to another computer which can be reached via network. For a large number of computers in a network, it may be sensible to create a backup server. This system is then connected to powerful tape machines, and possibly all computers of the network are backed up via this system.

This makes it possible to carry out a central backup, so that tape management need only take place at one location. Here, special measures such as safe storage of cassettes can also be organized relatively easily. Furthermore, it is no longer the individual user or the local system administrator who has to be responsible for backup, but backup can be established as a service of the computer center.

The disadvantages are the effort of coordinating and configuring the system plus the increase in network load. Furthermore, a backup may take significantly more time over the network than on a fast local tape drive. However, if you need to backup many (networked) computers, you should in any case go for a network-wide solution.

7.3.5 Special data media

In rare cases, removable disks, floptical disks or WORMS (Write Once Read Many times) are used for backup purposes. Because of their high cost, these data media are only seldom employed.

7.4 Backup strategies

Backup strategies are determined by many local factors. The system administrator must decide which data needs backing up at which intervals, and what number of backup media is needed for this purpose. Furthermore, the sequence of complete and incremental backups needs specifying. In complete backups, with a few exceptions, all files are backed up. In an incremental backup, the backup affects all files that have been modified since the last backup.

7.4.1 Extent and time of backup

First, the question should be answered what data needs backing up and at what intervals. For many LINUX and UNIX systems, the following gradients are the most likely.

The exact intervals and the affected directories or file systems should be determined by the system administrator on the basis of the local requirements.

As a rule, you should try to backup your data at low traffic time. On the one hand, less data is subject to changes; on the other hand, a backup involves a certain system load, so you should only interfere with the smallest number of users possible.

If you want to obtain a truly consistent backup, you should carry out the backup in single-user mode. In practice, this will not always be possible. Except for the backup of databases, however, you will be able to live with these problems.

7.4.2 Classes of files

Not all files need to be backed up on a daily basis. For many files which are only seldom changed, a weekly backup may well be sufficient. For other files, even a daily backup is not enough. Often, it is possible to classify the files according to the following structure. The final decision, however, is always left to the system administrator.

Backup of user data

User data which under LINUX are usually stored in the /home directory are continuously modified and should be backed up frequently. In commercial environments, we recommend a daily (incremental) backup of modified data. In addition, a complete backup should be carried out at least once a week. Loss of work done by several programmers or employees over a couple of days could cause substantial costs.

On privately used systems, a weekly or monthly backup can be sensible, according to the user's or system administrator's estimate. Depending on the amount of data, it might be possible to plan only complete backups which would greatly facilitate the handling. Longer intervals between two backups are seldom sensible if you work with your system on a regular basis.

Configuration files

The configuration files stored in /etc and /var are also subject to frequent changes. These files are often the result of extremely hard work and great knowledge, so this data should also be backed up regularly. This applies particularly to network and mail configurations.

These files should in any case be backed up before a system update. It is often sensible to copy these files into a new directory first (for example /etc.old), so that they can be directly accessed after the update. This allows many settings applied to a LINUX or UNIX system to be easily applied again to the updated version.

These settings are the ones that adapt the system to the requirements of the user and facilitate day-to-day work. If these adaptations have not been checked at least by the system administrator, the new installation is not yet a full replacement for the old one. Modern distributions such as Debian, Red Hat or SuSE are updateable, so that you can now in many cases avoid a new installation.

The /usr partition

The data and programs stored in the /usr partition are relatively static and can to a large extent be copied afresh from the installation medium. Nevertheless, it may be sensible to make backups at longer intervals, but certainly always before an update of important software packages.

The availability of the installation, for example on a CD, however, does not mean that this data can be read from the CD without problems. It is always too much of a gamble to rely on only one backup which could easily be affected by errors.

There are administrators who mount the /usr partition with the option ro for read-only. Since the system does not write to this partition, the probability of a data loss is lower; furthermore, no fsck is carried out after a system crash, so the system can be available again after a very short time. However, this procedure is only worth while if you exchange programs or make other modifications only in extremely rare cases.

Locally installed programs

In some cases, if a particularly large number of programs have been installed locally in the /usr/local partition and essential changes to the programs have been made, it may be sensible to backup this partition too, at least periodically. If only a few programs are present, it might be easier to reinstall them. Obviously, at this point, the program sources and/or the installation media should be kept.

Directories not worth backing up

The directories /tmp, /var/tmp, and other directories for the storage of temporary files (for example /usr/local/tmp), plus the pseudo file system /proc need not be saved. Therefore, these directories should always be excluded from the backup. At the system administrator's discretion, file systems such as /var/cache may also be excluded.

7.4.3 Sequencing of incremental and full backups

Execution of an incremental backup is sensible if only relatively few files are modified between the individual backups. Initially, you must begin with a complete backup, so that every file has been saved on at least one medium. Subsequently, only the modified files need to be backed up again.

Complete restoring of a backup is laborious if the last complete backup was made some time ago and in the meantime many incremental backups have been carried out. In case of data loss, the complete backup must be restored first, followed by all incremental backups in the correct order. Therefore, you should periodically carry out complete backups to limit the number of incremental backups. In practice, for example, one complete backup per week with daily incremental backups has proved to be an acceptable solution.

Another possibility is to carry out a complete backup every month, plus a weekly incremental backup of all data changed since the last monthly backup, plus a daily incremental backup with respect to the last weekly backup. If during an incremental backup nearly all files are backed up again, it is much more sensible to carry out a complete backup. The number of backup media required is almost the same, but handling is much easier.

7.4.4 Number of media required for the backup

In the next step, the number of media sets needed for the backup should be determined. As a minimum requirement, two independent sets of media should be used, preferably more.

The simplest variation is to use the media of the oldest backup for the current one. However, for reasons of data security, at least three media should be used. Imagine, for example, the following scenario: a backup is started, but aborted because of an error or a user intervention. Subsequently, a file from the last backup must be restored, but this medium is defective and causes reading errors. With only two tapes, there is no usable backup available – the data is lost.

If specific data must be kept for a longer time, for example, if monthly backups are kept for a year and at least one yearly backup is kept permanently, you obviously need more media. Enterprises that depend on electronic data processing often store selected backups in a fire-proof safe or with an external company to protect themselves against fire or other catastrophes. It is essential that magnetic media are stored in a cool dry place and kept away from magnetic fields.

7.5 Backup programs

In the following subsections, we present a series of backup programs. We differentiate between programs which only read data from a hard disk and write it to a backup medium and vice versa, and programs which also provide the administration of complete and incremental backups. These programs store a list of backed up files, so the corresponding medium can be requested directly.

7.5.1 Low-level programs

In the simplest case, the backup can be carried out by means of appropriate standard UNIX service programs. The individual programs are presented together with some examples which should make the internal procedures somewhat clearer; the same procedures are also used in a similar way in more complex backup systems.

These programs backup all data whether these are system, a partition, or a directory tree data. By means of an appropriate find command (see also Section 10.1.1) or other parameters, it is possible only to backup files that were modified since the last backup.

This involves a series of scripts intended to facilitate the handling of the program and the media. In most cases, however, it is preferable to use a dedicated backup program package. Many of these packages are freely available; the choice of a special system depends on a series of factors and should be made locally by the system administrator.

The tar program

The tar program (Tape Archiver) was originally only used to store archives of files on magnetic tapes. Today, diskettes, files, or network drives are supported too.

Older tar versions could only store files, directories, and links, but not the device files (devices in /dev). This was only implemented in the cpio program. GNU tar is also capable of storing special files (device files and pipes), so that cpio need no longer be used.

Unpacking of archives The tar program does not compress the data, but only combines the individual files into one archive. Compression can be activated (only) in GNU tar by means of the option –z, whereas with the standard tar, the input or output must be processed by an appropriate compression/decompression routine. A file name extension of .Z stands for compression with compress, the extension .gz for the use of gzip. For storage of compressed tar archives on DOS data media, the extension .tar.gz is abbreviated as .tgz. Similarly, archives packed with compress (extension .tar.Z) have the DOS extension .taz.

Many program packages are distributed in the tar format. To reduce the amount of data to be transferred, the files are usually compressed, by means of either compress or gzip. Since gzip compresses substantially better and can read data packed with compress, we only use the gzip program. The package bc-1.02.tar.gz is unpacked, when using the standard UNIX tar, with the command

```
(Linux):~> zcat bc-1.02.tar.gz | tar –xvf –
```

The options can be prefixed with a minus sign (–) or indicated directly. The option –x (--extract) means that the corresponding archive is to be unpacked. The option –v (--verbose) causes tar to output a list of the files contained in the archive on the standard output. After the option –f (--file), the file name of the archive is specified. The name – stands for the standard input when reading a file and for the standard output when writing. If no file name is specified, /dev/rmt0 is used as default. This value can be changed by means of the environment variable TAPE. If a floppy tape streamer is used, you will need the following command:

```
(Linux):~> setenv TAPE /dev/rft0
```

If a file name of the form *hostname:device* is specified, the backup is carried out on this network device. As with the rsh or rlogin programs, a corresponding entry in the file ~/.rhosts or /etc/hosts.equiv is required. If a different user ID is to be used on the remote computer, it can be specified with the same syntax as with the rcp program. In the following example, we use the floppy streamer of the computer atlantis with the user ID hein.

```
(Linux):~> tar –zxvf hein@atlantis:/dev/rft0
```

The archive can also be decompressed first and then processed with `tar`. However, this requires more disk space because the archive is present in uncompressed form.

```
(Linux):~> gunzip bc-1.02.tar.gz
(Linux):~> tar -xvf bc-1.02.tar
```

The additional option `-z`, which is only implemented in the GNU `tar`, causes the `gzip` compressor to be called internally. This makes the explicit call of the compression program superfluous.

```
(Linux):~> tar -zxvf bc-1.02.tar.gz
```

Creation of archives   For the creation of archives, the option `-c` (`--create`) is used. After the last option (mostly `-f`, followed by a file name), a list of the files and directories to be archived is specified. The above archive can be recreated from the files by means of:

```
(Linux):~> tar -zcvf bc-1.02.tar.gz bc-1.02
```

When backing up on magnetic tape, the tape should be left to run uninterrupted for as long as possible. Each new positioning costs a disproportionate amount of time. Therefore, it may be better to do completely without data compression, and to increase the block size (option `-b` or `--block-size`) instead.

An archive can be checked by means of the option `-t` (`--list`). If at the same time the option `-v` (`--verbose`) is specified, an extended list of the files contained in the archive is output.

```
(Linux):~> tar -ztvf bc-1.02.tar.gz
```

With the option `-M` (`--multi-volume`), archives are created that can span several data media. It is, however, not possible to compress such an archive. This would also not make much sense, because otherwise, after a read error on a backup medium, all further data would not be readable.

The `tar` program can also carry out incremental backups by means of the options `-g` (or `--listed-incremental`) and `--newer`. However, it is the task of the user to make a record of the last backup data and to manage a list of the backed up files. This is usually realized by means of scripts; there is a series of backup scripts which can easily be used. An example of a script for an incremental backup of the `home` directory is shown in Listing 7.5.

To check the backup, you should always specify the option `-W` (or `--verify`).

If individual files are to be excluded from the backup, you can use the option `-X` to specify a file that contains a list of regular expressions. The files whose names match the regular expressions are not included in the archive. In the example of Listing 7.6, all object and backup files are not backed up.

Special functions   The `tar` program can also be used to copy entire directory trees. Programs such as `cp` or `rcp` resolve the symbolic links during copying, and copy the file itself instead of the link. When using `tar`, these links are maintained.

```
#!/bin/bash
# Incremental backup
now=`date`
then=`cat date.dump`
tar --create --verbose - file /dev/rft0 --block-size 126 \
     --after-date "$then"\
     --label "Dump from $then to $now"\
  /home
echo $now > date.dump
```

Listing 7.5   Example of a script for incremental backup.

```
(Linux):~> cat exclude
*~
*.o
(Linux):~> tar -zcvXf exclude archiv.tgz .
```

Listing 7.6   Exclusion of files from the backup.

```
(Linux):~> tar -cf - . | ( cd /tmp ; tar -xvf -)
```

If you wish to avoid starting a new shell on the right-hand side of the pipe symbol, you need to switch to the specified directory by means of the option -C (-directory).

```
(Linux):~> tar -cf - . | tar -xvCf /tmp -
```

In a network, one tar can be started on another computer. This allows directory trees to be copied via a network.

```
(Linux):~> rsh host tar -cf - . | tar -xvCf /tmp -
```

Here, files are simply copied. To reduce network load, it may be sensible to compare directories and transfer only modified files or delete superfluous files. For this purpose, you can use the rdist program.

On various systems, the tar program is also capable of generating files with 'holes.' Here, null characters contained in the files are not stored, which can save some disk space, for example, in shared libraries. This is done by using the option -S (--sparse) which is, however, not implemented correctly on all UNIX systems.

The cpio program

Another widely used backup program is cpio. This program requires a list of the files to be backed up as its input. Therefore, cpio is often employed in combination with find (see Section 10.1.1). In the GNU distribution, the cpio package also includes the mt program. This program is used to control the tape drive (rewinding and deleting tapes, status inquiry of the streamer).

An archive on a floppy disk, for example, is created by means of the following command:

```
(Linux):~> find . | cpio -o -v -O /dev/fd0H1440
```

First, the find program generates a list of the files to be backed up. For the selection, all options are available that find can offer (see also Section 10.1.1). The combination of cpio and find is therefore very flexible. Here, we use the following options of the cpio program: -o (--create) for the creation of a new archive, -v (--verbose) for the output of the name of each backed up file, and -O followed by a file or device name. If the option -O is not specified, the archive is written to the standard output. Here too, it is possible to use a device in the network as output device. The syntax is the same as that discussed with the tar program.

The above archive can be read again by means of the following command:

```
(Linux):~> cpio -i -v -I /dev/fd0H1440
```

The option -i (--extract) means that an archive is to be read and the files contained in it are to be extracted. The option -I, followed by a file or device name, instructs cpio to read the archive not from the standard input, but from the specified file or device.

Here too, it would be sensible to obtain a contents list of the archive first. This is achieved by means of the option -t (--list).

```
(Linux):~> cpio -t -v -I /dev/fd0H1440
```

The afio program

The afio program is a significantly enhanced variation of cpio. The command line options are similar to those of cpio, so there is no need for an extensive presentation of the individual options.

An essential extension is that individual files can be compressed (with gzip) before they are included in the archive. This kind of compression, which is activated by means of the command line option -Z, is much safer than compressing the entire archive. If a reading error occurs, only the current file cannot be restored. The defective file is skipped, and the next file is extracted from the archive and subsequently decompressed. Because of the increased data security despite the compression, this program is used for backup by a whole series of packages.

The dump program

The dump program is known from other UNIX systems. Since it also accesses the internal structure of the file system, a specific version of dump is required for each file system. For LINUX, there are only ports for the Extended-2 file system and the Minix file system. The dump program for the Minix file system can only create complete backups and is not considered in the following discussion. Currently, there is only an alpha version of the port for the Extended-2 file system, which contains some known bugs. This version can be found on `tsx-11.with.edu` in the directory `/pub/linux/packages/ext2fs` under the name `dump-0.3.tar.gz`.

On the one hand, the `dump` program is a low-level program, since it is used by the `amanda` package, for example. On the other hand, it is a high-level program, since the file `/etc/dumpdates` stores the date and the level of the last backup, which are used to manage the different backup levels (incremental backups). The backup is restored by means of the `restore` program.

The `dump` program depends on the correct format of the `/etc/fstab` file. The entry `defaults` for options is not allowed; the program quits with a 'Segmentation fault' without displaying an error message.

A complete backup of the `home` directory to a floppy tape can be obtained by means of the following command:

```
(Linux):~> dump 0Bbuf 120000 1000 /dev/rft0 /home
```

The parameter 0 (dump level) stands for a complete dump of the file system. The different `dump` levels can be used for incremental and differential backups. The option u is used to update the file `/etc/dumpdates`, which keeps a list of all successful `dump` runs. This list is also used to carry out incremental backups.

When the `dump` program does not recognize the tape length correctly and requests a huge number of tapes, either the tape length and the recording density must be specified with the options s and d, or the size and number of blocks on the tape must be set with the options B and b.

Data restoring can be carried out interactively (i) or without user intervention (r). `restore` manages the incremental backups to be loaded on the basis of the dates stored in the file `/etc/dumpdates`.

```
(Linux):~> restore rf /dev/rft0
```

During interactive restoring, you work with a simple shell in which you can navigate by means of `ls` and `cd`. Individual files or directories can be requested with `add` or can later be deleted from the request with `delete`. The `extract` command reads the tape and restores the appropriate files.

7.5.2 High-level programs

The use of low-level programs has several disadvantages. Thus, the system administrator must write scripts for carrying out the complete and incremental backups, manage the different sets of media and, if at all possible, also keep a list of all backed up files so that for restoring individual files, it can immediately be specified which tape must be inserted.

The Linux Backup Utility

The Linux Backup Utility `lbu` is a script which provides an interface for the `tar` and `gzip` programs. This interface has been designed with the `dialog` program, which is also used in the Slackware installation scripts. Therefore, this package is easy to handle and sufficiently powerful for private LINUX systems, although no incremental backups are possible.

A special mention must be made of the extensive documentation (man page) for the use of this service program, and the possibility of preparing a backup and starting it at a later time. For this purpose, the UNIX service programs cron and at (see also Section 10.4) are used. No multi-volume backups are allowed for backups to be carried out later. These would require user intervention, but there is no guarantee that the user will actually be present at that time.

Installation is very easy because the program is a shell script. lbu is an interactive program; no configuration files need adapting. However, the program stores some settings in the file ~/.lburc, so not every value need be entered again.

```
(Linux):/# tar zxvf /tmp/Lnx-Bkp-Util-v1.10.tgz
```

The amanda backup system

amanda (Advanced Maryland Automated Network Disk Archiver) is a backup system designed for huge amounts of data stored on a large number of computers. Initially, the backup is carried out by means of standard programs such as dump and tar. The data is then transferred via network to the backup server. Here, the data can first be stored in a spool partition and then written to tape with the maximum possible speed.

A tape management system is implemented which is intended to prevent accidental overwriting of a tape and to ensure that the correct tape is inserted when restoring from a backup, .

This software is a complete, configurable backup system that consists of a series of individual programs. The programs are written in C and are portable. The programs are divided into server programs, which only need to be installed on the backup server, and client programs to be installed on the clients. Because of the system interfaces involved, the server programs are only portable to a limited extent. The client programs, in contrast, can run practically anywhere because they have already been ported to various UNIX derivatives.

For a private LINUX system, this software is certainly oversized. In large networks, amanda allows the backup of all connected workstations, even if they run under the most disparate UNIX variations.

The installation is significantly more complex than that of lbu, because special settings are required for the data transfer via the network. Furthermore, amanda consists of a series of programs for backing up and restoring data, together with a number of programs for system administration. Since a system administrator who is supposed to develop a backup concept for a network must delve much deeper into the matter than is possible in this book, installation and configuration are not described in any further detail. This is extensively done, however, in the amanda documentation.

The backup package backup

The backup package uses the afio program as an archiver. In contrast to tar, individual files are compressed before archiving. This procedure is significantly more secure than compressing the entire archive, since in the event of a tape or disk error only the affected file cannot be restored. In an archive compressed into one file with gzip, all data stored after the error position would be lost.

Various settings allow flexible backups of different partitions or directories, both complete and incremental, to be carried out. This package is easy to handle but it is also flexible and powerful. This system would be a good choice for a private LINUX system. The newly developed tob program (Tape Oriented Backup) by the same author is even easier to handle and to configure, and is intended to replace this package.

Installation is carried out by unpacking the archive and copying the required programs into the search path. Subsequently, you must configure the volumes that are to be backed up.

```
(Linux):~# cd /usr/local/etc
(Linux):.../etc# tar zxf /tmp/backup-1.03.tar.gz
(Linux):.../etc# cd backup
(Linux):.../backup# cp auxbin/afio /usr/local/bin
(Linux):.../backup# cp auxbin/icm* /usr/local/bin
(Linux):.../backup# rm -rf auxbin
(Linux):.../backup# echo /home > volumes/home.startdir
(Linux):.../backup# echo /home/lost+found > volumes/home.exclude
```

After these preparations, the backup system can be started by means of the backup command. If no parameter is specified, a help screen with the required parameters and short explanations is displayed. To start a complete backup of the volume home on a tape drive connected to the floppy disk controller, the system administrator would use the following command:

```
(Linux):~# backup -full home /dev/rft0
```

A (subsequent) incremental backup at a later time would be started by the following command:

```
(Linux):~# backup -incremental home /dev/rft0
```

A list of all backups carried out up to now is displayed by means of the option -backups. A list of all backed up files that match a pattern (regular expression, see also Section 10.3) can be created by means of the command

```
(Linux):~# backup -which pattern
```

If no pattern is specified, the list of all backed up files is displayed. Files can be read from the backup by means of the command:

```
(Linux):~# backup -restore /dev/rft0 pattern
```

The files are stored relative to the current directory, so files are not overwritten, unless the system administrator calls the command in the / directory. The extensive documentation in the file GENERAL.DOC is especially useful, also for other backup systems.

The tob package

For backups on magnetic tape, you can use the tob script (Tape Oriented Backup). This package originates from the above-mentioned backup package, which is no longer supported by the author.

This package is easier to install and better to configure than backup. A change is not difficult because the definitions of the volumes can still be used with some minor changes. This package is currently the best choice for a private user. Here too, the afio program is used as the archiver; it is possible to carry out both complete and incremental backups. The installation consists of the few steps shown in Listing 7.7.

```
(Linux):~# cd /usr/src
(Linux):/usr/src# tar zxf /tmp/tob-0.04.tar.gz
(Linux):/usr/src# cd tob
(Linux):/usr/src/tob# cp tob /sbin
(Linux):/usr/src/tob# cp afio /bin
(Linux):/usr/src/tob# rm -rf auxbin
(Linux):/usr/src/tob# mkdir /etc/tob
(Linux):/usr/src/tob# cd /etc/tob
(Linux):/etc/tob# echo /home > volumes/home.startdir
(Linux):/etc/tob# echo ^/home/lost+found > volumes/home.exclude
```

Listing 7.7   The installation of tob.

The *.exclude files differ from those of the backup package by the prefixed caret (^). Otherwise, the configuration files of this package can be used unchanged.

Prior to being used, this package also needs to be configured. The author has created a series of configuration files in the directory sample-rc. One of these files should be copied as /etc/tob.rc and then adapted to the system environment. The sample configurations differ in the archiver used and other settings, such as the device on which the backup is carried out. The following sample configurations are supplied:

- The configuration tob.rc.afioz uses the afio program for the creation of compressed archives. The files are compressed prior to being included in the archive. In the sample file, the module ftape.o is loaded prior to the backup and is removed from memory afterwards (see Listing 7.8).
- The file tob.rc.remote-afioz shows an example for a backup via the network. However, different options than those presented are conceivable.
- The configuration tob.rc.tar uses the tar program as archiver.

```
# The directory in which the volume descriptions
# and file lists are stored.
TOBHOME="/etc/tob"
# Device on which the backup is to be carried out
BACKUPDEV="/dev/rft0"
# Loading of the ftape module from /lib/modules/<kernel version>
PRECMD="insmod /lib/modules/'uname -r'/ftape.o"
# Deletion of the module after the backup
POSTCMD="rmmod ftape"
```

Listing 7.8   The file /etc/tob.rc using ftape.

- The file tob.rc.tarz contains a sample configuration for a compressed backup with tar.

For many of the possible settings, default values are defined. Therefore, a configuration file can be very short. In Listing 7.8, we show a configuration for a backup with afio on a floppy streamer.

There is a series of further possible settings, so tob can flexibly be adapted to different hardware and software environments. All possible settings are described in the (extensive) documentation, which can be found in the file doc/tob.txt.gz. This file can be displayed by means of the command zmore tob.txt.gz.[1] Usage is similar to that of the backup package. The volume home defined above is completely backed up by means of the following command:

(Linux):~# **tob –full home /dev/rft0**

With the option –fullcount instead of –full, no backup is carried out, but the size of the backup is calculated and displayed. A (subsequent) incremental backup is started by means of the following command:

(Linux):~# **tob –diff home /dev/rft0**

Here too, the size of the backup can be calculated by replacing the option –diff with –diffcount.

With the option –backups, a list of the executed backups is displayed. A list of all files that match a pattern (this is again a regular expression) is created and displayed by means of the following command:

(Linux):~# **tob –find *pattern***

If no pattern is specified, the list of all backed up files is displayed. Files can be read from the backup by means of the command:

(Linux):~# **tob –restore /dev/rft0 *pattern***

---

[1] In the Slackware distribution, the command is called zless.

The files are stored relative to the current directory, unless an additional parameter specifies the corresponding directory. Files are not overwritten, unless the system administrator calls the command in the / directory.

The tbackup program

The tbackup package was developed to allow simple backing up of large amounts of data on diskettes (!). A number of errors are recognized which would abort the backup with tar or make it unusable. Examples are read or write errors on diskettes or simply a forgotten disk change. It is possible to carry out incremental backups. As with all other packages, it is equally possible to restore individual files. This package too uses afio as the archiver.

Here too, a special mention goes to the extensive documentation supplied, which also includes instructions for the creation of emergency diskettes. Installation and configuration (/etc/tbackup/Config) are extensively described in the file /usr/lib/tbackup/README. The creation of an emergency diskette is described in the file /usr/lib/tbackup/rescue/CREATE. In the same directory, you will also find a series of programs which might help with the creation of an emergency diskette.

The tbackup package contains a separate program for practically every function and, in contrast to the other packages, is not controlled via command line options. A backup is started by means of the tbackup command; restoring is done by trestore. Further commands are tlist (recreate file list of a backup) and tguess (calculate size of a backup).

tbackup has not been developed for backup on magnetic tapes or in background operation. The use of magnetic tapes is possible to a limited extent; delayed backups via cron or at are not implemented.

The tkbackup program, which can also be found at sunsite.unc.edu, is a Tcl/Tk interface for the above tbackup package.

The KBackup program

The KBackup program by Karsten Balladuer is based on afio and tar. To enhance performance, the multibuf program can be employed. Backup on a tape drive connected to another computer is also supported.

As a user interface, KBackup uses dialog; thus, handling is quite easy. In my opinion, the most interesting special features are packing or encrypting of the backup. Furthermore, you can plan a backup by means of at and run it without supervision. If you look for a program that can be used easily and without configuration effort, KBackup is a good choice.

7.6 Conclusion and additional information

All programs presented here are well-documented and are suitable for carrying out backups. For private users who wish to backup their data on magnetic tape, `tob` is probably the best choice. When using diskettes as backup media, the `tbackup` package should be employed. For complex tasks such as setting up a backup server, `amanda` should be used.

Additional Information and Sources	
ftp server:	ftp.gnu.org
ftp path:	/pub/gnu
Package:	tar-1.11.tar.gz
Size:	about 210 Kbytes
Package:	cpio-2.3.tar.gz
Size:	about 110 Kbytes
ftp server:	tsx-11.mit.edu
ftp path:	/pub/linux/packages/ext2fs
Package:	dump-0.3.tar.gz
Size:	about 80 Kbytes
ftp server:	ftp.cs.umd.edu
ftp path:	/pub/amanda/
Package:	various files
Size:	about 150 Kbytes
ftp server:	sunsite.unc.edu
ftp path:	/pub/Linux/system/backup
Package:	afio-2.4.4.tgz
Size:	about 60 Kbytes
Package:	Lnx-Bkp-Util-v1.10.tgz
Size:	about 85 Kbytes
Package:	backup-1.03.tar.gz
Size:	about 75 Kbytes
Package:	tob-0.13.tar.gz
Size:	about 85 Kbytes
Package:	tbackup-0.9.tgz
Size:	about 150 Kbytes
Package:	tktbackup
Size:	about 20 Kbytes
Package:	KBackup-1.2.11.tar.gz
Size:	about 770 Kbytes

National Language Support $\boxed{8}$

*Anybody who has a mail gateway that isn't
8-bit clean these days should be shot.*

Linus B. Torvalds

The UNIX operating system was developed in the USA. Therefore, practically all available UNIX systems and programs are based on the use of (American) English as the language for messages, menus, and documentation, and on the use of the (US-) ASCII character set for interpretation of character strings and processing of texts.

The same can be said for LINUX which was developed as a UNIX-compatible system by an international community of programmers, using many of the existing UNIX programs.

For a worldwide diffusion of UNIX and LINUX it is necessary to remove these implicit dependencies and make them configurable for the user. This is achieved by means of the so-called *National Language Support* (NLS). The aim is to make a UNIX system behave as if it had been specially developed for the linguistic and cultural environment of the user.

The general support of NLS is also known as *internationalization*, whereas the translation of texts into a specific language and the adaptation of the system to a specific cultural environment is called *localization*.

The following pages briefly present the POSIX standard as far as it describes functions of the NLS. The emphasis lies on a general introduction to the terms and capabilities of the NLS, to give system administrators and users an idea of multi-language UNIX and LINUX operating systems.

Chapter 9 (*Localization*) then describes the configuration of individual programs for use with eight-bit characters sets, together with the use of the international A4 paper size for printed output.

Currently, there are only a few freeware programs that use NLS. Not all UNIX systems support NLS in the C library, although both the POSIX standard and the ANSI-C standard define most of the functions presented here. Also, many programmers and system administrators have only recently discovered the huge potential of the international market and the fact that an increasing number of foreign language users demand to interact with UNIX and LINUX applications in their own language, in the same way as they already do with Windows or MacOS systems and their associated applications.

Free software thrives on being ported to as many systems as possible, which is one of the reasons why up to now, because of its limited diffusion, NLS has seldom been employed. However, the Free Software Foundation has now recognized the importance of localizing the programs of the GNU project for international users and is currently implementing the necessary changes in its programs. Obviously, it will be some time before all the programs have been adapted.

The POSIX standard is going to be used by a rapidly increasing number of programs. Thus, the configuration of a UNIX/LINUX system to support a foreign language and its associated character set will be limited to setting a few environment variables with the commands `export` or `setenv`, depending on the shell being used.

8.1 ASCII and ISO character sets

The basic (US-)ASCII character set is a 7-bit character set containing 32 control characters (from 0 to 31), the upper and lower case letters (plain, without accents or umlauts), the digits from 0 to 9, and a number of special characters and punctuation marks (including the space).

Characters with the 8th bit set are (were) interpreted by many programs as special (or meta) characters (for example, by the `bash` or older versions of the Emacs editor), or considered as non-printable characters, either not to be output at all or to be coded by their ASCII value. Other programs (used to) simply cut the 8th bit with the consequence of outputting different characters from the ones required.

With the growing international diffusion of operating systems and application software and the growing demand for nationalized systems and user interfaces, the International Organization for Standardization (ISO) began in the late 1980s to set forth international standards for so-called 8-bit single-byte coded graphic character sets in the ISO-8859 group of standards. These character sets build on the original ASCII character set insofar as they share the first 128 codes (from 0 to 127).

This group of standards includes the following character sets:

–	8859-1	Latin 1, Europe, Latin America
–	8859-2	Latin 2, Eastern Europe
–	8859-3	Latin 3, SE Europe
–	8859-4	Latin 4, Scandinavia (mostly covered by 8859-1 also)
–	8859-5	Cyrillic
–	8859-6	Arabic
–	8859-7	Greek
–	8859-8	Hebrew

- 8859-9   Latin 5, same as 8859-1 except for Turkish instead of Icelandic

- 8859-10   Latin 6, for Eskimo/Scandinavian languages

ISO 8859-1, also known as ISO-Latin-1, is the most widely used standard and supports the following languages: Afrikaans, Catalan, Danish, Dutch, English, Faeroese, Finnish, French, German, Galician, Irish, Icelandic, Italian, Norwegian, Portuguese, Spanish and Swedish. ISO 8859-1 is also used by Windows (actually, Windows uses Unicode (ISO 10646, see below) truncated to 8 bit, which gives an equivalent encoding), VMS and (practically all) UNIX implementations. MS-DOS uses a different character set which can, however, be translated to this format with various tools.

Because of the wide diffusion of UNIX systems (which includes LINUX systems), an increasing number of application programs supports characters with the 8th bit set. These programs are called *8-bit-clean* and can obviously handle, for example, all characters of the ISO 8859-1 character set.

A character set of 256 characters is not sufficient to represent all (worldwide) possible characters. A further standard which tackles this problem area is Unicode which describes a 16-bit character set. In its current version, LINUX also supports the Unicode standard on the console, but most applications do not. More information on Unicode can be found under `http://www.unicode.org`.

A further problem is that very many programs must (still) be configured in a different way instead of evaluating the environment variables defined by the POSIX standard. However, a large number of programs are currently being revised with a view to being configurable following the standard defined by the POSIX group.

8.2 POSIX National Language Support

National Language Support provides a series of commands and functions of the C library to make programs independent from the language or the character set used. This requires that no program makes assumptions about characters sets or other locally different resources, but receives this information at runtime.

The central term in NLS is the *locale*. A locale describes all features that are significant for a country or a linguistic area and is used for adaptation of programs to locally different conventions. A locale is defined by a language, a country, and a character set. The complete specification of a locale can be expressed by a series of environment variables:

- The value of the environment variable LC_ALL, if this variable is set. This value takes precedence over all other variables described here. This variable defines the locale to be used for all categories.

- If the environment variable LC_ALL is not set, the value stored in the LC_*category* variable is used if the variable matching the category is set. A brief description of categories follows later.

- The value of the environment variable LANG for all categories which were not specifically configured and for the case that the variable LC_ALL is not set.

- Programs use the standard locale 'C' or 'POSIX', that is, the values defined in the ANSI-C standard, if none of the variables mentioned above is set.

8.3 Names of locales

Locales are selected by setting environment variables. The fundamental structure of a locale name is

`language[_country][.charset][@option][,version]`

LINUX uses the form `language_country.charset`. Table 8.1 shows some examples of locale names used under LINUX.

Locale	Language	Country	Character set
de_DE.646	German	Germany	ISO 646
de_DE.88591	German	Germany	ISO-8859-1
de_CH.88591	German	Switzerland	ISO-8859-1
de_AU.88591	German	Austria	ISO-8859-1
en_US.88591	English	USA	ISO-8859-1
en_UK.88591	English	United Kingdom	ISO-8859-1
C	English	Standard locale	US-ASCII
POSIX	English	Equivalent to C	US-ASCII

Table 8.1 Examples of locale names.

The `language` consists of two lower case characters. The abbreviations of the individual languages are defined in ISO 639.

The `country` consists of two upper case characters. The abbreviations of the individual countries are defined in ISO 3166.

The `charset` describes a character coding standard. If this field contains only digits, it stands for the number of the corresponding ISO standard. If no character set is specified, it can be safely assumed to be ISO-8859-1.[1] If it is not possible to describe the standard with digits alone, only additional lower case letters should be used, and no separators such as dot (.) or comma (,). If only one character set is used in a country, this field may be omitted.

---

[1] The ISO 8859-1 character set was defined about a dozen years ago; NLS was introduced, by AT&T for example, in the late 1980s and early 1990s with System V(/386) Release 4; and MIME as an 8-bit clean news and mail coding/decoding software became a standard as early as 1992. This should be a sufficient transition time to stop assuming that US-ASCII is still used as a default – or do our TV football league reporters go on talking about dark and light shirts because you might still own a b/w goggle box?

8.4 Categories used in NLS

This section presents a brief description of the different categories of a locale which are shown in Table 8.2. The names used for the individual categories are the names of the corresponding environment variables.

Variable	Description
LC_COLLATE	Sorting order of characters and character strings
LC_CTYPE	Assignment of characters to character classes
LC_MESSAGES	Language for messages and man pages
LC_MONETARY	Information on formatting of amounts of currency
LC_NUMERIC	Formatting of numbers
LC_RESPONSE	Language for responses
LC_TIME	Formatting of date and time

Table 8.2 Overview of locale categories.

8.4.1 The LC_MESSAGES category

The language of message texts of individual programs and the messages from the C library is defined by the environment variable LC_MESSAGES. This category has been implemented in the LINUX C library libc since version 4.5.26.

A change of this category has nearly immediate consequences for the user, because it significantly changes the behavior of the system, which now interacts with the user in the specified language instead of standard English.

Message texts are no longer directly output by the programs, but are read from a so-called message catalog. On the basis of the values assigned to the variables LANG (or LC_MESSAGES or LC_ALL), the corresponding catalog is opened and the messages are extracted. If no message catalog is present, the messages are output in the default language (generally in English). Messages in the default language are still present directly in the program, so no message catalog is needed if only the default language of a program is to be used.

Translation of the message texts of a program into another language does not require recompilation of the program. Indeed, the same program can be used on one system by different users in different languages if the appropriate message catalog exists for each of these languages.

The procedure of reading messages from message catalogs is not part of the ANSI-C or POSIX standards. Therefore, LINUX uses the standard proposed by X/Open. The creation of a message catalog is briefly described in Section 8.6.

With gettext, the GNU project uses a less complicated interface for the programmer to read messages from files at runtime. The package also includes a sophisticated specific Emacs mode for translation of messages.

Programs do not only output messages and text, but often require confirmation that a specific function is really to be executed. Such a question can be answered with 'yes' or 'no', or the equivalent in the selected language. Since there are different possibilities of answering (for example, 'yes', 'Yes', 'y', or 'Y'), the answer is internally handled by means of a regular expression. The program is responsible for checking whether the answer matches one of the regular expressions, as shown in Table 8.3.

Language	Yes answer	No answer
C/POSIX	[yY][[:alpha:]]	[nN][[:alpha:]]
de_DE.88591	[jJ][[:alpha:]]	[nN][[:alpha:]]
fr_FR.88591	[oO][[:alpha:]]	[nN][[:alpha:]]
it_IT.88591	[sS][[:alpha:]]	[nN][[:alpha:]]

Table 8.3 Possible regular expressions for yes/no answers.

8.4.2 The LC_CTYPE category (character classes)

The character set to be used is defined via the environment variable LC_CTYPE. The default character set should by now be ISO-8859-1 (ISO-Latin-1). However, this specification neither loads the appropriate character set nor does it use a corresponding font under X. It merely supplies the information on the required character set to all programs. Character sets for the console can be loaded by means of setfont. For X programs, you can select fonts with the xfontsel program and specify them directly to the programs as command line parameter or enter them in the X resources.

Up-to-date information on fonts for ISO-8859-x character sets can be found in the 'Finding Fonts for Internationalization FAQ' posted monthly in the newsgroup comp.software.international by mike@vlsivie.tuwien.ac.at.

In this category, the assignment of characters to character classes can be specified. This includes, for example, upper and lower case letters and printable characters. Thus, you can configure umlauts and accented letters as upper and/or lower case letters, so that, for example, conversion between upper and lower case will function properly.

Many programs, for example emacs, tcsh or less, do not interpret the set locale, but directly evaluate the value of the variable LC_CTYPE. The programs expect the value ISO-8859-1 if the ISO-Latin-1 character set is to be used and then apply their own routines. Also in the C library (libc5) the locale ISO-8859-1 is hard-coded for the category LC_CTYPE, so no further description of this locale is needed.

8.4.3 The LC_COLLATE category (sorting order)

The sorting order for characters and character strings is set via the variable LC_COLLATE. In the standard locale, sorting is performed by ASCII character code. This may sometimes be useful, because the procedure is very fast. Often, however, characters need to be sorted together that have completely different codes. In a phone book, for example, accented vowels and umlauts need to be sorted together with the corresponding plain vowels. Such behavior can be obtained by creating the appropriate locale. This specified sorting order will be used by the C functions `strcoll()` and `strxfrm()`, but not by the function `strcmp()`.

8.4.4 The `LC_TIME` category (date and time)

Another difference between different countries (independently of whether they use the same language) is the format of date and time indications. The rules to be used are determined by the variable `LC_TIME`.

In the USA, a date is usually indicated in the format `MM/DD/YYYY`, whereas in the United Kingdom `DD/MM/YYYY` is used. In Germany, for example, the template is `DD.MM.YYYY`. Thus, the date '9 June 1998' would be formatted in the different countries as shown in Table 8.4.

Country	Formatted date
USA	06/09/1998
United Kingdom	09/06/1998
Germany	09.06.1998

Table 8.4 Formatted dates in different locales.

This category is also used to translate the names of days and months and their three-letter abbreviations into the selected language.

8.4.5 The `LC_NUMERIC` category (number formats)

In the formatting of numbers, different symbols can be used as decimal point and thousands separator. Furthermore, grouping can be specified in different units than thousands. The variable `LC_NUMERIC` defines the rules to be applied.

Country	Amount
USA	1,234.56
Germany	1.234,56

Table 8.5 Examples of formatting of floating point numbers.

8.4.6 The `LC_MONETARY` category (formatting of amounts of currency)

In the formatting of amounts of currency, different countries have different separators and different symbols to mark the local currency. Valid currency symbols are specified in ISO 4217. A number of special features must be considered:

- Different characters can be used as the decimal point. This and the following setting correspond to those described for the LC_NUMERIC category.

- Different characters can be used as thousands separators.

- The formatting can deviate from the commonly used thousands separation and can prescribe a different number of digits for each group.

- The international symbol of the currency is unique for each country.

- A local currency symbol can be used as a short form if there is no possibility of confusion with other currencies. Thus, for example, DM for Deutsche Mark (DEM) can be used because it is still unique, whereas the Dollar sign ($) stands for USD in the USA, AUD in Australia, BBD on Barbados, CAD in Canada, and so forth.

- The number of digits after the decimal point can be different depending on the country.

- Different characters can be used as signs for (positive or negative) amounts of money.

- The position of the sign (before or after the amount) may vary depending on whether the amount is positive or negative; it is possible to insert a blank space between amount and sign.

In the GNU C library, the function strfmon is implemented which carries out the entire formatting according to the requirements of the programmer or the user.

8.5 Creating a locale definition

A locale definition is initially created as text and then translated into the internal representation by means of the program localedef. A locale definition file contains all of the information needed to create a locale and consists of a preamble containing general data and different sections, each of which describes a locale category.

Ready-made locale definitions are available for an increasing number of languages and countries. Therefore, no detailed description of the syntax will be given. For more information, you should refer to the man pages (locale(5), charmap(5)). For smaller adaptations, it is usually sufficient to look into the source code of the locale definition.

After a modification to the source text, the binary description of the locale must be recreated by means of the program localedef. The instructions in Listing 8.1, for example, create the Spanish es_ES.88591 locale.

```
(Linux):~# localedef -c -f/usr/lib/nls/charmap/ISO-8859-1 \
        -i /usr/lib/nls/src/es_ES es_ES.88591
```

Listing 8.1   Creation of a locale with localedef.

8.6 Creating message catalogs with GNU gettext

Internationalization and subsequent localization of programs require a significant effort by programmers and translators. The programs of the GNU project are often created and maintained by volunteers, so processes should be simplified as much as possible. For this reason, Ulrich Drepper (drepper@cygnus.com) developed the gettext package.

The library libintl contains the runtime routines needed for reading message catalogs. The message texts are automatically extracted by means of the program xgettext and stored in a file specially formatted for so-called 'portable object' data. This file initially only contains the original messages and placeholders for the translations. The translator can now manually translate the messages into the required language.

The command msgfmt converts the translated 'portable object' file into the internal representation ('machine object') file which is then used by the gettext() routines of the libintl library.

To accelerate adaptations of new versions of a program, two 'portable object' files can be compared with each other by means of msgmerge. Matching entries are preserved, deleted entries are commented out in the target file, and new entries are added. In cases where an exact match is not possible, msgmerge generates so-called 'fuzzy entries' which can then be easily edited by the translator.

Once again, a special mode which greatly facilitates dealing with 'portable objects' is provided by the Emacs editor. The first results of this method can already be seen in the current versions of many GNU programs.

Additional Information and Sources	
Newsgroups:	comp.software.international
	comp.std.internat
Mailing list:	LI-international@li.org
Package:	locale-tutorial-0.8.txt.gz
ftp server:	sunsite.unc.edu
ftp path:	/pub/Linux/utils/nls/catalogs/Incoming
Size:	about 15 Kbytes
Package:	gettext-0.10.tar.gz
ftp server:	pre.ai.with.edu
ftp path:	/gnu
Size:	about 400 Kbytes

8.7 Programming with NLS

This book is not intended to be a programming handbook. Nevertheless, I would like to give some hints on which functions can be used, always referring to the corresponding man pages.

8.7.1 General hints

Each program should begin by calling the function setlocale(LC_ALL,""). Thus, the program will use the locale set by the user. Without this function call, the program always uses the 'C' or 'POSIX' locale. In the development of programs that are to be relatively easily adaptable to national peculiarities, several things should be observed:

- Always define data fields that contain a character (char) as unsigned char. When compiling foreign programs it may be necessary to use the compiler switch -funsigned-char.

- Never assume that printable or usable characters are only seven bits long; that is, do not check whether the eighth bit is set or not. For example, the following code removes the eighth bit of a character (ch & 0x7f), or only characters in 7-bit code are accepted as input by checks like: if (ch <= 0177).

- Always use the standard functions isprint(), isgraph(), and so on, instead of implementing these functions yourself. Initially, the effort for a user-defined implementation seems slight, but it will significantly impair the portability of the program, the possibility of adaptation to local requirements, and the speed, because these functions are defined as macros both in the GNU libc and in the LINUX C library.

- Never use the (unportable) functions toascii() or isascii(), because these functions are not defined by a standard and furthermore prevent the use of 8-bit characters.

Table 8.6 shows some more functions that do not consider the set locale and others that do. For new programs, you should use these latter functions to facilitate further adaptations for National Language Support.

Without locale support	With locale support
strcmp()	strcoll(), strxfrm()
ctime()	strftime()

Table 8.6 Functions with and without NLS.

Other UNIX systems than LINUX have implemented the following functions in the C library as an X/Open extension to the ANSI-C standard:

- The function nl_langinfo() has the task of providing a uniform interface for access to the locales. Unfortunately, the POSIX.2 standard defines the effect of a locale, but not the C programming.

- The function rpmatch() checks whether the passed parameter is a character string that matches either the regular expression that describes a 'yes' answer or the regular expression that describes a 'no' answer. If the answer matches neither of the regular expressions, an error code is returned.

8.7.2 Message catalogs

For use with message catalogs, some functions were standardized by the X/Open Consortium:

- catopen() for opening a message catalog.

- catgets() for reading messages from the catalog. If a message is not found in the catalog, the text specified as the default text is returned as the message.

- catclose() for closing the message catalog after use.

The exact syntax and semantics of the function calls are described in the corresponding man pages.

8.8 Character set conversion

A number of programs exists for converting text files between different character sets. Probably the most powerful program is GNU recode which can convert texts from and to the most disparate character sets. These character sets include ASCII (IBM-PC-Codepage 437), ISO-8859-1 (ISO-Latin-1) and EBCDIC (IBM mainframes). Even text formats such as LaTeX or HTML (Hypertext Markup Language) can be used as possible coding. The mapping between characters of different character sets is controlled by means of tables. Changes to these tables, however, require recompilation of the program.

A simple use is the conversion of texts from and to DOS format. Two conversions must be performed:

- Under DOS usually the IBM code page 437 is used, under UNIX the ISO-Latin-1 character set. Letters that are also defined by the US-ASCII character set do not need conversion.

- Under DOS the line end of a text file is represented by the character sequence CR+LF (Carriage Return and Line Feed), under UNIX only by LF.

If you do not want to memorize the names of the associated character set tables, you can for example define the following aliases, which are completely sufficient for this purpose:

For the GNU bash:

```
(Linux):~$ alias fromdos='/usr/local/bin/recode ibmp:lat1'
(Linux):~$ alias todos='/usr/local/bin/recode lat1:ibmp'
```

For the tcsh:

```
(Linux):~> alias fromdos '/usr/local/bin/recode ibmp:lat1'
(Linux):~> alias todos '/usr/local/bin/recode lat1:ibmp'
```

You can find extensive documentation on implementation and functioning of `recode` in the Info documentation which you can, for example, read with the Emacs editor. The POSIX.2 standard requires the implementation of the `iconv` program. However, no free implementation of this program is available so far.

Additional Information and Sources	
Package:	`recode-3.4.tar.gz`
`ftp` server:	`ftp.gnu.org`
`ftp` path:	`/pub/gnu`
Size:	about 290 Kbytes

Localization

9

This chapter describes the remapping of the keyboard and the configuration of individual programs for use with foreign language special characters and the international A4 standard paper size. More generally, this chapter describes ways of obtaining a system-wide consistent keyboard mapping for special keys (such as BS, DEL, HOME and END), together with an 8-bit clean character representation on the console, in shells, and in application programs (including mail and news). The description is limited to general setup instructions; detailed information on individual configurations can usually be found in the documentation supplied with the programs. Detailed information on how to set up individual character sets for foreign languages can be found in the corresponding HowTos.

Two sections, namely the ones on console keyboard mapping and XFree86, describe LINUX-specific configurations. The remaining sections can also be applied to other UNIX systems.

9.1 Console keyboard mapping

A detailed description of keyboard mapping is given in Section 5.8. If you simply load one of the keyboard mappings presented there, you will not need any further information.

For most users, the national keyboard maps (whose names usually consist of the two-letter language code and the extension .map), plus the file *xx-latin1* and the variation nodeadkeys are sufficient. Nevertheless, you may want to redefine or newly assign a couple of keys. Fortunately, you do not have to create an entirely new keyboard map, it is sufficient to create a new file (for example /etc/keytables/local.map) which contains only the changes. In the rc scripts, this file is loaded with loadkeys and the keyboard is set up accordingly.

If, for some particular reason, you want to use a special pair of symbols as opening and closing quotes (such as the French guillemets), for example, you can compose these characters by means of a Compose key. Listing 9.1 shows an example of a possible Compose key configuration, in this case the right-hand ⎡Ctrl⎤ key which yields keycode 97 (as shown by the showkey program). The construction of

```
keycode  97 = Compose
compose '>' '>' to '»'
compose '<' '<' to '«'
```

Listing 9.1 Additional keyboard assignments with loadkeys.

the French opening quote « is achieved by pressing and holding the right-hand $\boxed{\text{Ctrl}}$ key and pressing the $\boxed{.}$ key twice, whereas the French closing quote » is obtained by pressing and holding the right-hand $\boxed{\text{Ctrl}}$ key and pressing the $\boxed{,}$ key twice.

9.2 Using the ISO-Latin-1 character set

Immediately after system start-up, LINUX uses a modified IBM graphics character set. This character set includes both some of the ISO-8859-1 characters from the range 127–255 and a series of graphical symbols which are used, for example, by the mc program for representation of frames. Thus, this character set cannot be used to represent all of the characters of the ISO-Latin-1 character set.

This can instead be achieved by loading the appropriate character set together with the corresponding conversion table, and subsequenly activating the newly loaded character set.

```
(Linux):~> setfont iso01.f14
(Linux):~> mapscrn trivial
(Linux):~> echo -e '\033(K'
```

Loading the character set and the conversion table applies to all virtual consoles, whereas switching character sets by means of the ESC sequence applies only to the current console. Unfortunately, the output of the mc program afterwards is hardly readable because the frames are not built out of the correct characters. Programs and character sets used can be found in the package kbd-0.89.tar.gz.

9.3 Keyboard assignment under X11

Since version XFree86 2.1.1, XFree86 reads the keyboard table of the LINUX kernel and, as far as possible, sets its own keyboard assignments to the same values. The only exceptions are special combinations and characters, such as the so-called 'dead-keys' (the tilde $\boxed{\sim}$ or the accent keys $\boxed{\acute{}}$ and $\boxed{\grave{}}$). To assign these keys, you must use the xmodmap program. When starting the X Window environment with startx, the following files are used, if present.

- The system-wide keyboard mapping under XFree86 is carried out in the file /usr/lib/X11/xinit/.Xmodmap.
- Every user can define a user-specific keyboard mapping in the file ~/.Xmodmap.

```
! Activation of the left-hand Alt key as the Meta key
keycode 0x40 =  Meta_L

! BackSpace generates BackSpace and Delete generates Delete
keycode 0x6B =  Delete
keycode 0x16 =  BackSpace
```

Listing 9.2 The file ˜/.Xmodmap for keyboard mapping under X.

Listing 9.2 shows an example of a user-defined keyboard mapping. To activate the left-hand ⟨Alt⟩ key as the Meta key and to use the right-hand ⟨Alt⟩ key as the ⟨AltGr⟩ key, you must include the entries shown in Listing 9.3 in the keyboard configuration section of the file XF86Config or, in older Xfree86 versions, of the file Xconfig. The xf86config program does this automatically.

```
Section "Keyboard"
Protocol "Standard"
AutoRepeat 500 5
ServerNumLock
LeftAlt Meta          # Left-hand Alt key is the Meta key
RightAlt modeShift    # Right-hand Alt key is AltGr
# ScrollLock modeLock # ScrollLock holds right-hand Alt key
# RightCtl Compose    # Right-hand Ctrl is the Compose key
EndSection
```

Listing 9.3 Keyboard adaptation in the file XF86Config.

To ensure that XTerm also interprets the ⟨Home⟩ and ⟨End⟩ keys as expected, you must insert the lines shown in Listing 9.4 in your ˜/.Xresources.

```
*vt100.translations: #override \
<Key>Home:        string(0x1b) string("[1~") \n\
<Key>Insert:      string(0x1b) string("[2~") \n\
<Key>Delete:      string(0x1b) string("[3~") \n\
<Key>End:         string(0x1b) string("[4~") \n\
Ctrl<Key>Left:    string(0x1b) string("b")\n\
Ctrl<Key>Right:   string(0x1b) string("f")\n
```

Listing 9.4 Keyboard assignment in xterm.

If, after this, programs such as joe or emacs do not react to these keys in XTerm, the file /etc/termcap must be adapted as well. For the xterm device, the following entries should be available in termcap:

```
:kh=\E[1~:kI=\E[2~:kD=\E[3~:kH=\E[4~:
```

To define your own keyboard assignments under X, you can use a program such as xkeycaps, for example, which allows you to create and test an input file for xmodmap under X in a menu-driven interactive way.

The program was contributed to the X Consortium to be distributed as a free extra with the X Window system. Therefore, it can be found on the ftp server ftp.x.org and all systems that mirror this server.

Additional Information and Sources	
Man pages:	xkeycaps(1x),
Package:	xkeycaps-2.25.tar.gz
ftp server:	ftp.x.org
ftp path:	/R5contrib
Size:	about 140 Kbytes

9.4 Use of foreign language characters at the shell level

After logging in to the LINUX system, a shell is started which accepts user input and launches programs. As a rule, no special characters such as umlauts or accented letters should be used in file names, because in many (older) UNIX systems, this can lead to problems as such files can be very hard to delete.

In some UNIX systems, first you must put the terminal device in question into the appropriate mode that allows transmission of 8-bit characters. Depending on the system, this is achieved with:

- stty pass8 in BSD systems;
- stty -istrip -8 in System V systems.

The corresponding initialization should, however, only be carried out if the input/ output of the shell is associated to a terminal because otherwise (for example in case of a rsh call) an error message is displayed. Depending on the shell, the following instructions are used:

- With the csh or tcsh:

```
tty -s
if ($status == 0) stty cs8 -istrip -parenb
```

- With the Bourne shell sh or its improved versions bash, ksh or sh:

```
tty -s
if [ $? = 0 ]; then
    stty cs8 -istrip -parenb >&0
fi
```

If you work under X, the terminal emulator must also be 8-bit clean, that is, leave special characters that are not contained in the US-ASCII character set unchanged. This applies to the xterm program. Older xterm versions, however, still need the settings specified in Listing 9.5 to be included in the ˜/.Xresources file.

```
XTerm*EightBitInput:    true
XTerm*EightBitOutput:   true
```

Listing 9.5   Forcing 8-bit mode for all Xterm windows.

Furthermore, an ISO-Latin-1 font must be used which is able to represent all of the special characters. You can choose an appropriate font by means of the xfontsel program and activate it with the following line, again in the ˜/.Xresources file:

```
XTerm*vt100*font: -adobe-courier-*-*-*-*-14-*-iso8859-1
```

The frequently used rxvt program is also 8-bit clean and in addition has the command line option -8 which explicitly activates this mode. Many terminal emulators of commercial operating systems, such as dxterm by DEC for the ULTRIX operating system, must be configured by means of the above stty commands.

9.4.1 GNU bash

The bash uses the GNU readline library which is also used in various other programs, such as the GNU debugger gdb. This library provides the programs with various functions that allow users to enter lines of input. In additions, different editing options (vi or Emacs mode) and a history function are available too.

The configuration presented here is supported by all programs that use the GNU readline library. To activate it, you must create a file ˜/.inputrc with the contents shown in Listing 9.6 in your home directory. These settings not only apply to the bash, but to all programs that use the readline library.

Additional Information and Sources	
Man pages:	bash(1)
Info system:	bash
Newsgroups:	comp.unix.questions
	comp.unix.shell
	gnu.bash
	gnu.bash.bug
Package:	bash-2.0.1.tar.gz
ftp server:	ftp.gnu.org
ftp path:	/pub/gnu
Size:	about 1.5 Mbytes

```
set meta-flag on
set convert-meta off
set output-meta on            # New with bash 1.14

# Keyboard mapping for the bash to make the cursor
# keys plus the Home and End keys function properly

"\e[1~": beginning-of-line  # Home
"\e[4~": end-of-line        # End
"\e[A": previous-history    # Cursor up
"\e[B": next-history        # Cursor down
"\e[3~": delete-char        # Delete
"\e[D": backward-char       # Cursor left
"\e[C": forward-char        # Cursor right
"\"": self-insert           # Double quotes
```

Listing 9.6   Adaptation of the readline library with the file ~/.inputrc.

9.4.2 The tcsh Turbo C shell

The tcsh is an improved variation of the csh. Substantial advantages for the user are a good history function and a user-programmable completion function. Current versions of the tcsh can handle foreign language characters without problems if the appropriate locale is installed and activated.

On several systems, the tcsh does not recognize the keys Ins, Del, Home and End correctly. This can be remedied by including the commands shown in Listing 9.7 in one of the initialization files of the tcsh. The following files are used for initializing the tcsh: /etc/csh.cshrc, /etc/csh.login, $HOME/.tcshrc, $HOME/.cshrc, and $HOME/.login. More detailed information on when an initialization file (and which file) is processed can be found in the online manual for tcsh (man 1 tcsh).

```
# Keyboard mapping for Home, End, Del, and Ins

bindkey ^[[1~ beginning-of-line        # Home
bindkey ^[[4~ end-of-line              # End
bindkey ^[[3~ delete-char              # Del
bindkey ^[[2~ overwrite mode           # Ins
```

Listing 9.7   Initialization of the tcsh.

The tcsh provides a series of functions, such as for example a programmable completion function for program names, file names, and options, and an automatic correction function for (supposed) typing errors. However, corrections are executed only after a prompt for confirmation. The text of this prompt can be individually edited by each user (Listing 9.8).

```
set correct=all
set prompt3='%BBetter like this?%b %R (y|n|e) ? '
```

Listing 9.8   Adaptation of the automatic correction prompt.

The sources of the `tcsh` include a sample configuration for programming the completion function.

Additional Information and Sources	
Man pages:	`tcsh(1)`
Newsgroups:	`comp.unix.questions`
	`comp.unix.shell`
Package:	`tcsh-6.06.tar.gz`
`ftp` server:	`tesla.ee.cornell.edu`
`ftp` path:	`/pub/tcsh`
Size:	about 525 Kbytes

9.4.3 Other shells

There are a number of other shells, some of which are designed for special purposes and thus represent sensible extensions to the system.

- The `ash` is a very small shell, often used on root or installation diskettes. Since shell scripts under LINUX often use features of the `bash`, these scripts are not always portable to other UNIX systems which have only implemented a simple `sh`. However, if you use shell scripts written for the `ash`, these scripts can often also be run under the standard shell `sh`. The `ash` man page describes the incompatibilities in more detail.
  The `ash` does not have command history, line editing features or completion and is therefore very small. Nevertheless, this shell can handle 8-bit characters without difficulties.
- The `zsh` is a very powerful shell which combines the features of the `bash` and the `tcsh`. The `zsh` is 8-bit clean.
- The `pdksh`, a free version of the Korn shell `ksh`, is 8-bit clean in `vi` mode, but not in Emacs mode. When you look into the source code, you will find that the eighth bit is removed in Emacs mode, without any apparent reason.
- The C shell (`csh`) is 8-bit clean. The sources ported to LINUX can be found on the `sunsite` ftp server.
- The `sash` is a stand-alone shell which makes many system utilities available as built-in commands. With a statically linked `sash` you can resolve many prob-

lems, for example, if a link to the current version of the shared libraries was deleted. This shell can handle foreign language special characters, but it does not provide a user-friendly interface with history or edit keys. The `sash` is 8-bit clean.

All of these shells can be found on `sunsite.unc.edu` in the directory `/pub/Linux/system/shells`.

9.5 Foreign language characters in editors

One of the essential application areas in which one would like to use foreign language special characters is text editing. For many users it is much easier to input umlauts or accented letters with single keystrokes than by means of some kind of transcription. It is therefore essential that editors are 8-bit clean or that they can be appropriately configured. This section briefly presents various editors and gives general hints on possible adaptations.

9.5.1 vi clones

Each and every UNIX system distribution includes a `vi` or a corresponding clone. No matter what you may think of `vi`, you should at least be able to use it to carry out simple functions. All widely used `vi` clones such as `elvis`, `vim`, and `nvi` (BSD `vi`) are 8-bit clean.

9.5.2 The GNU Emacs editor

Since version 19.26, Emacs has also taken the environment variable `LC_CTYPE` into account. Therefore, the only thing you have to do when using Emacs 19.26 and later versions, is to assign the environment variable `LC_CTYPE` the value `ISO-8859-1`. Things change with version 20, because this version integrates the Multi-Language Extensions (MULE). Listing 9.9 shows the settings I use with GNU Emacs 19.34.

Emacs provides some special modes for processing foreing language texts. Thus, the `iso-syntax` mode allows the use of word-related commands with words containing special characters. The `iso-cvt` mode stores texts containing TEX or news special characters, so that you need not worry about conversion prior to sending or using these files.

A modern Emacs version is XEmacs, formerly also known under the name of Lucid Emacs. This Emacs implementation has no problems with handling foreign languages.

```
(if (string-equal (getenv "LC_CTYPE") "ISO-8859-1")
(progn
(standard-display-european t)
(require 'iso-syntax)))   ; Foreign language characters in words
;
; Also for Emacs 19.27!
;
(set-input mode (car (current-input mode))
         (nth 1 (current-input mode))
         0)
```

Listing 9.9 Extension to the file ~/.emacs.

Additional Information and Sources	
Man pages:	emacs(1)
Info system:	Emacs
Newsgroups:	gnu.emacs
	gnu.emacs .help
	comp.editors
	comp.emacs
	comp.xemacs
Package:	emacs-20.2.tar.gz
ftp server:	ftp.gnu.org
ftp path:	/pub/gnu
Size:	about 12 Mbytes

9.5.3 The editor joe

The editor joe is largely compatible with WordStar and is thus more familiar to some newcomers than vi or Emacs. Since version 1.0.9, joe has been 8-bit clean, but still requires an entry in its initialization file ~/.joerc or /usr/lib/joerc to display 8-bit characters unchanged (Listing 9.10).

```
Comments begin after column 1,
commands in column 1 are active

-asis    Characters 160 to 254 shown as-is   (now active)
```

Listing 9.10 Adaptation for the editor joe.

Additional Information and Sources	
Man pages:	`joe(1)`
Newsgroups:	`comp.editors`
Package:	`joe23.tar.Z`
`ftp` server:	`ftp.std.com`
`ftp` path:	`/pub/gnu`
Size:	about 300 Kbytes

Another easy-to-handle editor for former DOS users is `pico`. This editor is 8-bit clean from its very design; it is located in the archive of `pine`, a mail and news reader.

9.6 Special characters in mail and news

In mail and news, foreign language (or any other 8-bit) characters can be sent directly, provided the transport route is 8-bit clean. The freely available programs `smail` and `sendmail` are either 8-bit clean by definition or can be configured accordingly. In the current `sendmail` version, you must include `O7false` in the file `sendmail.cf`. Older `sendmail` versions which can still be found under many commercial operating systems are not 8-bit clean and cannot be appropriately configured either.

Practically all news systems used today are 8-bit clean. The only news system still (rarely) used today that is not 8-bit clean is B-News. Therefore, one can safely assume that 8-bit characters will survive their transport via Usenet.

Although the following mail or news header does not correspond to the Internet standard defined in [rfc2045], it is de facto allowed and can help with the undisturbed transport of mail and news containing special characters via the different mail and news systems. The systems are simply advised that the message consists of text that contains 8-bit characters from the ISO-8859-1 character set.

```
Mime-Version: 1.0
Content-Type: text/plain; charset=iso-8859-1
Content-Transfer-Encoding: 8bit
```

If the transport route is not 8-bit clean, you can either substitute special characters with replacement characters or sequences of characters (which is a rather outmoded way of doing things), or you can leave their encoding to a MIME-capable[1] program which provides conversion in a way completely transparent to the user. However, this procedure only works without problems if both partners use MIME-capable programs.

MIME is rapidly becoming a standard, in particular because many Windows programs create such messages by default. It is only a question of time until all important programs under UNIX will also be capable of coping with MIME more or less directly.

---

[1] MIME=Multi-Media Internet Mail Extension

9.6.1 The mail reader `elm`

The program `elm` is an easy-to-use, but nevertheless powerful, mail user agent. In the first place, `elm` must be compiled correctly, which for a long time was not the case in the Slackware distribution. This allows special characters in incoming messages to be displayed by means of the built-in pager. Furthermore, the above-mentioned header lines can be included automatically in outgoing messages.

```
# elm.rc
# Transport of special characters
charset       = iso-8859-1
displaycharset= iso-8859-1
textencoding  = 8bit
pager         = builtin
```

However, `elm` can also cooperate with the MIME implementation `metamail`, so that MIME messages can be sent as well.

9.6.2 The mail and news reader `pine`

The mail and news reader `pine` (Pine Is No longer Elm) is a further development of `elm`. Pine is easy to use and is MIME-capable. Therefore, `pine` has no problems with representing or sending 8-bit characters.

9.6.3 The news reader `nn`

Yet another news reader is the program nn. nn represents 8-bit characters by means of the following entry in the file `~/.nn/init`:

```
# data-bits allows representation of
# 8-bit characters in nn
set data-bits 8
```

9.6.4 Emacs/`rmail`

Besides many other features, the Emacs editor also includes modes for creating and reading mail and news. A mode for mail is the `rmail` mode which can be started either directly by calling Emacs with `emacs -f rmail` or from inside Emacs with the command sequence `M-x rmail RET`.

If Emacs is configured appropriately, 8-bit characters can be used without problems if the transport route is 8-bit clean. If this is not the case, the minor mode `mime` can be used which can convert a message into MIME format before sending it. Such messages can also be read under Emacs by means of the MetaMail package. A possible configuration for `rmail` is shown in Listing 9.11.

Besides the description of the `rmail` mode in the Info system, you can find a series of helpful comments in the sources of the `rmail` mode, `/usr/lib/emacs/`*version*`/lisp/rmail.el`.

```
(setq mail-yank-prefix "> ")      ; text with " >" quotes
(setq mail-signature t)           ; signature from ~.signature
(setq mail-default-headers
"Mime-version: 1.0
Content-Type: text/plain; charset=iso-8859-1
Content-Transfer-Encoding: 8bit\n") ; use ISO-Latin-1
```

Listing 9.11   Configuration for Emacs/rmail (`~/.emacs`).

Additional Information and Sources	
Info system:	Emacs, advanced features, rmail
Newsgroups:	gnu.emacs
	gnu.emacs.help
	comp.editors
Package:	emacs-20.2.tar.gz
ftp server:	ftp.gnu.org
ftp path:	/pub/gnu
Size:	about 12 Mbytes

9.6.5 Emacs/gnus

Emacs not only provides a mail reader, but also the news reader gnus which allows you to read and write news inside the Emacs environment. Use of 8-bit characters is possible without problems by using either the ISO-Latin-1 character set or the MetaMail package in combination with the mime mode.

Like the rmail mode, the gnus mode can be started either from the command line or from inside Emacs. The latest versions of gnus use the tm package for displaying and creating MIME messages.

Additional Information and Sources	
Info system:	Emacs, advanced features, gnus
Newsgroups:	gnu.emacs.help
	gnu.emacs.gnus
	comp.editors
Package:	emacs-20.2.tar.gz
ftp server:	ftp.gnu.org
ftp path:	/pub/gnu
Size:	about 12 Mbytes

9.7 Adaptation of individual programs

In this section, configurations of programs are presented that do not belong to any of the categories discussed above. Further information on this subject can also be found in the various national language HowTos.

9.7.1 The program less

The GNU program less can display foreign language characters if the appropriate locale files are installed and activated. Older versions of less used to evaluate the environment variable LESSCHARSET, others the value ISO-8859-1 in the variable LC_CTYPE.

Additional Information and Sources	
Man pages:	less(1), lesskey(1)
Newsgroups:	gnu.utils.bug
Package:	less-257.tar.gz
ftp server:	ftp.gnu.org
ftp path:	/pub/gnu
Size:	about 150 Kbytes

9.7.2 The program package groff

The program groff is a text formatter which can translate texts set in nroff or troff format into a series of output formats. If you want to convert the text into a directly readable format, you must not select ascii as your output device, but latin1 (with the command line option -T latin1) to show foreign language characters in the output.

The formatting system includes a number of programs, such as for example gtbl for setting tables or geqn for setting formulae. Here too, the output device must be selected correspondingly.

A4 paper format

If you need to use A4 paper format (297 mm by 210 mm), you must set the environment variable PAGE to the value A4 before starting the configure script.

If the configuration file /usr/lib/groff/font/devps/DESC contains the line ^paperlength 841890, groff outputs in PostScript format on A4 paper. The same entry can be included in the file /usr/lib/groff/font/devdvi/DESC if the DVI[2] output too is to be formatted for A4 paper.

The setting of paper formats is not defined by standards, therefore manual intervention is required. This also applies to a number of other programs.

---

[2] DVI = Device Independent.

Additional Information and Sources	
Man pages:	`groff(1)`
Newsgroups:	`gnu.groff`
	`gnu.groff.bug`
Package:	`groff-1.09.tar.gz`
ftp server:	`ftp.gnu.org`
ftp path:	`/pub/gnu`
Size:	about 840 Kbytes

9.7.3 The man program

The `man` program is used for formatting and displaying individual pages of the online manual (also known as man pages). In the best UNIX tradition, various utilities are used to achieve this goal. With foreign language man pages, a couple of issues need to be considered:

- First of all, the man pages are formatted with the aid of `groff`. Therefore, the calls of `groff` and the other programs belonging to that package must be adapted as explained above.
- Subsequently, the text is displayed by means of `less` or `more`.

Thus, special characters in man pages are only displayed properly if all involved programs are configured correctly. The following information applies to `man-1.4`, a man program which can work with several languages by using message catalogs and displays the appropriate man page depending on the value of the variable `LANG`. Also `man-db`, which manages a list of the installed man pages in a database, is adapted to these conventions. Listing 9.12 shows an excerpt from the file `/usr/lib/man.config`.

```
TROFF        /usr/bin/groff -Tps -mandoc
NROFF        /usr/bin/groff -Tlatin1 -mandoc
EQN          /usr/bin/geqn -Tps
NEQN         /usr/bin/geqn -Tlatin1
TBL          /usr/bin/gtbl
COL          /usr/bin/col
REFER        /usr/bin/grefer
PIC          /usr/bin/gpic
VGRIND
GRAP
PAGER        /usr/bin/less -s -M -i
```

Listing 9.12   Excerpt from the file `man.config`.

9.7.4 Using A4 paper size in various programs

The dvips program

The dvips program is used to create PostScript files from DVI files generated by TEX, LATEX or groff. With the option -t a4, the dvips program can be configured to use A4 paper. You can, however, also set this option system-wide in the file /usr/lib/texmf/dvips/config.ps or for an individual user in the file ~/.dvipsrc. Listing 9.13 shows the corresponding section of the file config.ps. Users can also create this file as ~/.dvipsrc in their home directories.

```
% Paper size information. First definition is the default.
%
% If your default is a4 uncomment the following definition
% and comment out the LetterSize definition.
%
@ a4size 210mm 297mm
@+ ! %%DocumentPaperSizes: a4
@+ %%PaperSize: a4
@+ %%BeginPaperSize: a4
@+ a4
@+ %%EndPaperSize
%
%@ LetterSize 8.5in 11in
%
%@ Letter 8.5in 11in
%@+ %%PaperSize: Letter
%@+ %%BeginPaperSize: Letter
%@+ letter
%@+ %%EndPaperSize
```

Listing 9.13   A4 paper in the program dvips.

The xdvi program

The xdvi program displays a DVI file under X. The border of the paper is shown as a black line around the text. Therefore, you might want to configure xdvi as well for this paper size. You can do this either by means of the command line option -paper a4 or via a setting in the file ~/.Xresources (Listing 9.14).

```
! Setting for DIN A4
XDvi.paper:      a4
```

Listing 9.14   Adaptation for xdvi.

The Texinfo system

The Texinfo system can be used to read documentation online by means of the Info mode of the emacs editor or by means of external programs such as xinfo. It is, however, also possible to print the documentation in the form of a book. This format is the standard documentation format of the GNU project of the Free Software Foundation.

To use the A4 paper format for printouts, you must use the command @afourpaper at the beginning of the document. Thus, a TEXinfo documentation begins with the following lines:

```
\input texinfo    @c -*-texinfo-*-
@afourpaper
```

The GhostScript program (gs)

The GhostScript program (gs) is a PostScript interpreter which is capable of representing PostScript files on a number of non-PostScript printers and other output devices (X, LINUX console). This program too uses letter size paper as a default. The command line option -sPAPERSIZE=a4 switches to A4 format.

The ghostview program

The ghostview program is an X interface for GhostScript. Here, the paper format can be set either via the corresponding menu item or by means of the following entry in the file ~/.Xresources:

```
! Setting for DIN A4
Ghostview.pageMedia:  A4
```

9.7.5 termcap, curses, and ncurses

There are various libraries for portable control of terminals or the console which allow programming independently of the terminal actually in use. However, if such a library is not 8-bit clean, neither are the programs that use this library.

The termcap library is 8-bit clean, so special characters are processed correctly.

The BSD curses library, however, is not 8-bit clean. If a program uses the curses library, it should use the more powerful ncurses library instead.

However, even the ncurses library is not automatically 8-bit clean. You must specify the compiler switch -funsigned-char during compilation of the library. This switch should also be specified during compilation of all programs that use this library to prevent foreign language characters from being displayed as blinking special symbols. This switch ensures that 8-bit characters are treated as such and are not converted into negative number values.

9.7.6 The `ispell` program

The `ispell` program checks texts for spelling mistakes. On the Internet, you can find versions 3.1 and 4.0. The current and more powerful version is 3.1, since version 4.0 is not suited for foreign language texts.

Dictionaries for `ispell` are currently available for (at least) the following languages: Czech, Danish, Dutch, English (default), Esperanto, French, German, Greek, Italian, Portuguese, Romanian, Russian, Spanish, and Swedish.

Obviously, `ispell` can cope with ISO-Latin-1 characters, and it is also possible to use `ispell` from within Emacs. The call of Listing 9.15 makes the dictionary enclosed in the double quotes the default dictionary.

```
; Set default dictionary (with 8-bit characters)
(setq ispell-dictionary "dictionary8")
```

Listing 9.15   Default dictionary for `ispell` in Emacs.

Additional Information and Sources	
ftp server:	ftp.cs.ucla.edu
ftp path:	/pub/ispell-3.1
File name:	ispell-3.1.xx.tar.gz

UNIX tools

10

'Keep it simple, stupid'
One design goal of UNIX

One big advantage of UNIX is the large number of tools that facilitate working with the computer. Some of these are used to find files or execute programs on a periodical basis. Others can process text files relatively easily and quickly. There is an easy-to-use program for practically any (simple) task, and different programs can be flexibly joined together. All of this will be discussed in depth in this chapter.

The shell, the UNIX tools, and awk or other script languages can be used to write easy programs that may relieve the system administrator from boring routine tasks, such as periodical pruning of log files. Many other tasks, such as processing of text files, for example for ad-hoc evaluations, can be carried out by means of the UNIX utility programs with relatively little effort. However, this requires the user to be aware of the possibilities of the individual tools, at least in general terms.

A UNIX system can be seen as a 'tool box' containing a series of simple tools. The combination of different programs, which individually can only carry out a fraction of the work, can often save programmers or system administrators hours of dull, repetitive work. Individual programs are combined by means of control structures, for example, of the shell, and by means of data redirection via pipes. Several design decisions play an important role:

- Each program should perform one (simple) task.
- Programs read from the standard input. This can be a file, a pipe, or the user's terminal.
- Programs write their results to the standard output. This can be a file, a pipe, or the user's terminal.
- Programs must not generate additional output on the standard output. For error messages, the standard error output must be used.

The UNIX utilities can be easily combined with each other and thus carry out tasks that the utilities programmers never even thought of. For larger projects or programs, one should however consider programming in C or another programming language. Shell programs are slow and, in spite of all efforts, relatively error-prone, but they are very well suited for 'quick shots' and simple prototypes.

Most of the standard programs used under LINUX originate from the GNU project. The aim of the GNU project (GNU is Not Unix), which was initiated by Richard M. Stallman and is now managed by the Free Software Foundation, is the implementation of an improved, free UNIX operating system. The GNU programs are free reimplementations of well-known UNIX programs. Much effort is invested into removal of limitations, such as maximum line length or exclusive use of pure ASCII characters, present in the original implementations. Another essential goal is to achieve conformity to the POSIX standard.

This is the reason why GNU tools often behave slightly differently from their counterparts in other (older) UNIX systems (for example, BSD and System V derivatives). In case of incompatible extensions, GNU programs usually provide the option `--posix` or the environment variable `POSIXLY_CORRECT` which switch off the extensions and make the program behave exactly as set forth in the standard, even though this does not always correspond to what the user expects.

GNU extensions are often useful and convenient, even when they contradict the POSIX standard or are extensions of it. Therefore, on many commercial systems the GNU tools are installed in addition to the already existing UNIX versions. One further advantage is that the GNU tools are practically identical on all supported platforms. On various commercial UNIX systems one often finds different and incompatible versions of the various programs; here, the GNU programs can serve to create a uniform interface.

10.1 File management

A complete LINUX system consists of several thousand files. The search for a file may often seem futile. Luckily enough, there are tools that facilitate the search for files. There is the (UNIX) command `find` which can search the current directory tree for files that satisfy specific criteria. Another possibility is to use the GNU tool `locate`. This searches a database created with `updatedb` for the specified file name.

10.1.1 Searching for files with the `find` command

The `find` command can be used to search the files system for files that satisfy specific criteria. The output is a list of found files which can then be processed by other programs, such as `awk` (see Section 10.5). Alternatively, a UNIX command can be specified which is executed on every file found by the `find` command.

The `find` command can be passed the starting directory as the first parameter. All subdirectories of this directory are searched. The nesting depth can be restricted by means of the `-maxdepth` option; the whole search can be limited to a single file system with the option `-xdev`.

Various search criteria that the files must satisfy can be specified. Possible criteria are, for example, the file name (or a search pattern), the file type, or the last access, modification, or creation date. To search for a file name, the criterion would be input as –name *file name*.

Another parameter must tell the find command what to do if a matching file is found. Possible options are, among others, simply to output the file name (option –print) or to start other UNIX programs with the found file name as a parameter (option –exec). The GNU program find uses –print as default action if nothing different was specified; other UNIX systems may or may not do the same. If you want to remain portable, you should always explicitly specify –print. Listing 10.1 searches for all files in the directory /etc whose names match the pattern *net*.

```
(Linux):/$ find /etc -name '*net*' -print
/etc/rc.d/rc.inet1
/etc/rc.d/rc.inet2
/etc/inet
/etc/inetd.conf
/etc/networks
```

Listing 10.1   Searching for files with find.

The parameter /etc specifies the directory to be searched. The parameter –name '*net*' tells find to search for files whose names match the search pattern *net*. The file name to be searched for should be enclosed in single quotes so that the shell that calls find does not interpret the special characters. The –print parameter instructs find to output the complete file name.

When the –printf option is specified, the output can be modified by means of a format specification, for example, to include modification date, file owner, or file size in the output. The man page for find contains a complete overview of possible formats. Several additional output formats can be set, for example, –print0 inserts a null byte as a separator between the individual names instead of a line feed.

Instead of just listing the found file names, a UNIX command can be started with the file name as a parameter. This is obtained by using –exec which generates a new process for each found file. If the search result contains many files, it is recommended that one of the commands shown in Listing 10.2 be used, which generates only one or a few additional processes. These employ either a mechanism of the shell or the xargs program (see Section 10.1.6).

```
(Linux):~$ find . -name '*.bak' -exec rm -f {} \;
(Linux):~$ rm -f $(find . -name '*.bak')
(Linux):~$ find . -name '*.bak' | xargs rm -f
```

Listing 10.2   Execution of commands with find.

All examples in Listing 10.2 delete all files bearing the extension .bak. The –exec parameter executes the command rm –f for each found file. The curly brackets are placeholders for the found file name. The semicolon tells the `find` command where the `-exec` parameter ends. As the shell would also evaluate the semicolon, it must be masked with a backslash (\).

If you are not sure whether the specified command should really be executed for all files, you can use the option `-ok` instead of `-exec`. Here, for each found file, `find` prompts for confirmation to execute the specified command.

Another interesting purpose of the `-exec` option can be seen in its combination with the `grep` command. This makes it quite easy, for example, to find files in which a particular piece of text occurs. The example in Listing 10.3 lists all files that contain the host name. Depending on the extent of the file system, the example can take a while to run, because *all* directories are searched.

```
(Linux):/# find / -type f -exec grep -l `hostname` {} \;
/etc/profile
/etc/HOSTNAME
/etc/hosts
/etc/nntpserver
/etc/ftpaccess
```

Listing 10.3 `find` in combination with `grep`.

In combination with the `cpio` (page 175) or `afio` (page 176) commands, it is also possible to use `find` for the construction of a simple data backup system. A very rudimentary example can be found in Listing 10.4. As a rule, however, use of a complete backup system is the better choice (see also Chapter 7).

```
(Linux):~$ find . -print|afio -oZf /dev/fd0
././profile
././emacs
./diary
...
(Linux):~$ touch .backup
(Linux):~$ find . -newer .backup -print|afio -oZf /dev/fd0
././bash_history
```

Listing 10.4 Data backup with `find` and `cpio`.

After the installation of a LINUX distribution, several files must be adjusted manually, for example the `/etc/printcap` file. One after the other, more and more modifications are carried out to adapt the system to the specific requirements. This is either done manually or using the distribution tools. For a backup, to find out which files have been modified, one could create the file `Install_Date` in `/root` directly after the installation of a LINUX system (Listing 10.5).

```
(Linux):/root# date > /root/Install_Date
```

Listing 10.5   Creating a file that contains the installation date.

It is not necessary to save the date in a file; however, if the modification date of a file was inadvertently changed, for example with `touch`, it is always possible to restore the original date. Thus, all modified files can be retrieved whenever needed (Listing 10.6).

```
(Linux):/# find / -newer /root/Install_Date -print
/etc/profile
/etc/printcap
```

Listing 10.6   Finding all files modified after the installation.

Several current distributions can be updated to a new version without problems and a reinstallation. Nevertheless, this can still be a sensible way to create a backup of one's adaptations. All modified files could also be transferred to a new computer and be adapted there. Often, however, it is sufficient to know which files have been modified to learn more about the system.

Besides the options discussed above in more detail, `find` can also search for other criteria, such as file owner, access rights, or size. Furthermore, `find` can search for several criteria at a time, with the possibility of specifying several actions as well. The complete documentation of `find` can be found in the man page or in the Texinfo documentation.

10.1.2 Searching with `locate`

One disadvantage of the `find` command is that searching in large file systems or, worse, on network drives takes a very long time. Furthermore, there is a risk that in the case of incorrect symbolic links, `find` ends up in an infinite loop. There is, however, a second method of finding files, namely the GNU program `locate`.

Instead of the file systems, the `locate` command searches a database for the requested file name. This UNIX database must have been previously created by means of the `updatedb` command; only then can the `locate` command be employed. The search is now much faster than with the `find` command, but there is a chance that the database is not completely up-to-date, so that not all files are found, or files are shown that have been deleted. `locate` warns the user when the database is older than eight days. A further disadvantage in comparison with `find` is that only pattern search in file names is supported.

The `updatedb` command searches all directories specified in the environment variables SEARCHPATHS and NFSPATHS. The search pattern in the variable PRUNEREGEX can be used to exclude file names or whole paths from being included in the database.

By default, these are the directories /tmp, /usr/tmp, and /var/tmp. It is recommended that the /proc directory is included in this expression as well. The /proc file system contains only data that represent the internal status of the system, and such data change quite quickly.

To begin with, you should exclude the users' home directories from the search, because otherwise even unreadable directories would be searched by the system administrator. If you wish to provide your users with a database of all home directories, you should at least start this search run as user nobody. Otherwise, each user can create an additional database for his/her own directories and have it searched by locate by default. Listing 10.7 shows an example for creation and search of a user's locate database.

```
(Linux):~> updatedb --localpaths=/home/jochen \
? --output=update.db
(Linux):~> locate -d update.db:/var/lib/locatedb passwdtab
```

Listing 10.7   Creation of a user's locate database.

The updatedb command should be entered into crontab (for an example, see Listing 10.32), so that the database is periodically updated. Usually, the database is located in the /var/lib directory. The name of the database (locatedb), which is normally created by updatedb, can be overwritten by setting the variable LOCATE_DB. Thus, for example, a database can be created for each CD-ROM. With the –d parameter, you can also specify *several* colon-separated database names to be searched by locate.

In the following example (Listing 10.8) a database that contains the contents of the CD is created under the name cd_linux2_1.codes in the directory ~/locate. Once the database has been created, the locate command with the option –d ~/locate/cd_linux2_1.codes can be used to search this database.

```
(Linux):~# export LOCATE_DB=~/locate/cd_linux2_1.codes
(Linux):~# export SEARCHPATHS='/CD'
(Linux):~# export PRUNEREGEX=' '
(Linux):~# updatedb
(Linux):~# locate -d cd_linux2_1.codes ftape
```

Listing 10.8   Creation of a search database for a CD.

The disadvantage of this system is that the UNIX database must be updated as often as possible, because otherwise more recent files cannot be found or deleted files are still shown. The search itself is also not as flexible as that of the find command. You cannot search for date, owner, or the like, but only for file names. Furthermore, a run of updatedb is relatively costly because a find is carried out across the entire hard disk.

All in all, the use of locate is always worth while if you have many users on your system, and the computer enjoys enough 'quiet' periods during which the database can be updated. If you notice that on your system you frequently search for files by name, using locate is sensible even on a private system; on my own system, updatedb is called every four hours.

10.1.3 Where is program xyz?

If you are looking for the complete name of an executable file included in the search path(!), you can circumvent the longwinded search with find. Instead of the find program, you should use the which command. In the tcsh, which is an internal command of the shell. Users of the bash can use the alias type -path. In some UNIX systems, the command is also called ewhich, whereis, or whence.

The which command searches the complete path specified in the PATH variable for the name of the required file. The order in which the path is processed is exactly the same as the order that would be followed by the shell.

```
(Linux):/$ which gawk
/usr/bin/gawk
```

Listing 10.9   Using which.

With the whereis command, you can not only find programs, but also the corresponding man pages. The -b option searches only for programs, the -m option only for the man pages. Additional options and the search paths can be found in the man page for whereis.

The bash command type -all -path can be used to determine whether two different versions of a program exist in the path, for example in /usr/bin and /usr/local/bin, and which of these would be started. This can be useful in cases where a new program version was installed, but the old one is still being used.

Programs like which are always sensible when the path leading to a program is needed. This can be the case for installation and adaptation of shell scripts as well as for error detection. Programs such as strings or ldd work with files and not with programs from the search path.

10.1.4 What kind of file is this?

A UNIX system consists of a huge number of files. The number of file types is not quite as large, but still large enough: text files, binary programs, shell scripts, images, drawings, and many more. Often the file name or, more precisely, the extension can be used to determine the kind of file, but this trick does not always work.

The file program opens the file and tries to find a matching entry in the file /etc/magic. These 'magic IDs' and similar things are used to determine the file type. Sometimes, the output of file is surprisingly exact, other times, the program misses the mark. Listing 10.10 shows some sample output of file.

```
(Linux):~> file /vmlinuz /bin/ls announce
/vmlinuz: Linux/x86 kernel image, version 2.0.30
/bin/ls:  ELF 32-bit LSB executable, Intel 80386,
version 1, dynamically linked, stripped
announce: International language text
(Linux):~>
```

Listing 10.10   The `file` program.

The output of `file` is only as good as the underlying database in `/etc/magic`. Most commercial systems have relatively small and outdated versions, whereas modern LINUX implementations contain very good versions of this file. Often one also finds individual file types being defined in new programs, so that this file can be easily updated.

Additional Information and Sources	
ftp server:	`ftp.deshaw.com`
ftp path:	`/pub/file`
File name:	`file-X.YY.tar.gz`
Size:	about 80 Kbytes

10.1.5   Other little helpers

There are another couple of little helpers which are mainly used in shell programs. For writing efficient shell scripts, you should at least be familiar with the main possibilities. Usually, you can quickly look up the precise syntax of the commands in the man page, or you can just try it out. Do not worry if you are unable to memorize all the options – the online manual in the man pages was developed exactly for this purpose.

The basename of a file

The `basename` command separates the file name from the complete path. The command can, for example, be used in combination with the `find` command. As described above, the `find` command supplies the complete path of the sought file. If only the file name is to be output, then the `basename` command can be used (see Listing 10.11).

The `basename` command can also separate a specified extension from the file name. An example can be found in Listing 10.12. This allows you, for example, to give a series of files a different extension. However, for this purpose you could also use `mmv`, a program that provides a more flexible way of carrying out this kind of task.

```
(Linux):/$ find / -name '*.conf' -exec basename {} \;
ld.so.conf
syslog.conf
host.conf
inetd.conf
resolv.conf
lilo.conf
dosemu.conf
```

Listing 10.11   The first usage of basename.

```
(Linux):/$ find / -name '*.conf' -exec basename {} '.conf' \;
ld.so
syslog
host
inetd
resolv
lilo
dosemu
```

Listing 10.12   The second usage of basename.

The path of a file – dirname

The dirname command works in a similar way to the basename command, supplying the path name without the file name as output. If the name passed as a parameter does not contain a directory, a dot (.) is output that stands for the current directory. An example can be found in Listing 10.13.

```
(Linux):/$ dirname /etc/rc.d/rc.local
/etc/rc.d
(Linux):/$ dirname /vmlinuz
/
(Linux):/$ dirname vmlinuz
.
```

Listing 10.13   Using the dirname program.

10.1.6 Excessive length parameter lines

The xargs command generates a command line from the standard input which is passed to the specified command. If the command line exceeds the maximum length, the specified command is called several times in a row or simultaneously. With the use of `xargs`, the error message 'Command line too long' will never appear again.

If you want to search files for specific text using the `find` command in combination with the `grep` command, `grep` supplies the lines in which the sought text is found, but not the file name. There are several possibilities to solve this problem:

- You can pass `grep` the file `/dev/null` as an additional parameter.
- If the output of the file name is sufficient, you can pass `grep` the option `-l`.
- Several files at a time can be searched with `xargs`. An example can be found in Listing 10.14.

Because the `grep` command is not called separately for each file, as `find` would do with the `-exec` option, the file names are now output as well. Furthermore, this variation is 'friendlier' to other users since it employs less system resources in terms of processes, memory, and processor time.

```
(Linux):/# find /etc -type f -print | xargs grep LUENEO2
/etc/hosts:192.168.10.1 LUENEO2.goe.de LUENEO2
/etc/HOSTNAME:LUENEO2.goe.de
/etc/rc.d/rc.inet1:/sbin/ifconfig dummy LUENEO2
/etc/rc.d/rc.inet1:/sbin/route add LUENEO2
/etc/hosts,v:127.0.0.1          LUENEO2.goe.de LUENEO2
/etc/hosts,v:127.0.0.1  LUENEO2.goe.de LUENEO2
```

Listing 10.14   Using `xargs`.

Frequently, a series of files have to be renamed. Unfortunately, the command can rename only *one* file at a time (`mv *.c *.c.bak` does not work because of the expansion of the asterisks by the shell). Instead, you can use either a small `for` loop, or the `mmv` command, or the `xargs` command with the option `-n1 -i`. The examples in Listing 10.15 copy all files that end in `*.c` from the current directory to the directory `backups` and append the extension `.bak` to every file name.

This demonstrates that under UNIX several ways may lead to success. With regard to comfort and use of resources, however, these ways are often extremely different. True UNIX buffs combine the available tools quickly and elegantly, and try to save on system resources.

```
(Linux):~/src$ ls *.c | xargs -n1 -i cp {} backups/{}.bak
(Linux):~/src$ for i in *.c ; do
>      mv $i  backup/`basename $i .c`.bak ;
> done
```

Listing 10.15   Moving or renaming several files.

The option –n1 of the xargs command passes each file name separately to the cp command. The option –i instructs xargs to replace all curly brackets with the current file name (similar to the find command with the exec option). Instead of the copy command, you could also use a file comparison by means of diff.

10.2 Processing of text files

UNIX provides several programs for the processing of text files. Practically all configuration files, program sources, and text files are simple ASCII files that can be processed without special programs. This is one of the reasons why there are so many efficient tools in this area under UNIX. Text files can be easily processed by means of sed, tr, awk and other tools presented in this section. In addition, there are many other programs that can be useful, for example perl or Python.

awk and sed are tools which provide a script language for easy processing of text files. Depending on the specific task, one might prefer one or the other. If the task is to extract and further process specific data from text files, the choice would probably be awk. If certain parts of a text file are to be modified, this can best be done with sed. In principle, however, each task can be carried out by both tools.

The grep command can be used to search for text passages in text files. Other small tools, such as cut or tr carry out simple tasks that could also be performed by awk or sed, but often in a substantially shorter time due to the compactness of the programs.

10.2.1 Searching for text passages in files

The grep command (global regular expression print) searches arbitrary text files for a given search pattern, the so-called *regular expressions*. These search patterns are used in a similar form by various programs, therefore they are described in a separate section (see Section 10.3).

The grep command is line-oriented. This means that the input file or the standard input are checked line by line for a match with the search pattern. All lines that match the pattern are output on the standard output. The example in Listing 10.16 outputs all lines of the file /etc/services that contain the character string ftp.

```
(Linux):~$ grep ftp /etc/services
ftp          21/tcp
tftp         69/udp
sftp         115/tcp
```

Listing 10.16   A simple application of grep.

As with practically all UNIX tools, the grep command is case-sensitive. If grep is to ignore upper and lower case, the parameter –i must be specified. If all lines are to be output that do *not* contain the specified search pattern, the parameter -v must be used.

GNU grep implements two additional variations, egrep (or grep -E) and fgrep (or grep -F). The differences are that grep processes 'basic regular expressions,' whereas egrep can additionally handle 'extended regular expressions.' fgrep is the old 'fast' grep which only searches for constant strings.

With the option -n, grep can be instructed to output the line numbers in addition to the found lines. The option -l causes grep to output only the names of the files that contain the search pattern, but not the text contained in the line. When searching through texts, it is often sensible to show some lines of context around the found line, which can be achieved with the option -c. More about the command line options of grep can be found in the corresponding man page.

To search through files compressed with gzip, you can use the zgrep command. With this command, the file does not need to be unpacked first and subsequently compressed again. In the same way, compressed files can be displayed with zcat or zmore. Differences between compressed files can be displayed by means of zdiff.

10.2.2 Transforming characters with tr

The tr command can transform individual characters faster than sed or awk. However, tr is designed for processing single characters and does not utilize search patterns or context dependencies. If, for example, you want to output all lower case letters in a file as upper case letters, you can use the call shown in Listing 10.17.

```
(Linux):~$ echo 'Hello' | tr '[a-z]' '[A-Z]'
HELLO
(Linux):~$ echo 'Hello' | tr '[:lower:]' '[:upper:]'
HELLO
```

Listing 10.17   Using tr.

The parameters look like regular expressions, but represent only simple character strings. Please note that the second call is not possible if you are using a locale with the ISO-8859-1 character set (ISO-Latin-1) in which some accented letters and the German sharp s (ß) are classified as lower case letters with no corresponding upper case letter. In such a case, tr displays an appropriate message.

If, for example, all digits are to be filtered out of a file, the commands shown in Listing 10.18 can be used. The option -d ('delete') means that the specified characters are to be deleted from the input file. One frequently used application of tr is the deletion of the superfluous carriage returns (\r) in texts imported from Windows.

With tr you can not only modify readable characters, but also input characters as octal values. In addition, special symbols are defined for many frequently processed characters which consist of a backslash (\) followed by a character. Table 10.1

```
(Linux):~$ echo 'The secret number is 4711!' | tr -d '[0-9]'
The secret number is !
```

Listing 10.18   A further application of tr.

shows an overview of the most widely used special characters. A complete table of all special characters can be found in the man page for tr.

Character	Meaning
\f	Form feed, Control-F
\r	Carriage return, Control-M
\t	The tab character, Control-T
\\	A simple backslash
\ooo	Octal character representation

Table 10.1   Special characters for tr.

There are subtle differences between the tr programs in BSD and System V systems which complicate porting of shell scripts containing tr calls. These differences and the precise format of the parameter strings are extensively described in the man page for tr. It also includes a series of examples.

10.2.3 Processing fields in lines with cut

The cut command can be used to output specific parts of a line from a file. You might also use awk, but cut is often faster because it is not as flexible and powerful as awk. The cut command can isolate given fields that are separated from each other by a certain character (for example, a colon, as in /etc/passwd), or it can cut out fields character by character. The example in Listing 10.19 shows how to output the characters from position 1 to 11 of each line of a file.

The next example (Listing 10.20) shows how to obtain a list of the names of all users contained in the file /etc/passwd. The field containing the name is the fifth. All fields are separated by colons (:). The parameter -d sets the field separator ('delimitor'). The parameter -f5 selects the fifth field, which contains the user's real name.

```
(Linux):~$ cut -b1-11 articles.dat
11340556671
11366671332
30113434287
```

Listing 10.19   Characterwise cutting with cut.

```
(Linux):/$ cut -d: -f5 /etc/passwd
System administrator
New-Admin
James Kirk
Frank N. Furter
```

Listing 10.20   Cutting out fields from the file /etc/passwd.

10.2.4 Comparing text files

The contents of files can be compared by means of the diff program. Quite often, one would like to know if, where, and how two files differ from each other, for example, in the case of backup copies, different versions of a file, or changes and adaptations made by other users. Listing 10.21 shows the two files used in the following examples.

```
(Linux):~/examples> cat hello.c
#include <stdio.h>
main()
{
  printf("Hello World!\n");
}
(Linux):~/examples> cat hallo.c
#include <stdio.h>
main()
{
  printf("Hallo Welt!\n");
}
```

Listing 10.21   Sample files for the diff program.

The diff program can represent the differences between two files in a very flexible way. This concerns both the context of the differences (just the affected lines or some lines before and after) and the representation itself. The two files can be output next to each other on the screen. Some examples of how to apply the diff command are shown in Listing 10.22.

In the first example, a simple diff is used. The output is a sed script that can be used for automatic modification on other computers. A disadvantage of these scripts is that the context of the changes is not considered. Therefore, this function only makes sense with otherwise absolutely identical files.

A better solution is the creation of context diffs (-c) or unified diffs (second example in Listing 10.22). The generation of context diffs is part of the standard UNIX program, whereas unified diffs are an extension of the GNU version.

```
(Linux):~/examples> diff hello.c hallo.c
4c4
<   printf("Hello World!\n");
---
>   printf("Hallo Welt!\n");
(Linux):~/examples> diff -u hello.c hallo.c
--- hello.c     Sun Nov  2 10:44:09 1997
+++ hallo.c     Sun Nov  2 10:45:04 1997
@@ -1,5 +1,5 @@
 #include <stdio.h>
 main()
 {
-  printf("Hello World!\n");
+  printf("Hallo Welt!\n");
 }
(Linux):~/examples> diff -y --width=40 hello.c hallo.c
#include <stdio.h>              #include <stdio.h>
main()                         main()
{                              {
  printf("Hello World!\n");  |   printf("Hallo Welt!\n");
}                              }
```

Listing 10.22 Applying the diff program.

Personally, I think that unified diffs provide better readability; in both cases you can insert the changes by means of patch into slightly modified files.

The third example in Listing 10.22 shows the representation of both versions next to each other. This is often useful to get a quick overview of modifications, when dealing with files with short lines and a terminal with many columns.

The Emacs editor has special modes (ediff and emerge) to show the differences between files and, if needed, to adapt the files appropriately. Under X, differences are shown in different colors, and changes can be performed with a single keystroke. ediff can be used under Emacs for two or three files (ediff, ediff3), buffers (ediff-buffers, ediff-buffers3), or directories (ediff-directories, ediff-directories3). In addition, it is possible to compare revisions created by the Revision Control System (see Section 11.5).

When you call ediff, Emacs asks for two files to be compared with each other. These files are loaded into two buffers, buffer A and buffer B. You can now navigate through these files with single keystrokes. The ? key displays a menu with the available shortcuts. If you wish to try this out, just copy any file (for example /etc/profile) twice and modify one copy in arbitrary places. Then call ediff to make the same changes in the second file, if and where needed.

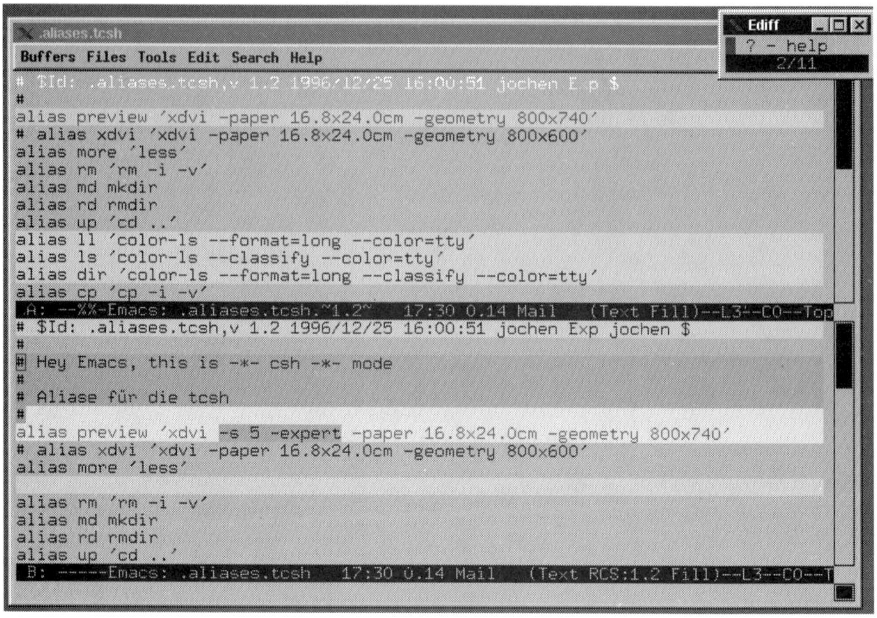

Figure 10.1 The Emacs `ediff` mode in action.

10.2.5 Creating and inserting patches

Many programs employed under LINUX are distributed in the form of source code. When an author releases a new version, the number of changes is often relatively small in comparison with the entire source code. In such cases it is sensible to publish only the changes, or to download only the changes from an `ftp` server in order to keep network load and transmission costs to a minimum. A file that contains only the changes between two versions is called 'diff' or 'patch.' Such changes can then be implemented automatically by means of the `patch` command.

Patch files are generated with the `diff` program. Either normal diffs, context diffs (`-c`), or unified diffs (`-u`) can be created. Normal diffs are smaller than context or unified diffs, but can be inserted only into otherwise absolutely identical files since the context of the changes is missing. Context and unified diffs contain (in slightly different formats) some lines of context around the changes, so that these changes can also be implemented manually if needed. Generally, however, changes will be implemented by means of the `patch` program.

Since the changes between individual versions of the LINUX kernel are published as patches, we are going to use these patches as an example. First of all, we look at the beginning of a patch file (Listing 10.23) by means of the `head` program (see also Section 10.7.4). The patch contains the names of the modified files in the `linux` path.

If the patch is carried out inside the directory /usr/src, the complete path must be preserved using the option -p0. Normally, this option could also be omitted, but if new files are created, they will be created in the wrong directory.

If the patch is carried out inside the directory /usr/src/linux, the first directory name can be removed using the option -p1. Setting the option -s causes screen messages to be displayed only in the event of an error.

```
(Linux):/usr/src# zcat 1.2-patches/patch-1.2.13.gz | head
diff -u -r -N v1.2.12/linux/Makefile linux/Makefile
--- v1.2.12/linux/Makefile       Tue Jul 25 12:39:54 1995
+++ linux/Makefile       Wed Jul 26 09:43:44 1995
@@ -1,6 +1,6 @@
 VERSION = 1
 PATCHLEVEL = 2
-SUBLEVEL = 12
+SUBLEVEL = 13

 ARCH = i386
```

Listing 10.23   Beginning of a kernel patch.

10.3 Search patterns (regular expressions)

A *search pattern* (also known as 'regular expression') is an expression, or a template, that is compared with a character string. Often, search patterns are employed to determine whether a given character string matches the pattern (for example, by the grep command), or to substitute one character string with another (for example, by the sed command).

Regular expressions are used by many UNIX programs, such as awk, sed, grep, and perl. Each of these programs uses some of the expressions described in this section, sometimes with a slightly different meaning. In your own programs, you can use the corresponding functions (regcomp(), regexec(), regerror(), and regfree()) of the C library. More about these functions can be found in the man pages for the individual functions.

A search pattern is a regular expression composed of characters. Some of these characters have a special meaning and they will be called 'wildcards' in the following text. Some of these wildcards stand for *an arbitrary* character, others for *a set* of characters. If these wildcard characters are to be used without their special meaning, they must be preceded by a backslash (\).

First, we describe those regular expressions that correspond to a single character. The most frequently used REs are one-character REs that correspond to themselves, such as for example the letter a. The example (Listing 10.24) shows the use of a pattern that consists of three such characters. All lines of the file `file` are output that contain the character string `abc`.

```
(Linux):~$ grep abc file
```

Listing 10.24   A simple regular expression.

The second most frequently employed character is the dot (`.`). This character is a wildcard character with a special meaning: it is the placeholder for *one* arbitrary character. The example in Listing 10.25 outputs all lines that contain the letter `a`, followed by an arbitrary character, followed by the character `c`. Thus, for example, `abc` and `afc`, but not `ac`.

```
(Linux):~$ grep 'a.c' file
```

Listing 10.25   Another simple regular expression.

If a check is to be made as to whether a character string contains an element of a specific set of characters in a certain position, this can be done by enclosing the characters in square brackets (`[` and `]`). The first example in Listing 10.26 outputs all lines of the file that contain the letter `a`, followed by either `d`, `e` or `f`, followed by the letter `c`. In the example, the regular expressions are now enclosed in single quotes – this is sensible if we want to avoid having to mask every special shell character individually.

```
(Linux):~$ grep 'a[def]c' file
(Linux):~$ grep 'a[a-z]c' file
(Linux):~$ grep 'a[^0-9]c' file
```

Listing 10.26   More examples of regular expressions.

The second example supplies all lines that contain a lower case letter between the `a` and the `c`. Ranges can be specified by means of a hyphen. Thus, the expression `[a-z]` stands for the ASCII lower case letters, whereas `[A-Z]` stands for the ASCII upper case letters. Ranges can also be combined: `[a-z0-9]` corresponds to all lower case letters and all digits.

In so-called extended regular expressions, such as those used by `egrep`, a set can also be specified by means of a character class, for example `[:lower:]` or `[:upper:]`. If a foreign language locale is used, these character classes also include special characters such as umlauts or accented letters. Please note that these character classes must be specified within a set, so that the resulting regular expression contains two opening and two closing square brackets each. Table 10.2 shows an overview of all character classes.

Character class	Meaning
[:alpha:]	All letters
[:upper:]	All upper case letters
[:lower:]	All lower case letters
[:digit:]	All digits
[:xdigit:]	All hexadecimal digits
[:space:]	All white space characters
[:punct:]	All punctuation marks
[:alnum:]	All letters and digits
[:print:]	All printable characters
[:graph:]	Printable characters excluding spaces
[:cntrl:]	All control characters
[:blank:]	Spaces or tabs

Table 10.2   Character classes in regular expressions.

The third example in Listing 10.26 supplies all lines of the file that have *no* digit between the letters a and c. The caret sign (^) placed as the first character of a character set (that is, immediately following the opening square bracket) means that the expression inside the square brackets is logically inverted.

Other very important wildcards are the asterisk (*) and the plus sign (+). These characters are repetition operators: the expression *in front of* the asterisk may occur an arbitrary number of times, including zero times (that is, it may also *not* occur at all), whereas the expression in front of a plus sign may occur an arbitrary number of times, but must occur at least once. The expression in Listing 10.27 lists all lines that contain the letter a, followed by an arbitrary number of digits, followed by the letter c. Obviously, the string ac is found as well, because the digits [0-9] may occur an arbitrary number of times (including zero).

```
(Linux):~$ grep 'a[0-9]*c' file
```

Listing 10.27   Repetitions in regular expressions.

Other useful special characters are the caret (^) at the beginning and the dollar sign ($) at the end of a regular expression. These two characters stand for the beginning and the end of a line. If you want to list, for example, all comment lines of a shell program, you can obtain this by means of the expression shown in Listing 10.28. To find all empty lines, you might use the expression ^$.

```
(Linux):~$ grep '^#.*'
```

Listing 10.28   The last example of regular expressions.

Expression	Meaning
.	*One* arbitrary character
[abc]	One element of a set of characters at this point
[^abc]	As above, but in the opposite sense
*	Repeats the preceding expression an arbitrary number of times
+	Repeats the preceding expression at least once
^	Beginning of line
$	End of line

Table 10.3   Regular expressions.

Table 10.3 shows an overview of the most important wildcards. Regular expressions are used frequently under UNIX (for example in the editor, at the shell prompt, or as parameters for grep). An intelligent use of regular expression substantially simplifies many tasks. On the other hand, regular expressions can become quite complicated and thus rather hard to follow.

10.4 Starting commands automatically

It is often required that CPU-intensive programs or programs that need exclusive access to the computer should be executed at a later point in time, for example, at night. This can be achieved by means of the at command. If specific programs are regularly to be started at a given time, we can use the crontab command, which manages the control tables for cron.

10.4.1 Executing commands at a later time (at)

The at command can be used to execute a command once at a specified time, for example, if you want to execute a program such as a complex database elaboration at a time when the computer is not too loaded. You could also use the batch command, which is particularly suitable for this purpose, because it executes the specified commands only if the system load has sunk below a specified level. The example in Listing 10.29 shows how to delete the file /etc/nologin.ttyS1 at 20:00.

The exact starting time of the at command depends on how frequently the atrun command is executed. On my system, for example, this command is only called every five minutes (see Section 10.4.3).

The at command expects the commands to be executed from the standard input. After entering the command, Ctrl+d must be pressed as end mark. This inserts the task into the job queue. To verify whether the at command has correctly stored the command, you can list the queue by means of the atq command (see Listing 10.30).

Date and time specify when the task is to be executed, and the owner of the task and an ID number are listed as well. If a job is to be canceled, it can be removed from the job queue by means of the atrm command (see Listing 10.31).

```
(Linux):~# at 20:00
> rm -f /etc/nologin.ttyS1
> Ctrl-D
Job c00c95ff4.00 will be executed using /bin/sh
```

Listing 10.29   Starting a program with at.

```
(Linux):~# atq
Date                    Owner    Queue    Job#
20:00:00 02/03/95       root     c        c00c95ff4.00
```

Listing 10.30   Output of the atq command.

```
(Linux):~# atrm c00c95ff4.00
```

Listing 10.31   Removing an at job with atrm.

The at command accepts time specifications in different formats. The time of day can be indicated as HH:MM or HHMM. Other legal values are midnight, noon, and teatime (16:00).

Besides the time of day, you can also specify the date on which at is to start the command. The date can be specified as DD.MM.YY or MM/DD/YY. Time specifications can also be indicated relative to the current time of day or the current date. If, for example, a command is to be started in two hours time, you can write this as +2 hours. With +2 days, you can start a command in two days time.

The at command usually reads the commands to be executed from the standard input. However, you can also specify a file (shell script) by setting the option -f file. If the command to be executed writes to the standard output or to the standard error output, this output is sent to the user who triggered the at command via UNIX mail.

The system administrator can control the use of the at command by means of the two files /etc/at.allow and /etc/at.deny. If the file /etc/at.allow exists, only the users who are listed in this file may execute the at command. If this file does not exist, but the file /etc/at.deny is present, *all* users may use the at command except those listed in /etc/at.deny. If neither file exists, only the system administrator (root) is allowed to use the at command.

10.4.2 Simulating batch processing with batch

The at program executes the given command at the specified time in practically all circumstances. If the computer's system load at that time is extremely high, it would sometimes be better to prevent execution of the process or to move it to a different time. The `batch` command schedules a program in the same way as `at`, but actually executes it only if the computer's load allows it. Otherwise, the handling is the same as the `at` command.

10.4.3 Executing commands periodically (`crontab`)

The `at` command executes a command only once. If given commands are to be executed regularly at specific times, they can be entered in the `crontab` table. This is done by using the homonymous command `crontab`. With `crontab`, periodically executed routine tasks can be carried out automatically. Examples of such tasks are generation of index files, monitoring the system on the basis of various criteria, or deletion of log files.

The `crontab` tables created with the `crontab` command are stored in the directory `/var/cron/tabs`. These files must not be modified directly, but should be edited by means of the `crontab` command with the option `-e`. This starts the editor specified in the environment variable `EDITOR` with the current `crontab`. The commands included in these files are periodically executed by the `crond` daemon.

Displaying a `crontab`

An existing `crontab` can be displayed by means of the `crontab` command with the option `-l`. The `crontab` shown in Listing 10.32 executes the `atrun` command every five minutes (see Section 10.4.1). In addition, the file `/etc/nologin.ttyS1` is deleted every day at 22:00 and recreated at 7:06.[1]

```
(Linux):~# crontab -l
# Run the 'atrun' program every 5 minutes
# This runs anything that is due to run from 'at'.
# See man 'at' or 'atrun'.
0,5,10,15,20,25,30,35,40,45,50,55 * * *    /usr/lib/atrun
00 22 * * * rm -f /etc/nologin.ttyS1
06 07 * * * touch /etc/nologin.ttyS1
# generate database for locate
0 04,12 * * * updatedb
```

Listing 10.32   Example of a `crontab` file for `root`.

During execution of the program, the environment variables `LOGNAME` and `HOME` are automatically set to the values of the file `/etc/passwd`, whereas the variable `SHELL` is always set to `/bin/sh`. The login scripts or other initializations of the shell are not processed.

Further variables can be set by means of the entry *variable* = *value* in the `crontab` table. The variable `MAILTO` is used directly by `cron` to determine the mail

---

[1] This file is evaluated by `mgetty`.

recipient of the program output. If no MAILTO is specified, the owner of the crontab is used; if the entry consists of the empty string, no mail is sent.

Structure of the crontab

All lines starting with the hash sign (#) are comment lines and are ignored by the cron daemon (crond). The first five words, separated by spaces, determine when the command is to be executed. The first number indicates the minutes, followed by the hours, followed by day, month, and finally the day of the week. An asterisk (*) means that the command is to be executed at any time. The time specifications are finally followed by the command to be executed. It is also possible to specify ranges, for example 20-23. If a program is to be executed every ten minutes, the crontab could contain one of the entries shown in Listing 10.33.

```
# The following command is started every ten minutes
# This entry is standard on System V computers
0,10,20,30,40,50 * * * * touch /tmp/cron_is_running
# Start every ten minutes, Vixie Cron extension
0-59/10 * * * * touch /tmp/cron_is_running.2
# And still somewhat simpler
*/10 * * * * touch /tmp/cron_is_running.3
```

Listing 10.33   Executing commands every ten minutes.

Some cron versions require an empty line at the end of the file, but do not support comments. If in doubt, you will find further information under /var/log/cron or the system log category daemon.

The use of the cron command can be controlled by means of the files /etc/cron.allow and /etc/cron.deny. If a file /etc/cron.allow exists, only the users who are listed in this file may use this tool. If the file /etc/cron.deny exists, those users listed in the file are excluded from using the cron command. If neither of the files exists, either every user or only root can use this tool, depending on the implementation of the cron daemon.

Further examples

In Listing 10.34, a program is to be started at 6:00 in the morning and at 22:00 in the evening, but only on working days (Monday to Friday). The same program can obviously be used again in further entries. Thus, you can easily define different patterns for working days and weekends.

As shown in Listing 10.35, a program is to be started on the 1st of every month at 02:00; obviously no restriction on special days of the week or public holidays is possible. If you specify a day of the week, for example Sunday, the program is executed *additionally* on each Sunday. There is no intuitive way of having jobs executed on the last day of every month.

```
0 6,22 * * 1-5 /usr/lib/uucp/uucico -r1 -spertron
```

Listing 10.34   Execution twice a day from Monday to Friday.

```
0 2 1 * * clean_logs
```

Listing 10.35   Monthly execution of a cron job.

To execute a program every Sunday, you can specify the entry shown in Listing 10.36. You can use either numbers or fully spelled out names to represent months and days of the week. cron recognizes the three-character abbreviations of the English names of months and days. If you use this notation, enumerations are no longer allowed.

```
0 1 * * sun clean_up
```

Listing 10.36   Executing a job once a week.

More information on cron and its possibilities can be found in the man page. LINUX generally uses the highly commendable Vixie cron by Paul Vixie which has several extensions with respect to the standard UNIX cron.

10.5 The AWK programming language

The awk command can be used to process structured files and output them, for example, as formatted tables. The name awk is composed of the initials of the inventors of this language: Alfred V. Aho, Peter J. Weinberger, and Brian W. Kernighan. The awk command provides an interpreter language which has some superficial similarities with the C programming language, although it is really completely different.

An awk program consists of function blocks that are, as in C, enclosed in curly brackets. Each function block can be assigned a condition as to when (and for which lines) this function is to be executed. This condition is a so-called regular expression. The function block is executed for each line that satisfies this condition. The function is passed the complete input line to be processed as parameter $0.

If no condition is specified, the instructions in the function block are executed for each line. If several conditions are satisfied, the function blocks of all matching conditions are executed.

There are two special conditions: BEGIN and END. The function block specified after BEGIN is executed before the first line of the input file is read. This is the place for initialization of variables and other preparations.

The instructions specified after the END condition are executed after having read the last line of the input file. This is the place where, for example, footers or calculated sums are output or other concluding operations are carried out.

10.5.1 A first sample program in awk

The whole description sounds more complicated than the process actually is. For a better understanding, Listing 10.37 shows a brief example. For all lines of the file /etc/services that contain the string ftp, the specified function block is executed, simply displaying the entire current line.

The example has the same result as described with the grep command. However, awk is able to process this line further. If, for example, only the service names are to be displayed and not the complete line, you simply replace $0 with $1 in the example. This causes only the first word of the line to be output.

```
(Linux):~$ awk '/ftp/ { print $0; }' /etc/services
ftp             21/tcp
tftp            69/udp
sftp            115/tcp
```

Listing 10.37 A first awk example.

You might think of the awk program as being enclosed in a loop that is cycled once for each line of input. In many cases, an awk program can even do without bothering about mundane things like opening and closing files or recognizing end-of-file codes.

10.5.2 Separating fields

awk splits the input line into words. These words can be accessed via the parameters $1, $2, $3, and so on. The separators used as boundaries between the words are stored in the variable FS (Field Separator). By default, words are separated by spaces, but this can easily be changed by the programmer.

The separator can be changed either in the special BEGIN function or via the command line parameter -F*character*. The example in Listing 10.38 outputs only the first word of the corresponding line. The words are now separated from each other by means of a slash (/). Another legal way of describing separators is by means of regular expressions. This makes awk easily adaptable to many different input formats.

You can also change the field separator without using the command line option -F. In this case, you use a BEGIN function in which the variable FS is set. The corresponding example can be found in Listing 10.39.

For more substantial awk programs, the awk command line is not the appropriate place because, on the one hand, there is no reasonable editor (such as Emacs in awk mode) and, on the other hand, the program may be no longer available at a later stage. Alternatively, an awk program can be executed either by means of awk -f *file* or,

```
(Linux):~$ awk -F'/' '/ftp/ { print $1; }' /etc/services
ftp             21
tftp            69
sftp            115
```

Listing 10.38   A second awk example.

```
(Linux):~$ awk 'BEGIN { FS="/" } /ftp/{ print $1 }' /etc/services
ftp             21
tftp            69
sftp            115
```

Listing 10.39   A third awk example.

if the #! mechanism is used and the script is readable and executable, directly. The example of Listing 10.39 could thus be rewritten as shown in Listing 10.40. For larger programs, this variation is also much clearer.

```
#!/usr/bin/awk -f
BEGIN {
    FS="/";
}
/ftp/ {
    print $1;
}
```

Listing 10.40   An awk script.

If you use Emacs as an editor for awk scripts, you will be assisted by the awk mode. Function blocks are automatically indented and comments that start with a hash sign (#) and end with an end-of-line are recognized. This mode is a slightly modified C mode, since awk and C are very similar. If you use the font lock package, comments, character strings, and keywords are also highlighted in different colors.

10.5.3 Internal variables

Besides FS and $n, awk recognizes additional internal variables with special meaning. These variables can be accessed read-only. Table 10.4 lists the most important variables with their meaning. The script in Listing 10.41 outputs the number of lines of the file /etc/services, using the internal variable NR.

With awk, you can simulate many other UNIX commands with little effort. This can be very useful if the system was damaged and only a few things can still be used. The info file for gawk contains some examples.

Variable	Meaning	Note
FS	Field separator	Default: space
NF	Number of fields	For output only
RS	Record separator	Default '\n'
NR	Number of records	For output only

Table 10.4 Internal awk variables.

```
(Linux):~$ awk 'END { print NR; }' /etc/services
184
```

Listing 10.41 Using the internal variable NR.

10.5.4 Output commands

Text can be output by means of the awk commands print or printf. The printf command can output variables in a formatted form, the syntax of the formatting instructions corresponds to those of the C function of the same name. An example for the formatting of numbers and character strings can be found in Listing 10.44. A complete overview of available formatting options can be found in the info pages and the man page for gawk.

10.5.5 Arithmetic operations

The awk programming language can handle most of the arithmetic operations known from C, such as +, -, *, ++, and +=. This allows you to perform even complicated calculations. awk does not have typed variables; thus you can use any variable for a calculation as long as it contains a number.

As in C, several conditions can be joined (|| for OR, && for AND, and ! for NOT). Together with the available control structures (if, while, do, and for), awk is a complete programming language.

awk always has a competitive advantage when texts are to be processed in a relatively simple way and the development has to be completed quickly. The disadvantage is the relatively low execution speed.

10.5.6 Internal functions

awk also has its built-in functions, both for arithmetic operations such as exp, sqrt and so on, and for operations on character strings such as substr or index. An extensive description of all internal functions, together with examples, can be found in the info documentation on GNU awk or in the man page gawk(1).

If you want to have an overview of the internal functions, just read through the info pages of gawk. You will obviously not be able to memorize them all, but you will get a feeling for which functions exist and how these are applied.

10.5.7 Associative arrays

In addition, awk implements so-called *associative arrays*. This means that the arrays do not use a numeric index, but an arbitrary value (no matter whether number or string). This makes it possible to program even complex search processes. Listing 10.42 shows an example of the use of associative arrays. Do not be alarmed: this example does use several functions that we have not yet discussed at all.

```
#!/usr/bin/awk -f
# Checking the hard disk for sufficient free space
# df -k -P | $0

BEGIN {
  FS = "[ \t]*";              # spaces or tabs
  while ( (getline < "/etc/freespace.conf") > 0 ) {
    if ( ($1 != "#") && ($2 != "")) {
      min_free[$1] = $2; # no comment
    }
  }
}


{
  fs=$1; size=$2; used=$3; free=$4; pct_used=$5; mount=$6;
  if ( min_free[mount] != "" ) {
    if ( free <= min_free[mount] )
      printf("%s has %d Kbytes free, wanted was %d Kbytes\n",
             mount, free, min_free[mount]);
  }
}
```

Listing 10.42   Associative arrays in awk.

In the BEGIN section, the configuration file /etc/freespace.conf is read and the data is stored in the internal array min_free. The name of a file system is used as an index – thus, even character strings can be used as indices in awk. Reading is carried out by means of the getline command; the end of the file is recognized by means of a while loop.

In the awk script, the output of the df -k -P command is expected as standard input. For each file system, a check is made with the aid of the associative array, whether a minimum free space was specified and if so, it is verified correspondingly.

In a program, you can always execute a loop over all elements of an array, no matter whether a numeric index is used or not. For error detection, I begin by using the END part shown in Listing 10.43.

```
END {
  for ( i in min_free )
    printf("FS %-30s min_free %d\n", i, min_free[i]);
}
```

Listing 10.43   A loop over an associative array.

10.5.8 A sensible application of awk

To conclude, here is a *sensible* application of awk which exemplifies for which purposes awk is suited best. We have used the SQL command 'unload' to retrieve data
from a database. As a field separator, the hash sign (#) was used. The data file has the
following contents:

```
134076#Skywalker#Luke#11256.01#
334521#Solo#Han#12.56#
422110#Vader#Darth#1198.00#
```

For a formatted output of the data, an awk script (Listing 10.44) is to be used.
In addition, the turnaround of the customers is to be summed up and output as well.
The output of the script can be found in Listing 10.45.

```
#!/usr/bin/awk -f
BEGIN {
FS="#";
  sum=0;
  print( "Cust.No.  Name            First Name       Turnaround");
  print( "--------  --------------- ---------------- ----------");
}
{
  printf( "%d  %-15s  %-15s  %8.2f\n", $1, $2, $3, $4);
  sum+=$4;
}
END {
  print( "--------  --------------- ---------------- ----------");
  printf("                                          Total:       %9.2f\n",sum);
  print( "                                                       ==========");
}
```

Listing 10.44   A last awk example.

Are you now in the mood for awk? Then just try it out. And do not forget that
GNU awk includes some (useful) extensions in comparison to standard awk. Besides
GNU awk, there is a series of other awk versions; thus, on many commercial UNIX
systems, you will find oawk (the historical program) and nawk (the corresponding new
version).

```
Cust.No.   Name              First Name            Turnaround
--------   ---------------   -------------------   --------
134076     Skywalker         Luke                  11256.01
334521     Solo              Han                      12.56
422110     Vader             Darth                  1198.00
--------   ---------------   -------------------   --------
                                           Total:  12466.57
                                                   ========
```

Listing 10.45   Output of the example of Listing 10.44.

10.6 Processing text files with sed

sed stands for 'stream editor.' sed is a genuine editor; however, as opposed to 'normal' editors such as emacs, sed is not interactive, but command-oriented. That is, a command file or the command line are used to give sed the editing commands which are then executed in the input file or in the standard input.

Listing 10.46 shows a brief sample application of sed. The ps command displays the currently running programs of the user. The first line normally consists of a heading which interferes with automatic processing.[2] This line is not to be displayed. Thus, the output of the ps command is redirected via a pipe to the sed editor. The sed command 1d means that the first line is to be deleted.

```
(Linux):~$ ps | sed '1d'
   95 p 1 SW    0:04 (bash)
11109 p 6 S     0:06 -bash
11110 p 5 SW    0:05 (bash)
11111 p b SW    0:04 (bash)
11811 p 5 S     2:02 emacs
12716 p 6 R     0:00 ps
12717 p 6 R     0:00 sed 1d
```

Listing 10.46   A simple example of sed.

All sed commands consist of only one letter. Individual commands are separated by an end-of-line in the command file or by a semicolon. Each command can be associated to an address or an address range. The address can be specified by means of line numbers – 1 in the above example – or by means of a search pattern (regular expression). The command is then executed for each line that matches the search criterion. The address specification is directly followed by the command, in the above example, the 'd' (delete) command. Some commands expect parameters, which are specified directly after the command in question.

---

[2] ps has an option (-h) for suppressing this line, but we will disregard it for the purpose of this example.

sed processes the input line by line. If a command is to be executed for a given line number, this number is specified in front of the command. It is also possible to specify a range of lines, with the first and the last line numbers of the range separated by a comma. Examples for the use of line numbers are shown in Listing 10.47. The output of the commands is not printed here for reasons of space – we suggest that you just try them out.

```
(Linux):~> head /etc/services | sed -e '1d'
(Linux):~> head /etc/services | sed -e '1,5d'
(Linux):~> head /etc/services | sed -e '$d'
```

Listing 10.47 Examples for the use of line numbers.

The first example in Listing 10.47 deletes the first line of the input, as explained above. The second command deletes lines 1 to 5 from the input, and the next example deletes the last line. As in vi, the dollar sign is a placeholder for the last line.

If the line number for which a sed command is to be executed is not known, a regular expression can be used as a search pattern. Here, you can also specify an address range by indicating two regular expressions separated by a comma. It is obviously possible to indicate the beginning with a line number and the end with a regular expression and vice versa. Listing 10.48 shows some examples for the use of search patterns in sed; the results are again not shown.

```
(Linux):~> head /etc/services | sed -e '/^#/d'
(Linux):~> head /etc/services | sed -e '/tcp/d'
(Linux):~> head /etc/services | sed -e '/[A-Z]/d'
(Linux):~> head /etc/services | sed -e '/tcpmux/,/ftp/d'
```

Listing 10.48 Search patterns in sed.

The first call in Listing 10.48 deletes all lines that contain a hash sign (#) in the first column from the input file. The second example deletes all lines that contain the string 'tcp', and the third example deletes all lines that contain at least one upper case letter. The last example deletes a block of lines from the input file whose first line contains the character string 'tcpmux', and whose last line contains 'ftp'.

Besides the 'd' (delete) command for deleting lines, there are further commands which will now be explained one by one. As described above, all these commands must be preceded by an address (range) for which the commands are to be executed. Only the most important commands are described; a complete overview can be found in the man page.

Additional information together with a practice-oriented introduction to awk and sed can be found in Dougherty (1990), which is a standard book on this subject and well worth reading.

- a\
  text (append)
  This command appends the text *text* to the specified address.
- d (delete)
  The complete line at the specified address is deleted.
- i\
  text (insert)
  The text *text* is inserted in front of the specified address.
- q (quit)
  When reaching the specified address, sed is terminated.
- r *file name* (read file)
  The contents of the file *file* is appended after the specified address.
- s/*regex*/*replacement*/*flags* (search and replace)
  This command corresponds to the 'search and replace' function of most text editors. The piece of text that matches the search pattern *regex* is replaced with the character string specified in *replacement*. This command is probably the most widely used sed command. In combination with the find command, the same changes can be made to several files.
  An example: you wish to change the host name, but you do not know in which files it occurs. Thus, you simply let sed change the old host name (spock) into the new host name (kirk) in all files found by find:

  ```
  (Linux):~$ find / -type f -exec sed 's/spock/kirk/g' {} \;
  ```

  The parameter *flags* can be used to specify whether this change is to be made globally (flag 'g') or at most zero to nine times. Flag 1, for example, only changes the first occurrence of *regex* into *replacement*.
- y/*char1*/*char2*/ (yank)
  All characters occurring in *char1* are replaced with the characters in *char2*. This allows you to transform characters in exactly the same way as with the tr command (see Section 10.2.2). One could think, for example, of a foreign language special character filter (umlauts, accents) from DOS character sets to ISO-Latin-1 or vice versa.

sed is often used to carry out changes in configuration files (for example when new software is installed) automatically. The configure scripts of the GNU project use sed to generate the system-dependent makefiles out of generic input files.

A further example for the use of sed is the dtree program. It shows a graphical representation of the file system hierarchy. The program, which is taken from the LINUX Journal September 1996, is shown in Listing 10.49.

At first sight, the way the program runs looks fairly confusing, but it is in fact quite easy at a closer look. In the first step, the name of the uppermost directory of the list is output. The second command searches the hard disk for directories that lie below the directory specified as a parameter. This list is sorted by means of sort and then processed by means of a series of sed commands.

```
#!/bin/sh
( cd ${1-.} ; pwd )
find ${1-.} -type d -print \
 | sort -f \
 | sed -e "s,^${1-.},," \
       -e "/^$/d" \
       -e "s,[^/]*/\([^/]*\)$,\'-----\1," \
       -e "s,[^/]*/,|       ,g"
```

Listing 10.49   The dtree program as an application of sed.

The first sed command deletes the (common) start path from all lines. This is constant in the whole list and, since it is already output, it is of no further interest. The second sed command (/^$/d) deletes all empty lines. The next two commands prepare the graphical representation: first, a horizontal line is generated for each new subdirectory; this is then complemented by a vertical line.

This program is not perfect, because the graphical representation is not always correct, but it does provide a good overview of the hierarchical directory structure.

10.7 Further useful utilities

The UNIX tool box is far from being exhausted. Many more programs can make life easier for UNIX users and administrators. These include further programming and script languages, such as perl (Practical Extraction and Report Language), python, or tcl (Tool Command Language), and utilities. A complete list or even a reference would exceed the framework of this book; we therefore limit ourselves to a brief presentation of only a few programs. The reference section gives some more hints about UNIX script languages and the corresponding literature.

Extensive descriptions of the options of the programs presented here can be found in the corresponding man pages. Here, the aim is to give an overview of the available programs so that you can choose the appropriate tool for a task. Subsequently, you can check the corresponding options and try them out (several times, if needed), for example, in a pipe, until you have reached the desired result.

The most important utilities can be found in the fileutils, sh-utils, and textutils packages of the GNU project. If you know that there is a program that might be suited to your task, you can get the appropriate options from the documentation. For this reason, you should have at least seen a rough outline of the programs of these packages, for example, the one contained in the whatis database.

10.7.1 Sorting files

One of the most frequent tasks in electronic data processing is sorting data. Sorted data is often clearer to handle, and in any case data often has to be sorted as a prerequisite for further processing. The `sort` program implements sophisticated sorting algorithms.

The `sort` program can sort and merge files, and check whether a file is already sorted. Sorting can be carried out by specified fields or columns which can also contain numeric values. Furthermore, the sorting order can be reversed. This allows you to carry out practically all sorting tasks in shell scripts as well.

Normally, the `sort` program sorts by fields (keys) that are separated by an empty string between a non-space character and a white space. The separator can be changed by means of the option `-t`. The sorting keys are specified with the option `-k`. You may specify the field, and inside the field an offset in the form `-k field[.offset]`. Obviously, you can also sort backwards (option `-r`) or by numbers (option `-n`).

`sort` has two further modes: `-c` to check whether a file is already in the correct sorting order, and `-m` to merge several sorted files. If you want to process large files, the available space in the `/tmp` directory may not be sufficient. You may want to specify a different directory by means of the environment variable `TMPDIR` or the option `-T`.

Currently, no sorting process is implemented that sorts umlauts, accented letters, and other foreign language characters correctly. In a future version, the sorting order stored in the description of the locale will be considered.

10.7.2 Finding or deleting multiple occurrences of lines with uniq

With several tasks it is not sensible for identical lines (with regard to a determined field) to occur repeatedly. Multiple lines can be deleted by means of the `uniq` command. Sometimes, only those lines are of interest that occur repeatedly (option `-d` or `--repeated`) or only once (option `-u` or `--unique`) in a file. The number of repetitions is output if the option `-c` or `--count` is set.

Various other options (among others, `--skip-fields` and `--skip-chars`, together with `--check-chars`) can be used to define more precisely the part of the line selected for comparison. The default compares the whole line.

This command is often used in combination with `sort`. When several files are merged, it is often annoying if lines occur more than once. In these cases, the lines are sorted and then cleaned up by means of the `uniq` program.

10.7.3 Modifying environment variables

In scripts or in programs that are to be started periodically (via `cron`), it is often necessary to set special environment variables. This can be done by means of the `env` program, which allows you to change environment variables temporarily for one process and its child processes without problems.

Listing 10.50 shows a simple example. It uses the `printenv` program, which can output individual or all environment variables. With this program, you can quickly get an overview of how the environment variables are set.

```
(Linux):~> printenv LANG
de_DE.88591
(Linux):~> env LANG=C printenv LANG
C
```

Listing 10.50   An example of the use of env.

Another application of the env command is dynamic linking with a special library. This allows you to set the variable LD_LIBRARY_PATH for individual programs which, for example, need an older libc version than the rest of the system. The dynamic linker uses this variable to load the required libraries, provided the program is not setuid or setgid. If the program were equipped with special rights and every user could specify another search path for shared libraries, then arbitrary program code could be executed with extended privileges.

Yet another application is a temporary deactivation of the 'National Language Support' by setting the variable LC_ALL to the value 'C'. This is sensible or necessary when individual programs do not use or incorrectly use NLS, but the rest of the system is set up properly. With time and practice, however, these measures should become unnecessary in most cases.

10.7.4 Displaying the beginning of files

It is often sufficient to display the beginning of a file to find out about the contents or the topicality of the file. The use of programs such as more or less is completely unnecessary. The tiny program head fulfills exactly this purpose and by default displays only the first ten lines of a file. With the option -n *lines* or, shortly, -*lines*, an arbitrary number of lines can be displayed. With the option -c *bytes*, a certain number of bytes can be displayed.

10.7.5 Displaying the end of a file

The counterpart of head is tail, which displays the end of a file. BSD versions of tail are capable of outputting relatively small files in reverse line order. The GNU project uses the tac program for this purpose.

In analogy to head, the option -n *lines* displays the last *lines* lines. If the option +n *lines* is specified, display begins starting with this line. Thus, tail can also be used to split a file into several parts. Usually, however, you would employ the split program for this task.

Frequently, one needs to look at a log file which continues to grow. Programs such as more read the entire file, so that newly added messages are not immediately displayed. With the option -f, tail, instead, always shows the up-to-date end of the file.

10.7.6 Displaying character strings in binary files

The `strings` program allows you to filter character strings out of binary files. This can be useful, for example, to establish which files the program is going to access, or to detect 'hidden' functions. The GNU `strings` (from `binutils`), by default, does not read all parts of a program, so the switch –a should be set.

10.7.7 Analyzing binary programs

The LINUX tool `strace`[3] is used to 'debug' compiled programs. All system calls are listed too. Thus, for example, you can find out which files are accessed by the program. By means of the command line parameter –o *filename*, the output of `strace` can be written to the specified file. Furthermore, it is possible to restrict the system calls to be listed by setting the option –etrace=*syscall*.

10.7.8 Displaying files in different formats

Sometimes it is necessary to analyze a file in more detail. In many cases, programs such as `strings` achieve good results, but sometimes you need an accurate view of the individual characters contained in the file. In such cases, you can employ the od program. By default, od displays the data in octal representation, but you may choose a different one. Listing 10.51 shows some simple examples of formatting output with od.

```
(Linux):~> echo 'Hello World' | od
0000000 044145 066154 067440 053557 071154 062012
0000013
(Linux):~> echo 'Hello World' | od -x
0000000 4865 6c6c 6f20 576f 726c 640a
0000013
(Linux):~> echo 'Hello World' | od -a
0000000   H   e   l   l   o   sp   W   o   r   l   d   nl
0000013
```

Listing 10.51   The program od.

10.8 The shell as a connecting link between various programs

Shells are not only a user interface, but are also relatively powerful programming languages. Every UNIX user has a login shell which is automatically started at login.

---

[3] Under Solaris, a similar program is called `truss`.

In principle, this is a normal program; often, for example, a business or another commercial package is automatically started at this point. For interactive use of a UNIX system, usually one of the most widely used shells is started, such as the Bourne or the Korn shell, or the C shell, or any of their descendants.

The shell takes over the interaction with the user and starts the required programs. Furthermore, all shells can also be used as programming languages – in the first place, to write initialization files, but also for further shell scripts.

Control structures, such as branches and loops, are implemented inside the shell itself. For nearly all other functions, the common UNIX programs are used. For reasons of performance, however, many functions, such as `echo` or `pwd`, are also implemented internally. Since these functions are described by the POSIX standard, internal and external commands are as a rule compatible with each other.

The following section introduces some functions for programming with the `bash` which are, however, also very useful for interactive control. Please note that often other UNIX systems only have an original `sh`, and therefore some extensions of the `bash` cannot be used on all systems.

Practically all modern UNIX systems support the `#!` mechanism for starting shell scripts. After this character sequence, the complete path to the interpreter must be specified. This restricts the choice of interpreter for scripts that are to run unchanged on different systems. Often the only remaining shells are the `/bin/sh` or the `/bin/csh`, where the `csh` should be avoided as a script language. The reasons for this position can be found in the text 'Why csh is considered harmful' by Tom Christiansen (`tchrist@mox.perl.com`). This text is periodically posted, for example, in the `comp.unix.shell` newsgroup, and can be found in the FAQ archive on `rtfm.mit.edu`.

On practically all modern UNIX systems, the Korn shell `ksh` is also available. The script language is compatible with that of the `sh`, under LINUX; however, the `bash` and the `tcsh`, an extended and improved version of the C shell, are employed far more widely.

For interactive use, interactive functions such as aliases, history, and a good command line editor are important. In shell scripts, these functions play practically no role. More about the choice of a login shell can be found in Section 4.6. In the following paragraphs, we deal with the use of the `bash` as a script language.

10.8.1 Input and output redirection and pipes

Functions for input and output redirection are often used both in the command line and in scripts, exploiting the fact that nearly all UNIX programs read from and write to the standard output. It is important that the programs stick to an essential rule: they must not generate additional output (for example, headings or suggestions). The shell provides several methods of intervention at this point.

The (standard) output of a program can immediately be used as input for the next program. This is indicated by means of a vertical bar (`|`) used to separate the commands. In Listing 10.52, the headline is removed from the output of `ps`. For this purpose, the ps command also has the option −h, so in practice tail would probably not be employed.

```
(Linux):~$ ps | tail −n +2
    143 v02 S      0:06 −tcsh
    144 v03 S      0:13 −tcsh
    145 v04 S      0:08 (tcsh)
    153 v04 S      4:47 emacs master.tex
    219 v03 R      0:00 ps
    220 v03 S      0:00 tail −n +2
```

Listing 10.52   Data transfer using a pipe.

Often you must keep the output of a command, for example, to include it in a text file. This function too is implemented in the shell by means of the greater than sign (>). If you specify /dev/null as file name, the output is ignored. Listing 10.53 shows an example for the use of a pipe and successive output redirection.

```
(Linux):~$ ps | tail −n +2 > ps.out
```

Listing 10.53   Using pipe and output redirection.

If you do not take any special measures, you can overwrite any file to which you have write access. But you do back up your data, don't you? Inside shell scripts, overwriting without prompt for confirmation is usually sensible; in interactive use, you can prevent accidental overwriting with the shell-option noclobber.

In the bash (and the sh and ksh), the standard error output, to which only error messages are written, can be handled separately, by using the character sequence 2> instead of the greater than sign (>). If you want to unify both output channels, you first redirect the standard output with >. Subsequently, you redirect the error output with 2>&1 to this channel. The character sequence &1 stands for the file descriptor of the standard output, &2 is the standard error output, and &0 the standard input. Here, the csh is not as flexible as the sh; this is one of the reasons why one should avoid writing csh scripts.

Another function is reading from a file instead of the standard input. This is indicated by the less than sign (<). Many programs use the standard input and the standard output instead of a file if a minus sign (−) is specified as file name. This is only required and sensible for programs which do not read from the standard input or write to the standard output by default. An example of such a program is tar, which uses a tape if no file name is specified.

In the example in Listing 10.54, the file .emacs is sent as an email to the user root. As Subject:, the text 'my .emacs file' is used.

In shell scripts, people often do not create a file if it is to be used as input in the next step. Instead, the text is directly incorporated in the script (as a *here document*).

```
(Linux):~$ mail -s 'my .emacs file' root < .emacs
```

Listing 10.54   Input redirection in the shell.

The character << followed by an arbitrary character string instructs the shell to use the text up to the next occurrence of this character sequence as the standard input. Shell variables are expanded, other special characters are not.

```
cat << EOF
The is the text to be output.
It can be of (almost) arbitrary length.
The script was started by user '$USER'.
EOF
```

Listing 10.55   An example of a 'here' document.

10.8.2 Expanding special characters

The shell uses a series of characters that have a special meaning in the input or in shell scripts. The fact is that the shell considers nearly everything as a string, which also applies to commands entered by the user and to shell scripts. Any of these strings is first searched for special characters, which are processed before the shell subsequently executes the required command.

The process of how the commands to be executed are generated from the input, and when specific substitutions are to be made is standardized. The POSIX standard describes the process that has developed over time together with the sh. Thus, some decisions have been established although now these would no longer be made in the same way.

File name expansion

When entering a command, you can either enter the file name(s) manually or you can use the file name expansion mechanism of the shell. Quite often one wants to process a group of files together, and this group is often identified by a common element in the file names. This is where you would normally use the shell's *file name expansion*.

Various special characters (wildcards) can be used for this functionality. First of all, an asterisk (*) stands for an arbitrary number of characters in a file name. As opposed to DOS, * thus stands for (nearly) all files, except those whose names begin with a dot (.). The question mark (?) stands for exactly one character in a file name. As opposed to DOS, the asterisk can appear at any position in the pattern, not just at the end. Except for the specific use mentioned above, the dot (.) has no special meaning under UNIX.

These expansions are carried out by the shell. Thus, when you enter ls *.c at the shell prompt, the ls command already contains a list of C files as parameter. In cases of emergency, for example, if no ls is present on an emergency floppy, you can still obtain a list of the files in the current directory by using the internal shell command echo *. This expansion by the shell is the reason why it is relatively difficult to rename a group of files with a single command. The best solution is to use the mmv tool.

If you want to prevent expansion, you can either deactivate each special character by means of a backslash (\), or you can enclose the character string in simple quotes. Otherwise, the program would contain expanded special shell characters as parameters and would not give the required result. If you are not sure whether a program is really being passed the correct parameters, you can use the echo command to find out.

In file name expansion, you can also specify sets of characters, for example with [A-Z]. These expansions are not regular expressions, but they are quite similar. If the expression is enclosed in double quotes, the shell variables are expanded, but not the special characters such as the asterisk.

File names under UNIX can contain nearly any character. You may even use spaces or wildcards, although this is not recommended. You should always take special care when using these characters, otherwise strange things may happen if the shell inadvertently expands them.

If you want to pass a file name that contains a space as a parameter, you must enclose this file name in quotes. Proper shells, such as the bash, do this automatically when expanding file names. The POSIX standard specifies that file names on POSIX compatible systems should consist of the letters from a to z, the corresponding upper case letters, the digits and some special characters such as the hyphen and underscore – foreign language characters must be handled with care in some programs or other UNIX systems.

Let us look at the problem of trying to create an expression that includes all files in a directory, but not the directories . and .. We have to think of how we would address a file whose name contains a space. A dangerous test for UNIX newcomers is to create and delete the file -rf *. Newcomers often forget to enclose the special characters in quotes and delete the entire directory, including all subdirectories. As a last consideration, although it has nothing to do with file name expansion, try deleting the file -i.

And now the solution to the above questions. A first attempt could be, for example, .* *, but this also involves the directories . and .. The second character of file names that start with a dot must be a non-dot character. Thus, the second attempt is .[^.]* * which, however, does not expand file names starting with two dots. Therefore, you need the additional search pattern ..?*. The full expression is therefore * .[^.]* ..?*, which also ensures that no file name is output twice.

A file whose name contains a space can be processed by the shell by enclosing the name in single or double quotes. Alternatively, you can deactivate the space by means of a backslash, but this quickly becomes messy. As stated above, during file name expansion, the `bash` automatically encloses file names containing a space in quotes.

In the third task, the `rm` program interprets the name `-i` as an option. The simplest way is the specification of a relative path to the file, such as `rm ./-i`. Alternatively, you can use the character sequence `--` to separate options and parameters. The resulting command is `rm -- -i`.

Shell variables

Besides the expansion of file names, the shell uses variables and parameters which are both marked by a dollar sign (`$`). Variables are identified by their names (for example `$PATH`), whereas parameters of shell scripts or shell functions are identified through their position in the input line (for example `$1` for the first parameter). Furthermore, there is a series of special variables; an overview can be found in Table 10.5.

In the man page for `bash`, you will find additional information for dealing with variables in shell programming. Section 10.8.4 contains further information on how variables are processed by the shell.

Variable	Meaning
`$*`	All parameters
`$@`	All parameters as individual words
`$#`	Number of parameters
`$?`	Status (return value) of the last command
`$$`	Process ID of the current shell, for example for temporary files
`$!`	Process ID of the last background process
`$0`	Name of the shell or of the shell script
`$1-$9`	First to ninth parameter,
	all further parameters can only be accessed after `shift`

Table 10.5 Special shell variables.

The meaning of the individual variables in Table 10.5 is quite clear, except for the difference between `$*` and `$@`. If you use `$*`, this corresponds more or less to a chain of parameters separated by spaces. If one of the parameters is, for example, `"I am here"`, this parameter is expanded into three words. If the shell variable `IFS` is set, the first character of this value is used as the separator.

The variable `$@`, in contrast, expands to `"$1" "$2" ...`, that is, the above example only expands into a parameter for the next call. The corresponding example can be found in Listing 10.56. Because of the double quotes, exactly one parameter is passed in the first call of the shell function `second`. The second call expands into two parameters, with the first parameter consisting of a character string with three words. The last call expands into a total of four individual words. If you write more substantial shell scripts with functions and nested calls, this information can be very useful.

```
(Linux):~$ second() { echo "$1 * $2 * $3 * $4" }
(Linux):~$ first() { second "$*"; second "$@"; second $* }
(Linux):~$ first "Here I am" "again"
Here I am again *  *  *
Here I am * again *  *
Here * I * am * again
(Linux):~$ IFS=/
(Linux):~$ first Here/I/am again
Here/I/am/again *  *  *
Here/I/am * again *  *
Here * I * am again *
```

Listing 10.56   Expansion of parameters and IFS.

Some variables are preset by the shell or by the system and can be used in login scripts or in personalized programs. A non-exhaustive overview can be found in Table 10.6. Special mention must be made of the variable IFS (Internal Field Separator). This variable determines, for example, if and where the shell separates parameters. The last call in Listing 10.56 shows a simple example.

Variable	Meaning
HOME	Home directory (sometimes also indicated as tilde (˜))
PATH	Search path for programs
USER	The user name
LOGNAME	The login name
SHELL	The shell used
PS1	Definition of the prompt
MAIL	The mailbox file
IFS	Internal field separator

Table 10.6   Preset shell variables.

There are further peculiarities in the expansion of variables. If the variables are to be followed immediately by additional text, the variable name must be enclosed in curly brackets (${PS1}text).

Brace expansion

The curly brackets ({}, 'braces') are another pair of special characters. The expansion (*brace expansion*) is carried out on a textual basis. With this function, it is relatively easy to generate a series of files with names that are described in that way. Listing 10.57 shows some examples for the use of this expansion.

```
(Linux):~$ echo file{1,2,3,4}
file1 file2 file3 file4
(Linux):~$ echo file{1,2,3}{a,b}
file1a file1b file2a file2b file3a file3b
```

Listing 10.57   Brace expansion.

Only after this expansion are other special characters, such as asterisks and question marks, or variables, expanded. For brace expansion, existing files play no role, in complete contrast to the wildcards * and ?.

Output of a command as a parameter

It is often useful or necessary to use the output of one program (for example of find) as the parameter of another program. For this *command substitution* there are two notations which are, in principle, equivalent to each other. Reversed simple quotes (backquotes, `) are usually easier to type, but have the disadvantage that they cannot be nested.

```
(Linux):~$ rm -f `find . -name \*.orig`
(Linux):~$ rm -f $(find . -name \*.orig)
```

Calculating in shell scripts

Although the shell essentially handles only strings, it is also possible to calculate in scripts or at the prompt. As with nearly all other functions, this too works at the cost of speed. If calculations reach a certain volume, you should think of employing a different script language, for example perl, or else you should implement a corresponding C program.

The first two examples in Listing 10.58 use the internal functions of the bash. Alternatively, the external command expr can be used, as in the third example. Here, the numbers and arithmetic operators must be separated by spaces. If you want to multiply, don't forget that the asterisk is a special character of the shell and must therefore be masked.

```
(Linux):~$ echo $[1+2]
3
(Linux):~$ echo $((1+2))
3
(Linux):~$ expr 1 + 2
3
```

Listing 10.58   Calculating in shell scripts.

10.8.3 **Control structures**

Besides management and expansion of variables, the shell can also be used for pro-gramming complex operations. The built-in control structures if, case, for, while, and until make the shell a powerful programming language.

The least evident control structure is the sequence. Individual commands are separated by semicolons (;). At the end of a line, no separator needs to be specified, since the shell usually interprets it as the end of the command. If you enclose a sequence of commands in round parentheses (), these commands are executed by a newly starting shell. Thus, changes to environment variables or directory changes have no effect on the shell or the script.

if **branch**

The if branch can be used to check a condition and deal with it accordingly. The condition is often, but not always, checked by means of the program test (or [). The decision criterion is the return value of the called program; therefore practically any UNIX program can be used as a condition, if the return value is set appropriately.

The test program can check several conditions and also connect them logi-cally. The most important options for test are listed in Table 10.7, and the complete function range of this program is documented in the man page.

Option	Meaning
-d *directory*	Does the directory exist?
-f *file*	Does the (regular) file exist?
-r *file*	Is the file readable?
-s *file*	Is the file bigger than zero bytes?
-w *file*	Is the file writable?
-x *file*	Is the file executable?
String1 = *String2*	The strings are equal
! *expr*	Logical NOT
expr1 -a *expr2*	Logical AND
expr1 -o *expr2*	Logical OR
expr1 OP *expr2*	Various numeric comparisons

Table 10.7   Excerpt of the options of test.

In many shell scripts, as in the example of Listing 10.59, the opening square bracket is used as an alias for test. In the file system, both programs are linked by means of hard links; the only thing you must remember is to close the opening bracket at some point.

Simple branches can also be realized by means of the control operators && and ||. Here, execution of the second command depends on the return value of the first command. The && operator only executes the following command if the first command was terminated with a return value of 0. The || operator starts the second

```
if [ -x /sbin/kerneld ] ; then
    echo -n "Starting kerneld "; /sbin/kerneld; echo "done"
else
    echo "/sbin/kerneld not found."
fi
```

Listing 10.59   Branching with if.

command only if the outcome of the first command is a non-0 return value. Some simple examples can be found in Listing 10.60; often these functions are used for error detection.

```
(Linux):~$ [ -f /etc/inittab ] && echo 'inittab exists'
inittab exists
(Linux):~$ false || echo 'is executed'
is executed
```

Listing 10.60   The operators && and ||.

Occasionally you need a program that always produces the same result. Under UNIX, you can use the programs true and false. If the task is permanently to output a given character string, the program yes can be very useful.

Multiple branching with case

As well as the simple branching based on the return values of programs, the shell also has *multiple branching* (case). This is based on *pattern matching*. A match between the specified variable and the search pattern is sought, and the corresponding case branch is cycled through. Listing 10.61 shows a simple example.

```
case "$1" in
    start|START)
        echo "start"
        ;;
    stop|STOP)
        echo "stop"
        ;;
    *)
        echo "Unknown parameter"
        exit 1
esac
```

Listing 10.61   Multiple branching with case.

If the character string start or START is specified as a parameter in Listing 10.61, the first branch is cycled through. If you want to specify as little as possible, you could indicate for example sta* as a pattern, so that effectively only three letters must be specified. The last pattern * is the branch that is cycled through if no matching search pattern could be found. In Listing 10.61, an error message is displayed and the program terminated.

Iterations and loops

Other constructions which a programming language must provide are iterations and loops. Here too, the bash offers a series of different possibilities.

Loops over enumerations   The for loop can be used to execute a sequence of commands for series of words. Listing 10.62 shows a simple example. First, the expression *.c is expanded into a list of the C files in the current directory. Subsequently, the commands in the loop's body are executed for each file.

```
for i in *.c ; do
    cp $i $i.old
done
```

Listing 10.62   The for loop in the bash.

The for loop iterates over words. A FOR loop like the one known from BASIC is not implemented in the shell. You can, however, first generate the required iteration values by means of an external program, such as seq, and then process them by means of a for loop.

Iteration until a condition is met   The shell commands until and while are used for the execution loops until (until) and while (while) the immediately following condition is satisfied (see Listing 10.63). Subsequently, the loop is terminated and execution is continued with the next command. The syntax of the commands is:

```
while list do list done
until list do list done
```

The loop can also be terminated by means of the break command. This can be useful if errors occur, or if the condition cannot be checked at the beginning or at the end of the loop, but can only be checked somewhere in the middle.

Shell functions

The bash offers *shell functions* which are, however, not supported by the standard shell sh. If, nevertheless, you wish to use functions, a very sensible thing to do for enhancing the clarity of shell scripts, you will lose the easy portability to other systems which do not (yet) have a POSIX-compatible shell like the Korn shell ksh.

```
(Linux):~$ cat example-of-while
#!/bin/sh
par=1
while [ $# -ne 0 ]; do
    echo "parameter $par: '$1'"
    par=' expr $par + 1'
    shift
done
(Linux):~$ ./example-of-while one two "three four"
parameter 1: 'one'
parameter 2: 'two'
parameter 3: 'three four'
```

Listing 10.63   A simple `while` loop.

Shell functions are also useful for interactive work. In an alias, you can only process the entire command line and not use individual parameters or append additional parameters. In such cases, a shell function is the solution, and you can even fit in additional functions, such as branches, easily and clearly. An example is shown in Listing 10.64.

```
(Linux):~$ alias abc='echo $* following
(Linux):~$ abc one two three
following one two three
(Linux):~$ unalias abc
(Linux):~$ function abc () { echo $* following }
(Linux):~$ abc one two three
one two three following
```

Listing 10.64   A simple shell function.

Variables used in shell functions are global, provided they have not been declared as local variables by means of the keyword `local`. The `bash` recognizes from the round parentheses that a shell function is being defined, so the keyword `function` does not need to be specified.

10.8.4 Variable substitution

Variables are expanded by means of the dollar sign (`$`). Instead of the variable name, the contents of the variable is substituted. The variable name can optionally be enclosed in curly brackets to mark the end of the name. However, the shell is also capable of influencing the expansion of variables.

- ${variable:-word}

  If the variable is not set or if it is empty, the value of the word is substituted. First, however, the shell carries out tilde expansion, variable expansion, command substitution, and arithmetic calculations.

- ${variable:=word}

  In addition to the functions indicated above, the variable *variable* is assigned the word after expansion of *word*.

- ${variable:?word}

  If the variable is not set or if it is empty, the text resulting from the expansion of the word is written to the standard error output. Otherwise, the value of the variable is substituted.

- ${variable:+word}

  If the variable is not set or if it is empty, nothing is substituted. Otherwise, the result of the expansion of *word* is substituted.

- ${#variable}

  The length of the variable contents in characters.

- ${variable#word}

  ${variable##word}

  The variable is expanded and, subsequently, the beginning of the text is removed if the pattern *word* matches it. In the # variation, the shortest matching string is removed, in the ## variation the longest.

- ${variable%word}

  ${variable%%word}

  In this case, it is the end of the string that is to be considered and not the beginning.

To conclude this chapter, Listing 10.65 shows some examples of variable expansion. Try to find out which command generates which output and why. Such knowledge can often be very useful if one needs to trace complex problems or errors in shell scripts or command lines.

```
(Linux):~$ export VAR="echo This is a test"
(Linux):~$ echo $VAR ; echo \$VAR ; echo "$VAR"
(Linux):~$ echo "\$VAR" ; echo '$VAR'
(Linux):~$ echo '\$VAR' ; echo `$VAR`
(Linux):~$ echo $VAR'abc' ; echo $VAR{a,b,c} ; echo $VARabc
(Linux):~$ echo ${VAR}abc ; echo ${VAR}{a,b,c}
```

Listing 10.65   Examples for quoting and variables in the shell.

10.8.5 Programming tips

Shell scripts are often used for automatic execution of repetitive tasks. Usually, you will at first carry out these tasks 'manually.' Later, when you know which commands are to be executed in which order (and under which conditions), you can begin creating a script.

When programming a script, proceed stepwise and periodically check the part created until then. This will enable you to track down errors such as incorrect or non-matching quotes in a relatively short time.

Break up program parts that are used several times into separate functions. Often there is a function that displays an error message and terminates the script (with a non-zero return value) and a function that explains the usage (syntax). Such functions should be stored in separate files and then 'sourced' (read) into the various shell scripts by means of `. file`.

Do not use fixed file names (for example, for temporary files), but use a unique variable. In this case, you can easily change the path and name of the file. For temporary files, you should in any case incorporate the process ID of the shell into the file name, so that several scripts can run in parallel.

If your script does not run as you expected, you can either execute the script with `sh -x script` or incorporate the option `-x` in the `#!` line. The shell then protocols every executed line, so you can get to the core of the problem relatively quickly. Alternatively, you can use the `set -x` command directly in the script.

This produces a relatively large output, and the execution of the script takes a fairly long time. It may therefore be sensible to write the output to a file by means of `script` or to store it in the shell mode of the Emacs editor. Once it is there, you can take your time to analyze the process and track the error.

10.9 Processes and jobs

Under UNIX, many programs of many different users can be active. Some of these are interactive programs used by logged-in users, programs started in the background by users that are no longer logged in, or system daemons for the provision of services. Both the UNIX system and the shell provide several functions for managing these processes.

10.9.1 Process management

Under UNIX, each process is uniquely identified by its *process number* (process ID, or PID). Process numbers are assigned by the kernel whenever a new process is generated by means of `fork()`. Usually, they are assigned in ascending order; however, on other systems, such as AIX, different procedures are sometimes used to generate the process numbers. Once the highest process number is reached, counting begins again from the start, obviously skipping numbers that have already been assigned. After a `fork()`, there are two nearly identical processes.

If after fork() another program is to be started, this is usually done by using a function from the exec family. These functions replace the currently running program with the one to be newly started, preserving the process number. Under UNIX, there is no C function to execute these two steps automatically.

The shell also has an exec command which replaces the shell with another program. If you get the error message no more processes when you call a command, you can at least use this command to start a program. After this, however, the shell is terminated, so you should use this command with great care. A useful tip would be, for example, to run top (table of processes), because you can use it to analyze the system and to terminate processes.

More recent LINUX and UNIX versions include the notion of *threads* as well as that of processes. Threads are execution paths inside a program. The use of threads is sensible, for example, with CPU-intensive tasks within an interactive program. Depending on the requirements, different system areas must be shared between the threads of a process; furthermore, synchronization by means of semaphores is needed. LINUX supports programming with threads via the clone(2) system call and the linuxthreads library.

Process status ps

The status and much more information on processes can be displayed by means of the ps (process status) command. Called without parameters, ps only shows the processes belonging to the user that are assigned to a terminal. The option -x also shows those processes that do not possess an associated terminal.

The processes of other users are displayed by specifying the option -a. With the option -w, the command line is shown in more detail. Frequently, commands like ps -aux | more[4] are used to gain an overview of the system and the running processes. The option -u displays the user, the starting time, and some other information.

Another important option is -w, which can be specified several times and displays more parameters of the command line. This is sensible if one needs to know with which parameters a specific background process has been started. On the other hand, every user can get to know the command lines of all running processes, which is often undesirable for security or data protection reasons.

The LINUX ps has an option -f which displays the process table as a tree. Alternatively, you can use the pstree command. In some cases, this kind of overview can be very useful.

Further options can be found in the man page for ps. Please note that UNIX systems derived from System V use different switches.

Process table

Together with some other programs, top (table of processes) is very popular. It displays the most active processes, so you can easily find out which currently active

---

[4] Under System V, the command is called ps -ef.

processes are occupying the CPU and the memory. Like `ps`, `top` uses the `proc` file system to display the process data.

Process tree

For each process, the kernel stores the ID of the process that generated it. This is also called the parent process. The newly started processes are called child processes. By means of the `pstree` command, which does not exist under other UNIX systems, you can gain an overview of the hierarchy in the process table.

Process management

A program that has a controlling terminal can usually be aborted with Ctrl-C (the interrupt character, see also `stty -a`). Many processes (for example network daemons) under UNIX have no associated terminal and cannot therefore be controlled with key combinations. It is obviously necessary to be able to address these processes as well; this is one of the applications of the concept of *signals*. If and how a program reacts to signals is implementation dependent and is usually documented in the man page. The default reaction to many signals is the termination of the program.

The `kill` program is not only used to abort programs, but also simply to send signals. Signals can be specified either numerically or symbolically. Table 10.8 shows the most important signals; all signals can be listed by means of `kill -l`.

Signal	Number	Meaning
SIGHUP	1	Hang-up, re-read configuration
SIGKILL	9	Unconditional program termination
SIGUSR1	10	User-defined signal
SIGUSR2	12	User-defined signal
SIGTERM	15	Normal program termination

Table 10.8   The most important signals.

It is often necessary to send a daemon a hang-up signal (`SIGHUP`); this causes many daemons to re-read their configuration file. You can find out the daemon's process number by means of `ps`. This process number must then be sent the signal with `kill -HUP PID`. Many daemons store their process ID in a file which can also be used directly to send the signal, for example with the command `kill -HUP `cat /var/run/syslog.pid``. The command `killall`, which is peculiar to LINUX, allows you to send a process a signal even if you only know the program name, for example `killall -HUP syslogd`.

In the shell and in shell programs, you can process signals by means of the `trap` command. This may be necessary if you want to prevent a user interrupting a shell script such as the login scripts. The example in Listing 10.66 shows the interactive use of `trap`.

```
(Linux):~$ trap 'echo sighup received' SIGHUP
(Linux):~$ kill -HUP $$
sighup received
```

Listing 10.66 Processing signals by means of the shell.

10.9.2 Jobs and job control

Under modern UNIX systems which have *job control*, many shells provide various functions for handling jobs more smoothly. Under UNIX, a job is a process that is started in the background. Job control is the name for the set of functions with which the jobs are controlled and managed. These terms have nothing to do with the 'Job Control Language' known from mainframe computers.

Programs can be sent to the background by means of an ampersand (&). Output, however, is displayed on the terminal from which the job was started. If the program expects an input, the program is halted and, depending on the shell and the configuration, the system displays an appropriate message.

The program can be pulled back into the foreground with fg. If you have started several jobs (you will obtain a list with jobs, see also help jobs in the bash), you can select a job by means of *%jobnumber*. The character sequence %% stands for the job started last. These character sequences can also be used in process management by means of kill.

If you have started a program and you want to continue with it later in the background, you can interrupt the program with Ctrl-Z (see also stty -a, suspend character), then you can shift it into the background with bg.

If you want to run larger programs which require much time and memory in the background, you can assign the program a lower priority by means of nice. Thus, other users' interactive work is considerably less affected.

The higher the nice value, the 'nicer' you are to other users. The user root is the only user who can also set a negative nice value. These processes are then privileged in the scheduling. If you forgot the call with nice, you can still change the priority at a later time by means of the program renice or top (but only the system administrator is allowed to increase the priority).

When a user of the bash logs out, background processes are sent the SIGHUP signal. Usually, this leads to termination of the program, which is often not desired. In such cases, the program must be started with nohup. This is always the case in the tcsh. If you forgot the nohup, there is unfortunately no other solution than to restart the program.

Examples of programs that run for a long time and are often started in the background are ftp transfers of large amounts of data, simulation programs or other CPU-intensive programs, and X clients. In all cases, you have the advantage of being able to log out and have the process continue, or at least you can continue using the shell.

Tools (not only) for programmers

Current LINUX distributions include a whole series of programs and packages from which the user can choose. Therefore it does not appear to make much sense compiling these or other programs oneself. But not all programs are readily available as binary versions, and in case of error corrections, changes are often available only to the source code. This chapter explains what the user can do concerning installation and development of programs. These possibilities are not only of interest to programmers, but also to users who have to carry out frequently recurring tasks.

A number of programming languages are available for LINUX. The most widely used one is C, because the kernel is mostly written in this language. Under LINUX, the installation of a C compiler is practically a must, since this is the only way to create a kernel properly adapted to individual hardware. Furthermore, most freely available UNIX programs are implemented in C.

Many other programming languages are available too: C++, Objective C, Pascal (GNU Pascal or Pascal-to-C), FORTRAN (GNU FORTRAN or FORTRAN-to-C), Lisp, and script languages such as Perl, Tcl, and Python. Programs are often implemented in one of these languages, so the corresponding interpreter or compiler must be installed if these programs are to be used. This is one of the reasons why the GNU project programs have usually been implemented in the C language.

11.1 The make program

The make program is primarily used for compilation of large programs that consist of many individual modules. When changes are made to the source code, only the modified program parts are recompiled. Compared to a complete compilation, this saves a lot of time; therefore the sources of nearly all programs are supplied with a Makefile which controls compilation.

GNU make uses one of the following files as control file for the compilation process, provided the file exists: GNUMakefile, Makefile, or makefile. Other files can be specified by means of the option -f. If you use special functions of GNU make in your Makefile, you should name this file GNUMakefile.

At the call of make, the default target specified in the Makefile file is created. If an additional parameter is specified, that target is created. Let us look at a simple example to explain this (Listing 11.1).

```
# A simple Makefile for prune
all: prune

prune: prune.c
    gcc -O -s prune.c -o prune

install: prune
    install -m 755 prune /usr/local/sbin/prune
    echo "edit /etc/prune.conf to suit your system"
```

Listing 11.1   A simple Makefile.

The make command creates the default target all. The default target is the first target in the Makefile. Targets are always written in the first column and are terminated with a colon. There is a dependency to the file or target prune. Dependencies are written to the right of the colon. Comments in a Makefile begin with a hash sign (#) and end with the end of the line.

In the target prune which depends on the file prune.c, the C compiler gcc is called if the file prune.c is more recent than the file prune. For this simple function, make already has a so-called default rule that would be applied if no command was specified at this point. The list of all default rules can be displayed with make -p. Commands are entered after a tab. If spaces are used instead of the tabs, some make versions show an error message.

The make install command executes the commands specified in the target install. First, however, it checks whether the program prune must be newly created. The install command copies the program to the location in the directory tree specified by the programmer and sets the appropriate access rights as well.

Listing 11.2 shows a slightly more complex Makefile, which uses both variables and default rules for compilation instead of the call of gcc.

This Makefile shows a certain resemblance to the commonly used Makefiles. In the first section, some variables are set which can later be used in the rules or dependencies. With the variable CFLAGS, the options for the C compiler are set. Here, it is the option -O2 for optimization. The variable LDFLAGS contains the options for the linker; here, the option -s is used.

In this Makefile, the prune program is created in two steps: first, the C source code is translated into the so-called object format (file name prune.o). Subsequently,

```
CFLAGS=-02
LDFLAGS=-s
INSTALLDIR=/usr/local/sbin

all: prune

install: prune
    install -m 755 prune $(INSTALLDIR)/prune
    echo "edit /etc/prune.conf to suit your system"

prune: prune.o

clean:
    rm -f prune.o prune
```

Listing 11.2   A slightly more complex Makefile.

this object file is linked with the standard C library to create an executable program. Both are default rules; the definition of all default rules can be displayed by means of the command make -p.

In the install target, the program is copied into the directory INSTALLDIR. A new member is the target clean, which deletes previously generated programs or object files. The next make call must then completely recompile the program, which makes sense, for example, in case of configuration changes. Another frequently used target is dist, which usually creates a tar file with the source code.

In larger programs, it is often necessary to adapt individual parameters before the compilation; for example, the names of configuration or lock files, or the installation directories. Usually, these variables can be found at the beginning of the Makefiles, where you can also often find comments on the meaning of the variables.

The make program has a series of options that can influence the operation of make. An important and useful one is the option -n, which causes make to display the necessary commands instead of executing them. Thus, it is possible, for example, to verify which files will be installed where by using the command make -n install instead of make install.

make can start several programs simultaneously, so that on computers with sufficient memory, the CPU can be charged to capacity as far as possible. The option -j allows parallel execution of several programs. If this option is followed by a number, the number of programs started simultaneously by make is limited to this number. Without this number, there is no limit.

With the start of many processes, the 'load,' that is, the number of processes competing for processor time, goes up. With the option -l, followed by a number, no new processes are started if other processes are still running and the load is greater than this number. If no number is specified, the load is not considered. Thus, if you start parallel make processes, you must keep an eye on the occupation of main

```
report.dvi: report.tex figure1.eps figure2.eps
    latex report

%.eps:%.fig
    fig2dev -L ps $< > $@
```

Listing 11.3 A Makefile for LATEX.

memory and processor load to obtain benefits in speed. Obviously, multi-processor machines have a special advantage.

Listing 11.3 shows an example for the use of make to generate the DVI file report.dvi. This file is dependent on the source text report.tex and the illustrations figure1.eps and figure.eps. These illustrations were generated with the xfig program and then converted into eps format (Encapsulated PostScript). The use of make automates the conversion of the illustrations and ensures that the most up-to-date illustrations are always included in the DVI file.

This example also shows some further functions of make. The symbol $< represents the files needed as input, the symbol $@ is replaced at runtime with the name of the file to be generated. These symbols are used in a rule which describes the general dependencies between illustrations (%.fig) and their eps format (%.eps). Thus it is not necessary to specify a rule for each illustration.

This information is intended to help you understand foreign Makefiles. Before you begin to develop your own Makefiles, you should read the manual for GNU make, which is distributed in Texinfo format. It provides extensive documentation on the use of make and the creation of Makefiles. If you frequently edit Makefiles, you can use the makefile-mode of the emacs editor, which provides a series of useful functions.

For the GNU project programs, the document standards.texi provides a sort of prescription which, as well as the C programming and the style to be employed, also outlines the most important functions for a Makefile. You may not agree with all of these prescriptions, but the document certainly contains a series of useful hints.

Additional Information and Sources	
Documentation:	make(1), Texinfo manual
ftp server:	ftp.gnu.org
ftp path:	/pub/gnu
File name:	make-3.72.1.tar.gz
Size:	about 550 Kbytes

11.2 The imake program

The imake program is a part of the X Window system and is therefore often used to compile X programs. For any such program, an Imakefile is created which describes the programs and libraries to be compiled. On the basis of system-specific configuration files, a `Makefile` is generated from the `Imakefile` which is then used for the compilation of the program.

Usually, the system-specific `Makefile` is generated by means of the `xmkmf` command. If the sources of the program are distributed across several directories, the Makefiles can also be automatically generated in the subdirectories by means of the `xmkmf -a` command. For this purpose, `xmkmf` internally starts `make Makefiles` and subsequently `make includes` and `make depend`.

The configuration files for the `imake` program can be found in the directory `/usr/X11R6/lib/X11/config`. The file `linux.cf` contains all necessary adaptations for LINUX. User-defined adaptations can be made in the file `site.def`, but usually none are required. A complete introduction to use and configuration of `imake` can be found, for example, in DuBois (1993).

11.3 Installation of programs

One recurrent task a UNIX system administrator is faced with all the time is the installation of new programs or new versions of existing programs. Practically all programs used under LINUX are free, that is, the source code is available. Since this software is generally also employed under other UNIX systems, it must allow compilation on different platforms. Thus, the programs must be portable between different systems.

11.3.1 Installation of GNU programs

The aim of the Free Software Foundation (FSF) is the creation of a free, UNIX-like operating system (The Hurd). All essential UNIX programs are developed and employed all over the world under the most disparate UNIX versions. Many of the programs employed under LINUX are GNU versions of the standard UNIX service programs. Therefore, LINUX is often described as a GNU system on a LINUX basis. Without these programs, LINUX would not be what it is today.

The GNU programs are portable and powerful, therefore they are installed on many computers in addition to the standard UNIX service programs. The portability is achieved by analyzing the system before the program is compiled and by adapting the program accordingly. The analysis of the system is started by means of the `configure` script. The GNU project has set some standards for the creation of programs and Makefiles which are observed by nearly all GNU programs. You can find the GNU coding standard on every GNU mirror in the file `standards.texi`.

The `configure` script analyzes the system and compiles a series of test programs. Subsequently, a `Makefile` is created which controls the compilation of the program. First, however, we have a look at some examples for the configuration of GNU programs. We begin with the configuration of `gzip`, the GNU replacement of UNIX `compress` (Listing 11.4). `gzip` packs substantially better and has the advantage that no license on the basis of existing patents is needed for its use.

```
(Linux):~> tar zxf /tmp/gzip-1.2.4.tar.gz
(Linux):~> cd gzip-1.2.4
(Linux):~/gzip-1.2.4> ./configure
```

Listing 11.4   Unpacking and configuring a GNU program.

The script displays a series of messages which allow you to follow the course of the configuration. More recent versions of GNU programs are distributed with con-figure scripts that also display the results of the analyses. At the end of the config-ure run, a Makefile is created with which the program can be compiled. The number of displayed messages can be influenced with the options --verbose or --quiet.

GNU programs are normally installed in the /usr/local directory. Under LINUX, the GNU programs are often installed in the /usr directory like the standard programs. This is achieved with the option --prefix (Listing 11.5). The command ./configure --help produces a list of all supported options. In addition, you can find the available options (for example, for setting the path to the X libraries) together with further explanations in the INSTALL or README files.

```
(Linux):~/gzip-1.2.4> ./configure --prefix=/usr
```

Listing 11.5   The option --prefix of the configure call.

Subsequently, the program can be compiled by means of make and installed by means of make install. GNU programs are normally compiled in such a way that a debugger can be used to detect errors. For the average system administrator, this is not needed, and it takes up a lot of space on the hard disk. There are two ways to remedy this. First of all, some environment variables can be set, for example by entering them in the initialization files of the shell (Listing 11.6).

```
(Linux):~/gzip-1.2.4> setenv CFLAGS=-02
(Linux):~/gzip-1.2.4> setenv LDFLAGS=-s
```

Listing 11.6   Additional flags for C compiler and linker.

The variables can also be specified at the call of the make program in addition to the corresponding target (Listing 11.7). For all GNU programs, you can store such settings in the file /etc/config.site, which is read by all configure scripts.

Now the program is installed. Depending on the shell, it might be necessary to rebuild the hash table in which the shell stores the paths to programs. In the tcsh, this is done with the command rehash, in the bash with hash -r.

Some GNU packages, such as the GNU C compiler (GCC) or the Emacs editor, can be configured with a series of additional options. Precise information on the

```
(Linux):~/gzip-1.2.4> make CFLAGS=-O2 LDFLAGS=-s
(Linux):~/gzip-1.2.4> su
(Linux):~/gzip-1.2.4# make CFLAGS=-O2 LDFLAGS=-s install
```

Listing 11.7 Passing special flags to `make`.

possible and mandatory options of the `configure` script can be found in the `INSTALL` file which is included in each package.

The standard format for the documentation of GNU programs is Texinfo. This allows you to create both printed and online documentation on the basis of the same source text. Man pages are also often installed for reference, offering a brief overview of the program's options.

11.3.2 Installation of other programs

Programs that are not part of the GNU project are installed in many different ways. Often, a precise description of the installation is given in the `README` or `INSTALL` files. Reading these files is essential before starting the installation. Frequently, there is also a file that contains tips and tricks for individual operating systems.

One possibility for compiling programs under different UNIX systems is the creation of a `Makefile` for each operating system. The appropriate `Makefile` must then be copied and, if needed, adapted. Other programs come with a huge `Makefile` which contains all configurations for the different systems. In this case, the correct setting must be activated by means of an editor.

In many cases, the programs are already prepared for compilation and installation under LINUX. Sometimes this is not the case, but often no changes are required for LINUX anyway. Usually, you can use the settings for a POSIX system. If the `Makefile` only considers System V and BSD-based systems, you should try the System V setting first. This should be sufficient to compile many of today's freely available programs. If you need to make substantial changes to the source code or the Makefiles, you should send these to the programmer. Thus, in a later version, other users can benefit from your experience.

Programs developed under BSD can be compiled with the aid of the compatibility library `libbsd`. This library contains a series of functions which are only available under BSD or which have different semantics in BSD. When linking, you must specify the `-lbsd` switch to include this library.[1] In addition, you must load the include files for this library by specifying the option `-I/usr/include/bsd` during compilation.

Currently, a relatively large number of programs is being adapted for use with GNU `configure`. This is a relatively expensive operation, but it significantly improves portability.

---

[1] Please note that the order of the libraries is relevant.

11.4 Editors

UNIX provides a very powerful environment for programmers. On the one hand, this consists of the kernel, which looks after the management of the CPU, the file system and the hardware. The kernel provides the programmer with almost all required functions. For reasons of portability and easier programming, the libc library represents a somewhat higher level of abstraction. Therefore, programmers of applications mostly use the functions of libc.

Another component of a UNIX system is the service programs. Each of these programs has been developed for a special function. By using combinations of these programs, a series of functions can be performed with relatively little effort. The link between these programs is constituted either by pipes or by functions of the shell.

Besides these service programs and compilers, programmers also need an editor to edit their programs. Such an editor should obviously be powerful and well integrated into the UNIX environment. On every UNIX system, you will find the editor vi (or a clone). This editor is relatively small, but is very powerful and well integrated into the UNIX environment. Some hints and tips, and the most important commands of this editor, are presented in Appendix A.

Here, we will first discuss some aspects of the emacs editor. Then, we will introduce two more editors, which can be useful to programmers.

11.4.1 The emacs editor

One of the most widely used editors is (GNU) Emacs. Because of its power and the variety of features, we have dedicated a whole chapter (Chapter 5) to this editor. Here, we will introduce some particular functions which are of special interest to programmers. All the information provided here obviously also applies to XEmacs.

Almost every programming language has its corresponding emacs mode. If no mode exists for the required programming language in the emacs standard version, you may still find this mode in an emacs Lisp archive (archive.cis.ohio-state.edu in the directory elisp-archive). In these modes, keys are assigned in such a way that editing source texts is made as easy as possible. Furthermore, functions are provided for compiling and testing programs.

A particularly useful feature is automatic indentation. This ensures that branches and loops are (almost) always indented correctly and allows you to recognize some logical errors from the indentation itself. If you use additional syntax highlighting, you will easily find your way even in foreign source texts.

To save typing effort, you may be able to use an abbrev-mode. For many modes, abbreviation tables have been created that contain the keywords of the programming language in question.

To keep a clear overview when dealing with more substantial projects, you can use the etags program to generate a TAGS file. This file contains a list of cross-references between source text files and implemented functions. With the aid of this file, arbitrary functions in arbitrary source files can be reached with a couple of keystrokes. An overview of the key combinations can be found in Table 11.1. Tags can be used, for example, in projects in C, Emacs Lisp, or LaTeX.

Key	Function	Description
M-.	find-tag	Search for tag
C-u M-.	find-tag	Next occurrence
	tags-search	Load files with tag
	tags-query-replace	Search and replace
M-,	tags-loop-continue	Continue search
	list-tags	Display tags
	tags-apropos	Search

Table 11.1 Key combinations for tags.

The tags mode can also use a TAGS file which is stored in a different directory. This file can either be loaded manually or selected on the basis of entries in the variable tag-table-alist. With the aid of the tags mode, you can get a good overview of the implementation of Emacs. Just create a TAGS file in the Emacs Lisp directory with the command etags *.el. You can then load this file with M-x visit-tags-table and use it. The command in the ~/.emacs file, shown in Listing 11.8, can be used to load the TAGS file automatically with every Emacs Lisp file.

```
(setq tag-table-alist
  '(
  ("\\.el$" . "/usr/local/share/emacs/19.29/lisp/")
))
```

Listing 11.8 Loading the TAGS file automatically.

After a program has been created, it must be compiled. For this, emacs also provides support when calling the compiler. With the command M-x compile, which can obviously be assigned to a key combination such as C-c C-c, the compiler (precisely, the command specified in the local variable compile-command) is started. If errors have occurred during compilation, you can use the key combination C-c C-` to jump to the next error position.

Once the program has been compiled, it can even be tested under emacs. This is done by means of an interface to the GNU debugger gdb. In one emacs window, the source text of the program is shown, with the current command highlighted. The source text can be edited directly in this buffer, if needed. In a second window, all commands of the debugger can be used.

For swapping modifications with other programmers or users, the diff program is used to create a patch which is then integrated into the source text by means of the patch program. If two or three versions of a program are to be patched, emacs provides support with the modes ediff and emerge. With the ediff mode, you can easily view individual changes and, if required, incorporate them. Under X, the differences are highlighted in color.

Furthermore, XEmacs has an integrated class browser for object-oriented programming languages. It functions in a similar way to the well-known Smalltalk browser and can handle several languages.

All this is only a very small sample of the possibilities Emacs offers programmers and experienced users. It is not always easy and it may take some time to familiarize yourself with all these functions, but you can always start with simple editing functions and acquire more proficiency when needed and when time allows it.

xcoral

The `xcoral` editor runs only under X. It is particularly suited for programming in C++, because it provides special browsers for the class hierarchy and the corresponding methods. This makes it relatively easy to gain an overview of a major project, and to maintain it.

Additional Information and Sources	
ftp server:	sunsite.unc.edu
Path:	/pub/Linux/X11/apps/editors
File:	xcoral-2.1.linux.tar.gz
Size:	about 380 Kbytes

Borland's IDE clone xwpe

In Hanover, an integrated development environment was implemented that functions in the same way as the interface known from Turbo Pascal or Turbo C. It is therefore well suited for a transition from these two compilers. This environment can be run both under X and on a terminal. Both the `gcc` compiler and the `gdb` debugger can be called from this interface.

Additional Information and Sources	
ftp server:	tsx-11.mit.edu
Path:	/pub/linux/sources/usr.bin.X11
File:	xwpe-1.4.2.tar.gz
Size:	about 340 Kbytes

11.5 The Revision Control System (rcs)

The Revision Control System (rcs) was written by Walter F. Tichy and manages different versions of text files. The rcs makes storing, retrieving, documenting, identifying and collating different versions of text files automatic. rcs can be used for text files that must be modified regularly, for example program, documentation, or configuration files. The rcs stores all modifications and version information in one file, the rcs archive.

In an rcs archive, only the differences between the versions are stored, not the complete files. Therefore, file management by means of rcs requires relatively little additional disk space. The latest version is always stored completely, so that it can be accessed very quickly. When accessing older versions, all changes must first be undone, which may take some time.

A similar (commercial) package is SCCS (Source Code Control System). Here, the first version is stored completely, and when accessing more recent versions, the alterations must be made first. The GNU program cvs (Concurrent Versions System) is based on rcs and includes some more useful functions, such as updates by several programmers without locking and the management of entire directory trees.

The main commands of the rcs are easy to learn. The two most important commands are ci and co. ci is an abbreviation for 'check in.' It stores the contents of a file in an rcs archive. co is the abbreviation for 'check out' and serves to copy versions from the rcs archive.

11.5.1 Functions of the rcs

- Old versions are stored in a space-saving manner, in a file that we refer to as 'rcs archive.' Modifications made to a text file no longer destroy the original, because previous versions are always available. Versions can be classified by version number, date, author's name, or status.

- Besides the changes to the text, the rcs stores the name of the author, the date and the time, and a log message. These messages make it easy to find out what happened to a file, without having to ask colleagues. This makes the complete history of modifications traceable at any time.

- If two or more programmers want to modify the same version, the rcs warns the programmers, thus preventing one modification from destroying the other.

- The rcs can be used to manage several versions of a project in the form of a tree. You start with one version, which may later be split into several different versions (test and production for several customers). These versions can later be merged again with the merge option.

- Overlapping changes in several versions of a tree are highlighted, so problems resulting from this can be eliminated manually.

- Files are automatically identified by versions with specification of file name, version number, author's name, date and time, and so on.

- The rcs requires little disk space for the archive. Only the differences between the versions are stored.

An example of the use of rcs

The use of rcs is much easier than one would have expected after having read the corresponding man pages. In the following paragraphs, we introduce the most important functions of the rcs with the aid of various examples. Listing 11.9 shows a file to be managed with rcs.

```
/* hello.c */
main( void)
{         printf( "Hello world\n");
}
```

Listing 11.9   A sample file for the use of rcs.

```
(Linux):~$ ci hello.c
hello.c,v  <-- hello.c
enter description, terminated with single '.' or end of file
NOTE: This is NOT the log message!
>> My first C program
>> .
initial revision: 1.1
done
```

Listing 11.10   Storing a file in the rcs archive.

This file is to be stored in the rcs archive in its original version. For this purpose, we will call the command ci (Listing 11.10). If you work with the Emacs editor, you can include a file in an rcs archive by means of the key combination C-x v v (vc-next-action). The mode line shows the text RCS: and the RCS version number of the file, so you can see at a glance that the file is under RCS control.

This command creates the rcs archive hello.c,v, stores the contents of hello.c as version 1.1 and deletes the work file. During the process, the user is prompted for a program description, which is also stored in the rcs archive. All further calls of ci will prompt for a log entry. There, the changes made should be described concisely and exactly. If at this point vague or erroneous descriptions are entered, the whole procedure becomes somewhat meaningless, but at least one still has access to the previous versions of the file.

rcs archives are the files whose names end with ,v. The v stands for version(s). The other files are the 'work files.' To read the work files of the previous example from the archive, you can use the command co (Listing 11.11).

```
(Linux):~$ co hello.c
hello.c,v  --> hello.c
revision 1.1
done
```

Listing 11.11   The use of co.

The co command extracts the last version from the rcs archive and generates the work file hello.c. If the work file is to be modified as well, the co command must be called with the option -l (for lock). A special version can be extracted from the archive with the option -r *version* (Listing 11.12).

```
(Linux):~$ co -l hello.c
hello.c,v  -->  hello.c
revision 1.1 (locked)
done
```

Listing 11.12   The use of co with locking.

Now the file hello.c has set write privileges for the user. In addition, a lock is activated which prevents another user being able to store a modified version in the rcs archive. If you use Emacs, you can read a file from the archive with the key combination C-x C-q (vc-toggle-read-only), modify it, and write it back into the archive with the same key combination. This information should be largely sufficient for a simple use of rcs.

After reading it from the archive, our sample file has been modified by translating the string to be printed into German. Listing 11.13 shows the file after modification.

```
/* hello.c */
main( void)
{       printf( "Hallo Welt\n");
}
```

Listing 11.13   The modified sample file.

The modified file is now to be incorporated into the rcs archive as a new version (see Listing 11.14). For this purpose, the ci command is called again. Now, the ci command prompts for a log message. The Emacs editor also asks for such an entry in a new window; the new version is included in the archive with the key combination C-c C-c.

```
(Linux):~$ ci hello.c
hello.c,v  <--  hello.c
new revision: 1.2; previous revision: 1.1
enter log message, terminated with single '.' or end of file
>> Translated into German.
>> .
done
```

Listing 11.14   Storing a modified file.

If the error message ci error: no lock set by *user* is displayed, the user has tried to insert a work file into the rcs archive that was not locked when reading the file out of the archive. The rcs command with the option -l creates a lock, so that the work file can finally be stored in the archive. The corresponding command can be found in Listing 11.15.

```
(Linux):~$ rcs -l1.1 hello.c
rcs file: hello.c,v
1.1 locked
done
```

Listing 11.15   The rcs command in use.

Management of versions by itself does not usually help a great deal. Above all, if a new error was introduced, it is sensible to know what exactly has changed between two versions. To display differences between two versions, you can use the rcsdiff command. The command in Listing 11.16 shows the differences between versions 1.1 and 1.2.

```
(Linux):~$ rcsdiff -r1.1 -r1.2 hello.c
rcs file: hello.c,v
retrieving revision 1.1
retrieving revision 1.2
diff -r1.1 -r1.2
3c3
< {        printf( "Hello world\n");
---
> {        printf( "Hallo Welt\n");
```

Listing 11.16   The rcsdiff command.

If only one version number is specified, the current work file is compared with the specified version. If no version number is specified, the work file is compared with the default version (this is usually the last version in the archive).

Since the rcsdiff command uses the UNIX command diff, it is for example also possible to create so-called 'unified diffs' (option -u) or 'context diffs' (option -c).

Within Emacs, you can use the function ediff-revision to compare different RCS versions of a file. This uses the ediff mode, with which you can also compare individual files.

rcs archives

rcs archives are files whose names end with `,v`; the 'v' stands for version(s). rcs archives are usually stored in the current directory. If you do not want to clutter your working directory with rcs archives, you can create a subdirectory `./RCS`, and all `*,v` files will be stored there. The rcs commands find this directory automatically and search it first for required archives. All commands described above continue to function as before. rcs archives and work files can be specified in three ways in the rcs commands:

- *Both* file names are specified.
  The name of the rcs archive is specified in the form *path1/file name,v*. The work file is specified with *path2/file name*. The paths *path1* and *path2* may be different.
- Only the name of the rcs archive is specified.
  In this case, the work file is expected to be found in the current directory. The name of the work file corresponds to the name of the rcs archive without the `,v`.
- Only the name of the work file is specified.
  If only the name of the work file is specified, ci searches for an rcs archive first in the specified path in the subdirectory RCS (*path2/RCS/file name,v*) and then directly in the specified path (*path2/file name,v*).

Contents of an rcs archive

An rcs archive usually contains several versions of a text file, an access list, a log of changes, and a text description.

At each inclusion of a version, the date and time, the file name of the work file, and the name of the user are automatically stored as well. If no version number is specified, it is automatically generated. In addition, the user can enter a message, which is also stored. The text file is stored as the difference from the previous version.

Furthermore, the rcs archive contains an access list which can be managed by means of the rcs command. This list specifies which users in the system are allowed to work with this archive and the file contained in it.

Automatic identification

The rcs can generate special markers in the work file, the so-called rcs markers. To insert such a marker into a file, the marker `$Id$` can be inserted into the text, for example, into a comment. This marker is replaced by the rcs with '`$Id: file name version date time author status $`'.

With this marker on the first page of each module, you can see at any time which version you are currently working on. The markers are automatically updated by the rcs. To get these marks into the object code of the program too, the ID must be embedded in a string. In the C programming language, for example, this can be done as shown in Listing 11.17.

```
static char rcsid[] =
"$Id: hello.c,v 1.18 1995/01/15 16:01:00 cschaba Exp $";
```

Listing 11.17 Embedding the RCS identification in binary programs.

The `ident` command extracts this marker from any kind of file, including, for example, object files, binary files, or core dumps. This allows you to find out which versions of which modules have been compiled into the program.

It might also be useful to include the marker `$Log$` in the source file. This marker collects all log entries that were entered during the storing processes of `ci`. Thus, the complete version history is stored in the source file as well. There is a whole series of such markers, which are listed in the man page of the `co` command.

rcs markers

`rcs` markers are character strings that begin with the character `$`, followed by the marker name, followed by, if the marker was already substituted, a colon and the value of the marker, followed by another `$`. At first, the user will enter the marker without a value; for example `$Id$`. `co` recognizes this marker and expands it with the current values. The following markers are recognized and substituted by `co` in the work file:

`$Author$`
The login name of the user who stored the version.

`$Date$`
The date and time in GMT of when the version was stored.

`$Header$`
A default header which contains the complete `rcs` file name, the version number, the date, the author's name, the status, and the name of the user who locked the file.

`$Id$`
A standard header like `$Header$`, but without specifying the path in the file name.

`$Locker$`
The login name of the user who locked the version.

`$Log$`
The log message that can be entered when storing a version. Existing log entries are not removed from the work file; the new entries are simply added.

`$rcsfile$`
The name of the `rcs` archive.

`$Revision$`
> The version number.

`$Source$`
> The complete pathname of the rcs archive.

`$State$`
> The current status of the version. Default status is 'Exp.' Reasonable status names in program development might be, for example, 'Alpha' or 'Beta.'

After this rather dry introduction, we will look again at an example. In Listing 11.18 you will find the header of a file before the rcs markers were expanded. Listing 11.19 shows the same header after rcs has expanded the markers.

```
/*
 * $Id$
 * $Revision$
 * $Date$
 * $Log$
 */
```

Listing 11.18   A file header for rcs.

```
/*
 * $Id: hello.c,v 1.18 1995/01/15 16:01:00 cschaba Exp $
 * $Revision: 1.18 $
 * $Date: 1995/01/15 16:01:00 $
 * Revision 1.18  1995/01/15  16:01:00  cschaba
 * The function now returns 0.
 *
 * Revision 1.17  1995/01/08  17:46:41  cschaba
 * Now uses the BSD header.
 * ...
 */
```

Listing 11.19   A file header with expanded rcs markers.

Access rights

The Revision Control System manages two kinds of access rights. First, a file can only be modified by one user at a time. This is achieved by file locks. Second, access can be restricted to authorized users in the sense of the rcs user management.

The access list   To enable a user to work with rcs, the user name must be registered in the access list, unless the access list is empty or the user is the superuser or the owner of the work file. Users can be entered into and removed from the access list by means of the rcs command.

File locks   Versions can be extracted from the archive when it is either locked or unlocked. If a version is locked, updates are prevented from overlapping. If the work file is to be made available read-only, it need not be locked.

To store a new version in an existing rcs archive, the last version must be locked by the user. This restriction does not apply to the owner of the rcs file if locking is set to 'no mandatory locking.' A lock of another user can be removed with the rcs command.

Locking prevents someone else being able to store the next update in the rcs archive. This is very important when several people are working on the same project.

If mandatory locking is not required, it can be deactivated. Then, the owner of the file can store and read the work file even without a lock by means of ci and co. Anybody else who wants to modify the file must, however, set the lock.

Branches

First you start with an implementation of one version of the program. After a while it may turn out that several versions need to be maintained in parallel. This may be the case, for example, with special adaptations for different customers or operating systems. It is also possible to 'freeze' a production version, which receives only the necessary error corrections, and to split off a developers' version. Each of these branches can obviously be split again.

A branch is created by incorporating the file into the archive under a new version number. This is done by calling the program ci with the option -rNewBranch. Thus, the command ci -r1.19.1 hello.c creates branch 1 in version 1.19.

11.5.2   rcs and other programs

We have already seen the cooperation between rcs and Emacs. The XEmacs editor includes the package pcl-cvs, which contains a substantial extension of the interface to cvs. cvs itself is implemented on the basis of rcs and has significant advantages over rcs, especially with developments involving several programmers.

The GNU make program has default rules to extract files from archives with rcs. It supports archives both in the current and in the ./RCS directory. This makes the use of rcs completely transparent even if you forgot to extract a work file for compilation.

11.5.3   Further rcs commands

rcs includes several other commands. In the following paragraphs, only a few functions of these programs can be introduced. The complete documentation can be found in the corresponding man pages.

Modification logs with rlog

The rlog program displays the modification history of a file. A series of selection criteria can be chosen, for example, modifying user (-w), versions (option -r), or periods of time (option -d). The precise format of the options and the corresponding parameters can be found in the man page for rlog.

Managing archives with rcs

The rcs program is generally used for management of rcs archives. Archives can be newly created or locked. The owner of an archive can deactivate locks set by other users or change the access rights to this archive. Furthermore, it is possible to use a symbolic name for a version. Because the rcs is central to the entire system, here is a complete description of all options.

-i

With this option, an rcs archive is created and initialized, but no versions are stored. If no path is specified, the rcs command creates the archive in the ./RCS directory or in the current directory. If the rcs archive already exists, an error message is displayed.

-ausername(s)

Appends the user name(s) *username(s)* to the access list. Several user names must be separated by commas.

-Aold_file

Copies the access list contained in the rcs archive *old_file* into the new rcs archive.

-eusername(s)

Removes the user name(s) *username(s)* from the access list. Several user names must be separated by commas.

-b[version]

This option changes the default branching to version *version*.

-ccomment

Sets the comment character to *comment*. This text is displayed in front of each log message line generated with Log. This is useful for programming languages that do not support multi-line comments.

-kmarker

This option can be used to change the substitution of the rcs marker. The precise meaning of the individual options is documented in the man page for co.

-l[version]

Locks a version with the number *version*. If no version number is specified, the last version is locked.

-u[version]

Removes the lock from version *version*. If no version is specified, the last lock of the user is used. Normally, only the user who has set the lock is allowed to remove it. If another user removes the lock, a mail message is sent to the creator of the lock. The user trying to remove the lock is prompted for a reason. This text and the specification of the version is sent to the creator of the lock.

-L

Sets locking to 'mandatory.' This means that the user must set locks for reading and writing. This is sensible if several users are working on one project.

-U

Sets locking to 'not mandatory.' This means that a user can read and write without setting a lock. This option should *not* be used if the files can be used by several users. Normally, locking is set to 'mandatory.'

-nname:version

This option assigns the symbolic name *name* to the version *version*. If the name is already assigned to another version, an error message is displayed. Omitting the version number removes the symbolic name.

-Nname:version

This option works exactly as the option -n. However, if a name is already assigned to the version *version*, this name is overwritten.

-orange

A range of versions is removed from the archive. The parameter *version1-version2* stands for the revisions *version1* to *version2* in the current branch. The parameter *-revision* means all versions from the beginning of the branch to this version. The parameter *-revision* deletes all versions from this version to the end of the branch.

-q

This option activates the 'quiet mode.' This suppresses the display of error messages.

-I

By specifying this option, the user is interactively prompted, even if the standard input is not a terminal.

-sstatus[:version]

This option sets the status of the version to *status*. If no version is specified, the last version stored in the archive is used. ci automatically uses the status Exp.

-t[file]

This option replaces the description of the work file in the rcs archive with the contents of *file*. If no file name is specified, the text is read from the standard input (keyboard). The input is terminated with a dot (full stop).

−t−*text*
   Replaces the description with the text *text*.

Merging of several branches

When working with several branches, modifications to one branch must often also be carried out on a second branch. Thus, for example, an error correction in the production version should also be incorporated into the developers' version, unless that point has not already been modified in some other way. This stressful and time-consuming task can be largely automated by means of the rcsmerge program. All options of rcsmerge can be found in the man page.

For a better understanding of the functioning of rcsmerge, we will look at an example. After we have delivered the program hello.c with version 2.2, we have opened a new development branch with version 3.3. Now, another programmer suggests some improvements to version 2.2, which you would like to incorporate into your current development version. To do this, you store the external modifications to version 2.2 in the file hello.c and start the rcsmerge command (Listing 11.20).

```
(Linux):~> rcsmerge -p -r2.2 -r3.3 hello.c > hello.merged.c
```

Listing 11.20   The rcsmerge command.

Subsequently, you will find all modifications, or at least those that could be carried out automatically, in the file hello.merged.c. However, since it is possible that changes were made to both branches at the same point of the program, you should check this file carefully.

Alternatively, you can place the external modifications in a separate branch and process them from there, as shown by the sample commands in Listing (11.21).

```
(Linux):~> ci -r2.2.1.1 hello.c
(Linux):~> co -r3.3 -j2.2:2.8.1.1 hello.c
```

Listing 11.21   Creation of a new branch.

With rcsmerge you can also remove less recent modifications from your program. You simply merge the changes between the two older versions in reverse order to your current working version. The example in Listing 11.22 removes the modifications between versions 3.2 and 3.1 from hello.c.

```
(Linux):~> rcsmerge -r3.2 -r3.1 hello.c
```

Listing 11.22   Another example of `rcsmerge`.

ident – identifying files

The `ident` command searches the specified file or the standard input for `rcs` markers. These markers are usually set automatically by `co`, but they can also be inserted into the file by hand. The option `-q` deactivates the display of the warning that no markers could be found. `ident` works with both text and binary files.

```
(Linux):~> ident hello
hello:
$Id: hello.c,v 1.18 1995/01/15 16:01:00 cschaba Exp $
```

Listing 11.23   Extracting RCS information from a file.

11.5.4 Additional information and programs

Additional Information and Sources	
Man pages:	`ci(1)`, `co(1)`, `rcs(1)`, `rcsdiff(1)`, `ident(1)`, `rcsclean(1)`, `rcsintro(1)`, `rcsmerge(1)`, `rlog(1)`, `rcsfile(5)`
Books:	Bolinger and Bronson (1995). *Applying RCS and SCCS*
`ftp` server:	`ftp.gnu.org`
`ftp` path:	`/pub/gnu`
File name:	`rcs-5.7.tar.gz`
Size:	about 280 Kbytes
File name:	`cvs-1.5.tar.gz`
Size:	about 1.1 Mbytes

11.6 Other version management systems

RCS processes each file individually. If you work on a project that consists of many files and you have made changes to more than one single file, you must check each file individually. Furthermore, RCS expects that only those files for which a lock was set were modified.

11.6.1 **The Concurrent Versions System**

In large projects it is often sensible to read or write the whole source tree with one command. This function is implemented (besides many other useful things) in CVS, the Concurrent Versions System. The authors have noticed that in most cases only one programmer works on a special function, so CVS does without locks.

If the system notes that modifications cannot be fitted in automatically, the programmer is prompted to remedy this conflict manually. This offers the advantage that programmers only very seldom get in each other's way.

Another useful function is a CVS archive, which is available on the Internet. This allows version control even for projects where no NFS access to the corresponding archives is possible. This function is used for several projects, such as `FreeBSD` or `lesstif`. Here, a distinction is made between read access, which is possible for many users, and the possibility of making changes, which is often restricted to only a few developers.

The CVS is implemented as a front end to RCS and can obviously also be controlled from within Emacs. For single configuration files or texts, RCS is normally sufficient, but for large projects I would currently recommend employing CVS.

11.6.2 **SCCS and CSSC**

Commercial UNIX systems often include SCCS for version management. If you employ this system in your projects, you can use the GNU implementation CSSC under LINUX. If you are beginning a new project, you should definitely look at RCS and CVS.

T̲E̲X and L̲A̲T̲E̲X under L̲INUX

12

This chapter deals with the installation and integration of a LaTeX system into an (existing) L̲INUX system.

12.1 The `teTeX` package

The standard T̲E̲X system for L̲INUX and other U̲NIX systems is `teTeX` by Thomas Esser (`te@informatik.uni-hannover.de`). This T̲E̲X can be installed into almost any directory, so the administrator has a free choice. `teTeX` includes the German hyphenation tables by default, which means that German users do not need to create a special format file. Hyphenation tables are available for a multitude of languages, such as Catalan, Croatian, Czech, Danish, Dutch, Finnish, Icelandic, Indonesian, Norwegian, Serbocroat, Turkish, Upper Sorbian, UK and US English, and many more, including languages that do not use roman character alphabets, such as Greek, Russian, Arabic, Japanese, and so on.

Currently, this T̲E̲X system is the most popular one, for the main reason that the author has made it available for other architectures and platforms too. A further advantage of this system is the use of the `kpathsea` library to search for styles and other files. This library manages an `ls -lR` directory of the T̲E̲X directory hierarchy which should always be kept up-to-date. Otherwise, T̲E̲X or LaTeX will possibly not find freshly installed files, since these programs exclusively use this file for searching. This greatly accelerates the search for styles.

The `teTeX` package can be installed into any directory. This directory is then automatically entered in the required configuration files by the installation routine. In the following text, the installation directory will therefore either not be specified at all, or it will be specified as the environment variable `TEXDIR` or as the current directory (`.`). Table 12.1 shows an overview of the `TEXDIR` directory.

TEXDIR	Directory contents
├─ dvipsk-5.58c	The dvips program
├─ gsftopkk-1.7	Converter for PostScript fonts
├─ kpathsea-2.4	Documentation on the kpathsea library
├─ kpsetools-0.2	Programs of the kpathsea library
├─ makeindex-2.12	Index generation
├─ scripts-0.2	Internally used scripts (for example MakeTeXPK)
├─ setup-0.2	Installation and configuration scripts
├─ texinfo-3.1	The Texinfo system
├─ texmf	The TEX and LATEX system
├─ texmf.cnf	The global configuration of teTeX
├─ web2c-6.1	The programs of the TEX system
└─ xdvik-18d	The xdvi previewer

Table 12.1 Structure of the installation directory of teTeX.

The installation of the programs into separate subdirectories makes the structure very clear. These directories are further subdivided into bin, man, etc (and other) directories. Integration into the search path of the user is carried out by symbolic links. The directory in which the links are to be created can be specified during the installation.

The ./texmf directory houses the very heart of the TEX or LATEX system, that is, formats, macros, styles, and fonts. This directory also contains a series of subdirectories which reflect the internal structure of the system. Table 12.2 shows an overview.

TEXDIR/texmf	Directory contents
├─ bibtex	BIBTeX styles
├─ doc	All available documentation
├─ dvips	Data for dvips
├─ fontmaps	Aliases for fonts
├─ fonts	Generated TEX fonts and METAFONT sources
├─ ls-R	Database for file search
├─ mf	Files of the METAFONT system
└─ tex	The TEX or LATEX system
├─ hyphen	Hyphenation tables
├─ latex	The LATEX system and additional styles
└─ plain	The TEX system and additional macros

Table 12.2 Structure of the ./texmf directory of teTeX.

Besides the TeX or LaTeX system, the directories `./texmf/plain` and `./texmf/latex` contain a series of extensions in the form of macro packages (for TeX) and styles (for LaTeX). These extensions can be found in additional subdirectories. The corresponding documentation can be found in the `./doc` directory shown in Table 12.1.

12.1.1 Integration of foreign language hyphenation tables into TeX

TeX is capable of switching between several hyphenation tables, so several languages can be used within a single text. Since the format file grows with each additional language, and thus becomes slower, only those hyphenation tables should be linked that are actually needed.

Within the TeX community, direct modification of the standard files, such as for example `plain.tex`, is not well received. Users should instead either adapt the appropriate configuration files or else should set the correct configuration in some other way. All used languages are entered in the file `$TEXDIR/tex/german/lhyphen.tex` (see also Listing 12.1). After loading the hyphenation tables, English must be set again as the default language.

```
\message{== Loading hyphenation patterns:}
\lefthyphenmin=2\righthyphenmin=3
%
\message{Loading hyphenation patterns for US English.}
\chardef\l@USenglish=\language
%% British English as "dialect"
\chardef\l@english=\l@USenglish
\input hyphen0
%
\message{Loading hyphenation patterns for German.}
\newlanguage\l@german \language=\l@german
\chardef\l@austrian=\l@german
\input ghyph31

%% Default hyphenation patterns: USenglish
\language=\l@USenglish \lefthyphenmin=2 \righthyphenmin=3
\endinput
```

Listing 12.1   The file `lhyphen.tex` for loading of different hyphenation tables.

The generation of the format file is then carried out by means of the commands shown in Listing 12.2. First, the English hyphenation table is copied under the name `hyphen0.tex`. The configuration is copied with the name `hyphe.tex`, so that `plain.tex` does not need changing.

```
cd /tmp
cp $TEXIDR/tex/languages/german/lhyphen.tex hyphen.tex
cp $TEXDIR/tex/languages/english/hyphen.tex hyphen0.tex
cp $TEXDIR/tex/languages/german/ghyph31.tex hyph1.tex
initex \\input plain \\dump
```

Listing 12.2 Creation of a TEX format file.

In teTEX, this is done in a different way. You can simply load additional hyphenation tables in the file `.../plain/local/tex.ini`. Subsequently, this file must be processed with `initex`. During installation, you can enter any hyphenation tables; the format file is then generated automatically (by means of the command `initex tex.ini`).

12.1.2 Integration of foreign language hyphenation tables into LATEX

A separate format file must also be created for LATEX. Here too, no standard file is modified, but the hyphenation tables to be loaded are entered in a configuration file (`/usr/lib/texmf/lib/tex/german/lhyphen.cfg`). This file corresponds exactly to the file shown in Listing 12.1. In addition, the file `hyphen.tex` must be copied as `hyphen0.tex`. Subsequently, `initex latex.ltx` can be used to generate a new LATEX format.

In TEX, the hyphenation tables to be loaded are entered in the file `../lplain/local/language.dat`. Subsequently, a new format file is generated (automatically by the configuration program) by means of the command `initex latex.ltx`.

The format file must then be copied to a directory which is automatically searched by `virtex`. You can also include an additional directory in the search path which is stored in the environment variable `TEXFORMATS`.

12.2 Local extensions of the TEX system

For a more sophisticated use of TEX or LATEX you need new, additional styles, although the distributions offer a good supply. These files can be integrated into the existing TEX installation. This has the advantage that all users can use these styles and no additional environment variables are needed. During a reinstallation or an update, however, one often forgets to backup these styles and copy them into the new installation.

Additional styles should be copied into the work directory, if they are only needed for one project. If these styles are for general use (for example letterheads), they should be installed either in the `~/TeX/Styles` directory or in

/usr/local/lib/texmf/tex/latex. Then, only the environment variable TEXINPUTS need be set. A similar procedure can be applied to Metafont files.

```
(Linux):~> setenv TEXINPUTS
$TEXINPUTS:$HOME/TeX/Styles
```

12.3 Efficient use of TEX and LATEX

LINUX provides a series of programs for the efficient use of TEX, including the previews with xdvi and ghostview under X. Furthermore, by means of the printing system and the installation of a printer filter, it is also possible to print PostScript files to non-PS printers. The use of different windows for editing, formatting, and viewing, when working with TEX under X, is quite convenient. In this context, multi-tasking proves to be very useful, because it allows you to compile one file, run the previewer on another, and eliminate the first syntax errors with your editor, all at the same time.

The use of emacs together with the installation of the AUCTEX package, however, can make the system much more powerful. AUCTEX provides an integrated environment for TEX under emacs. To begin with, you will probably use only a fraction of the features of AUCTEX. Even if AUCTEX cannot yet completely unleash its power, it is nevertheless of great help from the very beginning. Listing 12.3 shows a simple configuration of AUCTEX.

```
(require 'tex-site)              ; load Auc TeX if needed
(setq TeX-electric-escape t)     ; \ is active
(setq TeX-insert-braces t)       ; automatically append {}
(setq TeX-parse-self t)          ; analyze TeX files
(setq TeX-auto-save t)           ; store information
(setq-default TeX-master nil)    ; prompt for the master file
```

Listing 12.3 Excerpt from ~/.emacs for AUCTEX.

12.3.1 Installation of AUCTEX

The AUCTEX package consists of a series of emacs Lisp files and the lacheck program. The Lisp files are copied into the directory for local Lisp extensions by the Makefile. On most systems, this is /usr/lib/emacs/site-lisp. There, a subdirectory auctex is created in which all AUCTEX Lisp files are installed. System-specific adaptations (such as, for example, installed printers or additional style directories) are carried out in the file ./site-lisp/tex-site.el. By separating system-specific adaptations from the system itself, the adaptations can often be taken over directly or can be adjusted relatively easily when an update is made.

During the installation of AUCTEX, the system administrator generates all style files that are installed globally by means of the command `M-x auto-generate-global`. Thus, all TEX and LATEX commands are recognized and AUCTEX can support users during the input of their texts. AUCTEX has three different kinds of styles and macros:

- available system-wide, global macros, which AUCTEX finds in the path described by the variable `TeX-macro-global`;
- styles stored by the user in the `TeX-macro-private` directory;
- the TEX files or styles available in the current directory.

When reading styles, AUCTEX generates `elisp` files which describe the commands contained in the styles in `emacs` Lisp syntax. Depending on the origin of the styles, these Lisp files are stored in different directories. Here too, we find the subdivision into the above-mentioned categories:

- `TeX-auto-global` for globally available styles. These Lisp files should be regenerated by the system administrator by means of the `TeX-auto-generate-global` command when new styles or new versions are installed.
- `TeX-auto-private` contains the directory in which the user-defined styles are described.
- `TeX-auto-local` usually refers to the `./auto` directory in which the TEX files of the current directory are described.

However, automatic recognition of macros from styles is definitely not the most that AUCTEX can do. For example, a user can, without much difficulty, implement additional functions which, for example, prompt for additional parameters for macros and correspondingly insert them into the text. Here too, we find a distinction between the three macro categories:

- `TeX-style-global` for globally available styles.
- `TeX-style-private` contains the directory in which the user-defined styles are described.
- `TeX-style-local` usually refers to the `./style` directory in which the TEX files of the current directory are described.

Adaptations can initially be limited to simple functions which are already well known. With increasing experience with LATEX and `emacs` Lisp, more complicated adaptations can be carried out. In Listing 12.4, the parameter of a one-parameter macro is read into a minibuffer. There, the usual history is available.

```
\newcommand{\file}[1]{\texttt{#1}}          % file name
```

Listing 12.4   Excerpt from the file `aw-book.sty`.

The function `TeX-add-style-hook` appends the following commands when the style `aw-book.sty` is used. Here, AUCTEX receives additional information on the `listing` environment (where a Lisp function is called which carries out the prompting for parameters and their insertion into the source text) and on the `file` macro. This macro has one parameter which is read with the prompt 'file name.' The keyword `ignore` is used to convince AUCTEX that this definition is more up-to-date than the one extracted from the style. This is simply done by means of the number of specified parameters which is greater by one unit, namely the keyword `ignore`.

```
(TeX-add-style-hook "aw-book" (function
(lambda ()
(LaTeX-add-environments
    '("Listing" LaTeX-env-Listing))
(TeX-add-symbols
    '("file"     "file name"  ignore))))
```

Listing 12.5   Excerpt from the file `./style/aw-book.el`.

12.3.2 Usage of AUCTEX

To begin with, a LATEX source text can be created as usual with `emacs` and AUCTEX. You can familiarize yourself step by step with the features of AUCTEX; you need not master the whole package at once to be able to use it. Several functions, however, which are easy to remember, can significantly facilitate work with TEX or LATEX.

A very useful function is the automatic expansion of partially entered commands. In the standard version of AUCTEX, the key combination `M-Tab` (`TeX-complete-symbol`) is used for this purpose. AUCTEX also provides the possibility of activating the ⟨\⟩ key, so the input of the command is carried out in a minibuffer. In this minibuffer, the usual history functions are available, and completion of command names is done by means of the ⟨Tab⟩ key. To activate the ⟨\⟩ key, you should include the following section in your `~/.emacs` file:

```
(setq TeX-electric-escape t) ; \ is active
```

You need not leave your editor to translate your text with TEX or LATEX. The translation of your source text can be started by means of the key combination `C-c C-c` (`TeX-command-master`). To obtain a preview, you must enter `View` as a command after this key combination; for printing you must enter `Print`. AUCTEX always tries to propose the most probable command next. Thus, with LATEX files, AUCTEX begins with the command `LaTeX` which is repeated if another LATEX run is required. If the text contains a bibliography, AUCTEX proposes to carry out a BIBTEX run. Only at the end of all runs is the `View` command proposed.

If errors occur during a LATEX run, you can jump to the first (and each successive) error position with the key combination ⟨C-c '⟩ (`TeX-next-error`). The messages concerning 'Overfull' or 'Underfull' boxes, caused by problems with TEX during formatting, can be declared to be errors by means of the key combination `C-c C-w` (`TeX-toggle-debug-boxes`).

With long texts, it is often sensible to reformat only a part of the text. The key combination `C-c C-r` (`TeX-command-region`) allows you to translate only the active region. On the basis of the master file of the headers, AUCTEX recognizes which commands are to be incorporated into the dynamically generated preamble. This makes it possible to process bigger documents even on relatively slow computers. Alternatively, only the current buffer can be processed by TEX with the key combination `C-c C-b` (`TeX-command-buffer`).

AUCTEX recognizes many LATEX commands, and thus it prompts directly for the appropriate parameters. The key combination (C-c C-s) (`LaTeX-section`) inserts a new headline. The same level of hierarchy is proposed as was used in the last headline. Furthermore, AUCTEX recognizes the parameters of these commands, so they can be entered directly. Not only the headline can be inserted, but also a label, so it can be referred to from other sections. When creating the references, predefined labels are available in the form of `\ref` and `\pageref` to be completed with the (Tab) key.

A further function concerns insertion of environments with the key combination (C-c C-e) (`LaTeX-environment`). This function also recognizes the standard environments of LATEX and prompts directly for the corresponding parameters. Try to insert a `table` environment to see how AUCTEX proceeds.

These expedients alone can help prevent many trivial LATEX errors, such as a missing `\end` or a non-matching number of opening and closing brackets. In addition, the integration into the `emacs` editor allows all functions of `emacs` to be used as well. With longer texts, for example, the `outline` mode can be of great help for structuring and elaboration. Since the Revision Control System also has an interface to `emacs`, different versions of the text can easily be managed too.

Bigger documents frequently consist of several files. Furthermore, you will soon define your own macros or environments. The settings shown in Listing 12.6 instruct Emacs to recreate the appropriate Elisp descriptions of your files at each load or save operation.

```
(setq TeX-parse-self t) ; Enable parse on load.
(setq TeX-auto-save t)  ; Enable parse on save.
```

Listing 12.6 Automatic incorporation of LATEX macros in AUCTEX.

Emulators under LINUX

13

LINUX is a largely POSIX-compatible UNIX system. This compatibility, however, is limited to the portability of C source texts between different UNIX systems. This means that many UNIX programs run under LINUX if they are recompiled on a LINUX system. This is quite easy for free UNIX software, but the situation is different with commercial software or programs of other systems.

Nevertheless, it is possible to run many programs under LINUX that have been created for other operating systems or even for other computer architectures. This is done by means of so-called emulators, which map the functions of other hardware or other operating systems to the functions of the LINUX system.

Because of the great complexity of both LINUX and the other operating systems and processors, an emulation is often not complete. This is also because often functions must be emulated that are available and in use under other operating systems, but are not documented.

Under LINUX too, a series of emulators is available for different operating systems and computer architectures. Here, we will give a more detailed presentation of the emulators for DOS, Windows, and IBCS2-compatible programs. Additional emulators exist for more exotic systems, such as Macintosh, Apple II or Spectrum.

Additional Information and Sources	
ftp server:	sunsite.unc.edu
ftp path:	/pub/Linux/system/Emulators

13.1 The BIOS emulator DOSemu

The DOSemu is not a DOS emulator, as the name suggests, but a PC and BIOS[1] emulator. It emulates parts of the hardware and the most important functions of the BIOS.

---

[1] BIOS = Basic Input/Output System

Therefore, you need a DOS license to use it. The true DOS runs inside a user process under LINUX. You can use practically any DOS version, be it MS-DOS, Novell-DOS (formerly known as DR-DOS) or PC-DOS by IBM.

The DOS emulator is still under development, with the programmers calling it an alpha version. In each new version, many new functions are implemented and errors corrected (or introduced). Nevertheless, it is quite stable, and many DOS programs also function in the emulator. In many areas, compatibility with a true DOS system is surprisingly high.

Additional Information and Sources	
Man pages:	`dos(1)`
Info system:	`Dosemu`
Documentation:	`QuickStart`, `DANG`,[2] DOSemu HowTo,
	various `README` files, Novell HowTo
Mailing list:	`linux-msdos@vger.rutgers.edu`
Package:	`dosemu0.67.9.tar.gz`
ftp server:	`tsx-11.mit.edu`
ftp path:	`/pub/linux/ALPHA/dosemu`
Size:	about 1.5 Mbytes

13.1.1 Installation

Since the DOS emulator is still under development, no binary distribution is provided by the programmers. Some distributions include a binary version, in which case you should be able to use a relatively recent version. When you install a new kernel, problems may arise from the tight interlocking between `DOSemu` and the kernel.

When you install a new version of `DOSemu`, you must first unpack the sources on your LINUX computer and then compile and install the program. First, you should configure the emulator by means of the `default-configure` command and then compile it. Listing 13.1 shows an example.

```
(Linux):~# cd /usr/src
(Linux):/usr/src# tar zxvf /tmp/dosemu0.67.9.tar.gz
(Linux):/usr/src# cd dosemu-0.67.9
(Linux):/usr/src/dosemu-0.67.9# ./default-configure
(Linux):/usr/src/dosemu-0.67.9# make
```

Listing 13.1 Configuring `DOSemu`.

The script `configure-default` automatically recognizes whether the X Window system is installed on the system (with header files and libraries) and if this is the case, also generates an emulator than can run under X. Additional settings which

---

[2] **DANG** = DOSemu Altering Novice Guide, an introduction to the internal functioning of the emulator.

must be carried out at compile time are set to default values. Table 13.1 shows a
selection of the possible configuration options.

Option	Meaning
--enable-novm86plus	The new variation for switching into vm86 mode is not used
--with-x=[yes|no]	With/without X support
--enable-nomitshm	Do not employ shared memory during X access
--enable-dodebug	Activate debugging
--enable-nosbemu	Do not activate Soundblaster emulation
--anable-linkstatic	Link statically
--enable-runasroot	Installation as setuid program

Table 13.1   Options for the DOSemu configure script.

Any further configuration of the emulator can be carried out by means of the
configuration file /etc/dosemu.conf or ~/.dosrc, so that it is not necessary to make
changes to the Makefile file.

13.1.2 Configuring the emulator

After installation, only the configuration files for the emulator need to be adapted.
First of all, the names of all users who are allowed to start the DOS emulator must be
registered in the file /etc/dosemu.users. This allows use of the emulator to be restricted to 'trustworthy' users. For many functions, such as graphical output or access
to ports, it is necessary to start the emulator with root privileges. This restriction to
named users tries to alleviate this security problem.

With certain restrictions, which are essentially dictated by security considerations, users can carry out the configuration of the DOS emulator themselves by creating a file .dosrc in their home directory. The system administrator can carry out a
system-wide configuration for all users with the aid of the file /etc/dosemu.conf.
The syntax of both files is identical; the file ./examples/config.dist from the
source distribution of the DOS emulator can serve as an example.

The configuration can be carried out with any editor of your choice. It is also
possible to use the ./configure script, which can be found in the sources of the
emulator. In that case, however, the file will not contain all the comments which extensively describe the possible configuration options in the sample file. Furthermore,
you will not find the examples that have been commented out, so the possible entries
cannot immediately be recognized. Even a modification carried out at a later stage
becomes more difficult, because the configuration program does not read an existing
configuration file a second time. Only that part of the configuration that has been
modified by the user is newly stored.

Configuration should be carried out in several steps, so after each step you can
check whether the modifications still allow the emulator to run. You need a DOS
boot diskette, created with FORMAT A: /S, but without the files CONFIG.SYS and

AUTOEXEC.BAT. On this floppy disk, you will copy all programs and drivers from the directories ./commands, ./garrot, and ./periph.

- To begin with, you will use the simplest configuration possible. Thus, problems are less likely to arise. The following settings should be adapted in the configuration file /etc/dosemu.conf in the first step:

  - Setting up the national keyboard mapping for the start-up on the console, if required. You should avoid using the strongly hardware-related access in raw mode which may stop any more keyboard input from being accepted after a crash of the emulator. However, a login via a network connection or a serial terminal will still work:

    keyboard { layout en-latin1 keybint on rawkeyboard off }

  - Initially, only a simple, incomplete emulation of the screen output should be set up. An incompatible setting can lead to a crash of the emulator, after which no more screen output can be read. The system itself has not crashed, but only the screen output, which still allows the system to be shut down in an orderly fashion and then restarted, for example via a network connection or a serial terminal.

    video { vga console }

  - The DOS for the emulator should initially be booted from the first diskette drive:

    bootA

  - The only devices that can be accessed directly by the emulator are the diskette drives. These entries must be adapted to one's own hardware configuration. The first keyword defines drive A:, the second one, drive B:.

    floppy { device /dev/fd0 threeinch } # drive A:
    floppy { device /dev/fd1 fiveinch } # drive B:

  Now you can attempt to start the DOS emulator for the first time with the DOS boot diskette. No additional partitions, hard disks, or partitions mounted under LINUX are as yet made available. Also, it is not possible to access printers, hardware extensions or networks.

- In the next step, you can provide access to the normal DOS partitions. The most popular way to do this is to use the redirector LREDIR.EXE or the driver EMUFS.SYS. Both alternatives have the same functionality, drives can be assigned both in the file CONFIG.SYS and, later on, in the file AUTOEXEC.BAT, or from the command line. For DOS programs, the drive behaves as if it were a network drive.

  The call of the driver EMUFS.SYS has the syntax DEVICE=EMUFS.SYS LINUX *path* [r]. This assigns the specified path under LINUX to the next available drive letter. If, in addition, the parameter r is specified, the drive is write-protected.

```
DEVICE=A:\EMUFS.SYS /mount/dos/c
DEVICE=A:\EMUFS.SYS / r
```

The program LREDIR.EXE serves the same purpose and can also be used from the command line. The following commands would yield the same result as the above example:

```
A:LREDIR C: LINUX\MOUNT\DOS\C
A:LREDIR D: LINUX\
```

Drive assignments can also be deleted by entering the command LREDIR DEL *drive*. The LREDIR command without parameters displays an overview of the drive assignments.

This access alternative is always sensible if the corresponding partitions are also accessed by LINUX. If the partitions have not yet been mounted, now is a good time to do it.

If the partitions are not available under LINUX because they have been treated with a 'hard disk doubler' such as Stacker or DoubleSpace, the only way left is direct access either to an individual partition (direct partition access, DPA) or even to the entire hard disk (whole disk access, WDA). If at all possible, you should only use direct partition access. For this purpose, you can use an appropriately modified entry from the sample configuration.

```
#disk { partition "/dev/hda1" readonly }
#disk { wholedisk "/dev/hda" }
```

Warning: Never use DPA or WDA to access mounted partitions! This may lead to unrecoverable errors in the file system structure, with consequential loss of data.

It is useful if the drive letters under DOSemu correspond to those used under true DOS. Another good idea is the use of a boot diskette whose image is stored on the LINUX disk. This is configured by means of the keyword bootdisk, with the virtual drive being assigned the drive letter A:. However, by means of the BOOTOFF program, this drive can be switched to the configuration set via the first floppy, and the boot image is overwritten by the diskette drive. The opposite, that is, overwriting the diskette drive with the boot image, can be achieved with BOOTON. Programs such as MSD, which want to analyze the start-up files, need access to the boot image.

- Now, direct access to the graphic card can be released to enable use of graphic programs and games under the emulator. This is not necessary if only text programs are to be used. For this purpose, the emulator must obtain access privileges which are otherwise reserved to the system administrator. In the standard installation, this is done by setting the s bit. This starts the emulator with the privileges of the system administrator (setuid-root), but for all accesses that require only normal user privileges, the system switches back to the uid of the user who started the emulator.

Another important issue is that a possible shadow of the VGA-BIOS is switched off. Under the keyword `video`, the file `config.dist` lists a series of examples for different hardware configurations. There are, however, graphic cards which are not (yet) supported.

The configuration for screen output on a terminal or via a network begins with the keyword `terminal`. Examples can be found in the configuration file `./example/config.dist`. Configuration of screen output under X begins with the keyword `X`. Extensive documentation of the possible settings can be found in the sample configuration.

- Now, additional hardware can be configured, for example the mouse or the access to the serial interfaces. Extensively commented samples for all settings can be found in the configuration file.

System security considerations

Since the emulator carries out many accesses closely related to the hardware, it is installed as a `setuid` program. Thus, many accesses are executed with privileges of the system administrator `root`. In a true, networked multi-user system, this is not looked upon kindly. In this case, one should consider whether direct hardware access cannot be completely prevented by means of an appropriate configuration of the emulator. This, however, would also prevent access to the ports and thus make a direct emulation of the loudspeaker and a representation of graphics on screen impossible.

For this reason, the configuration files provide the option of making special settings dependent on the user name or the current computer . Thus it is possible for guest users to be allowed to use the emulator, but that the emulator does not provide all functions. Other, trustworthy users, on the other hand, may use all the emulator's possibilities. The sample configuration of `DOSemu` includes various examples.

Error detection support

The emulator is able to output different items of information for debugging purposes. On the one hand, you can trigger the corresponding output by specifying the keyword `debug` in the configuration file. Another option is the specification as a parameter. In the following example, all messages are displayed and stored in the file `dos.log`. This file can be of great help for debugging the emulator or the configuration file. Generation of debug output can be toggled by means of the `DOSDBG` program even with the emulator running. These files can become shockingly huge in a very short time if you activate *all* output as in the following command.

```
(Linux):~$ dos -D+a -o dos.log
```

13.1.3 Usage

As a user, you will start the DOS emulator with the command `dos`. This starts DOS in the virtual machine. After processing the start-up files, you can work as usual under DOS. However, several things must be noted:

- When starting the DOS emulator under X, currently no graphic output is possible. Applications that use text mode, however, run without difficulties. You should use the internal mouse driver to make the mouse available for DOS programs under X too.

- Programs which access an installed CD-ROM drive via the MSCDEX interface can be used if the CD is not mounted under LINUX, but the DOSemu driver cdrom.sys is loaded. This requires establishing a symbolic link /dev/cdrom to the corresponding CD-ROM device. More detailed information on this subject can be found in the file README.CDROM.

- The DOS emulator runs without problems on a serial terminal or via a network connection. However, no graphics are available, and the use of key combinations such as ⟨Alt⟩-⟨F1⟩ is not directly possible for all key combinations. The slang library for terminal control, however, allows you to assemble these special key combinations piecewise. Each of these sequences is initiated in the standard configuration with the key combination ⟨Ctrl⟩-⟨6⟩. With the keyword escchar in the terminal configuration, another character can be specified. If ⟨?⟩ is entered as the next character, a help page is displayed that explains the remaining key combinations. The string ^a stands for the key combination ⟨Ctrl⟩-⟨6⟩. Table 13.2 shows an overview of the implemented keyboard mapping (after ⟨Ctrl⟩-⟨6⟩) which is partly laid out for the US American keyboard.

Keys	Result	Keys	Result
⟨n⟩	Function key Fn (F1 to F9)	⟨0⟩	F10
⟨-⟩	F11	⟨=⟩	F12
⟨s⟩	Shift key	⟨S⟩	STICKY SHIFT KEY
⟨a⟩	Alt key	⟨A⟩	STICKY ALT KEY
⟨c⟩	Ctrl key	⟨C⟩	STICKY CTRL KEY
⟨Space⟩	Reset sticky keys	⟨Ctrl⟩-⟨Z⟩	Suspend DOSemu
⟨Ctrl⟩-⟨R⟩	Refresh screen	⟨Ctrl⟩-⟨L⟩	Refresh screen
⟨?⟩	Display help	⟨h⟩	Display help
⟨Ctrl⟩-⟨6⟩	The character ^a		

Table 13.2 Key combinations for the DOS emulator on a terminal.

- Network access is possible via a virtual packet driver. This applies to access to both TCP/IP and Novell networks with IPX as protocol. Since the LINUX kernel also supports the IPX protocol, DOSemu can use this protocol directly. More detailed information on emulator configuration in the network can be found on page 309.

- If the DOS emulator is started on a virtual console and the rawkeyboard setting is used, the virtual console is changed as under X with the key combination ⟨Alt⟩-⟨Ctrl⟩-⟨Fn⟩.

13.1.4 Techniques and internal procedures

The DOS emulator is a program that emulates the hardware and the BIOS of an IBM-compatible PC. This emulation is so powerful that any commercial DOS can be started in the emulator. To achieve this compatibility, programmers have used a series of special functions of the Intel processors from 386 onward and of the LINUX system.

Basics of an emulation

In a multi-tasking operating system, a user process may directly access the hardware only under very specific circumstances. Under DOS, on the other hand, practically every program not only uses the programming interface via interrupt 21h, but can also access the hardware directly. This applies to the access of video memory as well as to the programming of the remaining hardware, such as the serial interfaces.

   Therefore, the DOS emulator puts the processor into the so-called virtual 8086 mode. In this mode, every operation that would be illegal under a multi-tasking system triggers an interrupt, which in turn causes the operating system to trigger the DOS emulator to emulate the corresponding function. Privileged commands are, for example, access to I/O ports and triggering of interrupts.

Memory in the emulator

For the virtual system, the emulator can emulate any kind of memory known under DOS, that is, EMS (expanded memory), XMS (extended memory), UMB (upper memory blocks), HMA (high memory area) and access via DPMI (DOS protected mode interface). Since this memory is emulated in the virtual memory of the LINUX system, the emulator can use more memory than is actually available, obviously at the cost of speed, because this memory is only available via swapping.

   Memory below 1 Mbyte is used as usual under DOS. Therefore, the emulator is loaded into memory above the 1 Mbyte address. With the a.out binary format, this was achieved by means of a library which was loaded to a 'high' address. With the ELF binary format, this trick is no longer needed.

   It is also possible to map the physical memory area below 1 Mbyte directly into the address space of the DOS emulator. Then it is possible to read data from and store data into the data area of an expansion board. This memory assignment can be configured with the keyword hardware_ram.

   For all types of memory mentioned above, it is possible to fine-tune the configuration more precisely. Examples can be found in the configuration file. If you use EMS, you must load the EMS.SYS driver from the ./commands directory in your CONFIG.SYS.

Input devices for the emulator

Just like under DOS, the user has keyboard and mouse as input devices. The keyboard can be used in different ways, with a series of peculiarities to be found both with UNIX and with DOS.

The best emulation of the keyboard (on the console) is activated by setting the rawkeyboard mode in the file /etc/dosemu.conf. This allows DOS programs directly to access the keyboard connected to the console. Under X, the keyboard events are converted by the emulator into the corresponding scan codes of the keyboard. The DOS emulator can also be used via a network or on a serial terminal. Here, as under X, it is not possible to use the keyboard in the raw mode, so a conversion is required.

The mouse can also be used in different modes:

- Under X, the internal mouse driver should be used which, as under Windows or OS/2, ensures that X mouse events are translated into the corresponding DOS mouse movements.

- On the console, you can either use the internal mouse driver too, or you can release the corresponding serial interface for use by the emulator and then use a normal DOS driver. Since these drivers often react very sensitively to timing problems, you should use one of the drivers mentioned in the HowTo, if you need to.

- When using the emulator via a network or a serial terminal, no mouse can be used.

Output

The DOS emulator can use a series of output devices. This begins with the different possibilities for screen output:

- The DOS emulator can be used on the console, in both text and graphic modes, provided your graphic card is supported.

- Under X, only text mode can currently be used, but the mouse works 'seamlessly'[3] for DOS programs.

- The DOS emulator can be used both in the network and via a serial terminal. Here, a special terminal control (slang) is used, so that reasonable work is possible even via slow connections.

Another output device is the printer. In /etc/dosemu.conf, up to three printers can be configured. The output can either be stored in a file or immediately redirected to a program. One option is the use of lpr, so that printer output is managed by the LINUX spool system. There, GhostScript can be used to allow output of PostScript files even to non-PostScript printers. Because of the limited memory size, this is practically impossible under DOS itself. All printer output is processed that has been

---

[3] When the mouse pointer is in the XDos window, the mouse sends the mouse events to the DOS program.

generated via the DOS or the BIOS printer. This applies to most programs. Under Windows 3.0, you specify LPT1.DOS or LPT1.OS2 as the printer interface.

Diskettes and hard disks

The emulator only releases its full power when access to stored data and installed programs is made possible in the same way as under a directly starting DOS. All partitions should be available, and the assignment of drive letters in the emulator should correspond to the drive letters under DOS. Access to diskettes and hard disks is possible via a series of alternatives:

- The EMUFS driver and the LREDIR program are capable of creating a DOS drive which is treated by DOS as a network drive. No access outside the LINUX file system is needed. With this method, the DOS emulator can access all partitions mountable under LINUX, including read access to HPFS partitions of OS/2.
- Direct access to an individual partition (direct partition access, DPA) simulates a hard disk which consists only of this one partition. Partitions which are accessed via DPA or WDA must in no case be simultaneously mounted under LINUX – this may damage the file system!
- The emulator can also have access to an entire hard disk (whole disk access, WDA). Here too, no partition of this hard disk must be mounted under LINUX.
- Both the diskettes and the hard disks can be simulated by means of a file of appropriate size in the LINUX file system. This is called a disk image, which can, for example, be created with dd. One sensible use is as an image for the start of the DOS operating system, so that no floppy disk needs inserting. This greatly speeds up the start-up process.
- The diskette drives can be used directly.
- Provided they are supported by LINUX, CD-ROM drives can be used in two ways:
  - The CD can be mounted under LINUX and then be accessed via the network redirector (EMUFS or LREDIR).
  - A DOS driver exists which simulates a CD-ROM drive accessible via MSCDEX inside the DOS emulator.

External hardware, ports, interrupts

It is also possible to access hardware which is not supported by LINUX. For this purpose, the ports used must be released for the DOS emulator. This is done via an entry in the file /etc/dosemu.conf under the keyword ports. The kernel can forward a possible hardware interrupt to the emulator by means of the so-called silly interrupt generator. However, this requires a kernel patch. This is a possibility for accessing Novell or other networks by means of the DOS emulator. Virtualization of DMA (direct memory access) is under development.

Networks

With the DOS emulator it is also possible to access networks. Depending on the protocol, different procedures are needed, which will be explained in more detail in the following paragraphs.

DOSemu in a TCP/IP network   LINUX has a complete complement of network programs, such as ftp, telnet and others. Therefore, at first, running these programs under the DOS emulator does not appear to make much sense. There are, however, a series of functions which could hardly be implemented without a TCP/IP protocol stack in the emulator.

- The DOS emulator provides a complete packet interface. DOS-based network programs (clients and servers) can thus be implemented and tested on one computer, making use of a dedicated (virtual) subnetwork (see Figure 13.1). Thus, developers no longer need to have several computers at their disposal and there are no more consistency problems, since all programs can be stored on a shared disk.

- In the emulator, drives can be mounted via XFS (DOS-NFS client) and, for example, exported with Personal NetWare.

- Vice versa, Novell directories can be mapped to drive letters and then exported via SOSS (DOS-NFS server).

The latter two functions usually require the acquisition of (relatively expensive) Novell software. A true DOS computer running these functions could not take on any further tasks. A LINUX computer could, on the other hand, still be used as a print server or similar.

For these functions, several protocol stacks must be implemented on the LINUX computer. If one or two additional network cards are used, only a few additional stacks can be handled. Therefore, a virtual network is implemented in which packets are routed to the emulators. The emulators are assigned a separate subnetwork, which is then routed into the real network. The management effort must not be underestimated, but, on the other hand, DOS programs can now use all resources of the TCP/IP network without difficulties.

First, the emulators are to be assigned a separate subnetwork. A series of network numbers is available for an internal network whose data is not to be routed to the outside world (the Internet). From these networks, defined in [rfc2200], you should choose a Class C network. In this example, network 192.xxx.xxx.0 is used. The local computer has the address aaa.bbb.ccc.ddd.

On the local computer, you must now activate routing to the virtual DOS computers. First, a new (virtual) network device must be implemented via which the data is routed to the DOS emulators. The directory ./v-net contains a kernel module that implements the corresponding device. After compiling the module with make and loading it by means of the insmod program, the corresponding interface must be configured by means of ifconfig and the associated route created with route.

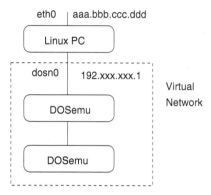

Figure 13.1   Network scheme for TCP/IP in the DOS emulator.

```
ifconfig dsn0 192.xxx.xxx.1 broadcast 192.xxx.xxx.255 \
 netmask 255.255.255.0
route add -net 192.xxx.xxx.0 dsn0
```

Listing 13.2   Configuration of the virtual network interface.

The emulator uses this interface only if the files `libpacket.c` and `pktnew.c` have been replaced with the files `libpacket.c.multi` and `pktnew.c.multi` in the `./net` directory. These modules assign each `tty` a virtual Ethernet address which can, for example, be used for the assignment of an Internet address via `bootp`. This assignment may cause problems if several emulators were started from the same window, for example under X. The virtual Ethernet address consists of one fixed and one variable part. The address has the form `64:62:variable:78:78:78`; the variable is calculated following Table 13.3 on the basis of the `tty` from which the emulator was started.

tty	Third address field
ttyn	n
ttypn	0xC0 + n
ttySn	0x40 + n

Table 13.3   Virtual Ethernet addresses.

If you want to use the emulator to access not only resources in your own computer, you must also adapt the routing tables on the other computer. There you can enter a static route to your computer for the virtual network assigned to the emulators.

```
route add -net 192.xxx.xxx.0 gw aaa.bbb.ccc.ddd
```

In the emulator, you can then use the standard programs that build on a packet driver, for example a multiplexer such as `PKTMUX`, or `SOSS` or `XFS`.

DOSemu in an IPX network DOSemu can employ two different ways of gaining access to a Novell network with IPX protocol. Novell uses three different frame types (Ethernet_II, Ethernet_802.2, Ethernet_802.3). The application areas and the possibilities of integrating LINUX computers are different, so you should contact your network administrator.

- Ethernet_II is used by Novell if the server supports the IP protocol. The IPX protocol too can be used with this frame type. This makes the connection of a LINUX computer relatively easy.

- The frame type Ethernet_802.3 was used by Novell before the VLM system or NetWare 4.x were introduced. With this frame type, no IP packets are routed.

- Today, Novell recommends the use of Ethernet_802.2, which is also the standard for newly created servers or networks. This frame type is not supported by the DOSemu packet driver, so you must either establish another frame type in the network or use LINUX IPX.

The configuration of LINUX IPX requires only a few paths and has proved more successful in practice through a significantly higher speed and the support of all frame types. To begin with, the kernel must support the IPX protocol. If no appropriate message is displayed at the start-up of LINUX, you must reconfigure and recompile the kernel. The prompt for 'The IPX protocol' must be answered with 'y.' You also need the programs that can be found in the ./ipxutils directory in the sources of the emulator. With the ipx_interface program, you can activate the IPX protocol on your network card.

```
ipx_interface add -p eth0 802.2
```

In the above example, you need to replace the device and the frame type with the device you are using or with the corresponding frame type (802.2, 802.3, or EtherII). As a last step, you need to enter the line ipxsupport on in the file dosemu.conf. This concludes the configuration on the LINUX side. After you have started the emulator, you only need to start the NetWare shell NETX.EXE or VLM.EXE. You do not need LSL, IPXODI, or any other program.

The second way to make a connection to an IPX network is via the virtual packet driver of the emulator. This requires no kernel support (except for the general TCP/IP). In the emulator, you must then start the following Novell programs:

```
LSL
PDETHER
IPXODI
VLM        # or NETX
```

The PDETHER program is an ODI driver which builds on a packet driver. This makes it possible to transmit IPX packets via the internal packet driver of the DOS emulator. This method only functions for the frame types Ethernet II and 802.3; for the latter, the line pktdriver novell_hack must be activated in the configuration. If you use an ODI driver, the file NET.CFG must be adapted accordingly.

DOSemu in other networks   The DOS emulator does not provide any special support for access to other networks. Nevertheless, it may be possible to access these networks by adding another network card to the computer and loading the DOS driver into the emulator. Such cards usually make use of interrupts for controlling the card and a RAM window for communication.

The DOS emulator can process hardware interrupts if the LINUX kernel forwards them to user processes. For this, you must load the 'silly interrupt generator' kernel module. Subsequently, the corresponding interrupt can be permitted in the DOSemu configuration by activating the line `silly interrupt`.

Access to the real memory of the computer can then be mapped into virtual DOS memory by means of the keyword `hardware_ram`. You can find commented examples for these settings in the sample configuration.

13.1.5 Further developments

Inspired by the great success of LINUX as a free operating system and by the need for a freely available DOS, a group was formed to work on the so-called `FreeDOS` project. This is intended to provide a free DOS which will still be maintained even after Microsoft and IBM will have discontinued active development of DOS. First programs and the operating system itself are already available.

Additional Information and Sources	
WWW server:	`www.freedos.org`

13.2 The Windows emulator `Wine`

The Windows emulator `Wine` (Wine Is Not an Emulator, or WINdows Emulator) converts calls of the MS Windows[4] API (Application Programming Interface) into equivalent X calls. This allows Windows programs to run under X.

The development of the Windows emulator `Wine` began when Sun announced the release of their Windows emulators `Wabi`. Some experienced LINUX programmers immediately began with the development of the emulator. Already the first versions of `Wine` were ported to the freely available *BSD systems. The first and most important application that ran under `Wine` was the good old Solitaire game from Windows 3.1.

This emulator is supposed to become a complete Windows emulation. Currently, however, it still makes use of several DLLs (Dynamic Link Libraries) from the Windows 3.1 environment. Besides the compatibility with this version, the Win32 interface is implemented as well; thus, programs for Windows 95 and Windows NT can also be run under `Wine`. A further goal is the development of a library (`libwine`) with which Windows programs can be easily ported to UNIX and X.

---

[4] In the following text, Windows stands for Microsoft Windows. X is a short form for the X Window system.

However, the Wine program is not a complete Windows emulator yet. The authors are step by step implementing all Windows APIs, including the Win32 API. Thus, Wine is one step ahead of the commercial Wabi which can only handle 16-bit programs. As long as not all Windows DLLs have been implemented completely and without errors, you can require loading of the original DLL via a command line option.

An important milestone is running the MS Office program suite. As yet, not all Windows programs are running, but the developers are working on it. Currently a patch is released about every two weeks, which is evidence of the visible progress of this development.

The Wine emulator is not subject to the GPL, but to the more liberal BSD or X copyright. The developers have made this decision deliberately because they do not regard the GPL as a suitable license for this project.

13.2.1 Compilation and installation

Wine does not exist as a binary distribution. Therefore you must have the C compiler installed to compile the source code. The installation of Wine also requires the X Window system to be installed together with the associated libraries and include files. An additional precondition is the libXpm library which is used for easy handling of bitmaps. The installation of Wine is as simple as that of the GNU programs and is limited to the use of ./configure and make.

Currently, in parallel with the emulator program wine, the compatibility library libwine is generated as well. This requires a certain amount of disk space, about 20 Mbytes. The general hope is that, in parallel with the development of the emulator, the library can be worked upon too, thus facilitating porting of Windows programs to UNIX on any hardware platforms.

13.2.2 Configuration of the emulator

Prior to its first start, the emulators need to be appropriately configured. As the default, the file /usr/local/etc/wine.conf is used. Individual users can configure the emulator according to their own requirements by means of the file ~/.winerc. Both files have exactly the same structure. You will also find a sample configuration with the name wine.ini in the Wine directory.

An important issue for starting your first programs is the assignment of drive letters to LINUX directories, and the search path for programs and DLLs. For this purpose, the file wine.conf, whose syntax recalls that of the .ini files of Windows, includes various sections:

- The assignment of drive letters to directories in the file system or devices such as diskette drives is carried out in one Drive section per drive. You can specify both devices and directories of the LINUX directory tree.

```
[Drive C]
Path=/home/dos
```

```
Type=hd
Label=DOS-DISK
```

- The search paths for programs, DLLs and other paths are configured in the wine section. The drives are assigned according to the specifications made in the Drive sections.

```
[wine]
Windows=c:\windows
system=c:\windows\system
Temp=c:\tmp
Path=c:\windows;c:\windows\system;C:\bin\win
```

- The configuration file contains additional sections for the selection of fonts (fonts), the serial and parallel interfaces (serialports and parallelports) and the control of output for debugging purposes (spy). Initially, these sections can remain unchanged; more detailed information can be found in the file ./documentation/fonts in the Wine sources.

This concludes the configuration for the time being, and the first Windows program can be started. One of the most popular Windows programs is Solitaire, a card game. Happy playing!

```
(Linux):~$ wine sol
```

13.2.3 The emulation technique

A series of problems must be solved to emulate the Windows API under LINUX and X. Here we try to explain the basic concepts underlying individual solutions. For a more in-depth view, you should read through the commented source code.

The Windows program must first be loaded into memory for them to be executed. Since LINUX and *BSD use completely different internal formats for programs (namely ELF and a.out), the necessary routines had to be developed from scratch. These routines load both the programs and the required DLLs into memory. All this takes place in the user space, so that here, in contrast to the iBCS2 emulator, no modification of the kernel is required. The individual segments of a Windows program are loaded into memory, and a selector which points to this segment is generated.

Windows programs can (and must) manipulate the descriptor tables of the Intel processor i386 and higher (or a compatible processor). This made it necessary to introduce a new system call by means of which the local descriptor table (LDT) can be modified. A normal process cannot do this directly without endangering the integrity of the entire system.

Furthermore, both the Windows program and the emulator must be able to access data areas such as the global or local Windows heap. Since Windows programs run in 16-bit mode and the emulator in 32-bit mode, an appropriate address conversion is required. The addresses of the corresponding memory areas can be directly converted into one another. Thus, for example, the segmented Windows address 1237:89AB is converted into the address 0x123789BA in the Wine process address space. This prevents Windows from accessing arbitrary addresses. Also, address zones that are apparently contiguous under Windows are fragmented in the emulator.

The 16-bit call of the Windows functions from within the Windows program are converted via a call-gate (a function that takes care of the entire handling centrally) into a 32-bit call of the corresponding function of the emulator. In these functions the parameters are converted into a suitable format for X calls and the corresponding X functions are called. Several things must be considered for passing parameters and returning results:

- Windows programs use a 16-bit stack; the Wine process a 32-bit stack. At the call of a Wine function, the arguments must be converted from the 16-bit stack and put on the 32-bit stack. The corresponding functions can be found in the ./if1632 directory.
- Wine functions that are called by Windows programs must lie in a memory area in which they can also be addressed by Windows programs.
- Functions which return their results in processor registers must (re)set the registers correctly when the function is terminated.
- Callback functions in application programs called by Windows must be allowed.

Wine manages the X windows itself, so that, on the one hand, the use of Windows programs under Wine is similar to the use under true Windows. On the other hand, this leads to problems with virtual window managers which provide several virtual desktops. There, the window of a Wine program can always be seen on the current screen. At the moment, it is possible to start the emulator with the parameter –desktop, so the X window manager manages one window containing a virtual Windows desktop (Listing 13.3).

```
(Linux):~$ wine -desktop 640x480 sol
```

Listing 13.3   Starting wine with the –desktop option.

If you do not appreciate one window in which the Windows programs frisk about, the option –managed may possibly help you (Listing 13.4). Here, the window-dressing is carried out by the window manager. However, since this procedure is not known under Windows, both options lead to some problems.

```
(Linux):~$ wine -managed sol
```

Listing 13.4   Starting wine with the –managed option.

This kind of control is a visible break in the use of the X Window system, but no better solution is currently in sight. One possibility would be the development of a Windows-compatible window manager. On my own system, I use `fvwm95`, which emulates the interface of Windows 95 together with the `-desktop` option.

13.2.4 Additional features

The development of `Wine` is not only aimed at creating a Windows emulator for LINUX and *BSD systems, but other operating systems too, which do not run on Intel processors. For this purpose, Bochs, a (shareware) CPU emulator for Intel CPUs, could be used.

A further function of `Wine` is the use as a library for porting Windows programs to arbitrary UNIX/X systems. This library has already been employed to implement a program manager and a help browser. Both programs are included in the `Wine` sources, but are not automatically installed.

For debugging purposes, `Wine` contains its own integrated debugger which can work in both 16-bit and 32-bit mode. Initially, the GNU debugger was used, but because of the GPL restrictions, it was replaced with the Mach debugger.

13.2.5 Further development

Many features are still to be implemented to complete the emulator. Important functions that are currently still lacking are the representation of different fonts, in particular TrueType fonts, a device-independent printer control, and functions such as DDE and OLE. Besides this, the implementation of the Win32 interface is being worked upon to allow processing of Windows 95 programs.

In addition, a manual is under development which is currently supplied in Texinfo format. It describes the internals of the emulator and documents the implemented API.

Additional Information and Sources	
Newsgroup:	`comp.emulators.ms-windows.wine`
`ftp` server:	`tsx-11.mit.edu`
`ftp` path:	`/pub/linux/ALPHA/Wine/development`
Package:	`Wine-date.tar.gz`
Size:	about 1.6 Mbytes
Homepage:	`http://www.winehq.com`

13.3 The iBCS emulator

For UNIX systems that run on Intel processors, iBCS (Intel Binary Compatibility Specification) is a standard which allows binary programs to be exchanged between different UNIX systems on Intel processors. LINUX itself is not compatible with iBCS because it uses a different method to execute system calls (`int 80` instead of `lcall 7`). Also, a series of internal kernel structures are organized differently, so direct access to kernel-internal data is not possible. Nevertheless, with the aid of the emulator, it becomes possible to use programs for other UNIX systems under LINUX as well.

First, the programs that are not present in LINUX binary format must be loaded into memory. This requires a new loading routine which can read and load these formats. The following binary formats are supported:

- a.out (with the standard LINUX loading routine)
- ELF, the standard format for LINUX and SVR4
- COFF (Common Object File Format) from SVR3
- XOUT from Xenix 386

Execution of programs of the following operating systems is made possible, partly in a limited form, by the introduction of personalities. These are rules for the conversion of system calls, signals, and error codes. The following personalities are supported:

- i386 BSD (386BSD, FreeBSD, NetBSD, BSDI/386) is currently being tested
- SVR4 (Unixware, USL, Dell, and so on)
- generic SVR3
- SCO (SVR3 with extensions)
- Wyse V/386 (SVR3 with extensions)
- Xenix V/386 (only 386 programs in the 'small model')
- Xenix V/286

Besides mandatory system calls such as `stat`, `exec`, and many more, a series of network functions and inter-process communication (IPC) are supported. The following areas of system calls are emulated:

- SYSV IPC allows communication between programs
- The device `/dev/socksys` which represents the socket interface for stream-based network implementations
- Wyse V/386 system calls for the socket interface
- The device `/dev/spx` which implements streams for local X servers

With this emulation, a series of commercial programs for other UNIX systems based on Intel 386 can also be run under LINUX. The sources of the emulator include a list of programs that can be used with the emulator under LINUX. There you can also find hints and tips on how to start some of these programs.

A further area is the emulation of shared libraries. Dynamically linked programs need the corresponding library at runtime. However, since the licensing conditions of the corresponding vendors are to be observed, which usually prohibit copying of the library to another (second) computer, programmers have begun to develop a corresponding free library. The sources of this library can also be found here.

13.3.1 Installation

The emulator is a module which must first be compiled and then loaded into the kernel space by means of `insmod` (see also Section 4.3). Prior to compilation, the configuration of the emulator can be checked and adapted, if required. This is done by copying the file `CONFIG.i386` under the name `CONFIG` and adapting it accordingly.

You must specify which processor architecture you are using (currently, Intel and SPARC processors are supported). In addition you must specify whether you have an SMP-capable kernel and whether your kernel works with symbol versions of modules (Listing 13.5).

```
# processor architecture
ARCH=i386
# SMP-kernel: 'yes' or 'no'
SMP=no
# version numbers for modules: 'yes' or 'no'
USE_VERSIONS=yes
```

Listing 13.5   Configuration of the `iBCS` emulator for the appropriate kernel.

Many emulations are automatically compiled and inserted into the kernel module. The emulation for BSD and Xenix programs may or may not be installed. This selection is carried out in the configuration file entries shown in Listing 13.6.

```
# BSD emulation (experimental): 'yes' or 'no'
EMU_BSD        = yes
# Xenix 286 emulation: 'yes' or 'no'
EMU_X286       = yes
```

Listing 13.6   Active emulations in the `iBCS` module.

Furthermore, you must configure the binary formats that can be loaded by means of the emulator. Listing 13.7 shows the corresponding entries in the `CONFIG` file.

```
# ELF programs: 'yes' or 'no'
EMU_BINFMT_ELF  = yes
# COFF (SVR3): 'yes' or 'no'
EMU_BINFMT_COFF = yes
# XOUT (Xenix): 'yes' or 'no'
EMU_BINFMT_XOUT = yes
```

Listing 13.7   Activating the binary formats for `iBCS`.

After compilation of the module by means of `make` and installation into the kernel with `insmod`, a series of devices must be created to enable different programs to run. For this purpose, you can use the script shown in Listing 13.8. Version 2.1 of the `MAKEDEV` program can create some of these devices if it is called with the parameter `ibcs2`.

```bash
#!/bin/bash
major=30
mknod /dev/socksys c $major 0
ln -s /dev/socksys /dev/nfsd
mknod /dev/inet/arp c $major 2
mknod /dev/inet/icmp c $major 2
mknod /dev/inet/ip c $major 2
mknod /dev/inet/rip c $major 2
mknod /dev/inet/tcp c $major 2
mknod /dev/inet/udp c $major 2
ln -s /dev/null /dev/XOR
mknod /dev/spx c $major 1
```

Listing 13.8 Generating the necessary devices for iBCS2.

For the execution of dynamically linked programs you will need the corresponding shared libraries. You may use the libraries of the corresponding UNIX system if the licensing conditions allow this. However, there are also free libraries in the `ibcs2` directory which enable many programs to run.

13.3.2 Emulation technique

The emulation of iBCS2 under LINUX has become necessary because of differences between LINUX and SVR4. Essentially, these differences consist in different binary formats for programs and internal data structures. Nevertheless, the emulation is suitable for many programs.

First of all, a decision is made on the basis of certain features about the operating system to which the program belongs. The recognition works similarly to the `file` program, which evaluates a database `/etc/magic` for this purpose. The recognized operating system is entered as a personality into the task structure. A personality is characterized by a series of settings that it modifies:

- LINUX uses a different method (int 0x80) to call a system call than other UNIX systems (lcall 7). The emulator redirects the 'incorrect' calls to the corresponding LINUX functions.

- LINUX uses different numbers for the system calls. Therefore, a table for each personality specifies how these calls are to be converted.

- The numerical values of the error codes are also different. Here too, the conversion is carried out by means of a table.

- Signals are processed analogously.

For a complete emulation of an SVR4 system, you will also need the corresponding shared libraries. Usually, however, the licensing conditions of commercial UNIX systems prohibit copying of the libraries to a LINUX computer. Therefore, a free version of the SVR4 and SCO libraries is under development.

13.3.3 Application of the emulator

This emulator makes it possible to use commercial programs which were, for example, developed for SCO. It is important to work with statically linked programs because the appropriate shared libraries are not available for LINUX and the licenses of the other UNIX systems often prohibit simply copying these libraries to the LINUX computer. Thus, for example, it is possible to obtain a statically linked SCO version of the WordPerfect word processing software which runs without problems under LINUX too. Software vendors often do not port commercial programs to the LINUX operating system, but the creation of a statically linked SCO version is often easy.

Additional Information and Sources	
Mailing list:	`linux-ibcs2@vger.rutgers.edu`
ftp server:	`tsx-11.mit.edu`
ftp path:	`/pub/linux/BETA/ibcs2`
Package:	`ibcs2-date.tar.gz`
Size:	about 200 Kbytes

LINUX in a networked environment

14

LINUX is often employed as a teaching system in the private domain. Because of its stability and power, LINUX is, however, also conquering the professional and commercial domains. Here, cooperation with other computer architectures and operating systems is of the utmost importance. But even in the private domain, LINUX systems are often networked with older computers which can, for example, serve as terminals.

A multi-user and multi-tasking operating system such as LINUX offers many advantages in a network. Many resources, such as a modem, can be used by several persons. You simply have to log in on the computer to which the modem is connected. However, this computer can still be used for other tasks, for example, as a file and printer server.

In the following chapters we present several possibilities for LINUX networking, with an emphasis on networking with MS Windows (in particular Windows for Workgroups) and Windows NT. Much space is also dedicated to security considerations, because with the installation of a network, the computer becomes more vulnerable.

LINUX, like other UNIX systems, uses TCP/IP (Transmission Control Protocol/Internet Protocol). This is a collection of protocols used for communication between different computers. They are the standard protocols in the Internet.

The specifications of the protocols are defined in so-called RFCs (Requests for Comment) which are freely available on the Internet. These RFCs are divided into proposals for further development and reports on problems with network implementation or administration, draft standards, and official standards. They do not constitute a standard of a national or international organization such as ANSI, DIN or ISO, but an agreement between Internet users.

Because of the free availability of the RFCs, an implementation is possible for everyone. This is one of the reasons for the large diffusion of the protocol and the good cross-compatibility between different implementations. The RFCs are developed by experienced Internet users and system administrators; the IAB (Internet Activities Board) manages these standards and their development.

RFCs can basically be written by any interested Internet user. The definition of a stable and secure protocol is, however, relatively difficult, so only a few users would stand the process of public discussion. Many of the RFCs are elaborated by the IETF (Internet Engineering Task Force). The process of how an RFC becomes an Internet standard is also defined in RFCs [rfc1311] and [rfc1602]).

If you want do delve deeper into the matter of UNIX networks, the Internet or Intranets, you must read the corresponding RFCs. A list of the most important RFCs can be found in the RFC directory in Appendix D; in addition, we always refer to the corresponding RFCs where necessary. The RFCs can be found, for example, under `ftp://ftp.nic.de/pub/doc/rfc` or `ftp://ftp.gwdg.de/pub/rfc`.

Because of the complexity of networks and the employed software, this book is not able to cover all aspects. A great deal of additional information can be found in the HowTo documents of the Linux Documentation Project, for example on SLIP, news or mail, and in the FAQs of the newsgroups that deal with these subjects. Many of the programs used under LINUX are not LINUX-specific and are therefore not discussed in the LINUX newsgroups, but in those on the programs or protocols. Furthermore, the bibliography in Appendix C contains a series of books on this subject area that are really worth reading.

The current Windows versions include clients for access via `telnet` and `ftp`; for practically all other protocols, free clients are available. Available, but relatively little known, are an NFS server (SOSS) and a client (XFS) for DOS.

The use of Windows as an Internet server is not to be recommended, but as a client, Windows is often an alternative to LINUX or UNIX. The latest versions of this popular PC operating system usually include all Internet clients needed.

14.1 Network software layers

The TCP/IP software consists of a number of layers that build on each other. Each layer is based on a well-defined interface with the underlying layers and can make use of their services without knowing which means are employed to provide these. Thus, it does not matter at all to an application program which medium is used to transfer its data. This subdivision into separate layers result in clean interfaces and facilitates implementation.

The Open System Interconnection (OSI) seven-layer reference model shown in Figure 14.1 defines seven layers. The tasks and functions of these seven layers can also be found (with a slightly different structure) in the layers of the TCP/IP protocols. Because of the different structure of the TCP/IP protocol, no direct mapping between the two models is possible.

A rough outline of the layers of the TCP/IP protocol is shown in Figure 14.2. Approximately, the OSI layers indicated for comparison purposes functionally correspond to the layers of the TCP/IP protocols. In the following chapter, we will work through these layers from bottom to top to obtain, in the end, an overview of the functioning of a TCP/IP network.

Application	Level 7
Presentation	Level 6
Session	Level 5
Transport	Level 4
Network	Level 3
Link	Level 2
Physical	Level 1

Figure 14.1   The OSI seven-layer model.

Application level (OSI: layers 5-7)	telnet	ftp	Mail	DNS	tftp	NFS
Transmission level (OSI layer 4)	TCP			UDP		
Internet level (OSI layer 3)	IP & ICMP					
Network level (OSI layers 1+2)	Ethernet		Token Ring		SLIP	

Figure 14.2   TCP/IP protocol layers.

14.2 Network hardware

A number of possibilities exists to connect a LINUX system to other computers, both locally and remote. One possible option is its integration into a local network (LAN) by means of Ethernet, ArcNet, or Token Ring. For connection to remote computers or networks, SLIP (Serial Line IP) and PPP (Point-to-Point Protocol) are available. Additional information can also be found in the corresponding HowTo documents.

This chapter deals with the integration of a LINUX computer into a local network; connections via modem are discussed in Chapter 24. As a first step, the computers must be connected by means of an appropriate cable. Today's most popular solution is Ethernet (CSMA/CD[1]), where three different types of cable are possible:

---

[1] Carrier Sense Multiple Access, Collision Detect; each user is allowed to send immediately, collisions are detected, and transmission is started again.

- Thick Ethernet (RJ-45 cable) is practically no longer used. The technical denomination is 10Base5.

- Thin Ethernet (coax cable) is frequently used in smaller installations and has a net throughput of 10 Mbits/sec. The Ethernet backbone is laid in the form of a bus and must be terminated at both ends with a terminating resistor (terminator). The individual computers are connected to the bus by means of a T-piece. Figure 14.3 shows a schematic representation of correct and incorrect (but widely used) connections.

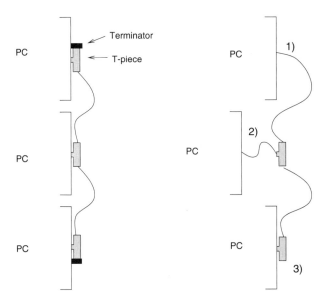

Figure 14.3   Cabling with Thin Ethernet – correct and incorrect.

The cable type is RG-58, the connectors are known by the term BNC. The technical denomination is 10Base2. When the bus is interrupted, problems may occur along the whole length of the cable, therefore this cable type is usually employed only in small installations. Furthermore, the cable length (without repeaters) is limited to about 180 meters.

- Twisted Pair (10BaseT) is often used in larger installations and allows speeds of up to 100 Mbits/sec, with suitable hardware. However, in addition to the network cards in the computers, a central concentrator or hub is needed, so this cable type plays practically no role in the private domain and in small installations. Cabling is laid out in the form of a star, with a separate cable connecting each computer to the concentrator. The maximum cable length is about 100 meters. If you do not have to worry about money, this is currently the best choice.

One problem with Thin Ethernet cabling is that a faulty connection to the network or a cable which is slightly too long can cause unexplained occurrences on other computers. If problems occur, you should therefore split the network into smaller parts and try to localize the fault in this way. Usual errors with connections are (see also Figure 14.3):

1. The end of the network cable is not connected to the computer by means of a T-piece, but directly to the network card.

2. A computer is not directly connected to the T-piece, but with an intermediate short cable.

3. The network cable is not equipped with a terminating resistor; it is not *terminated*.

In practice, the biggest problems are the limited cable length and thus the limited number of computers that can be connected, and the network load, which grows with the number of connected computers. The higher the network load, the higher the probability that a collision will occur and that both sending computers must wait for a short time and then retry transmission. In Token Ring networks, only the station that has the token is allowed to send.

If the network cable has become too long, the most varied, random problems occur. In such cases, it may be sensible to reduce the network and see whether this works. If the problems disappear, you should split the network by means of a bridge. In many network installations, meters for cable lengths and other important measures are available, but often one has to do without these devices.

In the simplest case, an Ethernet can be extended by means of a *repeater*. This device forwards all network packets on one cable to all other cables. Thus, the maximum cable length can be circumvented (but only to a certain degree, because the number of repeaters in a network is limited too). No load separation takes place, so the number of collisions is not reduced; therefore, repeaters are only seldom employed these days.

A more sensible thing to do is to employ a *bridge* which, on the basis of the network card addresses, decides to which of the cables the packets should be forwarded. LINUX can be used as a bridge in the same way as PC-Bridge, a DOS program. You can also buy hardware bridges. A *switch* is an enhanced bridge which can connect several networks in parallel and transmit several packets simultaneously. These devices are usually only worth employing in larger networks.

Routers too are used to separate networks and work on the next higher protocol level, for example with IP packets. Besides separating segments, routers can convert packets between different connection types (Token Ring, Ethernet, or SLIP). In practically all large networks you will find routers that can control remote connections. Routers, unlike repeaters, bridges, and switches, work on the protocol level and not at hardware level. Therefore, routers must be able to master all necessary protocols (such as IPX, AppleTalk, or SNA).

In the simplest case, an Ethernet card is built for exactly one type of connection. There are also combined cards that can be operated with several types of cable. If you are likely to change cabling in the near future, such cards may be a good choice. Otherwise, you will usually get by with a simple card. You will find a matching driver in the LINUX kernel for practically all widely used Ethernet cards from different manufacturers. More detailed information can be found in the Ethernet HowTo or, for Token Ring, in the Token Ring HowTo.

14.3 Network-related kernel configuration

After installation of the network card and connection to the network, the kernel must be configured for network operation, and the appropriate hardware drivers must be linked. The CONFIG_NET option generally activates the network capabilities of LINUX. Subsequently, the available protocols and options can be specified further.

To prevent the kernel from unnecessary growth, you should only activate the drivers and protocols that you will actually be using. Nearly all drivers can also be compiled as modules which are loaded into the kernel at runtime. Thus, the corresponding memory is only occupied when the drivers are actually needed. This can be interesting, for example, for temporary SLIP or PPP connections. More information on kernel modules can be found in Section 4.3.

For each configuration option there is a fairly extensive help text. Even for more recent options, this provides detailed information on the effects of this option, possibly required programs, and additional documentation such as HowTo documents.

14.3.1 Networking options

TCP/IP networking   allows the use of TCP/IP. This option is mandatory for using LINUX in a network. Even if you are not connected to a network, you should select this option. Some programs (for example syslog or lpd) need network functions to be activated.

Network firewalls   You should only answer 'yes' to this question if you want to use LINUX as a firewall. Later, you must also answer the question for IP: firewalling with 'yes.' Usually, you will answer 'no'; more information can be found in the Firewall HowTo.

Network aliasing   If your computer is supposed to handle several network addresses at a time and with different functions, you should answer 'yes.' This function is used, for example, by some http servers to allow Web hosting for several domains on one computer. Here too, you will later be asked for the protocols to be handled. More information on this subject can be found in the mini-HowTos on 'Virtual Web' and 'Virtual wuftp.'

IP forwarding/gatewaying   or routing is normally not activated. An Internet computer must not forward packets between different networks unless it is specially configured as a gateway or router. If you want to use your computer as a SLIP or PPP server, you must activate this option and set appropriate routes. Alternatively, you can answer 'no' and leave the data transfer to a firewall package.

IP multicasting The Internet protocol initially provides only two possibilities for addressing: addressing a specific computer, or addressing all computers in the local network (broadcast). With multicasting, several computers can be addressed individually. More details can be found in [rfc1112], [rfc1301], and [rfc1458].

IP accounting allows for userwise and packetwise accounting of the network load. This is sensible if you provide Internet access against payment, or if you need to account to your company for your network expenses. For this purpose you need special programs; sources of supply can be found in the help text for this option.

IP firewalling serves to protect a local network against attacks from alien networks via the Internet. Additional information on this subject area can be found in the Firewall HowTo and in Cheswick (1995). To employ LINUX as a firewall you need some utilities which you can find under ftp.tis.com.

Some settings follow, which, as a rule, should not be modified. Nevertheless, situations may occur in which the configuration options presented here are needed.

PC/TCP compatibility mode to be able to communicate with faulty TCP/IP implementations on MS-DOS computers.

Reverse ARP (RARP) is defined in [rfc0903] and serves a similar purpose as BOOTP (see also Chapter 23). This function is needed for some computers if they are to boot via the network.

Assume subnets are local is used for automatic determination of the MTU (Maximal Transfer Unit). For local networks, the MTU can be chosen higher than for SLIP connections, without any danger of loss of performance in interactive operation. Furthermore, the MTU can be set for individual interfaces or routes to achieve optimum data throughput.

IP: Disable path MTU discovery (normally enabled) Depending on the network connection, differently sized MTUs can lead to a higher network throughput. There is a method for automatic recognition of the best MTU which is usually employed.

Disable NAGLE algorithm (normally enabled) The Nagle algorithm is a heuristic that tries to prevent transmission of very small packets (for example single keystrokes in telnet) over slow lines by retarding the packet for a short time and trying to send it together with a second packet.

IP: Drop source routed frames Usually, the route to be followed in the Internet is determined by the routers. With source routing, the sender specifies the route the packet should follow. This can lead to security problems and is not required by the IP specification. As a rule, you should answer 'no.'

IP: Allow large windows (not recommended with less than 16 Mbytes of memory) If your computer has 16 Mbytes of memory or more, this option may improve network throughput.

The IPX protocol   is used by Novell servers and Personal NetWare. Besides the possibility of routing this protocol and of using it from `DOSemu`, LINUX can also be employed as a NetWare server or client. More information can be found in Section 20.1.

AppleTalk DDP   is a possibility for connecting Apple computers via Ethernet. Apple calls this protocol EtherTalk. This option is only sensible if you also use Apple computers in your network.

Amateur Radio AX.25 Level 2   is used for communication via amateur radio.

14.3.2 Network device support

Here, the appropriate hardware drivers are activated. You should only compile the driver that belongs to your card into the kernel, firstly to save memory and secondly to avoid problems with auto probing. Nearly all drivers can also be compiled as modules, so rarely used drivers need only be loaded when they are actually needed. If you want to install several network cards in one computer, for example, in order to use this computer as a router, you must either compile the addresses and interrupts of these cards into the kernel (`Space.c`) or pass them by means of a kernel command line.

Network device support?   Is it required to activate an additional driver? If the computer is supposed to use only the `loopback` device, no additional drivers are required. The `loopback` device is used for addressing your own computer, even when no network card is installed.

Dummy net driver support   The dummy driver can be used if the host is normally not integrated within a network, but is temporarily connected to a provider via SLIP or PPP connection. Here, the computer is assigned an IP address which is then assigned via `ifconfig` to the SLIP or PPP interface `sl0` or `ppp0`. If this connection is interrupted, the computer cannot reach itself via this IP address, which often leads to problems. Therefore, this address can be assigned to the dummy interface (`dummy` if compiled statically into the kernel or `dummy0` if the driver is loaded as a module), which then functions in the same way as the `loopback` device.

SLIP (serial line) support   Do you want to use SLIP? More information on SLIP (and PPP) can be found in Chapter 24 and in the SLIP HowTo.

PPP (point-to-point) support   Do you want to use PPP? More information can be found in Chapter 24 and in the PPP HowTo.

PLIP (parallel port) support   Do you want to use PLIP (Parallel Line IP)? This protocol is significantly slower than a local Ethernet, it functions only for a limited distance between two computers and it needs a special parallel cable.

Subsequently, you must identify the network card you are using to have the corresponding driver linked into the kernel. An updated list of the supported cards can be found in the Ethernet HowTo. There you will also find buying recommendations and warnings about certain cards.

After the kernel has been recompiled and the computer restarted, the network card should now be recognized and initialized by the kernel (output of I/O address and interrupt used, also DMA channel and hardware address of the card, if needed). Otherwise, no access to the network is possible. You will usually find the messages in the file /var/log/messages, or you can display them by means of the dmesg command.

In case of difficulties with autoprobing, the I/O address and the interrupt of the card can be specified by means of a kernel command line (for example ether=0x300,11) or entered in the file drivers/net/Space.c. If several Ethernet cards are installed on one computer, the corresponding parameters must either be entered in the file Space.c or passed as a kernel command line. This gives the system administrator full control over which kernel device belongs to which card.

14.4 Activating the network devices

Now the computer must be assigned an Internet address (and a host name), and the network connection must be activated. This allows computers to be addressed in the same subnet. Connection to the Internet is normally carried out via a router (also called a gateway), which forwards the data packets to remote computers that are not part of the local network. For this purpose, routes must be specified which indicate how the remote computers or networks can be reached.

In local networks, you are assigned the appropriate entries by the network administrator. If you are connected to the Internet via a provider, you will receive the corresponding data from there. In no case should you simply enter arbitrary addresses without asking first.

For each UNIX computer, the IP address 127.0.0.1 has a special meaning: it is used to address your own computer, the localhost. For this purpose, the lo interface (for loopback) is used. This allows you to develop and test network programs with only one computer. This interface is always activated when TCP/IP protocols are used. The loopback interface can be used, for example, by the port mapper, the syslog daemon, or the print system.

Initialization of the network interfaces is carried out by means of the ifconfig program. If called under LINUX without parameters, the current status of the network interfaces is displayed. If the name of a device is specified as a parameter, only the information on this device is displayed. On other systems, the status of all IP interfaces can be interrogated by means of ifconfig -a.

Listing 14.1 shows the configuration of the loopback interface. This is used for direct addressing of the local computer. The address 127.0.0.1 is reserved for this purpose. The address 127.0.0.0 describes the equally reserved corresponding network. Since it is used in normal operation, this interface must be configured on every TCP/IP computer.

```
# activate loopback interface
/sbin/ifconfig lo 127.0.0.1
# set route
/sbin/route add -net 127.0.0.0
```

Listing 14.1   Initialization of the loopback interface.

Listing 14.2 shows the configuration of an Ethernet card. If the computer is connected to a TokenRing, tr0 must be specified instead of eth0.[2] This not only activates the interface, but it also ensures accessibility of other computers by establishing the corresponding routes. The metrics indicate the 'costs' for these routes, so an economical route can be selected on the Internet.

```
# activate Ethernet interface
/sbin/ifconfig eth0 $IPADDR broadcast $BROADCAST \
     netmask $NETMASK
# set routes
/sbin/route add -net $NETWORK netmask $NETMASK
# default route via the gateway
/sbin/route add default gw $GATEWAY metric 1
```

Listing 14.2   Initialization of the Ethernet interface.

Listing 14.2 does not indicate the IP addresses, but only shell variables. The real values are either assigned to you locally by your provider or network administrator, or centrally by the Network Information Center. This central assignment of addresses ensures that each address is unique worldwide. In temporary connections to the Internet via SLIP or PPP, these addresses can also be dynamically assigned by the provider at each call. When using PPP, you do not have to worry about anything because the PPP daemons already contain this function.

The broadcast address specifies how all computers in the same subnet can be reached, whereas the netmask specifies how to determine whether a computer belongs to the local network or not. A detailed discussion can be found in Section 14.5.1.

After having made these settings, you should now be able to reach both your own computer and other computers connected to the network. The first test usually consists of a call to ping, as shown in Listing 14.3. You can (and should) address the loopback address, your own IP address, and other computers in the network. If you encounter problems, you should check the kernel messages to find out whether your network card was properly recognized. It is a good idea to use the IP addresses first in the first test to exclude problems with name resolution caused by the file /etc/hosts

---

[2] Under SunOS or Solaris the Ethernet interface is called le0, under AIX et0 or en0, sometimes also ed0 or wd0.

or the name server. In a second test, you can then make the same checks using the computer names.

The ping program uses a function (Echo) of the ICMP (Internet Control Message Protocol, [rfc0792] and [rfc0950]). It requests the other computer to send the received packet back. The throughput times should be around one millisecond for the loopback device and a few milliseconds in the local network. Lost packets indicate problems with the network installation, for example, broken cables or similar things. Running times to computers in the Internet can be significantly longer. Here you must also expect packets to be lost. These losses are, however, usually recognized by the applications and the corresponding packets are sent again.

As for IP packets themselves, here too no complete and reliable transmission is required, but only a 'best effort.' Thus, no system can rely on the reliability of ICMP messages and their forwarding. Many functions of the protocol can severely impair the network traffic, therefore only the user root is allowed to create ICMP packets. For this reason, the ping program is setuid.

```
(Linux):~> ping 127.0.0.1
PING 127.0.0.1 (127.0.0.1): 56 data bytes
64 bytes from 127.0.0.1: icmp_seq=0 ttl=255 time=1.6 ms
64 bytes from 127.0.0.1: icmp_seq=1 ttl=255 time=1.6 ms
64 bytes from 127.0.0.1: icmp_seq=2 ttl=255 time=1.6 ms
^C
--- 127.0.0.1 ping statistics ---
3 packets transmitted, 3 packets received, 0% packet loss
round-trip min/avg/max = 1.6/1.6/1.6 ms
```

Listing 14.3   The ping program for testing the TCP/IP configuration.

If you have problems with network access, you should check the correct initialization of your kernel interface by means of ifconfig and the set routes by means of route (only under LINUX) or netstat -r. Since you possibly have no access to a name server, you should additionally specify the option -n, so only the IP addresses are displayed and not the associated names.

14.5 Assignment of IP addresses

IP addresses consist (currently) of 32 bits and are usually written in 'dotted notation' (that is, one number per byte, separated by dots). The addresses are subdivided into a network part and a host part. Differently sized networks are available; an overview can be found in Table 14.1. In addition, there are addresses for special (experimental) services, such as multicasting (see also [rfc1112]).

The first bits of the IP address determine the membership in a network class. Depending on this class, the rest of the address is divided into a network number and a host number. Figure 14.4 shows this for the currently used address classes.

Class	Address range	Number of computers	Default netmask
A	1.0.0.0 – 127.0.0.0	About 1.6 million	255.0.0.0
B	128.0.0.0 – 191.255.0.0	65024	255.255.0.0
C	192.0.0.0 – 223.255.255.0	254	255.255.255.0
D	224.0.0.0 – 239.255.255.0	Multicast addresses	
E	240.0.0.0 – 255.255.255.255	Reserved	

Table 14.1   IP address ranges per network class.

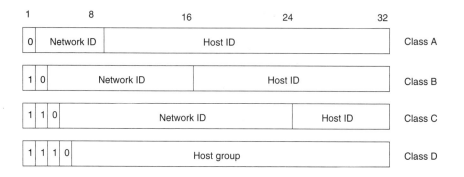

Figure 14.4   Structure of the subnet addresses.

Table 14.2 shows some examples. The network addresses are highlighted in bold. As a rule, only computers with the same network number should be connected to the same Ethernet cable. Equally, computers with the same network number should not be located on different sides of a router.

Class	IP address	Bit representation
A	10.0.0.32	**00001010**.00000000.00000000.00100000
B	128.14.58.60	**10000000.00001110**.00111010.00111100
C	192.9.150.202	**11000000.00001001.10010110**.11001010

Table 14.2   Examples of IP addresses from different network classes.

You can not only specify the IP address as a group of four bytes, but also as an integer number, for example, `telnet 2130706433` instead of `127.0.0.1`. On the basis of an IP address `a.b.c.d` this number is calculated via the formula $a * 256^3 + b * 256^2 + c * 256 + d$. Input of an IP address by means of this formula can confuse even hard-boiled system administrators.

If your internal network is not to be (continuously) connected to the Internet, it is often not possible to obtain an official IP address for all computers, because the available address space is limited and nearly exhausted through the rapid growth of the Internet. This situation will change with the introduction of IPv6, which significantly increases the address space.

For such cases, there are numbers reserved by [rfc1918] which are not routed in the Internet (see Table 14.3). These numbers can be used without problems in private networks, even if these are later to be connected to the Internet. For this case too, [rfc1918] gives some hints on how to prevent all computers having to be given a new IP address later on. [rfc1627], in contrast, points out the problems you can run into when using internal addresses.

Network size	Reserved IP addresses
Class A	10.0.0.0 – 10.255.255.255
Class B	172.16.0.0 – 172.31.255.255
Class C	192.168.0.0 – 192.168.255.255

Table 14.3   Reserved address ranges.

In the following chapters we will always use IP addresses that are reserved for internal use. The domain and host names we use are not officially registered either. This is meant to emphasize the sample character of the presented configurations.

The necessary IP addresses can be entered into the corresponding rc script or into a configuration file. In the Red Hat distribution, the IP addresses are stored in the file /etc/sysconfig/network; the SuSE distribution stores this information in the file /etc/rc.config.

The IP address can also be dynamically assigned during booting by means of a BOOTP interrogation [rfc0952]. For this purpose, a BOOTP server or a corresponding gateway must be configured in the local network which determines the IP address that corresponds to the hardware address and passes it to the client. RFCs worth reading on this subject are [rfc1497] and [rfc1542]. An extension of the BOOTP protocols is defined in [rfc2132] with the DHCP (Dynamic Host Configuration Protocol). More about set-up and operation of a BOOTP server can be found in Chapter 23.

Since the address space available on the Internet (with IPv4) is slowly becoming exhausted, the implementation of IPng (Internet Protocol, next generation; IP version 6) has begun, which greatly increases the address space. Through this change, the IP addresses are becoming significantly longer, so many more computers can be individually addressed.

14.5.1 Netmask and broadcast address

The Internet Protocol differentiates between local computers installed in the same subnet and remote computers. A computer is in the same subnet if its address matches all bits of the broadcast address that are specified by the netmask.

In this case, membership in the same network can still be directly seen by the user. If you use subnetting (see also [rfc0940] and [rfc0950]) you must look at the bit masks. Subnetting is used to subdivide an assigned network internally and to separate the subnets by means of a router. Such a separation is recommended for reasons of reliability of operation of networks that exceed a certain size. Another reason for subnetting could be that your provider has assigned you only 32 or 64 official IP addresses.

In subnetting, the boundary between network address and host address need not necessarily lie on a byte boundary. Thus, the network administrator is free to choose any arbitrary subdivision. This often has the unfortunate effect that already scarce IP addresses are given away (one network address and one broadcast address for each subnet), so employing private addresses in the sense of [rfc1918] should be considered instead.

The counterpart to the above is supernetting (see [rfc1518] and [rfc1519]). Because of the exponential growth of the Internet, the routing tables of the routers grew very rapidly too, since a separate route had to be entered for every Class C network. Later on, individual providers were assigned whole bundles of consecutive networks for which only one entry per provider is needed. Each provider then splits this range of numbers internally for the customers.

Also, companies and other organizations are assigned two or more contiguous Class C networks if one network is not sufficient. This structure can then be almost arbitrarily subdivided by means of subnetting, without any other network user having to take special measures.

14.6 **All about** `ifconfig`

The `ifconfig` program is used for management and activation of the appropriate kernel network interface. The first interface is `eth0` for Ethernet cards and `tr0` for Token Ring cards. The second interface is `eth1` or `tr1`. The kernel itself only recognizes the first interface automatically; the second one must be specified either by means of an adaptation in the file `drivers/net/Space.c` or by means of a kernel command line.

With `ifconfig`, interfaces can be stopped (`down`) or started (`up`). If `ifconfig` is called without parameters, it displays the status of the interfaces. If the name of an interface is specified as the parameter, only the status of this interface is shown. In addition, a series of further settings can be defined:

- `arp` specifies whether this interface uses ARP (Address Resolution Protocol). If ARP is not to be used, the option is prefixed with a minus sign (-). If you use Ethernet, you must use ARP, otherwise your computer cannot be reached in the network. This protocol is explained in more detail in Section 14.9.

- The Maximal Transfer Unit `mtu` is the maximum size of an IP packet transmitted via this device. For serial connections, a relatively small value should be specified because this reduces the answering times of interactive programs; for example, `telnet` transmits fewer bytes per character. For file transfer via `ftp`, however, a large MTU is better because it reduces the overhead, that is, the number of bytes used for headers and checksums instead of payload data.

  The MTU is determined by the employed medium. When using bridges between different network structures, the smallest MTU of all networks must be used. With the aid of fragmentation, routers can also transmit IP packets via media with a smaller packet size.

- On the basis of the specified IP address, `ifconfig` recognizes the network type and automatically determines the corresponding netmask. For purposes of subnetting, the parameter `netmask` can be used to specify your own netmask.

- The default value for the `broadcast` address is determined automatically, but it can equally be changed to allow subnetting. With the parameter `-broadcast`, the use of broadcasts on this interface can be deactivated.

- `pointopoint` followed by the IP address of the counterpart configures the specified interface for SLIP, PPP, or PLIP.

- With the parameter `hw`, the hardware (Ethernet) address of the adapter can be changed provided the corresponding driver supports this feature. This can be sensible in special network configurations if the partner needs to be configured on hardware addresses.

- As the last parameter, the interface can be assigned an IP address. If this is the case, the interface is activated automatically (`up` is executed).

Listing 14.4 shows a sample output of `ifconfig` on a computer with an active Token Ring connection (and obviously `loopback`). For each interface, various data is displayed: hardware address, assigned IP address (including netmask and broadcast address), status of the interface and MTU. The following two lines show the number of packets received (RX) and sent (TX), including the number of errors, dropped packets and overruns. As a rule, these numbers, compared to the number of successfully transmitted packets, should be very small for a computer under normal load.

```
(Linux):~# ifconfig
lo   Link encap:Local Loopback
 inet addr:127.0.0.1 Bcast:127.255.255.255 Mask:255.0.0.0
 UP BROADCAST LOOPBACK RUNNING  MTU:2000  Metric:1
 RX packets:0 errors:0 dropped:0 overruns
 TX packets:50 errors:0 dropped:0 overruns:0

tr0  Link encap:UNSPEC  HWaddr 10-00-5A-D2-62-F8
 inet addr:192.168.3.5 Bcast:192.168.3.255 Mask:255.255.255.0
 UP BROADCAST RUNNING  MTU:2000  Metric:1
 RX packets:10723 errors:0 dropped:0 overruns:0
 TX packets:5456 errors:0 dropped:0 overruns:0
 interrupt:3 Base address:0xa20
```

Listing 14.4   Output of the `ifconfig` program for loopback and Token Ring interfaces.

14.7 All about route

The route program is used for specification of static routes which ensure that other computers in the Internet can be reached. As explained above, direct connection of computers by means of Ethernet is only reasonable up to a certain network size. After this, separation into logically connected subnets must be carried out.

Connection between individual subnets is obtained through routers (formerly also known as gateways). A router works on the protocol level (for example IP, IPX, or SNA) and can establish a suitable connection on the basis of the information contained in the protocols. In the following sections, we only look at the routing of Internet protocols, or IP routing.

The route program is used to establish which computers or networks can be reached via which interface or which IP address is used as default gateway. Provided that the programs routed or gated are activated, routes can be modified by means of different routing protocols. In private local networks this is generally not needed.

A further possibility for changing routes dynamically is provided by ICMP redirect messages. A detailed description of this protocol can be found in [rfc0792].

The route command without parameters displays (only under LINUX) the kernel routing tables. The parameter –n causes IP addresses to be output instead of host names, so no name server needs to be interrogated. A better alternative, because it is available on practically all UNIX systems, is netstat –r. This command also displays the current routing tables of the kernel in a readable form. This information is provided by the kernel in the file /proc/net/route.

```
(Linux):~# route -n
kernel routing table
Destination Gateway      Genmask        Flags MSS  Window Use Iface
192.168.3.0 *            255.255.255.0 U     1872 0      5537 tr0
127.0.0.0   *            255.0.0.0     U     1872 0        41 lo
default     192.168.3.1 *              UG    1872 0         0 tr0
```

Listing 14.5   Output of the route program.

After activating an interface with ifconfig, the appropriate routes to computers and networks can be configured by means of route. A route is added with the parameter add. If the route leads to a computer, the corresponding address is prefixed with the keyword –host. If it leads to a network, –net is specified.

Each TCP/IP computer can address itself by means of the IP address 127.0.0.1 or the name localhost, which are reserved for this purpose. The corresponding network 127.0.0.0 is often called localnet. To be able to access the loopback interface, this must be activated by means of ifconfig, and the corresponding route must be established. This is done with the command:

```
route add -net 127.0.0.0
```

The route program automatically uses the netmask 255.0.0.0, because it classifies the address as belonging to a Class A network. You can use the parameter netmask to specify a different netmask. The network interface lo is also used automatically. With the parameter dev you can specify a different interface if the automatically determined value is incorrect.

The next example shows the creation of a route to a network via the Ethernet interface. The specification of the netmask could be omitted since the address used is a Class C address.

```
route add -net 192.168.3.0 netmask 255.255.255.0 dev eth0
```

The parameter default can be used to create a default route, which is used if no other routing entry is suited. If your network is connected to the Internet, you may want to enter the router to the Internet.

```
route add default gw router-3.veggies.org
```

In the above example, a host name was specified instead of the IP address. This works as long as the name can be resolved without access to a computer outside its own subnet. This is the case if the name of the gateway is contained in /etc/hosts or the name server is located in the same subnet. Usually, it is not a good idea to use a name instead of the IP address.

If you use your computer to connect to another network, you must enter the appropriate routes after activating the SLIP or PPP devices. In the first step, this is the route leading to the partner. In the second step you can specify which computers or networks can be reached via this gateway.

```
route add slipsrv sl0
route add -net 192.168.66.0 netmask 255.255.255.0 gw slipsrv
```

The first command looks after transport of packets from its own computer to the SLIP server, which is called slipsrv. In the second step, a route to the subnet 192.168.66.0 is entered which is transferred via the SLIP server. For this purpose, it must be configured as a gateway (IP forwarder). If you are not connected to a local network and connect to your provider (and thus the Internet) via SLIP or PPP, you must specify a default route.

A route can be deleted from the routing table, for example in case of problems or after termination of a dial-in connection, by means of the parameter del. The following command removes the routing entries of the SLIP connection used in the previous example.

```
route del -net 192.168.66.0
route del slipsrv
```

14.8 The netstat program

The netstat program is another alternative to obtain information on the current state of the network. It provides a number of options which display different kinds of information. `netstat` combines a series of utilities in one program. The different functions are selected via options.

- The option –a generates a list of all Internet sockets, that is TCP, UDP, RAW, and UNIX sockets, including the ports that are only listening. This command informs you about the existing connections and their status.

- –i displays statistics on the network devices. All sent and received packets are shown, together with the errors, drops, and overruns that occurred. A sample output can be found in Listing 14.6. In the last column, you will find a series of flags which describe the configuration of the interfaces in more detail. These flags are listed in Table 14.4.

```
(Linux):~> netstat -i
kernel Interface table
Iface  MTU Met RX-OK RX-ERR RX-DRP RX-OVR TX-OK TX-ERR TX-DRP TX-OVR Flags
lo    2000  0     0     0      0      0    89     0      0      0 BLRU
tr0   2000  0 10840     0      0      0  1000     0      0      0 BRU
```

Listing 14.6   Output of the `netstat -i` command.

Flag	Description
A	The interface receives all multicast addresses
B	Broadcasts are allowed
D	Debugging is on
L	This is a loopback interface
M	All packets are received (promiscuous mode)
N	No trailers are generated
O	This interface does not use ARP
P	The interface is a point-to-point connection
R	The interface is `running`
U	The interface is `up`

Table 14.4   Flags in `netstat -i`.

- –c regenerates the requested list each second, so that changes can be detected. The program must be terminated with [Ctrl]-[C].

- –n prevents the output of host name and service, so only the numerical values are displayed. Thus, the 'reverse lookup' in the name server is omitted, which may lead to long timeouts and increases network load.

- –o displays the timer status.

- Under LINUX, -r is equivalent to `route`, the kernel routing tables are displayed. Under other UNIX systems, where `route` cannot be used to display the routing tables of the kernel, you must always use `netstat -r`.
- -t displays information on TCP sockets.
- -u displays information on UDP sockets.
- -w displays information on RAW sockets.
- -x displays information on UNIX sockets.

As long as your computer is not networked, and no user is active at the console, you can shutdown your computer without problems. If a serial terminal is connected to your computer, you should verify before each `shutdown`, for example by means of `w` and `ps -aux`, whether a user is active on that terminal. If, however, your computer is employed as a network server, you must also consider other network connections. All active connections can be displayed via `netstat -a`.

14.9 The Address Resolution Protocol (ARP)

On the Ethernet level, there are two types of connections between computers: packets can be sent directly to a computer, that is, to the hardware address (MAC address or Media Access Control) of its Ethernet card, or to all computers in the local network (broadcast). If a computer is to be addressed directly, the Ethernet address[3] must be available. For transport within the local network, each IP packet is equipped with an additional header into which the hardware addresses of sender and receiver are entered.

Initially, however, only the IP address of the receiver is available. The sender sends a broadcast to all local computers and looks for the Ethernet address that belongs to the required IP address. The underlying *Address Resolution Protocol* is defined in [rfc0826]. The answer (the correlation between IP address and hardware address) of the required receiver is stored in the ARP cache, so this interrogation need not be continuously repeated. To ensure that, after replacing a card, this computer can still be addressed, the entries in the ARP cache expire after a short time and are then recreated.

The `arp` program can be used to display and modify this ARP cache. This can be useful if two computers (with different hardware addresses) think they can use the same IP address. With other means, such errors are difficult to diagnose. ARP cache entries are displayed by means of the option -a (see Listing 14.7). Entries can be deleted with -d and added with -s.

A further application of the `arp` program is the routing of IP packets, for example to a computer that is connected via SLIP (proxy ARP). The local computer

---

[3] Some drivers support the promiscuous mode in which all packets are read by the Ethernet. This is important for network monitoring, but it is also a security problem.

```
(Linux):~# arp -a
Address        HW type        HW address        Flags Mask
192.168.3.161 10Mbps Ethernet 00:00:83:21:D1:FA  C     *
192.168.3.150 10Mbps Ethernet 10:00:5A:B3:01:E9  C     *
```

Listing 14.7   The arp program.

accepts packets for the remote computer and forwards them via the SLIP connection. Thus, there is no more need to split off a subnet, which would be a waste of precious IP addresses.

On the computer that functions as a router between Ethernet and SLIP, the ARP cache is modified in such a way that it propagates its own Ethernet address as being also valid for the SLIP computer. This is obtained by specifying the parameter pub in the arp call. In the following example, a proxy ARP is set up for the computer slip-1 for its own Ethernet address (00:00:54:34:76:23).

```
arp -s slip-1 00:00:54:34:76:23 pub
```

You can also use LINUX to create proxy ARP for entire subnets, which can sometimes be sensible. If you want to create proxy ARP for several individual computers, you can enter the host names and the corresponding hardware addresses in a file, for example /etc/ethers, and specify the name of this file after the option -f.

TCP/IP basics

15

The previous chapter has shown how to configure a LINUX computer for participation in a TCP/IP-based network. This chapter intends to introduce the individual protocols and their use within the network. This should enable you to understand the functioning of a TCP/IP network. As already shown in Figure 14.2, the hardware connections form the basis for a series of protocol layers, whose interaction will now be explained in more detail.

15.1 Protocols

The Internet is based on a series of protocols which guarantee orderly data exchange between computers. The numbers of these protocols are defined in the file /etc/protocols (Listing 15.1). It is extremely improbable that you will ever be called on to modify this file.

Essentially, four protocols are used whose existence in the kernel is also signaled by LINUX during booting:

```
ip      0      IP      # internet protocol, pseudo number
icmp    1      ICMP    # internet control message protocol
igmp    2      IGMP    # internet group multicast protocol
ggp     3      GGP     # gateway-gateway protocol
tcp     6      TCP     # transmission control protocol
pup     12     PUP     # PARC universal packet protocol
udp     17     UDP     # user datagram protocol
idp     22     IDP     # WhatsThis?
raw     255    RAW     # RAW IP interface
```

Listing 15.1   Internet protocols (/etc/protocols).

- IP, the *Internet Protocol*, serves as a basis for TCP and UDP. It is a connectionless protocol which does not contain any mechanisms for guaranteeing data transfer. The only thing required from the implementation is a 'best effort' when forwarding the packets. Furthermore, the quality of a connection can be improved by means of ICMP. The protocol is defined in [rfc0791].

- ICMP, the *Internet Control Message Protocol*, is used for the exchange of messages between computers on a very low level. This protocol is often implemented in the kernel itself. The individual message types of ICMP are defined in [rfc0792]; the most important ones are ICMP echo (used by `ping`), ICMP redirect (changing of routes), and ICMP messages that signal refusal to establish a connection ('connection refused').

  You can use the `icmpinfo` program to display and protocol ICMP packets. Particularly on computers in very active networks, lots of messages are output, with the 'unimportant' ones only being displayed upon explicit request. More details about this program can be found in Chapter 26.

- TCP (*Transmission Control Protocol*, [rfc0793]), is a connection-oriented, reliable protocol which is, however, rather slow. Application programs can rely on the fact that all packets will be transmitted in the correct order. The kernel ensures completeness of data by means of retransmissions, acknowledgments, and timeouts.

- UDP (*User Datagram Protocol*, [rfc0768]), a connectionless, unreliable protocol which is faster than TCP. The speed advantage results from there being no requirement for a connection to be established, which takes three steps in TCP. On the basis of this protocol, applications can, however, implement reliable protocols, although the network layer cannot guarantee completeness of transmission.

Depending on the protocol, the application data are equipped with the appropriate header. These headers are defined in the corresponding RFCs. Each additional protocol layer adds its own management data so the overhead increases and an increasingly larger amount of data must be transmitted. Only in the last step are the packets converted into a format that suits the transmission medium; that is, they are equipped with an Ethernet or Token Ring header and then output to the transmission medium.

On the basis of TCP and UDP, further (application) protocols or services are defined (in the file /etc/services, Listing 15.2), which are then used by the individual applications, such as telnet or ftp. It is these applications that make a network useful. The file /etc/services assigns protocol names to the tcp and upd ports, through which communication finally takes place.

In the first column, the file /etc/services (Listing 15.2) contains the official name of the protocol. In the second column (separated by tabs or spaces) you will find the number of the port and the protocol used. A port can simultaneously be used for services on UDP and TCP; on the basis of the protocol numbers defined in /etc/protocols and used in the packet headers, the correct drivers are selected in the kernel and the data is forwarded to the correct program. Additional columns can be used to define aliases for the ports. Comments begin with a hash sign and end with the end of line.

```
tcpmux          1/tcp       # TCP port service multiplexer
echo            7/tcp
echo            7/udp
discard         9/tcp       sink null
discard         9/udp       sink null
```

Listing 15.2   Excerpt from the file /etc/services.

Many protocols, including their port numbers, are standardized Internet-wide. The officially reserved ports are administered by the Internet Assigned Numbers Authority (IANA). For general information, the numbers are published periodically, most recently in [rfc2200]. The port numbers should, if possible, be unique. Therefore, programmers should register the ports they are using with the IANA.

Port numbers can lie in the range from 1 to 65 535, where the ports from 1 to 1024 are reserved for the user root. This ensures that at the other end of a connection an authorized process is waiting, for example in a telnet or ftp connection through which a password is transmitted (without encryption).

C programs use port numbers internally; the port names can be converted into the corresponding numbers by means of the function getservbyname(3). In a large network keeping the services files consistent and up-to-date on different computers can be very costly. In such cases, the file can be distributed, for example, by means of NIS (Network Information System; see Chapter 22).

Communication between two computers takes place via these ports. At one end, a program must establish a connection via this port; at the other end, another program must monitor this port and carry out the necessary actions. There are two alternatives:

- The server is started (in the background) and listens on the port. Thus, the server is entirely responsible for the complete establishment of the connection.
- The server is started by inetd if a request arrives on the corresponding port. The ports to be monitored and the options and programs to be executed are configured in the file /etc/inetd.conf. A port cannot be simultaneously monitored with the two alternatives.

Whether an appropriate server is running on the other side of the connection can be determined in tcp applications by establishing a telnet connection to this port. Thus, for example, the echo service is used to check whether characters can be transmitted in both directions. You may also use telnet to activate application protocols such as smtp (Simple Mail Transfer Protocol) and test the server in this way.

Often, the protocols echo and discard are used for a first test. Listing 15.3 shows an example. On the other hand, these services can also be used for so-called

'Denial Of Service' attacks. For this reason these services are not available on many systems – and rightly so, because they are not normally needed in the first place.

```
(Linux):~$ telnet localhost echo
Trying 127.0.0.1...
Connected to localhost.
Escape character is '^]'.
This is a test
This is a test
^]
telnet> quit
Connection closed.
```

Listing 15.3   telnet as a test tool.

If you want to get an overview of the currently started services on your system, you can use the netstat -a command. This displays all existing connections, together with all ports on which a service is offered.

15.2 The inetd server

To be able to react correctly to clients' requests, a number of ports must be monitored on a server. If a separate background process (daemon) is to be started for each port, you will easily reach the system limit of running processes. Therefore, only the inetd server is started at system start-up. The ports that are to be monitored and the actions that are to be carried out when a request arrives are configured in the file /etc/inetd.conf.

```
#serv soc_typ prot flags   user server_path     args
echo   stream  tcp  nowait root internal
ftp    stream  tcp  nowait root /usr/sbin/tcpd /usr/sbin/wu.ftpd
talk   dgram   udp  wait   root /usr/sbin/tcpd /usr/sbin/in.ntalkd
```

Listing 15.4   Excerpt from the file /etc/inetd.conf.

Comments begin with a hash sign and end with the end of line. One line can be entered for each service from /etc/services, provided the corresponding daemon supports being started via inetd. The first column contains the name of the application protocol; here you should use the official name found in /etc/services.

The second column specifies the type of socket. Legal values are stream, dgram for datagrams, raw, rdm (reliably delivered message), and seqpacket (sequenced packet socket). If you want to add a new service to this file, for example because you install a new daemon, you will usually find the corresponding entry in the documentation of the program.

The third column contains a valid protocol from the file /etc/protocols. For TCP and UDP services, tcp or udp are entered. If you also want to manage RPC services with inetd, this can be entered with rpc/tcp or rpc/udp.

The next column indicates what the inetd server does after a connection has arrived. The differentiation between wait and nowait is only relevant for datagram sockets; for all others, nowait must be entered. When a connection is established (and the corresponding daemon supports this) the corresponding socket can again be monitored by inetd, and further requests can possibly be processed. For this, nowait must be entered. For services which are not multi-threaded, wait must be entered. If you want to limit the maximum number of connections that are processed within 60 seconds, you can specify this after a dot (.).

The fifth column contains the user name under whose ID the service is carried out. If you also want to change the group, you can specify this by separating it with a dot. Many daemons must be started with root privileges. For some of the services (for example finger) it may be sensible for security reasons to start the service as nobody or under another ID.

The next entry is the name of the program to be started, together with possible parameters to be passed. The parameters begin with argv[0]; that is, the program name itself. Older UNIX systems limit the parameters to five entries, so you may be required to start a script that calls the server with the appropriate parameters.

The inetd server provides some simple services internally (echo, discard, chargen, daytime, and time). For these, internal is entered as the program.

After modification of the file inetd.conf, the daemon must re-read this file. For this purpose, it can either be terminated and then started again, or it can be sent a SIGHUP signal, for example with the command kill -HUP `cat /var/run/syslogd.pid`.

Generally, the inetd server will allow any connection; authorization is the responsibility of the individual applications. Many applications, however, do not have such procedures; thus, a computer that provides Internet services is relatively vulnerable. Therefore, a local network is usually separated from the Internet by means of a firewall, which can also be installed under LINUX. The maintenance of a firewall requires much time and knowledge, and is usually too expensive for a private user.

15.3 The TCP wrapper (tcpd)

A measure of protection is implemented by the TCP wrapper (tcpwrap or tcpd). This program is started instead of the true daemon, checks whether the connection is legal on the basis of the files /etc/hosts.allow and /etc/hosts.deny, and starts the appropriate application server. This makes it possible to release or block specific protocols for specific computers or networks. However, this relies on the assumption that a computer actually has an IP address under which it wants to establish a connection. Feigning of another IP address is also known as IP spoofing. By means of targeted research, the TCP wrapper tries to exclude possible spoofing attacks. Additional information on these subjects can be found in the man page `tcpd(8)`.

The format of the entries in the files `hosts.deny` or `hosts.allow` is described in the man page `hosts_access(5)`. For each protocol, and for each host or domain or IP address range, whether a service is allowed or forbidden can be specified, and which actions are to be carried out. You can write log entries (with `syslog`), call 'safe' programs that execute the required function, or try to obtain the user name on the remote computer in accordance with [rfc0931] or [rfc1413] (see Section 15.4).

In Listing 15.5, an example shows the release of the `telnet` service. A distinction is made between internal connections that are made immediately and external connections. Internal connections (from the network `192.168.` or the domain `veggies.org`) are allowed without further actions. For external connections, a log file is written with `syslog`. Where the entries are found is specified in the file `/etc/syslog.conf` (see also Section 4.4).

```
# log "ftp" and "telnet" from outside...
in.ftpd: 192.168.
in.telnetd: .veggies.org
in.ftpd: ALL@ALL: severity = local0.notice
in.telnetd: ALL@ALL: severity = local0.notice
```

Listing 15.5   Example for the file `/etc/hosts.allow`.

Instead of the network number, you can also use a pattern for the domain name. Network numbers are closed with a dot, domain names must begin with a dot. If you use the Network Information System (NIS), you can use @ to specify a netgroup. The match can also be indicated by means of a combination of network number and netmask. Thus, the entry `192.168.72.0/255.255.254.0` stands for every address between `192.168.72.0` and `192.168.73.255`.

The entry `ALL` applies to all computers not yet covered by an entry. The keyword `LOCAL` stands for local computers. These are recognized because no dot appears in the host name that would initiate a domain name.

The example in Listing 15.6 shows simple ways of prohibiting specific connections of some or all computers or networks.

```
# Forbid TFTP to all further hosts
# (except those in /etc/hosts.allow)
in.tftpd: ALL
in.telnetd: 192.168.31.155
ALL EXCEPT in.fingerd: rtfm.with.edu, .com
```

Listing 15.6   Example for the file `/etc/hosts.deny`.

Besides creation of log files, any other shell command can be issued as well. This can be used to procure additional information or to provide the system administrator with information via mail. This can be useful if one wants to gather more information about the remote computer and its users. It does not, however, make much sense to react to an access made with the finger program with a finger in the opposite direction. If both administrators were to do this, both computers would be forever busy.

```
in.tftpd: ALL: (/usr/sbin/safe_finger -l a%h | \
        /usr/bin/mail -s %d-%h root) &
```

Listing 15.7   Starting shell commands from tcpd.

The example in Listing 15.7 shows one way to start shell commands. You should either use absolute paths or set the PATH variable accordingly. tcpd waits for the end of the command. If you want to allow the connection before that, you must start the shell command in the background by appending an ampersand (&) to the command. In the shell command, you can use some variables that are substituted by tcpd with the current values. An overview of these variables can be found in Table 15.1. Please note that not all information is always available; thus, for example, DOS computers do not recognize user IDs.

Variable	Substitution
%a	Address of the remote computer
%c	*user@host*, *hostname*, or address
%h	Host name (or address only) of the computer
%d	Name of the daemon to be started
%p	Process ID of the daemon
%u	User name (or unknown)
%%	A single % character

Table 15.1   Variable substitution by tcpd.

15.4 The ident daemon

Many protocols and tcpd do not provide the possibility of verifying user IDs. Often this is not possible, because DOC PCs, for example, do not have user IDs. The ident protocol [rfc1413], however, allows under some circumstances the user ID under which a connection was established to be determined. First of all, the identd daemon must be installed on the computer that has established the connection. This is only seldom the case.

The information supplied by this protocol only concerns existing connections between the two computers. Thus, it is not possible to learn anything about connections to other (alien) systems. In the best case, you can get the user ID of the person who established the connection. In the worst case, you will get completely meaningless information. Therefore, you should not employ this data for authentication, but should store it, for example, in log files and look at it with due caution.

Initially, the operation of an ident server appears to contradict elementary security considerations. Particularly in the Internet, a computer should provide only information and services that are absolutely necessary. The ident protocol itself, however, supplies information which often one does not wish to reveal to others (for example, names of user IDs).

But if a user of your system breaks into another computer or otherwise hampers its operation, the other system administrator can decide to deny establishment of connections directly to this user. Without ident, connection establishment would possibly be denied to the whole system, which would also affect other users. For you too it is easier to recognize and prevent attacks if the appropriate daemon runs on the remote computer.

By means of command line options you can restrict the data your computer is to output on demand. Thus, passing on of user IDs or other data can be prevented. Table 15.2 shows a selection of options for in.identd. All options are documented in the man page for in.identd(8).

Option	Meaning
-o	Do not supply information on the operating system
-e	Output 'UNKNOWN-ERROR' in case of errors
-n	Output numeric user ID instead of user name
-N	'HIDDEN-USER' if ~/.noident exists

Table 15.2 Some identd options.

The option -N allows users to decide for themselves whether information on their ID is to be passed on. Opinions on this are divided. There are identd programs which do not supply clear text messages, but a hash value of time and user ID. This has the advantage that no relevant data is passed on, but the system administrator can still reproduce this data from the log files. In this way, however, this method cannot be used to deny individual users of a computer access to specific services; but this was never the intention of this protocol in the first place.

The daemon should be started by inetd with the wait option. More about the different modes and call parameters can be found in the man page for identd(8).

15.5 Adding new services

Standard services such as telnet or ftp are installed on practically every UNIX system. However, new protocols keep being developed which enhance individual functions or make them possible for the first time. Installing more recent services as well is therefore a good idea, with respect to the work of your users or to system security.

Usually, these services are made available via a new daemon. After compilation and installation, the corresponding server must be configured. Some daemons can be started by `inetd`, others can be started directly. Both methods have their advantages and disadvantages which need to be carefully considered in each individual case:

- An additionally started daemon occupies an additional (otherwise unused) process slot. If many processes are already running on the computer, this may result in no further processes being started.

- The start of a daemon by `inetd` requires reading of the configuration files at each request. If the initialization takes a long time or takes up much CPU time, it may be better to start the daemon directly. An example for this is the `httpd` daemon.

A new application with a new protocol requires the following actions for its activation:

- The name of the services and the corresponding number must be entered in the file `/etc/services`. If you are in charge of many computers, this means a lot of work. Alternatively, you can distribute the file `services` by means of the Network Information System (NIS; see Chapter 22).

- The appropriate daemons and programs must be compiled and installed.

- The new daemons must either be called at system start-up (for example in the `/etc/rc.local` script) or entered in the file `/etc/inetd.conf`. Since this file has different formats on different computers, it can unfortunately not be distributed by means of the NIS (Network Information System). You could, however, employ a package such as GNU `cfengine`.

15.6 **Remote Procedure Call**

Remote Procedure Calls (RPC) are another widely used possibility of communication. This method was developed by Sun, among others; the specification was published in [rfc1057]. Services such as NFS (*Network File System*, Chapter 18, and NIS (*Network Information System*, Chapter 22) were developed on the basis of RPC.

Each version of an RPC protocol (for example `mount`, `ypbind`) is associated a version number. In case of incompatible changes to the protocol, the version number is increased. Each client specifies at the establishment of a connection which version of a protocol is to be used. Many servers support several versions and use the matching protocol. This makes it possible to install a new version first on the server and then on the clients in a network without disrupting the network operation.

Management of services is taken on, in analogy to `inetd`, by the port mapper. Under LINUX, the program is called `rpc.portmap` and can be found in the `/usr/sbin` directory. In `/etc/rpc`, the ports are assigned to individual applications. By means of the `rpcinfo` program you can find out which RPC services a computer provides

```
(Linux):~# rpcinfo -p
   program vers proto   port
   100000   2   tcp     111   portmapper
   100000   2   udp     111   portmapper
   100005   1   udp     668   mountd
   100005   1   tcp     670   mountd
   100003   2   udp    2049   nfs
   100003   2   tcp    2049   nfs
   100004   2   udp     698   ypserv
   100004   1   udp     698   ypserv
   100004   2   tcp     701   ypserv
   100007   2   udp     709   ypbind
   100007   2   tcp     711   ypbind
```

Listing 15.8 RPC services of a computer.

```
(Linux):~# rpcinfo -u localhost 100004 2
program 100004 version 2 ready and waiting
(Linux):~# rpcinfo -u localhost 100004
program 100004 version 1 ready and waiting
program 100004 version 2 ready and waiting
```

Listing 15.9 The rpcinfo program.

(rpcinfo -p *computer*, see Listing 15.8). If this function is called without a computer name, information on your own computer is displayed.

With the option -u (for UDP) or -t (for TCP) you can explicitly determine whether a computer provides a specific service (with a special version). To ensure functionality, the call is made to procedure 0 of the corresponding server.

If you are looking for a computer that provides a special service in the local network, you must use the option -b. This creates a broadcast which is answered by the server(s) providing this service. An example can be found in Listing 15.10.

```
(Linux):~# rpcinfo -b 100004 2
127.0.0.1 localhost
192.168.3.155.26 pea.veggies.org
127.0.0.1 localhost
192.168.3.155.26 pea.veggies.org
127.0.0.1 localhost
192.168.3.155.26 pea.veggies.org
```

Listing 15.10 The rpcinfo program.

15.7 Architecture-independent data format

Participation in network communication is open to almost any computer architecture. This creates a number of problems for the development of protocols and programs. One of the problems is the different coding of texts in various character sets (ASCII, ISO Latin-1 or EBCDIC).

Another problem is the different internal representation of integer numbers. Prior to their transmission (for example as port number), they must be converted into network order. This is achieved by the C language function htons(3). If on the currently used architecture the internal data format is equal to the network order, no conversion is performed. Figure 15.1 shows an example for the different representation of IP addresses on different computer architectures.

Network order (for example 68000 CPU):

192	168	31	155

Intel 80x86 CPU:

155	31	168	192

Figure 15.1   Internal representation of the IP address 192.168.3.155.

For the exchange of other data too, texts may have to be recoded or database files converted. A series of tools has been developed for these purposes, such as re-code for text files, or special libraries. More details on 'External Data Representation' can be found in [rfc1014].

IP addresses and computer names

16

Until now, we have almost exclusively used numerical IP addresses. These are used internally by the involved systems, but for human users, they are harder to remember than names. Therefore, in addition to its numerical IP address, each computer is also assigned a name under which it can equally be addressed. This will require an automatic bidirectional conversion between names and IP addresses.

The host name of a UNIX system is set at system start-up by means of the `hostname` command. There are thousands of computers in the Internet, which must all be uniquely addressable. Therefore, IP addresses *and* host names must be unique.

If only a single word is used as a name, as is common in the UUCP map, it will be difficult to find unique names. A solution is to use domain names. A domain is, for example, the organizationally homogeneous network of a company or a university. The domain name is set under LINUX by means of `dnsdomainname`.

The name space is subdivided by means of top-level domains (such as `.uk` [or any other two-letter national code], `.com` or `.edu`), and domains (for example `veggies.org` or `tuttifrutti.org`). The latter two domain names will appear in many examples in the following chapters. These names are not officially registered (as of August 1998) and are intended for demonstration purposes only.

A domain can be further divided into subdomains. Here, the organization `tuttifrutti.org` is divided into the subdomains `store.tuttifrutti.org` and `sales.tuttifrutti.org`. Thus, a host name must be unique only in its own (sub)domain; in practice, this can be relatively easily guaranteed. Normally, the network administrator who assigns the IP addresses also assigns the corresponding names.

A computer name is supposed to facilitate the users' work and should therefore be easy to memorize and should make sense. Some suggestions for assigning names can be found in the [rfc1178]. A summary is given on the next couple of pages. These hints reflect years of Internet experience with assigning names, though in practice they are quite often ignored.

- No computer types or operating system names because these can change.
- No 'important' terms which in a few months might no longer be important or may even have become offensive.
- No activities or projects because these can change quite quickly.
- No names of persons; this might lead to confusion about which is meant – the person or the computer? Furthermore, a computer is often transferred to someone else's desk.
- No long names which are hard to remember and take too much typing.
- No domain names (or similar) because this might confuse naive users.
- No offensive names.
- No digits at the beginning (or only hexadecimal characters).
- No special characters, such as underscores (_), umlauts, or accented letters.
- No distinction is made between upper and lower case.
- No randomly constructed names which practically nobody can remember.

What should you choose as a host name? Here too, you will find some suggestions in [rfc1178] which are, however, only seldom observed in real life. These ideas may help to circumvent the above-mentioned problems.

- Rare words.
- Thematically related names: colors, mythological characters, or the like.
- Easily spelt names.

Please note when choosing a name that this name will probably be used for the next few years to come. Changing the name of a computer is a relatively complex business, once all sorts of configurations have been set up. Thus, please choose the name of your computer with care.

In the Internet, the complete name (Fully Qualified Domain Name, FQDN) of an (arbitrary) computer consists of several parts that are separated by dots. For the computer name `apple.store.tuttifrutti.org`, for example, these are the following parts:

- `apple` is the name of the computer
- `tuttifrutti.org` is the domain of the computer
- `.org` is the top-level domain for 'organizations.' Further TLDs are, for example, `.com` for commercial businesses, `.edu` for universities, or `.mil` for military. For non-US Internet users, the top-level domain usually corresponds to the country code (for example, `.de`, `.fr`, `.uk` for German, French, and UK users, respectively).
- `store.tuttifrutti.org` is a subdomain of the domain `tuttifrutti.org`. It is possible to create further subdomains to extend the name space.

Because of this subdivision into domains, a computer name need only be unique in its own (sub)domain and can nevertheless be addressed in the whole Internet. You can obtain a domain either from your provider or through the Network Information Center (NIC), whereas you will assign the computer name by agreement with your network advisor (the person responsible for the name server) or your provider.

16.1 Correspondence between names and IP addresses in /etc/hosts

Normal users will usually address the computers by their host names. Among themselves, however, computers communicate using their IP addresses. Therefore, there must be an automatic procedure that allows names to be converted into IP addresses and vice versa.

In the simplest case, IP addresses and associated names are listed in the file /etc/hosts (Listing 16.1). Each entry begins with the IP address of the computer, followed by its name (FQDN, Full Qualified Domain Name), followed by its alias(es) if present.

The use of aliases allows you to address computers under names that describe their current function. Thus, many ftp servers can be reached under the alias ftp.*domain*. Further widely used aliases are www, gopher or news. If another computer takes over this function, only the alias is changed, but not the computer name itself. The change of an alias requires only a little effort, whereas the change of a computer name can be a very complicated business.

```
# IP address      Computer name      Aliases
127.0.0.1         localhost
192.168.3.155     pea.veggies.org    pea
```

Listing 16.1 Contents of the file /etc/hosts.

In a bigger network, the maintenance of a large number of hosts files is very labor-intensive and easily leads to inconsistencies because on different computers you will often find divergent and incomplete name tables. The correspondence between names and addresses should be unique so that on each computer the same hosts can be addressed under the same names. Here, centralized administration is needed to ensure this consistency.

The unique nature of host names can be ensured by means of the Domain Name Service (DNS) for which a so-called name server is set up. All data is centrally maintained on this computer and distributed via the network on demand.

Another alternative is the use of the Network Information Service (NIS), see Chapter 22). The use of NIS, however, only makes sense in UNIX networks since

DOS clients usually cannot handle NIS, whereas they can start DNS requests and use the answers.

16.2 Domain Name Service

Setting up a name server is a sensible thing to do for a variety of reasons. The administrative effort of synchronizing the name tables in a bigger network can be reduced, in particular when DOS and Windows clients are used which do not allow central administration of hosts files. For dial-up connections it may be sensible to set up a cache server. This avoids repeated requests to external name servers. More information on the DNS can be found in [rfc1033], [rfc1034], and [rfc1035].

A name server is responsible (authoritative) for a determined zone. Requests that the name server cannot answer are forwarded to the next higher server, which in turn may forward the request. Since the superior server does not have all of the data of the subordinate servers, it can also forward the request downward to the appropriate server. When you are connected to the Internet, it is therefore important to announce the existence of your own name server, for example to your local NIC. When you apply for your own domain, this is done either by the provider or the responsible Network Information Center.

To ensure fail-safe operation, there should be at least two name servers for each zone, one primary server and at least one secondary (backup) server. The primary server maintains databases which store information on computers and their addresses. The backup server copies this data at regular intervals and can thus take over the function of the name server in case of failure. For this purpose, the secondary server stores the data in a file which is then used as a basis for answering the DNS requests.

In many cases, your provider will operate the name server for you or at least provide a secondary server. Often two or three customers of a provider mutually operate a secondary server.

Please ensure the presence of a DNS backup server in your network. If this service breaks down, it looks to many users like a total breakdown of the network – the DNS is a very central service in a TCP/IP network. For this reason, the protocol requires secondary servers that fetch their data automatically from the primary server. With respect to the clients, you simply enter several name servers into their configurations.

16.3 Using a name server with LINUX

This section deals with the use of an already existing name server as a client. The configuration of a name server is extensively described in Chapter 21, where you will also find additional hints for its operation.

If you still use libc-5, the configuration of a DNS client is initially carried out by means of entries in the file /etc/host.conf. An example of this file can be found in Listing 16.2.

The keyword `order` specifies the order in which the information sources are interrogated. Legal values are `hosts` for the file `/etc/hosts`, `bind` for a request to a name server and `nis` for a request to a NIS server (Network Information System). More about NIS can be found in Chapter 22.

```
order hosts, bind
multi on
```

Listing 16.2   Entries in the file `/etc/host.conf`.

The entry `multi on` allows a computer to be assigned several IP addresses. Such computers are also known as 'multi-homed.' It is sensible to assign a computer several IP addresses if it is used to provide specific services for different addresses. Often a computer is employed as a Web server by different companies or departments and is supposed to display a different home page for each `http://www.company.cc` address. Another example of application is a change of machine of the name server which then additionally serves the old IP address as well.

If you are already using GNU `libc` (also known as `libc-6`), linkage to a name server is configured in the file `/etc/nsswitch.conf`. This file has the same format as under Solaris; an example can be found in Listing 16.3.

The name `nsswitch` stands for 'Name Service Switch' and is used not only for configuration of the DNS client, but for many other configurations. If application programs only use the `libc` functions for reading this file, the call of remote services is completely transparent for programmers and users. More information on this subject can be found in the Info documentation on GNU `libs` version 2.0 or higher.

```
passwd:     files nisplus nis
shadow:     files nisplus nis
group:      files nisplus nis

hosts:      files nisplus nis dns
```

Listing 16.3   The file `/etc/nsswitch.conf`.

In the first column, you will find the name of the (local) configuration file, followed by a colon (`:`). The following columns specify the services to be interrogated when data are to be read from the corresponding configuration files. An overview of the possible entries can be found in Table 16.1.

The last entry in Table 16.1 is only an example of a possible reaction. Possible statuses are `success`, `notfound`, `unavail`, and `tryagain`. The interrogation can be negated by means of an exclamation mark (`!`); furthermore, several interrogations are possible. Available actions are `return` and `continue`. More about these functions and default entries can again be found in the Info documentation of GNU `libc`.

Keyword	Meaning
file	Read the corresponding local file
nisplus	Fetch the data from an NIS+ server (NIS version 3)
nis+	As nisplus
nis	Fetch the data from an NIS server (NIS version 2)
yp	As nis
dns	Interrogate the name server
db	Read from a local database
[NOTFOUND=return]	Terminate search if not found

Table 16.1 Possible entries in the file /etc/nsswitch.conf.

In the next step, the name server to be used must be entered in the file /etc/resolv.conf (Listing 16.4). The name of the file is derived from the resolver library (libresolv) which is responsible for name resolution. On some UNIX systems (as under LINUX) this library is an integrated part of libc, whereas on other systems and with the GNU libc version 2, the resolver library must be explicitly linked with the option -lresolv.

Up to three nameserver entries are allowed in the file /etc/resolv.conf. The servers are addressed in the specified order, so the local (or most reliable) server should occupy the first position.

```
nameserver 192.168.3.150
domain store.tuttifrutti.org
search store.tuttifrutti.org tuttifrutti.org
# sortlist sort-list
# options option-list
```

Listing 16.4 The file /etc/resolv.conf.

If no name server is registered in resolv.conf, your own computer is used as a name server. However, the IP address should be specified instead of the host name to prevent recursion (name server or NIS requests) or deadlocks. If possible, the name server's IP address should not be changed because this would involve a major configuration exercise if no bootp is employed.

Furthermore, you can specify the domain name in resolv.conf. Otherwise, the part after the first dot (.) is used in the host name. The domain used in Listing 16.4 is store.tuttifrutti.org.

The search list (keyword search) specifies how to construct a possibly existing computer name out of an incompletely specified host name (without domain). By default, only the domain name is appended rather than all parts of the domain separated by dots, as in older versions. An inconsiderate entry in the search list can lead to a number of unanswerable DNS requests to alien computers, which are not well looked upon. The following example is intended to clarify the process.

In the sample file /etc/resolv.conf (Listing 16.4), the search list is entered as store.tuttifrutti.org tuttifrutti.org. Now, a user tries to establish a connection with the computer corn. To resolve the name into an IP address (with the aid of a name server, see the file /etc/host.conf), a search is made for the computer name itself. If it is not found in the name server, the string store.tuttifrutti.org is appended with a dot (.) to the computer name, and the name server is asked again. If this request is also unsuccessful, the next entry of the search list (tuttifrutti.org in the above example) is tried.

If the top-level domain (for example .uk, .edu or .com) were also part of the search list, a further request is added to the above-mentioned requests which would, for example, for the computer somehost.somewhere.org be forwarded to the name server of the (possibly existing) domain org.uk. This kind of domain name is no longer assigned, and neither are two-letter subdomain names.

For individual processes, you can overwrite the configuration of search and option with the environment variables LOCALDOMAIN or RES_OPTIONS. More detailed information on the keywords sortlist and options can be found in the man page for resolver(5).

16.4 Testing a name server

Several programs are available to test the connection to a name server or its configuration. Some of the most widely used tools are presented in the following sections.

Above all, the name server must be reachable in the network. You can verify this by means of a quick test with the ping program. The employed name server is not required to be located in the local subnet; therefore, the necessary routes must be set up too.

16.4.1 Interactive DNS requests with nslookup

With the nslookup program, DNS requests can be made in two modes: interactive and non-interactive. In interactive mode, different requests can be made one after the other. In non-interactive mode, only the required information is displayed and the program terminated.

Additional options can be specified with a leading minus sign (-) either before the host name or before the address. Furthermore, default values can be stored in the file ~/.nslookuprc. An example for a non-interactive call of nslookup can be found in Listing 16.5.

The interactive mode is used if either no parameter is specified or a name server (name or IP address) is specified after a minus sign (-). Subsequently, requests can be started by entering a host name or an IP address. The command set type=any can be used to request all information on a computer. An example can be found in Listing 16.6. More detailed information on nslookup and a list of all possible request options can be found in the man page for nslookup(1).

```
(Linux):~> nslookup ftp
server:  carrot.veggies.org
Address:  192.168.3.150

name:    pea.veggies.org
Address:  192.168.3.155
Aliases:  ftp.veggies.org
```

Listing 16.5 nslookup in non-interactive mode.

```
(Linux):~> nslookup
Default server:  carrot.veggies.org
Address:  192.168.3.150

> ftp
server:  carrot.veggies.org
Address:  192.168.3.150

name:    pea.veggies.org
Address:  192.168.3.155
Aliases:  ftp.veggies.org

> set type=any
> ftp
server:  carrot.veggies.org
Address:  192.168.3.150

ftp.veggies.org canonical name = pea.veggies.org
veggies.org      nameserver = carrot.veggies.org
pea.veggies.org      internet address = 192.168.3.155
> exit
```

Listing 16.6 nslookup in interactive mode.

The nslookup program can also be used to carry out a so-called reverse lookup, that is, a request for the name belonging to a specific IP address. In this case, you simply specify the IP address instead of the host name.

The nslookup program can interrogate different name servers and analyze the sent and received packets. Since this program is also available under other systems, such as Windows NT, it is very widely used for testing name servers.

16.4.2 Name server requests with host

The host program also allows you to analyze data stored in a name server. Here, a useful feature is that the data can be output in the format required for name server database entries (option -v). With the option -t, the required entries can be selected (for example ns, cname, soa, hinfo, mx, and any or * for all entries). The meaning of the entries is explained in more detail in Chapter 21.

The option -a is a short form for -t any. A more detailed description of all entries can be found in the man page host(1) and in the 'Bind Operators Guide' which is supplied together with the sources of bind. Listing 16.7 shows some examples of the use of host.

```
(Linux):~> host pea
pea.veggies.org has address 192.168.3.155
(Linux):~> host -v pea
Trying domain " veggies.org"
rcode = 0 (Success), ancount=1
pea.veggies.org        86400 IN         A      192.168.3.155
For authoritative answers, see:
veggies.org      86400 IN          NS       carrot.veggies.org
Additional information:
carrot.veggies.org        86400 IN         A     192.168.3.150
(Linux):> host -a pea
Trying domain "veggies.org"
rcode = 0 (Success), ancount=3
pea.veggies.org  86400 IN          A     192.168.3.155
pea.veggies.org  86400 IN          HINFO  IBM-PC/AT        UNIX-PC
pea.veggies.org  86400 IN          TXT "Test with text"
For authoritative answers, see:
veggies.org 86400 IN          NS       carrot.veggies.org
```

Listing 16.7   Name server requests with host.

16.4.3 Name server requests with dig

Another tool for the analysis of a name server is dig (Domain Information Groper). This program can also be used interactively and in batch mode. Many TCP/IP packages contain only this program and not nslookup or host.

The options and functions of dig are extensively described in the man page. Please note that for a 'reverse lookup' you must specify the option -x in addition to the IP address.

16.5 **Reliability of name servers**

Until now, the Internet protocols have been developed and implemented with a view to implementation techniques and functionality. This was no problem so long as only a few and reliable users participated in the Internet. In the past years, the number of Internet computers and users has grown substantially, so the number of 'baddies' among them has also increased.

For this reason, Internet computers – particularly the best-known ones – are subject to all sorts of attacks. Depending on protocols, programs, and other environment features, there are different types of attack and defense. A vast amount of information on this subject can be found, among others, in the CERT Advisories on `http://www.cert.org` or `ftp://ftp.cert.org/pub/cert_advisories`.

One widespread type of attack is the faking of name server responses. Many programs (for example `rlogin`) admit users or access in dependence on the computer name. In an incoming connection, however, only the IP address of the sender is available, if this has not already been falsified by means of so-called IP spoofing. Thus, for authentication, a reverse lookup is carried out which is processed by the responsible name server.

Since the responsible name server might be under the control of the attacker, any falsification is possible. Defense measures consist of improved programs that countercheck DNS responses a second time, new protocols (for example `ssh` instead of `rsh`), and by not using any vulnerable services.

The use of a DNS is also very useful in the Intranet, because it is relatively laborious to maintain the host tables on all computers. Here, the essential advantage of the DNS is that there is an ultimate instance whose data is available everywhere. Alternatively, in a UNIX network, you can also use the NIS to distribute the host tables, but only to UNIX systems.

Network applications

On the basis of TCP/IP, a number of applications have been developed that can be useful for running a network. The following sections present a small selection of these applications, without any pretense at completeness. Furthermore, new protocols are continuously being developed, implemented, and enhanced, so a definitive reference is practically impossible.

Many of these applications were developed under BSD and then ported to LINUX. Therefore, many of these programs can be found on every BSD system and in more recent times also on various System V computers. However, some of the programs presented here are not contained in the standard installations of LINUX and UNIX systems, so system administrators must compile and install these themselves. Hints on installation of programs and network services can be found in Chapters 11 and 15.

17.1 The `telnet` program

The `telnet` program (Terminal EmuLation over NETwork) allows you to log in on a remote computer. The program (and the protocol of the same name) define a 'Network Virtual Terminal' via which programs can be controlled or other services requested.

For this purpose, the `telnetd` daemon must be started on the remote computer, which is usually done by means of the `inetd` super server. Furthermore, you must have a valid user ID (user name and password) on this computer. Besides this normal application, `telnet` can also be used for testing other TCP protocols. The `telnet` protocol is defined in [rfc0854] and following.

In the simplest case, the call `telnet` *hostname* is used to establish a telnet connection with the specified computer. If you call the `telnet` program without parameters or send the escape sequence (usually Ctrl-]), you enter the command mode. In this mode you can, at the `telnet>` prompt, open a connection (`open`), close a connection (`close`), or send a special character (`send`). Extensive help information on all commands can be found in the man page `telnet(1)`; a brief overview is displayed when you enter `help` in command mode. Please note that the command mode is terminated after each command if a connection with another system exists.

You can establish a connection to a port other than the `telnet` port by specifying the required port as the service name or number after the host name. Thus, you can use the command `telnet localhost smtp` or `telnet localhost 25` to establish a connection to the `smtp` port (Simple Mail Transfer Protocol) and then communicate directly with `sendmail` or `smail` of the remote computer.

Apart from testing individual services, `telnet` can also be misused to test the connection. Usually, the ports `discard` (9) and `echo` (7) are used for this purpose. With `discard`, all entered characters are ignored, whereas `echo` sends all entered characters back unchanged (line by line).

At start-up, the `telnet` program reads the file `~/.telnetrc`. In this file you can specify various settings to adapt `telnet` to your requirements. The example in Listing 17.1 shows some possible configurations; a complete description can be found in the man page for `telnet`.

```
# configuration of the telnet program
localhost toggle binary
corn       toggle binary
  set interrupt ^K
```

Listing 17.1   The file `~/.telnetrc`.

Comments begin with a hash sign (#) in the first column and comprise the whole line. Empty lines are ignored. Valid entries begin with a host name in column one, followed by options and commands. An entry can span several lines provided that the continuation lines begin with a white space (blank or tab).

In Listing 17.1, binary transmission mode is set for the computers `localhost` and `corn`. In addition, the interrupt character is changed on computer `corn`. Upon activation, all options are protocolled by the `telnet` program.

17.2 The File Transfer Protocol (`ftp`)

With `ftp`, files can be exchanged between computers. The underlying protocol is defined in [rfc0959]. Two basic alternatives must be distinguished when exchanging data between two computers:

- You have a user ID on the remote computer and can either log in via `telnet` or transfer files with `ftp`.[1]

- You have no user ID on the remote computer, but the computer is set up as an `anonymous ftp` server. There you can log in as `anonymous` or `ftp`, usually

---

[1] There are also `ftp` servers for operating systems that do not have user IDs or `telnet` connections.

specifying your email address as the password. Often you can also use the short form *name*@ which is automatically recognized by the ftp server.

Subsequently, you can download files from this computer, or upload files to special directories, which are usually called incoming. After the administrator has integrated these files into the ftp directory, other users can access these files. In the Internet, this method is used for exchanging programs and documentation. Additional information on this subject can be found in [rfc1635]. The installation of an anonymous ftp server is described in Chapter 19.

You can either start the ftp program with a computer name as the parameter, so that a direct connection with this computer is established, or you can start ftp without a parameter which brings you into command mode (with ftp> as prompt). help displays an overview of the available commands. Listing 17.2 shows a brief example of an ftp session.

```
(Linux):~> ftp corn
Connected to corn.
220 corn FTP server (version wu-2.4(1)) ready.
name (corn:jochen): jochen
331 Password required for jochen.
Password:
230 User jochen logged in.
Remote system type is UNIX.
Using binary mode to transfer files.
ftp> bin
200 Type set to I.
ftp> hash
Hash mark printing on (1024 bytes/hash mark).
ftp> prompt
Interactive mode off.
ftp> lcd /tmp
Local directory now /tmp
ftp> get .emacs
200 PORT command successful.
150 Opening BINARY mode data connection for .emacs.
##########
226 Transfer complete.
11557 bytes received in 0.0184 secs (6.1e+02 Kbytes/sec)
ftp> quit
221 Goodbye.
```

Listing 17.2   File transfer with ftp.

In the first step, the connection to the computer corn is established. The login is carried out with user name (jochen) and password, since the remote computer does not allow anonymous ftp. Data transmission is to be in binary mode (input bin), because otherwise the protocol would attempt a character set conversion. This would usually make archives and other files unusable.

The prompt command suppresses requests for confirmation of the ftp clients during the following mget. The cd command changes into another directory on the ftp server, whereas the local directory is changed with lcd. In the last step, the file .emacs is transferred and the connection closed.

The ftp program can be configured by means of the file ~/.netrc. In this file you can, for example, define a series of commands for each host which are executed after the (possibly automatic) login. Listing 17.3 shows an example of an initialization file. For connections with the computer corn, jochen is used as the user name. On all other computers, anonymous ftp is attempted. All options and commands of the ftp client are documented in the man page ftp(1).

Special features of a particular ftp server are usually documented in a README file which explains special functions, such as transfer of entire directory trees and repacking of files, together with possibly existing mail servers which send the required files by email.

In these files or in the messages displayed during login, users are often advised that all commands and transfers are protocoled. People who do not like this to be done should not use such servers. Since the provision of an ftp server is often understood as a 'service' for the users, one should accept the rules and behave accordingly.

```
# Entry for the computer corn
machine corn login jochen
macdef init
bin
hash

# Default for anonymous ftp
default login anonymous password jochen.hein@li.org
macdef init
bin
hash
```

Listing 17.3 Example of a ~/.netrc file.

If you have problems logging in via ftp, you should check whether your login shell is listed in the file /etc/shells. There are ftp daemons which refuse the login if the user does not have a valid shell. Furthermore, the user may well be registered in the file /etc/ftpusers. This file contains the user IDs for which ftp connections are not allowed.

Besides the standard ftp program, there is the more powerful ncftp which has a more user-friendly interface. A useful function is the transfer of entire directory trees which is here implemented in the client. Also for X, there are other, more usable, ftp clients such as xftp or mxFtp. Furthermore, Emacs possesses an ftp mode (`ange-ftp`) with which you can search, view, and transfer files inside your usual `dired` environment.

If you have no online access to the Internet, but only exchange mail and news via UUCP, you can still obtain files from `ftp` servers. Some servers also send files by email; the corresponding instructions can usually be found in the `README` file of the server. Then there are servers which, controlled by commands and email, transfer files from other computers and send them (uuencoded) by email. Appropriate addresses can be found in the FAQ 'Accessing the Internet by mail.'

17.3 Searching for files with `archie`

There are many `ftp` servers on the Internet on which even more files and programs are available ready to be called. Now, if you are looking for a specific program, but do not know any `ftp` server that makes this program available, you can look for it by means of the programs `archie` or `xarchie`. For handling the `archie` client, an additional Emacs mode called `archie.el` is available.

If these programs are not available on your computer, you can log in via `telnet` to an Archie server (for example `archie.rutgers.edu` with the user name `archie`) and start your requests directly there. If you have no online access, you can also send your requests by email, for example, to `archie@archie.rutgers.edu`. Instructions for use can be obtained by entering `help`.

A big disadvantage of the `archie` service is that you can only search for names (substrings or regular expressions) of files. But how do you know which cryptic name is hiding that program for which you have been desperately looking for ages? If you are searching for a program that performs a specific function, it is often worth looking into the FAQs (Frequently Asked Questions) of the corresponding newsgroup.

Sometimes, you can also locate programs by searching on an `ftp` server that is ordered by groups. Recently, search by means of the various search engines on the WWW has proved very useful. There are many different search engines, which differ by extent and topicality. Therefore, if you do not achieve what you wanted with your search terms, you can use another search engine and/or other search terms. If you do not want to search online, you can obviously do this via mail as well. Just send the commands to the corresponding mail Archie. Listing 17.4 shows an example.

```
(Linux):> mail archie@archie.rutgers.edu
Subject:
prog bbdb-1
quit

.
```

Listing 17.4   An Archie request by means of email.

If you send mail containing the word `help`, you will get the instructions on how to use Archie. In the example of Listing 17.4 a program is sought whose file name contains bbdb-1. In this case, I have been searching for the Emacs package bbdb (Big Brothers Database).

Listing 17.5 shows a connection with the European Archie server located at the Technical University of Darmstadt, Germany. For reasons of clarity, the server output is shown in abbreviated form.

```
(Linux):> telnet archie.th-darmstadt.de
Trying 130.83.22.1...
Connected to archie.th-darmstadt.de.
Escape character is '^]'.

Welcome to archie.th-darmstadt.de

login: archie
# terminal type 'ansi-bbs' is unknown to this system.
# 'erase' character is '^?'.
# 'search' (type string) has the value 'sub'.
th-archie> pager
th-archie> set term vt100
# terminal type set to 'vt100 24 80'.
th-archie> prog bbdb
# Search type: sub.
# Your queue position: 1
# Estimated time for completion: 10 seconds.
working...

host ftp.th-darmstadt.de    (130.83.47.112)
Last updated 06:18  8 Dec 1996

Location: /pub/editors/GNU-Emacs/elisp-archive/packages
-rw-rw-r-- 155377 bytes 22:00 13 Jan 1994 bbdb-1.49.tar.Z
...
th-archie> quit
# Bye.
Connection closed by foreign host.
```

Listing 17.5   Protocol of an Archie request.

The pager command ensures that the search results are not displayed directly, but with the aid of a paging utility such as more. Otherwise, you would often not be able to analyze the output before it disappears from the screen. Since the Archie server does not recognize the ansi-bbs terminal which is emulated by Minicom, set term vt100 was used to change the type of terminal.

Obviously, Archie can also be accessed via the WWW. Another very popular service offered in the WWW is FTPSearch. There, you can easily search for files on `ftp` servers without having to plunge into the complexities of handling `archie`.

17.4 The r tools

One disadvantage of the `telnet` and `ftp` protocols is that at each login the password is transferred unencrypted via the network, thus, via potentially insecure connections.[2] This can be prevented by means of the r tools, although then you are depending on the reliability of the system administrators. Furthermore, these tools, which originate from the BSD world, exist only on UNIX systems. It is true that some NT servers have installed these services too, but they do not belong to the normal contents of the distribution.

As a further restriction, the corresponding daemons must be running on the remote computer. On many systems, this is not the case for reasons of security. Security can be jeopardized, for example, by users including a plus sign (+) in the file `~/.rhosts`, thus opening their user ID to the whole world. There are daemons which simply ignore this kind of entry. The protocol itself is open to IP and DNS spoofing and only really sensible in environments that are under single administration.

The r tools were developed at the University of California in Berkeley, when the TCP/IP system was implemented under BSD. Besides the already standardized protocols such as `telnet` and `ftp`, additional protocols were developed and some local UNIX commands adapted to be used in networks and on remote computers. The r is an abbreviation of `remote`.

17.4.1 Execution of programs on remote computers

The program `rsh` (remote shell, not to be confused with the restricted shell which is sometimes also called `rsh`) can be used to start programs on remote computers. For this purpose, the file `~/.rhosts` (see Listing 17.7) must be created on the remote computer. Each line of this file contains a computer name. Thus, the user can directly log in from the alien computer by means of the r tools without having to specify a password.

Listing 17.6 shows an example for the use of the `rsh` command. The first parameter (`--`) prevents the options of the `ls` command from being evaluated by `rsh` on the local computer. This is a peculiarity of the GNU `getopt` function which is used for evaluation of command line options and parameters. On some systems, the program is also called `remsh` to avoid the name clash with the 'restricted shell.'

If users have different accounts (for example `hein` on one and `jhein` on the other computer), they can use the option `-l` to specify another user ID before the computer name from which a login should be possible. Further useful options are `-8` for an 8-bit-capable session and `-E` for switching off the special treatment of the

---

[2] With the `tcpdump` tool, the system administrator can view any TCP packet in the local network. Similar programs also exist for DOS computers.

```
(Linux):~> rsh -- pea ls -l -d bin
drwxr-xr-x   2 hein      staff         512 Jul 26 16:22 bin
```

Listing 17.6 Execution of programs on remote computers with `rsh`.

escape character (usually, the tilde). The option `-e` can be used to specify a replacement character for this.

Some `rlogind` daemons allow specification of `+` in `.rhosts` files. This allows users with the same user name to log in, no matter from which computer they are calling `rlogin`. For reasons of security, this kind of entry should be avoided; furthermore, there are daemons that ignore this entry.

Listing 17.7 shows an example of the file `~/.rhosts`. This file should only be readable for individual users. Each line describes a computer from which a `rsh`, `rlogin` or `rcp` without password is possible. As the computer name, you should specify the first entry from the file `/etc/hosts` or the Fully Qualified Domain Name (FQDN). If you have different user IDs on the computers, you can then enter a user name.

```
corn.veggies.org hein
pea.veggies.org jhein
```

Listing 17.7 An example of the file `~/.rhosts`.

The system administrator can set up computers (in a local network) as having equal rights by entering the names of all local computers in the file `/etc/hosts.equiv` (Listing 17.8) of each computer. However, this makes sense only for networks in which computers and user IDs are centrally managed.

The file `/etc/hosts.equiv` is not used for accesses by the user ID `root`, so in this case an additional `~/.rhosts` file is required. In a local network which is to be centrally managed, this can significantly facilitate things, because, for example, it allows use of `rdist` (see Section 17.7).

```
corn.veggies.org
-carrot.veggies.org
cabbage.veggies.org    sven
```

Listing 17.8 The file `/etc/hosts.equiv`.

The first entry in Listing 17.8 ensures that every user (except for `root`) can log in from `corn.veggies.org` using `rlogin` without a password. The second entry requires a password for each login from `carrot.veggies.org`, no matter what individual users have entered in their `~/.rhosts`. The third line allows user `sven` on `cabbage.veggies.org` to log in without a password as an arbitrary user (except as root).

This method is based on the fact that by means of the incoming IP packets (namely the sender's address) the correct sender (computer) can be identified. However, this is not always the case, because with so-called IP or DNS spoofing another sender's address or another host name can be specified. Thus, if security considerations play a major role, this method can certainly not be recommended. This applies in particular if the access is carried out on or from the external computer.

A disadvantage of `rsh` is that no `tty` is associated with the program. Thus, programs such as `vi` cannot be started directly with `rsh`. Instead, you need to log in, for example, with `rlogin`. If you receive error messages such as '$TERM is not defined' (from `setterm`) or 'stty: standard input: invalid argument' (from `stty`) when using `rsh`, you must adapt your login scripts accordingly. Listing 17.9 shows some sample adaptations for the `tcsh`, Listing 17.10 the corresponding adaptations for the `bash`. This can be used to prevent the commands `stty` or `setterm` being called although no `tty` is available.

```
tty -s
if ( $status == 0 )
    stty pass8
endif
```

Listing 17.9   Adaptations in `~/.login`.

```
tty -s
if [ $? = 0 ]; then
    stty pass8
endif
```

Listing 17.10   Adaptations in `~/.profile`.

On the basis of `rsh`, a protocol called `rstart` was developed for X which facilitates the start of X programs on other computers. Both the current value of the `DISPLAY` variable and the authorization (see Section 6.6) for the X server are transmitted. This, however, requires the `rstartd` daemon which is usually running only on very few computers.

Another alternative is provided by the `xon` program which is also based on `rsh`, but does not require an additional daemon. However, if you want to use `xauth` for authorization of X accesses, this must be done separately. An example is shown in Listing 17.11.

If you are using `ssh` (see Section 17.5), it is no longer necessary to use `xhost` or `xauth`. Display redirection and authentication are taken over by the secure shell.

```
xauth extract - $DISPLAY | rsh RemoteHost xauth merge -
```

Listing 17.11 Transferring the X authority by means of rsh.

This method is very comfortable and stable. It is not easy to generate and manage the correct DISPLAY variable by means of a shell script.

The protocol used in the rsh was documented a posteriori in [rfc1258]. In this case, the RFC is only used for the documentation of an implemented and used protocol.

17.4.2 Login on remote computers

With the rlogin (remote login) program, you can run an interactive session on a remote computer. If no command is specified with rsh, a login is carried out automatically, thus assigning the shell a tty. If you specify a program with rsh that needs a tty (such as vi), you will receive an appropriate error message.

Logins with rlogin instead of telnet are used on UNIX computers because with an appropriate configuration (as with rsh) no password need be entered. The rlogin program is the only one of the r tools that asks for a password if a login without password is not possible.

The security considerations are the same as with rsh. This protocol is defined in [rfc1282].

If the rlogin program is called with the name of a computer, a connection to this computer is automatically established. Thus you can, for example, create a symbolic link to the rlogin program for each target computer. In my own login scripts, I define an alias for each frequently used computer.

17.4.3 File transfer

The program rcp (remote copy) is used to copy files between two computers on each of which you need a valid user ID. The computer name of the remote computer is followed by a colon (:) and the name of the file or the target directory. A different user ID can be specified by prefixing the computer name with the user name followed by an at sign (@) (see Listing 17.12). The authorization is carried out via the same mechanism as with rsh or rlogin.

```
rcp .netrc pea.veggies.org:.
rcp .netrc user@pea.veggies.org:.
rcp user1@host1:file1 user2@host2:file2
```

Listing 17.12 Copying files in the network with rcp.

On older UNIX systems, where the cp command is not capable of copying subdirectories recursively, the rcp −r command can be used instead.

rcp always copies all specified files. For the purpose of synchronization between directories on different computers, the rdist program can be used. This program deletes files which no longer exist on the source computer and transfers only files that have changed. Especially when updating larger directory trees in which little has changed, the network load with the use of rcp is much higher than it should actually be.

17.4.4 Logged-in users in the local network

Often, a network consists of a number of computers. If you are looking for a specific user, for example to address this person by means of talk, it is difficult and long-winded to issue a w on all computers or to start the finger program for all possible computers.

If the administrator has started the rwhod daemon on all computers of the local network, you can use the rwho command to obtain a list of all active, logged-in users (Listing 17.13). With the command ruptime (Listing 17.14) you get an overview of the computers in the local network and their workload. Only computers located in the same subnet are included, that is, computers which match the broadcast address.

```
(Linux):~> rwho
hein      pea:tty2     Aug  1 13:43 :21
jochen    pea:tty3     Aug  1 13:25 :10
jochen    pea:tty4     Aug  1 13:22 :55
katrin    corn:ttyp1   Aug  1 14:30 :47
katrin    corn:ttyp2   Aug  1 14:30 :41
```

Listing 17.13 Logged-in users in the network.

```
(Linux):~> ruptime
carrot    up     22:05,    2 users,  load 0,02, 0,03, 0,04
pea       up      0:58,    4 users,  load 0,00, 0,01, 0,00
corn      down    3:45
```

Listing 17.14 Overview of active computers in the network.

Often the rwhod daemon is not started because the regular exchange of logged-in users and the workload cause a fairly high network load. This is particularly the case where diskless computers are employed. After each rwhod broadcast, the rwhod programs are loaded via network into the main memory of all workstations, and then the appropriate entries are made in the files. This is again done via the network, so a high data volume is produced in a relatively short time.

As an alternative to `rwho`, Sun developed the programs `rusers` and `rstat`. These programs communicate with the corresponding servers (`ruserd` and `rstatd`) which were implemented by means of RPC. Under LINUX, the programs are usually called `rpc.userd` and `rpc.rstatd`. Here, the network load only comes into being if a user is actually interested in the data.

For reasons of data protection or security, there is often a need to prevent access to login and working times of the users. In these cases, the `finger` service and `rwho` will definitely not be started.

17.5 The secure shell `ssh`

Many protocols used in connection with TCP/IP were initially designed with a view to functionality and performance. Aspects of safety against failures and redundancy also played a role, but the aspect of data protection was still considered marginal. Today, this subject is often more important than was initially expected.

In many programs, passwords are transmitted in clear text. Examples for this are `telnet` and `ftp`. When a connection is established in a local network, you can use a packet sniffer like `tcpdump` to protocol the entire session including the login. Remedy can be brought by methods such as one-way passwords (such as S/Key), but the whole connection is still transmitted in clear text, including further passwords.

The r programs, for example `rlogin` and `rsh`, can be configured by means of the files `/etc/hosts.equiv` (system-wide) or `~/.rhosts` in such a way that no password is required. This method of authentication is, however, not particularly safe and can, for example, be hoodwinked by means of IP or DNS spoofing. Here too, the connection is not encrypted, although some `rlogin` programs have the option `-x` for encryption of the session by means of DES.

This can be remedied by the `ssh` package which contains (nearly) all r programs in a more secure version. This begins with the programs `ssh` and `slogin` as replacements for `rsh` and `rlogin` and ends with a more agreeable version of `rcp`, namely `scp`. Once these programs are set up on your network, you can quietly delete the (unsafe) r programs from your system without any user noticing any change.

The s programs are based on a series of key methods. First, each computer has a host key which exists in one private and one public variation. Computers can authenticate each other by encrypting a challenge with the public key of the other computer and sending it to that computer. Only this computer can decrypt and answer the challenge and send it back (encrypted).

Furthermore, a so-called session key is generated for the encryption of each session. This key is not stored on the hard disk, but exists only in RAM. For security reasons, this key is periodically discarded and generated afresh.

Besides the host-based authentication, users can define their own individual confidential relationships that allow logging in without password. First, however, we will install and configure the programs. We will first consider a series of computers under unique administration. Formerly, the file `/etc/hosts.equiv` was used in such a computer pool, so users could switch between different computers by means of rlogin.

As already known from many other programs, the ssh package is compiled with ./configure and make and installed with make install (in /usr/local; this can be changed by means of the option --prefix in configure). This automatically creates a host key (by means of ssh-keygen). If you install the programs on a shared disk (/usr/local is shared via NFS), you must manually create a pair of keys for each computer.

The host keys are stored in the /etc directory, the file ssh_host_key containing the private key and the file ssh_host_key.pub the public key. The configuration files are /etc/ssh_config for the client programs and /etc/sshd_config for the server.

For reciprocal authentication, each host must know the public keys of all other computers, together with its own private key. These are stored in the file /etc/ssh_known_hosts. Since the keys are very long and cryptic, they are usually not entered manually, but generated by means of the program make-ssh-known-hosts. This program can ask all computers in the domain for their public keys and store them. This requires the sshd process to be already running on all computers.

The sshd process should be started once and for all at system start-up, for example in the file rc.local, because the generation of the keys may well take several seconds, which can be inconvenient if the process is started by the inetd super server. In the last step, the computers that are to be allowed direct access must be entered in the file /etc/shosts.equiv. This file functions exactly as the file /etc/hosts.equiv, except that the identity of the alien computer is ensured by cryptographic methods. The file /etc/hosts.equiv is used even if no shosts.equiv file exists.

Each user can additionally create the file ~/.shosts, which will then also be used for authentication. Here too, the file ~/.rhosts is used as a fallback. However, in my opinion, the more specific shosts files are more suitable, because the r services are not (inadvertently) released if they have not (yet) been switched off.

As with the r tools, the system-wide file /etc/shosts.equiv does not allow a login as root. If you want this to be possible, the entry PermitRootLogin in the file /etc/sshd_config must have the value yes and the file ~/.shosts of the user root must be set up accordingly.

On my own system, no /etc/hosts.equiv or ~/.rhosts exist any longer. Even if by chance a rlogind were started again, this would hardly compromise the security of the system. For the ssh, I have obviously set up the file /etc/shosts.equiv accordingly.

Now, all users can use the above-mentioned programs ssh, slogin and scp without password as long as they keep inside the limits set by the administrator. They will experience a number of positive surprises. If an attempt is made to copy a file with scp, the user is prompted for a password if this is required. The rcp program would display an error message. If a user tries to log in to a system that has no sshd process, the user is informed that the session will not be encrypted.

As a countermove, the user is warned if the host key has changed. This can become necessary, for example, in case of a hardware replacement or other major action, but it should make you suspicious because it can also indicate a break-in. A further advantage of the ssh is that X redirection takes place automatically. Again, the whole session is encrypted, and authentication is carried out by means of the ssh and not by means of xhost or xauth.

As you can see, the secure shell offers a significant increase in security and improves handling of the system. In my view, these programs belong to the standard equipment of every UNIX system, since they are not only available for LINUX, but also for almost all other UNIX systems.

If you have problems with the programs, you should start the daemon with the option -d (for debugging) and the client with the option -v (for verbose). Both programs will then generate extensive protocols in which all steps that were carried out can be viewed. With these instruments, you should be able to track down all problems quite quickly.

Besides authentication via host name and RSA key as described above, there are several further options. An even more secure one is the exclusive use of RSA for authentication, where only the pair of keys is used (in combination with a password group). For the rest, a certain confidence is put in the remote computer.

Every user can use the ssh-keygen command to create an individual private key which is stored in the file identity in the ~/.ssh directory. The corresponding public key is stored in identity.pub. For authentication, the local computer must transmit the public key to the target computer in the file ~/.ssh/authorized_keys.

If you use this method, the password must be freshly entered for each connection. This is quite annoying and in the long run relatively dangerous. For this reason, you can start the tool ssh-agent as the first program after the login (for example, instead of the window manager). This program then becomes the parent process of all further programs and can pass them the authentication via an inherited file descriptor.

For this purpose, you must replace the call of the window manager with the program ssh-agent, for example in the file ~/.xsession, passing the names of the programs to be started as parameters. Please note that processes started earlier in the file ~/.xsession have no access to the agent.

The password that belongs to the file ~/.ssh/identity can be entered once and for all by means of the program ssh-add; its management is then taken over by the ssh-agent tool. You can add or delete individual identities, or remove all existing ones from memory if you happen to have to leave your office for a longish period of time.

Practically all programs you can use in combination with rsh can also be employed with the ssh. Individual adaptations exist for rdist, which uses the ssh internally, and screen, which normally closes all file descriptors. In my view, this program package should not be missing from any UNIX system.

Yet another function of ssh is the possibility of redirecting arbitrary TCP connections and encrypting them at the same time. First, you must start ssh with the additional parameter *target_computer* with the option -L *port:host:hostport*. Thus, ssh establishes a connection between the local port *port* and the port *hostport* on the computer *host*. The connection section between the local computer and *target_computer* is then encrypted.

In your application program, you do not use the actual computer as target computer and port, but the specified port on the local computer. Everything else is handled internally by the ssh.

Additional Information and Sources	
ftp server:	ftp.cs.hut.fi
ftp path:	/pub/ssh
File name:	ssh-1.2.20.tar.gz
Size:	about 1 Mbyte
WWW page:	http://www.cs.hut.fi/ssh

17.6 Sending warnings to remote computers with rwall

On the local computer, warnings or messages can be sent to all users by means of the wall command. This happens, for example, at the call of shutdown. When a server is shut down, it might be a good idea to inform the users of other computers as well. This can be done by means of the command rwall *computer*. However, the rwalld daemon must be running on the target computer. Under LINUX, this is the program /usr/sbin/rpc.rwalld. Whether and on which computers this service is running can be determined by means of the command rpcinfo -b 100008 1.

17.7 File transfer with rdist

The rdist program can be used to synchronize directory trees in the network. Thus, it is possible to install a master server with programs which are then forwarded to other computers (local file servers). Only new or modified files are transferred, and (possibly) superfluous files are deleted. The login on the remote computer is carried out via rsh. It is, however, possible to use the ssh. In this case, you must either replace the rsh program with a copy of the ssh or compile rdist accordingly.

The rdist program can be controlled both via parameters and options and by means of files. Especially with more complex tasks and therefore more voluminous parameters, it is a good idea to use rdist scripts. For this purpose, you will need to create an input file and enter the rdist program as the interpreter in the first line. Here, you can also specify additional parameters.[3] A rdist file consists of entries that conform to one of the three following formats:

- *variable = list*
  A variable which is used in the further course of the script is assigned a value.

- *source_files -> destination commands*
  The specified *source_files* are to be transferred to the computers whose

---

[3] On older operating systems, for example Ultrix, this may cause problems.

```
HOSTS = ( pea.veggies.org injhe@corn )

FILES = ( ~/.emacs ~/.gnus ~/.vm ~/.project
  ~/.plan ~/.custom.el ~/.fvwmrc ~/.netrc
  ~/.rhosts ~/.elm ~/.tin  ~/.emacs
  ~/emacs-lisp ~/emacs.init ~/insert ~/work )

$FILES -> $HOSTS
install -R;
```

Listing 17.15   Example of the use of rdist.

names are specified in *destination*. The specified *command* is used for the transfer. Legal commands are presented in more detail in this chapter. However, only those files are transferred which are older or not present on the remote computer.

• *source_files :: timestamp_file commands*
In this format, the files to be transferred are determined by the *timestamp_file*.

Inside rdist scripts, a series of commands can be called to transfer files or trigger other actions.

• install copies the files to be transferred to the target computer(s). Additional options can be specified, which are documented in the man page.
• The notify command causes rdist to send a list of the transferred files and possible error messages to the specified user. If the user name does not contain an 'at' sign (@), the corresponding user on the target computer is used.
• except copies all files that are *not* specified. This is an easy way of transferring a directory with the exception of a few files.
• except_pat is similar to except, with the difference that patterns for file names are specified. Patterns are expanded in the same way as in the sh.
• special can be used to call external commands for each transferred file.
• The command following cmdspecial, in contrast, is executed only once, after all affected files have been transferred.

The example in Listing 17.15 copies the most important configuration files of a user to another computer. This is a relatively simple solution to configure a unique environment even on computers without a shared home directory. This is only a simple example. All options and features of rdist are extensively described in the man page, where you can also find a more detailed example.

17.8 Conversation between users with talk

Two logged-in users can talk to each other, even via a network, by means of the talk program. For this purpose, the corresponding talk daemon must be installed on the communicating systems. Unfortunately, there are two different and incompatible protocols (talk and ntalk), so communication is often not possible.

After the establishment of a connection, shown in Listing 17.16, the screen is split. The upper field displays one's own input. Below this, one or more fields are shown which display the texts of the talk partners. With four or more partners, the screen soon becomes garbled.

In the standard talk, communication is limited to two users. A more powerful and flexible program is ytalk which can handle both talk protocols and, in addition, allows communication with several partners. Users with ytalk can view the texts of all other ytalk users in the corresponding screen areas, but not the texts of users only using the standard UNIX talk.

A talk connection is opened with ytalk *user@host*. The corresponding user receives a message with an invitation for a talk. If the user issues the command specified in the message (see Listing 17.16), the connection is established. All further input is transmitted to the interlocutor, whose input is in turn displayed in the dedicated screen area. The connection is terminated with Ctrl-C.

```
Message from Talk_Daemon@pea at 11:56 ...
talk: connection requested by hein@pea.veggies.org
talk: respond with:  talk hein@pea.veggies.org
```

Listing 17.16   Invitation to a talk.

In comparison with the UNIX talk, the ytalk program offers a series of additional features. These functions are called via a menu, which appears when you press the Esc key. With a German keyboard mapping, for example, the Alt key sends an 'Escape' before the second key, so that these functions can be directly called with Alt-*key*. This keyboard setting can be configured by means of the setmetamode command.

- The a key (add) is used to add a new interlocutor.
- The d key (delete) terminates the connection with a partner.
- Additional options can be changed by means of the o key. These options can also be permanently configured in the file ~/.ytalkrc.
- A useful feature is the call of a shell by means of the s key, so you can enter commands whose output is transmitted to the interlocutor.
- An overview of all active users can be obtained by means of the u key (user).

- You can protocol the text of an interlocutor in a file by means of the $\boxed{\text{w}}$ key (write), so this text is available for future use.
- The $\boxed{\text{q}}$ key terminates ytalk.

In local networks, communication with talk is quick and easy. If the interlocutor is further away, long waiting times accumulate because each keystroke is transmitted individually.

17.9 Internet Relay Chat (irc)

When communicating with several partners via ytalk, screen space runs out rather quickly. Furthermore, each partner must have the ytalk program, which is not, however, available as a standard under many UNIX variations. Another protocol for communicating with several partners is Internet Relay Chat (IRC). In IRC, you will find a large number of channels on which online discussions take place on the most varied subjects.

The backbone of the system is a series of IRC servers which exchange the messages entered by the users. These computers are usually connected via fast lines to keep waiting times to a minimum. The servers forward the messages to the logged-in clients, which in turn handle the user interaction.

If you are unwilling or unable to operate an IRC client on your system, you still have the possibility of accessing IRC via a telnet gate. Detailed information on IRC can be found in the documentation of the IRC client ircII-*. Alternatively, more user-friendly clients are irchat for Emacs and Zircon for X.

The in thing is to set up chat rooms on one's own Web server. The advantage is that only a Web browser is required and no other client. On the other hand, the user circle is very limited because no use is made of the worldwide infrastructure of the IRC. For many companies, however, this is a striking argument, because only in this way can they have exclusive control over the chat room and, for example, stuff it with advertising.

17.10 File transfer with sendfile

In a network with several users it is often necessary to exchange files between users and computers. If only a text file is to be sent, this can often be done by means of the standard mail program:

```
(Linux):~> mail user < file
```

If the file contains 8-bit coded text (foreign language special characters) or if it is a binary file, it must be converted into a format that survives transport as mail before it is actually transmitted. This can be done by means of programs like uuencode, or you can use MIME encoding.

However, this method is quite laborious, particularly if the mail system in addition limits the length of messages. With sendfile one or more files can be sent to a user. The transmitted files can then be received by means of receive.

(Linux):~> **sendfile** *file User@host*

This program uses the SAFT protocol (Simple Asynchronous File Transfer) for which a port has already been officially reserved. An RFC for this protocol is in preparation. Besides transmission of files, a function for sending messages is also implemented. This allows you to send short texts via the network (locally, you can use write) to a logged-in user without having to log in on another computer.

sendfile can only be used if the appropriate server is running on the target computer, which currently is only seldom the case. Furthermore, the computer must be directly reachable via TCP/IP. If you send files via mail, the target computer does not even need to be online, provided a corresponding MX entry exists for the computer in the DNS.

The system administrator can prohibit the use of this service to individual users in the file /usr/local/etc/nosendfile. Each user can create a file with aliases for destinations. Furthermore, transmission of files and messages from alien computers can be prohibited.

Another function often missed under UNIX is sending a short message to a logged-in user. If this user works on the same computer, you can use the write command. However, if the user is logged in on another computer, you cannot use write. If sendfile is installed, you can send a brief message with sendmsg which is immediately displayed to the user.

Additional Information and Sources	
Author:	Ulli Horlacher
email:	framstag@rus.uni-stuttgart.de
ftp server:	ftp.uni-stuttgart.de
ftp path:	/pub/unix/comm/sendfile/
File:	sendfile.tar.gz
Size:	about 300 Kbytes

Network File System (NFS)

18

With the Network File System (NFS), files can be accessed and used by different computers. Thus, for example, users can have their home or mail directories, data and configuration files on all computers, which greatly facilitates their daily work. Another sensible thing is a unique server installation of programs in /usr/local or /usr, in particular of voluminous packages such as X11 or TEX. This also reduces the administrative effort of updates.

The computer on which these directories are locally available is called the NFS server; the computer that uses data from a remote computer is called an NFS client. For the user, it does not matter at all whether files are stored locally or on a remote computer since the remote directory tree is integrated into the local directory tree. Directory trees exported by the NFS server are also known as NFS volumes.

The Network File System is implemented on the basis of Remote Procedure Calls (RPCs, see also Section 15.6). This protocol was developed by Sun and is published in [rfc1094]. NFS is the standard protocol for sharing directories between different UNIX systems. In the PC world, you will also find Novell NetWare (IPX, see Section 20.1) and Server Message Block (SMB, LAN manager, Windows for Workgroups, Windows NT; see Section 20.2).

As already mentioned in Chapter 15, the Sun RPC system is mandatory for the operation of an NFS client or server.

Currently, the NFS performance under LINUX is worse than under comparable systems. Olaf Kirch is working on an implementation of NFS version 3 and an NFS server that is integrated into the kernel. Both promise a significant increase in speed. Furthermore, several parameters will allow a higher throughput to be achieved.

18.1 LINUX as NFS client

Frequently, NFS servers already exist in local networks for the home directories of the users or, for example, for sharing CD-ROM drives. In particular, since many

383

operating system vendors no longer supply printed documentation with their systems, the latter has often become necessary. Usually, in these cases, LINUX will initially be configured as an NFS client. The following conditions must be satisfied:

- The network must be configured; that is, a `ping` to the NFS server must be possible.
- The NFS file system must be compiled into the kernel or loaded as a module. You can check this by looking at the output of the command `cat /proc/file systems` in which `nfs` must appear. Otherwise, you must either load the module `nfs.o` or reconfigure and recompile the kernel.
- The RPC system must have been started. You can view the services registered with the port mapper by means of the command `rpcinfo -p computer`.
- Another computer in the network must export data to this computer. Which directories are exported can be determined by means of the command `showmount -e nfs-server`.

The command `mount -t nfs nfs-server:NFS-Volume /mnt` can be used to append the path exported by the server `nfs-server`. The type (`-t nfs`) need not be specified because the `mount` program recognizes from the colon (`:`) that it is dealing with an NFS volume. The command `showmount -e nfs server` displays a list of directories exported by this server.

When mounting these directories, several options can be specified which are sensible to keep the network secure or allow work to be continued in case of failure of the NFS server. As with local file systems, these options can also be specified in the file `/etc/fstab` (Listing 18.1). The following list contains only the most important options. A complete description of all options can be found in the man page `nfs(5)`.

```
nfs-server:/home /home       nfs rw,auto         0 0
nfs-server:/cd0  /mount/cd0 nfs ro,noauto,user 0 0
```

Listing 18.1   Excerpts of the file `/etc/fstab`.

- The option `rsize` specifies the block size for read access. The current default is 1024 bytes; other systems support block sizes of 2048, 4096 and 8192 bytes. In case of performance problems, it may be necessary (and sensible) to change these sizes; often a block size of 8192 bytes is used.
- The option `wsize` specifies the block size for write access, in analogy to what has been said about the option `rsize`.
- The option `timeo` is used to set the time, in tenths of a second, to a timeout and thus a retransmission of the request. The default value is 7 (which corresponds to 0.7 seconds). This is a 'minor timeout.'
- The option `retrans` (default 3) specifies the number of retransmissions after a 'minor timeout,' but before a 'major timeout.'

- It can be specified how the NFS client behaves in the event of a 'major timeout':

  - hard displays the message 'server not responding' and repeats the attempts indefinitely. This setting is the default.
  - soft signals an I/O error to the program.
  - intr allows interruption of the request by means of Ctrl-C for volumes mounted with the hard option. The program is sent the error code EINTR.

Frequently, the NFS is seen as a great security problem. This is due, on the one hand, to the use of Remote Procedure Calls, and on the other to the implementation of the protocols. You should consider various issues before deciding to employ the NFS (also known as 'Nightmare File System'):

- Only export to known computers.
- If at all possible, only export read-only.
- Keep an eye on the log files of the system.

Sun has developed an enhanced version of the NFS, the so-called Secure NFS. This is based on an extension of the RPC interface, the Secure RPCs. Other manufacturers have licensed this technology, but currently implementations are only available for very few platforms. Thus, this excludes application in heterogeneous networks.

18.2 Linux as NFS server

A LINUX computer can also be employed as an NFS server. An NFS server provides other computers with disk space that can be used in common. For the application of a LINUX system as NFS server, some conditions must be satisfied:

- The network must be configured (ping from server to client and vice versa).
- The port mapper rpc.portmap must be started. In the Slackware distribution, this happens in the file rc.inet2. Modern distributions which use the System V boot concept usually contain a separate script for this purpose in the /etc/rc.d/init.d directory.
- The daemons rpc.mountd and rpc.nfsd must be started. In the Slackware distribution, this is equally done in the file rc.inet2, with the System V init again in a separate script.
- When PC/NFS is used, the daemon rpc.pcnfsd must be started. This daemon is required for authentication and provision of printer services in connections involving DOS and Windows PCs.
- The NFS protocol assumes that the uid and gid numbers are the same on both computers. This can be obtained through identical /etc/passwd files or by means of NIS (see Chapter 22). If neither is possible (or sensible), the rpc.ugidd can be used.

Which directory trees are made available to other computers is specified in the file /etc/exports. There, the access to individual computers or networks can be restricted or only read-only access allowed. This is achieved by means of several options, the most important of which are:

- Volumes can be exported write-protected (ro, default) or writable (rw).

- The option root_squash redirects the user ID 0 to the user nobody (uid -2). The default value is no_root_squash.

- The user IDs of server and client are equal to map_identy (default) or are assigned via rpc.ugidd (map_daemon).

A complete list of the possible options can be found in the man pages for exports(5) and nfs(5). Listing 18.2 contains an example for the file /etc/exports. The volume /home is exported to all computers in the domain veggies.org. The volume /opt is exported only to nfsclient. Accesses by user root are redirected to the user nobody. The volume /project can be used by all project-related computers whose names begin with proj. The volume /pub can be mounted worldwide.

```
/opt         nfsclient(ro,root_squash)
/home        *.veggies.org(rw,root_squash)
/project     proj*.veggies.org(rw)
/pub         (ro,insecure,root_squash)
```

Listing 18.2   Excerpt from the file /etc/exports.

Additional Information and Sources	
Man pages:	mount(8), nfs(5), exports(5), rpc.nfsd(8), rpc.mountd(8), rpc.pcnfsd(8)

18.2.1 Problems with the use of NFS

NFS is implemented on the basis of RPCs. Usually, a statusless protocol (UDP) is used. This means that the server has no history for the current requests and that, therefore, caching functions can only be realized to a very limited extent. An advantage of NFS is that the client can be sure that the data is stored on the server disk after the corresponding call is terminated.

Sharing files is only possible in a reasonable way if the user names and the corresponding user IDs on the participating computers match. When you activate NFS for the first time, you will notice that users sometimes have different UIDs on different computers or that one UID belongs to several users. Before you employ NFS, you should therefore clean up the password files (and assign the files to the correct users).

First, you should create a list of the files that are owned by a user, for example by means of find / -uid *userID*. Then you adapt the password file and convey these files to the new ID by means of `chown`. Manual synchronization of the password files is laborious and error-prone. You should therefore think about using NIS (see also Chapter 22). The use of the `uigdd` program which adjusts the user IDs at runtime on the basis of the names must only be seen as an emergency solution.

During data exchange via NFS, the internal clocks of the participating computers should be synchronized relatively exactly to prevent problems that might be very hard to trace. When files are created, they receive a time stamp by the server. When the same files are read (maybe directly afterwards) this time stamp is interpreted on the basis of the local time of the client. If the times differ, programs such as `make` get confused.

Apart from these problems, it is also less confusing for the user if the internal clocks do not differ. Since PC clocks in particular are very inaccurate, you must take special measures. Relative divergences can be corrected locally by means of the `adjtime` program. To synchronize the clocks in the network, you can employ various methods, all of which have their raison d'être:

- You can request the time from the NIST Network Time Service via the Internet (for example, from `http://www.time.nist.gov`). The service responds in several formats, including the DAYTIME, TIME, and NTP protocols.

- If a time server exists in the network, you can fetch the time from there by means of program `xntp`. Some RFCs (for example [rfc1305] and [rfc1769]) describe appropriate protocols for time synchronization.

- You can use the programs `netdate` or `rdate` to obtain the time from one or all computers in the network.

In the management of data and program files, NFS is almost completely transparent to the user. The situation is different for device files and named pipes. Here, communication with the kernel or an application program on the other side of the pipe is to be established. Practically neither can be realized via the NFS.

You should make sure that the NFS server is connected to the same subnet and network segment as the clients. Otherwise, the router may be (over)strained through the rather high network load and bridges cannot separate loads between individual segments. In the long run, neither is good for the safe operation of the network and thus for the satisfaction of the users.

Currently the SMB protocol is being further developed to become the *Common Internet File System* (CIFS). Besides Microsoft, the Samba team also participates in the development, which is intended to provide better performance and better semantics than NFS.

18.3 The automounter

In a local network in which many directories are mounted back and forth between different computers via NFS, it is often not sensible to do this directly at the start-up of the computer. On the one hand, each mounted volume occupies one of 32 superblocks in the LINUX kernel; on the other hand, the corresponding server must be available for the mounting process. If the NFS server can no longer be reached during active operation, then, depending on the type of data used, operational restrictions must be expected. Furthermore, the `fstab` files continue to grow and, in case of a change, must be adapted on all computers.

These problems were the background for the development of the automounter. Here, the corresponding directories are only mounted into the directory tree when they are actually needed. If the data is not used for a certain period of time, the volume is unmounted. In addition, the automounter is flexible enough to ensure that, in the event of failure of a server, another computer can take its place.

Because of the flexible (and therefore somewhat more complex) syntax, one configuration file can be used for all computers in the local network. This significantly reduces management effort, in particular if this file is distributed by means of NIS (see Chapter 22).

18.3.1 Internals of the automounter

In the local network, each exported volume receives a unique name. Under this name, all computers in the local network can address this volume. This makes it possible to have the same home directory on all computers. Frequently, the mail directories are mounted in the same way.

However, depending on the computer architecture or the operating system used, the automounter can also mount different volumes that fulfill the same purpose (for example the TEX path for different architectures).

Besides this, local devices such as a CD-ROM drive or diskette drives can be mounted as well. This allows you to do without the `usermount` program.

18.3.2 Conditions for using the automounter

The automounter is implemented internally as an NFS server. Therefore, as with an NFS server or client, the RPC port mapper and the other NFS daemons are required. In addition, the `amd` must obviously be started as well. The sources of the `amd` include a sample script (`./text/amd.start.ex`) which calls the daemon with the correct parameters.

Furthermore, the appropriate volumes must be configured. This can be done, for example, by means of the file `/etc/mount.amd`, whose name must be passed to `amd` as a parameter. Listing 18.3 shows an example for a simple configuration of the automounter.

The volumes `fd0` and `dos` are made available for local use only. The volume `cdrom` is mounted locally on the computer. On all other systems, the corresponding volume of the CD server is addressed via NFS. `amd` has many additional functions and configuration options, which are explained in the info documentation.

```
/defaults opts:=intr

fd0      host==$host;type:=ufs;\
         dev:=/dev/fd0;\
         opts:=type=msdos,gid=6,uid=0,umask=002,noexec,nodev

dos      host==$host;type:=ufs;dev:=/dev/hdc1;\
         opts:=type=msdos,gid=120,uid=0,umask=002,noexec

cdrom    host==cdserver;type:=ufs;dev:=/dev/sr0;\
         opts:=type=iso9660,ro \
         host!=$host;type:=nfs;rhost:=cdserver;\
         rfs:=/mount/cdrom;opts:=ro,rsize=4096,wsize=4096
```

Listing 18.3   The map file for the automounter `amd`.

Additional Information and Sources	
ftp server:	ftp.cs.columbia.edu
ftp path:	/pub/amd
file name:	amd-upl102.tar.gz
Size:	about 530 Kbytes

18.3.3 The LINUX autofs

Kernel version 2.1 and later versions include the `autofs` file system. This is an alternative to the BSD automounter (`amd`) and is intended to take its place in the foreseeable future. In addition to `autofs` in the kernel, you will need the appropriate utilities. A source is given in the info box at the end of the chapter.

The configuration of the `automounter` is carried out in two steps. First, the list of maps to be managed is stored in the file /etc/auto.master (Listing 18.4). The format of this file is documented in the man page for `auto.master`. Each individual map is located in a separate file.

```
# The file /etc/auto.master. The format of this file is
#    mountpoint mapfile [options]
/mount  /etc/auto.mount
```

Listing 18.4   The file /etc/auto.master.

If a file or subdirectory is sought in the /mount directory, the `automounter` finds additional information in the file /etc/auto.mount. An example for this file can be found in Listing 18.5.

```
# The file /etc/auto.mount has the format
#   key [ -mount-options ] source
kernel    -ro                    ftp.kernel.org:/pub/linux
cdrom     -fstype=iso9660,ro  :/dev/scd0
floppy    -fstype=auto        :/dev/fd0
dos       -fstype=vfat,uid=0,gid=100,umask=002 :/dev/sda1
```

Listing 18.5   The file /etc/auto.mount.

The first entry mounts the NFS volume ftp.kernel.org:/pub/linux when the directory /mount/kernel is referenced. The other three entries have no host names specified in the third field, therefore a local mount is executed. After five minutes, the file system is removed.

Here too, it is possible to work with different keys and architectures. However, this is only required in very large installations. More information can be found in the man page autofs(5). In the near future, the amd will be replaced by autofs at least under LINUX.

Additional Information and Sources	
ftp server:	ftp.kernel.org
ftp path:	/pub/linux/daemons/autofs
File name:	autofs-0.3.14.tar.gz
Size:	about 50 Kbytes
Mailing list:	autofs@linux.kernel.org
	Subscribe quoting 'subscribe autofs' with
	majordomo@linux.kernel.org

Anonymous FTP servers

19

The `ftpd` daemon is installed on practically every networked UNIX system. In the standard version, each authorized user can transfer files to and from the system. Users are authorized if they have a valid user ID (which also presumes that the login shell is registered in the file `/etc/shells`) and is *not* registered in the file `/etc/ftpusers`.

For a computer in a local network, this is quite acceptable. However, users without an ID may often need to view or transfer certain files. To make this possible, a so-called anonymous `ftp` server can be installed. This is a sensible solution if you want to distribute freeware programs or if you want to provide information or program patches or other similar items to the general public. Frequently, `http` servers (Web servers) are employed for this purpose, but they have several disadvantages: uploads of users must be implemented by means of special constructions; the protocol has not been developed for the transfer of larger amounts of data; and after a transmission failure, the transfer process must be started all over again.

When setting up an `ftp` server, several issues must be considered to prevent alien users from having full access to all files of the computer. Of course you want to make the relevant data accessible in the easiest possible way, but you certainly do not wish to neglect all security aspects.

There are various `ftp` daemons, which are in part configured in a different manner. When choosing your server, you should make sure that you can monitor all actions by the users, if at all possible, so that you can trace what happens on your computer. This is an important tool for ensuring the security of your computer and for preventing its misuse as an intermediate storage place for pirate copies or other unauthorized files. Furthermore, it might be a good idea to deactivate specific commands and to provide useful features such as a searchable index.

When a user logs in under the user name `anonymous` or `ftp`, a special directory (for example `/home/ftp`) is usually made the current directory. For this purpose, the system call `chroot(2)` is used which declares this directory to be the new root directory for this process (and for all of its child processes). This is used to prevent anonymous ftp users from having access to files outside this directory.

After entering the user name ftp or anonymous, the email address of the user is often expected to be entered. Often, a login is refused if the address is not correct, for example, if it does not contain the 'at' sign (ⓐ). Many servers also try to find out the name of the computer by asking for the name server.

Another alternative is the use of ident to determine the identity of the user more precisely. However, this leads to frequent problems with PC users, since no user IDs exist on these systems. Furthermore, data protection issues which might prohibit surrendering of the user ID, have not yet been clarified either.

In the whole directory tree under ˜ftp, all directories and files should be available for anonymous users in read-only mode. This is intended to prevent, for example, storage of a file .rhosts on the computer that allows interactive access. The simplest solution is that no directory is owned by the user ID under which the ftp server is running.

Some special directories (such as incoming) should be exempted from these restrictions to allow users without ID to make files publicly available as well. However, these files should be made available to other users only after they have been checked by the system administrator. This will hopefully be sufficient to prevent unauthorized distribution of data via your computer.

In unauthorized use, files with the name ... or with names that contain control characters are very popular. Therefore, you should search the transfer statistics for unusual names, so that you can at least exercise some control (a posteriori).

A very helpful feature for users is the use of special functions such as the automatic combination of all files in a directory into one archive. This allows users to transfer a complete directory tree with a single command. You may deactivate this function for individual directories, which would be a sensible thing to do, for example, for the root directory.

In some clients (such as ncftp), this function is integrated; in most programs, however, it is not. Another useful feature is to restart an interrupted transmission where it left off by means of the reget command. Unfortunately, most WWW browsers do not use this function. A further reason for using a 'normal' ftp client is that it will allow you to issue special commands such as search in the index file or change of permissions. These commands are initiated with QUOTE. Depending on the ftp server, different commands are supported; help can be obtained by means of the command QUOTE HELP.

19.1 Installing the wu-ftpd

As mentioned above, there are various ftp daemons. Many ftp servers on the Internet use the wu-ftpd, because it provides many special features for an anonymous ftp server, carries out extensive monitoring, and allows corrected versions to be quickly installed in the event of security problems. The striking argument in its favor is the availability of the source code, which allows local adaptations to be made.

For the system administrator, installing this ftp daemon is slightly more laborious than using the one supplied as a standard with UNIX.[1] Nevertheless it is sensible to use a daemon whose source code is available, if you wish to be able to react rapidly to possible problems. The wu-ftpd can be installed on almost all UNIX platforms, so some adaptations in different files are required.

The paths to important configuration files must be set prior to compilation in the file src/pathnames.h. Here, you enter the specific paths that are used on your system. Development of this daemon does not take place under LINUX, so you will have to make several changes. The following list indicates the paths used on my own system:

- _PATH_FTPUSERS   "/etc/ftpusers"
  This file contains the names of those users who are not allowed to log in via ftp. Usually, these are the users root, bin, and some other system IDs.

- _PATH_FTPACCESS "/etc/ftpaccess"
  Here is where the central configuration of the ftp server takes place. The contents of this file, which is evaluated at runtime, is described in more detail in the man page ftpaccess.

- _PATH_FTPHOSTS   "/etc/ftphosts"
  This can be used for admission or refusal of individual users of various computers.

- _PATH_EXECPATH   "/bin/ftp-exec"
  This specifies the path under which programs are sought. For anonymous users, chroot() is used to switch to the ~ftp directory, so this path is relative to it. For all other users, you may have to create an appropriate symbolic link. This is meant for the security of your server; therefore you should *not* specify a system directory.

- _PATH_PIDNAMES   "/var/run/ftp.pids-%s"
  Users can be subdivided into different classes (for example, users in the local domain and other users). For each class, restrictions can be entered and monitored, which is done using these files.

- _PATH_CVT   "/etc/ftpconversions"
  The ftp daemon can pack or unpack files during the transfer. For this purpose, the appropriate programs must be present in ~ftp/bin/ftp-exec and the file /etc/ftpconversions must be set up accordingly.

- _PATH_XFERLOG   "/var/log/xferlog"
  This file stores the transmission statistics, which you can evaluate, for example, with awk or perl. You should check this file regularly for unusual events.

- _PATH_PRIVATE   "/etc/ftpgroups"
  This is the password file for the site group and site gpass commands.

---

[1] Many LINUX distributions already include the wu-ftpd; commercial UNIX systems, on the other hand, do not.

- _PATH_UTMP   "/var/run/utmp"
  This specifies the path to the utmp file, which contains the names of the users currently logged in to the system. You can then use the usual UNIX commands (for example last) to find out which of these users are currently using the ftp server.

- _PATH_WTMP   "/var/log/wtmp"
  This specifies the path to the wtmp file. This file contains a log of the user logins.

- _PATH_LASTLOG   "/var/log/lastlog"
  This file contains the data of the last login of a user.

Finally, you need to check the settings in the files ./src/config/config.lnx and ./src/makefiles/Makefile.lnx. Subsequently, you can compile the daemon with ./build lnx. After a short lapse of time, you will find the programs in the subdirectory ./bin, and you can terminate the installation with ./build install.

To activate the new daemon, you need to modify the file /etc/inetd.conf and re-initialize the inetd server with the signal SIGHUP. This is done by means of the command killall -HUP inetd. Subsequently, an ftp daemon is available for the users of this computer. The setup of an anonymous ftp server is described in the next section.

19.2 Administration of an ftp server

The operation of an anonymous ftp server, more than other services, raises some security problems. Some of them are taken into consideration in the implementation of the ftp daemon. Many other issues affect the security of your server. Before you make the server available to other users, you should take time to read the man pages and the CERT advisories on this subject.

To keep programs as small as possible, LINUX normally uses shared libraries. After the chroot to the ~ftp directory, access to the libraries stored in /lib is no longer possible. Therefore you must either copy the required libraries (ld.so and libc.so) together with the required files from /etc (ld.so.cache, group, and passwd) into the ~ftp/lib directory, or you must use statically linked programs, which as a rule should be the simplest solution.

For a simple ftp server without special features you will only need the ls program. If you want to provide automatic packing of directories and files, you will also need tar and compress or gzip. These programs must be copied into the directory ~ftp/bin/ftp-exec. Additional programs that ftp users are allowed to execute by means of the site exec command must be copied into the ~ftp/bin/ftp-exec directory. Here, one frequently finds a search program for the file index. Please use special care when deciding which commands alien users are allowed to execute on your computer.

When setting up the server, you must definitely ensure that you do not make any files or directories writable for alien users. The only exception should be the incoming directory. Transmissions into or from this directory always need special monitoring since ftp servers are often misused as intermediate storage for pirate copies or other illegal material.

To display the file owner, the ls program needs the files ~ftp/etc/passwd and ~ftp/etc/group. You should not, however, use the system password file, but a specially elaborated one in which no passwords are stored. If you so wish, you can also change the user IDs (and their names) to prevent them from being revealed to the whole world.

In the next step, you can set up the special functions of the server in the files ftpconversions, ftpusers, and ftpgroups. In the file /etc/ftpconversions, you can specify which conversions can be carried out during the transfer and which programs can be used for that purpose. Each line of this file consists of eight colon-separated columns that describe one conversion method. An example is shown in Listing 19.1.

```
:.Z : :    :/bin/compress -d -c %s:T_REG:O_UNCOMPRESS:UNCOMPRESS
:    : :.Z:/bin/compress -c %s:T_REG:O_COMPRESS:COMPRESS
:.gz: :    :/bin/gzip -cd %s:T_REG:O_UNCOMPRESS:GUNZIP
:    : :.gz:/bin/gzip -9c %s:T_REG:O_COMPRESS:GZIP
:    : :.tar:/bin/tar -cf - %s:T_REG|T_DIR:O_TAR:TAR
:    : :.tgz:/bin/tar -czf - %s:T_REG|T_DIR:O_COMPRESS|O_TAR:TGZ
```

Listing 19.1   The file /etc/ftpconversions.

The meaning of the individual fields is shown in Table 19.1. Please note that currently the prefix options are not yet implemented. You must copy the required programs (statically linked, if needed) into the directory ~ftp/bin to make them executable by anonymous users too.

Field	Description
1	Name prefix to be removed
2	Name suffix to be removed
3	Name prefix to be appended
4	Name suffix to be appended
5	Command to be executed
6	File types: T_REG, T_DIR or T_ASCII
7	Options: O_COMPRESS, O_UNCOMPRESS or O_TAR
8	Description

Table 19.1   Description of the entries in the file /etc/ftpconversions.

The file /etc/ftpusers contains the names of the users who are *not* allowed to log in with ftp. Usually, these will be the users root, bin, and other system IDs. The file /etc/ftpgroups can be used to set up various user groups and provide them with a password.

The most sophisticated configuration file, however, is the file /etc/ftpaccess. You can find extensive examples in the directory ./doc/examples and documentation that is well worth reading in the man page ftpaccess(5).

A simple check as to whether the installation is correct can be carried out by means of the program ./bin/ckconfig. This program, however, does not point out security problems that might have been created through your configuration.

Once the server is configured and only a few problems arise in day-to-day operations, you should nevertheless carefully check the log files. ftp servers can be attacked via the network and sometimes used for distribution of pirate copies or other illegal actions. Besides the transfer statistics, the log files of the servers are an important source of information.

Further information on operation and configuration of ftp servers can be found in several CERT advisories. Also, packages such as COPS or Tripwire which search systems for known security gaps or unauthorized changes may help you ensure secure operation of an ftp server.

Never take the security of a server for granted. You bear the responsibility for your computer, particularly if the system is used for illegal purposes such as the distribution of pirate copies.

Additional Information and Sources	
Man pages:	ftpd(8), ftpaccess(5), ftphosts(5), xferlog(5) ftpcount(1) ftpwho(1), ftpshut(8), ftpconversions(5)
ftp server:	sunsite.unc.edu
ftp path:	/pub/Linux/system/Network/file-transfer
File name:	wu-ftpd-2.4.fixed.tar.Z
Size:	about 185 Kbytes
Mailing lists:	wu-ftpd and wu-ftpd-announce, subscribe with email to listproc@mail.wustl.edu without subject with subscribe *list name*

LINUX in a heterogeneous network

All TCP/IP-based protocols and applications discussed until now are a standard for UNIX systems of all manufacturers. In UNIX networks, these protocols are usually sufficient. Things change, however, if a UNIX system is to be linked into an existing local network composed of PCs and Macintosh systems. There, you often find an unruly growth of protocols, and each computer is supposed to communicate with every other directly and with as little effort as possible.

Besides the TCP/IP protocol, LINUX speaks a number of other languages widely used in local networks. Thus, once again, LINUX proves to be an economical and powerful solution for connection of different network platforms. Comparable commercial packages are often prohibitively expensive for smaller businesses or private users.

A widely-used protocol in PC networks is the IPX protocol (Internet Packet Exchange) by Novell NetWare. Usually, well-equipped PCs are used as servers; the speed is somewhat higher than with TCP/IP, which is why this protocol is very popular in pure PC networks. Clients exist for DOS, Windows, OS/2, and MacOS, either directly included in the operating system or available from Novell.

Novell also offers a TCP/IP package for its servers, but it does not attain the functionality of a UNIX host. Furthermore, this package, which also includes NFS, is relatively expensive. With IntraNetware, Novell too is slowly opening its doors towards TCP/IP-based networking.

Another protocol is Server Message Block (SMB). This is used by the LAN manager (by IBM and Microsoft) and by Windows NT, Windows for Workgroups, and Windows 95. Under LINUX, the samba package is used as a server. This package can also be employed on many other UNIX platforms. As a client, you can use the smbfs file system for accessing Windows shares. Authorized printers can be addressed by means of the smbclient program from the samba package.

For communication with Apple Macintosh computers, the AppleTalk protocol is employed. Here too, there is an implementation under LINUX. With this, LINUX is a truly open and communicative operating system. This is also due to the fact that practically the whole source code is available and any interested party can make appropriate changes and adaptations.

20.1 LINUX as a NetWare client and server

In local PC networks, Novell NetWare is very popular. The implementation is stable and somewhat faster than the TCP/IP protocols. Several years ago, when PCs were much less powerful, this was often the only reasonable way of networking. Today, also because of the Internet and Intranet strategies, TCP/IP is gaining a growing importance.

IPX is used as the lowest protocol layer. This protocol is documented and has been implemented in the LINUX kernel for some time. Thus, LINUX can also be used as an IPX router, and NetWare services can be accessed in the DOSemu.

NetWare services, that is file and print services, are however based on the Net-Ware Core Protocol (NCP) which builds on IPX, but was not officially documented by Novell. This documentation is now (at least partly) available, so that LINUX can be employed in NetWare networks both as a client and as a server. Only the Bindery of NetWare 3.x is emulated. Access to the NetWare Directory Services (NDS) is only possible with the commercial NetWare client contained in the Caldera OpenLinux standard distribution. Also, the NetWare servers for LINUX only represent Bindery servers.

First of all, the IPX protocol must be compiled into the kernel. This implementation has been carried out among others by Caldera, a company initially financed by former Novell CEO Ray Noorda. After a reboot, the kernel signals the presence of this protocol with a message such as the following:

```
Swansea University Computer Society IPX 0.34 for NET3.035
IPX Portions Copyright (c) 1995 Caldera, Inc.
```

Subsequently, similar to TCP/IP networks, the interface must be configured. Currently, this is still done by means of a separate program. These functions could in future be integrated into the ifconfig program. Configuration of the interface can be carried out either automatically or manually. With the command ipx_configure --auto_primary=on --auto_interface=on you will automatically create a primary IPX interface when an IPX packet arrives.

Automatic recognition is only possible if you want to operate LINUX only as a client in the network. Otherwise, you will need an internal IPX network number, which is assigned to you by your network administrator. If your network includes computers running Windows 95 as the operating system, you should equally do without automatic recognition. Because of a bug in the system, these computers send packets with a different frame type than otherwise used in the network, which prevents safe operation with automatic recognition.

If automatic creation is not possible, you can create the interface manually with the command `ipx_interface`. For this, you must specify the network device (for example `eth0`), the frame type, and the network number. You can obtain frame type and network number from your network administrator. Table 20.1 shows an overview of common frame types and their standard use.

Frame type	Use
802.2	Ethernet 802.2
802.3	Ethernet 802.3
ether_ii	The Ethernet-II protocol
802.2TR	Token Ring encapsulation

Table 20.1   IPX frame types and their use.

Today, most (new) networks are operated with frame type 802.3; this is also the standard for many commercial products. In existing installations, however, types 802.2 and ether_ii are still being used. If you have a Token Ring network, you must employ frame type 802.2TR.

The command shown in Listing 20.1 creates an IPX interface for frame type 802.2. The network number is 2A. If you specify zero (0), the kernel tries to read the network number from the incoming IPX packets. Please note that you may severely hamper the entire network operation in the event of collisions or errors in the assignment of IPX network numbers.

```
(Linux):~# ipx_interface add -p eth0 802.2 2A
```

Listing 20.1   Creation of an IPX interface under LINUX.

Information on the current status of the IPX subsystem can be found in the /proc file system in the files `ipx_interface` (Listing 20.2), `ipx` (Listing 20.3), and `ipx_route` (Listing 20.4) in the /proc/net directory.

The file /proc/net/ipx_interface contains one line for each configured interface. The example in Listing 20.2 comes from a LINUX computer which is both NetWare server (via `mars_nwe`) and NetWare client (via `ncpfs`).

```
Network    Node_Address   Primary  Device    Frame_Type
00000030   10005AD2813C   No       tr0       802.2TR
10000106   000000000001   Yes      Internal  None
```

Listing 20.2   The file /proc/net/ipx_interface.

The external network interface `tr0`, a Token Ring network card, is connected to the network 30, using frame type `802.2TR`. The node address is the hardware address of the network card which is automatically inserted by the kernel. The interface is not primary.

Each NetWare server has its own (internal) network. The number assigned to this must be unique and should therefore be centrally managed. If you are in doubt, please ask your network administrator. In this network, the server has the node address 1. In the above example, the internal interface is also the primary one.

Listing 20.3 shows an example of the file /proc/net/ipx. As soon as your computer participates in the IPX network, this file fills up automatically.

```
Local_Address   Remote_Address  Tx_Queue   Rx_Queue   State Uid
10000106:4000   Not_Connected   00000000   00000000   07    000
10000106:0452   Not_Connected   00000000   00000000   07    000
10000106:0453   Not_Connected   00000000   00000000   07    000
10000106:4001   Not_Connected   00000000   00000000   07    000
10000106:4002   Not_Connected   00000000   00000000   07    000
10000106:0451   Not_Connected   00000000   00000000   07    000
10000106:4003   Not_Connected   00000000   00000000   07    000
10000106:4004   Not_Connected   00000000   00000000   07    000
```

Listing 20.3   The file /proc/net/ipx.

Listing 20.4 shows an excerpt from the file /proc/net/ipx_route. In this file, the routing table for IPX packets is shown in a readable form. For each reachable network, the table indicates the network through which the routing takes place and which computer acts as a router. Since all IPX servers usually also function as routers and publish this information periodically in the network, this table fills up rather quickly. If you have many NetWare servers, this (pseudo) file will contain lots of entries.

```
Network    Router_Net    Router_Node
10000411   00000030      00001D17C1F9
25031995   00000030      00805F189164
...
00000030   Directly      Connected
10000106   Directly      Connected
```

Listing 20.4   The file /proc/net/ipx_route.

After use, the interface can be deleted by means of the ipx_interface program (Listing 20.5). Here too, the frame type must be specified. Usually, the interface is created by the start-up scripts of your distribution and deleted at system shutdown. However, if you need to test the individual functions, it may be more sensible to call them manually.

```
(Linux):~# ipx_interface del eth0 802.2
```

Listing 20.5 Deletion of an IPX interface.

More recent distributions are already prepared for use as NetWare clients (and servers), so the corresponding start/stop scripts are readily available. The following sections deal with the configuration of the corresponding applications.

Additional Information and Sources	
Man pages:	`ipx_configure(8)`, `ipx_internal_net(8)`, `ipx_interface(8)`, `ipx_route(8)`
HowTo:	`IPX-HOWTO`
Author:	Greg Page, `greg@caldera.com`
`ftp` server:	`ftp.caldera.com`
`ftp` path:	`/pub/ipx`
File name:	`ipx-1.0.tar.gz`
Size:	about 8 Kbytes

20.1.1 LINUX as a NetWare client

The `ncpfs` package provides an implementation of the NCP which can be loaded into the kernel as a module. As the name suggests, it is (among others) a file system based on the NetWare Core Protocol. In addition, print services are provided and exploited.

The source code of the `ncpfs` itself is contained in the standard kernel and can be selected during kernel configuration. In addition, you will need the `ncpmount` program, which you can use to mount volumes exported by NetWare servers in a LINUX system. Since the Novell volumes differ significantly from the file systems normally used under LINUX, this function has not yet been integrated into the normal `mount` program.

The `ncpfs` package was developed by Volker Lendecke, who also implemented the `smbfs` for accessing Windows shares. More details on this package can be found in Section 20.2.1. Currently supported is the access to volumes of NetWare 3.x servers and of NetWare 4.x servers with the aid of Bindery emulation.

In the current implementation, LINUX can use not only disks, but also printers connected to NetWare servers. The corresponding file system (`ncpfs`) is integrated into the standard kernel. You only need to select the IPX protocol and this file system during kernel configuration. The above-mentioned mandatory programs (possibly in more recent versions) can be found under `ftp://ftp.gwdg.de/pub/linux/misc/ncpfs`.

After the network interfaces have been activated as described in the previous section, you can obtain a list of the active NetWare servers by means of `slist`. If this command displays an error message, you will need to check the kernel and network configurations. First, you should check the boot messages of the kernel for the existence of the IPX protocol (using the `dmesg` command; often these messages are also stored in the file /var/log/kernel). Next, you should have a look at the /proc/net/ipx* files.

Subsequently, you can use the ncpmount command (Listing 20.6) to mount a volume of a NetWare server. For this, you will need the name of the server (see the output of slist), a valid user ID on this server (for example guest), and maybe the associated password. If no password is required, you can specify the option -n, so no user interaction is needed. If a password is required, you can specify this after the option -P (however, in the process list it becomes readable to all users) or you are prompted for it interactively.

```
(Linux):~# ncpmount -S server /mnt -U guest -n
```

Listing 20.6   Mounting of a NetWare volume under LINUX.

Practically all programs of the ncpfs package require this information for logging in to a NetWare server. Therefore, the options -S followed by a server name and -U followed by a user name are implemented in practically all programs of the ncpfs package.

You can store some settings, together with the NetWare user ID and password, in the file ~/.nwclient. For reasons of security, this file must only be readable for its owner; this is verified by the programs of the ncpfs package.

An entry in the file consists of two or three parts, the name of the server, the user ID, and maybe the password. Comment lines begin with a hash sign (#) in the first column. The formats of server name and user ID follow the usual NetWare conventions.

```
# The "preferred server"
NW311/HEIN
# A guest access with password
FS-DEMO/GUEST GUEST
# An access without password
FS-DEMO/GAST -
```

Listing 20.7   An example for the file ~/.nwclient.

The first entry in the file (Listing 20.7) has a special meaning: it describes the 'preferred server.' If no server name is specified in a call to one of the programs of the ncpfs package, this entry is used. At the call nwuserlist, the program logs in on server NW311 as NetWare user HEIN and asks for the password.

In the second entry, the specified password is GUEST, so the program can log in on the NetWare server without interaction. For the user in the third entry, no password is specified in the NetWare server; this is represented by the minus sign (-).

Besides many other tools known from NetWare, this package also includes programs (pqlist and nprint) which can be used to access printers connected to the Novell network from LINUX. It also includes a simple print server (pserver). A useful feature for many administrators will be the access to objects from the Bindery by means of command line tools. The Novell programs are colorful and relatively user-friendly, but not suited for mass changes or script control.

Currently, only access to servers of NetWare versions 2.x and 3.x is supported. Logging in to NetWare-4 servers is only possible if all necessary data (user IDs, print queues) are stored in the Bindery emulation. Access to the NetWare Directory Services (NDS) is not supported; here, a suitable solution is the commercial NetWare client by Caldera. Furthermore, Novell has released the NDS technology for use by third parties, so an implementation could come into being.

Additional Information and Sources	
Author:	Volker Lendecke
Email:	lendecke@math.uni-goettingen.de
ftp server:	ftp.gwdg.de
ftp path:	/pub/linux/misc/ncpfs
File name:	ncpfs-2.05.tgz
Size:	about 130 Kbytes

20.1.2 LINUX as a NetWare server

Besides the implementation of a NetWare client, two implementations of NetWare servers are available. Both servers currently provide the possibility of exporting volumes for NetWare clients. However, since both servers are still under development, other functions may become available. Detailed information on the installation of both the IPX subsystem and the server can be found in the IPX HowTo of the Linux Documentation Project.

Of the two products, mars_nwe is probably the one that is currently used most. Development is actively going on, and support in the mailing list is good. Please note that, as with the NetWare client, you must also activate IPX support in the kernel. Support for 'Full internal IPX network,' on the other hand, must not be set.

If you have a large number of NetWare servers in your network (over 40), you must adapt the file config.h before you can compile mars_nwe. In addition, you can define further constants although this is not usually needed. After compilation with make and installation with make install you need to adapt the file /etc/nwserv.conf.

This file is subdivided into individual sections, which are again numbered. These numbers are followed by the individual entries. The file /etc/nwserv.conf is extensively commented, so you should need additional information only in very rare cases.

The only entry that can impair the functionality of your network is the internal network number. Thus, you will need to ask your network administrator for a free IPX network number. Then, you copy the well-commented file examples/nw.ini as /etc/nwserv.conf and adapt the entries to your requirements.

Before the first start, you should also set up the NetWare administrator and further users. This too can be done by adapting the file /etc/nwserv.conf, this time in sections 12 and 13. In section 12, the NetWare SUPERVISOR is set up. If no entry is specified, there will be no SUPERVISOR in the emulated NetWare server. Therefore, prior to the first start, you should enter an appropriate user and assign this user a password. After the first start, mars_nwe will have written this password in an encrypted form into the internal Bindery, so you can delete the clear text from /etc/nwserv.conf.

In section 13, a correspondence between NetWare names and LINUX users is established. For each NetWare user there must be one LINUX account; this can however be marked with an asterisk (*) as the password, so that only access via IPX is possible. Alternatively, in section 15, you can have the NetWare accounts generated automatically. This, however, entails several disadvantages in security. Simply read the comments in the file /etc/nwserv.conf.

Subsequently, you can start the nwserv program, and you have a NetWare server under LINUX. You can terminate this server by means of the command nwserv -k. If you have problems, you will find the debug log in the file /tmp/nw.log. The quantity of information to be output can be specified in the file nwserv.conf. With mars_nwe, your LINUX computer is a small, Novell NetWare 3.x compatible server. Besides enjoying the stability and speed of LINUX, you will gain independence from the licensing policy of Novell where for practically every user an expensive Novell license must be purchased.

You cannot, however, perform any Novell server tasks in the form of so-called NetWare Loadable Modules (NLMs). These require a true Novell server as their running environment. Neither is it possible to gain access to the Novell Directory Services (NDS).

Additional Information and Sources	
ftp server:	ftp.gwdg.de
ftp path:	/pub/linux/misc/ncpfs
File:	mars_nwe.tar.gz
Size:	about 80 Kbytes
File:	lwared-0.95.tgz
Size:	about 92 Kbytes

In addition to the programs presented above, you still need the client programs for other operating systems (for example DOS or OS/2 clients). These are included in Novell NetWare and are not freely available. There are free implementations of some programs (for example LOGIN.EXE) which could possibly be used. Some of these programs can also be found in the above-mentioned directory.

A LINUX computer can also be employed as an IPX router. For this, you need the programs ipxripd and/or ipxd, which you can also find in the above-mentioned directory. More details about their configuration are included in the IPX HowTo by Terry Dawson.

20.2 LINUX as an SMB client and server

The implementation of the SMB protocol (Server Message Block) in Windows for Workgroups and its wide diffusion have greatly facilitated the networking of individual computers. All you need is a network card for each computer, and you are in business. Particularly for private users and small businesses, it is beneficial that no special server need be acquired to share hard disks and printers between users.

Intensive use, however, may turn this situation into the opposite. If one computer is used by many users as a file and print server, reasonable interactive work on that computer is no longer possible. Since, for example, Windows for Workgroups has not been designed as a server operating system, problems will now occur with the maintenance of this computer, which is probably now standing in a locked room.

The SMB protocol is used by many products; besides the Windows family, the most widely used ones are LAN manager (by Microsoft and IBM) and Pathworks (by DEC).

20.2.1 LINUX as an SMB client

If a workgroup or a domain already exists in your network, you can use LINUX to participate in this group. The smbfs file system required for this is implemented in the kernel. In addition, you will need the smbmount program, which mounts the exported volume into the LINUX file system. If you use the kerneld to load this file system, you must yourself deactivate the call for loading the module in the smbmount program.

To set up the smbfs, you will need root privileges. Also, this file system is not portable to other systems. In exchange, the shares are integrated into the normal LINUX directory tree. For the user, it does not matter at all whether the files are stored locally, on an NFS server, or on an SMB server.

The samba package includes an SMB client (smbclient) which is handled in a similar way to the ftp program. This program can be used without special privileges; help is obtained by means of the help command inside the program. On other UNIX systems, this is a simple way to access SMB shares.

The syntax of the share names is exactly as under Windows: first two backslashes, then the computer name, and, separated by another backslash, the share name. Please note, however, that you must quote the special characters of the shell (backslash) (Listing 20.8).

```
(Linux):~> smbclient -L pea
(Linux):~> smbclient '\\pea\jochen'
```

Listing 20.8 The use of smbclient.

With the option **-L**, you get a list of the shares available from this server (disks and printers). You can obtain access to these shares if you specify their names as in the second example.

This method is available for practically every UNIX system. Under LINUX, however, an SMB share can be directly inserted into the directory tree. For this purpose, the smbfs must be compiled into the kernel or loaded as a module, and the smbmount program must be installed. An example for mounting of a share is shown in Listing 20.9.

```
(Linux):~> /usr/sbin/smbmount //pea/jochen mnt -C
```

Listing 20.9 Mounting of an SMB share.

In the smbmount program, normal slashes instead of backslashes are used as separators inside the share names. Thus, the user does not need to bother about quotes or other special characters. The share name is expected as the first parameter, the mount point as the second. If the smbmount program is installed setuid-root, every user can use this program.

The program smbmount has a number of options which are used to influence the behavior of the program. If you have problems with logging in, you should try the option -c which prevents the password from being converted into upper case before it is transmitted to the server.

Additional Information and Sources	
ftp server:	ftp.gwdg.de
ftp path:	/pub/linux/misc/ksmbfs
File name:	smbmount-1.3.tar.z
Size:	about 32 Kbytes

20.2.2 SMB servers under LINUX

With samba, a powerful SMB server is available for UNIX systems. The program can also be compiled and installed under LINUX without any problems. Modern distributions include preconfigured versions of this package; however, it may be sensible to install it yourself.

Distributions exported from the USA normally do not include packages that use cryptographic methods. Thus, the samba package is usually compiled without password encryption. With the Service Pack 3 for Windows NT 4.0, however, transmission of encrypted passwords has become the default under NT, which leads to the consequence that these computers can no longer log in to a samba server.

Weigh the advantages and disadvantages of using the libdes library yourself. The advantages are:

- NT computers can log in to a samba server without reconfiguration of the registry.

- No passwords are transmitted that could be read with a password sniffer.
- Windows NT can then also browse via a `samba` server.

There are also well-known disadvantages; the following list will hopefully help you make your decision:

- A 'password equivalent' is stored on the hard disk of the server.
- The UNIX server and `samba` no longer use the same passwords from the file `/etc/passwd` or `/etc/shadow`.
- Do you use services such as `telnet` or `ftp`? Then the passwords are transmitted via the network in clear text anyway, and you do not gain much.

If you have Windows NT 4.0 computers in your network, you should use encrypted passwords. This is the default since Service Pack 3. You can, however, also reconfigure the Windows NT clients by inserting the entry `EnablePlainTextPassword` with a value of 1 (as type `REG_DWORD`) into the `HKEY_LOCAL_MACHINE` tree of the registry under `\system\currentcontrolset\services\rdr\parameters`. This setting must be carried out separately on every client.

You can only use encrypted passwords if the SMB server was compiled with the `libdes` library. This is not the case with distributions exported from the USA. In this situation you should compile the program yourself. You need to activate the entries for the `libdes` library and obviously also install it. Furthermore, you must include the entry `encrypted passwords = yes` in the file `smb.conf`, section `[global]`. More information on the subject of encryption can be found in the file `ENCRYPTION.TXT` in the `samba` package.

For the compilation of `samba`, you must activate the settings for LINUX in the file `./source/Makefile` and maybe adapt the paths to be used. Subsequently, you can compile `samba` with `make` and install it with `make install`. You must include the lines shown in Listing 20.10 in the file `/etc/services` if they are not yet included.

```
netbios-ns      137/udp
netbios-ssn     139/tcp
```

Listing 20.10 New entries in the file `/etc/services`.

You can start the daemons `smbd` and `nmbd` either directly (for example in `rc.local`) or by means of the `inetd` server. For this, you must include the two lines shown in Listing 20.11, adapted to the paths specified in the `Makefile`, in the file `/etc/inetd.conf` and restart the `inetd` server. This is certainly sensible for testing, since a new `samba` process is started for every new connection which newly reads the configuration.

Subsequently, the server must be configured with the file `smb.conf`. You can release directories and printers for use by clients. The directory `./example` contains some examples for the configuration of the server. Finally, you should check the syntax of the configuration file by means of the `testparm` program.

```
netbios-ssn stream tcp nowait root /usr/local/bin/smbd smbd
netbios-ns dgram udp wait root /usr/local/bin/nmbd nmbd
```

Listing 20.11   New entries in the file `/etc/inetd.conf`.

Many distributions include this package in a preconfigured form. For reasons of speed, the daemons are usually not started by the `inetd`, but in the start-up scripts.

In practice, you will probably start with exporting the home directories of your users. For this, you will need the entry shown in Listing 20.12 in the file `smb.conf`. You can carry out a first test with the `smbclient` program locally under UNIX. All possible settings are extensively documented in the man page for `smb.conf`.

```
[homes]
  comment = home directories
  browseable = no
  read only = no
  create mode = 0750
```

Listing 20.12   Exporting the home directories.

Some clients always send the password to the server in upper case. Under UNIX, however, upper and lower case spelling in passwords is significant. `samba` converts the password into lower case and attempts the login. If the password contains one or more upper case letters, the attempt fails. In the file `smb.conf`, you can enter `password level = N` in the `[global]` section to specify that all combinations with up to N upper case letters in the password are to be tried. For larger values of N, this can, however, take up large amounts of CPU time.

In addition, `samba` can be used as a print server for SMB networks. For this, you must include the section `[printers]` in the file `smb.conf`. You need not define each individual printer; `samba` exports all printers and aliases from the `/etc/printcap` file. In the example of Listing 20.13, guests are not allowed to print, and the printers are not displayed in the browse list.

You can, however, also define private printers for individual users. An example for this can be found in the `samba` sources.

If you use Windows for Workgroups, you should ensure that during login the 'store password' box is not activated. Otherwise, anybody having access to your PC can login on the server under your name without a password. Personally, I consider this 'comfort function' a security problem, but it may often be difficult to enforce acquisition of products that allow a secure single login on the network.

Additional, very extensive documentation on `samba` can be found in the `./docs` directory; most distributions also store these files under `/usr/doc`. Many questions are also answered in the `samba` FAQ. Furthermore, there are mailing lists to which you can subscribe. Besides the functions briefly introduced above, `samba` can also be

```
[printers]
 comment = all printers defined in /etc/printcap
 path = /var/spool/samba
 browseable = no
 printable = yes
 public = no
 writable = no
 create mode = 0700
```

Listing 20.13   Printer definition for samba.

used as a WINS server or client, or as a master browser for the domain. You are not familiar with this? You should thank your lucky stars! But if you wish to find out, browse through the documentation directory.

Additional Information and Sources	
Man pages:	smbd(8), nmbd(8), smbstatus(1), smb.conf(5), smbclient(1), testparm(1), testprn(1)
ftp server:	nimbus.anu.edu.au
ftp path:	/pub/tridge/samba
File name:	samba*
Size:	about 400 Kbytes
WWW server:	http://lake.canberra.edu.au/pub/samba/
libdes:	a general library containing the DES algorithm
ftp server:	samba.anu.edu.au
ftp path:	/pub/libdes/
File name:	libdes.tar.gz
Size:	about 300 Kbytes

Configuration and operation of a name server

## 21

The Domain Name Service (DNS) is defined in [rfc1034], [rfc1035], and [rfc1183]. It is used to manage an up-to-date and flexible database in the entire Internet, which has the purpose of converting computer names into IP addresses and vice versa. In the early stages of the Internet, this task was fulfilled by the file HOSTS.TXT, which was centrally maintained and then copied by the administrators to their local computers.

Such a method, however, is only practicable in relatively small networks, so a new service, namely the DNS, was developed. Today, the client side of this service is an integrated part of all TCP/IP implementations; today's Internet could not even be thought of without DNS. Local networks from a certain size onward also benefit from the use of a name server, even if they are not connected to the Internet. The administrative effort created by many (different) hosts files and problems arising from inconsistent entries can thus be prevented.

Detailed information on configuration and operation of a name server can be found in the sources of BIND (Berkeley Internet Name Domain). The official source of supply is given at the end of this chapter. Additional tips and tricks together with hints on frequently committed errors can be found in [rfc1536] and [rfc1912]. The program that manages the database and answers the requests of the clients is called named. On the client side, use is made of the Resolver library, which communicates with the name server.

21.1 The concept of Domain Name Service

The administration of names in the Internet is structured as a hierarchy. At the very top, we find the so-called root name servers. These computers are primarily responsible for the resolution of names, and they keep the register that specifies which other name servers are responsible (or constitute the authority) for individual zones. In other words, these zones are delegated.

A domain as we know it from the host name is not in all cases identical with a DNS zone. An example for different zones is shown in Figure 21.1.

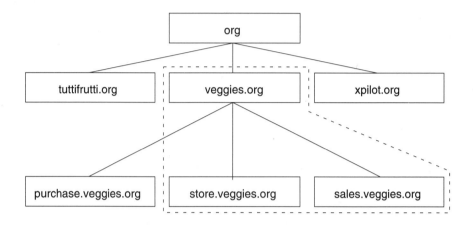

Figure 21.1   Examples of DNS zones.

The top zone, which is not considered any further at this point, is .org. Here, the zones tuttifrutti.org, veggies.org, and xpilot.org are delegated to other name servers. In our sample domain, the purchasing department runs its own name server. Therefore, the subdomain purchase.veggies.org is not part of the zone veggies.org. This zone is marked in Figure 21.1 by means of the dotted line.

Technically, a zone is determined by an NS data record in the superior name server. This zone can be identical with the domain, but further name servers which in turn manage separate zones may be defined as being responsible for subdomains. This separation often originates from organizational factors, such as different responsibilities for network administration or geographical separation of individual departments or branches.

Users generally use computer names, and no IP addresses, because well-chosen names are easier to remember. Therefore, a failure of the name server is often equivalent to the failure of the whole network. Consequently, there should be several name servers active in each zone, of which one should be the primary name server and all others secondary name servers. It may be sensible to distribute these computers across several network segments, so that at least one name server remains reachable even in the event of a router or hub failure. A secondary server is practically maintenance free because it automatically fetches its data from the primary server. You should, however, occasionally check the log files.

21.2 General remarks on configuration of a name server

In comparison with a DNS client, the file /etc/host.conf can remain unchanged, as well as the file /etc/resolv.conf. In this case, the server is also its own client, although this is likely to be required in most cases anyway. It is also possible to use a name server other than the one on the local computer.

First, the file /etc/named.boot must be adapted to your own zone. An example for a primary name server can be found in Listing 21.1. This file specifies the domain and other global data, such as the working directory of the named. In addition, the names of the underlying files are determined.

After the change in the database, the named must re-read the data. For this purpose, you can send the daemon a SIGHUP signal (for example with kill -HUP `cat /var/run/named.pid`) or you can use the named.reload script. With the named.restart script, the daemon can be terminated and restarted. For simple name server management, you can also use the ndc program instead.

Another important signal is SIGINT, which causes the daemon to output its database in the file /var/tmp/named_dump.db. This is sometimes necessary for debugging. Several other signals exist to control the daemon; they are documented in the man page.

21.3 Primary name servers

There are a number of name server types. In each zone, there must be one primary server which manages the authoritative data for that zone. For reasons of safety against failures, at least one more name server should exist which is operated as a secondary server. The required configuration for a secondary server can be found in Section 21.8. For computers that are only temporarily connected to the Internet, for example via SLIP or PPP, it might be sensible to set up a caching-only name server.

The operation of a name server requires additional computing power and memory on the corresponding computer together with a greater administrative effort in comparison with simple editing of the file /etc/hosts. Essentially, there are two (compelling) reasons for installing your own name server:

- You apply for a new domain. Talk to your provider about who will be operating the name server for this domain. If you want to operate the name server yourself, your provider must configure his site accordingly. Often, your provider will initially operate the name server for you.

- You want to set up a new name server for an organizational zone inside an already existing domain. You must discuss this with your network administrator, otherwise your new server will not be recognized as authorized.

Your own name server, however, also has its advantages, no matter whether you are connected to the Internet or not:

- In a local network, all computer names are always known on all other computers.
- The database is always up-to-date and consistent on all computers. The `hosts` files otherwise needed on the different computers tend to become obsolete and possibly contradictory fairly quickly.
- Assignment of names and IP addresses is consistent.
- If you operate the name server yourself, you can change data without having to bring in your provider.

Listing 21.1 shows an example of the file `/etc/named.boot` on a primary name server. `directory` specifies the directory in which the files of this name server are stored. A computer can be the primary and/or secondary name server for several zones. The only requirements are that the `primary` lines are entered in the file `/etc/named.boot` and the corresponding data is available.

```
;     boot file for name server
directory /var/named
; type      domain                  source      backup
cache       .                       named.root
primary     veggies.org             named.hosts
primary     0.0.127.in-addr.arpa    named.local
primary     168.192.in-addr.arpa    named.rev
; secondary
```

Listing 21.1 The file `/etc/named.boot` for a primary name server.

Each name server should create a cache of requests and answers. This can be done by means of the keyword `cache`. At the start of the name server, all data from `named.root` that is still correct is reloaded into the cache. A name server becomes a cache-only server if no `primary` or `secondary` keywords are contained in the file `named.boot`.

The name server must know where to find the authoritative name server for the root domain of the network. This information is stored in the file `named.root`. In many documents, this file is also called `root.cache`, although this does not describe its purpose.

This file, like all other data files, is stored in standard Resource Record (RR) or Masterfile format. A detailed description of this format can be found in the BIND Operators Guide; an introduction is given in the following paragraphs.

The name server is a `primary` name server for the zone `veggies.org`. The database is located in the file `named.hosts` in the directory `/var/named`. In addition, the server is a primary server for the zones `0.0.127.in-addr.arpa` and `168.192.in-addr.arpa`, which are used for 'reverse lookup.'

In the next step, the data of the individual computers whose names were specified in the file `/etc/named.boot` must be entered in the corresponding files. The format of these files and the most important entries are explained in more detail on the following pages.

21.4 The file `named.hosts`

The file `named.hosts` stores the data of all computers in the zone. The format and the individual entries are described in the following section, since they are also used in the other name server configuration files. In this file, you must enter all hosts of the zone for which you are an authorized name server. Listing 21.2 shows an example.

```
a        IN    SOA   carrot.veggies.org. hostmaster.veggies.org. (
                     1997040101      ; Serial
                     28800           ; Refresh      8 hours
                     7200            ; Retry        2 hours
                     604800          ; Expire       7 days
                     86400 )         ; Minimum TTL 1 day
         IN    MX      10 bean
         IN    NS      carrot.veggies.org.

carrot   IN    A          192.168.3.150
corn     IN    A          192.168.3.151
cabbage  IN    A          192.168.3.152
bean     IN    A          192.168.3.154
pea      IN    A          192.168.3.155
         HINFO IBM-PC/AT   UNIX-PC
         IN    TXT         "Test with text"
```

Listing 21.2 The file `named.hosts`.

21.5 The Masterfile format

A name server data file consist of several records called Resource Records (RR). The format is defined in [rfc1035] and is called Masterfile format. A data record consists of the following parts:

```
{name}  {ttl}  addr-class  Record Type  Record Specific data
```

In the `name` field you will find the name of the computer or domain belonging to the entry. The field `ttl` contains the 'time to live,' which specifies for how long this data will be kept in the database. If no value is specified, the default value is the one specified in the `SOA` record. In the Internet, `IN` is used as the address class. The fourth field contains the record type, followed by the data required for that record type.

A number of characters have a special meaning in Masterfile format files:

- The dot (.) stands for the current domain to which the data shall apply.
- The 'at' character (@) stands for the origin, that is, the zone for which the name server is responsible.
- The characters .. in the field name stand for the null domain.
- The character sequence \X, where X is one of the special characters, masks this special meaning and stands for the character itself.
- The character sequence \DDD, where D is a digit, stands for the character with the ASCII code DDD.
- A data record can stretch across several lines if the data is enclosed in parentheses ( ).
- A semicolon ; initiates a comment which reaches to the end of the line.
- An asterisk (*) in the field name has a special meaning with some of the RR types (for example MX). This special meaning does not apply to the data area.

21.5.1 Start Of Authority (SOA)

An SOA record (Start Of Authority) marks the beginning of a zone. The name (@, the origin) stands for the name of the zone. Here, the fundamental information on a zone is specified. The origin is the name of the computer that provides the data. An example of an SOA record is shown in Listing 21.3. There is at most one SOA record for one zone.

```
name {ttl} addr-class SOA Origin      Responsible
@         IN    SOA  carrot.veggies.org. hostmaster.veggies.org. (
                     1997040101   ; Serial
                     28800   ; Refresh    8 hours
                     7200    ; Retry      2 hours
                     604800  ; Expire     7 days
                     86400 ) ; Minimum TTL 1 day
```

Listing 21.3   An SOA record (Start Of Authority).

The responsible person is the manager of the name server, who should be contacted in case of problems and questions. Here, the email address of this person is specified; the at character (@) is replaced with a dot. Usually, a mail alias is used, such as hostmaster or dnsadmin.

An additional item of information to be managed is a serial number, which should be incremented with each modification. If several changes are made within one day, you should use the date in combination with a version number. A possible serial number for 26 February 1996 would then be, for example, 1996022601. On the basis of this serial number, a secondary server recognizes that new data is present and that it must carry out a zone transfer.

The value indicated for refresh specifies the number of seconds after which the slave server should again check and maybe transfer the data. Retry specifies how long a zone transfer is to be waited for before a failure is assumed. Expire specifies how long data are at most considered to be valid. Minimum specifies the default value for the 'time-to-live' (ttl) of the individual records.

Suggestions for the choice of these values can be found in [rfc1912]. Long timeouts and expire times ensure little network load during data update, but increase the waiting time before changes are transferred to the secondary server. Frequently, these times are reduced when major changes are imminent. After all secondary name servers have fetched their data, you can return to the previous values.

Please note that the `named` appends the origin to all names that are not terminated with a dot (`.`). Because of this, a missing or superfluous dot is one of the most frequent errors in DNS configuration.

21.5.2 Name Server (NS)

Here, one entry must exist for every name server in the zone. With this entry, a new zone is created and delegated. The first entry is the name of the zone being processed; the last entry is the name of the responsible name server.

Each zone should at least have two name servers (one primary and one secondary), so that in the event of a computer failure the name service continues to function. A popular constellation is to operate a name server that is not authorized, that is, for which no `NS` record exists in the superior name server (or parent name server) or a computer registered as a (secondary) name server although no `named` is running on it.

```
{name}    {ttl}   addr-class   NS   name servers name
                  IN           NS   carrot.veggies.org.
```

Listing 21.4   Name Server Record.

21.5.3 Address (A)

An `A` record contains the IP address of a computer. For computers with several IP addresses (multihomed hosts), one record is needed per IP address. Further information stored in the record types explained below is not required for the operation of a name server, and is often not even maintained. The only exception is the `PTR` records which are needed for 'reverse lookup.'

For each IP address assigned in the zone, there should be exactly one `A` record. For computers that have several IP addresses, the corresponding number of `A` records must be created. As shown in Listing 21.5, the same name can be used. In some cases, however, it is sensible to set up an additional name which, for example, describes the corresponding interface.

{name}	{ttl}	addr-class	A	address
pea		IN	A	192.168.3.155
corn		IN	A	192.168.31.151
		IN	A	10.0.0.78

Listing 21.5   Address record in the DNS.

The names in the first column are specified without domain. Since the name is also not terminated with a dot, the name server automatically appends the zone. Thus, the computer is registered in the name server under its full name (FQDN). The client, that is, the Resolver library, initially searches the name server for names with appended domain, so users inside the local network usually need not specify it.

21.5.4 Host Information (HINFO)

A HINFO record can be used to store information on the hardware and operating system of the computer. The values that you can enter are specified in an RFC on Assigned Numbers, for example [rfc2200]. Usually, this data is not maintained and, if present, is not up-to-date. In most cases, the use of SNMP is much more efficient for the network administrator.

{name}	{ttl}	addr-class	HINFO	Hardware	OS
		IN	HINFO	IBM-PC/AT	PC-UNIX

Listing 21.6   Host Information.

21.5.5 Well Known Services (WKS)

In the DNS it is possible to store additional information on services offered by a computer. Usually, this data is not maintained, so one cannot rely on these indications. The best thing to do is simply to try these services out. If the connection can be established, the computer provides the corresponding service, otherwise it does not.

21.5.6 Canonical Name (CNAME)

As already mentioned in Chapter 16, a computer name should not be assigned on the basis of the computer's function. Nevertheless, it is often sensible to be able to reach a computer under a suitable name. This applies, for example, to ftp servers, which can also be reached under the name ftp. Further services that often use aliases (or nicknames) are www, gopher, and news.

If another computer takes over this function, you need not change the name of the computer, but only the corresponding nickname. This makes it obvious for the user which computer has actually taken over the service. If no CNAME is used and the computer must be renamed instead, this often entails a certain configuration effort and creates a possible source of errors.

If a computer is renamed, it is often sensible to keep the old name as an additional nickname. However, no MX record (Mail Exchange) should ever point to a CNAME, since mail transfer agents are not required to make inquiries there (named issues an appropriate warning).

```
aliases    {ttl}   addr-class   CNAME   Canonical name
pea                IN           CNAME   ftp
```

Listing 21.7   Canonical Name.

21.5.7 **Domain Name Pointer (PTR)**

A PTR record (Domain Name Pointer) allows you to determine the host name belonging to a given IP address. This function is used in the IN-ADDR.ARPA domain, thus, for example, in the file named.rev. This makes it possible to display a name even if initially only the IP address of a computer or a gateway is known. This function is used, for example, by the netstat and traceroute programs.

The PTR records are required by the function gethostbyaddr(3), which is responsible for the conversion of IP addresses into names. Each name in the PTR record is terminated with a dot to prevent BIND from appending the domain IN-ADDR.ARPA. You should include *all* network users that have an IP address in the name server to avoid having to wait for a name server timeout only because no entry is available for reverse lookup.

```
name    {ttl}   addr-class   PTR   real name
155.31          IN           PTR   pea.veggies.org.
151.31          IN           PTR   corn.veggies.org.
```

Listing 21.8   Domain Name Pointer.

Please note that *all* names must be terminated with a dot. Otherwise, the domain IN-ADDR.ARPA would be appended.

21.5.8 **Mail Exchange (MX)**

If a computer cannot be reached at the moment of sending mail (or the computer is not connected to the Internet, but via UUCP), another available computer can be entered for receiving the mail. If the original computer becomes reachable again, the mail is forwarded. Lower preference values correspond to lower 'costs.'

This function is often employed to enable only one or two computers in the network to accept mail. This concentrates configuration efforts and availability problems to a few computers only. You should check with the administrator of the computer before you have an MX record point to another computer. Otherwise, this computer will be bombarded with unexpected mail which might possibly get lost.

```
name            {ttl} addr-class MX preference mail exchange
pea.veggies.org.    IN          MX 0          bean
```

Listing 21.9   Mail Exchange.

21.5.9 Text (TXT)

For each computer, arbitrary text can be stored as additional information. Apart from the fact that this text must be enclosed in double quotes ("), no further restrictions apply.

```
name            {ttl}  addr-class  TXT   string
pea.veggies.org.       IN          TXT   "A text"
```

Listing 21.10   Text.

21.5.10 Responsible Person (RP)

Besides the person responsible for the name server, a contact person for this computer can be stored for each additional entry. Here again, the 'at' character (@) in the mail address is replaced with a dot.

If, however, you manage your computer with the aid of SNMP (Simple Network Management Protocol), you should enter this information into the Management Information Base (MIB).

```
owner  {ttl} addr-class RP mbox-domain-name TXT-domain-name
pea  IN RP jochen.veggies.org. sysadmins.veggies.org.
sysadmins.veggies.org. IN TXT "Tel: 4711"
```

Listing 21.11   Responsible Person.

21.6 The file named.local

The file named.local (see Listing 21.12) which is located in the /var/named directory contains the data pertaining to your own computer or the current localhost. This file consists of only a few entries which are important if users also want to use the entry localhost in their ~/.rhosts files.

```
@ IN SOA carrot.veggies.org. hostmaster.veggies.org. (
                  1986012101 ; Serial
                  3600     ; Refresh
                  300      ; Retry
                  3600000 ; Expire
                  14400 )  ; Minimum
   IN NS  carrot.veggies.org.
0 IN PTR loopback.
1 IN PTR localhost.
```

Listing 21.12   The file named.local.

21.7 The file named.rev

The file named.rev stores the computer names belonging to given IP addresses. This makes it relatively quick and easy to find a corresponding name for an IP address; this function is also called reverse lookup. The file named.rev is stored in Masterfile format. An example is shown in Listing 21.13.

```
@ IN  SOA carrot.veggies.org. hostmaster.veggies.org. (
                     1986020501 ; Serial
                     10800    ; Refresh 3 hours
                     3600     ; Retry   1 hour
                     3600000 ; Expire   1000 hours
                     86400 ) ; Minimum 24 hours
          IN     NS      carrot.veggies.org.
0.0       IN     PTR     veggies.org.
          IN     A       255.255.255.0
151.31    IN     PTR     corn.veggies.org.
155.31    IN     PTR     pea.veggies.org.
```

Listing 21.13   The file named.rev.

Please note that you must terminate each host name with a dot. Otherwise, the domain in-addr.arpa would be automatically appended. Also, you should ensure consistency between the files named.data and named.rev.

21.8 Secondary name servers

For reasons of safety against failures, at least two name servers should be operated in each zone. In the event of the failure of one computer, the second name server can still answer all requests. To keep the data consistent at any time, only one (authorized) master server must exist per zone.

Besides this, one or more secondary name servers may be configured. A secondary name server fetches its data from the primary server. If this is not available, the data stored in backup copies (*.bak) is used. If the life cycle of the data has expired, an attempt is made to fetch this data afresh from the primary server. Listing 21.14 shows an example of the file /etc/named.boot of a secondary name server.

```
;     boot file for secondary name server
directory /var/named
; type     domain                   source        backup
cache      .                        root.cache
secondary veggies.org               192.168.3.150 named.bak
primary    0.0.127.in-addr.arpa named.local
secondary 168.192.in-addr.arpa 192.168.3.150 named.rev.bak
```

Listing 21.14   The file /etc/named.boot for a secondary name server.

On the basis of the serial numbers registered in the SOA records of the name server data, a secondary name server can determine whether it still has the current data of a zone. If not, a new transfer can be triggered. If you specify a smaller serial number in the primary data, the secondary name server will react with an appropriate message. You should therefore keep an eye on the system log entries of all name servers to exclude this kind of error. Otherwise, secondary servers are completely maintenance-free.

21.9 Slave name servers

A slave server does not manage zone-related data, but only a cache, and forwards requests that cannot be answered on the basis of the cache contents to specific name servers (forwarders). This allows this computer to build up a good cache from which all users can benefit.

In principle, every name server can be configured for use of forward. This is sensible if, for example, the name server is not directly connected to the Internet. If the router or firewall is entered as a forwarder, this can forward the requests. A further advantage is the formation of a large cache so eventually fewer requests need be answered by other name servers.

Forwarders ask the registered servers in addition to the known root name servers. In a slave server, only the forwarders are asked. If these cannot supply an answer, the host name cannot be resolved. Since these computers possibly need to

procure data themselves, you should enter the addresses several times in the file
`/etc/named.boot`. An example is shown in Listing 21.15.

```
;     boot file for slave name server
directory /var/named
; type       domain          source host/file backup file
cache        .               named.root
slave
forwarders xxx.xxx.xxx.xxx yyy.yyy.yyy.yyy ...
```

Listing 21.15   The file `/etc/named.boot` for a slave name server.

In the first place, you should enter the fastest (and most stable) name server.
Since it is possible (and even probable) that this computer must initially procure the
data itself, you should place the entry for this computer again once or twice between
the other forwarders.

21.10 Further information on the DNS

The most important information on how to operate a name server is given by the
Name Server Operations Guide for BIND, which is included in the sources of `bind`.
A highly recommended book is Albitz and Liu (1992).

Additional Information and Sources	
ftp server:	`ftp.vix.com`
ftp path:	`/pub/bind/release`
File name:	`bind.tar.gz`
Newsgroup:	`comp.protocols.tcp-ip.domains`
Mailing list:	`bind-users@vix.com`, subscribe with
	mail to `bind-users-request@vix.com`
Man pages:	`named(8)`, `ndc(8)`, `resolver(5)`
Further documents:	Various texts in the BIND source distribution

Network Information Service

## 22

The Network Information Service (NIS) is used for managing a number of computers centrally, at least in part. Several files are no longer maintained locally on each computer, but centrally on the NIS server. NIS is also known under the name of YP (Yellow Pages[1]). The use of NIS is sensible if a series of UNIX computers are to be placed under central administration.

With NIS, a series of files (Table 22.1) can be managed centrally, which significantly reduces administrative efforts. This applies in particular to the application of NFS, where at least the files /etc/passwd and /etc/group must be synchronized between participating computers. As well as standard files, an arbitrary number of databases can be managed.

File name	NIS maps
ethers	ethers.byname ethers.byaddr
hosts	hosts.byname hosts.byaddr
networks	networks.byaddr networks.byname
protocols	protocols.bynumber protocols.byname
rpc	rpc.byname rpc.bynumber
services	services.byname
passwd	passwd.byname passwd.byuid
group	group.byname group.bygid
netid	netid.byname
shadow	shadow.byname
gshadow	gshadow.byname

Table 22.1 Standard NIS maps.

---

[1] Trademark of British Telecom.

The maps are a central concept of the NIS. In a map, a database is managed with the aid of a key. If a file (for example /etc/passwd) can be searched by several keys (for example, by user name and user ID), more maps are created accordingly. This data is managed by means of a hash table so that larger maps too can be handled in a reasonable way.

The LINUX Documentation Project contains a HowTo on NIS. Besides this, Stern (1991) is *the* standard work on NFS and NIS administration.

22.1 Using NIS services as a client

First of all, to be able to use a NIS server, the port mapper rpc.portmap must be started. If you use NFS, this is already done. Otherwise, you can use the command rpcinfo -p to determine which RPC services your computer provides. More information on RPC can be found in Chapter 15.

Prior to starting the ypbind program, you need to set the name of the NIS domain. This is done by means of the command domainname *NIS_domain*. The NIS domain has nothing to do with the domains of the DNS; its task is the subdivision of the network into groups of commonly managed computers. Besides this, the domain name is sometimes regarded as a password for accessing the NIS server which does not, however, represent any additional data security.

The ypbind program either searches for a suitable NIS server by means of broadcasting, or it reads the file /etc/yp.conf. This file contains the NIS server to be used and/or the NIS domain name. An example of this file can be found in Listing 22.1. If you enter a host name there, you must also enter it in the file /etc/hosts, and you must establish the correct search order in the file /etc/host.conf if name resolution is also to be carried out by means of the NIS.

You can use the rpcinfo program to search for a NIS server (rpcinfo -b ypserv) or to check whether the server actually reacts (rpcinfo -u *NIS_server* ypserv 2). Similarly, you can also use this command to search for NIS clients which have started the ypbind service. This can be helpful for debugging.

```
# Use of a fixed NIS server
# and setting of the domain:
#domain NIS_domain server NIS_server
# Setting of the domain and searching for a NIS server
#domain NIS_domain broadcast
# Use fixed NIS_server
ypserver NIS_server
```

Listing 22.1 The file /etc/yp.conf.

After a NIS server has been linked in with ypbind, individual maps can be displayed by means of the ypcat command. For frequently used maps, such as passwd.byname, aliases are defined (here, passwd). All known aliases are displayed by means of the command `ypcat -x`. You can search a map by its key with the command `ypmatch`. Examples for this are shown in Listing 22.2.

```
(Linux):~> ypcat -x
Use "passwd" for "passwd.byname"
Use "group" for "group.byname"
Use "networks" for "networks.byaddr"
Use "hosts" for "hosts.byname"
Use "protocols" for "protocols.bynumber"
Use "services" for "services.byname"
Use "aliases" for "mail.aliases"
Use "ethers" for "ethers.byname"
(Linux):~> ypcat passwd
dosemu:*:409:10:DOS-disk:/home/dos:/usr/bin/true
jochen:pNnKshbkY1gvk:405:6:Jochen:/home/jochen:/bin/tcsh
(Linux):~> ypmatch jochen passwd
jochen:pNnKshbkY1gvk:405:6:Jochen:/home/jochen:/bin/tcsh
```

Listing 22.2   Examples of the use of NIS.

If you want to get the files `/etc/passwd` and `/etc/group` from the NIS server, you must append a plus sign (+) in the last line of the files. You can overwrite the entries for password, real name, home directory, and shell for all NIS users by entering the appropriate values in this line. If you want to change the value for an individual user, you must enter the user with *-user* followed by the required values into the file. Some examples that can be appended at the end of the password file are shown in Listing 22.3.

```
+jochen:::::::/bin/bash
-dosemu
+
```

Listing 22.3   Entries in the file `/etc/passwd`.

A user name that begins with a plus sign (+) is appended to the password file together with the possibly changed values. If a name begins with a minus sign (−), this user ID is removed from the NIS map of this computer.

With NIS, the password file is no longer locally available, so a user can no longer change password by means of the `passwd` command. This is now done by means of the `yppasswd` command, which communicates with the corresponding daemon (`yppasswdd`) on the NIS server. This server modifies the NIS database. To make use of NIS transparent to the users of the system, the system administrator should rename the `passwd` program (for example to `passwd.old`) and create a (symbolic) link from `yppasswd` to `passwd`.

If you want to distribute the file /etc/hosts via NIS, you must enter this into the file /etc/host.conf. A sample entry is shown in Listing 22.4. Please note that in order to avoid recursion (during name resolution the name of the server must be resolved, ...), you should not indicate the name of the NIS server in the file /etc/yp.conf.

```
order hosts, yp
multi on
```

Listing 22.4 The file /etc/host.conf.

With the ypwich command, you can determine which NIS server is currently being used. If ypwhich is called without parameters, the binding of the local computer is displayed. If you specify a host name as a parameter, the binding of this computer is displayed. You can change NIS servers by means of the ypset program.

Additional Information and Sources	
ftp server:	sunsite.unc.edu
ftp path:	/pub/Linux/system/Network/admin
File name:	yp-clients-2.2.tar.gz
Size:	about 20 Kbytes

22.2 NIS servers

If no NIS server exists in your network, you can create one (even) under LINUX. For this purpose, you need the program ypserv. Currently, there are two versions for LINUX, the yps package and the ypserv package. Which of the two packages you use is very much a matter of taste, at the end of the day.

Prior to the start of the server, the NIS domain must be set by means of the command domainname *NIS_domain*. The databases for this domain are stored in the /var/yp/*NIS_domain* directory. In the sources of the NIS server you will find the file ypMakefile, which you must copy as Makefile into the /var/yp directory. The databases are created by entering the make command in this directory.

In the Makefile you can enter the system files that are to be used as masters for the NIS databases. In some cases, it is sensible to use the system files (for example /etc/services); sometimes a new file will need creating (for example passwd). If you do not want to distribute all files via NIS, you can remove the unwanted entries from the Makefile or can simply comment them out.

If you use this NIS server to start ypserv and ypbind on your server, then the server is also its own client. This is sensible if the server is not supposed to be clearly distinguished from the clients.

Additional Information and Sources	
`ftp` server:	`ftp.funet.fi`
`ftp` path:	`/pub/OS/linux/BETA/NYS`
File name:	`yps-0.21.tar.gz`
Size:	about 30 Kbytes
File name:	`ypserv-0.11.tar.gz`
Size:	about 35 Kbytes

22.3 Toward the future with NIS+

With the implementation of NIS+, Sun has presented an extension of the NIS concept. The appropriate routines are already contained in `libc`, but they are not compiled into the binary version. Therefore, you must compile `libc` yourself and link it with NYS. NYS contains the implementations of both traditional NIS and NIS+.

The bootp protocol

23

When TCP/IP is used for network communication, each computer or network component must be assigned a (worldwide) unique IP address. These assigned addresses are best managed by the person responsible for the network. When the distribution of addresses is changed or other adaptations are made, it is necessary to carry out these changes on all network devices affected. Depending on the type of change, for example if a new name server needs to be set up, a large number of computers may be involved.

Where DOS and Windows clients are employed, central maintenance by means of `telnet` or `rlogin` is not possible, so the administrator must physically visit each computer. With the introduction of `bootp`, it is possible to manage many TCP/IP configurations centrally on the `bootp` server. Thus, the clients receive all required data at start-up from the `bootp` server.

The `bootp` protocol (defined in [rfc0951], [rfc1542], and [rfc2132]) allows you to assign a computer an IP address, the netmask, the name server, and many other things, in accordance with the hardware address of its network card. This is useful for booting diskless devices (for example X terminals) and for application of TCP/IP under DOS, to keep the configuration effort at the DOS computers as low as possible. Even some network computers (NCs) use `bootp` for configuration.

The `bootp` protocol is often used to start and configure a computer from scratch. At each stage, only a little information is available, which is however sufficient to start the next stage. It is possible to use `bootp` even before loading the operating system, for example to find the server from which the operating system for a diskless device is to be loaded. In this case, the network card must be equipped with an additional EPROM which understands the `bootp` protocol.

Often the operating system is installed locally on the hard disk of the client and only the network configuration is carried out with `bootp`. This reduces only the configuration effort for the network settings; all other (operating system dependent) elements must still be set in the usual way. A `bootp` request and its processing will usually take place as follows:

431

- The client broadcasts a bootp request on the (local) network. The only information known at that point is the hardware address of the network card of the client.

- The bootp server(s) receives the request. On the basis of the hardware address of the sender's network card, the required information can be read from the /etc/bootptab and sent back to the client. This is not yet done using the true IP address of the client, but on a slightly lower level, because the client does not yet know its own IP address.

- On the basis of the response of the bootp server, the client can configure its network, including netmask and broadcast address, together with name server, log host, and print server. The answer reaches the client because the server knows the hardware address of the client and sends the answer directly to this address.

- If the operating system is not yet loaded on the client computer, it can, for example, be loaded from a server via tftp. Otherwise, the boot process is continued as usual.

In the course of time, the bootp protocol was extended to become the *Dynamic Host Configuration Protocol* (DHCP, [rfc1531]). A similar purpose is fulfilled by the older *Reverse Address Resolution Protocol* (RARP, [rfc0903]), which is still used today for booting workstations or X terminals. Usually, bootp is employed, but some DOS clients and many X terminals still prefer RARP.

Currently, bootp is still employed in most cases; therefore only the highlights of DHCP are presented. Essential advantages of DHCP are automatic assignment of (permanent) IP addresses and dynamic address assignment for a limited time. In addition, as with bootp, the address can be manually assigned by the system administrator.

On the bootp server, the bootpd daemon must be started. This can either happen under control of the inetd server or by starting the bootpd as a daemon. In the test stage, starting via inetd is the better solution because at each restart of the bootpd daemon, the file /etc/bootptab is read again. If bootpd runs as an autonomous daemon, it must be freshly started after each change.

With a voluminous bootptab, that is, when many clients are to be managed, rereading this file requires quite a lot of CPU time, so the start as a daemon is more sensible. To do this, you must enter the bootpd program, for example, in the file rc.local. With System V init, you can also create a separate start/stop script with which you can manage the daemon directly.

If you want to have bootpd started by the inetd, you can specify by means of the option -t *minutes* that the daemon must run for at least the specified number of minutes. For a start via inetd, you need to incorporate the line from Listing 23.1 into the file /etc/inetd.conf on the server.

If the bootp server is not in the same subnet as the client, the requests would not be transmitted via the router, because broadcasts are carried out only within the local network. Therefore, in each (sub)network in which bootp requests are carried out and no bootp server exists, a gateway (bootpgw) must be installed or the router

```
bootps  dgram  udp  wait  root  /usr/sbin/tcpd  bootpd
```

Listing 23.1 New entries in the file /etc/inetd.conf.

appropriately configured. For this purpose, you need to incorporate the line from Listing 23.2 into the file /etc/inetd.conf on a computer that will then function as a gateway. Some routers have this function built in, so you may only have to enter the corresponding server.

```
bootps dgram udp wait root /usr/sbin/tcpd bootpgw server
```

Listing 23.2 A bootp gateway.

The whole remaining configuration is done in the file /etc/bootptab (Listing 23.3). The structure of this file is somewhat similar to /etc/termcap, see also Section 4.5. The individual fields are separated by colons (:); commands can be spread across several lines by terminating the line to be continued with a backslash (\) as last character.

```
.default:hn:sm=255.255.255.0:dn=veggies.org:\
        :ds=192.168.3.150:

# Reference entries for each subnet
.subnet31:sm=255.255.255.0:gw=192.168.31.1:tc=.default:
.dosemu   :sm=255.255.255.0:gw=192.168.31.1:tc=.default:

# TCP/IP in the DOSEmulator
dosemu-1:tc=.dosemu:ha=646201907878:ip=192.168.31.101:
dosemu-2:tc=.dosemu:ha=646202907878:ip=192.168.31.102:
dosemu-3:tc=.dosemu:ha=646203907878:ip=192.168.31.103:

# Real (DOS) computers
pea.veggies.org:tc=.subnet31:ht=ieee802:\
        :ha=10005AD262F8:ip=192.168.3.155:
```

Listing 23.3 Excerpt from the file /etc/bootptab.

An entry (also known as stanza) consists of a name and the associated values. The keyword tc (table continuation) can be used to refer to a template. These references can be multiple, so the definition of a reference may in turn contain a reference. Listing 23.3 first defines a default entry (.default) which contains the domain (dn), the name server (ds), and the default netmask (sm). Entries that remain unchanged in the subnet are defined in an additional template (.subnet31). The name of a template should begin with a dot (.).

Finally, entries are created for each computer. Entries that differ from computer to computer are `ha` (hardware address) and `ip` (IP address) which are used for dynamic assignment of IP addresses. The name of an entry is sent to the client as host name if this has been specified in the `hn` configuration.

With some DOS clients it may be necessary to specify the additional entry vm=rfc1084. By doing so, these clients are presented the answer in a format in compliance with [rfc1084], even if they have made their request in another format. Normally, answers are given in the format in which the client has sent the request.

For diskless devices that are booted remotely, you can specify where the appropriate boot files can be found. Furthermore, there is some additional data that can be transmitted to a client. An overview of the most important entries is shown in Table 23.1; a complete list of all entries can be found in the man page `bootptab(5)`.

Entry	Meaning
ds	DNS server addresses
gw	List of gateway addresses
ha	Hardware address
hn	Transmit host name to client
ht	Hardware type of client, see for example [rfc2200]
ip	Client's IP address
sm	Client's subnet mask
vm	Vendor Magic Cookie
tc	Reference entry (template)

Table 23.1   The most important entries of the `bootptab` file.

After configuration of the network programs, some X terminals and diskless workstations fetch the kernel and all further programs from a boot server. Usually, the `tftp` protocol (Trivial File Transfer Protocol) is used to load the kernel.

Since this protocol does not have any form of authentication, special caution must be applied with the configuration. Thus, it should be mandatory to specify in /etc/tftptab which files may be transmitted, and the daemon should only have access to the directory containing the boot image. Furthermore, you can use the TCP wrapper to allow access to only a few specific computers. More details can be found in the man pages for `tftp` and `tftpd`.

It is also possible to configure computers under LINUX by means of `bootp`. You will need the appropriate client (`bootpc`), and you must adapt the network configuration scripts accordingly. Examples for these scripts can be found in this package, which also includes a program (`bootptest`) with which you can test the configuration of your `bootp` server.

The `bootpd` daemons currently available for LINUX can only handle part of the DHCP functions. There is a free DHCP server which has now also been ported to LINUX. In the same way, you can carry out the IP configuration of your LINUX computer by means of DHCP. The supply source is given in the info box below.

In a commercial network, fail-safe operation is paramount. It is therefore possible to operate several bootp servers in one (sub)network. They should, however, all be configured with the same bootptabs. This can be achieved by making a copy on both computers (for example by means of rdist) or by using NFS.

Additional Information and Sources	
ftp server:	tsx-11.mit.edu
ftp path:	/pub/linux/packages/net/netboot
File:	bootpd-2.4.tar.gz
Size:	about 40 Kbytes
ftp server:	tsx-11.mit.edu
ftp path:	/pub/linux/packages/net/netboot
File:	bootpc.v061.tgz
Size:	about 40 Kbytes
ftp server:	ftp.fugue.com
ftp path:	pub
File:	DHCPD-BETA-5.14.tar.gz
Size:	about 180 Kbytes
ftp server:	sunsite.unc.edu
ftp path:	/pub/Linux/system/Network/daemons
File:	dhcpcd-0.5.tar.gz
Size:	about 32 Kbytes
ftp server:	ftp.isc.org
ftp path:	/isc/dhcp
File:	dhcpcd-1.0.0.tar.gz
Size:	about 180 Kbytes

Connection via SLIP and PPP

24

Larger business networks are usually connected to the Internet (via a provider) by means of a router or firewall. If you need to connect only one or a few computers to the Internet, you will usually employ a modem or ISDN connection. Under LINUX, several alternatives are available. Which of these you can use is a matter of discussion with your provider, who will also be able to supply you with sample configuration files or scripts. Even if your provider cannot provide direct support for LINUX, you should still check the usually available scripts for Windows – this may possibly help you.

Please note that during an online connection your computer is a nearly fully-fledged Internet computer. This means that alien users can gain access to your computer and the services provided by it. Many problems can be easily solved, others require great effort. Some hints are listed in the following overview:

- You should employ the TCP wrapper to prevent access by alien computers via its access protection mechanisms. More details about the TCP wrapper can be found in Section 15.3.

- You should provide as few network services as possible. Check the file /etc/inetd.conf for unnecessary services and deactivate them.

- You should use well-chosen passwords and mark unused user IDs with an asterisk (*) in the password field.

- You should watch the log files of your system. Here you can find traces of failed 'attacks'; sometimes, however, the cause for log entries can also lie in one's own carelessness.

Before you begin to use SLIP or PPP, you must at least configure the loopback device. Furthermore, you must compile the appropriate driver for SLIP, CSLIP, or PPP into the kernel or load it as a module. Modules can be loaded into memory on demand by means of the `kerneld` daemon; they are removed when they are no longer needed. By means of the `diald` daemon, you can automatically dial your provider as soon as a program needs to use a network service.

This chapter can only give a simple introduction to a rather complex subject. You should in any case consult the man pages and HowTo documents of the LDP project, together with the indicated RFCs, which may also be helpful reading.

24.1 Serial Line Internet Protocol (SLIP)

Initially, the Serial Line Internet Protocol (SLIP), which allows transmission of Internet protocols via a modem connection between two computers, was developed under BSD. These protocols are usually limited to interactive work via `telnet`, file transfer with `ftp`, or network surfing with a Web browser. Protocols like NFS are not designed to be used via SLIP, although this is possible. You can even transmit the X representation, but this makes sense only with really fast connections.[1]

After the diffusion of SLIP within BSD UNIX, the protocol was a posteriori documented in [rfc1055]. In the Internet protocol, the header values transmitted during a connection are mostly the same. If you use CSLIP (Compressed SLIP, van Jacobsen Compression), identical header fields are not transmitted repeatedly, and this greatly reduces the protocol overhead. This method is described in [rfc1144]. If you have a choice between SLIP and CSLIP, you should choose CSLIP. If your provider also offers PPP (see next section), you would be well advised to use this latter protocol.

Support for SLIP must be compiled into the kernel or loaded as a module. In addition, you need the programs `dip` or `slattach`, which should be included in every distribution. If your provider also offers PPP, you should skip the following pages – SLIP is only used in exceptional cases.

24.1.1 LINUX as a SLIP client

Once you have established a connection with your provider, for example with Kermit, you log in with the ID assigned to you. Instead of starting a shell, the SLIP interface is configured. You must do the same on your computer. Please ensure that you use the same SLIP variation (SLIP or CSLIP) as your counterpart, otherwise no usable connection can be established.

A serial interface is put into SLIP mode by means of the `slattach` program. You need to specify the name of the interface to be used as a parameter. In addition, you can specify the protocol to be used (`slip` or `cslip`) by means of the option `-p`. Additional options, for example for debugging, can be found in the man page. The `slattach` program is well suited for leased line connections; for dial-up connections, you should employ `dip` (Dial-Up IP).

The first interface prepared for SLIP gets the name `sl0`, the next one `sl1`, and so on. This interface must now be configured and activated. Furthermore, the routes

---

[1] With the LBX extension (Low Bandwidth X) this should function better.

must be set up by which the provider and the remaining Internet can be reached. This can be done, for example, by means of the commands shown in Listing 24.1.

```
(Linux):~# slattach -s 19200 /dev/ttyS1 &
(Linux):~# ifconfig sl0 peaslip pointopoint slipsrv
(Linux):~# route add slipsrv
(Linux):~# route add default gw slipsrv
```

Listing 24.1   Activating a SLIP connection.

With the first command, the interface is prepared for use with SLIP. The second command activates the corresponding network interface, specifying that it is a point-to-point connection. Instead of the names (peaslip and slipsrv) you may also specify the corresponding IP addresses; if you have not properly maintained the file /etc/hosts, you must do so. At this point, no access to an external name server is as yet possible. Depending on the provider, these addresses are often dynamically assigned with each connection.

In the next step, you must enter the necessary routes. This is done by means of the last two commands of Listing 24.1. First, only a route to the provider (slipsrv) is established. In the second step, a default route is entered with the provider as a gateway.

After you have terminated the connection, you must delete the routes and deactivate the network interface. The corresponding commands are shown in Listing 24.2.

```
(Linux):~# route del default
(Linux):~# route del slipsrv
(Linux):~# ifconfig sl0 down
(Linux):~# killall slattach
```

Listing 24.2   Terminating a SLIP connection.

If you use the address registered in the internal network and if you always have that same address with your provider, you can permanently configure the SLIP interface for this address. However, if SLIP is not active, you cannot reach your computer under this address. In this case, you can activate the dummy device with this address so long as no SLIP is started.

In the test and configuration stage, it is sensible to enter these commands manually at first. Later, this method will become thoroughly boring and can be made automatic by means of the dip program. Listing 24.3 shows an example.

In the dip script, several connection parameters are specified. In Listing 24.3, these are modem port and baud rate. Furthermore, the MTU (Maximum Transfer Unit) and the netmask are specified. Subsequently, the modem is initialized (reset).

```
# Set modem port and baud rate
 port modem
 speed 38400
# Specify netmask and MTU
 netmask 255.255.255.0
 get $mtu 296
# Beginning of the chat script
 reset
 if $errlvl != 0 goto error

 dial provider_number
 if $errlvl != 1 goto error
 wait Username: 30
 send user_ID\n
 wait Password: 3
 password
 send \n
 wait Prompt 5
 if $errlvl != 0 goto login
 send slip\n

 wait Your 5
 if $errlvl != 0 goto slip-error
 get $locip remote
 print SLIP connection established with address $locip
 default
 mode CSLIP
 exit

error:
 print An error occurred during establishment of the connection
 beep
 exit 1
```

Listing 24.3 SLIP login with dip.

Then, a chat script begins. The parameters of the send command are sent to the modem. wait is used to wait for the corresponding answer. The second parameter of wait is the time in seconds after which a timeout is triggered. In the script, you might also think of automatic redialing (even with several numbers).

Once the connection is established and the login carried out, SLIP is started on the remote computer by means of the slip command. Your provider can (and must) tell you the exact procedure. CSLIP is activated on the local computer by means of mode CSLIP. If the dial-up line is busy, automatic redialing could be carried out.

The connection is shut down by means of the command `dip -k`. Extensive documentation can be found in the SLIP HowTo and in the man page for `dip`. The sources of `dip` also contain various `dip` sample scripts.

24.1.2 LINUX as a SLIP server

You can also employ LINUX as a SLIP server. For this purpose, you must enter the `diplogin` command as a login shell for the SLIP accounts. Further configuration takes place in the file `/etc/diphosts`. This file contains one line of colon-separated values for each SLIP login.

```
user:password:IP_address:netmask:text:parameters
```

The field *user* contains the user name of the SLIP account as specified in the file `/etc/passwd`. In the second field, an additional (encrypted) password can be entered. The next field contains the IP address or the host name under which the SLIP client is managed. After this field, a network mask can be specified. The sixth field may contain arbitrary text. In the last field, the parameters of the connection can be specified, including the protocol (SLIP, CSLIP, or PPP) and, separated by a comma, the MTU.

If the remote computer is also to have access to the local network or the Internet, the SLIP server must forward the corresponding packets. This can be done either by activating IP forwarding in the kernel or by using a firewall. In recent times, SLIP is increasingly being replaced by PPP, therefore no further explanations will follow.

24.2 Point-to-Point Protocol (PPP)

With the use of SLIP, several problems remain unresolved. These concern the negotiation of connection parameters, which is not standardized, and the exchange of the IP addresses to be used. This protocol does not even provide any authentication mechanism by means of which the identity of the communication partner can be verified.

These and other problems led to the development of the Point-to-Point Protocol (PPP) which is described in [rfc1661]. This protocol is based on the experience gained with implementation and application of SLIP. Today, practically every provider supports PPP, so you should use this protocol. In addition, PPP can be used to transmit other protocols besides IP, such as IPX or AppleTalk. Further information on PPP can be found in the PPP HowTo of the Linux Documentation Project and in the man page for `pppd`.

For using PPP, you will need the appropriate kernel support (compiled into the kernel or as a module). In addition, the `pppd` daemon that suits your kernel version must be installed on your system.

24.2.1 Dial-up IP with PPP

If the connection to the PPP server is already established and the PPP driver is loaded on the server, the PPP link is opened with the following command:

```
(Linux):~# pppd /dev/ttyS1 38400 crtscts defaultroute
```

The serial interface `ttyS1` is put into PPP mode, and the speed is set to 38 400 bps, using hardware handshake. This link is installed as the default route; this is one of the reasons why `pppd` must be started by `root`. If non-privileged users too are to be allowed to open a PPP link, you must start the `setuid` program (see `chmod(1)`). You can restrict execution rights to a group of users, see also Section 4.4.

Before payload data can be transmitted via this connection, you must specify the connection parameters, such as the IP address and MTU. If you have not specified any special settings, these are negotiated with the server with the aid of the IP Control Protocol (IPCP), which is a dialog between computers in which the use of individual settings is proposed and accepted or refused. The log file shows the exchange of the corresponding parameters, in particular if `pppd` is started with the `debug` option. The log file is managed by the `syslogd`, using the facility `daemon` and the priority `debug`. Subsequently, the PPP interfaces (`ppp0` for the first, `ppp1` for the second, and so on) are initialized and configured.

The parameters of the connection can be further restricted through the use of a configuration file. In the file `/etc/ppp/options`, global options for the system can be specified. Listing 24.4 shows a simple example.

```
# Global PPP options
auth      # Authentication required for each connection
lock      # Create UUCP-like lock files
```

Listing 24.4 The file `/etc/ppp/options`.

With the keyword `auth` you can specify that an authentication is required for each PPP connection. Thus, a connection can be established only to computers which are known locally. There are two protocols named Password Authentication Protocol (PAP) and Cryptographic Handshake Authentication Protocol (CHAP) which can be used by PPP. If you can, you should used CHAP because it is more secure than PAP, but in no case should you do without any authentication.

This kind of authentication can be requested both from the server and from the client. Thus, both sides can be relatively sure that the partner really is what it actually claims to be. This problem area is not solved by SLIP.

Various options of this file can be overwritten by other settings, for example in the file `~/.ppprc`. However, options that are particularly relevant for security can no longer be changed, therefore you should definitely create a global option file.

24.2.2 Establishing a connection with `chat`

As with SLIP, the connection can be established by means of a `chat` script. An appropriate script language with which you can make the establishment of a connection automatic, in general terms, is already integrated in the `pppd` daemon.

In many examples (for example the `ppp-on` script), the `chat` script is passed as a command line option. This script contains user name and password. With the command `ps -auxwww`, each user can create an extensive process list and read the password so long as the `pppd` process is not swapped out of the memory. A better solution is to store the `chat` script in a file and pass the `chat` interpreter the option `-f` *Chat file*.

This `chat` script is structured similarly to UUCP chats. A string that comes from the modem alternates with a string to be sent to the modem. The first string to be received must be empty; further empty strings may follow later. After the test stage, you should not specify the `chat` script in the command line of the `pppd`, as suggested in Listing 24.5, but should store it in a separate file. For reasons of space and simplicity of presentation, this is not shown here.

```
pppd connect 'chat -v "" ATDT5551212 \
             CONNECT "" \
             ogin: ppp \
             word: password' \
  /dev/ttyS1 38400 debug crtscts modem \
  defaultroute 192.168.99.2
```

Listing 24.5   Establishment of a PPP connection.

On my own system, a normal shell script is started as a `connect` script instead of a `chat` script. This attempts a `CONNECT` for the different phone numbers of my provider. If it succeeds, the script is terminated with `exit 0`, otherwise an error is returned to the `pppd`. This script is shown in Listing 24.6, whereas Listing 24.7 shows an example for a called `chat` script.

The messages of the `pppd` are managed via `syslog`, using the facility `daemon`. The file where you will find these messages is specified in the file `/etc/syslog.conf`. Here you will find the debug protocol which is requested by means of the parameter `debug`. This protocol helps you trace configuration problems; in addition, start and end times of the connections are stored.

After successful establishment of a connection, the `pppd` program starts the script `/etc/ppp/ip-up`. As parameters, this script is passed the name of the network interface, the modem device, the speed of the connection, plus the personal and the remote IP address. Here, for example, mail can be automatically fetched by means of `fetchmail`. On my own system, mail and news are exchanged via UUCP, so `uucp` is started via a TCP connection. Similar scripts exist for terminating a connection (`/etc/ppp/ip-down`) and for other protocols (`/etc/ppp/ipx-up` and `/etc/ppp/ipx-down`).

```
#!/bin/sh
MAXTRIES=3                         # number of attempts
host=`basename $0`                 # how were we called

# repeat until number of attempts is reached
for i in `seq 1 $MAXTRIES`; do
    # one chat script for each phone number
    for j in /etc/ppp/chat/$host-*; do
        chat $CHATFLAGS -f $j # and dial in
        rc=$?
        if [ $rc = 0 ]; then  # successful?
            exit 0            # yes, then get out of here
        fi
    done
done
exit 1   # all numbers tried without success
```

Listing 24.6   A chat script with retries and several numbers.

```
TIMEOUT 5
ABORT "NO CARRIER"
ABORT BUSY
ABORT "NO DIALTONE"
ABORT ERROR
"" ATZ
OK ATDTphone_number
CONNECT ""
sername: username
word: password
"Your IP" "\d\d\d"
```

Listing 24.7   A chat script as an input file for chat.

Extensive documentation on PPP can be found in the man pages for pppd(8), chat(8), the PPP HowTo of the Linux Documentation Project, and the README files included in the pppd package.

24.2.3 Termination of a connection

To terminate a PPP connection, you must send the pppd a SIGINT signal with a kill command. The PPP drivers will then shut down the connection in an orderly fashion, and the modem hangs up. You can find the process ID of the PPP daemon in the file /var/run/pppN.pid where N stands for the number of the PPP device.

24.2.4 Authentication

As a rule, you must identify yourself with your provider with your user ID and password before the PPP drivers are started. The caller cannot be sure that the counterpart is indeed the provider. Authentication in the opposite direction is seldom used (this also applies to everyday life). Thus, everybody assumes that a cash machine behaves correctly, but there is no guarantee for this. If someone has set up a fake machine, it is only after having entered your PIN that you notice that the machine does not distribute cash but was only used to get hold of your PIN.

If `auth` is present in the option file, a PPP link can only be established after authentication of the partner. Two methods are implemented, the Cryptographic Handshake Authentication Protocol (CHAP) and the Password Authentication Protocol (PAP). If at all possible, you should use CHAP, although PAP will do.

Cryptographic Handshake Authentication Protocol

The Cryptographic Handshake Authentication Protocol is based on the exchange of secret phrases. Each partner, no matter whether calling or called, can request authentication. By means of options, you can insist on CHAP being used, or you can also allow PAP.

When partners need to authenticate themselves, they select the appropriate phrase from the file `/etc/ppp/chap-secrets`. Both partners need both phrases to be able to identify each other. Some ISDN routers support configuration of only one phrase; you can obtain more precise information from your provider or network administrator.

If the computer `pea` establishes a PPP link with `corn` and CHAP is used for authentication, the secrets file must be structured as shown in Listing 24.8.

```
#remote  local  secret                     IP address list
pea      corn   "Hey, what's the password?" 192.168.3.155
corn     pea    "Ken sent me"               192.168.31.151
```

Listing 24.8   The file `/etc/ppp/chap-secrets`.

In CHAP, a 'challenge' is sent which is encrypted by means of the 'secret.' If the partner's answer is identical to the locally calculated result, the authentication was successful. The `IP address` field can be used to activate the connection definitely only with specific IP addresses.

Password Authentication Protocol

If authentication with CHAP is not possible, you should at least use the Password Authentication Protocol (PAP). In this file too, both the personal and the remote passwords are stored.

```
#account remote    password        IP address list
pea      corn      "kw9n3k"        10.10.10.2
corn     pea       "auemf6"        10.10.10.1
```

Listing 24.9   The file /etc/ppp/pap-secrets.

The first entry in Listing 24.9 is used for logging in on the computer corn. If the computer corn authenticates itself by means of PAP, the second line is used for verification. Please note that some systems only have one password or secret for each communication partner. In this case, the password is the same for both directions.

Additional Information and Sources	
Man page:	pppd(8)
HowTo:	PPP-HowTo
Newsgroup:	comp.protocol.ppp
ftp server:	sunsite.unc.edu
ftp path:	/pub/Linux/system/Network/serial
File name:	ppp-2.2.0f.tar.gz
Size:	about 210 Kbytes

24.3 Automatic connection with dialter

The procedures described up to now require the connection to be manually established and terminated by the user. This is not very functional and it may lead to 'forgetting' an open connection which goes on accruing telephone charges. It is much more useful if the connection is dynamically established when needed, without the user having to intervene. If the connection is not used for a certain lapse of time, it can also be automatically terminated. Since establishing and terminating connections are initiated from a root process, the pppd program in this case does not need to be made setuid.

With the previously presented programs, this is not possible; you will need to use the dialter program by Eric Schenk (schenk@cs.toronto.edu). dialter uses a proxy interface (this *must* be a SLIP interface) to which all requests are redirected. If a program wants to access a remote computer, then this is recognized by dialter. The connection with the provider is established in the background, and the packets are forwarded to the true PPP or SLIP interface. Thus, one precondition for the use of dialter is a kernel that contains both SLIP and PPP.

The dialter program is configured by means of the two files /etc/dialter.defs and /etc/dialter.conf. In the file dialter.defs, symbolic names are defined for individual fields of the IP packets. These can be used in the file dialter.conf to store rules for individual protocols. On the basis of these rules, the decision is made when a connection must be established and when it can be closed again. The file

`/etc/diald.conf` is extensively commented and provided with workable default settings for nearly all protocols.

The man page contains extensive documentation of all options and various examples for calling of `diald`. In addition, the distribution includes the `diald` FAQ which answers many frequently asked questions.

Additional Information and Sources	
`ftp` server:	`sunsite.unc.edu`
`ftp` path:	`/pub/Linux/system/Network/serial`
File name:	`diald-0.13.tar.gz`
Home page:	`http://www.cs.toronto.edu/~schenk/diald.html`
Mailing list:	`linux-diald@vger.rutgers.edu`
	`subscribe linux-diald` to
	`majordomo@vger.rutgers.edu`

24.4 ISDN instead of a modem

In recent times, digital ISDN connections have been gaining a growing share of the international telecommunications market, replacing traditional analog phone connections. For computer users, ISDN has the advantage that up to 64 kbits per second can be transmitted in each direction. All you need is an ISDN line in your home or office and an ISDN card in your PC.

Unlike the use of a modem, the data is directly transmitted digitally and therefore does not need to be modulated onto a carrier signal. Therefore, ISDN connections are usually very stable and have a constant speed. If the transmission rate of one ISDN channel is not sufficient, channel bundling is possible in some cases. Furthermore, establishing connections is extremely fast, so 'dial-on-demand' can easily be implemented without causing noticeable delays for the user.

There are two different ISDN subsystems for LINUX, the (older) Urlichs ISDN based on the BSD network code, and the current ISDN-4-LINUX which is integrated into the standard kernel. It supports the most popular ISDN cards, including Teles, AVM, and Elsa. The kernel configuration contains a dedicated submenu for this subsystem.

In the U.S., the telephone company will be providing its customers with a *U interface*. This is a two-wire (single pair) interface from the phone switch. It supports full-duplex data transfer over a single pair of wires, therefore only a single device can be connected to a U interface. This device is called a *Network Termination 1* (NT-1). The situation is different elsewhere in the world, where the phone company supplies the NT-1. The NT-1 converts the 2-wire U interface into the 4-wire *S/T interface* to which several devices, such as ISDN cards, can be connected. Some devices also have NT-1s built into their design.

Furthermore, you must select the driver for your specific ISDN card. These integrated ISDN drivers allow different kinds of connection. First of all, there is a 'modem emulation' (X.75) which can, for example, be used with `minicom`, `kermit`, or uucp. Via this connection, you can also transmit SLIP or (asynchronous) PPP. The only difference to a modem configuration is that a ttyI* device is used instead of ttyS*. The term 'modem emulation' refers to the fact that the local computer can control the ISDN card by means of the usual AT commands known from the traditional modem. Unfortunately, no connection is possible with systems that only have a modem.

If your provider provides X.75, the PPP configuration hardly differs from the configuration used with a modem. Therefore, this type of connection will not be discussed in more detail.

A second type of connection is synchronous PPP (syncPPP). Here, the connection is not carried out via an emulated modem, and thus no authentication is possible via user name and password in a chat script. CHAP or PAP are used instead; in addition, the connection can be configured in such a way that only calls from known numbers are accepted.

It may well be that your provider cannot tell you which kind of PPP is supported. In such cases, you have to rely on educated guesses ('Is a chat script required? Then it will be asynchronous PPP.') and experiments.

For the direct PPP connection, you will need a special PPP daemon, the ipppd. Its configuration is practically identical to that of the normal pppd. All essential configurations are carried out by means of the isdnctrl program. Listing 24.10 shows some important parameters; more can be found in the corresponding man page.

```
# Creation of the ISDN interface ippp0
/sbin/isdnctrl addif        ippp0
# Which number shall be dialed?
/sbin/isdnctrl addphone     ippp0 out 4711
# Setting of the own 'multiple subscriber number' (MSN)
/sbin/isdnctrl eaz          ippp0 4712
# Hangup after 60 seconds without data traffic
/sbin/isdnctrl huptimeout ippp0 60
# Use synchronous PPP
/sbin/isdnctrl encap        ippp0 syncppp
```

Listing 24.10 Application of the isdnctrl program.

An important parameter is huptimeout which by default is set to 10 seconds. If you do not change this, the connection will be closed after only 10 seconds without data traffic. With isdnctrl, you can also select additional connection parameters such as encapsulation and ISDN protocol.

Subsequently, the ISDN subsystem automatically establishes a connection with the provider if an IP packet is to be sent. The selection options are not (yet) as sophisticated as with diald; on the other hand, connection can be established much more quickly.

The network interface /dev/ipppN is managed by a specially adapted PPP daemon, namely the ipppd program. Listing 24.11 shows an example of the corresponding call.

```
# Configure interface
/sbin/ifconfig ippp0 192.168.99.5 \
    pointopoint 192.168.99.2 -arp metric 3
# Set route
/sbin/route add default dev ippp0
# Start ipppd, one process can handle many interfaces
/sbin/ipppd name zeus remotename ppp.provider.de -bsdcomp \
    debug -pred1comp \
    -vj 192.168.99.5:192.168.99.2 /dev/ippp0
```

Listing 24.11   Starting the ipppd daemon.

Further connection alternatives are, among others, Raw IP, Ethernet via ISDN, and Cisco HDLC. This makes LINUX prepared for all sorts of requirements.

The ISDN-4-LINUX package also includes a number of additional programs which can only be briefly mentioned. The iprofd program is used for storing the settings for modem emulation. A useful feature is the imon, which displays the status of the ISDN lines. With isdnlog you can display and store a great deal of information concerning start and termination of connections; this also allows telephone cost auditing.

Additional Information and Sources	
ftp server:	ftp.franken.de
ftp path:	/pub/isdn4linux/v2.0
Newsgroup:	de.alt.comm.isdn4linux

LINUX and the World Wide Web

25

The Internet is a loose association of many different networks. Universities in particular began relatively early to offer services such as anonymous `ftp` to other users. This kind of service, however, is not easy to handle, and the search for information (and its visually appealing elaboration) used to be difficult.

A first step in the direction of an integrated information system was the development of the `gopher` protocol, see [rfc1436], which allowed text documents to be hierarchically structured. Besides this, it was also possible to refer to documents on other `gopher` servers. These references were practically unnoticeable for the user, so a distributed database was developed, which was transparent and usable without complicated manipulation.

Data preparation was carried out personally by the author, and no images could be (directly) displayed. There was a possibility of calling external programs such as `telnet`, and references to `ftp` servers could also be specified.

With the World Wide Web, the Internet has found its 'killer application,' because practically all Internet services can be controlled with ease within one user interface. Many of its functions are also of interest in local networks, so-called Intranets, for example as a documentation system.

25.1 History and concept

The World Wide Web (or WWW, Web, or W3) is a distributed hypertext and hypermedia system. This system was developed from 1989 mostly at CERN (Centre Européen de Recherches Nucléaires) in Geneva. Its critics interpret the abbreviation also as 'World Wide Waiting' or 'Multi-Media Muddle.'[1] Why this is so, and what you as an information provider or user of the Web can do about it, is one of the things discussed in the following sections.

The prefix 'hyper' suggests that hypertext or hypermedia is a phenomenon that goes beyond normal text or normal media – namely the connection of different items

---

[1] All you need to do is 'multimedially' stand the character string WWW on its head.

of information with each other. A word which occurs in a text, for example, can at a click of the mouse[2] call up the associated lexicon entry on screen, or the click on a note on a sheet of music shown on screen can cause this note to be played via a loudspeaker. Also, the opposite is possible in many cases: clicking on a specific word generates a list of the texts or text passages where it occurs. In texts that are displayed on screen, for example, such connections between two elements are often highlighted by underlining.

The aim of the WWW developers was not only to improve the availability of information in the field of High Energy Physics (HEP) and other areas of science, but also to improve communication between scientists by extending computer-based ways of communication beyond mail and news. The WWW was also supposed to provide the possibility of common elaboration of texts and documents in the direction of so-called Computer Supported Cooperative Work (CSCW). Early steps in this direction were made with the possibility of drafting annotations to documents. Because of the overwhelming success of the information component, however, this aim has become of secondary importance in the development.

The central concepts in hypertext systems are nodes (= information units, such as texts, menus, graphics, and so on) and links (= references from one information unit to another). The point in a document which contains the reference to another document is also known as an anchor. Expressed in terms of information science, the hypertext implementation of the WWW is a system of directed graphs.[3]

25.2 The WWW and the Internet

As the name suggests, the World Wide Web is designed as a worldwide and thus distributed information system – that is, the individual texts, graphics, databases, and so on *can* be located on completely different computers, provided the references include the corresponding computer name or number.

Ideally, users will not be able to notice that a document is just being fetched from somewhere across the ocean – only the transmission takes longer than with data coming straight from their own machine, the LAN or a WAN.

The representation of information on screen is organized by means of a so-called browser with which the users interact. Data supply is ensured by other programs on your own or other computers, so-called servers. What and where these are is usually of no interest; users do not have to bother about computer addresses and file names. The WWW follows the client/server principle in its functioning: the client program or browser provides the representation of the information on the screen of the local computer; one or more servers supply the documents on demand.

---

[2] Mouse and graphics screen are not necessary conditions for a hypertext application. There are a number of non-graphical tools for representation of hypertext; only the representation of non-textual information is then greatly restricted.

[3] Edges can only be traced back in the opposite direction insofar as every browser can 'return' to the previous node by means of a `Back` button.

Since the Internet Protocol (IP) was the most widely used of all networking protocols, it was chosen as the basis for a new data transmission protocol, the so-called HyperText Transfer Protocol (HTTP). The HTTP defines a series of procedures that must be followed by browsers and servers to guarantee successful exchange of information.

Individual nodes or information units (documents) are indicated in the WWW by means of URLs (Universal Resource Locators, see [rfc1630]). The reference or URL itself represents a link, the specified document represents the node. The syntax of a URL looks as follows:

protocol://address[:port]/filename

- *protocol* stands for the Internet protocol used; this mechanism allows integration of various other Internet protocols (such as `ftp` or `news`) into the uniform format of the WWW and thus into the uniform interface of the application programs.

- *address* specifies the numeric or symbolic Internet address of a computer. It is common to use an alias `www`, so that many addresses can be reached, for example, as `www.company.cc` where `cc` stands for the country code.

- *port* is an optional specification which is used to address servers which do not provide the service in question on the port reserved, for example, by [rfc2200], but on a non-standard port.

- *filename* specifies path and file names of the document.

Besides simple access to files available locally or via NFS (`file`), other important Internet services are integrated into the WWW as protocols. Some examples of URLs are shown in Listing 25.1.

```
file://localhost/default.html
ftp://www.cern.ch/pub/hypertext/WWW/Daemon/Status.html
nntp://www.gwdg.de/comp.infosystems.www.misc
telnet://info.cern.ch
gopher://
wais://
archie://archie.rutgers.edu
```

Listing 25.1   Examples of Universal Resource Locators.

Usually, URLs are of no importance for the user, since you travel click by click from one page to the next. Interesting URLs can be found in a number of indexes or by means of search engines. For those who find this procedure too expensive (for example because they are connected to the Internet only via a 64 kbit [or slower] line), every browser provides the possibility of entering URLs via the keyboard – therefore, these more technical details are also relevant to end users.

A disadvantage of this method is that you must know the location where a document is stored to be able to access it. This location will probably change if the user uses a different computer, changes provider, or simply changes the organization of the pages. This problem will possibly be addressed in a new protocol version; currently, it is a problem you must live with.

Up to now, Web pages used to be relatively static. Either the pages were displayed as they were stored on the hard disk of the server, or they were dynamically created by scripts (for example, answers of search engines).

With the development and implementation of the Java language, Sun has gone up a step in the ladder as far as use of the Internet is concerned. Now, browsers can not only display pages, but also execute programs (Applets) written in the Java programming language. These programs can be requested by a server if they are not yet stored on the local disk.

Thus, new and significantly better possibilities of using the Internet are opened up. On the other hand, the execution of programs from unknown and possibly untrustworthy sources can lead to security problems. For this reason, Java is only modeled on C++ and does not include many operations (such as pointer arithmetic). Nevertheless it is expected that with the development of so-called Java Applets, the Internet will receive a new push for further development. Appropriate browsers and development environments are also available for LINUX.

25.3 Web browsers

For the user, the so-called browser is the user interface of the World Wide Web. By means of user-friendly programs which virtually hide all technical details, many Internet services have become accessible even to novice users. Almost all browsers have a 'Bookmark' function. Here you can store interesting addresses which can later be called back with a mouse click or a keystroke. However, there are some very big differences in handling and functionality.

The licensing conditions of the browsers are quite different and do not correspond to the GPL. Often, commercial application or distribution is not allowed. Therefore, these programs can only be found on CDs in isolated cases, and you may have to download them yourself from an `ftp` server.

25.3.1 NCSA Mosaic

With Mosaic, the American National Center for Supercomputer Applications provided the first graphical browser for the WWW. As well as a version for UNIX and LINUX, there are also versions for MS Windows and Macintosh. Mosaic uses Motif, so you must either have Motif or employ a statically linked version.

Because of its easy handling, Mosaic was for a long time the standard browser. Recently, however, its use has continued to decrease, although the sources are freely available and Mosaic can thus be installed on practically all platforms. But Mosaic is no longer the technological frontrunner it once used to be. Nevertheless, many commercial browsers are based on the source code of Mosaic.

25.3.2 **Netscape Navigator**

Currently, the standard browser under UNIX is 'Netscape Navigator.' In the current version it supports frames, tables, Java, and JavaScript. Besides Microsoft's Internet Explorer, it is a beacon for new technologies which, however, can also have disadvantages.

Netscape has implemented many HTML constructions that were not yet standardized. Many users employ these features when creating their own WWW pages, so you are often forced to use this browser. Frequently, you can hardly read such pages with other browsers.

Netscape also tries to keep waiting times for the user as short as possible. Therefore, several simultaneous connections to the server are established. This puts an unnecessary load on both network and server.

The only real competition for Netscape is the 'Internet Explorer' by Microsoft. It has been only recently released under Sun's Solaris version of UNIX, but is not yet available for any other platform and therefore no alternative. As in Netscape's Navigator, here too we find that many extensions vis-à-vis the standard HTML are implemented which (obviously and unfortunately) are used by many information providers.

As a reaction to Microsoft's supremacy in the battle for market share in the browser market, Netscape now distributes its browser free of charge. The next version will also be available as source code; with this strategy, Netscape expects the help of many developers and thus hopes to gain an advantage over Microsoft.

25.3.3 **The text browser** Lynx

Many users associate a graphical interface with the WWW. In the definition of the standards, however, this is not described as a necessary condition. For many purposes, exclusive use of text is a much better alternative, because transmission of images, particularly via slow lines, can take a long time.

The lynx program is a simple browser, which can be used without graphics on any text terminal. Unfortunately, commercial distribution of lynx is restricted, so this browser cannot be found on LINUX CDs (the same applies to Netscape). For me, lynx is the most important browser because it is very fast and stable, and even more because it can be controlled via the keyboard, essentially by means of the cursor keys.

However, many Web pages are designed in such a way that they cannot be read or controlled by means of a text browser, or only to a very limited extent. In such cases, you should not hesitate to contact the author of the pages (by email) who has probably tested the pages only with a graphical browser.

The latest versions of lynx can display frames. However, this possibility strongly depends on a good site layout. If frames and links are only equipped with non-descriptive names (such as [LINK]) and images are only represented by [IMAGE], then the site operator has not taken text browsers into consideration. lynx can also use colors and thus represent pages in a more readable form.

25.3.4 The w3 mode in Emacs

Emacs also provides the possibility of operating a Web browser. The corresponding major mode is the w3 mode. You can start the browser with M-x w3. The most important settings, such as the use of a proxy cache and the home page, can be stored in the file ~/.emacs (Listing 25.2).

```
; asynchronous transfer
(setq-default url-be-asynchronous t)

; proxies
(setq-default url-proxy-services
'(("http" . "www-proxy.veggies.org:8080/")))

; default home page
(setq-default w3-default-homepage
"http://www.veggies.org/")
```

Listing 25.2   Initialization of the w3 mode.

Inside XEmacs, display of images is possible directly if the tools from netpbm or pbmplus are installed on the system. These convert the images loaded from the server into a format readable by XEmacs. However, a disadvantage of this procedure is that it is slower than other browsers and, because of the images, XEmacs uses a great deal of memory.

25.3.5 Other browsers

Besides the browsers mentioned up to now, there are others which will be presented briefly. The best thing to do is to try out some browsers and then decide which is your favorite program.

- tkwww is a browser which is implemented in the Tcl/Tk language. Thus, the appropriate interpreter must be installed to run this program.
- chimera is a simple browser for X.
- Together with the development of Java, Sun has developed a sample browser (hotjava). With the implementation of Java into other browsers, this will probably not be developed any further.
- The file manager of the KDE project kfm can also be used as a Web browser.
- The Mnemonic project implements a browser which can easily be extended with the aid of plug-ins. Currently, no published version exists, but similar to 'The GIMP,' this program could get a large number of extensions.

25.4 Providing information

The Web lives on its ability to make information available and to link it together. One of the reasons for using the Internet as a basis for the implementation of HTTP was certainly the fact that a large number of information resources and potential information providers are already available which 'only' need linking together. On the other hand, many users are connected who would like to use this information in an easy way.

Besides the creation of text documents in appropriate formats with the aid of special editors, the dynamic creation of information is also important, for example, as the result of a keyword search in a database, or as a synchronous display of a simulation in some field of science. The latter purposes require employment of an HTTP server or, in the UNIX jargon, an HTTP daemon.

For many purposes, it is sufficient to rent disk space on a WWW server and deposit one's pages there. The advantage is that you do not need to operate your own server. A disadvantage is that the address does not relate to the contents of your pages. Alternatively, you can install the `apache` WWW server in such a way that it reacts differently to connections with different host names. This allows a computer to be shared by several providers as if it were a separate system for each of them (virtual Web hosting).

If your company wants to appear in the Internet as an information provider, you have again various alternatives if you want to operate your own WWW server. You can place the computer with an Internet provider, but then you must transfer modified pages to this computer, for example, by means of `ftp`. For major maintenance work, one of your technicians must then physically go down to the provider's site. Alternatively, the computer can be connected with the provider, for example, via an ISDN (leased) line. The exact possibilities and costs depend on the provider and the expected activity of the server. This is a point where you should take extensive expert advice to avoid expensive mistakes in your investment or high running costs.

25.4.1 The HyperText Markup Language

Documents to be used in the WWW must be formatted in the HyperText Markup Language (HTML, see [rfc1866]). The HTML format is a special form of the Structured Generalized Markup Language (SGML) which is defined in an HTML-specific Document Type Description (DTD).

The structure of SGML and HTML recalls some aspects of TEX or LATEX: there are text markers that mark the beginning and end of a specially formatted text passage. Each of these modes (such as a different font size) must also be switched off again. Inside such a marked environment, further marks can be used. The most important of these marks or `tags` will be discussed briefly in the following paragraphs:

- `<TITLE>` ... `</TITLE>` specifies the title of a document.
- `<NEXTID xyz>` is a 'goto' tag inside a document.
- `<A NAME=xxx HREF=yyy>` ... `</A>` is an anchor or link to another document.

- `<P> ... </P>` marks a paragraph.

The Internet is full of pages that deal with the subject of HTML. Furthermore, there are many books exclusively dedicated to this subject; therefore I will not go into any more detail here.

The HTML language is, however, not as powerful as required for various purposes. Therefore, in further versions such as HTML 3.0 the language is extended. Here, for example, tables are defined. These are already frequently used, although not all browsers support these tags.

When creating HTML documents, one must abandon the idea that one is going to be able to influence the appearance of the document at the user's end. HTML is (still) only used to mark the logical structure of the document. If, in spite of this, you try to achieve a specific effect with a particular browser, the result may look appalling on other browsers.

In addition to the possibilities mentioned above, you can also create documents dynamically by means of the so-called CGI-BIN (Common Gateway Interface/Binaries) programs. For example, you could send the result of a database inquiry back to the client in HTML format. This functionality is supported by all commonly used Web servers.

25.4.2 HTML converters

Several converters allow automatic conversion of text documents that were created, for example, with TEX, FrameMaker, WordPerfect, WinWord (RTF), AmiPro or others, into HTML format. In many programs, the appropriate tools are included with the distribution.

The conversion of man pages or info files of the GNU project into an HTML-specific form is particularly interesting. This allows you to visualize all the documentation of your LINUX system with only one program. The SuSE distribution includes the corresponding programs.

25.4.3 Netiquette for the construction of a home page

The 'netiquette' describes rules of behavior in the network. Even though no sanctions are envisaged for a violation of these rules, you should assume that you are certainly not winning people's hearts. The network lives on reciprocal acceptance by all users.

With a home page, you should consider a couple of things that can make life easier for you and your provider, but also for other users. The following list does not claim to be exhaustive, but is intended to give some hints.

- Do not include large graphics in the home page. Use reduced, clickable images to transmit the large image later.
- Pages should be readable with as many browsers as possible. Test your pages, for example, with `lynx`, `netscape` and one other browser.
- Equip your images with an `ALT` tag, so that `lynx` users can view at least a brief text instead of the image.

- Do not use non-standardized tags, such as `netscape` extensions or new tags from a draft standard.

25.4.4 HTML editors

You can create HTML pages with any ASCII editor. In this case, you must, however, check the syntax yourself (for example via display in a browser). Furthermore, you must know the appropriate tags. For an average user, this is far too complicated, so in the course of time some special editors were developed. Furthermore, there are HTML checkers which check the pages for compliance with a selectable HTML standard.

Since HTML is only an application of SGML, you can create correct HTML pages with any SGML system. For Emacs, there is the package `psgml` which in XEmacs is part of the standard implementation. A few keystrokes are sufficient to insert tags, check for correct syntax, and verify the representation with a browser.

25.4.5 Web servers

If you want to provide a Web server on a central computer or on the Internet, you need an `http` daemon. Through the provision of services on this computer, security problems may occur. It is often sensible to place the Web server outside the local network which is separated by means of a firewall. In this case, only publicly accessible data should be stored on the Web server.

Many servers can simultaneously exercise the function of a proxy or cache. If this was configured in the browser, requests are first put to the proxy, which may answer them from the cache. Particularly if many images or other vast amounts of data must be transmitted, a cache can significantly reduce the network load. If, however, many users with different interests are active, the hit rate is low, and a relatively large amount of disk space is occupied.

In the Internet you can find a number of servers, practically all of which are very powerful and easy to configure. The corresponding instructions can be found in the documentation of the server. Very popular under UNIX is the freely available Apache, which is already contained in current distributions.

Additional Information and Sources	
Web server:	`www.apache.org`

25.5 The use of LINUX in the Internet

LINUX is used at many points in the Internet. There are LINUX computers which provide anonymous `ftp`, for example `ftp.gwdg.de`. This computer has a disk space of 40 Gbytes and daily handles an immense volume of data.

Other organizations use LINUX as a Web server. It is particularly suited for Web hosting, since several virtual domains can be set up on one system. In parallel, a WWW proxy cache can be installed, or the system can be used as a mail server.

In principle, LINUX can be used, in exactly the same way as all other UNIX systems, as a fully-fledged Internet server. Recently, many servers are initially operated under Windows NT, but if such a computer is placed with the provider, it cannot be managed particularly well.

LINUX can be used as a dial-in point by inserting ISDN cards and connecting modems. In contrast to NT systems, you cannot only offer PPP, but also a shell account. This can be quite useful for many services.

But also on the client side LINUX is becoming popular. Dialing the provider can be carried out automatically on demand, and the system can be employed as a firewall or a 'masquerading host.' Obviously, you can also use LINUX as a desktop system. All important clients are available and are usually fully developed and stable.

25.6 Sources of information

Additional Information and Sources	
Newsgroups:	comp.infosystems.www.browsers.misc
	comp.infosystems.www.browsers.x
	comp.infosystems.www.misc
	comp.text.sgml
WWW servers:	http://ncsa.uiuc.edu/
	http://info.isoc.org/home.html
	http://info.cern.ch/
	http://www.apache.org/
	http://www.w3.org

Network administration

26

*The only trouble with troubleshooting
is that the trouble shoots back.*

Anonymous troubleshooter

Any local network will continue to develop. New computers are connected, old computers are removed or equipped with a new operating system. These changes and many others affect the network too. Usually, a network administrator is responsible for an ordered and carefully managed development. Together with these 'easy-to-plan' activities, finding and eliminating errors (troubleshooting) is an important component of the network administrator's activities. For both kinds of requirements, there are a number of programs designed to support the administrator. Some programs will be presented in this chapter, many others are mentioned in [rfc1470].

26.1 Troubleshooting in the network

A local network is a complex entity which is relatively prone to errors. It consists of different hardware components from different manufacturers which nevertheless must work with each other. Often, the structural issue must be given serious consideration. Further complications are different network protocols under various operating systems.

Although these protocols are standardized, there are still implementations that cannot cooperate with all other versions. In the Internet, regular contests are organized in which cross-compatibility and stability of different programs are tested. Valid and invalid packets are sent out to check the reactions of the system.

As well as these, there are a number of error situations where it is not at all evident where the cause of the error lies. In such cases, the only thing that can still help is a well-targeted search for the cause. In many companies, the network is of strategic importance, and there are enterprises that depend on their network today in the same way as they depended on their mainframe computers in the old days – without, however, taking the appropriate precautions.

The stability and fail-safety of a network can be augmented by using twisted pair cabling for the Ethernet instead of coax cables. As a concentrator, a switch should be employed instead of a simple hub because it can carry out load separation between the various segments. Individual network segments can be separated by bridges or routers. Furthermore, there should be at least one backup unit for each central component.

The network administrator should be familiar with tools such as logic analyzers and should periodically check the network to be able to detect differences from the normal behavior. If you do not know what is normal, you cannot recognize what is different in a particular situation.

If you have problems, you should try to circumscribe them, for example by isolating individual computers or network segments and carrying out relatively local tests. Problems such as forgotten or dropped terminators, in particular, are not easy to localize.

26.1.1 Configuration errors of the local system

Even in the configuration of a single computer one can commit a number of errors which prevent its functioning in the network. Thus, when problems occur, you should first check the configurations of the involved computers. Detection of the following errors is particularly easy:

- Has the network card been recognized by the kernel? You can use the `dmesg` program to view the kernel messages. At system start-up the messages may have been stored in a file (usually `/var/log/dmesg`, `kernel`, or `messages`).

- Has the network interface been assigned the correct IP address? Here, the output of the `ifconfig` command can be of help. This program also shows netmask and broadcast address, which you should check as well.

- Have the appropriate routes been set? For this, you need to use the commands `route` or `netstat -r`. If you have problems with name resolution, you must use the additional option `-n`.

- Does `ping localhost` work? Do `ping IP address` or `ping host name` work? Does a `ping` come from another computer?

- Does the network card transfer data? Many network cards are equipped with LEDs which show outgoing and incoming packets. Sometimes, you can obtain this information via a `tcpdump` on another computer.

- Does the port at the repeater or hub show 'red'? Maybe the cable is damaged.

- If present, can the name server be addressed? Does a `ping` work? Can you issue requests by means of `nslookup` and do you receive answers?

- Does the `inetd` run, and have the correct daemons been entered in the file `/etc/inetd.conf`? Can you see any peculiar entries in the log file of the `inetd`?

- Have the necessary RPC daemons been started? You can check this by means of `rpcinfo -p`.

- Does the kernel display strange messages? You can view past messages again by means of dmesg, but without time stamps. In this case, you should look into the corresponding system log.

Depending on installation and use of the computer, further easily verifiable functions can be added or individual functions can be dropped. Especially with cabling problems, software alone does not get you far enough in your search for sources of trouble. For larger networks, acquisition of a network analyzer is highly recommended. With such an instrument, you can detect collisions, broken cables or missing terminations.

26.1.2 Bottlenecks in the Internet

Often, individual computers in the Internet cannot be reached at all or can only be reached with difficulty. By means of the traceroute command, you can gather an overview of all routers or gateways via which the data transfer is likely to be carried out. The result is not 100 percent sure because a different route may be dynamically chosen for each individual packet. traceroute makes use of functions of the IP and ICMP to obtain this information. The program also exists for NT, where it is called tracert.

The program sends an IP packet which has only a limited life cycle. This life cycle is stored in the field ttl (Time To Live, Max Hops in IPv6) in the IP header. The first packet is sent with a ttl of 1, the destination is a port number which is probably not used. The gateway that removes the packet from the network because it has exceeded its time to live, sends an ICMP message of the type 'time exceed.' On the basis of this message, this gateway can be identified. Subsequently, the ttl is increased by one, and the packet is sent again. If the program receives the ICMP message 'port unreachable,' the sought computer has been reached.

With the option −n, you prevent a reverse DNS request for each gateway, so only the IP addresses are shown. If you are experiencing problems with your network or name service, you should activate this option in any case. Additional settings can be carried out by means of various command line parameters which are explained in the man page. An sample output of traceroute is shown in Listing 26.1.

```
(troubadix):~> traceroute −n ftp.gwdg.de
traceroute to gwdu32.gwdg.de (134.76.12.1) 30 hops max, 40 byte packets
 1  139.174.2.254  4 ms  2 ms  3 ms
 2  139.174.254.2  3 ms  3 ms  3 ms
 3  * 188.1.132.13  3156 ms  1310 ms
 4  134.76.12.1  519 ms  1066 ms  1188 ms
```

Listing 26.1   An example of the use of traceroute.

If a computer cannot be reached within the waiting time, an asterisk (*) is output instead of the response time. The waiting time can be specified with the command line option −w. Complete documentation of all options can be found in the man page.

traceroute can generate a fairly high network load, in particular if the network is already reaching capacity. As a rule, you should only employ traceroute for error detection and not in (automatically starting) scripts. Furthermore, several firewall systems forward no or a only few ICMP packets, which makes the use of traceroute impossible.

traceroute only gives information on computers that can be reached by means of ICMP. Often, you can reach systems located behind a firewall with this protocol, whereas other (application) protocols are filtered out. This is another reason why the output of this program should be looked at with due caution. Other seemingly erratic output can probably be explained by an incorrect implementation of the TCP/IP stack.

Additional Information and Sources	
Man page:	traceroute(1)
ftp server:	sunsite.unc.edu
ftp path:	/pub/Linux/system/network/management
File name:	traceroute-4.4BSD.tar.z
Size:	about 25 Kbytes

26.1.3 Protocolling of ICMP packets

Besides its use as a diagnostic tool (for example in ping and traceroute), ICMP fulfills some important tasks for the reliability of the protocols. Most ICMP messages are evaluated and processed by the kernel in silence. Sometimes, it can be useful to analyze these packets.

The analysis can, for example, be carried out by means of tcpdump, which is presented in more detail in the next section. However, if you are only interested in ICMP packets, icmpinfo is easier to handle.

You must start icmpinfo as root (or install setuid-root); the output can either be written to the standard output or further processed by means of syslog (option -l). By default, only unusual ICMP packets are protocolled. With the option -v, all packets are analyzed except ICMP_ECHO_REPLY, whereas the option -vv definitely displays all packets. You will be surprised how many ICMP packets your computer has to process.

An interesting option for very particular cases is -vvv which displays the packets completely. If you want to avoid name server requests, you should specify the option -n. Since the program needs only very little memory and consumes practically no CPU power, you can let it run in the background for longer periods of time.

Additional Information and Sources	
ftp server:	hplyot.obspm.fr
ftp path:	/net
File name:	icmpinfo-1.11.tar.gz
Size:	about 13 Kbytes

26.2 Programs for network management

Many of the problems mentioned above or in the previous chapters can be antici-
pated or easily recognized with the appropriate tools. The following section presents
several programs which you can use to analyze the network on different levels. For
this purpose, the network card is often put into *promiscuous mode* in which *all* Ethernet packets are accepted by the card and not only the packets directed towards this
computer. Thus, the whole network traffic can be observed and analyzed.

This function is also of interest to intruders into the local network because for
example in `telnet`, the password is transmitted unencrypted and can thus be read.
Remedy can be brought by programs and protocols like `ssh` which do not transmit
passwords in clear text. Furthermore, you should periodically check your systems
for network cards operated in promiscuous mode. The `ifconfig` program shows this
information.

26.2.1 Analyzing TCP packets

Many problems arise because faulty TCP packets may be traveling through the network. Such packets can be analyzed by means of the `tcpdump` program. Individual
protocols or packets from or for specific computers can be displayed. Packets that
are to be looked at in more detail can be flexibly restricted so that even for a network
under full load the output of the program does not become too large.

The `tcpdump` program puts the Ethernet card into promiscuous mode, in which
all packets of the network are read. This allows the system administrator to follow all
connections that are established or accepted by computers in the local network. In the
default setting, `tcpdump` only shows the headers of the packets. You can also record
all data and thus, for example, follow the course of establishing an `ftp` or `telnet`
session. In this case, you can also determine the password of the corresponding user
from the data.

The `tcpdump` program can only be used by `root`, because it must put the network card into promiscuous mode. Similar packages also exist for DOS systems,
where this does not represent a restriction.

After this introduction, we show some examples of the use of `tcpdump`. Initially
the data was stored completely in a file which was then used as input for the `tcpdump`
commands, even though the necessary options have been omitted for space reasons.
Furthermore, the IP addresses were replaced by addresses reserved for internal use.

A reasonable application of `tcpdump` assumes an intensive understanding of the
protocols to be observed, particularly if you want to make your selections on the basis
of the data transported in the packets. If you want to work more in-depth with this
program, you should have the corresponding RFCs at hand. Later, you will certainly
create scripts for the different applications. The first example (Listing 26.2) shows all
`tcp` connections.

The option `-n` prevents reverse lookup by the name server. The option `-t` suppresses the display of the time of day and `-q` provides a shorter output. The first
column specifies the source computer and its port. The next column (after the greater

```
(Linux):~# tcpdump -n -t -q
192.168.31.150.23 > 192.168.31.155.1808: tcp 1
192.168.31.155.1808 > 192.168.31.150.23: tcp 0
192.168.31.150.23 > 192.168.31.155.1808: tcp 47
192.168.31.155.1808 > 192.168.31.150.23: tcp 0
192.168.31.155.513 > 192.168.31.151.1023: tcp 47 (DF) [tos 0x10]
192.168.31.151.1023 > 192.168.31.155.513: tcp 0 [tos 0x10]
192.168.31.155.1808 > 192.168.31.150.23: tcp 0
192.168.31.151.1023 > 192.168.31.155.513: tcp 0 [tos 0x10]
```

Listing 26.2   Display of all `tcp` connections in the network.

than sign) shows the target computer with the target port. For port numbers contained in the file `/etc/services`, the symbolic name is shown, otherwise only the port number. After the colon, additional information from the packet header is displayed.

The next example shows only the connections with the `login` port. If you compare the output of Listing 26.3 with that of Listing 26.2, you will find fewer packets. Besides the limitation to ports, you can also make selections by computers (`host`), networks (`net`), or gateways (`gateway`). Furthermore, you can limit the display to incoming or outgoing packets (`dst` or `src`) and individual protocols (`udp`, `tcp`, or `icmp`).

```
(Linux):~# tcpdump -n -q -t port login
192.168.31.155.login > 192.168.31.151.1023: tcp 47 (DF) [tos 0x10]
192.168.31.151.1023 > 192.168.31.155.login: tcp 0 [tos 0x10]
192.168.31.151.1023 > 192.168.31.155.login: tcp 0 [tos 0x10]
192.168.31.155.login > 192.168.31.151.1023: tcp 40 (DF) [tos 0x10]
192.168.31.151.1023 > 192.168.31.155.login: tcp 0 [tos 0x10]
```

Listing 26.3   `rlogin` connections only.

Listing 26.4 shows an example of logical combination of several features. Here, only the `rlogin` connections with a specific computer are shown. Instead of `and`, conditions can also be combined with `or` or negated with an exclamation mark (`!`). You may also enclose these expressions in round parentheses to force a specific order of evaluation.

```
(Linux):~# tcpdump -n -q -t port login and host 192.168.31.152
192.168.31.153.1023 > 192.168.31.152.login: tcp 0
192.168.31.152.login > 192.168.31.153.1023: tcp 0 (DF)
192.168.31.153.1023 > 192.168.31.152.login: tcp 0
192.168.31.153.1023 > 192.168.31.152.login: tcp 1 (DF)
192.168.31.152.login > 192.168.31.153.1023: tcp 0 (DF)
192.168.31.153.1023 > 192.168.31.152.login: tcp 25 (DF)
```

Listing 26.4   `rlogin` connections with only one host.

The last example (Listing 26.5) shows the access to data stored in the packet. Here, packets are displayed that were sent during establishment or termination of a connection. If you record packets of a sufficient size (option -s), you can access arbitrary data fields of the packet. These functions require a profound knowledge of the protocol definitions as found in the appropriate RFCs.

```
(Linux):~# tcpdump 'tcp[13] & 3 != 0 and not src and dst net 192.168.31'
192.168.31.151.1094 > 192.168.3.151.23: tcp 0
192.168.3.151.23 > 192.168.31.151.1094: tcp 0 (DF)
192.168.31.151.1022 > 192.168.3.150.514: tcp 0
192.168.3.150.514 > 192.168.31.151.1022: tcp 0 (DF)
192.168.31.151.1022 > 192.168.3.150.514: tcp 0
192.168.3.150.514 > 192.168.31.151.1022: tcp 0 (DF)
```

Listing 26.5   Beginning and end of connections only.

The tcpdump program is supplied together with some simple awk scripts which can be used for evaluation of the collected data. In practice, you will create appropriate scripts for frequently recurring tasks to be able, for example, to react quickly in case of problems without having to leaf through the man pages first.

For everybody really interested in the internals of the TCP/IP, the series 'TCP/IP illustrated' by Richard W. Stevens is a true bonanza. Particularly in the first part, many protocols are analyzed and observed by means of tcpdump.

Additional Information and Sources	
Man page:	tcpdump(1)
ftp server:	sunsite.unc.edu
ftp path:	/pub/Linux/system/network/management
File name:	tcpdump-3.0.2.tar.z
Size:	about 200 Kbytes

26.2.2 Network performance

A frequent complaint of network users is that data throughput over the network is much too slow. Usually, users store all their data centrally on one (or more) servers. This has the advantage that data can easily be backed up and exchanged between various colleagues. Transmission via the network is slower than storage on a local hard disk, but the advantages usually outweigh this disadvantage.

Network throughput becomes even more important when, in addition, operating systems and programs are loaded from the network servers. The advantage is again easier and centralized management; the disadvantage is the high network load. Further network killers are X programs and swapping via NFS (for diskless devices). There may be several causes for the fall in data throughput rates.

Collisions in the network

First of all, the network load may simply be too high. The Ethernet protocol (CSMA/CD, Carrier Sense Multiple Access/Collision Detect) is defined in such a way that each computer can access the network at any time. In case of a collision (several computers have simultaneously sent data over the network), data transmission is repeated.

After each collision, the computer waits a short time and then retries transmission. If another collision is detected, the waiting time is increased. These delays are set at random to avoid the two colliding computers causing a new collision at the next attempt.

One disadvantage of the Ethernet protocol is that from a certain network load onward, the net transfer rate falls because of the number of collisions. This problem is not shared by the Token Ring protocol. Here, a special character (token) circulates around the ring. Each station that has this token can then work with the network. After transmission, the token is handed over to the next station. If the ring consists of a large number of stations, this can also lead to a fall in throughput (although only much later than with the Ethernet). If the token disappears, for example, because the computer that had the token has just crashed, then after a certain waiting time, a new token is generated by one computer in the ring.

Remedy can be brought principally by two actions: the network load can be reduced, for example by copying and processing data locally. However, this contradicts the fundamental idea of a network, namely that data are stored centrally and only once. Thus, this option is usually not an option at all. The second alternative is to split the network (for example, by means of an 'intelligent' bridge, a switch or even a router) and to separate loads between the two networks. When data is transmitted between two computers in one network segment, the other segment is free.

This method functions satisfactorily only if the network load is relatively local. If all packets must pass the bridge or the router, these devices quickly become bottlenecks. A further disadvantage is that the latency time (or round-trip time in `ping`) increases with each device.

Unfortunately, no program is available under LINUX that can show the number of collisions. Thus, you can only guess from the network load that many collisions occur. For larger, commercially used networks the acquisition of an analyzer is recommended, which can check these cases.

Server overload

A further cause for a fall in network throughput can be a server overload. In many networks, a single computer initially becomes a server for many services. In the course of time, these services are increasingly exploited, so that soon the (processor and/or disk) power of the server is no longer sufficient. Symptoms for this cause can be a high load (shown, for example, with `uptime`), swapping (`vmstat`), or little free memory (`free`).

The only thing to do in this case is to transfer individual services to another, less used computer. Here you will find it very useful to have registered an alias for each service on this computer. After changing the alias in the name server, the service is taken over by another computer. Thus, it is not necessary to make changes to system configurations or even user configurations. Each modification to computers or the network should be as transparent to the user as possible.

The network card can also represent the eye of a needle. In a server, a high-quality fast card should be used which takes the load off the CPU. If the data throughput through the card itself is a bottleneck, a second network card may help.

Performance measurements with spray

The spray program can be used to determine the possible throughput over the network with relatively simple means. On one computer, the sprayd daemon must be started. Subsequently, you can use spray to test the connection with this computer. The packets are transmitted by means of the UDP protocol.

If you know the values for an empty and a normally loaded network, you may be able to get an idea of the state of the network. Please bear in mind that with this program, you can hamper other users in their work, because the network is fully loaded. At the end, the spray program displays a statistical overview of sent and received packets. By means of the options –c and –l, the number and size of the packets can be modified. Additional options are explained in the man page.

Listing 26.6 shows a sample output of spray. The program was run only for a short time to avoid disturbing other users in the network. Please note that with many of the programs presented here, you can actually increase the network load substantially, thus worsening the situation.

```
(Linux):~> spray pea
sending 1162 packets of length 86 to pea...
in 2.36 seconds elapsed time,
0 packets (0.00%) dropped.
Sent:   491 packets/sec, 42.3 KBytes/sec
Recvd:  523 packets/sec, 45.0 KBytes/sec
```

Listing 26.6   The spray program.

spray uses UDP as a protocol. This does not ensure reliable transmission of the packets, and the measurement strongly depends on the speed difference of the two computers. Therefore, the TCP-based tcpspray is usually better suited to make meaningful assertions about network performance.

Additional Information and Sources	
Man page:	spray(8), sprayd(8)
ftp server:	tsx-11.mit.edu
ftp path:	/pub/linux/packages/net/attic/Other
File name:	spray-1.0.tar.z
Size:	about 12 Kbytes

Performance measurements with `tcpspray`

As an alternative to `spray`, you can also use `tcpspray`. Here, TCP is used for data transmission instead of UDP. Again, all caveats mentioned above apply. As a counterpart, `tcpspray` uses the internal `discard` service of the `inetd` on the computer specified as the parameter. Alternatively, you can also use the `echo` port if you specify the option `-e`.

Additional Information and Sources	
Man page:	`tcpspray(1)`
ftp server:	`sunsite.unc.edu`
ftp path:	`/pub/Linux/system/network/admin`
File name:	`tcpspray.1.1a.tar.z`
Size:	about 4 Kbytes

26.2.3 Testing of TCP services

For testing a TCP service, you can use the `telnet` program. To do this, you must establish a connection directly to the required port, after which you can test the service directly. We suggest that you begin by trying `telnet localhost smtp`. If you know how this protocol works (this is defined in [rfc0821]) you can now test this service manually.

It is often possible to start a new version of a daemon under a different port and check it through before replacing the old version. If a system is already utilized by users, care should be taken that such changes are kept as far as possible transparent to them.

26.2.4 Fault detection in RPC services

When you are using RPC services, additional errors can occur besides the problems already mentioned above. First of all, you should check whether the port mapper is running. Subsequently, you can use `rcpinfo -p host name` to find out which services are registered with the port mapper. As a last step, you can test the individual daemons by means of `rpcinfo -u hostname service`.

26.2.5 Network File System

The Network File System is based on RPCs, so that you should first check the items mentioned above in connection with RPC services. You can use the `showmount` program to determine which volumes are exported by the computer in question. You can also find out which client has mounted which directories.

If you have problems with data throughput via NFS, you can try increasing the buffer sizes for write and read access to 4 and 8 Kbytes, respectively. This should usually result in a significant improvement in reading and writing speed.

26.2.6 Network statistics

A statistical display of the network load, similar to the output of `top`, can be obtained by means of the `Netstat` or `tcptop` programs. You will also find some additional programs on the `ftp` server mentioned below.

	Additional Information and Sources
Man page:	`tcptop(1)`
`ftp` server:	`sunsite.unc.edu`
`ftp` path:	`/pub/Linux/system/network/admin`
File name:	`netstat`
Size:	about 4 Kbytes

26.3 IP network management

In many companies, the IP network is managed with the aid of *SNMP* (*Simple Network Management Protocol* [rfc1157]). Each device managed with SNMP (including workstations, routers, switches, printers, and many others) organizes its information in the Management Information Base (MIB). The MIB is defined in the Internet Standards [rfc1441] to [rfc1450]. Besides (static) information on the device (for example location, person responsible), dynamic data are managed too. This includes, for example, routing tables, interface statistics or general information on the device (for example, the load of UNIX workstations or the available disk space).

Access to the information stored in the MIB is managed via the *Community*. The default Community is `public` and allows read access to the data. Modification of the data should only be permitted to another Community. Furthermore, it may be sensible to limit access to the MIB to the IP address of the network management station.

Individual devices can register with the network console by means of an SNMP trap and thus trigger different actions. A great disadvantage in heterogeneous networks is, however, that only IP devices are included. Other protocols cannot be handled, so you might need an additional tool for this purpose.

LINUX as an SNMP client

One available package for LINUX is, for example, the `smnp` package of Carnegie-Mellon University (CMU). This can be used to call upon various items of information on a LINUX computer from a network management station. This information reaches from data via the network connection of the computer down to CPU load or occupation of the hard disks.

This package includes some simple programs used to display entries from the MIB (or the whole MIB). For day-to-day use, however, these programs are certainly not user-friendly enough.

LINUX for network management

At the Technical University of Braunschweig, the tkined package was developed for network management with SNMP. This program package was written in Tcl/Tk (with extensions for network access); the source code can be found on the ftp server of the TU Braunschweig.

With this program, you can generate a map of your network. Based on this map, you can carry out various management tasks and create statistics (also as graphics). This tool is an inexpensive alternative to commercial packages available, for example, from IBM, Sun or HP.

Figure 26.1 shows the representation of a simple map. The center is constituted by a switch which connects the different network segments with each other. Here, these segments are represented as icons, which can be expanded if required; then, access is possible to all devices of that segment. Here, each segment is associated a statistical representation of the network load.

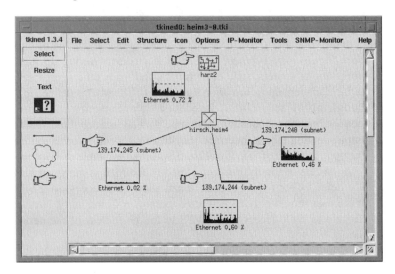

Figure 26.1 Network management with tkined.

Additional Information and Sources	
ftp server:	sunsite.unc.edu
ftp path:	/pub/Linux/system/Network/admin
File name:	cmu-snmp2.1.2l4-src.tar.gz
Size:	about 400 Kbytes
ftp server:	ftp.tu-bs.de
ftp path:	/pub/local/tkined

The standard editor vi

Hated by many and loved by some, vi has become *the* standard editor for UNIX systems. Prior to vi, there were only line editors (such as ex or ed), now (meaning from around 1978) you can edit 'visually,' that is, you can view a large section of the text and all modifications you make are shown immediately. This was when the environment variable VISUAL came into being which, together with EDITOR, is used to select the standard editor.

Most LINUX distributions include one of the two popular vi clones elvis or vim. Both editors are largely compatible with their archetype, but have some extended functions. vim, for example, can mark text columnwise and has a macro recorder. In the context of freely available systems (*BSD and GNU), nvi is employed as a vi clone. Here, the aim is to develop a truly compatible vi clone which even has the bugs of the original.

It is highly recommended that you make yourself familiar at least with the basic functions of vi. vi is usually the only editor to be found on boot or emergency diskettes because of its reduced size (about 100 Kbytes). Furthermore, this editor, in contrast to Emacs and other free editors, is available on every commercial UNIX system. vi stands for 'visual editor' because changes to the text are immediately displayed on screen. If the program is called with the name ex, only the line mode is used. If you only want to view a file, you can load it read-only into the editor by means of view.

The simplest call is vi *filename*. The vi editor works in different modes (command mode, insertion mode, and command line mode) in which the keyboard is differently mapped. This differentiation originated from the requirement to be able to use vi in a reasonable way even with slow terminals and network connections. Today, this kind of handling looks rather antiquated, but as soon as the keyboard commands come straight from your fingers rather than from your memory, working with vi is quite easy.

After loading the text, you will normally be in command mode. In this mode, commands are triggered by simple keystrokes. Thus, pressing the ⌧ key does not cause the letter x to be displayed on screen, but the character under the cursor to be deleted. In command mode, nearly every key calls a specific command. Some commands are expressed as upper case letters, in which case the character key must be pressed together with the (Shift) key. Other commands require simultaneous pressing of the (Ctrl) key.

Other more complex commands can be input in command line mode which you enter by pressing the colon ((:)). Therefore, this mode is also known as colon mode. An overview of the most important commands is shown at the end of this appendix in Table A.1.

From the command mode, you can switch to other modes by pressing specific keys. The most important modes are the insertion mode, which is activated by pressing the (i) key, and the command line mode, which is reached by pressing the colon ((:)). To return from insertion mode back into command mode, you must press the (Esc) key. If you do not know in which mode you (or vi) are, you should simply press the (Esc) key. The worst that can happen is that you hear a beep.

If existing text is to be overwritten, this is best done in overwrite mode. This mode is accessed by pressing (Shift)-(r). If you only want to replace a single character, you can do that in command mode by pressing (r) followed by the new character. Text can be deleted characterwise by pressing the (x) key. If a whole line is to be deleted, you need to press the (d) key twice.

If you want to move around your text file, you can usually do this using the cursor keys, but only in command mode (this may, however, differ depending on version and terminal used). If the terminal adaptation does not match, you can still move around the document in command mode, namely by pressing (h) to move left, (l) to move right, (j) to move down and (k) to move up. Pagewise leafing through a document is possible with (Ctrl)-(f) to move forward and (Ctrl)-(b) to move backward. A disadvantage of the cursor keys is (depending on the compatibility of the vi clone) that they trigger a command. Afterwards, you can neither undo your last command with (u) nor repeat it with (.).

To save the text file, you need to enter (:), (w) in command mode. This saves the file under its current name. If the file is to be saved under a different name, this name can be specified, for example, (:)w *filename*. If the file is write-protected, you can overwrite it in spite of this by means of (:), (w), (!).

You can quit vi by entering the command (:), (q). If the text document was changed, you are advised of this by the message 'Use q! to abort changes, or wq to save changes'. You have the possibility of saving the document and terminating vi ((:), (w), (q)) or of discarding the changes to the document and simply terminating vi ((:), (q), (!)).

Many commands can be executed repeatedly by means of a numeric prefix. The key combination (5), (x) in command mode, for example, deletes the next five characters. There are also simple shortcuts for many functions, such as for example (c), (w) or (d), (w) for 'change word' or 'delete word' respectively.

Obviously, vi can also search and replace. The notation used for this recalls that of sed (see Section 10.6). First of all, search and replace is a colon command, that is, it must be entered in command line mode. Then you need to specify the range in which replacement should take place; this can be done by means of line numbers (here, the :set nu command is very helpful) or search expressions.

The command for search and replace is s, followed by the search term and the replacement. If the replacement is to be executed repeatedly, a g must be appended. This sounds complicated, therefore here is a brief example.

```
1,$ s/sought/replaced/g
```

In the whole text (from line 1 to the end), the character string sought is replaced with the character string replaced. This syntax, which initially appears quite complicated, makes vi very flexible for this kind of task.

If the built-in functions of vi are not sufficient, you can call external programs. Here, the whole file or only the current paragraph can be used as input, and the output of the program replaces the input. Furthermore, in command line mode, you can call any program directly by means of ⏸.

Users can define their own macros or adapt vi to their own requirements. The configuration file for vi is ~/.exrc. Here you can define (your own) function keys and carry out other settings.

This certainly does not exhaust the power of vi. For example, vi is able to cooperate with auxiliary programs, such as ctags, and is therefore employed by many programmers and system administrators. Recommended documentation includes the vi tutorial supplied with nvi or the tutorial supplied with vim, together with the vi FAQs. Table A.1 shows an overview of the most important vi commands in command mode.

Additional Information and Sources	
Man pages: FAQ:	vi(1), elvis(1), vim(1), nvi(1) vi-FAQ
ftp server: ftp path: File name: Size:	ftp.fu-berlin.de /unix/editors/vim vim-3.0.tar.gz about 470 Kbytes
ftp server: ftp path: File name: Size:	ftp.cs.berkeley.edu /ucb/4bsd nvi-1.3.4.tar.gz about 1.4 Mbytes

Key(s)	Function
h	Cursor left
l	Cursor right
j	Cursor down
k	Cursor up
Ctrl-f	Page forward
Strg-b	Page back
i	Activate insertion mode
r	Overwrite one character
Shift-r	Activate overwrite mode
x	Delete character
.	Repeat last command
u	Undo last command
d d	Delete line
/ search_term	Search for search term
n	Search again
: line_number	Goto line line_number
: $	Goto last line
: q	Terminate v i
: q!	Terminate v i without saving
Shift-z Shift-z	Save and terminate v i
: wq	Save and terminate v i
: w filename	Save file
: r filename	Load file

Table A.1   The most important v i commands.

Generating passwords

The security of most computer systems relies on the security of the passwords used. In special high-risk areas, chip cards and other hardware solutions are employed, but for standard security, this is not necessary.

As a rule, users should be able to choose their passwords themselves so that they can remember them easily. As the administrator, you should however make sure that your users choose adequate passwords. Programs such as `npasswd`, `passwd+`, or `crack` may help you with this task. Furthermore, you should convince your users to change passwords periodically. In the shadow password suite, this function is already included.

However, even in normal environments, it is sensible to choose especially secure passwords for special user IDs. This is, for example, useful for all administrator IDs to prevent them from being guessed by means of a `crack` attack. Unfortunately, UNIX has no finer subdivision of administrator privileges, like that in VMS. This means that a compromised `root` user has the consequence that the whole system is no longer trustworthy.

A simple method of generating a password is to throw the dice. This excludes the uncertainties of using a random number generator and prevents easy guessing of the password. This kind of password is particularly indicated for privileged user IDs such as `root`. The table on the following page was kindly supplied by Jörg Czeranski (`czeranski@informatik.tu-clausthal.de`).

For each character of the password, you throw three dice (or one die three times). The first die (or throw) specifies which table is to be used. The second die (or throw) specifies the row in which the character is located and the third one the column. Thus, one character is randomly defined. This procedure is repeated for each subsequent character, until you have collected six or eight characters. A password that consists of fewer than six characters is generally too short to be really secure. However, passwords should not exceed eight characters, first because you will need to remember them and second because several programs accept only the first eight characters anyway.

If you manage several computers with different keyboard layouts (for example, with US American and German layouts), you should admit only those characters that can be found in the same position on both keyboard layouts. Also, using the space bar is not a good idea in a password, because this key is quite conspicuous both for the eye and for the ear.

1	1	2	3	4	5	6
1	o	p	3	l	a	%
2	1	k	M	B	7	m
3	D	B	w	m	v	0
4	e	R	8	z	2	u
5	d	x	4	M	C	Z
6	2	$	i	N	0	g

2	1	2	3	4	5	6
1	j	V		A	u	2
2	x	t	9	S	4	r
3		C	P	j	o	J
4	d	-	T	K	n	#
5	8	9	X	E	,	e
6	6	U	3	k	!	b

3	1	2	3	4	5	6
1	8	b	Q	C	W	.
2	f	Z	P	0	g	q
3	s	X	*	7	0	q
4	Z	&	N	y	6	W
5	I	P	n	J	l	7
6	y	F	S	A	;	c

4	1	2	3	4	5	6
1	<	U	s	R	D	K
2	v	c	"	G	=	)
3	g	i	5	;	3	b
4	x	c	=	f	M	a
5	f	(	G	z	I	t
6	/	?	v	5	p	Q

5	1	2	3	4	5	6
1	i	I	d	^	h	/
2	N	y	n	E	T	e
3	H	>	U	t	L	E
4	_	9	r	1	A	h
5	+	j	W	s	H	q
6	o	B	r	K	V	w

6	1	2	3	4	5	6
1	z	J	L	w	5	H
2	0	6	Y	,	F	X
3	Q	S	I	p	Y	V
4	4	G	F	.	l	k
5	m	D	1	T	u	R
6	0	L	Y	-	h	a

Table B.1   Relation between cast dice and characters of a password.

References

The aim of this Reference Section is to give an overview of available books on LINUX and UNIX. Many a good book has been written about the subject areas addressed here. Therefore, only relatively few titles can be presented. Within the framework of the LINUX Documentation Project, you can also find a HowTo, which presents literature that is both useful and worth reading.

The LINUX Documentation Project

The LINUX Documentation Project (LDP) originates from the insight that in spite of all similarity with other (commercial) UNIX systems, LINUX-specific literature is needed. In the spirit of the GPL, the books written within the framework of this project are freely available, but for a variety of reasons, they are not subject to the GPL.

Besides the books presented in this section, which constitute the main work of the LDP, there are short, practice-oriented introductions to nearly all subjects relevant for LINUX users, the so-called HowTo's. You will find these documents in most current distributions, and they are periodically posted in the newsgroup `comp.os.linux.answers`.

Johnson, M. K. (1995). *The Linux Kernel Hacker's Guide*. Linux Documentation Project

The LDP's manual for kernel hackers. This book is freely available, but obsolete in its current version 0.5. At the moment, only an interactive online version exists at `http://www.redhat.com/khg`.

Kirch, O. (1995a). *Linux Network Administrator's Guide*. Linux Documentation Project

An extensive description of how to install a LINUX network. A revised version is published by O'Reilly.

Welsh, M. (1995). *Linux Installation and Getting Started*. Linux Documentation Project

The LDP's freely available installation and user manual for LINUX.

Wirzenius, L. (1995). *The Linux System Administrator's Guide*. Linux Documentation Project

The LDP's equally freely available system administration manual.

LINUX literature

In the course of the past years, a good and ample selection of LINUX books has been published. Since it is impossible to quote them all, only a very short selection is presented here.

Beck, M. *et al* (1997). *Linux Kernel Internals*, 2nd ed. Addison-Wesley

This book extensively describes the structures and functions used in the LINUX kernel (version 2.0). The book contains practically no information on system administration or application and is therefore of real interest only to C and kernel programmers.

Kirch, O. (1995b). *Linux Network Administrator's Guide*. O'Reilly

An extensive description of how to install a LINUX network. This text originates from the Linux Documentation, but has been revised for the O'Reilly publication.

Kofler, M. (1997). *Linux – Installation, configuration, and use*. Addison-Wesley

An introduction to LINUX; the enclosed CD also contains the Red Hat distribution. This book is mainly addressed to newcomers.

Welsh, M. and Kaufman, L. (1995). *Running Linux*. O'Reilly

Introduction to use and administration of a LINUX system. Networks setup and management is dealt with rather too briefly, but the book is easy to read. It has originated from the LDP's *Linux Installation and Getting Started*.

GNU project documentation

The GNU project was brought into life by Richard Stallman, in order to develop a free operating system. This was supposed to be largely compatible with UNIX, but also contain extensions and improvements. Today, the programs of the GNU project are used on nearly every UNIX system, because they are powerful, quick, and stable.

Besides the programs as such, Richard Stallman puts great emphasis on adequate documentation. In contrast to other UNIX systems, the GNU system practically uses no man pages, although they often come in handy when you only want to look up some call parameters. Instead, the Texinfo format is employed, which can be displayed on screen (for example, by means of `info` or Emacs), but also printed out in form of a book by means of TEX.

Since the GNU system is compatible with the POSIX standard, the corresponding books can often also be used for work with commercial UNIX systems. Usually, extensions of the programs with respect to the POSIX standard are specially marked, so besides the programs, the documentation too is relatively portable.

Practically all GNU manuals put a strong emphasis on an extensive and easily understandable introduction to concepts and handling of the programs. Only in the second part of such manuals are the functions documented extensively, so both beginners and experienced users can benefit from these books.

As a user, you can print out the documents yourself, or you can order them with the Free Software Foundation, Inc., 59 Temple Place - Suite 330, Boston, MA 02111, USA. The money earned through the sales of books (and magnetic tapes or CD-ROMs) is used for implementation and improvement of the GNU system. Here too, you will only find a selection of titles which are usually distributed together with the corresponding programs.

Loosemore, S., Stallman, R. M., McGrath, R., and Oram, A. (1994). *The GNU C library*. Free Software Foundation

The GNU C library manual explains all functions of the library, ordered by subject areas. This is neither a C language primer nor a reference manual, but an extensive description of all `libc` functions. Since LINUX uses an adapted GNU `libc`, this manual is also of interest for LINUX users.

Stallman, R. M., and McGrath, R. (1994). *GNU Make manual*. Free Software Foundation

The GNU make manual, available as Texinfo file, is an introduction to the use of `make`. All functions of `make` are discussed extensively, together with the differences against other `make` programs.

Stallman, R. M. (1994). *The Emacs Editor*. Free Software Foundation

The GNU Emacs manual, available as Texinfo file, is an extensive introduction to configuration and use of GNU Emacs. The manual is also available online in the Info system.

Stallman, R. M. (1994). *Using and Porting GCC*. Free Software Foundation

The GCC manual, available as Texinfo file, is not an introduction to the C programming language, but to the peculiarities of porting and using GCC.

General UNIX literature

Although LINUX differs in some details (positively) from other UNIX systems, one can frequently and without doubts or problems resort to existing UNIX literature. Here too, you will only find a (subjective) selection of good books.

Bolinger, D., and Bronson, T. (1995). *Applying RCS and SCCS*. O'Reilly

An extensive introduction to the use of RCS und SCCS.

DuBois, P. (1993). *Software portabililty with imake*. O'Reilly

The use of imake as a tool for compiling and installing platform-independent programs. Currently the only book on imake, which treats installation and configuration of imake as well as writing and testing of Imakefiles.

Dougherty, D. (1990). *sed & awk*. O'Reilly

A practice-oriented introduction to the use of sed and awk.

Garfinkel, S., and Spafford, G. (1991). *Practical UNIX Security*. O'Reilly

This book deals particularly with the security of UNIX systems, including some aspects of network security.

Intel. *iBCS – Intel Binary Compatibility Specification*. McGraw-Hill, Inc.

ANSI/IEEE (1966). *ISO/IEC 9945-1:1996 (ANSI/IEEE Std 1003.1, 1996 Edition), Information technology–Portable Operating System Interface (POSIX) Part 1: System Application Program Interface (API) [C Language]*, 896 pages, ISBN 1-55937-573-6, IEEE order number SH94352-NYF. Price: 120 USD.

The much-quoted (first part of the) POSIX standard. This is where the programming interface of UNIX is specified in detail. The other parts define other system issues (for example shell, utilities, and so on).

Lamb, L. (1993). *Learning the vi Editor*. O'Reilly

An introduction to the use of `vi`.

Lewine, D. (1991). *POSIX Programmer's Guide*. O'Reilly

An instruction manual for writing POSIX-compatible programs. The introduction to problem areas is well done with hints on frequent error sources. An easy-to-read book, as opposed to the POSIX standard itself.

Montgomery, J. (1995). *The Underground Guide to Unix*. Addison-Wesley

Loads of hints and tricks for UNIX users who want to set up their own working environment, without bothering about system administration. The book is written in a refreshing American English style.

Nemeth, E., Snyder, G., Seebass, S., and Hein, T. R. (1995). *Unix System Administration Handbook*. Prentice Hall

Oram, A., and Talbott, S. (1991). *Managing Projects with make*. O'Reilly

An introduction to the use of `make` in small and large projects.

Stevens, W. R. (1992). *Advanced Programming in the UNIX Environment*. Addison-Wesley

The book is *the* standard reference ('The Bible') for UNIX programming. It discusses both BSD and System V-based systems.

Strang, J., Mui, L., and O'Reilly, T. (1988). *Termcap & Terminfo*. O'Reilly

This book, addressed to UNIX system administrators, contains information on developing and testing terminal descriptions for the two common approaches.

Peek, J., Loukides, M., O'Reilly, T., *et al* (1994). *Unix Power Tools*. O'Reilly

This book consists of a presentation of hints and tricks related to UNIX. It describes many popular auxiliary UNIX programs.

Wall, L., and Schwartz, R. L. (1991). *Programming perl*. O'Reilly

The standard book on PERL is co-authored by the author of this language himself.

General TEX/LATEX literature

The big advantage of TEX and LATEX lies in the portability of documents. You can process your texts under DOS, UNIX or on a mainframe, and the same functions are available everywhere. The printout too is identical on every TEX system. Thus, especially in heterogeneous environments, TEX has extreme advantages, in particular when documents must be processed by various people. These advantages are obviously also reflected in the literature available on this subject.

Goossens, M., Mittelbach, F., and Samarin, A. (1994). *The LATEX Companion*. Addison-Wesley

Extensive presentation of LATEX 2$_\varepsilon$ and many other macro packages (styles) for LATEX. Part of the money raised by this book is used to support the LATEX3 project.

Knuth, D. E. (1986). *The METAFONT book*. Addison-Wesley

The METAFONT book is *the* standard book on METAFONT. Not easy to read, it requires commitment.

Knuth, D. E. (1986). *The TEXbook*. Addison-Wesley

The TEXbook is *the* standard book on TEX. Not easy to read, it requires commitment. With this book, however, the reader will acquire a very good knowledge of the TEX system.

Lamport, L. (1994). *LATEX – A Documentation Preparation System – User's Guide*. Addison-Wesley

With the new, even more powerful standard version LATEX 2$_\varepsilon$, the original manual of the system developer Leslie Lamport has been re-edited. The new edition contains additional sections on production of books and slides, subject indices with MakeIndex and reference lists with BibTeX, together with a section on electronic exchange of LATEX files.

Literature on UNIX networks

In the past years, the TCP/IP protocol has become a standard used in a growing number of networks. Here again, there are many books LINUX users can resort to.

Albitz, P., and Liu, C. (1992). *DNS and BIND*. O'Reilly

This book extensively describes installation, configuration, and maintenance of DNS. For administrators of this service, this book is practically a must.

Costales, B., Allman, E., and Rickert, N. (1993). *sendmail*. O'Reilly

This book is an extensive reference for `sendmail` and discusses the various versions employed under different systems.

Cheswick, W. R., and Bellovin, S. M. (1994). *Firewalls and Internet Security*. Addison-Wesley

The standard book on Internet security.

Hunt, C. (1992). *TCP/IP Network Administration*. O'Reilly

An extensive and well-written introduction to installation and administration of a TCP/IP network. Particularly useful are the hints on network security and error detection.

Santifaller, M. (1994). *TCP/IP and ONC/NFS: Internetworking in a UNIX environment*, 2nd ed. Addison-Wesley

Detailed introduction to implementation and protocols of TCP/IP and RPC services. Nevertheless, the book is easy to read and very lively and practical.

Stern, H. (1991). *Managing NFS and NIS*. O'Reilly

The standard book for network administrators operating NFS and NIS. Concepts, functions, and programs are discussed in great detail. In addition, the book includes extensive advice on error detection.

Stevens, W. R. (1994). *TCP/IP Illustrated*. Addison-Wesley

Three-volume opus excellently explaining structure and implementation of the TCP/IP protocol.

Todino, G., and O'Reilly, T. (1992). *Managing UUCP and Usenet*. O'Reilly

This book explains installation and management of UUCP and news. Unfortunately, it does not discuss the more modern and easier Tylor configuration, but only the HBD format.

Washburn, K., and Evans, J. (1994). *TCP/IP: Running a Successful Network*. Addison-Wesley

An excellent introduction to set-up and operation of a TCP/IP network. The basics are explained in an understandable manner, taking into account the problems of a continuously growing and developing network. Another point in favor is the presentation of protocols and data exchanged by the programs.

The World Wide Web

Bush, V. (1945, August). As We May Think. *The Atlantic Monthly*, 101-108.

Engelbart, D. C. (1975). NLS Teleconferencing Features: The Journal, and Shared Screen Telephoning. *Digest of Papers, IEEE Computer Society Conference (CompCon75)*, 173-176.

Goodman, D. (1987). *The Complete HyperCard Handbook*. Bantam Books.

Nelson, T. (1981). *Literary Machines*. Swarthmore, PA 19081: T. Nelson, P.O. Box 128.

Trigg, R. H., Suchman, L., and Halasz, F. G. (1986). Supporting Collaboration in NoteCards. it Computer Supported Collaborative Work (CSCW '86) Proceedings, 216-227. Portland, OR.

Miscellaneous references

Schulman, A., Brown, R., *et al.* (1993). *Undocumented DOS*. Addison-Wesley
The standard book on undocumented DOS functions.

Schulman, A., and Maxey, D. (1992). *Undocumented Windows*. Addison-Wesley
The standard book on undocumented Windows functions.

List of important RFCs

The Internet RFCs (Requests for Comment) are the definitive descriptions of the Internet protocols. Each RFC, no matter whether it is a standard or is intended as a basis for discussion or for information, has a unique number. When documents are modified, they receive a new number, and the old number is marked as obsolete.

Often one RFC is integrated with a further RFC containing changes or additional information. This too is registered in the file `rfc-index.txt`. Recently, many new RFCs have been created, so you should check the latest news, for example under the URL `ftp://ftp.gwdg.de/pub/rfc`.

The following list is intended to give you an overview of some of the most important RFCs. The texts are relatively readable although they are definitions of standards. In particular, they are a cornucopia for the interested network or system administrator.

[rfc0768]   **User Datagram Protocol**, *J. Postel*, Aug-28-1980.

[rfc0791]   **Internet Protocol**, *J. Postel*, Sep-01-1981.

[rfc0792]   **Internet Control Message Protocol**, *J. Postel*, Sep-01-1981.

[rfc0793]   **Transmission Control Protocol**, *J. Postel*, Sep-01-1981.

[rfc0821]   **Simple Mail Transfer Protocol**, *J. Postel*, Aug-01-1982.

[rfc0826]   **Ethernet Address Resolution Protocol:** Or converting network protocol addresses to 48.bit Ethernet address for transmission on Ethernet hardware, *D. Plummer*, Nov-01-1982.

[rfc0827]   **Exterior Gateway Protocol (EGP)**, *E. Rosen*, Nov-01-1982.

[rfc0854]   **Telnet Protocol specification**, *J. Postel, J. Reynolds*, May-01-1983.

[rfc0855]   **Telnet option specifications**, *J. Postel, J.K. Reynolds*, May-01-1983.

[rfc0903]   **Reverse Address Resolution Protocol**, *R. Finlayson, T. Mann, J.C. Mogul, M. Theimer*, Jun-01-1984.

[rfc0931]   **Authentication server**, *M. St. Johns*, January 1985.

[rfc0940]   **Toward an Internet standard scheme for subnetting**, *Gateway Algorithms and Data Structures Task Force*, April 1985.

[rfc0950]   **Internet standard subnetting procedure**, *J. Mogul, J. Postel*, August 1985.

[rfc0951]   **Bootstrap Protocol**, *W.J. Croft, J. Gilmore*, September 1985.

[rfc0952]   **DoD Internet host table specification**, *K. Harrenstien, M. Stahl, E. Feinler*, October 1985.

[rfc0959]   **File Transfer Protocol**, *J. Postel, J.K. Reynolds*, Oct-01-1985.

[rfc1014]   **XDR: External Data Representation standard**, *Sun Microsystems Inc.*, Jun-01-1987.

[rfc1032]   **Domain administrators guide**, *M.K. Stahl*, Nov-01-1987.

[rfc1033]   **Domain administrators operations guide**, *M. Lottor*, Nov-01-1987.

[rfc1034]   **Domain names – concepts and facilities**, *P.V. Mockapetris*, Nov-01-1987.

[rfc1035]   **Domain names – implementation and specification**, *P.V. Mockapetris*, Nov-01-1987.

[rfc1055]   **Nonstandard for transmission of IP datagrams over serial lines: SLIP**, *J. Romkey*, June 1988.

[rfc1057]   **RPC: Remote Procedure Call Protocol specification: Version 2**, *Sun Microsystems, Inc.*, Jun-01-1988.

[rfc1058]   **Routing Information Protocol**, *C. Hedrick*, June 1988.

[rfc1084]   **BOOTP vendor information extensions**, *J. Reynolds*, 12/01/1988.

[rfc1094]   **NFS: Network File System Protocol specification**, *Sun Microsystems, Inc.*, March 1989.

[rfc1112]   **Host extensions for IP multicasting**, *S. Deering*, August 1989.

[rfc1122]   **Requirements for Internet hosts – communication layers**, *R. Braden*, 10/01/1989.

[rfc1123]   **Requirements for Internet hosts – application and support**, *R. Braden*, 10/01/1989.

[rfc1144]   **Compressing TCP/IP headers for low-speed serial links**, *V. Jacobson*, February 1990.

[rfc1157]   **Simple Network Management Protocol (SNMP)**, *J. Case, M. Fedor, M. Schoffstall, C. Davin*, May 1990.

[rfc1178]   **Choosing a name for your computer**, *D. Libes*, August 1990.

[rfc1183]   **New DNS RR definitions**, *C. Everhart, L. Mamakos, R. Ullmann, P. Mockapetris*, October 1990.

[rfc1258]   **BSD Rlogin**, *B. Kantor*, Sep-01-1991.

[rfc1282]   **BSD Rlogin**, *B. Kantor*, December 1991.

[rfc1301]   **Multicast Transport Protocol**, *S. Armstrong, A. Freier, K. Marzullo*, February 1992.

[rfc1305]   **Network Time Protocol (v3)**, *D. Mills*, 04/09/1992.

[rfc1311]   **Introduction to the STD Notes**, *J. Postel, ed.*, March 1992.

[rfc1340]   **ASSIGNED NUMBERS**, *J. Reynolds, J. Postel*, July 1992.

[rfc1413]   **Identification Protocol**, *M. St. Johns*, February 1993.

[rfc1436]   **The Internet Gopher Protocol (a distributed document search and retrieval protocol)**, *F. Anklesaria, M. McCahill, P. Lindner, D. Johnson, D. John, D. Torrey, B. Alberti*, 03/18/1993.

[rfc1441]   **Introduction to version 2 of the Internet-standard Network Management Framework**, *J. Case, K. McCloghrie, M. Rose, S. Waldbusser*, April 1993.

[rfc1442]   **Structure of Management Information for version 2 of the Simple Network Management Protocol (SNMPv2)**, *J. Case, K. McCloghrie, M. Rose, S. Waldbusser*, April 1993.

[rfc1443]   **Textual Conventions for version 2 of the Simple Network Management Protocol (SNMPv2)**, *J. Case, K. McCloghrie, M. Rose, S. Waldbusser*, April 1993.

[rfc1444]   **Conformance Statements for version 2 of the Simple Network Management Protocol (SNMPv2)**, *J. Case, K. McCloghrie, M. Rose, S. Waldbusser*, April 1993.

[rfc1445]   **Administrative Model for version 2 of the Simple Network Management Protocol (SNMPv2)**, *J. Galvin, K. McCloghrie*, April 1993.

[rfc1446]   **Security Protocols for version 2 of the Simple Network Management Protocol (SNMPv2)**, *J. Galvin, K. McCloghrie*, April 1993.

[rfc1447]   **Party MIB for version 2 of the Simple Network Management Protocol (SNMPv2)**, *J. Galvin, K. McCloghrie*, April 1993.

[rfc1448]   **Protocol Operations for version 2 of the Simple Network Management Protocol (SNMPv2)**, *J. Case, K. McCloghrie, M. Rose, S. Waldbusser*, April 1993.

[rfc1450]   **Management Information Base for version 2 of the Simple Network Management Protocol (SNMPv2)**, *J. Case, K. McCloghrie, M. Rose, S. Waldbusser*, April 1993.

[rfc1458]   **Requirements for Multicast Protocols**, *R. Braudes, S. Zabele*, May 1993.

[rfc1470]   **FYI on a Network Management Tool Catalog: Tools for Monitoring and Debugging TCP/IP Internets and Interconnected Devices**, *R. Enger, J. Reynolds*, 06/25/1993.

[rfc1497]   **BOOTP Vendor Information Extensions**, *J. Reynolds*, August 1993.

[rfc1519]   **Classless Inter-Domain Routing (CIDR): an Address Assignment and Aggregation Strategy**, *V. Fuller, T. Li, J. Yu, K. Varadhan*, 09/24/1993.

[rfc1518]   **An Architecture for IP Address Allocation with CIDR**, *Y. Rekhter, T. Li*, 09/24/1993.

[rfc1523]   **The text/enriched MIME Content-type** *N. Borenstein*, September 1993.

[rfc1524]   **A User Agent Configuration Mechanism For Multimedia Mail Format Information**, *N. Borenstein*, September 1993.

[rfc1531]   **Dynamic Host Configuration Protocol**, *R. Droms*, October 1993.

[rfc1536]   **Common DNS Implementation Errors and Suggested Fixes**, *A. Kumar, J. Postel, C. Neuman, P. Danzig, S. Miller*, October 1993.

[rfc1542]   **Clarifications and Extensions for the Bootstrap Protocol**, *W. Wimer*, October 1993.

[rfc1602]   **Internet Engineering Steering Group. The Internet Standards Process – Revision 2**, *Internet Architecture Board*, March 1994.

[rfc1627]   **Network 10 Considered Harmful (Some Practices Shouldn't be Codified)**, *E. Lear, E. Fair, D. Crocker, T. Kessler*, July 1994, obsoleted by [rfc1918].

[rfc1630]   **Universal Resource Identifiers in WWW: A Unifying Syntax for the Expression of Names and Addresses of Objects on the Network as used in the World-Wide Web**, *T. Berners-Lee*, 06/09/1994.

[rfc1635]   **How to Use Anonymous FTP**, *P. Deutsch, A. Emtage, A. Marine*, 05/25/1994.

[rfc1661]   **The Point-to-Point Protocol (PPP)**, *W. Simpson, ed.*, July 1994.

[rfc1739]   **A Primer On Internet and TCP/IP Tools**, *G. Kessler, S. Shepard*, December 1994.

[rfc1769]   **Simple Network Time Protocol (SNTP)**, *D. Mills*, 03/17/1995.

[rfc1866]   **Hypertext Markup Language – 2.0**, *T. Berners-Lee, D. Connolly*, 11/03/1995.

[rfc1912]   **Common DNS Operational and Configuration Errors**, *D. Barr*, February 1996.

[rfc1918]   **Address Allocation for Private Internets**, *Y. Rekhter, B. Moskowitz, D. Karrenberg, G. J. de Groot, E. Lear*, February 1996, obsoletes [rfc1627].

[rfc1983]   **Internet Users' Glossary**, *G. Malkin*, August 1996

[rfc2007]   **Catalogue of Network Training Materials**, *J. Foster, M. Isaacs, M. Prior*, October 1996.

[rfc2015]   **MIME Security with Pretty Good Privacy (PGP)**, *M. Elkins*, October 1996.

[rfc2045]   **Multipurpose Internet Mail Extensions (MIME) Part One: Format of Internet Message Bodies**, *N. Freed, N. Borenstein*, November 1996.

[rfc2046]   **Multipurpose Internet Mail Extensions (MIME) Part Two: Media Types**, *N. Freed, N. Borenstein*, November 1996.

[rfc2047]   **MIME (Multipurpose Internet Mail Extensions) Part Three: Message Header Extensions for Non-ASCII Text**, *K. Moore*, November 1996

[rfc2048]   **Multipurpose Internet Mail Extension (MIME) Part Four: Registration Procedures**, *N. Freed, J. Klensin, J. Postel*, November 1996.

[rfc2049]   **Multipurpose Internet Mail Extensions (MIME) Part Five: Conformance Criteria and Examples**, *N. Freed, N. Borenstein*, November 1996.

[rfc2060]   **INTERNET MESSAGE ACCESS PROTOCOL – VERSION 4 rev1**, *M. Crispin*, December 1996.

[rfc2068]   **Hypertext Transfer Protocol – HTTP/1.1**, *R. Fielding, J. Gettys, J. Mogul, H. Frystyk, T. Berners-Lee*, January 1997

[rfc2083]   **PNG (Portable Network Graphics) Specification**, *T. Boutell*, January 1997.

[rfc2100]   **The Naming of Hosts**, *J. Ashworth*, April 1997.

[rfc2131]   **Dynamic Host Configuration Protocol**, *R. Droms*, March 1997.

[rfc2132]   **DHCP Options and BOOTP Vendor Extensions**, *S. Alexander, R. Droms*, March 1997.

[rfc2151]   **A Primer on Internet and TCP/IP Tools and Utilities**, *G. Kessler, S. Shepard*, June 1997.

[rfc2182]   **Selection and Operation of Secondary DNS Servers** *R. Elz, R. Bush, S. Bradner, M. Patton*, July 1997.

[rfc2200]   **INTERNET OFFICIAL PROTOCOL STANDARDS**, *J. Postel*, June 1997.

Index

/ partition   13
/bin directory   15
/boot directory   16
/dev directory   17
/dev/lp1   91
/etc directory   17
/etc/auto.master   389
/etc/bootptab   432
/etc/conf.modules   70
/etc/cshcshrc   115
/etc/csh.login   115
/etc/csh.logout   115
/etc/dosemu.conf   301
/etc/dosemu.users   301
/etc/dumpdates   177
/etc/exports   386
/etc/fstab   89
/etc/ftpaccess   396
/etc/ftpconversions   395
/etc/ftpusers{   79
/etc/gettydefs   103
/etc/group   33, 74, 80
/etc/host.conf   **356**, 413
/etc/hosts   355
/etc/hosts.allow   345
/etc/hosts.deny   345
/etc/hosts.equiv   173, **370**, 375
/etc/hosts.lpd   94
/etc/inetd.conf   343, 344
/etc/inittab   49
/etc/magic   **221**, 319
/etc/motd   109
/etc/mtools.conf   88
/etc/named.boot   413, 414
/etc/named.hosts   415
/etc/nsswitch.conf   357
/etc/nwserv.conf   403
/etc/passwd   33, 72, 74
/etc/printcap   93
/etc/profile   115

/etc/protocols   341
/etc/rc.d   17
/etc/rc.d/rc.serial   68
/etc/resolv.conf   **358**, 413
/etc/rpc   349
/etc/securesingle   50
/etc/services   342
/etc/shadow   75
/etc/shells   73
/etc/shosts.equiv   **375**
/etc/singleboot   50
/etc/skel   17, 72, 113
/etc/syslog.conf   96
/etc/termcap   110
/etc/X11/xdm/Xaccess   151
/etc/XF86Config   148
/home directory   18
/lib directory   19
/mnt directory   19
/proc directory   20
/root directory   20
/sbin directory   21
/tmp directory   22
/usr directory   22
/usr/bin directory   24
/usr/include directory   24
/usr/info   112
/usr/lib directory   25
/usr/lib/joerc   117
/usr/lib/terminfo   111
/usr/local directory   25
/usr/man directory
    see /usr/share/man directory   27
/usr/sbin directory   26
/usr/share directory   26
/usr/share/man directory   27
/usr/src directory   28
/usr/X11R6 directory   24
/var directory   28
/var/cache/man directory   30

/var/games directory 31
/var/local directory 31
/var/lock directory 31
/var/log directory 31
/var/mail directory 32
/var/opt directory 32
/var/run directory 32
/var/spool directory 32
/var/tmp directory 33
/var/yp 33
/var/yp directory 33
[258
~/.xmodmap 152
~/.bashrc 116
~/.bash_login 115
~/.bash_logout 116
~/.bash_profile 115
~/.cshrc 115
~/.dosrc 301
~/.dvipsrc 211
~/.emacs 128
~/.fvwmrc 154
~/.joerc 117
~/.login 115
~/.logout 115
~/.mtoolsrc 88
~/.nwclient 402
~/.ppprc 442
~/.profile 115
~/.rhosts 173, 369
~/.rhosts 375
~/.shosts \mainindex{375
~/.tcshrc 115
~/.telnetrc 364
~/.winerc 313
~/.Xresources 152
~/.xinitrc 150
~/.xserverrc 150
~/.xsession 150
~/.xsession-errors 150
~/.emacs 117

A
a.out 317
abbrev mode 142
Access Control List 85
ACL 85
Address 417
Address Resolution Protocol 334, 339
adduser 17
administration 57
afio 176
alias 163
amanda 178
amd 91, 387

ange-ftp 140
anonymous ftp 364
apache 457
API 312
app-defaults 152
Applets 454
apropos 112
archie 367
ARP 334, 339
arp 339
ARP cache 339
associative arrays
    see awk 242
at 234
at.allow
    see at 235
at.deny
    see at 235
atq 234
atrm 234
atrun 234
auto-detect 47
auto-probing 47
AUTOEXEC.BAT 302
autofs 389
automounter 91, 387
awk 238

B
backup 163
basename 222
bash 113
batch 234, **236**
bdflush 48, 55
Berkeley Internet Name Domain 411
BIND 411
BIOS 35
boot sector 37
BOOTOFF 303
BOOTON 303
BOOTP 327, 333, 431
bootpgw 432
bootptest 434
Bourne shell 115
brace expansion 256
bridge 325
broadcast 333, 339
BSD 363
buffers
    see Emacs 123

C
Caldera 7
Canonical Name 418
case 259

CDE   146
cdeject   68
CFLAGS   268
CGI   458
character set conversion   195
character classes   190
character set   187
chat   443
chat script   443
chattr   85
chfn   73
chgrp   80
chimera   456
chmod   82
chown   80
chsh   73, 114
ci   277, 278
CIFS   387
CNAME   418
co   277, 278
COFF   317
command substitution   257
Common Desktop Environment   146
Common Gateway Interface   458
Common Internet File System   387
Community
      see SNMP   471
computer name   353
config.ps   211
CONFIG.SYS   302
configuration   57
CONFIG_MODVERSIONS   69
cpio   175
crack   75
crond   236, 237
crontab   236
crypt   73
csh   114, 115
CSLIP   438
ctags   475
ctrlaltdel   56
cut   227
cvs   277

D
DAT streamer   168
data media   88
Debian   7
depmod   69
DHCP   333, 432
diff   228
dig   361
dip   438, 439
dired
      see Emacs   139

dirname   223
distribution   1
DLL   312
dmesg   47, 462
DNS   355, 356, 411
dnsdomainname   353
Document Type Description   457
Domain Name Pointer   419
Domain Name Service   355, 356, 411
domainname   426
DOS emulator   299
dosemu   299
dpkg   7
DTD   457
dump   176
Dynamic Host Configuration Protocol
      333, 432

E
e2fsck   165
EDITOR   116
editors
      see vi   473
ELF   317
elisp   119
elm   207
      elm.rc   207
elvis
      see vi   473
Emacs   119
      call   125
      operation   125
      buffers   123
      dired mode   139
      ediff mode   229
      frame   123
      hook   130
      major mode   124
      mark   123
      minibuffer   124
      minor mode   124
      mode   124
      modeline   124
      point   123
      region   123
      tutorial   128
      window   123
Emacs Lisp   119
emacsclient   134
EMUFS.SYS   302
emulators   299
env   248
etags   274
eth0   330
Ethernet   323

ex   473
exec   114
expr   257
Extended-2 file system   85

F
false   259
FHS   11
file   **221**, 319
file name expansion   253
file system   88
File System Hierarchy Standard   11
File Transfer Protocol   364
files
    processing
        with awk   238
        with sed   244
    search
        with find   216
        with locate   219
find   175, 216
finger   73, 347, 373
firewall   326
for   260
fork   263
FQDN   354
frame
    see Emacs   123
fsck.ext2   165
FSSTND
    see FHS   11
ftp   364
ftp server   391
ftpd   391
Fully Qualified Domain Name   354
function   261
fvwm   154

G
gated   336
gateway   326, 329
gecos   73
General Public License   3
getty   **101**
getty_ps   107
getuid   100
GhostScript   212
gid   73
GNU/Linux   7
gnuattach   135
gnudoit   135
GNUMakefile   268
GPL   3
grep   225
groff   112

group   33
groups   80
GRUB   44
grub   39
gs   212

H
halt   56
hardware   57
head   230, **249**
here document   252
HINFO   418
hook
    see Emacs   130
host   361
host information   418
host name   353
hostname   353
hotjava   456
HTML   457
HTTP   453
http daemon   459
hypertext   451
Hypertext Transfer Protocol   453
Hyptertext Markup Language   457

I
IAB   321
iBCS   316
ICCCM   153
ICMP   331, 342
ICMP redirect   336
icmpinfo   342, 464
id   80
IETF   322
if   258
ifconfig   329, 334
imake   270
Imakefile   270
immutable   85
inetd   343, 344
Info   196
info   112
infocmp   111
INFOPATH   112
init   38
    simpleinit   50
    System V init   52
    System V-like init   51
insmod   68
internationalization   185
Internet address   330, 331
Internet Control Message Protocol   331, 342
Internet Engineering Task Force   322

Internet Packet Exchange   398
Internet Protocol   321, 342
Internet Relay Chat   380
IP   321, 342
IP accounting   327
IP address   330, 331
IP addresses   353
IP firewalling   327
IP forwarding   326
IP gatewaying   326
IP multicasting   327
IP next generation   333
IP spoofing   371
IPC   317
IPng   333
IPv4, 333
IPv6, 333
IPX   398
ipx   399
ipx_configure   398
ipx_interface   399
ipx_interface   399
ipx_route   399
IRC   380
ISO-8859-1, 187
ISO-Latin-1, 187

J
Java   454
jmacs   117
job control   266
jobs   266
joe   117, 205
joerc   117
jstar   117

K
kernel   57
kernel modules   68
kerneld   59, 70
keyboard assignments   117
kill   265
killall   265
ksyms.c   69

L
LAN   323
lbu   177
LC_COLLATE   190
LC_CTYPE   190
LC_MESSAGES   189
LC_NUMERIC   191
LC_TIME   191
ld.so   100
ld.so.cache   100

ld.so.conf   100
ldconfig   100
ldd   100
LDFLAGS   268
LDP   3
LD_LIBRARY_PATH   113
LD_LIBRARY_PATH   100
LD_PRELOAD   113
less   117
libc   73
LINUX Documentation Project   3
LINUX loader   39
    LILO   39
    LOADLIN   44
    SYSLINUX   45
loadkeys   117
locale   187
localhost   329
localization   185
locate   219
locatedb   220
LOCATE_DB
    see updatedb   220
login   101
loopback   328, 329
lp1   91
lpc   93
lpq   93
lpr   93
lprm   93
LREDIR.EXE   302
lsattr   85
lsmod   68
lynx   455

M
Mach   68
magnetic tape   168
Mail Exchange   419
make   267
MAKEDEV   17
Makefile   267
makeinfo   112
man.config   112
MANPATH   112
manpath.config   112
mark
    see Emacs   123
Master Boot Record   37
Masterfile format   415
Maximal Transfer Unit   327, 334
MBR   37
message catalog   189
Meta key   126
micro kernel   68

minibuffer
    see Emacs   124
mknod   17
mmv   222, 254
mode
    see Emacs   124
modeline
    see Emacs   124
modprobe   69
module   68
monolithic kernel   68
more   117
Mosaic   454
Motif   146
mount   89
MSCDEX   305
mt   176
mtools   88
MTOOLSRC   88
MTU   327, 334
multicasting   331
multiple branching   259
MX   419

N
Nagle algorithm   327
name server   356, **411**, 417
    primary   413
    secondary   422
named   411
named.hosts   414
named.local   421
named.root   414
National Language Support   185
NCP   398
ncpfs   401
ncpmount   401, 402
ncurses   111
ndc   413
netdate   387
netmask   333
Netscape   455
Netstat   471
netstat   331, 337
NetWare   398
NetWare Core Protocol   398
network   321
Network Information Center   330
Network Information Service   33, 76, 355, **425**
newgrp   80, 81, 84, 85
NFS client   383
NFS server   383, 385
NFS volume   384
NFSPATHS

    see updatedb   219
NIC   330
nice   266
NIS   33, 76, 355, **425**
NIS map   426
NIS+,
    see NIS   76
NLS   185
nmbd   407
noclobber   164
nohup   266
Novell   398
nprint   96, 402
nroff
    see groff   112
NS   417
nslookup   359
ntalk   379
nvi
    see vi   473
NYS   429

O
od   250
open   101
OpenLook   146
OSF/Motif   146
output redirection   164

P
PAGER   117
PAM   76
passwd   33, 72
password   72
password generator   477
patch   229, 230
PATH   221
pdksh   114
perl   247
personality   317
pg   117
PID   263
ping   330
PLIP   328, 335
Pluggable Authentication Modules   76
point
    see Emacs   123
Point-to-Point Protocol
    see PPP   323
port   342
port mapper   349, 385
POSIX   185, 187
POST   36
PPP   323, 328, 335, **441**
pppd   441

printenv 248
printer 91
PRINTER 94
process 263
process ID 263
process management 263, 265
process number 263
process status 264
process table 264
promiscuous mode 339, 465
proxy ARP 339
prune 99
PRUNEREGEX
    see updatedb 219
ps 264
pserver 403
pstree 265
PTR 419
python 247

Q
QIC 168
quota 18
quota 62

R
r tools 369
RARP 327, 432
rc.inet2 385
rc.serial 68
rcp 372
rpc.nfsd 385
RCS 276
rcs 276
rcsdiff 280
rcsmerge 287
rdist 175, 373, 377
readline 201
reboot 56
recode 92, 195
recover-file 126
recover-session 126
redirect 336
redirection 164
region
    see Emacs 123
regular expression 174, 179, 190, 225, **231**, 238
remote copy 372
Remote Procedure Call 349
remote shell 369
renice 266
repeater 325
Request for Comment 321
resolver 358

Resolver 411
Resource Records 415
Responsible Person 420
restore 177
Reverse Address Resolution Protocol 432
Reverse ARP 327
Revision Control System 276
RFC 321
rlog 285
rlogin 372
rmmod 68
root partition 13
root.cache 414
route 336
route 331, 336
routed 336
router 325, 326, 329
RP 420
RPC 349
rpc.mountd 385
rpc.pcnfsd 385
rpc.portmap 385
rpc.portmap 349
rpc.rstatd 374
rpc.rwalld 377
rpc.ugidd 385
rpc.userd 374
rpcinfo 349
rpm 6
rsh 369
rstart 371
rstartd 371
rstat 374
rstatd 374
runlevel 51
ruptime 373
ruserd 374
rusers 374
rwall 377
rwalld 377
rwho 373
rwhod 373

S
S.u.S.E. 5
samba 406
SCO 317
screen 101, **108**
script 263
SCSI streamer 168
search pattern 231
SEARCHPATHS
    see updatedb 219
secure shell 374
sed 244

sendfile   380
sendmail   364
seq   260
Serial Line IP   323
setmetamode   379
setserial   68
setuid   82, 89, 100
SGML   457
shadow passwords   74
shared libraries   99
shell   200
shell function   260
showmount   384
shutdown   55
signal   265
Simple Mail Transfer Protocol   364
Simple Network Management Protocol
      420, 471
simpleinit   50
single user mode   49
Slackware   5
slattach   438
SLIP   323, 328, 335, **438**
slist   401
smail   364
SMB server   406
smbclient   96, 405
smbd   407
smbfs   405
smbmount   405
smtp   364
SNMP   420, 471
SOA   416
socket   338
sort   247
sorting order   190
Space.c   329
split   249
spoofing   371
spray   469
standard locale   188
stanza   433
Start Of Authority   416
startx   150
strace   250
streamer   168
streams   317
strings   250
Structured Generalized Markup Language
      457
su   74
sudo   86
superblock   165
SVR3, 317
SVR4, 317

switch   325
sync   55
syslogd   96
System V init   52
system log   96
system.fvwmrc   154
system start   35

T
tac   249
TAGS   274
tail   249
talk   373, 379
tar   173
tcl   247
TCP   342
TCP wrapper   345
tcpip   321
tcpd   345
tcpdump   465
tcpspray   470
tcpwrap   345
tcsh   113, 115
telinit   51
telnet   343, 363
telnetd   363
TERM   110
TERMCAP   110
terminal capabilities   110
terminal configuration   110
terminator   324
terminfo   111
TERMINFO   111
test   258
teTeX   291
text   420
text processing   225
threads   264
tic   111
tkined   472
tkww   456
tob   180
Token Ring   323
top   264
tr   226
tr0   330
traceroute   463
Transmission Control Protocol   321,
      342
trap   265
true   259
tune2fs   18, 43
tunelp   92
twm   154
TXT   420

U
UDP   342
uid   73
umask   84, 99
undelete   164
Unicode   187
Universal Resource Locator   453
until   260
update   55
updatedb   219
URL   453
User Datagram Protocol   342
user groups   80
user ID   71
useradd   72, 113
usermount   89
uugetty   107

V
vi   **473**
vim
    see vi   473
vipw   72
VISUAL   116

W
w   373
W3, 451
wall   377
Web server   459
Well Known Services   418
whatis   112
whence   221
whereis   221
which   221
while   260
wildcard   253
window
    see Emacs   123
window manager   145, 153
Windows emulator   312
wine   312
WKS   418
World Wide Web   451
WWW   451

X
X   145
X client   145
X Consortium   147, 200
X display manager   18, 150
X resources   152
X server   145
X terminal   145, 151
X Window system   145

X/Open   189
xarchie   367
xargs   223
xauth   371, 376
xbanner   109
xcoral   276
xdm   18, 109, 150
xdvi   211
XEmacs   119
Xenix   317
xev   151
XF86Config   148
XF86Setup   148
XFree86, 148, 198
xhost   376
xinfo   112
xinit   150
xkeycaps   151
XKeysymDB   152
xmessage   109
xmkmf   271
xmodmap   151
xmotd   109
xntp   387
xon   371
XOUT   317
xrdb   152
xserverrc   150
XSERVERRC   150
xset   153
xterm   113
xwpe   276

Y
Yellow Pages
    see NIS   33, 76
yes   259
YP
    see NIS   33, 76
ypbind   426
ypcat   426
ypmatch   427
yppasswd   427
ypserv   428
ypset   428
ypwhich   428
ytalk   379

Z
zcat   226
zdiff   226
zgrep   226
zmore   226
zsh   114